John Platter

SOUTH AFRICAN

WINES

2 0 0 1

THE GUIDE TO CELLARS, VINEYARDS

WINEMAKERS, RESTAURANTS

AND ACCOMMODATION

The John Platter SA Wine Guide (Pty) Ltd
www.platterwineguide.co.za

Publisher
Andrew McDowall

Editor
Philip van Zyl

Consulting editor
Erica Platter

Associates
Michael Fridjhon • Colin Frith • Dave Hughes • Tim James • Angela Lloyd • Tony Mossop • Jabulani Ntshangase • Neil Pendock • John Platter • Dave Swingler • Irina von Holdt

Contributors
Hymli Krige • Kim Maxwell • Lindsaye McGregor • Wendy Toerien-Bristow

Sales
Alison Worrall

Co-ordination
Ina de Villiers • Meryl Weaver • Helene Scott

Maps
Tim James

Photography
Dennis Gordon

© The John Platter SA Wine Guide (Pty) Ltd 2001
PO Box 53212, Kenilworth 7745

E-mail: publisher@platterwineguide.co.za; editor@platterwineguide.co.za
Website: www.platterwineguide.co.za
Tel: (021) 761-8773
Fax: (021) 762-5914

ISBN 0-9583898-8-8

Typeset by Zebra Publications, Hout Bay
Printed and bound in South Africa by National Book Printers, Goodwood

Contents

How to use this guide

Ratings

(Subjective choices in a South African wine context.)

🏵🏵	Superlative. A Cape classic	🏵🏵	Outstanding
🏵	Excellent	🏵	Very good/promising
🏵	Good everyday drinking	🏵	Pleasant drinking
★	Casual quaffing	☆	Plain and simple
★	Very ordinary	No star	Somewhat less than ordinary
✔	Good value	😊	Exceptionally drinkable and well priced

Symbols & abbreviations

- 🍷 Bottles own wine on property
- 🍷 Visiting hours, tasting details (no tasting fee unless noted)
- 🍴 Restaurant/refreshments
- 🏨 Accommodation
- 🍷 Other tourist attractions/amenities on the property

Veritas	SA National Bottled Wine Show
VVG	Veritas double-gold medal
VG	Veritas gold medal
SAYWS	SA Young Wine Show
SAA	Selected for South African Airways (first & business class)
IWSC	International Wine & Spirit Competition

For details about some of the above competitions, see page 426.

Wine 🏵	Stars in South African *Wine* magazine
CWG	Cape Winemakers Guild (pvsly Cape Independent Winemakers Guild)
WO	Wine of Origin
Bdx	Bordeaux
MCC	Méthode cap classique; sparkling wine by méthode champenoise (see page 425)
NLH	Noble Late Harvest
SLH	Special Late Harvest
LBV	Late Bottled Vintage
NV	Non-vintage. Year of harvest not stated on label
Malo	Malolactic fermentation (see page 425)
g/ℓ	Grams per litre
% alc	Percentage of alcohol by volume

Assumptions

Unless stated otherwise, the following are implied:

- Cabernet = cabernet sauvignon; pinot = pinot noir; chenin = chenin blanc; sauvignon = sauvignon blanc; riesling = Rhine/weisser riesling; touriga = touriga naçional; tinta b = tinta barocca; tinta r = tinta roriz; tinta f = tinta francisca
- Red wines oaked; white wines not
- Case = 12 × 750 ml bottles
- All wines are dry unless noted

See also Editor's Note opposite for more about using the guide

Editor's note

JOHN AND ERICA PLATTER launched this book 21 years ago as a guide "for the average wine drinker, for the aspiring enthusiast — and for the confused; confused by the proliferation of wines with labels often bewilderingly vague about what's inside the bottle". With the exception of 1981, a 'Platter' has appeared every year since 1980, always with the same purpose.

The current edition follows previous guides in trying to include every SA-made bottled/boxed wine currently available. While we make every effort to cover the full spectrum, a number undoubtedly have slipped past us. We will try to reflect these, as well as fresh entrants to the market in the next edition.

Descriptions and ratings can be found in the A–Z, with details such as release dates (where none is mentioned, it's safe to assume wines are already obtainable via retail, ex-cellar or in the hospitality trade), quantities produced and general style indicators. Technical details — alcohol, acid, sugar levels, time in wood etc — are provided only where they are useful in giving clues to the character of the wine.

A word about our rankings: the star-rating system of the previous guide has been expanded to include, for the first time, zero-star ratings for wines considered 'somewhat less than ordinary' (previously wines with no stars were 'not tasted'). Further, to better reflect their 'good everyday drinking' attributes, wines rated ✿✿ are now included in the 'run-on' listing of more modest wines at the end of each entry. Wines rated ✿ and higher — 'very good/promising' to 'superlative' — are listed first, with a general rating in the margin. Vintages deviating from the general rating are individually starred in the text. The ▼ icon highlights ✿ and better wines offering exceptional quality for their price. In the quaffing category (✿ and below), exceptionally drinkable and well-priced wines are flagged with the friendly 😊 symbol, and now grouped for easier identification.

Also in the book are brief notes on some recent vintages, listings of top performing wines, wine terms used and more. Tucked into the colour section from page 49 is the photo gallery which features some young blood transfusing Cape wine in the 21st century.

Because of early deadlines, a significant number of wines in the guide were tasted freshly-bottled or as works-in-progress. Where wines were considered too embryonic or bottle-shocked to rate, a note to this effect is included in the text. The wines generally were slightly younger when tasted for this guide than previously — something to consider in relation to the star-ratings (these, in any case, should not be read in isolation, but with the tasting notes and the results of other professional tastings mentioned in the descriptions).

New in this edition is the Stay-over section, featuring upmarket guest lodges, hotels, country inns, B&Bs and self-catering cottages in the winelands. This joins the popular Eat-out collection of wine country restaurants, cafés and bistros.

Wines featured in the guide were assessed by a team of seasoned tasters whose professionalism and unflagging enthusiasm we gratefully acknowledge: Michael Fridjhon (for the five-star taste-off), Colin Frith, Dave Hughes (barefoot, weather permitting), Tim James, Angela Lloyd, Tony Mossop, Jabulani Ntshangase, Neil Pendock, John Platter, Dave Swingler and Irina von Holdt. Warm thanks, too, to our contributors Hymli Krige, Kim Maxwell, Lindsaye McGregor and Wendy Toerien-Bristow; co-ordinators Meryl Weaver, Helene Scott, Ina de Villiers and Linda Hunt; sales consultant Alison Worrall, photographer Dennis Gordon; layout/design guru Gawie du Toit, and map-maker Tim James. Special thanks to the wine producers, without whose support the book could not be produced. Personal thanks to Cathy and Luke. And most importantly, to Erica, our consulting editor, and John Platter, who started it all. Siyabonga.

Finally, for updates and extra information not included in this guide, an invitation to visit our soon-to-be-expanded website, www.platterwineguide.co.za.

Preface

PURE OENOLOGICAL VIAGRA, the new-wave Cabernets, Syrahs, Chardonnays and Merlots tumbling out of Cape cellars in ever-greater profusion: riper, silkier, more giving than most of their predecessors, and so captivating anyone would want to take them out to dinner. And the chic 'new' varieties — mourvèdre, nebbiolo, sangiovese, viognier — and imaginative combinations and interpretations of old-Cape standards like cinsaut and chenin. Plus freshly energised (and about-to-be-revitalised) styles like rosé and — thanks to a recently formed producers' association — traditional fortified muscats. And, not least, the grapes and styles spotlighted annually by the Diners Club competition: chenin this year, pinotage in 2002 and, over the horizon, innovative reds and semillon blends.

Beguiling, too, are the new-Cape winegrowers — an inspirational blend of oenology graduates, naturally, but also advocates, dentists, sometime airline pilots, after-hours philosophers and surfers. Thoughtful, travelled, unapologetic; pouring out their passion in cellars which range from marbled showpieces to converted milking sheds, and appellations that stretch the old bureaucratic boundaries into promising new shapes, often nearer the moderating ocean. Counselling, cajoling and otherwise contributing global perspectives and fresh ideas are a cast of foreign consultants, merchants, Masters of Wine, journalists, flying winemakers and tourists lured by — British winewriter Susy Atkins' phrase — "the jaw-dropping, heart-stopping, full-on beauty" of our vineyards.

And a steady stream of investors and joint-venture partners, which is quickening the pace of Cape internationalisation.

In cyberspace, a parallel universe of allures: on-line shopping, virtual tasting, and, soon, digitised wine bouquets to download and sniff while you browse. Plus, already, the ability to be more than just a voiceless consumer: in the democracy of the Internet, you can also be an armchair critic and judge.

It's no wonder that wine is so hip right now. And it's coolest among women, particularly 18–34-year-olds who, according to a *Decanter* survey of the bellwether UK market, are buying more *and* drinking more than older age groups or earlier generations. More than half of their purchases are 'budget' wines costing less than £4; almost 40% of the balance are medium-priced at under £7. Already about 70% of all UK wine purchases are from supermarket shelves, and amid the trolley-fication, supermarkets and grocery chains are cutting back on the number of wine suppliers to negotiate better prices and simplify logistics. Meanwhile merchants and producers are gobbling up competitors in a bid to grow big enough to keep shopping carts (not just in Britain, but in all target markets) filled with their own brands. Which is no easy thing: most shoppers, by their own admission, don't have a particular marque or style in mind when standing before the often dizzying selection on the supermarket gondola.

So while it's wildly encouraging that many of SA's top wines are garnering international recognition (recent major accolades include the Burgundy & Pinot Noir Trophy from the International Wine Challenge; a gold medal in the Chardonnay du Monde competition, held in Burgundy; an invitation from *Wine Spectator* to its ultra-swish New York Wine Experience; and excellent ratings by international reputation maker/breaker Robert Parker), it isn't at all helpful that the *general* perception of Cape wine remains, to quote British winewriter Simon Woods, "tired whites and overbaked, high acid reds".

"The South African wine industry has not evolved fast enough," challenges the British *Financial Times* newspaper. "[Which is] a shame," the *FT* continues, "for South Africa has, or will have, so much to offer the world . . . the pot of gold awaits."

In the old Cape, such an assessment would not have gone over particularly well. But now there's a refreshing, grown-up capacity to absorb and learn and even criticise what is wrong with SA wine. Which is a lot. Not just apartheid-era hang-overs — viti/vinicultural, social, wine-political — but a number of newer issues: over-blown, excessively alcoholic styles (the old *dikvoet* numbers masquerading as 'optimally picked' or 'phenolically ripe'); swashbuckling, oaky wines which shine at shows but pall after the first glass; pretentious (and naïve) packaging; arrogant claims trumpeted from back-labels; gimmicky pricing; and sometimes an emphasis on spin over substance.

But also extraordinary, even revolutionary progress. Our wines are better, on the whole, than 10 or even 5 years ago; our producers more focused, our wine laws more conducive. We're on a roll, and there's more than enough bright-eyed enthusiasm — and beady-eyed realism — to keep moving.

Our next challenge — and opportunity — is to create a common focus and identity, a defining vision for SA wine, capable of simultaneously informing, reassuring and exciting consumers in the manner 'Brand Australia' has done with such enormous, enduring success. What, we need to ask, do we want to be in global wine? And is there an essential South Africanness that we can identify and package and broadcast? Is it, after all, our diversity, our rainbowhood, our midwayness, geographically and stylistically, between Old World and New? South Africa is different, and in a McDonalding wine world, maybe that's a flavour worth propagating internationally.

Locally too. The success of some new, slickly marketed value-brands, 'Cape reds', pinotages, Rhône-style blends and unusual varietal bottlings suggests there is enormous scope for innovation and creativity and a good dollop of pizzazz. So, let's gather our next-generation wines, our charismatic winegrowers and our star appelations, and sieze the pot of gold that waits.

Philip van Zyl

The Cape's top performers

The following are the leading South African wines in 1998–2000, as measured by their showing in some of the leading annual local wine awards, as well as this guide. These awards are: Veritas — here we indicate only double-gold medallists (score of 17/20 or higher by 5 of the 7 judges); SAA Selections (only 1st/Business Class Top Ten red and white wines, as well as trophy winners indicated); and *SA Wine* magazine's panels (only four star and above indicated; 'What's New' ratings not included). Our own ✕✕ ratings also flagged. ○ indicates SAA Trophy winners: the top-scoring red, white, sparkling and 'port' wines that year. Results of other local and international competitions are included in the A–Z section under individual producers and brands. Be aware that some wineries do not enter competitions, thus they might not be represented here. Also see page 426 for more about SA wine competitions. *Note:* this is not a comprehensive list.

	Year	Veritas Dbl Gold	SAA	Wine 4-5 Stars	Platter 2000	Platter 2001
Cabernet Sauvignon						
Allesverloren	96		●			
Bellingham Spitz	97	●				
Beyerskloof	97			●		
Beyerskloof	96			●		
Blaauwklippen	96		●			
Boekenhoutskloof	98					●
Boekenhoutskloof	97	●				
Darling Cellars	97		●			
Delheim	98	●				
Fleur du Cap	97			●		
Goede Hoop	97			●		
Hartenberg	96		●			
Hartenberg	95	●	●			
Hoopenburg	98		●			
Jordan	96		●			
Kaapzicht Reserve	96			●		
Knorhoek	97	●		●		
KWV Cathedral Cellars	96		●			
L'Avenir	97		●	●		
Laborie	98		●			
Laborie	97		●			
Le Bonheur	97	●				
Le Bonheur	96		●			
Le Bonheur	95	●	●			
Le Riche Reserve	99					●
Le Riche	98		●			
Le Riche Reserve	97		●	●		
Lievland	94	●				
Longridge	98		●			
Môreson Pinehurst	98		●			
Morgenhof Reserve	98					●
Neil Ellis	96			●		

	Year	Veritas Dbl Gold	SAA	Wine 4-5 Stars	Platter 2000	Platter 2001
Neil Ellis Reserve	97	●			●	
Rustenberg Peter Barlow	97			●		
Saxenburg	97		●			
Saxenburg Private Collection	97			●		
Saxenburg Private Collection	96			●		
Signal Hill	97			●		
Steenberg	96			●		
Stellenbosch Vineyards Genesis	97		●			
Stony Brook Reserve	98	●				
Thelema	97			●		●
Thelema	95		●			
Uitkyk Carlonet	96			●		
Cabernet Franc						
Bellingham Spitz	96			●		
Blaauwklippen Cabernet Franc	98		●			
KWV Cathedral Cellar Cabernet Franc	96		●			
Merlot						
Boschendal	97		●	●		
Boschendal	96			●		
Delheim	96			●		
Fleur du Cap	97	●				
Fleur du Cap	96		●			
Glen Carlou	97		●			
Hartenberg	96			●		
Hartenberg	95		●			
Jordan	96			●		
KWV	96		●			
Longridge	98		●			
Meerlust	96		●			
Overgaauw	96			●		
Saxenburg Private Collection	97				●	
Spice Route	99					●
Spier IV Spears Reserve	98	●		●		
Steenberg	96			●		
Thelema	95		●			
Uiterwyk	96			●		
Veenwouden	97			●		
Zevenwacht Reserve	96			●		
Mourvèdre						
Fairview	98			●		
Pinotage						
Bellingham Spitz	98		●			
Bellingham Spitz	97	●				
Bouwland	98		●			
Bouwland Reserve	98			●		
Cape Indaba	98		●			
Cape Levant	96		●			

	Year	Veritas Dbl Gold	SAA	Wine 4-5 Stars	Platter 2000	Platter 2001
Darling Cellars Groenkloof	98		●	●		
Diemersdal	98		●	●		
Douglas Green	98		●			
Graham Beck	98		●			
Hidden Valley	96			●		
Jacobsdal	95	●				
JP Bredell	96			●		
JP Bredell	98			●		
Kaapzicht	96			●		
Kaapzicht Reserve	97	●				
Kaapzicht Steytler	98			●		
Kanonkop	98	●	●	●	●	
Kanonkop	97		●			
KWV Cathedral Cellar	96	●	●	●		
L'Avenir	96	●				
L'Avenir CWG Reserve	96			●		
L'Avenir	97	●				
Neethlingshof Lord Neethling	97	●				
Newton Johnson	98			●		
Savisa Athlone	97		●			
Saxenburg Private Collection	96			●		
Simonsig	97		●			
Simonsig	95	●				
Simonsig Red Hill	97		●			
Slaley Broken Stone	98			●		
Spice Route Flagship	98			●	●	
Stellenzicht	98			●		
Uiterwyk	96	●	●			
Uiterwyk Top of the Hill	96			●		
Villiera	97	●				
Villiera Reserve	97		●			
Pinot Noir						
Bouchard Finlayson Galpin Peak	97		●			
Shiraz						
Boekenhoutskloof	97			●	●	
Boschendal	97	●		●		
Cordoba	94			●		
De Trafford	98			●		
Delheim	98			●		
Gilga	98			●		
Graham Beck	98		●			
Graham Beck Coastal	98	●				
Graham Beck The Ridge	98		●	●		
Hartenberg	96		●			
JP Bredell	97			●		
Kanu Limited Release	98			●		
Kevin Arnold	98			●		

	Year	Veritas Dbl Gold	SAA	Wine 4-5 Stars	Platter 2000	Platter 2001
Klein Constantia	97	●	●			
KWV Cathedral Cellar	97	●	●			
KWV Cathedral Cellar	96	●	●			
Lievland	98	●		●		
Longridge Bay View	98		●			
Neil Ellis	98		✪			
Rickety Bridge	97			●		
Saxenburg Select	98					●
Saxenburg Private Collection	96		●			
Sentinel	98	●				
Simonsig Merindol Syrah	97			●		
Simonsig Reserve	97			●		
Simonsvlei Hercules Paragon	97	●	●			
Slaley	98			●	●	
Spice Route Flagship Syrah	98	●				
Stellenzicht	97		●			
Stellenzicht Syrah	98	●			●	
Vergenoegd	97			●		
Red Blends						
Bertrams Robert Fuller	96	●				
Beyerskloof	96	●				
Bouwland Cabernet-Merlot	98		●			
Cederberg Cederberger	97	●				
Clos Malverne Auret	97	●				
Clos Malverne Cabernet-Merlot	98		●			
Delaire Cabernet-Merlot	98		●			
Douglas Green St Augustine	96	●				
Fort Simon Merlot-Pinotage	98	●				
Glen Carlou Grand Classique	96	●	●			
Graham Beck Cabernet-Merlot	97		●			
Kanonkop Paul Sauer	96	●		●	●	
Kanonkop Paul Sauer	95		●			
KWV Cathedral Cellar Triptych	96	●	●			
KWV Cathedral Cellar Triptych	95	●	●			
KWV Cathedral Cellars Triptych	97			●	●	
Le Bonheur Prima	96	●				
Le Bonheur Prima	95		●			
Louisvale Cabernet Sauvignon-Merlot	96	●				
Meerlust Rubicon	95		●			
Middelvlei Pinotage-Merlot	96	●		●		
Morgenhof Première Sélection	95				●	
Morgenhof Première Sélection	96			●		
Overgaauw Pinotage-Cabernet Franc	97			●		
Rickety Bridge Paulinas Reserve	96	●				
Rust en Vrede Cabernet-Shiraz	96	●				
Rustenberg Stellenbosch	96		●			
Simonsig Frans Malan Reserve	97	●	●			

	Year	Veritas Dbl Gold	SAA	Wine 4-5 Stars	Platter 2000	Platter 2001
Slaléy Broken Stone Cabernet-Shiraz	98	●				
Stellenzicht Merlot-Cabernet Franc	95	●				
Uiterwyk Estate Wine	96			●		
Uitkyk Cabernet-Shiraz	96		●			
Veenwouden Classic	98					●
Veenwouden Classic	96			●		
Vergelegen	98					●
Vergelegen Mill Race Red	98		●			
Vergelegen Mill Race Red	97		●			
Villiera Cru Monro	96	●				
Warwick Trilogy	96	●				
Zevenwacht Cabernet-Merlot	96			●		
Chardonnay						
Agusta	97		●			
Agusta Haute Provence Reserve	98	●				
Avontuur Reserve	99					●
Berg & Brook	97		●			
Constantia Uitsig	97	●	●			
Constantia Uitsig Reserve	98		●			
Constantia Uitsig Reserve	97			●		
Count Agusta	98			●		
De Wetshof Bon Vallon	98	●				
De Wetshof Finesse	98		●			
Delaire	97			●		
Eikendal	98		●	●		
Glen Carlou	98		●	●		
Glen Carlou	97		●	●		
Goedgeloof Kanu	98		●			
Hartenberg	97		●			
Hartenberg Reserve	97		●			
Haute Provence	98			●		
Jordan	98		●			
L'Ormarins	98		●			
Longridge	98			●		
Longridge	97		●			
Môreson Premium	97	●				
Mulderbosch (wooded)	98			●		
Neil Ellis Elgin	98				●	
Nitida	98	●		●		
Paul Cluver	98		●			
Rock Ridge	99	●				
Simonsig	98		●			
Simonsig	97		●			
Springfield Méthode Anciènne	97		●			
Stellenzicht	98		●			
Stellenzicht	97		●	●		
Stellenzicht Cuvée Hans Schreiber	98				●	

	Year	Veritas Dbl Gold	SAA	Wine 4-5 Stars	Platter 2000	Platter 2001
Thelema	97		●	●		
Vergelegen	98		●			
Vergelegen Reserve	98		●			
Vergelegen Reserve	97		●	●		
Warwick	99		●			
Weltevrede Oude Weltevreden	98			●		
Zandvliet	97			●		
Chenin Blanc						
Glen Carlou Peter Devereux	95			●		
Kleine Zalze Barrel Fermented	98		●			
L'Avenir	97		●			
Morgenhof	98		●			
Mulderbosch Steen op Hout	98			●		
Simonsig	98		●			
Villiera	99		●			
Villiera	96		●	●		
Gewürztraminer						
Nederburg Gewürztraminer	97		●			
Neethlingshof	98		●			
Villiera Gewürztraminer	99		●			
Pinot Blanc						
Nederburg Reserve	98		●			
Riesling						
Groot Constantia Weisser Riesling	99					●
Hartenberg Weisser Riesling	98		●			
Klein Constantia Rhine Riesling	96		●			
Simonsig Weisser Riesling	98		●			
Weltevrede Rhine Riesling	98		●			
Sauvignon Blanc						
Agusta	98		●			
Amani Blanc Fumé	98	●				
Backsberg	99		●			
Cape Indaba	98		●			
Groote Post	99				●	
Jordan	99				●	
Jordan Blanc Fumé	98		●			
Klein Constantia	99		●			
Klein Constantia	98		●			
Klein Constantia	97		●			
Klein Constantia	96		●			
L'Avenir	99		●			
Mulderbosch	98		●			
Neil Ellis Elgin	99		●			
Neil Ellis Groenekloof	99				●	
Neil Ellis Groenekloof	98			●		
Paul Cluver	98		●			
Spier IV Spears	99		●			

	Year	Veritas Dbl Gold	SAA	Wine 4-5 Stars	Platter 2000	Platter 2001
Springfield Life From Stone	99		●			
Steenberg	98		●			
Steenberg Reserve	99		✪			
Steenberg Reserve	98		●			
Vergelegen	99			●		
Vergelegen	98		●			
Vergelegen Reserve	99		●			
Vergelegen Reserve	98		●			
Villiera	99		●			
Villiera Bush Vine	99		●			
Welmoed Reserve	98			●		
Semillon						
Boschendal Jean le Long	99			●		
Constantia Uitsig	98			●		
Constantia Uitsig Reserve	98		●			
Landau du Val	98			●		
Steenberg	99			●		
Steenberg	98		●	●		
Steenberg (oaked)	98			●		
Stellenzicht Reserve	98			●		
Viognier						
Fairview	99			●		
White Blends						
Jordan Chameleon	99		●			
L'Avenir Vin d'Erstelle	98		●			
Longridge Capelands Classic	98		●			
Nederburg Private Bin S333 Muskadel/Steen	97	●				
Neil Ellis Inglewood	99		●			
Stellenzicht Sauvignon Blanc-Semillon	97		●			
Vergelegen Vin de Florence	98		●			
Desserts						
Avontuur Above Royalty	99					●
Beaumont Goutte D'Or	97			●		
Buitenverwachting Noblesse	95			●		
De Wetshof NLH	00					●
De Wetshof NLH	98			●		
Fairview La Beryl	99			●		
Fleur du Cap NLH	96			●		
IV Spears NLH	98			●		
Klein Constantia Vin de Constance	96					●
Klein Constantia Vin de Constance	95			●	●	
Klein Constantia Vin de Constance	94			●		
Klein Constantia Vin de Constance	93			●		
L'Avenir Vin de Meurveur	97					
Lievland NLH Reserve	97	●		●		
Meerendal	98			●		
Nederburg Edelkeur	95			●		

	Year	Veritas Dbl Gold	SAA	Wine 4-5 Stars	Platter 2000	Platter 2001
Nederburg Eminence	96			●		
Nederburg NLH	97			●		
Neethlingshof Weisser Riesling NLH	98				●	
Neethlingshof SLH	97			●		
Simonsig Bukettraube	96			●		
Stellenzicht Weisser Riesling NLH	98			●		
Méthode Cap Classique						
Graham Beck Brut	NV		✪			
JC le Roux Chardonnay	90			●		
JC le Roux Pinot Noir	89	●		●		
Krone Borealis Brut	94			●		
Laborie Brut	93			●		
Pongrácz	NV	●				
Weltevrede Philip Jonker Brut	95			●		
Fortified desserts						
Kaapzicht Hanepoot Jerepigo	98	●				
Nuy Rooi Muskadel	97	●				
Weltevrede Ouma se Wyn	97	●				
'Port'						
Allesverloren	93			●		
Axe Hill	98					●
Axe Hill Cape Vintage	97			●	●	
Boplaas Cape Vintage Reserve	96			●		
Boplaas Cape Vintage Reserve Touriga Naçional	95			●		
Die Krans Cape Vintage Reserve	97	●		●	●	
Die Krans Cape Vintage Reserve	95			●		
Glen Carlou Cape Vintage	96			●		
JP Bredell Cape LBV	96	●		●		
JP Bredell Cape Vintage Reserve	98					●
JP Bredell Cape Vintage Reserve	97			●	●	
JP Bredell Cape Vintage Reserve	95			●		
KWV Full Tawny	NV	●		●		
KWV	97		✪			
Landskroon	96	●				
Landskroon	95			●		
Masters Cape Vintage Reserve	98			●		
Monis VO Tawny Port	NV	●				
Morgenhof	94			●		
Morgenhof Centenaire Cape Vintage	98			●		
Overgaauw Cape Vintage	97			●		
Overgaauw Cape Vintage Reserve	98			●		
Swartland	97			●		
Vergenoegd	95			●		
Vergenoegd Cape Vintage	94			●		
Villiera	95	●				

Maps

THE MAPS on the following pages show wineries and other locales where wine may be tasted (at times indicated under the relevant entries). The areas covered by the individual maps are not necessarily those of the official Wine of Origin areas — which are indicated on a separate map. Note that the maps are not to the same scale, and a few are not to scale at all.

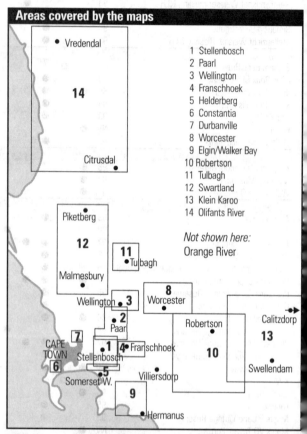

Areas covered by the maps

• Vredendal	1 Stellenbosch
	2 Paarl
14	3 Wellington
	4 Franschhoek
	5 Helderberg
	6 Constantia
	7 Durbanville
Citrusdal •	8 Worcester
	9 Elgin/Walker Bay
	10 Robertson
	11 Tulbagh
	12 Swartland
	13 Klein Karoo
	14 Olifants River

Not shown here:
Orange River

Piketberg •

12

Malmesbury •

11 • Tulbagh

Wellington • **3**

8 Worcester •

• Paarl **2**

Robertson •

Calitzdorp →

13

7

CAPE TOWN

1 **4**• Franschhoek

10

Stellenbosch •

6

5

Villiersdorp •

Swellendam •

Somerset W. •

9

• Hermanus

Some distances from Cape Town (kilometres)

Calitzdorp	370	Paarl	60	Tulbagh	120
Franschhoek	75	Robertson	160	Worcester	110
Hermanus	120	Stellenbosch	45	Vredendal	300

Key for maps

—— Main access roads		R62 R60	Road numbers
—— Roads		◆ ●	Towns
········· Gravel roads		**18**	Tasting facilities

Constantia

1 Ambeloui
2 Buitenverwachting
3 Constantia Uitsig
4 Groot Constantia
5 High Constantia
6 Klein Constantia
7 Steenberg

To Hout Bay
To Cape Town
M41
Kendal Rd
M42
Klein Constantia Rd
Ladies Mile Rd
Main Rd
M3
N
Map not to scale
Not all roads shown
M42
Tokai Rd
To Ou Kaapse Weg
To Muizenberg

Durbanville

1 Altydgedacht
2 Bloemendal
3 Diemersdal
4 Durbanville Hills
5 Havana Hills
6 Meerendal
7 Nitida

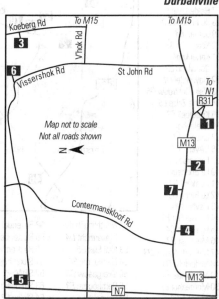

Koeberg Rd
To M15
To M15
V'hok Rd
St John Rd
Vissershok Rd
To N1
R31
Map not to scale
Not all roads shown
N
M13
Contermanskloof Rd
M13
N7

Stellenbosch

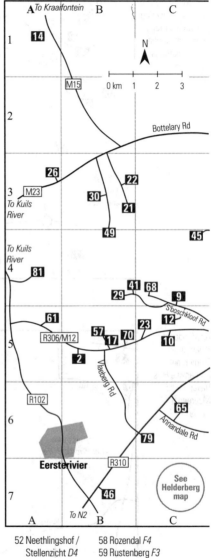

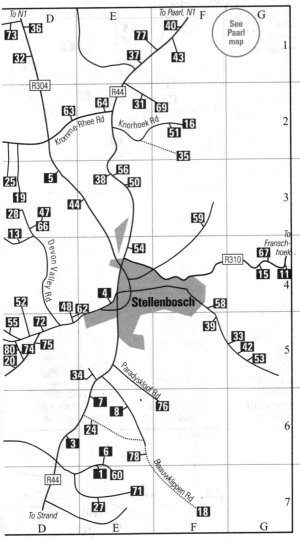

65 Spier Cellars/
  Savanha *C6*
66 Sylvanvale (Devon
  Valley Hotel) *D3*
67 Thelema *G4*
68 Uiterwyk *C4*
69 Uitkyk *F2*

70 Uitzicht *B5*
71 Uva Mira *E7*
72 Verdun *D5*
73 Villiera *D1*
74 Vlottenburg *D5*
75 Vredenheim *D5*
76 Vriesenhof/Talana Hill *F6*

77 Warwick *E1*
78 Waterford *E6*
79 Welmoed / S'bosch
  Vineyards *C6*
80 *Wineways D5*
81 Zevenwacht *A4*

Wellington

1 Bovlei
2 Claridge
3 Hildenbrand
4 Jacaranda
5 Linton Park
6 Mischa
7 Mont du Toit
8 Oude Wellington
9 Upland
10 Wamakersvallei
11 Wellington
12 Welvanpas

Paarl

1 Avondale *G6*
2 Avondvrede *D7*
3 Ashanti *G4*
4 Backsberg *D8*
5 Bernheim *F3*
6 Bodega *A7*
7 Boland *E3 + F3*
8 Brenthurst *E6*
9 Coleraine *E9*
10 De Meye *A7*
11 De Villiers *E3*
12 De Zoete Inval *E6*
13 Diamant *E6*
14 Fairview/Spice Route *D6*
15 Glen Carlou *D7*
16 Hoopenburg *B7*
17 Joostenberg *B7*
18 Kleine Draken *E6*
19 Klein Simonsvlei *D7*
20 Koelenhof *A8*
21 KWV *E5*
22 Laborie *E6*
23 Landskroon *D5*
24 Mellasat *G5*
25 Mont Destin *D7*
26 Muldersvlei *C7*
27 Nederburg *G4*
28 Nelson/New Beginnings *E2*
29 Perdeberg *D2*
30 R & R *E8*
31 Rhebokskloof *E3*
32 Ruitersvlei *D5*
33 Seidelberg *D6*
34 Signal Hill *D8*
35 Simonsvlei/ Lost Horizons *D7*
36 Sonop *D1*
37 Veenwouden *F3*
38 Vendôme *D7*
39 Villiera *A8*
40 Welgemeend *D7*
41 Windmeul *D3*
42 Zanddrift *F6*

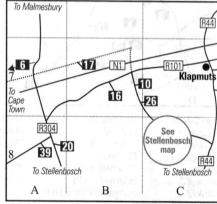

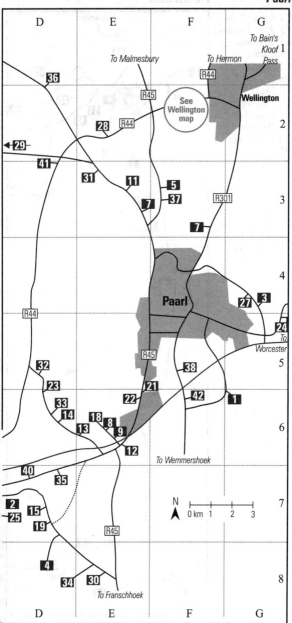

Franschhoek

1 Agusta Wines
2 Boekenhoutskloof
3 Boschendal
4 Cabrière
5 Cape Chamonix
6 Dieu Donné
7 Eikehof
8 Franschhoek
  Vineyards / La Bri
9 L'Ormarins
10 La Bourgogne
11 La Couronne
12 Landau du Val
13 La Motte
14 La Petite Ferme
15 Mont Rochelle
16 Môreson
17 Plaisir de Merle
18 Rickety Bridge
19 Stony Brook
20 TenFiftySix
21 Von Ortloff

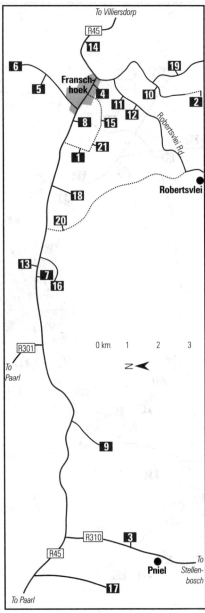

Helderberg

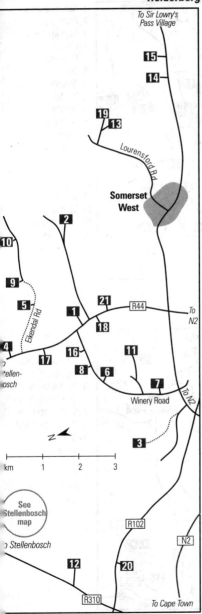

To Sir Lowry's
Pass Village

15

14

19 13

Lourensford Rd

**Somerset
West**

2

10

9

5

Eikendal Rd

21 R44

1

18   To
N2

4

Stellen-
bosch   17

16

8   6   11

7   To N2

Winery Road

N

km   1   2   3

See
Stellenbosch
map

3

o Stellenbosch

R102

N2

12   20

R310

To Cape Town

1 Avontuur
2 Cordoba
3 Dellrust
4 Eikendal
5 Grangehurst
6 Helderberg/
  Stellenbosch V'yards
7 JP Bredell
8 Ken Forrester
  (96 Winery Rd)
9 Longridge
10 Lushof
11 Lyngrove
12 Meerlust
13 Morgenster
14 Mount Rozier
15 Onderkloof
16 Post House
17 Somerbosch
18 Stonewall
19 Vergelegen
20 Vergenoegd
21 Yonder Hill

Worcester

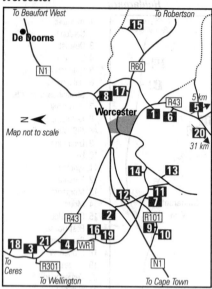

1 Aan-de-Doorns
2 Badsberg
3 Bergsig
4 Botha
5 Brandvlei
6 Cilmor
7 Deetlefs
8 De Wet
9 Du Preez
10 Du Toitskloof
11 Goudini
12 Groot Eiland
13 Louwshoek
14 Merwida
15 Nuy
16 Opstal
17 Overhex
18 Romansrivier
19 Slanghoek
20 Villiersdorp

Elgin/Walker Bay

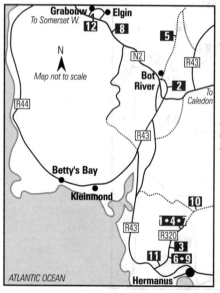

1 Bartho Eksteen
2 Beaumont
3 Bouchard Finlayson
4 Cape Bay
5 Goedvertrouw
6 Hamilton Russell
7 Newton Johnson
8 Paul Cluver/Thandi
9 Southern Right
10 Sumaridge
11 WhaleHaven
12 Wildekrans
*(Orchard Farm
Stall)*

Robertson

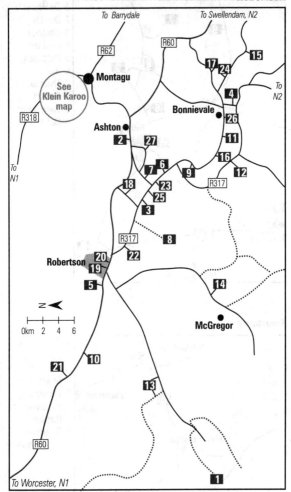

1 Agterkliphoogte	11 Jonker	21 Rooiberg
2 Ashton	12 Langverwacht	22 Springfield
3 Bon Courage	13 Le Gr. Chasseur	23 Van Loveren
4 Bonnievale	14 McGregor	24 Van Zylshof
5 Clairvaux	15 Merwespont	25 Viljoensdrift
6 De Wetshof	16 Mooiuitsig	26 Weltevrede
7 Excelsior	17 Nordale	27 Zandvliet
8 Fraai Uitzicht	18 Rietvallei	
9 Goedverwacht	19 Robertson	
10 Graham Beck	20 Roodezandt	

Tulbagh

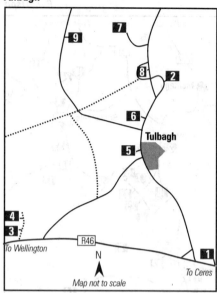

1 De Heuvel
2 Drostdy
3 Kloofzicht
4 Lemberg
5 Paddagang
6 Rijk's
7 Theuniskraal
8 Tulbagh
9 Twee Jonge
  Gezellen

Tulbagh

To Wellington
R46
N
Map not to scale
To Ceres

Swartland

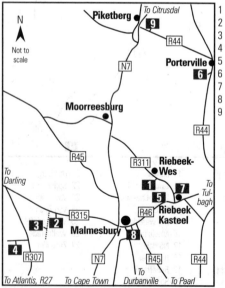

1 Allesverloren
2 Darling Cellars
3 Groene Cloof
4 Groote Post
5 Kloovenburg
6 Porterville
7 Riebeek
8 Swartland
9 Winkelshoek

N
Not to
scale

Piketberg
To Citrusdal
R44
Porterville
N7
Moorreesburg
R44
R45
R311
Riebeek-Wes
To Darling
R315
Riebeek
Kasteel
R46
To Tulbagh
Malmesbury
R307
N7
R45
R44
To Atlantis, R27
To Cape Town
To Durbanville
To Paarl

Klein Karoo

1 Barrydale
2 Bloupunt
3 Boplaas
4 Calitzdorp
5 Die Krans
6 Die Poort
7 Dom. Doornkraal
8 Grundheim
9 Ladismith
10 Mons Ruber
11 Montagu
12 Uitvlucht

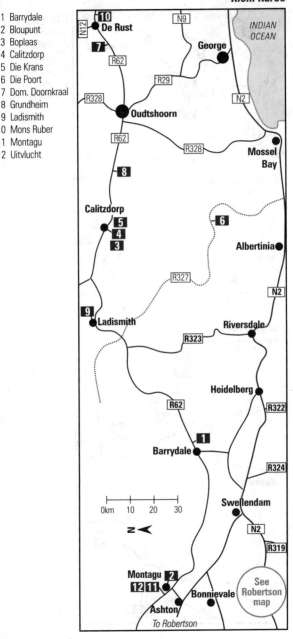

Olifants River

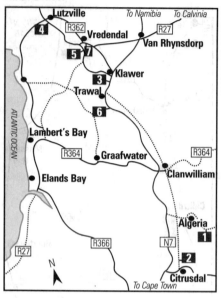

1 Cederberg
2 Goue Vallei
3 Klawer
4 Lutzville
5 Spruitdrift
6 Trawal
7 Vredendal

Orange River

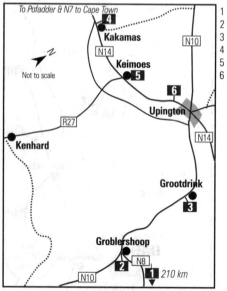

1 Douglas
2 Groblershoop
3 Grootdrink
4 Kakamas
5 Keimoes
6 Upington

A Few Good Men see Arlington

. . . .

African Dawn

WILDLIFE-THEMED RANGE by Breede River valley partnership including Groot Eiland and Louwshoek–Voorsorg wineries (see those entries). Features 'Big Five' front label painting by Cape artist Tony Butler. Available from above cellars, game parks, guest houses, duty free shops and some retailers, the current range includes a Cabernet Sauvignon and a Chardonnay, both untasted.

. . . .

African Legend see Sonop
African Sky see Drostdy
African Sunset see Clairvaux

. . . .

African Wines & Spirits

Constantia • Directors Mike Cox, James McLachlan, André van Wyk, Chris Weeden • PO Box 389 Constantia 7848 • Tel (021) 794-6697 • Fax (021) 794-3990

MARKETING COMPANY which owns a number of established brands such as Craighall, Mondial, Bertrams wines, sherries and ports, Cinzano sparklers and vermouths. Also new S/SW (South/South West) easy drinkers, and international rights for the Alphen range, made by AWS from Robertson grapes (see separate entries).

. . . .

Agulhas see Merwespont
Agulhas Bank see Winecorp

. . . .

Agterkliphoogte Winery

Robertson (see Robertson map) • Tasting, sales, cellar tours Mon—Fri 8—12.30; 1.30—5 • Owners 22 members • Winemaker Helmard Hanekom (since 1986) • Consulting viticulturist Stephan Joubert (VinPro) • Vineyards 398 ha • Production 6 500 tons (500 cases own label) 67% white 11% red 22% fortified & other • PO Box 267 Robertson 6705 • Tel (023) 626-1103 • Fax (023) 626-3329 • E-mail akhwyn@lando.co.za

A BIT CRUMPLED after the 2000 harvest — "a weak year, dry and very hot, some hail damage" — but certainly not crushed, one-man-show Helmard Hanekom has been busy putting together some nifty new packaging for the co-op's own wines (these now bottled under new Wandsbeck label for export and the local market). And keeping a beady eye on the revamp of the cellar complex, tucked into the secluded Agterkliphoogte Valley. All this between diving for perlemoen and crayfish on weekends in Kleinbaai. Note: wines below all **00**.

Wandsbeck range

> **Ruby Cabernet** ✿ 😊 Helmard Hanekom coaxes extra gulpability from this grape, with soft, mouthfilling mint, cherry, mulberry tastes. Med-bodied, unoaked. 300 cases.

Shiraz ‡ Lightish toned/bodied, dominated by Am oak (chip fermented), some understated vanilla/pepper hints. 300 cases. **Chardonnay** ✿ Tasted young, already good notch up on pvs. Now oaked; bright citrus flavour with hint of vanilla. High-kicking 14,6% alc. **Sauvignon Blanc** ‡ Tank sample tasted mid-2000 still closed, needing time. 300 cases. **Red Muscadel** ‡ Fresh, attractive fortified dessert; light, uncomplicated. Pour over crushed ice, recommends winemaker. 300 cases.

Agusta Wines

Y Y W ⴴ Y

Franschhoek (see Franschhoek map) • Tasting & sales daily 9—5 Tasting fee R5 for 5 wines • Cellar tours by appointment • Le Provençal Restaurant (see Eat-out section) • Luxury 5-bedroom guest house • Conferences • Facilities for children • Tour groups • Wheelchair-friendly • Owner Count Riccardo Agusta • Consulting winemaker Jean-Luc Sweerts (since 1999) with Ilse van Dijk (since 1999) • Viticulturist Niel Marée • Vineyards 40 ha • Production 1 000 tons, 60 000 — 80 000 cases 85% white 15% red • PO Box 393 Franschhoek 7690 • Tel (021) 876-3195 • Fax (021) 876-3118 • E-mail orders@agustawines.co.za

JEAN-LUC SWEERTS, consultant at this merger of La Provence and Haute Provence — he also does the flying winemaker bit in Madagascar and France — is perking up. Owner Count Riccardo Agusta has added a "lovely" farm across the road to his Franschhoek interests; 40 ha of red varieties have just been planted; the conversion of a largely white wine operation to red has begun. A currently fairly bewildering array of wines — this is a property in transition — is to be pared down to the top-quality Count Agusta range, and Angels' Tears, the popular Haute Provence label, will be expanded to include a bubbly and a red. Then there's Agusta's own gourmet restaurant, Le Provençal. All silver-lining stuff. Which of course means there's a dark cloud, and even the perennially droll Sweerts is unable to mask his dismay at the cellar, all R17-million of it, which was the venue of a national cheese festival in 2000, but due to all sorts of design faults has turned out a winemaker's nightmare. "A farce," he sighs. "A catastrophe." (This last word to be pronounced in the Sweerts French manner, and with extra accent on the last syllable for maximum effect.) Ongoing rescue/renovation operations left Sweerts without electricity, cooling and water at various times during the harvest.

Count Agusta range

✿ **Cabernet Sauvignon** Festooned with young wine show ribbons: national champ in **98**, **97**; local competition hero in **96**, **95**. Barrel sample of **99**, packed with ripe cherry fruit, should follow these footsteps. **98** not ready for tasting. **97**, from 'imported' St'bosch grapes, offers fine blackcurrant flavour, dark berry colour and scent, cool minty finish. Good now and over next 1–2 yrs. French old oak matured 14 mths.

✿ **Chardonnay** Opulent style with obvious tropical (melon, pineapple, mango) fruit in **99** ✿, tempered by twist of sweet/sour apricot. Ripe, almost overblown palate, though alc is moderate 12,5%. 6 mths new oak. Notch down from **98** VG, which 85% barrel fermented in Fr/Am oak, 15% unwooded portion for freshness. **97** SAA.

✿ **Sauvignon Blanc** Lively zip of crisp, dry **99** (first time own grapes) has faded to figgy, nettle character. **00** ✿ tank sample has tight green acid and "fox pee" (a Sweerts-ism) tempered by cantaloupe flesh.

✿ **Semillon 99** has developed its potential (and gained star luminosity): inviting golden tinges, tropical/peachy aromas now secondary to luscious lanolin, waxy layers which pervade full, flavoursome palate. Oak vanilla rounds it out. Lengthy finish from touch of bottle age.

Muscat du Provençal ✿ New Intriguing savoury fullness to this **NV** honeycomb bouquet, rich sweetness lifted by touch of lime and 16,5% fortifying alc.

Angels' Tears range

Angels' Tears Red ‡ (Pvsly Agusta Rosso) Light, undemanding **NV**, multi-vintage cab. Preview of **00** contribution suggests Sweerts' knack with soft, docile-tannined fruity reds will emerge. **Angels' Tears** ‡ Ever popular, not too sweet hanepoot dominated **NV** blend. Spicy nose filled out with delicate petal nuances, grapey mouthful just beyond off-dry.

Agusta range

Chardonnay ✱ Quiet **99** nose redeemed by soft citric flavours, maturing palate. Unwooded. **Sauvignon Blanc** ✱ **99** short, lacks grassy aromatics of fuller **98**. **Brut** ✱ Two versions of this dry carbonated sparkler: blue label, from chardonnay; red label, from sémillon; light, no-frills refreshment. **Bianco NV** Sharp, thin.

Haute Provence range

To be phased out.

✿ **Chardonnay Reserve 98** VVG continues to gain complexity in bottle: golden patina, tropical fruit woven with into creamy full-flavoured mouthful, extended finish; suggestion of sweetness adds to appeal. 20% barrel fermented, rest wood chip exposed; through malo. Creditable performance (R75/bottle) at 2000 Nederburg Auction.

Blanc Fumé ✱ Cooked vegetable aroma in fatigued **98** VG. **Semillon Reserve** ✱ Subdued **98** finishes briskly. **Semillon ★ 97** Well past its best.

. . . .

Angels' Tears see Agusta Wines

. . . .

Allesverloren Estate

Swartland (see Swartland map) • Tasting & sales Mon—Fri 8.30—5 Sat 8.30—12.30 On public holidays phone (022) 461-2589 • Cellar tours by appointment • Owners/winemakers Danie & Fanie Malan • Vineyards 160 ha • Production 1 400 tons • PO Box 23 Riebeek West 7306 • Tel (022) 461-2320 • Fax (022) 461-2444

DANIE MALAN'S Diners Club victory lap around France included a close encounter with the fabled soils of Bordeaux. "I was driving through Pomerol," says gravel voiced Malan, who regards himself primarily as a grape grower who also makes wine, "when I saw some labourers digging a trench on either side of the road. I got quite excited when I realised one ditch was 'across the border' in St Émilion. I thought, I've heard the soils differ completely; here's a chance to see for myself. Man, those trenches must have been 2,5 m deep, but I tell you, you'd have needed a microscope to tell the difference!" Fortunately some other aspects of French viticulture proved to be more enlightening: he "learnt a lot" about plant density and the importance of low cropping. "We tend to calculate yield in terms of litres per hectare. The French look at litres per *vine*." Expect these insights to inform future releases of Malan's ever popular Port (a new Vintage **97** in the pipeline) and his robust red wines.

✿ **Shiraz** Highly rated example, usually deeply flavoured with satisfying shiraz aromatics — black pepper, spice, woodsmoke — big, mouthfilling, high alcs, though latest **98** ✿ relatively slimline ('only' 13,6% alc), distinctly lighter feel, more refined, probably earlier peaking. But pleasing, good mouthfeel, balanced, oak well judged (6 mths, 30% new Fr/Am casks). Pvs **96** ✿✿ Diners Club champ, blockbuster style, but not as challenging as 14,4% alc would suggest. This a stayer: likely peak around 2004, then hold several yrs. No **97**.

✿ **Cabernet Sauvignon** Latest **97** ✿ reflects cooler yr in lighter colour, body (11,8% alc). Peppery/herbaceous tones quite dominant, some frisky tannins which probably better with Danie Malan's culinary preference, roast beef ("Now that's what I call food!"). 19 mths Fr oak, 50% new. **96** SAA, *Wine* ✿ among most substantial, promising cabs from this often ethereal yr. Potential 8—10 yrs' development.

✿ **Tinta Barocca** Now in extrovert fruity style, no hint of porty decadence. **97**, with good whack new oak, attractively complex: whiffs rhubarb/black pepper/ earth in dense, layered mulberry/redcurrant palate. Lower (though not insubstantial) 13,4% alc from cooler vintage. Now and over 4—8 yrs. 14 mths oak, ±30% new Fr/Am. **96** SAA.

⚝⚝**Port** Consistent, ready on release Late Bottled Vintage, ubiquitous in SA restaurants/pubs etc with close to 20% of total fortified dessert market. Super complexity in current **93** *Wine* ⚝, SAPPA/Peter Schultz trophy: ripe berry fruit, wild scrub/herbaceous whiffs with mint/liquorice and marzipan hints in extra-smooth, lightly spirity palate. Good now, elbow room for 10-15 vintages' development. Tintas francisca, barocca, roriz, with souzão, pontac, malvasia rey. 57 mths 20 yr old Limousin casks. 18,9% alc, 108 g/ℓ sugar.

Alphen Mondial

BELOW are the first fruits of a collaboration between the Cloete-Hopkins family, original owners of the old-Cape Alphen label, and African Wines & Spirits to re-launch Alphen as a quality brand. To follow is a premium range from Constantia vineyards.

> **Pinotage** ⚝ 🆕 🏆 Lots of plummy pinotage juiciness (and some tannins, so no pushover); tasty med-bodied **99**. 13% alc.

Chardonnay ⚝ Higher orders of zinginess in **99** compared to pvs; tastebud-perking citrus fruit. **Sauvignon Blanc** ☆ 🆕 **99** not knock your socks off style, but amiable quick quaffing.

Alto Estate

Stellenbosch (see Stellenbosch map) • Tasting & sales Mon—Fri 9—5 Sat 9—12.30 Closed Sun • Owner Lusan Holdings • Winemaker Schalk van der Westhuizen (since 2000) • Vineyards 100 ha • Production 459 tons 33 174 cases • PO Box 118 Lynedoch 7603 • Tel (021) 881-3884 • Fax (021) 881-3894

HEMPIES DU TOIT and Schalk van der Westhuizen, veritable Cape institutions (du Toit almost a quarter century at Alto, van der Westhuizen a lifetime at Neethlingshof — he was born on the property 47 vintages ago), suddenly got the fidgets in 2000 (a millennium condition?) and ended up each in a different cellar. Du Toit moved down the road to run his own Annandale operation while van der Westhuizen rose to these high Helderberg slopes (owned, like Neethlingshof, by Lusan Holdings, so the change of scenery is within same group). Though Alto is a smaller cellar, this is no downsize for the gentle giant who's probably best known for his gorgeous NLH desserts. "Being able to dedicate all my time and attention to red wines" is what vdW now regards as his most exciting opportunity.

⚝**Cabernet Sauvignon** Ageworthy, top rated cab, classically structured, needing time to reach peak. Cassis and plums, with hints of mocha and almond, bursting from deep ruby **97**, announcing concentrated and well balanced palate with fine, silky tannins and satisfying finish. Still tight — give it time. 13,2 alc; 20 mths new Fr oak. **96** ⚝ reflects troublesome vintage with vegetal nose, lighter body (12,5% alc), but well balanced. **95** ⚝⚝ *Wine* ⚝ opulent, massive, mouth-expanding concentration. No **92–94**.

⚝**Rouge** Many variations on the grape theme for one of the grand old Cape wine institutions, with merlot now playing a more central role in what was a shiraz-driven blend up to **84**. Latest incarnation **97** has merlot at 65%, cab 24% shiraz 11%: fragant, spicy fruit-packed, high-toned nose. Well balanced, with modest 12,5% alc. **96** VG has bigger body (13% alc) yet somewhat lighter effect, showing acid bones (49% merlot, 25% cab, 17% cab f, 9% shiraz). These 18 mths Fr oak — new for the cab, remainder 2nd fill.

⚝**Port** Modern and rather delicious. **97** approaching Portuguese-style balance (18,2 alc; 92 g/ℓ sugar), but Cape-style varietal composition: 100% shiraz. Nose flaunts prunes, smoky aniseed; dark chocolate and burnt orange-peel held in tight grip of alc and acid. Lingering finish. First in old 300 ℓ barrels 36 mths, now in chic 500 ml bottles. Available only from cellar.

Altydgedacht Estate

Durbanville (see Durbanville map) • Tasting & sales Mon—Fri 9—5 Sat 9—1 • Cellar tours by appointment • Owners Parker family • Winemaker Oliver Parker (since 1980) • Viticulturists John Parker (since 1976) & Gerhard Fourie (since 1997) • Vineyards 130 ha • Production 1 000 tons (5 500 cases own label) 50/50 red/white • PO Box 213 Durbanville 7551 • Tel (021) 976-1295 • Fax (021) 976-8521

THE PARKER FAMILY'S fine winemaking motivation is probably more pressing than most: their 415 ha estate is an oasis amid spreading suburbia, and winemaker Oliver Parker echoes neighbours in the same position when he defines their future goals: "To ensure, through the successful production of premium quality grapes and wine, that the Durbanville area can survive increasing urban pressure." There's a joint strategy (see Durbanville Hills entry) to achieve this end, but it starts in each farm's vineyards. Here, on 3 centuries old Altydgedacht, brother John Parker has been overseeing the conversion of grainland and pasture ("some of our best soils") to red wine varieties; 130 ha are now under vines, and the estate's first Merlot will be released during 2001. This range has always been notable for its character and individuality — no little grey wines from these dryland vineyards, air-conditioning courtesy of nearby Table Bay.

- **Merlot** New "A wine to enjoy with good food, or for that matter, to add sparkle to a not-so-good meal," says John Parker, wearing his marketer's hat. We say **99** also good on its own: silky milk choc, sweet violet scents, fine charry oak backdrop and enough svelte tannins for 3–6 yrs' keeping. 8 mths new Nevers casks. 175 cases.

- **Pinotage** Accessible, new-style pinotage since **93**, lifted by Am oak, ±30% new. **97**, **95** Wine best of recent vintages; latest **98** promising, though perhaps a late bloomer. Usual fleshy plum, banana tones, vanilla spice and choc. Easy, open, soft tannins for now and 4–6 yrs. 6 mths barrelled. 13,7% alc. 580 cases. **96** more understated, in line with vintage.

- **Shiraz** Fast forward to **99** (pvs version rated was **96**) where signature smoky, charry tones greet you, long quite grippy tannins hold your attention. Fragrant menthol, wild scrub add to spicy allure, which on past form should last 6 yrs or longer. 8 mths Fr/Am casks. 13% alc. 500 cases.

Gewürztraminer Dry version, rare in Cape. Unusually subdued in **00**, perhaps slow off the blocks (in any case, these better after yr); signature litchi and rose petal, plus whiffs of lime. Lightly chilled, good aperitif, or with curries, Cape Malay cuisine. Med/full-bodied. 552 cases. **Sauvignon Blanc** Classic Dbnville sauvignon aromatics of capsicum, cat's pee, green tea in **00**; ripe guava materialises unexpectedly in palate, carries into arrestingly dry finish. Individual style. 13,4% alc. 841 cases. **Chatelaine** Delightful floral/spicy semi-sweet white, bukettraube/gewürz combo invariably smooth, fragrant, inviting. Anyone/where/time wine. **00** bit drier than pvs at 13 g/ℓ sugar. Med-bodied.

Also available, not tasted for this ed: **Cabernet Sauvignon 98** Last (95) rating in the guide, **Barbera 98** Pvs 96.

Amani

Stellenbosch (see Stellenbosch map) • Tasting & sales daily 10—4 (Dec-Apr) otherwise Tue—Fri 10—4 Sat 10—1 • Cellar tours as above • 'Sit down' tastings, including cellar tour/barrel tasting by arrangement (max 20 people) • Bring your own picnic (tables/umbrellas provided) • Views • Gallery of authentic African artefacts, paintings, sculpture • SA fine-art exhibitions year-round (featured artist/exhibitor rotated bi-monthly) • Wheelchair-friendly • Owners Mark &

Hillary Makepeace • Winemaker Mark Makepeace (since 2000) • Consulting viticulturist/winemaker Rod Easthope (since 2000) • Vineyards 32 ha • Production 160 tons 8 000 cases (4 000 own label) 85% white 15% red • PO Box 12422 Die Boord 7613 • Tel (021) 905-1126 • Fax (021) 905-4404 • E-mail wine@amani.co.za

MARK AND HILLARY MAKEPEACE are delighted by their mention, twice during 2000, in reputation-make-or-break US magazine, *Wine Spectator*, as a South African new-comer with the potential to produce world class Sauvignon Blanc. But decidedly not copy-cat stuff. Here's a winery (with a Swahili name) which celebrates its African roots. Which showcases the creativity of the continent in exhibitions of African arts and crafts. Which disassociates its architecture from the colonial Cape-Dutch style Amani is in the "urban African contemporary genre not another thatched gable". The Makepeaces urge: "Forget about the Loire, Napa Valley and Marlborough district. This is a truly African winery." And on the cellar's roof terrace, with its Imax-impact sea, mountain and vineyard wrap-around, who'd hanker after anywhere else? Mark Makepeace marks the new millennium with a new challenge — he's taken over the winemaking from French/US-trained Cathy Marshall; brilliant New Zealander Rod Easthope (ex-Rustenberg, now consulting) is holding his hand in vineyard (4 ha of shiraz newly planted) and winery. "He put together a 'paint by numbers' winemaking spec for me."

✿ **Merlot** New Impressive first appearance, though **99** deserves yr or so for con-siderable charms to fully emerge. Complex plum, spice array, extra berry inter-est from splash cab, sprinkle earth in firm dry finish. This a 'once-off': fruit ex-Cordoba and one of its neighbours; from 2000 Amani grapes exclusively. 13,8% alc. 1 000 cases.

✿ **Chardonnay** ▽ Elegant style, trademark peachy succulence introduced with **98**, sold out after one showing at US trade show. Snatches of toast, cinnamon in understated follow-up **99** ✿, plus yellow peach in broad, satiny, lingering palate. Low 3 t/ha yield. Barrel fermented/aged 9 mths, 1st/2nd fill Fr oak. 13% alc. 1 000 cases.

Chenin Blanc Lightly oak-aged, characterful example of this ubiquitous-in-Cape variety. Self-imposed 'declassification' in 2000 means no follow-up to attractive debut **99** ✿. **Sauvignon Blanc** ✿ ▽ Partially barrelled version offers good spread of herbaceous, lime, fig flavours in **00** mouthfilling palate with clean bite of acid. Mark Makepeace's gourmet serving suggestion: Norwegian salmon parcels and green pepper sauce. 13% alc. 2 000 cases. **Sculpted Blanc** ✿ Pocket friendly varietal allsort, good everyday dry quaffing (±R12 from cellar door). Latest **99** also the last. **Charlotte** ✿ New After the Makepeaces' 4-yr-old daughter. Successful "first attempt at making a 'sticky'". **00** from lightly botrytised chenin, Fr oak aged; fragrant dried apricot, crystallised pineapple in zestily sweet palate. 14,8% alc. From tasting locale only. 500 cases.

. . . .

Ambeloui Wine Cellar ▼

Hout Bay (see Constantia map) • Tasting, sales & cellar tours "by appointment but very welcome" • Groups welcome • Owners Nick & Ann Christodoulou • Winemaker/viticulturist Nick Christodoulou • Vineyard 0,6 ha • Production 400 cases 100% MCC • PO Box 26800 Hout Bay 7872 • Tel (021) 790-7386 • Fax (021) 790-7873 • E-mail ntc@icon.co.za

FINANCIAL INDUSTRY exec (and keen sailor) Nick Christodoulou bought a plot to build a home near the sea. Then sparkling wine became an overriding passion and in true Champagne style he excavated a cellar under the family's Hout Bay home. What the *cave* lacks the traditional chalky walls, it more than makes up in atmospheric vaulted ceilings and traditional riddling *pupîtres*. And with total production of just 400 cases, there's a distinct European *garagiste* air about the place. Local interest is spreading, and a neighbour on a smallholding is now growing bubbly grapes for Christodoulou. Holding some base-wine in reserve, he's hoping to realise a dream of ultimately releasing sparklers with 3 or more years on the lees — adding yet more authenticity to this boutique winery *sur mer*.

🌟 **Miranda Brut MCC** These serious, classic (pinot noir/chardonnay) méthode champenoise bubbles honour the Christodoulou daughters. First **98**, still available, named after oldest Lisa, "released for the millennium with great success". Follow-up **99** 🌟 features marginally higher pinot fraction (70%) but same delicate, almost dainty feel. Lovely youthful floral bouquet, some light redcurrant/strawberry and good crisp finish. 300 cases.

Annandale
New 🍷

Stellenbosch • Tasting & sales by appointment • Owner/winemaker Hempies du Toit • Tel (021) 881-3560/1 or 082 895 8960 • Fax (021) 881-3562 • E-mail annandale@telkomsa.net

THERE AREN'T ENOUGH hours in the day for Hempies du Toit since he took up residence on his own Annandale property. This rugged ex-Springbok was winemaker at nearby Alto for over two decades, and his departure cuts a deep family tie (father Piet was Alto's cellarmaster and later co-owner from 1959 to 1988, when his son took over). Part of the Annandale property, some of which Hempies du Toit has owned since 1982, was originally planted to broccoli: "The fact that veggies were grown here really built up the soil. You can already see it in the new growth of the vines," he beams. It's a red wines only operation: an earthy Cabernet Sauvignon premiered in 96, the horse on the label reflecting the farm's proud equestrian past as the Annandale Riding School. Shiraz and a blend will be next, followed eventually by port.

🌟 **Cabernet Sauvignon** A horse of a different colour — not an Alto clone, though there's recognisable breed and promise, plus plenty of interest and substance for those who can't wait the 5–6 yrs **97** needs to give its best. Ripe, fairly chewy blackberries, toast/woodsmoky whiffs recurring in palate with tobacco, flecks of choc. 18 mths 300 ℓ Fr casks. 1 500 cases. Not a blockbuster yr, and this reflects it, though at 13,2% alc weightier than **96** 🌟, which *is* a clone — of **97** — in somewhat lighter, lower keyed form, with more pronounced tobacco/straw character.

Apostles Falls see International Wine Services

Arlington Beverage Group

Stellenbosch • Managing director Richard Addison • Production 100 000 cases (40 000 own labels) • PO Box 1376 Stellenbosch 7599 • Tel (021) 794-6697 • Fax (021) 794-3990 • E-mail avi@arlingtnbeverage.com abg@adept.co.za • Website www.arlingtonbeverage.com

ARLINGTON is involved in product development, sales, marketing and export of SA wines to European and, more recently, American outlets and restaurants. The following own-label wines, unavailable for tasting, are made by Riebeek Winery and Darling Cellars: A Few Good Men, Hutton Ridge, Millbrook, Landsdowne and Rocheburg (the latter both New). Arlington also represents a number of top SA wine properties in the international market.

Arniston Bay see Vinfruco

Ashanti
🍷 🍷 🍷 🍷

Paarl (see Paarl map) • Tasting & sales Mon—Fri 9—5 Sat 10—4 Tasting fee R5 refundable with purchases • Cellar tours by appointment • Il Casale Restaurant (see Eat-out section) • Views • Wheelchair-friendly • Owner Ashanti Estates (Pty) Ltd • General Manager Charlto Opperman • Winemaker Sydney Burke (since 2000), with Nelson Buthelezi, Johan Fortuin, Willie Claasen • Viticulturist Louis Hitchcock (since 1992), with Jacob Fortuin • Vineyards 96 ha • Production

500 tons 34 000 cases 65% red 25% white 5% rosé • PO Box 934 Huguenot 7645 • Tel (021) 862-0789 • Fax (021) 862-2864 • E-mail info@ashanti-wines.com sales@ashanti-wines.com • Website http://ashanti-wines.com

WHAT'S NEW in this cosmopolitan corner of Paarl? Let's see, that would be Sydney Burke, who's stepped into the energetic shoes of Frenchman Jean-Vincent Ridon, now making his own-label Signal Hill range from the Agusta cellar. Unassuming Bourke has been making wine since the age of 10, initially in dad's garage — "really awful" — and more fruitfully at Steenberg in Constantia. Also new is a permanent local residence for Swiss-born Manfred Schoeni, the Chinese art-dealer and restaurant owner who's been a mostly long-distance presence here since he and a syndicate bought the Languedoc farm from Nederburg and gave it its present chic Swahili name. Also fresh on the property are Alsatian sommelier-patron Marc Friederich and the Il Casale restaurant with its new wave Cape-Mediterranean cuisine, the epitome of culinary cool. New, too, are regraftings of voguish red varieties like mourvèdre, zinfandel and sangiovese, which will bring the eventual red:white ratio to 75:25. In the works is a flagship red, Ashanti Dôme, after Schoeni's swanky Shanghai restaurant (where Ashanti wines are popped faster than many international high-flyers).

Premium range

- ✿**Cabernet Sauvignon 98** cassis/blackberry fragrance elegantly woven with oaky spice. Some quite austere background tannins noted in pvs ed coming to fore, so suggest enjoy over next yr or 2 while still at peak. Yr oaked, 60% new casks. 13,7% alc. 4 000 cases.

- ✿**Malbec** Sweetly ripe **99** features good cassis/mulberry concentration, long yielding tannins. By contrast, unoaked **00**'s ✿ astringency needs taming by strong/rustic food. 14% alc. 424 cases.

- ✿**Pinotage** ▼ Establishing itself as one of the top examples in Cape. **99** reprise of luscious mulberry fruit, velvety texture, satisfyingly long finish of pvs. Bigger tannin structure should extend the pleasure over good 4–6 yrs.

- ✿**Zinfandel** New Some floral aromas, concentrated flavours of sweet strawberry jam in full-bodied **00**, one of very few new zinfandels in Cape. Juicy, supple, with good dry tannins. Drink now or keep 2–3 yrs. Not oaked. 13,2% alc. 400 cases.

Shiraz New Too young to rate, **00** seems set for a fine ✿ debut. Super shiraz aromatics — some wild scrub, swirling woodsmoke — over ripe mulberry fruit, big supple tannins. Promising. 13,6% alc. 525 cases. **Chardonnay** Untasted for this ed. Pvs **98** rated ✿. **Chenin Blanc Reserve** ✿ New Showy, muscular barrel fermented **99** ripples with alc (14,8%), mouth expanding tropical flavour (mango/banana/papaya), backed by sweet vanilla, aromatic charry oak. Statement wine which needs rich food (casserole of guinea fowl could be good) to match its weighty intensity. 1 400 cases.

'Second label' (to be named)

Red Dragon ✿ Sappy mulberry/plum fruit tweaked for easy/early drinking, yet under **99**'s upfront juiciness are some chunky tannins which won't be intimidated by robust or spicy food. Unusual blend cab/mourvèdre/pinotage. 13,4% alc. 1 700 cases. **Blush** ✿ **00**, like pvs, smoothly dry blend pinotage/cab. Lightly chilled, chic with a fresh salad, curry or BBQ (though beefy 15% alc could almost be a meal in itself). **Peak** ✿ sophisticated white aperitif, very different in **00** to previous: now unwooded, off-dry, with gentle peachy tones from chenin, guava from colombard (new in blend), citrus tailnotes from chardonnay. 13% alc. 4 500 cases.

Ashbourne

THESE are Hamilton Russell Vineyards' premium priced, single vineyard 'terroir' wines, grown and vinified to reflect the specific site chosen for each variety. See also Hamilton Russell Vineyards.

✿✿Pinot Noir Unmistakable family resemblance between these and HRV siblings, but greater amplitude, depth and complexity here — with HRV's inimitable restraint. **99** delivering all-round greater intensity of flavour, more extract and presence (though slightly less weight at 13,1% alc — vs 13,6%). Terrific broad, truffly palate layered with ripe cherry/berry, still closed mid-2000 (as was the pvs **97** *Wine* ✿ at same stage of development). 2 mths' extra Fr oak (11 mths) impart the now familiar densely packed tannins, which promise super development. Only 280 cases. No **98**.

✿✿Chardonnay 99 to be kept back extra yr before release (bottled with elevated sulphurs). Serious oaking — 100% new Fr, 8 mths — gives pleasing mid-palate glycerol 'sweetness', keeps the lemon/lime flavours in warm embrace. This well-balanced by quite a tight acid line, giving impression of more acidity than the HRV counterpart. Statement wine with excellent ageing potential. 12,6% alc. 280 cases. First was **96**, no **97**.

Ashton Co-operative ♀

Ashton (see Robertson map) • Tasting & sales Mon—Fri 8—12.30; 1.30—5 Sat 9—12.30 • Cellar tours by arrangement • Wheelchair-friendly • Owners 94 members • Winemaker Marna Brink (since 1995) • Consulting viticulturist Leon Dippenaar (VinPro) • Vineyards 1 200 ha • Production ±20 000 tons (10 000 cases own label) 21% white 10% red 69% distilling wine/concentrate • PO Box 40 Ashton 6715 • Tel (023) 615-1135 • Fax (023) 615-1284

"BLOCK SELECTION" — earmarking prime parcels, designated for specific wines — is no small task when you're drawing on 1 200 ha of vineyards in the Robertson valley, farmed by 94 co-op members. But winemaker Marna Brink is undaunted in the quest for "better quality grapes and wine", and has the assistance of VinPro viticultural consultant Leon Dippenaar. The friendly range represents only a third of the grapes handled here — the bulk is destined for distilling and fruit concentrate — but expansion of the red wine cellar heralds an upcoming adjustment of this ratio.

> **Chardonnay** ✿✿ 😊 Look here first for good value quaffing — but note, too, strapping 14% alc which not all that apparent in latest **00**, with light vanilla spice from barrel fermentation/ageing in new 300 ℓ Fr/Am casks. Plenty of tropical melons, some citrus and bracing dry finish. 300 cases. **Colombard** ✿✿ 😊 Unfettered by oak, perfumed tropical fruit pops out of the glass in briskly dry-finishing **00**. Bigger than pvs at nearly 13% alc. 1 250 cases.

Cabernet Sauvignon ✿ Usual big grippy palate, brisk acidity in med-bodied **00**; good for cutting the fat on a barbequed chop. **Ruby Cabernet** ✿ New Unpretentious, light-toned quaffing style (though substantial 13,5% alc), some undemanding tannins in **98**. 500 cases. **Shiraz** ✿ Current **98** not developing in bottle nearly as well as previous. 13,2% alc. 750 cases. **Satyn Rooi** ✿✿ 50/50 ruby cab/pinotage. Some light black berry tones in current **99**, which not as generous, inviting as pvs. Unwooded. 13,5% alc. 1 000 cases. **Colombar-Chardonnay** ✿ **00** relaxed summer swigging; very lightly oaked; full bodied. Good dry finish. **Pétillant Blanc** Lightly spritzy semi-sweet white from **99** muscat de frontignan/colombard. Screwtop. 1 000 cases. **Bukettraube Late Harvest** ★ Warm vintage mirrored in prematurely aged, fairly subdued **99**. Some light muscat tones. Low level 11% alc. 500 cases. **Special Late Harvest** ✿✿ Particularly well priced **00**, light, airy semi-sweet white; lovely spring-blossom fragrance, good sugar/acid ratio. Muscat de frontignan. Lowish 11,4% alc. 750 cases. **Red Muscadel 98** ⚡ Bright copper-pink fortified dessert, no longer so fresh, forwardly muscatty as last yr. 750 cases. **White Muscadel** ⚹⚹ Buttercup yellow tropical toned **97** loosing its youthful spirity zing, though still a good, soft raisiny mouthful. **96** SAYWS gold. **Port** ⚡ Pleasant jerepigo style **98**, soft easy, fairly dry-tasting. Ruby cab fortified with 3 yr old brandy. 98 g/ℓ sugar, 17,5% alc. **96** gold on SAYWS.

- -

Ashwood Wines

Franschhoek • Not open to the public • Owners Mike Wishart, Paul & David Meihuizen, Brett Paxton, Barry Cock, Neville Carew, David Kenny • Winemaker Clive Hartnell (since Jun 1998) • Production 250 000 cases 50% red 50% white • PO Box 62 Simondium 7670 • Tel (021) 874-1050 • Fax (021) 874-1867 • E-mail info@ashwood.co.za • Website www.ashwood.co.za

NICELY SETTLED into a R3,2-million new Simondium premises, is this very stable, mainly export (65-70%) negociant business. And that's just as well because the "enthusiastic group of wine fanatics" is making sure the SA wine industry and their popular ranges are promoted to all corners of the globe. They put their wines together with "passion influenced by the intended markets", which include the USA, Europe and, more recently, Japan, Thailand, Malaysia and Singapore. Even their winemaker, Clive Hartnell, clocks up air miles, with *three* harvests a year (Zimbabwe, SA and Hungary). And when they take a tea break, they still mean business: wine sales are supplemented by the 600 tons of rooibos and honeybush tea exported annually.

Ashwood range

Medium/upper priced wines. **Cabernet Sauvignon** ⚡ Full-bodied highly individual **99** — exotic pomegranate (!) taste which you'll either love or leave. 13,6% alc. 700 cases. **Chardonnay** ⚹⚹ **99** has some toasty tones from partial oak barrelling; gentle lemony tang gliding into sultry peach in smoothly dry finish. Full-bodied. 13% alc. 750 cases.

Copper Creek range

Uncomplicated, medium priced wines offering "character and drinkability".

> **Ruby Cabernet-Merlot** ⚹⚹ 😊 Honest everyday tipple; good plummy fruit and whiff of vanilla in lightly oaked **99**. ±13% alc. 1 000 cases.

Chardonnay ⚡ Subdued cling-peach aromas in crisp finishing **99**. 13,2% alc. 1 000 cases.

Fairhills range

Buy now, drink tonight wines. Budget priced. **Garnet Red** ⚡ Unpretentious med-bodied varietal allsort. Alternate with mouthfuls of boerewors, winemaker recommends, unpretentiously. Unwooded **NV (99)**. 3 000 cases. **Dry White** ⚡ Smoked Scottish salmon is winemaker's culinary tip for this med-bodied drink-soon **00** quaff, with brisk acidity. From colombard. 1 000 cases.

- -

Astonvale see Zandvliet

Audacia Wines

Stellenbosch (see Stellenbosch map) • Tasting & sales Mon—Fri 9—5 Sat 9.30—5 Sun 12—4 Open public holidays except Christian religious days and New Year Tasting fee R2/wine • Cellar tours by appointment • Bring your own picnic • Walks • Views • Wheelchair-friendly • Owners Trevor & Diane Strydom • Winemaker/general manager Elsa Carstens (since 1999) Viticulturist Elsa Carstens assisted by Willem Booysen • 3 ha (rising to 15) • Production 60 tons 100% red • PO Box 12679 Die Board 7613 • Tel (021) 881-3052 • Fax (021) 881-3137 • E-mail audacia@icon.co.za • Website www.wine.co.za

THE FAMOUS FIVE Bordeaux classics, plus shiraz, make up the blend of varieties slated to revive this property's old red wine reputation. Replanting to bring the vineyard tally up to 18 ha will be completed in 2001, driven by former Elsenburg staffer Elsa Carstens, who's a pro on the farm's tractor (a substitute for the vehicle of her dreams; she's taken a 4x4 driving course in preparation). She names the Malans of Simonsig where she worked as a student as mentors, and a 1999 working season in Napa has added Californian accents to her experience. A tasting room with huge Helderberg views is a new attraction here, and she promises visitors: "We'll always have something audacious up our sleeves."

Cabernet Sauvignon ✿ Unpretentious, undaunting cab (with price tag to match); two vintages available: **98** more relaxed, chocolaty with soft mulberry fruit, **97** bit firmer, more sinewy. Both satisfy. Fr oak aged, 8–14 mths. 500 cases each.

Chardonnay ✿ New Well priced and, like everything here, characterful. Current release is **98** (though **97**, first white under relaunched Audacia label, still available). Later vintage is richer, fuller, more harmonious; citrus/butterscotch attractions amplified by creamy oak and honey. 13,3% alc. 2 500 cases.

- -

Autumn Harvest

FORERUNNER OF MEDIUM-PRICED WINES in SA; by Stellenbosch Farmers' Winery. Includes dry to sweet wines, all boxed except the perlé Crackling, available in screwtops and 1,5 ⌀packs. All NV.

Grand Cru ✫ Bit bland but properly dry; some low key guava freshness. **Crackling** ✿ Colombard-based blend with tingly petillance; balanced, soft, slightly sweet finish. **Stein** ✿ Everything a Stein should be: soft, fruity, semi-sweet, smoothly clean and easy. **Late Vintage** ✫ Ripe, honeyed flavours, smooth and surprisingly long. Better than many bottled versions.

- -

Avondale

Paarl (see Paarl map) • Tasting & sales Mon–Fri 8–5 • Wheelchair-friendly • Views • Owner Avondale Trust • Winemaker Dewaldt Heyns (since 1998) • Viticulturist Peter Sewell (since 1999) • Vineyards 60 ha • Production 400 tons (4 000 cases own label) 80% red 20% white • PO Box 602 Suider-Paarl 7620 • Tel (021) 863-1976 • Fax (021) 863-1534 • E-mail wine@avondalewine.co.za

ULTRA-PHLEGMATIC Dewaldt Heyns caused consternation in this Grieve family owned winery by declaring himself "excited" about the new Cabernet. "We nearly collapsed," laughs Ginny Grieve, who celebrated the millennium planting merlot with husband John and their children. "We were convinced we'd spawned a First Growth." Not quite, as it turns out, but young Elsenburg trained, Rust en Vrede seasoned Heyns certainly has reason to be pleased with the releases from this beautifully restored Paarl farm, portions of which date from around 1813. Since 1996 it's been the Grieves' property (they're the people behind the Vital health products empire), and though gnashingly close to losing the vineyards and atmospheric old cellar in a devastating bushfire (the local *brandweer* arrived, Hollywood like, literally at the last gasp), they're energetically pursuing their goal "to develop this farm as a leader in quality production in Paarl and then in South Africa".

- ✿ **Cabernet Sauvignon 99** delivering on youthful potential spotted in pvs guide: mouthfilling tannins offset by densely 'sweet' mulberry, dark cherry fruit. Decidedly dry finish and good weight add to impressive debut. Aged in all-new oak. Alc close to 13%.

- ✿ **Shiraz** Too young to rate for pvs ed, new barrel fermented/aged 99 (with splash cab) has matured into the classy young adult envisaged. Woodsmoke, char, black fruit, plus violets, oak-spice and Rhônish wild scrub in complex, long mouthful. 13,4% alc. 650 cases.

❉ **Dry Red 99** Don't be fooled by the afterthoughtish name: this generous Paarl red obviously VIP-treated — and nudging four stars. 80% expensively new Fr oaked, remainder 2nd fill. Seriously tasty: some piquant raspberries, blackberries, satisfying satiny tannins. Cab, ruby cab, cab franc (52/42/6). 13,7% alc. 1 200 cases.

❉ **Chenin Blanc 99** has become more luscious with bit of bottle age: peaches and cream texture; drop lemon for instant freshness, drinkability (though 13,3% alc needs watching). 300 cases. Preview of **00** probably finer, ultra-youthful leesy/sherbety tone shows promise.

❉ **Sauvignon Blanc** In pvs ed we urged you to give Fr accented **99** time to fulfil its promise. For the patient, good rewards: forward cut grass, ripe gooseberry now richly expressed; broad fruity with zesty finish. Lightly wooded. 300 cases. Follow-up **00** unoaked; sampled young (so unrated), similar mould to pvs: intense tropical/leesy palate, pear/gooseberry richness. 13,2% alc.

❉ **Eclipse** (Blanc de Blanc in pvs ed) "Bottled during last eclipse of the millennium." All good chenin/sauvignon/chardonnay (54/38/8) characters upfront in **99**, unobtrusively oaked. Cut grass, tropical guava, pineapple in smooth, expansive palate. 300 cases.

❉ **Muscat du Cap** New Individual limited release (210 cases) sweet fortified dessert from top performing, low cropping vyd (4 t/ha). **00** arrives with fragrant basket Seville orange, honeysuckle and freesia, hint vanilla in luscious, unexpectedly zippy palate (despite low 4 g/ℓ acid, powerfully sweet 238 g/ℓ sugar). Good ripple of spirit keeps tastebuds refreshed. Dewaldt Heyns' after-dinner tips: crème brulée, crème caramel or lightly salty cheese.

Chardonnay This **00** still incubating in oak when sampled mid-2000 but already hinting at ❉ future. Headily ripe (14,5% alc) but somehow not too demanding: peach/citrus layered with almond, marmalade, vanilla oak; yeast and lemon zest to finish. Winemaker's table arrangement is perfect: grilled tuna steaks with aubergine, tomato and sweet-pepper ratatouille.

. . . .

Avondvrede ♈

Stellenbosch (see Stellenbosch map) • Tasting & sales by appointment • Owners Enthoven family • Farm manager Dorothea Crafford • Winemaker Gerda van Zyl • Vineyards 8,2 ha • PO Box 152 Klapmuts 7625 • Tel 083-658-0595/ 082-854-5953 • Fax (021) 875-5609

JOHN and Christine Enthoven have been keeping their produce all to themselves since they bought this small wine farm in viticulturally glossy Simonsberg in 1995. Now we know why: their Cabernet is exceptional — on par with the neighbours' (Le Bonheur, Lievland, Warwick included) — and though they're now parting with a small portion (only from the farm, by appointment, so phone ahead for the password), they admit they'd most like to drink the wine "on our own" (and, presumably, with a tiny smattering of customers in John Enthoven's country of origin, Belgium, to which a few cases are exported).

❉ **Koningshof Noble Red** "Classical Bdx type wine" — John Enthoven's phrase — encapsulates the first public release of this label, though **99** initially more 'giving', less reclusive than the Old World model (and certainly far more punchy at 14%+ alc). Supple, almost juicy fruit, elegant cherry fragrance with hints fennel/vanilla, gentle oak which persists into smooth dry finish. Low 4 t/ha yield, 14 mths new Fr oak. 125 cases.

. . . .

Avontuur Estate ♈ ♈ ♏ ♈

Stellenbosch (see Helderberg map) • Tasting & sales Mon—Fri 8.30—5 Sat 9—12.30 Tasting fee R5 for 4 samples • Buffet lunches (served on terrace weather permitting) • Views • Wheelchair-friendly • Owner Tony Taberer • Winemaker Lizelle Gerber (since 1999) • General manager Pippa Mickleburgh (since 1999) • Vineyards 50 ha • Production

± 370 tons (± 300 tons, 25 000 cases own label) 65% red 35% white • PO Box 1128 Somerset West 7129 • Tel (021) 855-3450 • Fax (021) 855-4600 • E-mail avonwine@mweb.co.za

"DEFINITELY a good year for reds," reports Lizelle Gerber, "but the 2000 whites were a challenge." Not the sort to huddle in the trenches when there's a good battle to be fought (Elsenburg-trained Gerber was set for a career in the military when wine-making winked), the cellar captain of this Helderberg wine and thoroughbred farm hung in and eventually completed the "awfully dry and warm" harvest. No doubt her all-female colleagues, and proprietor Tony Taberer, retired tobacco baron and passionate golfer (he's the developer of one of the splashiest links around: Zimbabwe's famous Leopard Rock), are hoping the jockey-sized winemaker will repeat the success of her Sauvignon and Merlot, which garnered respectively silver and bronze medals at the Singapore International Wine Challenge. The wine line, meanwhile, is being refocused into a premium reserve, emblazoned with the Taberer crest (a Bordeaux blend soon to join these upper ranks), with the regular range identified by its own handsome livery. In the vineyard, groomed by GM Pippa Mickleburgh (who also looks after the stud), a new parcel of shiraz has been established.

Merlot 98 VG developing with distinction: initial tannic grip relaxing, generous cassis/blueberry spilling into med-bodied palate seasoned with cinnamon, clove and oak spice. Yr Fr oak, some new. Better than **97** ✿, from fine, cool red wine vintage.

Pinotage 99 hasn't lost its fruity punch in yr since first tasted. Textbook varietal flavours — 'sweet' raspberry, redcurrant topped with cinnamon; still lightly raspy tannins should soften within yr. 14% alc. 12 mths in casks, some new. ± 1 000 cases. Follows **98** ✿ with soft, ripe fruit. **97** under Reserve label, more gamey, nutty flavours, *Wine* ✿.

Chardonnay Reserve (Le Chardon name discontinued) Bold, showy style, but well controlled. Initial **99** oakiness from 100% new barriques now seamlessly woven into super-dense lime/lemon texture. Butterscotch, expensive smoky/toasty oak and some rich lees add sophistication. 14% alc. 350 cases.

Above Royalty (Noble Late Harvest in pvs ed) **99** full blown botrytised dessert from riesling, barrelled 9 mths, two-thirds new oak. Arresting pale orange colour; dried apricot intensity, heady whiffs of muscat; sumptuously sweet palate and quivering acidity. Lingering rich finish. 8,3 g/ℓ acid, 113 g/ℓ sugar.

MCC 2000 Fine example of the méthode champenoise sparkling style. Classic cuvée pinot noir/chardonnay, 5 yrs on lees imparts yeasty richness, toasted nuts intensity; these more apparent in creamy, leesy palate; delicate, superfine mousse refreshes, invigorates. This **NV** improving in bottle (which worth considering when choosing bubbles to ring in the 'real' millennium).

Cabernet Sauvignon ✿ **97** lacks dense cassis, tannic grip of pvs, but some good wild berry fruit, bit of honey/bottle age, good dry finish. Yr oaked, some new casks. ± 900 cases. **Pinot Noir** ♣ Two vintages available, each highly individual, divergent: **97** reeky, farmyardy; **99** with curious wild pomegranate fragrance. 13% alc. 350 cases. **Frantage** ♣ Intriguing cab f/pinotage blend. Latter fills out linear economy of former, though current **97** more herbaceous, vegetal, rustic. Yr oaked, no new casks. **Avon Rouge** ✿ Eminently quaffable, juicy red berry fruit shoe-horned into easy drinking package, broke the Cape mould of austere dry reds a decade ago. To drink rather than store, more pleasure than challenge (pleases palate and pocket). Latest **99** a cab/merlot blend, bit more tannic than pvs, but good raspberry/redcurrant fruit. 13,% alc. **Dolcetto** ✿ Confusingly, not the Piedmontese grape but a semi-sweet red blend (varieties not revealed), unwooded, in tall frosted bottle with colourful, cheeky label. Sappy plums from start to finish. Individual style which will have its adherents. **NV**. 13,5% alc. **Sauvignon Blanc** ✿ Med-bodied, just off-dry **99** ♣ has grown pleasant grassy, animal-like smells. Michelangelo gold. Follow-up **00** marginally finer, drier yet quite fleshy. 580 cases.

Avon Ridge range

Cabernet Franc ✿ Decision not to blend away lightly oaked **99** (Lizelle Gerber's first vintage here) into Frantage was a good one: mouthfilling raspberry, redcurrant ripeness, smoothed/broadened by dollop sugar. **96** (under Avontuur label) *Wine* ✿. **Ruby Blush** ☆ Startlingly pink semi-sweet **99** rosé; high toned 'pink sweets' bouquet. 14% alc. **Chardonnay** ✿ Some muted oaky/caramelised tastes in **99**. Full bodied (14% alc). 2 000 cases. **Sauvignon Blanc-Chardonnay** ✿ Nicely judged off-dry **NV** blend, sauvignon contributing fresh-cut grass/passionfruit aromatics, chardonnay weighing in with broad peachy/oaky tones. 13% alc. **Insensata** ✿ New to this ed. **99** gentle semi-sweet chenin, med-bodied, honeyed tastes freshened by clean acidity.

· ·

Axe Hill

Calitzdorp (see Klein Karoo map) • Not open to the public. Sales from Queens Bottle Store, Voortrekker Road (R62), Calitzdorp • Owners Tony & Lyn Mossop • Winemaker Tony Mossop (since 1996) • Vineyard manager Sydney Cooper (since 1996) • Vineyard 1 ha • Production 6–8 tons 400 cases 100% 'port' • PO Box 43942 Scarborough 7975 • Tel (021) 780-1051 (farm 044-213-3585) • Fax (021) 780-1178 • E-mail tony@axehill.co.za

ONE VERY GOOD REASON to diarise the annual Calitzdorp Port Festival is that it's the only time of the year when this, the Cape's only specialist port cellar, is officially open to the public. Tony and Lyn Mossop, he a top tannery technology consultant (and taster for this guide), she boss of the classy Executive Caterers company, lead hectic lives in Cape Town and are super-frequent flyers abroad — a lengthy stay in Australia most recently. And though you're also certain to find them in the Little Karoo round about Valentine's Day, don't even think of visiting then — they and friends will be up to their knees in touriga nacional and tinta barocca, hand-harvesting and foot pressing the fruits of this 1 ha vineyard. Their property on a dry, rocky hillside — named after the many ancient stone tools uncovered in the planting process — may be minuscule, but its impact has been huge. The first 1997 vintage, quite the most elegantly presented in the country (a Grape 2000 Packaging Award to prove it), instantly earned 5 stars in this guide and sold out in a flash (just a few cases have been kept back, and could pop up at a Nederburg Auction). The 98 — see below — is another marvel. But the Mossops continue to raise the bar — they've acquired another patch of land (with much needed water rights) where they'll plant a few rows of souzão "to complete the cocktail".

✿ **Axe Hill Cape Vintage Port** ▽ **97**, first release of this powerful, individual dessert ("the most traditionally made SA 'port'") bypassed the little leagues and leapt straight into the majors. Follow-up **98** ✿ — fractionally sweeter, touch more tinta b, though still 'correct' varieties, properly foot trodden, old-oak aged, fortified around 20% alc, per the Douro — confidently restates claim to be one of the Cape's finest. Reveals itself in waves: thumbnail floral perfume initially, then cherries and plums, pepper, wisps of smoke. Pattern repeats in palate: ethereal, spirity sensation to start, followed by whoosh of ripe fruit and exotic spice, fanning into long, tangy dry finish. Deeper layering of tannin suggest this a longer term wine than pvs; Mossop ventures 5–10 yrs. But already sensational. Touriga nacional/tinta barocca, yr 500 ℓ old oak, plus yr tank; alc 20%. 7 000 bottles. **97** *Wine* ✿.

· ·

Baarsma see Lyngrove
Babbling Brook see Makro

· ·

Backsberg Estate

♆ ♆ ♆ ♆

Paarl (see Paarl map) • Tasting & sales Mon–Fri 8.30–5 Sat 8.30–1 Tasting fee R5 p/p • Self-guided cellar tour with audio-visual presentation • Tastings for groups of max 20 by arrangement • Bring your own picnic basket • Play area for children • Gifts • Wheelchair-friendly • Owner Michael Back • General manager Charles Withington • Winemaker Hardy Laubser (since 1988) Viticulturist Clive Trent • Vineyards 160 ha • PO Box 537 Paarl 7624 • Tel (021) 875-5141 Fax (021) 875-5144 • E-mail info@backsberg.co.za • Website www.backsberg.co.za

"WE'RE TRYING to do everything better, faster, cleverer and more professionally for our customers," says Michael Back, owner and hands-on cheerleader of this well established wine team, radiating an air of bonhomie and relaxed informality which contradicts their breathless work rate. Mindful that "it's not just the Currie Cup we're playing now, it's the World Cup", over the past 8 years they have sought to become "as viticulturally advanced as possible". To this end a great deal of time is spent analysing the performance of the grapes". A major plus here has been the relationship with itinerant US consultants, Phil Freese and Zelma Long. This has blossomed into a wine partnership, Simunye ('we are one'). To date there has been only a Sauvignon from bought-in grapes (see separate entry), but the range may well be expanded. Meanwhile the Freedom Road project to fund housing on full-ownership basis for long employed staff has proved a long winding road — rocky at times and not yet at its end. Michael Back has been emphatic from the start that the houses should not place a burden on the new owners, who should be able to move in without the added burden of debt. Bureaucratic tangles have tied him up for years, and though funds are already available, not a brick has been laid. Back is optimistic that by the time this edition is published all obstacles will have been cleared. We'll drink to that.

Merlot Steadily improving label ("If I had my way this would be a merlot-only farm!" enthuses Laubser). Elegant, compact rather than blockbusting style. **97** mulberry-fruity, quaffable. **98** notch up, waft of sweet cassis fruit, touches of choc-mint (which should please merlot-philes). Excellent concentration, fine-grained tannins and fresh acidity — a structure which both approachable and long-lasting.

Pinotage Showcases increasing new-clone component (young vines onstream from 98, delivering ±20% of total now, rising to 35%; balance from 33-yr-old vyds). Latest **99** with more intense, focused fruit ('sweet' red cherry, raspberry, wilder forest berries) for more vibrant, exciting effect. Edgy pinotage tannins need some bottle ageing.

Shiraz Old vyds very consistent on this farm though current **98** less exciting. Good whiff of smoky, leathery fruit as befits older clones, smooth rounded fruit, good ripeness from warmer year, some juiciness, the wood supportive and subservient, but fruit curiously unyielding. May yet open out and bloom, so give yr or 2. **97** richer, perhaps most intense Backsberg red of yr.

Klein Babylonstoren A Cape classic and this estate's flagship red. Always a Bdx blend, 50/50 cab/merlot in **98**, with waves of blackcurrant, eucalyptus and fragrant new oak. Dense yet elegant, tannins ripe but still youthful, clean 'pencil shavings' in finish. Well balanced but needs another 2–3 yrs. **95**, standout red wine vintage, extra complexity, gamey whiffs, sweet fruit. **96**, in troubled yr, friendly rather than intense.

Chardonnay Reserve New Seriously good chardonnay, characterised by beautifully integrated oak (only possible with highly concentrated fruit, courtesy of Backsberg's mature chardonnay vyds, among most senior in Cape). Ripe citrus with sniffs of aromatic vanilla, expansive, buttery flavours which spread across the palate. Estate's first Reserve label; selection of **99** barrel (two coopers, Seguin Moreau and François Frères, all new casks). Only 200 cases, released Dec 2000.

John Martin Barrel fermented (80%) sauvignon, one of first in Cape. Broad, bold flavours more typical of farm's sauvignon. Dry, full bodied but not rich or heavy. Excellent food wine, especially with grilled yellowtail. Cloves, vanilla in **00**, plus citrus/gooseberry ripeness. Grown-up, individual, with ability to age a bit.

❀ **Special Late Harvest** Higher star wattage in lovely, lively **00**, sweetness leavened by fresh, cleansing acidity. Pineapple, honey, mimosa, though no botrytis ("We've tried everything but this farm never gets it," laments Laubser). 90% chenin, 10% hanepoot.

❀ **Sparkling Brut** ▼ Distinctive cap classique yeasty/toasty freshness in this new, more sparkly bottling, a 98, first since 93. Lively, almost aggressive attack, tapering to pleasant creaminess, fullness in mid-palate. 2 yrs on lees, further time in your cellar will enhance richness and flesh out the palate. 50/50 chardonnay/pinot noir. Disgorged as necessary.

Chenin Blanc ❀ 😊 Invariably charming, quaffable. **00** made off-dry, tweaked with splash hanepoot for extra perfume. Lightly fruity, dainty and fresh.

Cabernet Sauvignon ❀ One of Cape's most enduring favourites, with solid following. Whistle-clean **98** with cool, green herbaceous fruit, cedarwood whiffs which translate easily into palate, joined by some cassis. Lightish body/texture, some greenish tannins. **Malbec** ❀ A curiosity, one of very few in Cape, only produced when tiny, 1 ha vyd generous enough to produce a crop! Current **97** lovely smoky, oaky fruit, lighter style from cooler vintage. Easy drinking with lighter tannins to match, dry but not austere. **Dry Red** ♣ **00** means what it says: really dry, with some sticky-out tannins and a bit of juice. Blend of all farm's reds plus some volume-extending chenin. Popular as ever. **Rosé** ♣ Semi-sweet style with high-toned cherry fruit, brush of tannin; blend pinotage, merlot, chenin. **NV. Chardonnay** ❀ One of the Cape's first, and still reliable. Ripe lemon-lime in newest **99**, backed by dusty oak, touches of butterscotch. Partially oak fermented, some new casks. Combines freshness with weight. **Rhine Riesling** ❀ Latest semi-dry **00** scented with musky evening flowers and honey. Lively fruit, smooth acidity with just enough plumping sugar to achieve balance. **Sauvignon Blanc** ❀ Tropical whiffs, melons and some gooseberry aroma/flavour; very dry, brisk, but **00** lacks the usual varietal punch. **99** SAA. **Semillon 00** tasted pre blending/bottling, so unrated (pvs barrel fermented **98** ❀). Exotic ginger/pineapple combo, attractive spiciness which persists in juicy, fruity palate to bone-dry finish.

Freedom Road range

Label of Backsberg worker-management project (see intro above). To date a **Sauvignon Blanc 99** (❀).

Simsberg range

Includes **Pinot Noir**, **Cabernet Sauvignon-Merlot** and **Chardonnay**, for export.

. . . .

Badsberg Winery ⚲

Worcester (see Worcester map) • Tasting & sales Mon—Fri 8—7 Sat 10—1 Tasting fee R5 p/p for groups of more than 10 • Cellar tours by arrangement • Wheelchair-friendly • Owners 26 members • Manager/winemaker Willie Burger (since 1998) with Hugo Conradie (since 1996) • Viticulturist Pierre Snyman (VinPro) • Vineyards 1 000 ha • Production 15 000 tons 94% white 6% red • PO Box 72 Rawsonville 6845 • Tel (023) 349-3021 • Fax (023) 349-3023 • E-mail badsberg@lando.co.za

THIS RAWSONVILLE CO-OP celebrates its centenary this year, prompting Willie Burger and Hugo Conradie (who confess to being somewhat homesick during their recent swing through UK and Europe) to reflect on some of the recent changes and achievements. These include producing the champion wood matured Chardonnay at the Young Wine Show. Released under the in-house Chardonnay Sur Lie label,

. . . .

it's available for sampling in the new tasting locale — handily just a brisk walk from the hot springs at Goudini.

⚜Hanepoot Jerepigo Delicate, pretty sweet fortified dessert, **99** wafting narcissus/musk/fresh grape scents with some pine nut/herby surprises in silky, long palate. Balanced. 17,5% alc.

Pinotage ⚜ Pinotage at its most slurpable (though sturdy 13,9% alc certainly needs watching). **99** packed with pure red cherry/raspberry fruit, fresh, polished, not a jagged edge in sight.

Badsberger ⚘ Fresh, lightish summer white, **00** flowery/herby scents and lighter acidity for undemanding sunset sipping. **Chardonnay Sur Lie** ⚜ Breakfast-in-bed **99** spreads marmalade on buttered toast with zesty lime on the side. Med-bodied; chalky/yeasty extras, attractively packaged. 13% alc. **Vin Doux Sparkling** ⚜ Pleasing floral tones, spread with honey, fresh acidity prevents **99** from lapsing into tiring sweetness. **Port** ⚘ Some underripe green tones, little port character. **Special Late Harvest** ⚘ Lighter bodied **99**, overly sweet though somewhat leavened with tangy grapefruit/lime.

Bakenskop see Jonkheer

Barefoot Wine Company

Stellenbosch • Tasting & sales by appointment • Owners Catherine Marshall, Jeff Jolly, Greg Mitchell, Peter Oxenham • Winemaker/logistician Catherine Marshall (since 1997) • Production 20 tons 1 400 cases 100% red • PO Box 13404 Mowbray 7705 • Tel/fax (021) 887-9910 • E-mail wine@barefoot.co.za • Website www.barefoot.co.za

THE SHAREHOLDERS of this small winery may not have a permanent address (or vineyards or cellar), but they don't lack enthusiasm or drive to stay focused. 'We're producing 20 tons now and looking to more than double that in 2 years," says Cathy Marshall, ex-Amani winemaker and now flying solo. After hosting Barefoot tastings at her dining room table, she's looking forward to settling into proper business premises someday. "My office is in the boot of my car," she laughs. A change of grape supplier for the 2000 Pinot should see a step up in quality ("such complexity and depth"), and a new Devon Valley source should further pump up the Shiraz. New is the Pineau des Charentes, which adds a Cognaçais note to the Barefoot friends' French toned repertoire.

⚜Shiraz Rhônish characters lurking last yr now shouting and waving their arms in bold, striking **99**, grown-up and handsome in ebony bottle with Hannetjie de Clercq artwork. Liquorice, woodsmoke, fennel, cracked pepper all distinctly Fr, as is fine tannic edge which cuts incipient ripe-fruit sweetness. Fr oak, 6 mths 3rd–4th fill, then 6 mths new. 13% alc. 275 cases.

⚜Pinot Noir Growing more confident, expansive, by the vintage; acquiring complexity, too, as in **99**, now with smoky oak swirling through cherry/strawberry fruit. Fr oaked, Burgundian cooperage. 13% alc. 800 cases. **98** gentle, spicy, whiffs of mushroom, sweet loam. Follow-up **00**, fruit ex-Muratie, most serious, finest of these; structured to grow into ⚜ with time.

Pineau des Charentes New Courting French ire (?) with name borrowed from traditional Cognac aperitif: grape juice fortified with brandy. Too young to rate, though strawberry/fresh hay tones, sweet/dry palate sensations suggest **00** could crack ⚜.

Barrydale Winery

Tradouw Valley (see Klein Karoo map) • Tasting & sales Mon—Fri 8—5 Sat & public holidays 9—1 • Cellar tours by appointment. • Picnic baskets by arrangement (24 hours' notice needed) or BYO • Gift shop • Garden with outdoor tasting area • Walks • Views • Play area for children • Tour groups • Owners 53 members • Manager/winemaker Riaan Marais (since 1999) • Consulting viticulturists Stephan Joubert, Briaan Stipp (VinPro) • Vineyards 350 ha • Production 3 400 tons (400 tons, 25 000 cases own label) 25% white 10% red 5% rosé, 60% spirits • PO Box 59 Barrydale 6750 • Tel (028) 572-1012 • Fax (028) 572-1541 • E-mail barrywine@dorea.co.za

THE ONLY CAPE CO-OP which has also been a distillery for 60 years, this Little Karoo cellar has successfully remodelled itself as a fine wine producer. The cool Tradouw valley, source of its premium range, was pounced upon by Aussie Robin Day when snuffling out prime fruit for Pernod-Ricard's international Long Mountain label. So is winemaker-manager Riaan Marais going backwards when he does a song and dance about a brandy? Decidedly not. It's just that the time has come to show off some of the skills that for years have disappeared anonymously into merchants' bottles. The 5-year-old Joseph Barry Cape Potstill Brandy released in 2000 is a first for Barrydale, right in step with its quality mission, and the current drive to buff up the image of this underrated and ruggedly beautiful wine region.

Tradouw range

✿ Cap Classique 𝗡𝗲𝘄 Impressive debut with elegant blanc de blancs style brut méthode champenoise sparkler; authentic brioche tastes and fresh, lemony sea-spray bouquet. Fine, almost-creamy texture from all-chardonnay fruit. **NV** (95). 400 cases.

Reserve ✿✿ First Bdx style from this area. Current **97** cab/cab f/merlot blend probably needs drinking while it still has some juice. Yr Fr oak. 500 cases. **Merlot ✱** Herbal/tobacco notes carry into **98** palate, which finishes dry and austere. 13% alc. 180 cases. **Chardonnay Sur Lie** ✿✿ Newest **99** continues New World path broken by **98** VG. Latest with coconut, buttered toast richness, contrasted well with citrus piquancy. Enjoy young. **96** VG.

Barrydale range

Blanc de Noir ✿✿ Barely blush-pink semi-sweet **99**, muscat/jasmine scents, tangy raspberry flavour. Red muscadel. 13% alc. 500 cases. **Chardonnay-Chenin Blanc** ✿✿ Peaches and cream aromas, uncomplicated but mouthfilling dry **99**. 500 cases.

Misty Point range

Red ✿✿ (Pvsly Village Red) "Braai, braai, braai!" Riaan Marais wants to be sure you understand this **00** fuchsia-coloured, fleshy ruby cab/merlot is a BBQ slurper. Got that? 13,5% alc. 2 000 cases. **White ✱** Tropical/floral sniffs in off-dry **99**, fresh lemony tastes. Good simple quaffing. 1 200 cases.

....

Bartho Eksteen Wines   🍷 🍷 🍷

Walker Bay (see Walker Bay map) • Tasting & sales Mon—Sat 9—5 (also Sun 11—1 during school holidays) at Wine & Company, Shop 3, Village Square, Marine Drive, Hermanus • Wide range of hand made cheeses for sale • Picnic baskets by arrangement • Owners Bartho Eksteen & Ailsa Butler (UK) • Winemaker Bartho Eksteen • Production 23 tons 1 500 cases 84% white 16% red • Suite 47 Private Bag X15 Hermanus 7200 • Tel (028) 313-2047 • Fax (028) 312-4029 • E-mail winenco@mweb.co.za

"ADVICE for those who make sauvignon but aren't totally serious and dedicated: rather don't!" Bartho Eksteen knows whereof he speaks. Since leaving nearish-by Wildekrans he's made his reputation on the back of this notoriously fastidious grape. And though he appears mellow, even offhand, there's passion and focus beneath the surface (he names Cloudy Bay's Kevin Judd among the wine people he's most pleased to have met). Now Hermanus-based 'Mr Sauvignon' is branching into shiraz (having compared notes with, among others, Henschke Wines' Prue Henschke during a swing through Australia). Contemplating an own cellar, for now Eksteen uses Dave Johnson's facilities in Hemel-en-Aarde valley when not operating from Eksteen family HQ: the trendy Wine & Company shop managed by equally wine-minded wife, Suné.

....

✿ **Sauvignon Blanc** ✔ Here's the bottom line: buy **00** (because it's good) and drink soon (with — Eksteen's suggestion — grilled salmon drizzled with lemongrass butter). Now read on: **00** reverts to classic flinty raciness after detour into plump tropicality in **99** ✿. Transfusion of soupçon semillon (ex-Beaumont), supercharged in new Fr oak, 2 mths, plus dab sugar (3,9 g/ℓ), broadens **00** palate without deflecting focus from Loire-like dusty grass/cat's pee/capsicum trio. Clever winemaking but, winemaker agrees, this needs drinking in bloom of youth. Grapes ex-Vrede farm (Hemel-en-Aarde valley), Elandsrivier (Villiersdorp). 13,5% alc. 1 300 cases.

Shiraz 〖New〗 Difficult to definitively measure this **00** toddler, sampled ex-barrel mid-2000, but all signs point towards ✿ adulthood perhaps 3–5 yrs away. Intense shiraz fruit (choc-mulberry, red berry), eye-catching plum colour with black/purple centre, supple long tannins all augur well for future good development.

....

Bay View see Longridge

....

Beaumont Wines

Walker Bay (see Walker Bay map) • Tasting, sales, cellar tours Mon—Fri 9.30—12.30; 1.30—4.30 Sat morning by appointment • Tasting/tours for groups by appointment (picnic-style lunches available) Fee quoted on enquiry • Bring your own picnic on special open days (also art exhibits on these days) • Self-catering cottages • Walks/hikes by arrangement • Wheelchair-friendly • Owners Raoul & Jayne Beaumont • Winemaker Niels Verburg (since 1995) • Viticulturist Sebastian Beaumont (since 1999) • Vineyards 50 ha • Production 250 tons • PO Box 3 Bot River 7185 • Office tel (028) 284-9194 • Cellar tel (028) 284-9450 • Fax (028) 284-9733 • E-mail beauwine@netactive.co.za

'CHARM' is a dodgy word. In some hostelries it's used to cover cracks in the walls, livestock in the bed. If it oozes it's too much, if it's too thinly applied it's a veneer. Here, on this Bot River farm, it's unaffected, and comes in exactly the right dose, apt for the Beaumont family, the wines they started making in 1993, the atmospheric old cellar, the stay-over cottages, the lot. Add 'unconventional' and 'individual' and you'll get the full flavour. Here's the cast of characters, and we mean characters: Jayne Beaumont (artist, wine stylist, market-force), Raoul Beaumont (farmer, biker, yachtsman), Sebastian Beaumont (viticulturist, epitome of young cool), Niels Verburg (winemaker, Rhône ranger, chenin fanatic). Below are the wines — attractive personalities all, with the Pinotage a special wow with the eminent tasters from *Decanter* magazine. Here's the latest news: the Mourvèdre is an original (which follows at Beaumont), the first unblended bottling of this variety in the Cape; the 50 ha vineyards are in the throes of replanting, with the emphasis on more shiraz. And here's the weather report: 3 days before Christmas 1999, disaster wrapped in the form of huge hailstones rocketed down, wiping out two-thirds of the grapes — and all Raoul Beaumont's pears. Only the bravest survived, which means the 2000 vintage wines will be very scarce indeed "but outstanding quality" Verburg stresses. Fans had better place orders very quickly.

✿ **Pinotage** ✔ New-wave SA pinotage incorporating cool Walker Bay influence, quite different to Stbosch/Paarl variants. Individuality heightened by naturally fermented portion. **99**, very good yr, youthfully vivid purple; big, bold fruit — spicy plums and brush of honey — chunky tannins contrasting with touch Am oak (8%) for interesting sweet-dry effect. 8 mths oaked, some new casks. 12,9% alc. 3 000 cases. Peek into **00** barrel reveals good 'sweet' fruit, fine concentration, coffee/choc from higher proportion (20%) Am oak. 675 cases (only).

✿ **Mourvèdre** 〖New〗 Collector's item: first varietal bottling in SA. Debut **99** amazingly intense for mere 2 yr old vines: striking inky, almost black colour; dense, oaky, shiraz like fruit cocooned in big mouthcoating tannins. 1 t production, 4 mths all-new Am barrels ("ran out of tank space"). 12,5% alc. 75 cases. Preview of **00** ✿ intense, perfumed with black plum/mulberry evocative of Fr syrah. Single (Fr) barrel, oaked "as long as possible". Future to be blended with Shiraz.

✿ **Shiraz** ✅ Move to spicier, more elegant mode inaugurated with **98**. Continues with Rhône like **99** ✿, lightish tone and weight (12,7% alc), avoids New World brashness ("shiraz should be like pinot noir"). No shortage of savoury tang (smoky bacon, salt and pepper). Portion fruit ex-Kaapzicht, Stbosch. 8 mths oaked, mainly Fr 1 500 cases. **00** barrel sample markedly richer, weightier (14% alc) yet elegant, fine grip.

✿ **Hope Marguerite Chenin Blanc Barrel Reserve** ✅ Designer chenin, tweaked in vyd/cellar to appeal to "serious chenin fans"; intense and ageworthy. Current **98** reflects vintage's warm generosity; toasted almond richness deserves yr at least to gain full opulence (will give pleasure for further 5). 12,5% alc. 140 cases. Softer, creamier than **97**, with racy, fresh acidity. These from extra-mature (40 yrs) single vyd, low-cropped (4 t/ha), entirely barrel fermented/aged ±18 mths on lees. Upcoming **99** waxy; finely structured, good carrythrough from mid to end palate. Standard **Chenin Blanc** ✅ From old low yielding vines on own farm. Signature 'wet wool' character in med-bodied **99**; high natural acidity gives fresh feel, clean citrus finish. Lightly wooded. "Goes really well with Indian/Thai cuisine". 500 cases. Next-up **00**, with new barrel fermented portion, remarkably intense. Retains house's tauter, more classic style.

✿ **Chardonnay** ✅ Returns to steely elegance after meander into **98** billowing fatness. New Burgundian clone making presence felt in **99**, filling mid-palate with bigger, purer fruit. Fermentation with champagne yeast gives racy grip to honey/butter richness. Best in 2–3 yrs and then with oysters. 1st crop from new vines. Barrel fermented/aged 9 mths. 560 cases. **00**, from barrel, bigger than usual, clean acid gives nice zing.

✿ **Sauvignon Blanc** ✅ **00** best yet, more intense than any pvs. Racy, big, mouthfilling; pungent cut grass and tropical fruit, grapefruit tang. Sweetish feel from generous 13% alc. Good match for rich linefish. 350 cases.

✿ **Goutte d'Or** Honeyed botrytis dessert, wood matured, which rare in Cape. Infusion of 40% semillon, extended oaking in **99** helps raise the quality bar (and star wattage to ✿). Lovely marmalade viscosity with an edgy sherbet finish. Less botrytis, substantially drier tasting (though sweeter in analysis) than all-chenin **98** ✿, with pineapple/lime flavours and strong noble rot character (25%). These ±300 cases. 375 ml. **97 VG** *Wine* ✿.

Ariane ✿ Dry red blend inaugurated with **98**, with dash tinta b. Current **99** conventional Bdx cuvée (cab/merlot/cab f, 42/33/25) offering generous dark chocolate cloaked in firm, almost austere tannins. These need 4–6 yrs to become velvety. 8 mths Fr oak, some new. **Raoul's Old Basket Press Rustic Red** ✿ Spicy ripe, earthy flavours, muscular tannins. **00** mainly tinta with splodge pinotage. 1 000 cases. **Jayne's Old Basket Press Walker Bay White** ✿ (Jayne's Walkabout White in pvs ed) Easy drinking unwooded chenin. **00** with charming fruit basket (apricot, peach, pineapple), zippily fresh. 13% alc. 350 cases. **Vintage Port** ✿ Gives new meaning to the term 'home made': foot-pressed (at end-of-harvestparty), bottled directly from barrel, hand labelled. **99** 70/30 tinta/pinotage, two yrs in old wood; fruity 'cake mix' flavours, quite dry finish. 100 cases.

· ·

Bellevue Estate New

Stellenbosch • Not open to the public • Owner Houdamond Trust • Winemakers/viticulturists Dirkie Morkel (since 1979), with ACF van der Merwe (since 2000) • Vineyard manager J Pypers (since 1985) • Vineyards 190 ha • Production 1 200 tons (± 113 tons own label) 75% red 25% white • PO Box 33 Koelenhof 7605 • Tel (021) 882-2055 • Fax (021) 882-2899

THE NEW MILLENNIUM sees this member of the elite corps of wineries along the Bottelary Hills marching out in public for the first time, and immediately looking like

... *continued on page 66*

· ·

SupremeCorq.® The closure that keeps wine exactly as the winemaker *intended*.

Introducing SupremeCorq, a revolutionary

cork that opens with a regular corkscrew, won't

break, and virtually eliminates the leakage and

off-flavours associated with traditional closures.

Which explains why SupremeCorq is used by

hundreds of wineries worldwide. To learn more,

please visit our Web site at www.supremecorq.com

or call us at tel+27 21 872 8082, or fax+27 21 872 8863.

SUPREME**CORQ**®

THE NEW TRADITION ™

Above: **Marianne Katts** has been breaking new ground: first female assistant winemaker at Nederburg; first winner of the Patrick Grubb Scholarship (jointly funded by veteran auctioneer Grubb and the Nederberg Auction, it gives aspiring winemakers/viticulturists overseas opportunities). A qualified nursing sister, Katts started as a lab assistant (sidelining in first aid), completed two winemaking courses, then popped up in Australia at the University of Adelaide's Murray Institute via her sponsorship. Eikendal's cellar supervisor **Leonard O'Rein**, who won the 2000 scholarship, jetted off to Stimson Lane Vineyards to pick up some California know-how.

Left: Winemakers **Schalk-Willem Joubert** (centre) and **Clive Radloff** (on his left) with cellar staff at R&R are reaping the benefits of global networking. Benjamin de Rothschild and Anthonij Rubert are the Rs behind this new-generation partnership; the French connection is strengthened by consulting wine guru Michel Rolland and flying winemaker Yann Buchwalter (third from right).

Below left: Racing ahead on the road to empowerment is the **Thandi** initiative, solidly backed up by the **Paul Cluver Estate** team (Cluver, second from left back, was the original motivator). Their winning formula: serious intent bolstered by their company credo: "With love we grow together".

Below: **Carmen Stevens**, SFW's diminutive assistant winemaker, makes the wines for Tukulu (an innovative joint venture between SFW, the local community and a group of black liquor retailers), the first 'woman of colour' to hold such a position in SA. There's a lot resting on her slender shoulders but she responds with charm and grace – and wines which stand up and get noticed.

Above: Father to son: **Adi** and **André Badenhorst**. This youngster's solid Cape roots (grandfather was farm manager at Groot Constantia, father is wine director at Constantia Uitsig and chair of the Constantia Wine Route) have helped him to branch out confidently at the revitalised Rustenburg property, with its brand new spirit embodied in the motivated and empowered staff.

It's irresistible if it's in glass.

Consol
glass

Right: **Johan Reyneke**, artist wife **Mila** and Scotsman **James Farquharson** (whose day-job is winemaker at Lievland) with their shareholders in Reyneke Wines (staff are involved in a profit-sharing initiative). This eco-friendly extended family shares a commitment to preserving the natural environment - and a penchant for surfing.

Left: **Jenny Ratcliffe** (assistant selector), **Alan Mullins** (selection manager) and **Ivan Oertle** (senior buyer) select and buy the wines for local super-chain Woolworths. Tasters and trend spotters of note, their combined talents will now be obvious to everyone, with specialist wine stores in every branch by 2002. Trained and motivated staff complete the package, which is stamped with Woolies' special brand of credibility.

Actively involved in the S

We like to think of ourselves as more than just supporters of the So
prestigious Diners Club Winemaker or Winelist of the Year Awards,
Wine Society, our hands-on involvement helps in the creation of m

...th **African** wine industry.

...frican Wine Industry. In fact, whether it's the
...ine tasting dinners, or even our Diners Club
...orld class wines for you to enjoy.

Diners Club
International

A Fairview feast . . . available at our farm and fine retailers countrywide.

FAIRVIEW

FOR FURTHER INFORMATION
TEL: (021) 863 2450
e.mail: cheese@iafrica.com
Website: http://www.fairview.co.za

Below: Financial wizard **GT Ferreira** (FirstRand banking group), accomplished cellarmaster **Gyles Webb** and winemaker **Miles Mossop** (son of port-producing CWM Tony) are the public faces of the stunning new Tokara property – and some of the Cape's most eagerly-anticipated wines. Fans will have to wait just a bit longer . . .

Wine-X-Press. An air express service introduced first by DHL. Its specialised wine bottle packaging makes it the safest, fastest way to send wine from and across Africa. Because good things come to those who don't have to wait.

National Customer Service: **0860 345 000** Paarl: **021 872 4717** www.dhl.co.za

DHL
WORLDWIDE EXPRESS®

We keep your promises

officer material. Dirkie Morkel has ample space on this nearly 300 ha spread to indulge his interests of horse-riding and growing fynbos (wild Cape flora), but its 190 ha vineyards are his particular passion (his post-graduate studies at Stellenbosch University were in viticulture). And there's plenty of scope for variety in this love-life — the plantings feature 16 (mostly red wine) varieties: all the usual noble suspects, plus petit verdot, and newly bearing malbec and pinot noir. A new red wine cellar has swung into action, bristling with the latest hi-tech equipment, and first fruits of all this activity are a joint venture range with KWV for export, and the trio of local releases below, including a rare (in the Cape) standalone Malbec.

☆☆ Pinotage ▼ This pioneer — world's first commercial pinotage, SA national champ of 1959 — still showing the way in latest **99**. Sampled pre-bottling, showed potential for eventual five star rating in huge, complex evening-flower bouquet with whiffs peach melba/caramel/coffee/prune. Ripe, fleshy raspberry palate spiced with fragrant vanilla oak; silkily dry finish. Drink-now accessibility with promise of good 3–7 yrs ageing. 50/50 Fr/Am oak, half new. SAYWS gold. First SA pinotage release from this estate. 13,8% alc. 650 cases.

☆☆ Tumara ▼ Fine, beautifully made dry red balancing Old World restraint and New World fruity hedonism. **99** Bdx blend of cab (from top performing block), merlot, cab f (75/15/10) — though some pvs included dashes shiraz, malbec. Heady cedar/capsicum/eucalyptus fragrances for starters; for main course well-fleshed blackcurrant fruit harnessed by long tannins, good dry finish. 13,8% alc unobtrusive. Sampled pre-bottling, could well attain higher rating with time. All Fr oak, 50% new. Very well priced. 1 000 cases.

✿ Malbec ▼ Rich, massive (14% alc), fragrant; intense eucalyptus scents with hints woodsmoke/smoked meat. Concentrated plummy flavours and very smooth, satiny texture with understated oak. Ready, but should easily go 3–5 yrs. 8 mths 300 ℓ Fr casks, 2nd fill. 1 000 cases. All above very modestly priced.

. . . .

Bellingham

Franschhoek • Closed to the public • Owner DGB (Pty) Ltd • Oenologist Jaco Potgieter (since 2000) Wines made by Charles Hopkins at Graham Beck Coastal • Production 350 000 cases • PO Box 79 Groot Drakenstein 7680 • Tel (021) 874-1011 • Fax (021) 874-1680 • E-mail exports@dgb.co.za

"To continue the trend and vision started by Charles Hopkins" is the aim of Jaco Potgieter, the oenologist who now oversees this venerable Cape brand. Potgieter's freshly created post enables him to work more closely with Bellingham's widely-flung contract growers, ensuring only tip-top grapes are delivered to the cellar. Though Bellingham's previous owner, Graham Beck, has sold his interest to DGB management, Graham Becks' dynamic co-winemaker, Charles Hopkins, continues to imbue the Bellingham range with style and quality.

Premium range

✿ Cabernet Franc Beautifully refined wine, unusual and very satisfying on release with potential to develop. Aromatic elegance in **98**, with eucalyptus/nutmeg/ripe plum; a gentle explosion of fruit and spice in palate sustained by long ripe tannins to lingering crisp dry finish. 13% alc. **95** VVG, **96** SAA, *Wine* ✿.

✿ Pinotage Spitz Has never looked back since first **96** VVG, Perold Trophy for best Pinotage on 1997 IWSC. **97** VVG. **98** Labelled 'Limited Edition', signed by Charles Hopkins, possibly in a trough mid-2000, ✿ on present form though might perk up to heights of pvs. Tasted for last ed, **98** revealed gorgeous spicy, raspberry headiness highlighted by Am oak. Fine tannins extend ripe, dry finish. From old, low-yield Bellingham vyd. 13,2% alc. Yr Am oak, mainly new. 4 000 cases.

'Big Six' range

✿ Shiraz Big, warming **99** has plenty of development potential, but our guess is you won't resist the generous spicy flavours with mulberries and plums, touched with just the right amount of fragrant oak for a sophisticated yet accessible effect. 13,2% alc.

❀ **Merlot** First a sniff of smoked bacon, then perfumes of violets/coffee trailing into palate with plums and fruitcake hints. **99**'s fairly stern tannins give a long, firm finish thats good at table. 13% alc.

Pinotage ❀ Quality in quantity here — 33 000 cases of lingering ripe-fruity flavour with appetising vanilla/choc dimensions and a subtle hint of oak in **99**. 13,4% alc. Available but not ready for tasting: **Cabernet Sauvignon, Chardonnay.**

'Blended' range

Sauvenay ❀ 😊 Popular sauvignon/chardonnay blend which at home practically anywhere. **00** med-bodied, bright, fresh, tropical with a really long lip-smacking finish.

Sauvignon Blanc ❀ Medley of tropical notes in **00**, soft on the tongue but not lacking character or zest. Med-bodied. **95** VVG; **94** VG, SAA. **Classic** Uncomplicated dry red blend. **98** not available for tasting. ± 13% alc. **Rosé** ❀ **00** proper rosé colour, not a pale excuse; some floral introductions and then lightish, sweetly ripe fruit rolls across the palate to very nice clean, dry finish. 11,4% alc. **Premier Grand Cru** ❀ SA's first dry table wine, still top seller in its class. 31 000 cases. **NV** Rousingly fresh — a real palate wakener blowing cut-grass/dried herbs/tropical fruit into the far corners of the mouth. Crisp, dry finish. Sauvignon/chenin/Cape riesling/colombard blend. Try with smoorsnoek, traditional spicy braised fish. **Johannisberger** ‡ Launched 1957, still SA's best selling semi-sweet — 100 000 cases. (Export label Cape Gold) Light-bodied **NV** gentle, light, sweetly tropical and fresh finishing. **Brut** ‡ Refreshing generous mousse, clean across the palate, fresh and rather moreish. **NV** charmat.

. . . .

Benguela Current see Winecorp
Berg & Brook see Winecorp

. . . .

Bergkelder 🍷 🍷

Stellenbosch (see Stellenbosch map) • Tasting Mon–Fri 8–5 Sat 9–1 Tasting fee R10 p/p Sales Mon–Fri 9–4.30 Sat 9–12.30 • Cellar tours Mon–Sat 10, 10.30, 3 (in French, German, Afrikaans and English) • Cellarmaster Callie van Niekerk • Senior winemakers Coenie Snyman (reds, since 1995) Karl Lambour (whites, since 2000) • Chief viticulturist Dawid Saayman • PO Box 184 Stellenbosch 7599 • Tel (021) 888-3400 • Fax (021) 887-5769 • Website www.bergkelder.co.za

OWNED BY DISTILLERS CORP, Bergkelder (literally 'Mountain Cellar', after the maturation halls cut into Stellenbosch's Papegaaiberg) is responsible for various ranges listed separately in this guide: Fleur du Cap, Grünberger, Here XVII, Kupferberger, Stellenryck.

. . . .

Bergsig Estate 🍷 🍷 🍷

Worcester (see Worcester map) • Tasting & sales Mon–Fri 8–5 Sat 9–1 • Cellar tours by arrangement • Portion of farm is sanctuary for rare suurpootjie tortoise • Wheelchair-friendly • Owners Lategan family • Winemaker De Wet Lategan (since 1992) • Vineyards 230 ha • Production ± 3 000 tons, ± 30 000 cases (15 000 cases own label) 70% white 30 red • PO Box 15 Breede River 6858 • Tel (023) 355-1603/355-1721 • Fax (023) 355-1658 • E-mail wine@bergsig.co.za • Website www.bergsig.co.za

IN THEIR QUIET, unassuming way, the younger generation Lategans — Louis, De Wet and Wilhelm — are setting the lone-ranging cat among the mainly co-operative pigeons in this scenic neck of the Breede River valley. Mind-melding with Kobus Deetlefs, owner of one of only a handful of registered estates in the region, they've departed from the high-cropping road and broken a path for quality: planting classic varieties in poorer hillside soils, lavishing R1-million on a state-of-the-art Italian bottling line, sprucing up the appearance of the range (new Cape LBV livery lauded by judges of Grape's 2000 Packaging Awards). With quality on the up and exports booming (first 1 000 case order from Switzerland something to yodel about), the brothers are encouraging others in the valley to break the mould. "Co-ops, if well managed, are necessary and valuable," says De Wet Lategan. "But a few boutiques would enhance our image immeasurably, even if they continue to sell the bulk of production to the collectives."

❀ **Pinotage** Modern, perfumed style drawing strength from venerable extra-low cropping (3 t/ha) 30-yr-old vyds. **99** deeply flavoured, ripe red fruit infused with vanilla spice by 14 mths new Fr/Am small oak. Built-in staying power from firm tannins, body (13,5% alc). De Wet Lategan excited about this ("For us a benchmark"). 1 800 cases.

❀ **Sauvignon Blanc Brut** ✔ Lovely **NV** carbonated dry sparkler, bargain priced, youthfully fresh. Sprig of herb adds extra dimension to sauvignon green-grassy bite. Deserves its VG accolade. Lowish 11,9% alc.

❀ **Soet Hanepoot** Radical facelift for this sweet fortified dessert in **99**, emphasising quality within. Now manageable 375 ml 'after dinner drop', vintage dated; really charming light, bright lemony tone throughout, non-cloying, clean. Step in right direction for this underrated style. Appropriately moderate 17,5 alc.

❀ **Edel Laatoes** Long-lived NLH, made intermittently; latest **99** chenin/gewürz/sauvignon/riesling. Dried apricot creamy sweetness, livened by good vein of acidity. Needs time for botrytis dimension to develop. 375 ml.

❀ **Cape Ruby** New Promising entrant to this genre, dismissed by sniffy purists but at best satisfying with some complexity. And ready on release, not in need of ageing. All of which this **NV** is; ripely fruity with fragrant mocha/tobacco/prune and lingering, dryish, spirity finish.

❀ **Late Bottled Vintage Port** ✔ Rich, subtle, potentially long lived **97** rises to heights of some pvs (**94**, **92** VG). Christmas pud density against tangy spirit backdrop, good spice hints in firm, dryish finish. Low cropping block tinta b, fortified with brandy spirit. 3 yrs large 3 000 ℓ vats.

Cabernet Sauvignon ❀ ☺ Highly drinkable **99** wears yr Fr/Am oak ageing lightly, so interesting tobacco/capsicum spicing shines through. Med/light-bodied but not slight. 3 000 cases. **Ruby Cabernet-Merlot** New ☺ ❀ Ruby cab spice, merlot plumminess combine tastily in soft, slurpable **99**, which received best value awards from two local wine clubs. Med-full bodied. **Chenin Blanc** ❀ ☺ Worker-bee variety (in Cape) takes flight in charming, quaffable **00**, juicy lemonade flavour freshened by zingy acid. Chill and drink soonest. 13% alc.

Blanc de Noir ★ Lighter bodied semi-sweet **99**, boiled sweets/pears losing their freshness. From pinotage. 10% alc. **Chardonnay** ❀ Much-improved **99** of pvs ed has acquired gentle honey/vanilla glaze; citrus/tropical fruit still firmly focused. Partial barrel ferment/malo. **00** preview in different league. **Sauvignon Blanc** ‡ Non-megaphoning poolside tipple, lightish bodied. **99** fresh, citric; some earthy background tones. **Gewürztraminer** ‡ Fragrant semi-sweet, though **00** drier tasting than pvs, fresher too, more expressive with forward honeysuckle fragrance. 13% alc. **Chenin Blanc Special Late Harvest** ‡ Apricot-toned **99** has improved in bottle, acquired extra smoothness. Drop of acid ensures there's no stickiness. Lowish 11,6% alc.

Bernheim

Paarl (see Paarl map) • Tasting, sales & cellar tours Mon—Fri 8.30—5 Sat/Sun by appointment • Light snacks by arrangement • Birding (official avian sanctuary faces onto this Berg River-fringing farm) • Owners Schwulst Family Trust • Winemaker Gisela Kolar • Viticulturist George Schwulst • Production 60 tons 4 000 cases 70% red 25% white 5% rosé • PO Box 7274 Noorder-Paarl 7623 • Tel/fax (021) 872-5618 • E-mail bernheim@iafrica.com • Website www.wine.co.za

KITCHEN chairs and bathroom scales — the wine cellar at Bernheim is blatantly unconventional and passionately hands-on. Winemaker Gisela and her viticulturist husband, Norbert Kolar, have made their second vintage reds (all bottled, corked and labelled by hand) to join a selection of white wines, which Gisela Kolar confesses have "very sentimental names and lovely stories". Not surprisingly, in the same creative shoestring style, an old cement reservoir on the farm has been turned into a tasting room-cum-pub called Dop en Dam. Gisela Kolar describes it as "very humble — a rustic atmosphere where people can relax".

> **Philip's Pinotage** ☺ Good vinous qualities in **00**, big (13,8% alc) but quaffable, "to be enjoyed, not aged". 1 000 cases. **Rosé** ☺ Rose bud pink semi-sweet **00**, with raisin/currant aromas, very easy to drink. Pinotage/chenin, lowish 12,2% alc. 600 cases. **Reminisce** ☺ Light-bodied, delicately fruity **99** offers gentle dried peach tastes. Uncomplicated. honest and rather fun. Unwooded chenin. 1 000 cases.

Cabernet Sauvignon ☺ Usual chunky, full throated style (14,5% alc), **00** made off-dry "to help those still learning to enjoy red wine". Not oaked. 900 cases. **Abendsglück** (pvsly Colombard) ★ Sweetish **00** dedicated to Gisela Kolar's father, as this is "one of only few colombards he can drink". Lower 11,5% alc. **Morgentau** ☺ Very ripe picked, naturally sweet chenin (no concentrate added); fragrant orange blossom, honey in early drinking **00**. Easy 10,5% alc. 500 cases. **Wilhelm V Port** ☺ New Honours quartet of Wilhelms in this close-knit family. Some dried fig, caramel tastes. **NV** from cabernet. 200 cases.

Bertrams Wines

VENERABLE BRAND — established by Robert Fuller Bertram at the end of the 19th century — now under aegis of African Wines & Spirits, which acquired the southern African agency from Gilbeys. Also good, reliable Medium Dry, Medium Cream and Full Cream 'sherries'.

> **Shiraz** Still best of Bertrams. Current **98** usual warm, soft-centred self. Spicy, full, woodsmoke and strawberries in smooth mouthfilling finish. Charms won't fade for another 4–5 yrs. 13% alc. **96** *Wine* ✿.

> **Robert Fuller Reserve** Bdx blend, classically styled for elegance rather than high-kicking display. Fair grasp of tannin in **97**, some spice, blackberries which deserve bit of time to soften, grow. 12% alc.

Cabernet Sauvignon ☺ Skips a vintage to **98**, which fairly compact compared to pvs **96** VG. Latest med/full, spicy, definite tannic grip in dry finish. **Bertrams Ruby Port** ☺ Likable example of older Cape style. Developed tones; sweet spice/Demerara sugar flavours, clean spirity grip. 19,5% alc quite high for style. **NV**.

Beyerskloof

Stellenbosch (see Stellenbosch map) • Tasting & sales Mon—Fri 9—4.30 Sat by appointment • Wheelchair-friendly • Owners Beyers Truter, Johann & Paul Krige and partners • Winemaker/viticulturist Beyers Truter (since 1989) • Own vineyards ±5 ha • Production 70 000 cases 100% red • PO Box 107 Koelenhof 7605 • Tel (021) 882-2135 • Fax (021) 882-2683

HUGE market and critical successes have happily not impinged on this miniature farm's charms. With just 5 ha under cabernet and merlot vines, and a tasting room as atmospheric as its winemaker, Beyers Truter, it's a delight to visit: Vineyard Ventures' Gilly Stoltzman, who guides VIP oenophiles through the winelands, always includes it on her itinerary. Truter and partners Johann and Paul Krige all do their fulltime thing at Kanonkop; off-duty Truter is an inveterate crayfish/perlemoen diver, angler, hunter and sports spectator. Where he manages to squeeze this cellar into his diary, let alone find enough time there to make the exceptional flagship blend below, winner of countless awards, is hard to imagine. And so — *'n boer maak 'n plan* — various cellars help out with the pinotage. By Appointment to the King ?…

Beyerskloof "He gets it right every time," says Paul Krige, admiringly. No more so than in stunning **97** *Wine* ✿, Air France–Preteux Bourgeois trophy. Deeper, fuller, (dare we say chunky?) fruit, intensely pleasurable. Interestingly, 'older style' than current Kanonkop Paul Sauer 'stablemate'. Replete garnet colour reflects rich, enveloping bouquet of plush dark berries, folded into wide, wonderfully ripe palate layered with deep fruit, chewy muscle. Hint of choc in extended finish. Roundly delicious. Oh so accessible now, will further reward those who can resist for 5 yrs or so. Mainly cab, with 23% merlot. 91 rating in Robert Parker's *Wine Spectator*. Next **98** inky black, loaded with ripe cassis, full plummy palate, fleshy finish. Difficult to resist swallowing at tasting! 2 yrs new Nevers oak. 13% alc. 1 000 cases. Track record: **96** VVG, Air France–Preteux Bourgeois trophy, *Wine* ✿; **95** still excellent potential; **94** best cab on IWSC, 5 stars UK *Decanter* SA cab tasting.

Pinotage ✓ Huge success, especially in local restaurants where offers exceptional value. Quality maintained, improved even, despite volume growth to 60 000 cases. **00** sample features clean sweet fruit, pinotage character more overt than **99** best to date: deep blue/purple colour, ripe banana/plum/raspberry finished in spicy oak. Delicate violets leaven dark toasty wood in palate. Silky, sweetly ripe, but fine tannins end classically dry. **96** ABSA Top Ten trophy. From unirrigated bushvines, 20–40 yrs old; fruit/wine sourced from 'quality partners'.

. . . .

Bianco see De Heuvel

. . . .

Bilton Wines   New ♆ ♆ ♆

Stellenbosch (see Stellenbosch map) • Tasting & sales Mon—Fri 8.30—1 or by appointment • Light refreshments • Bring your own picnic • Conferencing for 20—25 delegates • Walks • Mountain biking • Views • Wheelchair-friendly • Owner Mark Bilton • Consulting winemaker Pierre Wahl • Viticulturist/farm manager Adrean Naudé (since 1996) • Vineyards 60 ha • Production 500 tons (24 tons, 140—1 200 cases own label) 70% red 30% white • PO Box 60 Lynedoch 7603 • Tel (021) 881-3714/082-804-2224 Fax (021) 881-3721 • E-mail blyhoek@mweb.co.za

INTRODUCING A NEWCOMER to a rather classy neighbourhood — Rust en Vrede, Stellenzicht etc are just up the road. Meet owner Mark Bilton, formerly grower of gourmet salads for Woolworths and company, who has a lot here to conjure with — 400 ha of prime land. And meet Adrean Naudé, the ex-industrial chemist (with Denel) and deciduous fruit expert who's magicked up the first wines from the property's 60 ha vineyards. He answered Bilton's ad which mysteriously stated "no knowledge of vineyards required" — this despite grapes being the main crop, delivered to a nearby co-op and later to SFW. But all serendipitous in the end. His chemistry background was a plus in the vineyards, and scientific curiosity drew him magnetically into the old (1824) cellar, where he began to make a splash of wine "by trial and error, for fun", calling on Stellenbosch University's Eben Archer for advice. A 98 Merlot turned out so well that suddenly they were in business. Name registered, salad production stopped, pear orchards pulled out, more wine made

(in a Franschhoek cellar while theirs was being revamped) and a planting programme launched — 10 ha annually of fashionable varieties, including mourvèdre,
between 2000 and 2004, to bring the vineyard total to 104 ha. "The bug bit," says
Naudé. "My interest started out of inquisitiveness, now it's a passion." .

🌸**Merlot** Just 80 cases made, so maiden **98** sure to be hotly fought over. Modern, full throated style (berries harvested at 27 °B), open choc-charry black cherries and cassis, just enough glossy tannins for pleasurable drinking now or over
2–4 yrs. 14% alc. Follow up **99** (500 cases) not ready for tasting.

Cabernet Sauvignon On form of roommate above, consider the 🌸 rating for first
release **99** a provisional one. Freshly bottled mid-2000, and clearly still woozy, quiet
on nose, yet some good mulberry, expensive smelling cedary oak, fine structural
acid already apparent and boding well for good development over min 2–3 yrs.
13,5% alc. 500 cases.

. . . .
Birdfield see Klawer
. . . .

Blaauwklippen

Stellenbosch (see Stellenbosch map) • Tasting & sales Mon–Fri 9–5 Sat 9–1 Tasting fee R10 • Cellar tours
Mon–Thu 11, 3; Fri 11 • Three-course coachman's lunch Mon–Sat 12–2.30 • Gift shop • Permanent museum of
antique carriages, cars & furniture • Owner Farmers Markt Landhandel Gmbh • Winemaker Hein Hesebeck (since
1997) • Vineyard manager Kowie Kotze (since 1987) • Vineyards 100 ha • Production 600 tons (500 tons, 35 000
cases own label) 60% red 40% white • PO Box 54 Stellenbosch 7599 • Tel (021) 880-0133 • Fax (021) 880-0136
• E-mail mail@blaauwklippen.com

A GERMAN POTTER was the first owner of this property, clearing virgin forest to plant
vines. Now, after more than three centuries, with the suburban sprawl of Stellenbosch fast approaching these 100 ha vineyards, a German transformation is again
underway. Stefan Schörghuber, the owner of the Münich-based Schörghuber Corporate Group, with interests in construction, real estate, beverages and the service
industry, plans to relaunch Blaauwklippen as "one of the great red wine estates of
the world". Bulldozers swarm all over the place, uprooting old vines, planting new.
Serious money is being poured into new barrels. A recently acquired brandy potstill
heralds a spot of diversification. The historic manor house and farmyard are being
restored. New GM Frank Meaker (his CV spans the industry, from Bergkelder to
co-op winery to private estate), says the holding company, Farmers Markt Landhandel Gmbh, "has committed itself to making Blaauwklippen the jewel in its
crown". Günter Brözel-protege Hein Hesebeck, the winemaker charged with stirring this label from hibernation, has an exciting challenge on his hands.

Chardonnay-Semillon 🌸 😊 Partial barrelling adds buttered toast dimension to fresh, citrus-fragrant **00**. Bit of time for needed for semillon portion to
get up to speed, fill out palate. "Enjoyed by everyone, everywhere," reports
Hein Hesebeck. 13% alc. 1 300 cases.

🌸**Pinotage** Am oak aged **99** 🌸 less generous than pvs; honey/bottle age overlay
already apparent. Drink soon to catch the smoky mulberry/raspberry fruit. 14%
alc. 1 000 cases. **98** more serious, individual, longer-lived. *Wine* 🌸.

🌸**Zinfandel Reserve** Rich, concentrated version of this cellar's signature wine.
98 smoother, more lushly fruity now than when tasted for pvs ed. Sweetening
effect of sturdy alc, dollop sugar, Am oak barrelling well contained by dry tannins. 14% alc, 6,9 g/ℓ sugar. 1 100 cases.

Bordeaux Blend 🌸 NEW (To be named.) Lighter style, sweetish *and* savoury
impressions from ripe cherries, green/black pepper. Cab/cab f/mer 50/25/25; yr
small casks. 5 000 cases. **Cabernet Sauvignon** 🌸 After fresh-fruity explosion in
98 🌸, latest **99** relaxes into lower-wattage, more comfortable style. Red berries,

cherries, some light vanilla tones. Distinctly fresh finish calls for rich/rustic food. 13% alc. **96** SAA. 13,8% alc. 740 cases. **Cabernet Sauvignon Reserve 99** marks return of this top-rated label, pvsly for CWG auction, noted for its expansive palate, classic dusty dry finish. Latest shows great promise; tasted from barrel rated ✿, but could well top ✿ on release in Mar 2001. New barrique treatment sets up good spicy vanilla backdrop for layered mulberry, black cherry assembly, fine long tannins. One to watch. 13,2% alc. 875 cases. **Cabernet Franc** ✿✿ Gentle minty blackberries in **98** SAA, understated vanilla oak. 13,5% alc. 1 600 cases. **Shiraz** ✿✿ Perfumed, smoky **98** gaining harmony. Fairly-finish indicates this not for long keeping. 14,2% alc. 2 500 cases. **97** dry, slightly lean. **Chardonnay** Barrel fermented/aged **00**, mid-2000 still too young to rate but showing good potential. Should match **99**'s ✿✿ at least. 13% alc. Release date Feb 2001. 1 300 cases. **Chardonnay Reserve 99** ★ unexpectedly insubstantial, tired. **Sauvignon Blanc** ⚐ **00** reprises no-worries, lightly tropical style of pvs. Some delicate mango, muscat fragrances, crisp dry finish. 2 600 cases. **White Landau** ⚐ Long time member of range returns in undemanding, semi-dry **99** quaffer. Keep-'em-guessing blend now set at sauvignon, semillon, pinot blanc, muscat ottonel. 1 800 cases.

Bloemendal Estate ⚑ ⚑ ⚑

Durbanville (see Durbanville map) • Tasting & sales Mon–Fri 9–5 Sat 9–1 • Bloemendal Restaurant tel (021) 975-7525/75 (also conferences) • Owner/winemaker Jackie Coetzee • Vineyards 150 ha • Production 1 000 tons (5 000 cases own label) 80% red 20% white • PO Box 466 Durbanville 7551 • Tel/fax (021) 796-2682

IT SOUNDS much better in Afrikaans, Jackie Coetzee's reason for choosing a career in wine: *"Ollo Parker het gesê ek lê te veel op die beach"*. That is, boy-next-door wine farmer/maker Oliver Parker gave his old mate a pep talk: get off your back, get off the beach, get real. It's impossible to avoid becoming a bit of a beach-boy (or in Coetzee's case more than a bit) if some of the world's finest waves and silveriest strands wink at you from your vineyards, but Coetzee resigned himself to responsibility and began to turn out wines of (naturally) individuality and aplomb. He still keeps a much better balance than his peers between chilling out and working manically, and remains the winelands' best reminder that there is life — a lot of good, soul feeding life — outside the cellar. And when the sea calls, he'll take the wine along. "The pop of a cork on a deserted beach, with your family, is rather beautiful." Note: the wines below were tasted pre-final blending and ratings are provisional.

Cabernet Sauvignon As individual as its maker. Slow starting, usually best 5–7 yrs after vintage (and can still be exceptional after 15). Latest **98** still tight-wound; violets, some black/red berries in subdued bouquet, dry tannins which are going to need time. Potential ✿. **Merlot 99** could grow into the finest of the recent vintages. Excellent extract, long ripe tannins and deep red/black cherry plushness. Good weight (13,7% alc) and structure yet already quite soft, approachable. Fine ✿ promise. **Sauvignon Blanc** On this farm shows distinctive dusty pungency, usually with capsicum/green fig overtones, depending on vintage. In **00** some passionfruit exotica, too, contrasting with fresh-cut grass. Too young to rate conclusively, but shows ✿ potential. Good on release, but pvs have aged with interest. From 'Suider Terras' vyd. Also available (not tasted for this ed): **Semillon 99** (pvs rating ✿✿) **Brut** Sparkling MCC, **NV** (✿✿).

Bloupunt Wines ⚑ ⚑ ⚑

Montagu (see Klein Karoo map) • Tasting & sales Mon–Fri 9–5 Sat 9–4 Nominal tasting fee for tourgroups • Cellar visits by arrangement • Views • Owner Phil Hoffman • Winemakers/viticulturists Paul & Phil Hoffman (since 1997) • Vineyards 3 ha • Production 55 tons (±4 000 cases own label) 100% white • 12 Long Street Montagu 6720 • Tel/fax (023) 614-2385 • E-mail bloupunt@lando.co.za

THE Hoffman family's 2 ha of very closely planted chardonnay on the Montagu riverside are bulging at the seams, so supposed retirees Phil and Dixie, with ex-financial whiz son, Paul, are busy preparing another 3,5 ha of merlot and more chardonnay. And considering a Ruby Cabernet under a different label — all to supply a newly established market in the UK. "Frightening" is how Phil Hoffman describes the export formalities and bureaucracy that they as newcomer exporters had to deal with. Fortunately nothing has yet managed to even remotely deter his "deep down ambition to be in the wine industry". Meanwhile Paul Hoffman flies remote controlled helicopters in his (not so) spare time. "No they're not lifesize. We're not making that much money you know!'"

⚜**Chardonnay** 🏆 Two versions, both attractive, reasonably priced: **Wooded** Always a big, weighty wine, alc in 13–14% range which better (and very versatile) with food, especially richer cuisine; charming, fragrant peachy fruit well embroidered with clean, spicy vanilla oak, good dry finish. Current **99** fermented/aged Nevers barrels/staves. 1 100 cases. **98** mellowing nicely, some gentle vanilla tones. **97** double gold on regional show. **Unwooded** Peachy aromatics as above, more straightforward. **99** with brisk citrus palate, dry finish. 13,8% alc. 1 900 cases. **98** gold on regional show. These from ±9 yr old vyd on the property.

Merlot New First release **99** flew out of the cellar, and follow-up **00** barely 4 weeks in oak (out of envisaged 52) when sampled mid-2000, too young to rate; but promising, good concentration of fruit. Bought-in grapes. 13,2% alc. 300 cases.

· ·

Blueberry Hill

FRANSCHHOEK'S Brian and Lindy Heyman call on medico-turned-winemaker Nigel McNaught to make this wine at his next-door Stony Brook cellar. PO Box 580 Franschhoek 7690 • Tel (021) 876–3362 • Fax (021) 876-2114

Sauvignon Blanc ‡ Individual (Nigel McNaught's middle name) **99** with sweet/sour tussle in palate after low key ripe gooseberry/pineapple introduction. For the adventurous palate. 13,5% alc. 350 cases.

· ·

Blue Creek   🏆 ℞ 🏆

Stellenbosch (see Stellenbosch map) • Tasting, sales, cellar tours Mon—Fri by appointment • Tourgroups • Views • Wheelchair-friendly • Owners Rabie & Piet Smal • Winemaker Piet Smal (since 1998) "with a little help from my friends" • Consulting viticulturist AndrewToubes • Vineyards 5 ha • Production 20 tons 1 000 cases 100% red • PO Box 3247 Matieland Stellenbosch 7602 • Tel (021) 887-6938/880-0522 • Fax (021) 886-5462

AFTER a 5-year spell abroad, and many visits to the wine areas of Europe, dentist Piet Smal realised: "You don't need huge grounds and vast vineyards to make wine." In fact, you need no more than the 5 ha of cabernet and pinotage (merlot to follow) here on the Smal family's smallholding in the Blaauwklippen valley bordering Stellenbosch. The first 96 vintage was a promising newcomer. And it's simply got better since then, the 98 — lavished with the individual attention such a hands-on, boutique sized operation makes possible — making it to the top 10 (out of 405 entrants) in the Air France-Preteux Bourgeois Classic Wine Trophy. Any other new developments? Indeed: the Smals have been busy sprucing up their cellar and adding a tasting area — "it must be a pleasure to visit us; the wine and the surroundings must complement each other."

⚜**Cabernet Sauvignon** In pvs ed we foresaw a bright future for this polished Stbosch cab, now made by father and son Smal (first **96**, **97** with Jacques Kruger). That starry potential now fully fledged in **98** ⚜. Dense, ripe mulberry/mint supported by oaky vanilla, seamless firm tannins. Approachable, with good few yrs development ahead. Own grapes, with some Helderberg, Devon Valley,

Bottelary fruit. Yr Nevers barriques, mainly 2nd fill. Unfiltered. 13,4% alc. 600 cases.

. . . .

Blue Ridge see Villiera
Blue White see Old Vines Cellars

. . . .

Bodega

Paarl (see Paarl map) • Tasting & sales by appointment • "Occasional" B&B • Bring your own picnic • Walks • Wheelchair-friendly • Owners Julianne Barlow & Jeremy Squier • Winemaker/viticulturist Julianne Barlow advised by Eugene van Zyl, Paul Wallace • Vineyards 14 ha • Production ±40 tons (±1 500 cases own label) 100% red • PO Box 590 Kraaifontein 7569 • Tel (021) 988-2929 • Fax (021) 988-3527 • E-mail austinwine@iafrica.com

JULIANNE BARLOW'S involvement here initially was from at least an arm's length. But in 1994 she jumped in feet first, learning everything from pruning to pressing "from the bottom rung up". Weighing in with advice and the occasional visit is UK-based brother Jeremy Squier, a retired farmer. Friends and consultants help unravel "winemaking chemistry and other mysteries". Merlot and Cabernet are the only wines made on the property (you'll find them on selected winelists here and in the UK and US); pinotage is grown in minute quantities, too, but sold off to ensure the own-label reds stay focused.

✿ **Cabernet Sauvignon** Opens with sweetish prune, aromatic liquorice notes with hints of green olive; in palate, **98**'s initial fruity ripeness beginning to fade, growing a shade porty with some chunky tannins. Single vyd. 9 mths new Fr oak. 14% alc. 450 cases.

✿ **Merlot 98** marked by striking plum/purple depths — very inviting. Sniffs of meat and mouthwatering savouriness meld with power packed berry fruit persisting in finish. Unusual, characterful style which satisfies. 9 mths new Fr barriques. 13,5% alc. 800 cases.

. . . .

Boekenhoutskloof

Franschhoek (see Franschhoek map) • Tasting by appointment • Sales Mon–Fri 9-5 • Owner Boekenhoutskloof Investments (Pty) Ltd • Winemaker Marc Kent (since 1994) • Viticulturist Pieter Siebrits (since 1997) • PO Box 433 Franschhoek 7690 • Tel (021) 876-3320 • Fax (021) 876-3793 • E-mail boeken@mweb.co.za

A CORNER of the Côte Rôtie is being carved out of the mountain face behind the venerable pioneer homestead on this farm. Terraces are being co-planted with viognier and syrah: look and you might be in the Rhône; taste the Syrah and you'll still be there (even though consulting viticuluralist Di Davidson is Australian). Winemaker Marc Kent's gurus are the Guigals, Jaboulets and other Gallic legends, and while *le tout* Franschhoek trumpets its historic Huguenot connections, it's here, so deep into this valley of vines that you can go no further, that you'll find the most authentic French flavour. Though not great splashes of it — the flagship Boekenhoutskloof range (the 7 chairs on its — superb, Grape packaging award winning — label denoting the 7 partners in the venture, including Kent) did not reach the 2 000-case level until, appropriately, the year 2000. It's Porcupine Ridge — second-label but decidedly first-class — spreads its charms more broadly. (If you can't find it locally, head to London, where the Conran restaurants have listed 4 vintages of the Cabernet.) A new barrel cellar is in the making here, and a tasting room — though visits will still be by appointment. "There will be no hard sell," Kent assures. "I want people to come here to enjoy the beauty and not be intimidated."

✿ **Syrah 98** ✿ probably the year's most anticipated release, after much-acclaimed/talked-about **97** Air France–Preteux Bourgeois trophy, *Wine* ✿. Could Marc Kent, single-minded syrah fanatic, repeat or even top his superbly individual first vintage? Happily he's pursued a totally different route, preferring to contrast rather than complement that magnum opus (though, in a sense, he had no choice: the original Somerset West vyd grubbed up to make way for an industrial park). **98** and future vintages, through long-term contract, sourced from single Wellington. So, while **97** dazzled with generous shake of white pepper, sappy tannins (subliminal nod to Crozes-Hermitage icon, Alain Graillot?), **98** projects altogether darker, deeper rumblings, still around the upper quality reaches of the Rhône. Kent suggests it has the unyielding nature of a young Cornas. Not quite, but we get his gist: tight, structured palate — gripped by grape rather than oak tannins (traditionalist Kent finishes his wine in all older, Fr oak) — embracing waves of still unveiled, glycerol rich flavours: smoky salami, roasted nuts, minerally/earthy notes. Unlike **97**, with its delicious immediacy; the drama comes from **98**'s massiveness (14,8% alc) and still cryptic fruit core.

✿ **Cabernet Sauvignon** Unfairly overshadowed by hype surrounding above wine; latest, brilliant release should rescue it from cinderellahood. 'Claret' is the immediate, unequivocal impression voiced by **98** ✿ sleek, perfectly ripe blackberry smells with expensive cedary wrap. 'Lightness', too, defining character of palate; concentration, complexity achieved via fruit purity, minerally chic rather than piled tannins (this also downplays generous 13,9% alc.). Despite present agreeable harmony, packed, compact feel promises greatest future of any of three vintages to date. **97** VVG unusually delicate despite powerful thrust, complexity. Finish yields balanced tannins; uncommon achievement in Cape cab. All from single, F'hoek hillside vineyard. All new-oak polished, Sylvain chateau (extra thin stave) barrels, 24 mths; no filtration. (Very slow) malo in barrel.

✿ **Semillon** ✔ Vinosity, rather than clearly-defined fruit, sets the tone here (making this the ideal food style). **99** lively, still quite oaky nose; true potential revealed in silkily viscous palate with mouthcoating extract, persistence. From original F'hoek 'groendruif' (green grape) bushvines, harvested slighter earlier than pvs to capture greater freshness (still weighs in at 13% alc.). **98** gives idea of development year down the line: typical (of older vines) slightly austere baked sponge pudding character with lanolin/lemon/honey sidelights. Fermented/aged new Burgundy casks; through malo.

Porcupine Ridge range

✿ **Cabernet Sauvignon** ✔ One cabernet that doesn't need hanging on to. **99** styled for greatest possible fruit appeal, without loss of cab structure. Real European-hedgerow character: soft, dark berry-fruit purity enhanced by portion spontaneous ferment. Accessible; ripe, supple tannins. Oak matured; portion Klapmuts grapes.

✿ **Syrah** New Be seduced by this **99**! Real 'comfort food' served up with a generous dose of southern Rhône sultry appeal (smoky/gamey infusions brushed with sun-warmed garrigue) over palate of fleshy tannins. For insouciant, French pavement café enjoyment with suitably hearty peasant food. 14,5% alc. Wellington/Stbosch grapes.

✿ **Pinotage Reserve** New **99** "made for fun". Marc Kent not a big pinotage fan, but old bush vines offered a challenge (as did Makro buyers, for whom this an exclusive) — answered convincingly. Inky crimson, characteristic dried banana/fig whiffs not totally bowed by earthy, smoky gusts. Creamily mouthfilling; lively yet fine minerally tannins. Traditional vinification (spontaneous fermentation, open vats, extractive punching down of skins). More serious, ageworthy than other reds in PR range.

✿ **Sauvignon Blanc 00** whips up gastric-juices; non-stop flavour waterfall — and just as fresh — featuring F'hoek's moderate varietal nettly tang. "Good lunchtime sauvignon," reckons Kent. 90% F'hoek grapes, balance Stbosch.

Merlot ✦ **99** voluptuous plum/prune volume washes around mouth in juicy waves; minimal tannin hindrance. Non-challenging drinking partner, with pasta. Mainly own fruit, some Stbosch. Oak aged. 13,5% alc.

. . . .

Boland Wine Cellar

Paarl (see Paarl map) • Tasting & sales Mon—Fri 8—5 Sat 8.30—1 • Cellar tours by appointment • Picnic baskets during Dec holidays. Or bring your own year-round during tasting/sales huurs • Subterranean cellar for private receptions • Winter cultural evenings • Play area for children • Views • Wheelchair-friendly • Owners Boland Vineyards International (114 shareholders) • Winemakers Naudé Bruwer, Daljosafat cellar (since 1999); Johan Joubert, Northern Paarl cellar (since 1997) • Viticulturist Jurie Germishuys (since 1998) • Vineyards ± 2 000 ha • Production 17 100 tons 78% white 22% red • PO Box 7007 Noorder-Paarl 7623 • Tel (021) 862-6190 (Daljosafat) (021) 872-1747 (Northern Paarl) • Fax (021) 862-5379 • E-mail boland@wine.co.za • Website www.bolandwines.co.za

THIS CO-OP turned company is so dynamic, it needs two cellars in which to work off its energy: one nearer Wellington at Daljosafat, the other scenically perched on a knoll below Paarl mountain. With Charl du Plessis transferring to Rijk's Cellar at Tulbagh, his No 2 Naudé Bruwer gets a turn as co-captain with stalwart Johan Joubert. Their wines are regular try-scorers in Britain, Germany, Belgium and the US. And in the Netherlands, retail chain Gall & Gall recently sold an all time record-breaking 12 000 cases of their Pinotage-Cinsaut in just one month. This comes on the back of a surprise Veritas gold for their Bon Vino dry white. Probably the biggest coup is the joint-venture with the DM900-million German wine marketing group, WIF, to further bolster exports. It's just a matter of time before the Boland squad has their new partners shouting for more of their famously delicious potjiekos casseroles.

✿**Cabernet Sauvignon** ▼ Upward trend continues in **99**, with classic ripe-cassis and new-clone infusions of eucalyptus/dark choc; vibrant creamy finish. Light green tones of pvs significantly absent. SAYWS gold. **98** SAA.

✿**Red Muscadel** ▼ Balanced, silky example of this traditional Cape fortified dessert; **99** striking garnet hue and rich mocha taste with dried herb/tea leaf contrasts. Very low 3,1 g/ℓ acidity.

✿**White Muscadel** ▼ Fine interplay between extra-ripe, viscous muscat fruit and tangy-smooth spirit in **97**. Beautiful rich perfume of grape, honeysuckle, rose mirrored deep, bright orange-gold lights. 17,5% alc.

Pinotage-Cinsaut ✦ New ☺ Charming fresh take on this old-Cape varietal duet in ultra-sappy, unoaked **00**, with satisfying sweet/savoury tones. Real pour-'n-party stuff, so watch the high 13,3% alc. **Chenin Blanc** ✦ ☺ Easily swiggable style, usually big hit with consumers. Supple, succulent **00**, super-charged guava aromas, milder tropical tastes. Gently dry, full-bodied (13% alc). **99** SAYWS class winner. **Brut** ✦ ☺ Carbonated **NV** from sauvignon sparkles in a light, friendly way; some soft peachy/green grass, non-aggressively dry.

Merlot ✦ Disciplined oaking doesn't overwhelm the demure plum-jam, dark choc tones in full-bodied **98**. Well-made wine for standalone sipping. 13,4% alc. **Pinotage** ✦ Swaggering style with full frontal fruit exposure (mulberry/plum), plus fragrant wood-spice notes in **99**. **97** *Wine* ✦. **Shiraz** This cellar really going places with this ultra-chic variety. **00** (sample) reprises super smoky/aromatic fireworks of pvs, plus creamy strawberry/plum, oaky vanilla flavours. Solid ✦ with promise of development. **99** SAYWS class winner. **Chardonnay** ✦ Cellar's flagship, clanks with show medals. Exceptionally juicy, drinkable **00** SAYWS gold, sweet melon/caramel/toast with leesy touches in soft, dry, med/light body. 8 mths on lees in cask. **99** best SA white at International Wine Challenge, Hong Kong. **98** Concours Mondial gold; best value chardonnay in local wine mail-order club tasting. **97** SAA.

Sauvignon Blanc ★ **00** well constructed but not as punchy as pvs. Some green pepper/kiwifruit in broad, full, dry palate. **Riesling** ☆ Lacks zing, but compensates in herb/haystack/lemon-cream complexity, all mingling in light/med-bodied dry palate. **Bukettraube** ☆ Variety's pear/herbal aromas on display in **00**, made off-dry for soft, easy solo sipping or with spicy foods. **Noble Late Harvest** ★☆ Gorgeous turquoise teardop bottle catches the eye, intense apricot/jasmine/botrytis flavours arrest the palate in **00**, soft, lightish and cordial-like but lacking acid raciness. White muscadel. **Vin Doux** ☆ Sweet version of Brut above, more tropical tastes, honeyed to the end. **Port** ☆☆ Low cropped (5 t/ha) ruby cab imparts intensity to **97**, sweeter toned with pleasing smoky choc/leather accents. 16,7% alc. Yr in oak.

Bon Vino range

In 500 ml glass dumpies, 2 ℓ and 5 ℓ packs. All **NV**.

Dry Red ☆☆ ☺ The king of quaffers, neither over-full nor too tannic. All the softies squeezed into service here — cinsaut, merlot, ruby cab — with cab propping it all up quite delightfully. Almost free at R7 per 500 ml bottle.

Dry White ☆☆ Crisp, just-dry, well balanced aperitif with herb/citrus and lemon grass tang. Works well with Oriental food. Chenin/sauvignon/Cape riesling. VG. **Semi-Sweet** ☆ Soft, easy, light; delicate talcum/honeysuckle scents from soupçon muscat (remainder chenin).

Bon Courage Estate

Robertson (see Robertson map) • Tasting & sales Mon–Fri 8.30–5 Sat 9.30–1 Tasting fee for groups of more than 10 • Cellar tours by appointment during tasting hours • Light meals, coffees during tasting hours, "inside or under the pepper tree" • Conferences • Walks • Views • Birdlife • Play area for children • Tourgroups • Cheese made on premises • Owner André Bruwer • Winemaker Jacques Bruwer (since 1992) • Viticulturists André & Jacques Bruwer • Vineyards 150 ha • Production 1 700–2 000 tons • PO Box 589 Robertson 6705 • Tel (023) 626-4178 • Fax (023) 626-3581 • E-mail boncourage@minds.co.za

THIS FAMILY ESTATE, run by the engaging Bruwer family, with wines to suit every pocket, palate, season and occasion — the NLH currently, perhaps, the cracker of the range — has always been a pleasure to visit. Now a coffee shop adds to its charms, offering salads and sandwiches, cakes and desserts, and (how can we resist?) Platters with a capital P. Another new attraction is cheese made on the farm. A pepper tree outside provides more than shade — here's where to team a bit of birdwatching with a glass of house bubbly, or Jacques Bruwer's current preoccupation, Shiraz, and eyeball the fish and other sorts of eagles, owls, hamerkops, etc roosting above. Other recent developments at this enterprising 200 ha estate (150 ha under vines) include elegant new labels and the introduction of a second-tier range, Three Rivers.

☆ **Shiraz** "A wine worth watching," we said in pvs ed, after sniffing future star qualities in **98**. These now convincingly expressed in follow-up **99** ☆☆, evoking the Rhône in aromatic hillside scrub, woodsmoke and red fruit richness, smoothed with licks of creamy chocolate. Good advertisement for this farm's red wine potential. Yr small Am oak. 13% alc. 700 cases.

☆ **Cabernet Sauvignon** ✔ Steadily improving label, shifting from old Cape greenness towards riper, purer fruit. Plus new-found subtlety, claret-like mineral grip in latest **99**, with strawberry/cassis abundance and spicy oak. **98** ★☆, with green olive/cassis array, drinking well now. 700 cases.

☆ **Cabernet Sauvignon-Shiraz** ✔ Among the highlights of this resurgent range, **98** harmonious from further yr bottle maturation, cab cassis and shiraz pepper now seamless. Next up (step up, too) is unoaked **99**, lively hedgerow scents, fine shiraz spiciness. 13% alc. 1 500 cases.

✿**Chardonnay Prestige Cuvée** Two **99** versions: *4 mths oaked:* ✿, fruit salad aromas/tastes with light buttered toast in dry finish. 13% alc. 500 cases. *Yr oaked:* similar style but finer, needs some time to fill out, good toasty vanilla in finish. 300 cases. Pvs **98** "more serious wine," explains Jacques Bruwer (though only 4 mths oaked). Toasty butterscotch/ripe melon, tight yet harmonious farewell. 13,5% alc. 180 cases.

✿**Noble Late Harvest** Luscious botrytised riesling dessert, evolving into one of the Cape's standouts. Made intermittently, pvs **97**, **99**; newest **00** ✿ undoubtedly best of these. Super-intense, almost overwhelming apricot/crushed orange rind/botrytis scents, concentrated dried fruit palate, exhilarating acidity tapering to crisp, extra-long finish. Lowish 11% alc. 150 cases.

✿**Wit Muscadel** ⭐ A classic of this style, frequent VG. **99** up to customary top form after quiet start. Attention-grabbing pale orange-gold colour, exotic beeswax/barley sugar bouquet, hints of (attractive) varnish resonate in sweet, ripe raisiny palate. 300 cases.

Pinot Noir ✿ **New** Gamey nuances in **99**, some green stalky whiffs, fragrant plums. Earthy dry finish. 11 mths oak, mainly Fr. SAYWS gold. 300 cases. **Sauvignon Blanc** ✿ Usually big, gutsy, yet **00** not quite as flamboyant as pvs. Tangy guava/passionfruit, piquant finish. 500 cases. **Colombard-Chardonnay** ✿ Estate's most exported label. No-ceremony **00** cork popper, med-bodied, lots of lemony fruit, brush of honey/oak, creamily dry. 6 000 cases. **97** VVG. **Gewürztraminer Special Late Harvest** ✿ Diners Club award-winning sweet dessert, showing usual fine form in **99**. Perfume counter fragrances (roses/jasmine/orange rind/apricot), lightly brushed with botrytis. Ethereal floral finish. Moderate 11,5% alc. 500 cases. **Jacques Bruére Brut Millennium** ✿ Classically-styled **NV** MCC sparkler from pinot/chardonnay, individual and well priced. Current (**97**) brisk lemon/apple tones with suggestion of oak, very dry finish. 10% wood aged. Lowish 11,5% alc. 400 cases.

Three Rivers range

Ruby Cabernet-Pinotage ✿ 🙂 Arresting fuchsia colour tells you all you need to know about this **99** snappy swigger. Bright red berries, wisps of smoke, juicy to the end. 13% alc. 1 000 cases. **Chardonnay** ⚥ 🙂 **99** quick quaff showcases dusty apple/pear aromas and compact, almost austere palate which marks this as a versatile food companion. 13% alc. 800 cases. **Riesling** ✿ 🙂 Satisfying, compatible everyday Cape riesling with instant swiggability. Semi-dry **00** quite luscious; broad quince nuances, creamy finish. Drink young. 500 cases.

Bonfoi Estate 🍷

Stellenbosch (see Stellenbosch map) • Tasting & sales by appointment • Owner/winemaker/viticulturist Johannes van der Westhuizen (since 1990) • Vineyards ±100 ha • Production 700 tons (30 tons, 500—1 500 cases own label) 65% white 35% red • PO Box 9 Vlottenburg 7604 • Tel/fax (021) 881-3604 • E-mail bonfoi@mweb.co.za

THIS family-owned Stellenboschkloof property appears in the guide for the first time since 1994, when their limited release own-range — a semi-sweet and a barrel-aged chenin (the latter something of a pioneer in the Cape) — was discontinued. Now Stellenbosch University-trained Johannes van der Westhuizen, the present owner, is unfurling the flag. He's extensively replanted the 100 ha vineyards, establishing shiraz, chardonnay and merlot. Sauvignon blanc, at 350 m above sea level, for now has the best view. And cabernet, planted in 91, makes its debut in the wines below. The original cellar has been revamped, and in 2000 additional mini-tanks were wheeled in to "maintain quality by keeping small quantities separate". A tasting room is on the cards.

❀ **Cabernet Sauvignon** Ripe brambleberries send you soaring in **97** ❀, but some dusty, dry tannins quickly reel you in. Old-clone tautness not so evident in promising **98**, with broader, more relaxed palate tone, though still chunky tannins need a few yrs or food (Johannes van der Westhuizen's swing through the foodhall often turns up oxtail or richly sauced fillet/rump steak). Med-bodied, Fr oak aged, 18 mths. 1 200/500 cases.

Bonnievale Cellar

Bonnievale (see Robertson map) • Tasting & sales Mon—Fri 8—5 Sat 10—1 • Cellar tours by arrangement • Views • Wheelchair-friendly • Owners 60 members • Winemaker Henk Wentzel (since 1999) • Vineyards 790 ha • Production ±12 000 tons (5 000 cases own label) 80% white 20% red • PO Box 206 Bonnievale 6730 • Tel (023) 616-2795/ 2359 • Fax (023) 616-2332 • E-mail bonnie@cybertrade.co.za

THERE'S always a buzz at this co-op in quiet Bonnievale. These days much of the action is orchestrated by home-boy Henk Wentzel, who grew up on a farm in the area and knew he wanted to be a winemaker since school days. Now he's at the controls of the "very modern cellar with some of the best equipped crushing facilities in SA". A red wine making hall is being created while, out in the 790 ha vineyards, young rows of mainly red varieties march into the future. For shiraz, bottled for the first time in 2000, tomorrow's already here. Next up is sauvignon, set to flow from selected plots in 2001. The range, not available for tasting (pvs rating in brackets) includes: **Riggton Red 00** (❀), **Cabernet Sauvignon 99** (❀), **Shiraz** 𝐍𝐞𝐰 **00**, **Kelkierooi 00** (❀), **Pinotage** 𝐍𝐞𝐰 **00**, **Chenin Blanc** 𝐍𝐞𝐰 **00**, **Sauvignon Blanc** 𝐍𝐞𝐰 **00**, **Pik 'n Wyntjie** 𝐍𝐞𝐰 **00** (colombard), **Riggton White** (❀) **00** (chenin-colombard), **Kelkiewit ‡ 00** (colombard), **Special Late Harvest** 𝐍𝐞𝐰 **00** (chenin).

Boplaas

Calitzdorp (see Klein Karoo map) • Tasting & sales Mon—Fri 8—5 Sat 9—3 • Cellar tours by appointment • Tourgroups • Views • Permanent exhibition of San artefacts • Carel Nel part owner of 47 000 ha Rooiberg Conservancy nearby • Owners Carel & Jeanne Nel • Winemaker Carel Nel • Viticulturist Pieter Terblanche • Vineyards 67 ha • Production 900 tons 25 000 cases 50/50 red/white • PO Box 156 Calitzdorp 6660 • Tel (044) 213-3326 • Fax (044) 213-3750 • E-mail boplaas@mweb.co.za

WHY DID THE EEC make such a fuss about South African wines labelled "Port"? Perhaps, we suspect, it all started with the burly, bike-riding, microlight-flying Cape Wine Master who energises this remote cellar. Such wines had been made in the Cape for generations, but it was Carel Nel who dragged them out of the wings in the late 80s, called Lights! Cameras! Action! and led from the front. He proudly declared port his speciality, initiated exchanges with the great winemakers of the Douro, transplanted traditional Portuguese varieties in the arid Klein Karoo soil, drove the establishment of a South African Port Producers' Association, spearheaded Calitzdorp's annual Port Festival, led the trend towards drier, higher alcohol styles. Put the passion into port. Local colleagues were infected, local standards soared. Suddenly, here was competition for the Portuguese, for Europe; the sacred title of "Port" was under threat … So, the Cape must drop the name. This skirmish was lost. But the well-travelled Nel and his cohorts are convinced they've won the campaign. "Our ports are world-class," he says, matter-of-factly.

❀ **Pinotage Reserve** Complexity, balance, supple tannins make this the standout table wine of range. Stbosch grapes provide **99** deep mulberry colour, ripe plum-and-spice stuffing, wisps of smoky vanilla oak. 10 mths Fr oak. 250 cases. 4 stars (Highly Recommended) in UK *Decanter*'s pinotage review. Regular **Pinotage**, from C'dorp grapes, ❀. Unlike pvs which unoaked, **99** aged 8 mths Fr barriques. Not much wood pickup, though; ripe strawberry/earth tones remain the focus.

Cabernet Sauvignon Reserve Tall Bdx bottle distinguishes **99** from other reds in range, as does loftier quality. Blackcurrant, ripe plum fleshiness, some mocha enticement, soft tannins and tapering finish; from Stbosch grapes, vinified in C'dorp, 10 mths Fr oak. Regular **Cabernet Sauvignon** **99** finer, more serious than pvs, though similar mulberry, green olive hints with pinch pepper. 8 mths Fr barriques. Sub R20 price ex cellar.

Merlot Reserve This variety, elsewhere in Cape often plump, expansive, here more sinewy, almost austere, even when grapes ex Stbosch as again in **99**. Initial aromatic burst of violets, cherries, mocha contrast with dry, tannic palate. Time (or food) needed to tone down present astringency. 10 mths new Fr oak (Nevers med-toast). 250 cases. Regular **Merlot**, from C'dorp vyds, reveals trademark lean gaminess in latest **99**, Fr oaked 8 mths.

Muscadel Soet Usual fragrant potpourri wafting away in **00** fortified white dessert, overall delicacy reflected in velvety sweet, raisiny palate with gentle spirity tang.

Cape Vintage Reserve Port Impressive, long-lasting Cape 'port', made only in exceptional yrs. Pvs **96** almost molasses-like in fruit density, cinnamon spice intensity. Current **97** great example of what region and cellar can produce in 'reserve' year. This flagship now blend touriga, tinta b, souzão (60/30/10), oak aged 2 yrs. 18,8% alc, 94,5 g/ℓ sugar. Deep plum with russet rim; inky, dusty aromas with hints fennel, bluegum; rich dark chocolate, plum, nutmeg flavours, which with grippy tannins promise good development over next decade at least.

Cape Tawny Port Cape benchmark for this style. Wood-matured **NV**, mainly tinta b, some touriga; avg age 8 yrs; freshened before bottling with dash younger touriga. Extraordinarily pale colour, almost orange, pink hints; comfortable aromatic array of cinnamon, caramel; dried apricot, coffee, toffee in satiny palate with hint wild scrub. VG, regional show double-gold. 18,8% alc, 109 g/ℓ sugar.

Blanc de Noir Chirpy rose bud pink semi-dry alfresco wine; highly rated by quaffnoscenti. **00** again pinotage, cab, shiraz trio; flowers, strawberries, pears in trademark firm, dry-tasting palate. Lowish 11% alc. **Golden Harvest** Light-bodied Natural Sweet white, signature grapefruit aromas broadened by honeysuckle, lime in **00**; zippy acidity ensures uncloying finish. Colombard, muscadel. 10% alc.

Sangiovese Creditable first performance from this classic grape, transplanted from Italy, aged 10 mths new Fr oak; champion red table wine on regional show. Cinnamon, black pepper, ripe plum and fresh-earth richness not quite matched by lean, lightweight palate, though good savoury finish hints at future potential. 11,9% alc. **Shiraz Reserve** Second vintage **99** mirrors pvs Rhône spicy/peppery profile, some gamey savouriness. Stbosch grapes. 10 mths new Fr oak. 250 cases. **Red** Varietal allsort with soft, light-bodied dried fruit, appetising savoury tang. Honest everyday stuff. **Chardonnay** Changes to unoaked in **99**; very quiet, some vague tropical/citrus tastes, brisk finish. **Sauvignon Blanc** Very popular in s-Cape restaurants, reports Carel Nel. **00** not a table-thumping style. Light bodied/toned, gentle boiled sweet/peardrop easiness, fresh finish. **Late Harvest** Technically sweet but dry-tasting, **00** offers delicate flowers, fairground sweets. Usual low 10,5% alc. **Pinot Noir Sparkling** **00** first certified SA wine of millennium. Palest blush colour, animated mousse, light, refreshing pear/strawberry flavour and bracing, lightly earthy finish. Ungreedily priced at under R20 ex farm. Carbonated. **Vonkelwyn Soet** Finely carbonated, sweet grapey **NV** bubble, from hanepoot, colombard. Low 9,5% alc. **Red Dessert** Russet-ruby **NV** blend of tinta b, muscadel. Unusual combination sweet jasmine, 'savoury' stewed fruit. Soft, smooth, clean-finishing. **Hanepoot Soet** **00**, second showing of this white fortified dessert, features familiar burnished gold colour, ethereal grapey sweetness, good thread of acidity which lightens, freshens. **Cape Vintage Port** ✿ This 'regular' version produced annually, usually tinta b, souzão, touriga mix, aged 18–24 mths old 500 ℓ Portuguese pipes. 'Correct' lower level sugars. Latest **97** unusually grippy, needs yr or 2 for spicy fruitcake flavours to fill out, dry tannins to soften. Not over-priced. **Cape Ruby Port** ✿ SA's best selling ruby, **NV**, in drier Portuguese style, satisfying and attractively priced. Latest bottling only tinta b (no touriga); sappy cherry/'dusty' prune nose, woodsmoke notes. The whole harmonious, some nice long dry tannins. **Cape White Port** ✿ Not too sweet **NV** fortified, from colombard; popular (lightly chilled) as aperitif. Newest bottling honeyed, spicy, some dried apricot richness and feint 'sherry' hints. Double gold on regional show.

Boschendal Wines ᵧ ᵧ ᵧ ᵧ ᵧ

Franschhoek (see Franschhoek map) • Tasting & sales Nov–Apr: Mon–Sat 8.30–4.30 Dec/Jan: Sun 9.30–12.30 May–Oct: Mon–Fri 8.30–4.30 Sat 8.30–12.30 Tasting fee R5 p/p • Combined cellar/vineyard tour Nov–Apr 10.30, 11.30 (weather dependent) • Restaurants, picnics (see Eat-out section) • Children's' picnics Nov–Apr • Tourgroups • Gifts • Views • Tours of restored 1812 manor house • Wheelchair-friendly • Owner Anglo American Farms (MD: Don Tooth) • Senior winemaker JC Bekker (since 1996) • Winemaker Raymond Greyling with Lionell Leibrandt & Henry Kotze • Viticulturist Spekkies von Breda (since 1995) • Vineyards 344 ha • Production 210 000 cases 49% white 32% red 14% pink 5% sparkling • PO Box 1 Groot Drakenstein 7680 • Tel (021) 870-4274 • Fax (021) 874-1864 • E-mail reservations@boschendal.com • Website www.boschendal.com www.boschendalwines.co.za

IT MIGHT SEEM SURPRISING to advise: watch this place. Boschendal is so well known, such a fixture, haven't they been growing vines here since forever, or at least 1685? That's the point. Familiarity and longevity have not bred contempt — the wines are far too professional for that — but there has been something of a 'good old Boschendal' fog hanging over its label, a sense that the centre of winemaking gravity has moved beyond this 3 500 ha farm stretching from Simonsberg to the Groot Drakenstein mountains. Upstart smaller wineries have become rave-age sex symbols. And the dog eared "where the Huguenots first made wine" slogan obscured the fact that Boschendal has actually been turning out wines which chant the current market mantras of 'modern' and 'new-wave' as fervently as any others. The Shiraz is a stunning example, and as for innovation — well, for a start, it was here that the Cape's first still Pinot Noir-Chardonnay was pioneered. The big empire is now fighting back, mustering its forces to correct inaccurate perceptions and stake out prime territory. Owners Anglo American have shed their other farming interests to concentrate on quality wine, and new Amfarms MD Don Tooth has the nose for business and wine this will take (an accountant by day, British Wine Master student by night). The well travelled in-house team (veteran winery assistant Lionell Leibrandt has just spent a month in Australia on a Wine Industry Trust scholarship) is very impressive, focused and committed to its mission. Senior winemaker JC Bekker sums up: "Wines to compete with the best in the world." His recent shiraz-study visit to his favourite area — the Northern Rhône — reflects Boschendal's contemporary commitment to red wines.

✿ **Grand Reserve** ⃞New⃞ Statement claret, beautifully, classically crafted to be this resurgent cellar's flagship. **97** VG cask selection of equal parts merlot, cab f; echoing blackberry fruit bound in cabernet franc austerity; trademark herbaceous stamp in lengthy finish. Will reveal splendid elegance with time. Extra width from 14% alcohol. Yr new Fr oak. Upcoming **98**, Médoc profile with cab s/merlot/cab f (50/30/20), nudges ✿✿ with bigger, succulent cassis, choc, bramble; generous, juicy flavours and ripe tannin layered in textured palate; oak a supporting act.

✿ **Merlot** 'Runner up' to above in listing order, but no less serious — perhaps more so when present dense, tight-furled **98** tannins open up with maturation. Gamey/meaty fruit in terrific superstructure, luscious plums, cherries beckoning below. 13,9% alc. Latest more perfumed — wafting violets — but altogether more intense, mouthfilling than **97**, which garnered enough awards (SAA, Michelangelo gold, *Wine* ✿) to set the pace. These single vyd wines, 12 mths Fr oak, 30% new.

✿ **Jean le Long Pinot Noir** NEW Vaults into front ranks of bigger, more gutsy Cape pinots in excellent debut **97**. Strong colour, raspberry/cherry fruit intensity in palate, excellent velvet texture, soft tannins, some exotic spiced cherries to mull over. Will bloom over next 2 yrs. Hint residual sugar (3,8 g/ℓ) adds final softness. From mother-block Dijon clone 113; 6 mths seasoned barrels, 13,5% alc. 170 cases from farm only.

✿ **Shiraz 98** sees change to curvaceous Rhône bottle (**97** square-shouldered Bdx), yet paradoxically contents are further from northern France in feel than pvs. Latest cocks an ear to Australia — showstopper style; full, robust; fat fruit reflecting hot vintage, juicy berries with black pepper whiffs. 100% oaked, 30% new, 14% alc. **97** VVG, *Wine* ✿, no less fine but not as voluminous. Enticing mix of upper Rhône (black pepper/pimento/cinnamon) and Californian late-palate choc/mint fillip. Remaining parcel of this bottling held back for Nederburg Auction. Both from single vyd. Still slumbering **00** set to wake to ✿ applause.

✿ **Lanoy** ✔ Once perhaps a convenient pasture for end-of-run (though by no means charmless) wines, recent releases much more serious. This reflected in more thoughtful oaking, as in **98**, 25% new wood, rest 2nd/3rd fill, 12 mths. Easier garnet colour, pungent thatchy/'fynbos' aromas — "That's Boschendal," shrugs JC Bekker, content with the unmistakable stamp of the land — savoury spice, pepper melded with pulpy cherry fruit. Sturdy tannins need food, time. Merlot/cab s/shiraz/cab f (60/22/15/3), 13,8% alc. **97**, Diners Club 1999 finalist. Named for Nicolas de Lanoy, 17th century owner of 2 farms now part of the property.

✿ **Pinot Noir-Chardonnay** ✔ A double-take: styled and packaged as a red, but when poured, it's white! Local drinkers may be confused, but Europeans aren't — major success in Holland's Indonesian restaurants. Mainly pinot (one-third cask fermented), which adds strawberry/cherry fruit, broad texture; splash chardonnay, 100% oaked, brings fullness to this **98** non-aggressively dry party. 13,8% alc. No **99**; next is **00**. Limited production, the undiscovered/undercover gem here.

✿ **Chardonnay Reserve** ✔ JC Becker's endeavours to settle the stylistic see-saw thwarted by vintage: intended restraint undone by bold **99** (and equally bumptious **00**, resting in cellar). Current **98** more in envisaged elegant mould: shimmering golden patina, complex apple pie nose, smooth peaches-and-cream mouthful. Zesty litchi lifts palate to integrated chalky finish. Barrel fermented/aged 9 mths, 40% new; third through malo. These characterised by increasing use of natural fermentation. Usually 14% alc, production stabilising at 1 000 cases. Standard **Chardonnay** ✔ has been through all sorts of name changes; now simply what it is. Partially oaked (40%, remainder stainless steel), **99** creamy vanilla nose hauled in by arresting tart lime/lemon twist; enduring tropical (mango, pines) finish. 14% alc. Complex, enveloping range of nuts, nougat in **98**, creamy vanilla, buttery palate shows 60% barrel-aged predominance (reverse of **99**). Exotic food note: topped UK *Wine* magazine line-up of matches for risotto of crab with piquillo peppers!

✿ **Chenin Blanc** Reflects vagaries of nature: protracted 4 week fermentation in **00** ✿ left off-dry natural residual sugar (winemaker would have preferred dry) but good depth to otherwise simple guava flavours. 4 mths on lees helps fill out palate. **99** rich, aromatic array of passionfruit, pineapple, peach, dusted with exotic spice.

✿ **Jean le Long Sauvignon Blanc** Grapes from 2nd highest block on farm, 21 yr old dryland vines which consistently produce the best fruit. **99** refined, inimitably Boschendal: herbaceous nettle/green pea/heather wafts; blooming tropical fruits on tongue. Excellent flavour concentration. 14,25% alc. balanced with length. Pvs. was **96**.

🔆 **Sauvignon Blanc** 🍷 Thoughts of a re-rating after generally troubled sauvignon **99** year comprehensively put to rest by unique, herbaceous, intense **00**. Tropical melon/soft pear followed by reductive grassy palate, with heather/wild scrub intensity, enduring length. 13,4% alc. Maintains super mineral/chalk thread of **99**. All-farm fruit: low yielding, high altitude vines.

🔆 **Jean le Long Semillon** New Single vyd's miniscule 2 t/ha yield an unheralded **99** opportunity for a 'reserve' under the JdL label (always a single vyd wine, after the property's Huguenot founder). "Very, very special" and close to JC Bekker's heart. 50/50 Fr/Am casks fermented/aged 6 mths. Green shards in straw colour; intriguing melange of citrus, herbs, candlewax, full but tapered palate ends crisply. Hints rounded oiliness add dimension. *Wine* 🔆. 13,9% alc.

🔆 **Grand Vin Blanc** Intended once-off for 300th anniversary in 1985 has endured (wining/dining public won't let go), though now a different basket of berries: mainly sauvignon (85% — and subtitled Sauvignon Blanc on label — 15% chardonnay). **99** quintessential 'Boschendal buchu' — grassy/herby flavours, extra weight from 30% cask fermentation. 13% alc. 20 000 cases.

🔆 **Vin d'Or** 🍷 Gentle, meticulous handling reflected in elegance of **98** (first since **94**). Induced berry concentration (stems lightly crushed) preserved by harvesting in small, export-grape lug boxes, small batch pressing, wood fermentation. Attention to acid balance shows in crisp twist to redolent peach-pip/dried apricot mouth intensity. 100% semillon. 103 g/ℓ sugar contained by 8 g/ℓ acid, lemon-zest tang. 13,5% alc.

🔆 **Brut 2000** Premium MCC bubbly to launch Y2K fireworks — though wise winelovers will hold it back for the 'true' millennium changeover end 2000, or beyond (a 2010 anniversary sparkle?). 50/50 chardonnay/pinot, fruit selected bunch-by-bunch, low sulphuring; complexity geared up by further yr on lees: rich, creamy but still closed; austere backbone to exceptional complexity. Bonedry. Appropriately, 2 000 bottles. VG, *Wine* 🔆.

🔆 **Brut** Latest **95** showcases all best features of house style: plush biscuity texture, black-grape length, bready/yeasty richness from 4/5 yrs on lees. More generous (now) than millennium fizzkid above, partly thanks to 9,2 g/ℓ sugar, marginally higher than pvs **93**, which stylish, mouthfilling; delicious toasty dimension. 50/50 chardonnay/pinot. No **94**.

Blanc de Noir 🔆 Versatile, venerable food partner (Boschendal pioneered this blush style in Cape in **80**) gets a revamp with grubbing up of old vines, nearly 40% cut in production to enhance quality. Consistent blend pinot/merlot (65/35) maintained in latest salmon pink, off-dry **00**, undemanding succulent red cherries, easy mouthful filled out with 6,5 g/ℓ residual sugar. 13,5% alc. **99**, featuring pinotage, plummier. **Blanc de Blanc** 🔆 Brand builder extraordinaire — and still shipping 30 000 cases with regularity. Refreshing white quaffer sees big change in **00**: sauvignon now dominates (70%); shows in grassy, heather aromas/flavour. Breadth, depth from splash chardonnay (pvsly in this driving seat); unoaked; ± 13% alc. **Riesling** (Cape) 🔆 **99**, made by Lionell Leibrandt, will be swansong — casualty of sweeping upgrade which slashed production from 250 tons to zero in a yr. Still crisp; straw character leavened by hints pepper/spice. **Le Bouquet** 🔆 Evergreen semi-sweet, now in drier, more obvious mode; upcoming **00** more emphatically muscat (hanepoot, morio), less spicy (reduced gewürz, no riesling). Pungent aromatic muscat esters, honeyed pineapple bouquet amplified in mouth. 13% alc.

Le Pavillon range

🔆 **Le Grand Pavillon** Now more serious MCC style; latest **NV** 70/30 cuvée chardonnay/pinot (with subtle name change: 'Blanc de Blancs' correctly dropped); extra pinot weight but still easy drinking, excellent value for money; 'entry-level' quality to be proud of (and not overpriced). Creamy mousse resonates in the mouth, toasty notes, fine lees stuffing for extra elegance. Properly dry at 7,9 g/ℓ sugar.

> **Rouge** ⚜ 👓 Bouncy cassis/cherry, milled pepper in **99**, some claret character in tarry nose from touch more wood (25%). Good grip without being hard. 45% each cab/merlot, drops pinot/shiraz/ruby cab. Value at under R20. **Blanc** ⚜ 😊 'Boschendal' returns to label — and rightly so: the public know it as such — in **99**. New livery reflects provenance and quality within; vitality will carry through into 2001. Chardonnay/chenin/riesling (40/35/20), drizzle semillon; easy, flavourful: lemon/lime, ripe peach. Satisfying, even more so at gentle price.

....

Boschkloof Wines

Stellenbosch (see Stellenbosch map) • Tasting, sales, cellar tours Mon—Sat 8—6 by appointment • Play area for children • Views • Wheelchair-friendly • Owners/winemakers Reenen Furter & Jacques Borman • Viticulturist Reenen Furter • Vineyards 16 ha • Production 180 tons • PO Box 1340 Stellenbosch 7599 • Tel (021) 881-3293 • Fax (021) 881-3032 • E-mail boschkloof@adept.co.za

"WHY did you choose a career in wine?" was our question. "My chosen career was medicine," is Dr Reenen Furter's answer. "Farming and wine were chosen as a way of life." And now he's seen through the trials and tribulations and unpredictability of 5 vintages, is this retired radiologist — now fulltime vineyardist and winemaker (under the consultant eye of son-in-law Jacques Borman of La Motte) — happy with this way of life? He certainly sounds so: "We have survived another year in good health and even better spirits," he remarks when we ask him about recent personal milestones. Perhaps hard work is the secret of this upbeat attitude: he's expanded the vineyards to 16 ha with plantings of shiraz and cabernet. Less strenuously, a new label has been created, and the US and Canadian markets now feature on Boschkloof's growing export list.

⚜ **Cabernet Sauvignon** Handsome in its new livery, this flagship classically styled for measured contemplation/maturation — no shortcut to pleasure here. Spartan approach epitomised by **97**, which needed 5 yrs from release to begin revealing its charms. Current **98**, back-tasted mid-2000, possibly in a trough. Much quieter than last yr, ⚜ on current form, though retains signature elegance. Some juiciness indicates this just a phase, but suggest regularly check on progress. Own/Paarl fruit, 50% new Nevers oak. **96** ⚜ VG.

⚜ **Boschkloof Reserve** Old World reticence, firmness cornerstones of this Bdx-style blend; with wraparound dry tannins, sinewy build needing ample time to grow. **98** (cab/merlot 77/23) easing somewhat but nowhere near peak; stewed plum/tobacco/eucalyptus and some earthy tones, classically dry finish. Yr oaked, 50% new Nevers. 13% alc. 2 000 cases. Follow up **99** (sample) broader, more intense; greets with nearly opaque plum colour, dense sweet cassis/fruitcake lingering to ripe conclusion. Potential ⚜. 13,6% alc. 2 000 cases.

⚜ **Chardonnay** Vaults into a different class with latest **99**, barrel fermented with real 'grapefruit marmalade on toast' aromas; palate more tropical (melon/passionfruit) finishing with butterscotch tang. "Excellent with fillets of sole 'bonne femme', reports Reenen Furter. 2 000 cases. 13% alc.

Merlot ⚜ Hints at 'right bank' Bdx. **99** tinged with fennel/earth, some savoury touches **98** similar but lighter, seemingly less body though also 13,5% alc. ±Yr Fr oak. 13,5% alc. **96** VG. ±2 500 cases.

....

Botha Wine Cellar

Worcester (see Worcester map) • Tasting & sales Mon–Fri 7.30–12.30; 1.30–5.30 Sat 9–12.30 • Cellar tours by appointment • Bring your own picnic • Tour groups by appointment • Views • Owners 32 members • Manager/cellarmaster Dassie Smith (since 1996) • Winemaker Johan Linde (since 1996) & Michiel Visser (since 2000) • Consulting viticulturists VinPro • Production 24 000 tons (10 000 cases own label) 83% white 17% red • PO Box 30 Botha 6857 • Tel (023) 355-1740 • Fax (023) 355-1615

To MARK its 50th anniversary, this solid Worcester co-op (there've been only three winemakers heading the cellar in all those years) unveiled a range of specially packaged magnums of Port, Cabernet Sauvignon and Sparkling. These are available only at the cellar, which conveniently opens at the crack of dawn so you can happily pick up some of the collectables before breakfast. Super-experienced cellarmaster Dassie Smit and winemakers Johan Linde (son of Nuy's equally seasoned Wilhelm) and newcomer Michiel Visser strive for soft, flavourful and above all easily drinkable wines.

Dassie's Reserve range

Cabernet Sauvignon These ready on release but could go 2–3 yrs. Warmer vintage reflected in 98's extra-concentrated raspberry/mulberry fruit, absorbing toasty oak with ease. Long sweet-fruity finish with peppery aftertaste. 13,4% alc. 97 SAYWS gold.

Special Late Harvest Continues high standard set by 99 first release in beautifully fresh, âppealing 00, with botrytis hints and citrus zest to well-fleshed ripe tropical fruit. Lightish 10,4% alc. Fine drink-soon aperitif.

Pinotage 97 drinkable but past its best. **Shiraz** Earth-toned, mouthfilling **98** offers quite rich coffee/choc/treacle flavours and a spiral of smoke to tickle your nose. Good now but could develop into something more interesting. **Chardonnay** **00** pleasing youthful citrus with fresh grip of acidity, which cushions the high 13,7% alc. For early enjoyment. **Colombard** Delicate semi-dry **00**, fresh, very delicate tropical flavours. Good lightish everyday fare.

Standard range

Merlot Higher-vaulting than pvs in **99**, with deep piles of fruit and distinct but supple tannins for now and for 2–3 yrs. Raspberries, soft red cherries, hints of choc; drier than pvs, bigger alc too (± 14% alc).

Hanepoot Jerepigo This traditional Cape fortified dessert a speciality of the house; seldom fails to please. Variety's honeysuckle joined by grapefruit and tropical aromas in **99**, all echo in palate with unusual bitter-marmalade tang. Solo in winter, over crushed ice in summer. 17,1% alc.

Cabernet Sauvignon Style change here from firm to fun. Latest **99** jolly and swiggable, sweet sappy fruit with blackberries and some good charry notes; long undaunting tannin. Drink before the next release. 13,2% alc. **Pinotage** Ripe banana/mulberry in **98**, uncomplicated, med-bodied, lightly oaked. Smoothing dollop sugar for effortless glugging. **Dassie's Rood** Slurpable **99** with bright strawberries, hints green pepper, light grip of tannin for standalone enjoyment or with pastas, pizzas, barbecues etc. 13% alc. **Sparkling Chardonnay Demi-sec** New Appealing peachy carbonated fizz with exuberant, creamy bubbles and not overpoweringly sweet finish. **NV.**

Blanc de Blanc No-worries med-bodied **00**, agreeable mango/dry hay flavours, just off-dry. Best in yr of harvest. **Chardonnay Brut Sparkling** Good ripe peach/tropical aromas/flavours, full-bodied and fine-moussed; some pear in gently dry finish. Striking black and silver livery. Carbonated **NV**. **Red Jerepigo** Plums and bananas in **00**; concentrated, smooth but heavily textured compared to white muscat version. 16% alc. **Port** Attractive, ruby style; **97** still going strong, drinks well now though could go couple more yrs. Peppery/herby tastes and not oversweet. Pinotage/shiraz. 19,5% alc, 100 g/ℓ sugar.

Bouchard Finlayson

Walker Bay (see Walker Bay map) • Tasting & sales Mon—Fri 9.30—5 Sat 9.30—12.30 Closed public holidays • Fynbos tours by arrangement • Owner Klein Hemel-en-Aarde (Pty) Ltd • Winemaker/viticulturist Peter Finlayson (since 1990) • Vineyards 15 ha • Production 12 000 cases 85% white 15% red • PO Box 303 Hermanus 7200 • Tel (028) 312-3515 • Fax (028) 312-2317 • E-mail info@bouchardfinlayson.co.za • Website www.bouchardfinlayson.co.za

'PASSION is too mild a word to convey Peter Finlayson's feelings for this Burgundian grape. He's obsessive about it, practically a stalker, relentlessly pursuing its charms on this 125 ha farm under the Glen Vauloch mountains in the Hemel-en-Aarde valley near Hermanus. "Once you taste a good Pinot, you don't move on," he explains. "You spend the rest of your life searching for the perfect Pinot." On his own terms, even the much admired 97 Tête de Cuvée Galpin Peak — described by assistant winemaker Norman Hardie, formerly a top sommelier in Canada, as "a perfectly formed ballerina" — isn't nearly the end of the road, it's merely a milestone on a life-long route. (It was one of only 3 South African wines awarded a gold medal at the 2000 International Wine Challenge in London.) So it's pinot which dominates the 15 ha vineyards and will soon spread into a bigger *pied-a-terre*. This won't encroach on the property's beautiful wilderness area (*fynbos* tours can be arranged by appointment). The idea is small scale, but highly compressed expansion — planting even more tightly than the current, Burgundy inspired 9 000 vines/ha, which already make the Cape's usual 5 000/ha look very greedy indeed. Finlayson believes that limiting pinot's space maximises its fruitiness and colour: struggle-grapes are better grapes. This Franco-Cape venture — Burgundy bred Paul Bouchard waves the *tricolore* in the 10 year long alliance — has recently picked up a smattering of Greek. Finlayson spent 2 weeks at the Gentillini winery on the island of Cephalonica — invited by the Cosmetatos family, who are at the forefront of Greece's modern wine revival, to share his experience in coastal winemaking and viticulture.

⚜️ **Galpin Peak Pinot Noir** Path blazing SA pinot, from home vyds overlooked by Galpin Peak. Tone here is distinctly, determinedly French: fruit of Burgundian clone 113, densely planted/pruned in Fr double guyot mode, crushed to release less tannin; oaking regime set at 25% new oak to not overpower fruit. Some Burgundian initial tautness needs ±5 yrs to settle, relax — even in current-release **99**, which among softer, more immediately approachable of these. This latest achieves difficult feat of substance and structure without resorting to alcohol kick. Fine vinosity, Old World complexity, richness, with light touch of volatility which lifts the fruit; mid-palate further fleshed by invisible grain of sugar (3,2 g/ℓ). Long, elastic tannins for good keeping. 12,8% alc. **98** ⚜️ reflects a difficult year (for pinot, being hotter): quieter nose, ripe (13% alc.) but less commanding fruit concentration and grip than exceptional **97** ⚜️ from a super vintage (see also below).

⚜️ **Tête de Cuvée Galpin Peak Pinot Noir** Limited release barrel selection, only from the greatest years. To date only **96**, mere 20 cases; **97**, 120 cases, 300 magnums, triumphant IWC gold. Latter with profound colour, almost black; and sweeping flavours, plum and berries predominating. Rich rather than intense, overall lushness enhanced by exceptional viscosity which literally glides across the palate. Nowhere near its best — keep another 3–4 yrs. 13,5% alc.

⚜️ **Missionvale Chardonnay** Flagship white from own grapes, harvested for flavour intensity without breathtaking alcs. Crackles with excitement in **99**, triumph of balance and finesse. Everything in its place, in the right proportion, especially the oak dimension which exceptionally well judged — delicate lemony flavour, chalky texture vividly highlighted. Notch up scale from **98** which in turn marked a new high for this label

* ✿ **Kaaimansgat Chardonnay** 'Crocodile's Lair', from Villiersdorp vyd, barrel fermented. Statement Cape chardonnay — bold and broad, where above stablemate is more delicate and compact. Oak impact slightly reduced in **99** (9 mths vs **98**'s 10), so fresher lemony profile, wide spectrum of long citrus flavours. Glorious yellow colour, honey nose, broad mouthfeel. **98** openly oaky, yeasty fullness in palate. More ample than usual at 13,4% alc.

* ✿ **Sans Barrique Chardonnay** "Designed for chardonnay-philes who resist oak". First was **97**; latest **99** Chablis style; big wine (±13% alc) with graphic varietal flavours, yet well controlled. Good with Mediterranean food. **98** more buttery, more New World

* ✿ **Pinot Blanc-Chardonnay** New **99** A different take on Burgundy (pinot blanc originated from — through is no longer widely planted in — that Fr wine region). Here, it is ⅔ of the blend, which features some arresting acidity (gravitating naturally to food, so watch for it on upscale restaurant wine lists) plus ripe 'melon skin' flavours. Lay some down for 2–3 yrs and wait for flavours to develop. Partially oaked. 12,8% alc. Not oaked.

Sauvignon Blanc ✿ **00** Pale yellow/green colour, grassy nose, green fruit palate, sweetish finish. Best with food. **Blanc de Mer** ✿ Unwooded white blend, made for table (so good with oysters, Knysna Oyster Company is biggest customer). **99** basket of fruit flavours, simple, fresh. Blend riesling, chardonnay, gewürz, sauvignon plus rare (in Cape) kerner.

. . . .

Bouwland

Stellenbosch (see Stellenbosch map) • Not open to the public, but tasting & sales at Kanonkop, Beyerskloof (see those entries) • Owners Johann & Paul Krige, Beyers Truter • Winemaker Beyers Truter • Viticulturist Koos du Toit (since 1996) • Vineyards 80 ha • Production 30 000 cases 100% red • PO Box 74 Koelenhof 7605 • Tel/fax (021) 882-2447 • E-mail wine@kanonkop.co.za

UNDERLINING the potential and performance of the Bottelary area is the investment in this property by red wine wheeler-dealers, makers and shakers Johann and Paul Krige and Beyers Truter, of Kanonkop and Beyerskloof. These canny three know good vineyard prospects when they see them (there are 80 ha here), and they've been busy redeveloping since 1997, planting mostly pinotage with a dash of cabernet and merlot. Meantime, even before their vines grow up, this is a success story: buying in fruit from nearby farms, which produce the same sort of personality-packed wines their own vineyards will eventually deliver, the Bouwland brand name is already established in 20 countries.

* ✿✿ **Pinotage Reserve** ✔ Aim here is to produce pinotage that can stand up to 'cousin' Kanonkop: big but still beautiful. **98** *Wine* ✿✿ has great presence, from its inky purple colour and heady, complex nose to mineral and lead nuances refining the juicy fruit. Mulberries, blackcurrants, touches of ripe banana jostle with oak vanilla in big soft palate. Runner up SAA red wine trophy.

* ✿ **Cabernet Sauvignon-Merlot** ✔ Eminently quaffable, but at a quality level that demands more genteel sipping. 60/40 blend in **99**, shiny garnet colour, meaty nose, then soft mouthful fruit (plums, blackberry, cherry, kumquat) given gravitas by chewy tannic corset. Delicious. Med-bodied **98** SAA also super-juicy-fruity, flavours ripe and succulent. Interesting green pepper spice. Footprints made by **97**, 8 mths oaked.

. . . .

Bovlei Winery   ♈ ♈

Wellington (see Wellington map) • Tasting & sales Mon—Fri 8.30—12.30, 1.30—5 Sat 8.30—12.30 • Views • Wheelchair-friendly • Owners ±50 members • Manager/cellarmaster Marthinus Broodryk (since 1980) • Winemaker Hendrik de Villiers (since 1996), with Albertus Louw (since 1998) • Consulting viticulturist Dawie le Roux (VineWise) • Vineyards 560 ha • Production 7 500 tons, 135 000 cases 60% red, 40% red • PO Box 82 Wellington 7654 • Tel (021) 873-1567/864-1283 • Fax (021) 864-1483/873-1386

THE SECOND-OLDEST CO-OPERATIVE winery in South Africa (est 1907), Bovlei is also one of the most progressive. Its winemakers regularly work a European harvest (Albertus Louw in Hungary, for example). Its multi-continental export destinations now include the market every producer dreams of cracking — China. And it's among the few co-ops which can list reds (shiraz, cabernet, merlot and pinotage) as its main varieties; with a 60–40 red–white ratio, from 560 ha of members' vineyards, Bovlei meets modern consumer demand much more closely than the national ratio, which is still weighted the other way. Here's where to call for affordable and affable Cabernet in particular — and, a bonus, the splendid view of the Hawequa mountain range from the tasting room.

❁ **Cabernet Sauvignon** ▼ This cellar's flagship, accessible on release but with enough stuffing for short-term maturation (2–3 yrs). Latest **99** should add to string of awards: layers of cassis, tobacco, cut grass reverberate in juicy palate to mouthcoating but not rough tannic finish. **92** VVG and VG; **91** VG. **Merlot** ✿ This **97** cork needs to be popped before the firm tannins overwhelm the muted earthy fruit. Unwooded.

> **Grand Rouge** ❁ ☺ Easy, med-bodied everyday fare. Quick-quaffing **97** notch up on pvs. Cab f's herby leafiness plumped by merlot's red berry flesh. **Chardonnay** ✿ ☺ Slick of honeyed bottle-age adds interest in med-bodied **99**; bright citrus fruit uncluttered by oak.

Shiraz ❁ **99** sees return to darker toned style after lively **98** ❁. Latest offers coffee, tar, earth hints and some fairly dry tannin. Unwooded. **Pinotage** ❁ Unoaked **97** still fresh and juicy, 'sweet' red-berry flavours provide convincing argument for not wooding this variety. Lower level 11,5% alc. **Chenin Blanc** ✿ Some understated floral, waxy notes in dry-finishing **00**, uncharacteristically quiet. **Riesling** ✿ From Cape riesling. Light honeyed tones in **99**, clean dry finish. Gentle 11% alc. **Sauvignon Blanc** ❁ Attractive everyday sauvignon, well priced, best enjoyed young. Dusty nettles, bell peppers in **00**, fuller than pvs, very dry. 13,5% alc. **Bukettraube** ★ Muscat-scented semi-sweet; **99** (NV in pvs ed) not for further keeping. Lightish 11% alc. **Gewürztraminer** Usually among more respectable local versions. Semi-sweet. **00** not ready for tasting. **Blanc Imperial** Lightish-bodied stein-style chenin, now **NV**. Bottling tasted mid-2000 past its best. **Special Late Harvest** Usually from chenin; smooth, clean dessert. **00** not ready for tasting. Following **NV** bubbles from semillon/chardonnay: **Baynsvalley Brut Sparkling** ❁ Extra dry fizz with wake-up freshness; like plunge into an ice-cold mountain pool. **Sec Sparkling** ✿ Latest bottling not quite as sparkly as pvs; quite a harsh finish. **Demi-sec Sparkling** ✿ Fresh grapey flavours, not oversweet. **Red Hanepoot** ❁ Current release of this fortified dessert is **90**! Lighter, lively style (no signs of flagging); billows raisins from nose to clean, non-cloying tail. **Muscat d'Alexandrie** ❁ (White Hanepoot in pvs ed) Oldie **90** still golden in all respects: brilliant 24-carat sheen, penetrating molten barley sugar sweetness, brisk finish. **Port** ★ Pvs highly individual charms of cab f-based **97** fortified dessert appear to be fading; emerging malty/savoury impressions less alluring. In **NV** 'Wellington Dumpies': **Vin Rouge** ✿ Earth-toned dry swigger. **Vin Blanc** Not ready for tasting. **Stein** Semi-sweet white, tasting very tired now. In 5 ℓ casks: **Dry Red** ✿ Unpretentious, quaffable. **Dry White** ★ Light, dry, dauntingly fresh.

. . . .

Bradgate see Jordan
Brampton see Rustenberg

. . . .

Brandvlei Winery

Worcester • Tasting & sales Mon—Fri 8—12.30; 1.30—5 • Cellar tours by arrangement • Reception facilities for ± 150 guests • Wheelchair-friendly • Owners 32 members • Winemaker Jean le Roux • Viticulturist Pierre Snyman (since 2000) • Vineyards 1 270 ha • Production 20 000 tons (4 000 cases own label) 90% white 10% red • PO Box 595 Worcester 6849 • Tel (023) 349-4215 • Fax (023) 349-4332 • E-mail brandvlei@cybertrade.co.za

A DRY WHITE 2000 season for this Worcester winery ended with "rot in the late summer", reports winemaker Jean le Roux. Situated some 23 km from Worcester on the Villiersdorp road, this co-op has been one of the area's consistent bulk wine producers — 90% of its vineyards planted with white grapes. The appointment of Pierre Snyman as viticulturist coincides with the introduction of new packaging and construction of a 400-ton red wine cellar to receive the 2001 harvest. Recent plantings by the 32 active members have focused on chenin, colombard, pinotage and merlot.

Bacchante ✵ 😊 Charming, fragrant semi-sweet quaffer with mimosa/honey sniffs. **00** lightish, for drinking now. Unusual (in Cape) semillon/hanepoot blend. 250 cases.

Ruby Cabernet-Merlot ‡ Juicy, quaffable **99** smoothed by vanilla from fermentation with Am oak chips. 13% alc. 750 cases. **Chardonnay** ✵ Well defined chardonnay fruit with intriguing smokiness (though not oaked), so **00** probably good with one of Jean le Roux's culinary favourites, BBQed leg of lamb. 13,2% alc. 500 cases. **Chenin Blanc** ‡ Lightish **00** offers marzipan whiffs, brisk, firm acidity. 750 cases. **Sauvignon Blanc** ‡ Insubstantial, dry **00** from very young vines, early-picked. 750 cases. **Hanepoot Jerepigo** ✵ Attractive **99** fortified dessert tastes — rather unexpectedly — of lemon meringue pie. Light, smooth with citrus zesty finish. Nice. 280 cases.

. . . .

Bredasdorp see Sonop

. . . .

Bredell & Nel Cape Vintage Reserve

THIS STARTED OFF AS A LARK, with two of the Cape's leading 'port' exponents, Anton Bredell and Carel Nel, disputing the merits of their respective vintage reserves. As a compromise, the two were combined and the blend judged better than the sum of the parts. The result is the collector's item (only 225 cases) below. Enquiries Boplaas tel (044) 213-3326 JP Bredell Wines tel (021) 842-2478.

✿ **Bredell & Nel Cape Vintage Reserve** Limited release **97** blend of finished wines made in Calitzdorp (Boplaas), Helderberg (JP Bredell). Inky black appearance reflects the intriguing, complex wine within, which quite different to the constituents. Damson plums in nose and palate, with almonds and peach pip kernels. 2 yrs Fr oak. 19% alc, 95 g/ℓ sugar.

. . . .

Bredell see JP Bredell

. . . .

Brenthurst Winery

Paarl (see Paarl map) • Tasting & sales by appointment • Owner Adv SA Jordaan • Winemaker Adv SA Jordaan, with consultants • Consulting viticulturist Johan Wiese • Vineyards 5 ha • Production 50—70 tons 3 000—5 000 cases 100% red • PO Box 6091 Main Road Paarl 7622 • Tel (021) 863-1154/424-6602 • Fax (021) 424-5666

"THIS WHOLE WINE THING is a hobby that got out of hand," says a rueful José Jordaan. This senior counsel hangs up his gown to leap into the cellar (assisted by expert consultants) on his Paarl property, from where he runs a tight export operation in his spare time. Inspired by some top Bordeaux blends, he has now included petit verdot in the Cabernet-Merlot blend, which was joined by an impressive Cabernet Reserve released last year. An exceptional 2000 harvest augurs well for this boutique winery.

🌺 **Cabernet Sauvignon-Merlot** Classically styled claret with dash, elegantly packaged and tasty. Sophisticated bitter choc the signature here (and below), with more conventional cassis, fragrant mint in **97**; deep plummy layers well contained by ripe tannin. **98** virtual clone of pvs, perhaps bit richer, fuller (though actually lower in alc), more generous. These aged yr in seasoned Fr barriques, Stbosch fruit. Dash cab f for complexity. ±13% alc. Strings of accolades, of which latest include 91/100 rating in UK Wine's tasting of SA wines.

🌺 **Cabernet Sauvignon Reserve** This **97** VG almost spitting image of Bdx blend above; though very slightly sterner, more grippy but still balanced and most attractive. Vinification/analysis as above.

....

Broken Stone see Slaley

....

Buitenverwachting

Constantia (see Constantia map) • Tasting & sales Mon—Fri 9—5 Sat 9—1 • Cellar tours by appointment • Buitenverwachting Restaurant Tel (021) 794-1012 Also light lunches/cakes & coffee served on terrace, picnic lunches in summer • Play area for children Views • Jazz concerts • Teddy Bear Fair May 1st • Valentine's Picnic • Owner Richard & Sieglinde (Christine) Mueller, Lars Maack • Winemaker Hermann Kirschbaum (since 1992) • Farm/vineyard manager Peter Reynolds (since 1997) • Own vineyards 100 ha • Production 70 000 cases 82% white 17% red 1% MCC • PO Box 281 Constantia 7848 • Tel (021) 794-5190 • Fax (021) 794-1351 • E-mail buiten@pixie.co.za

IT'S A BATTLE, every edition, to write about this Constantia property. A battle against the irresistible urge to gush; a battle against the magnetic pull of superlatives; a battle against drowning readers in a stream of adjectives. Elegant, sophisticated, refined, and so on and on. And that's just the wines! We've not got onto the setting, the 100 ha vineyards, the staff (and worker-policies), the 1796 manor house, the gourmet restaurant and all the other features which further define its personality profile. Trouble is, they're all sheer class. And how to convey this without sounding ridiculously effusive? On the other hand, it would be quite unfair to co-owner/director Lars Maack and winemaker Hermann Kirschbaum to downplay their achievements here. The sober judgment simply has to be that this historic, rejuvenated property and its wines are brilliant gems of the Cape, and that Maack's relaxed management style and Kirschbaum's intense perfectionism make up a premium blend. Though many of these wines' devotees (Japanese the latest) wouldn't want to change a thing, multiple experiments are underway in the cellar, including testing new yeast strains and cooperage. The sauvignon blanc vineyards are being renewed with the latest clones. Young malbec and Burgundian clone pinot noir plantings are starting to deliver. And the runaway fires which raged over the mountains shadowing these vineyards during the harvest of 2000 were kept at bay. "We survived the fire, the drought and the after-harvest party," Maack notes as the milestones of the season.

⭐⭐ **Christine** For over a decade, squarely in the vanguard of SA claret blends pursuing international form and class. Individual, neither new wave nor Old World, rather its own style. Released annually on Sep 18th, birthday of owner Christine Mueller, to intense competition for allocation. Composition vintage-dependent — usually 80% cab, 15% cab f, splash merlot. Lighter **96** 🌺 vintage reflected in restrained style — no rooftop shouting here. Barrel sample shows dense ruby brilliance, fantastic fleshy fruit already peering out from behind nerve-tingling structure. Accessible rather than austere. Adherents won't be put off — will be open earlier than last **95**, swathed in quiet, unmistakable class. Vibrant vermilion colour prelude to silky cassis/blackberry fruit, dark choc/plum notes on measured oak palate, firm tannic grip finishes with style. Marvelous structure, discretely brilliant balance. 13,5% alc. upholsters the plush ensemble. Softening but far from ready on tasting mid-2000, needs another 4 years to surrender all its charms. **94** excellent, spicy scents, ripe plums, cassis. Core opening, revealing minerally fruit, gravelly ring, sustained finish, immaculately synchronised. These from low-yield vyds. 18 mths small barrel-maturated, much in new oak.

✿ **Merlot** ❦ Jean Daneel, during his sojourn here, won the Diners Club Winemaker of Year award for brilliant **91**. So this **95** not really New, but first fresh release in four yrs. Will be loudly applauded by fans; even usually even-toned Hermann Kirschbaum's fired up: "This could easily be in the Christine!" Compact, shimmering garnet colour, waves of smoked wild meat, cocoa, lifted by floral violet scents; superb tannin structure heralds intense, lingering finish. Wonderfully welcome return. Soft but manicured, this is serious stuff.

✿ **Cabernet Sauvignon** Another old friend returns from sabbatical. Last was cracking **92** VVG, SAA. Comeback kid **95**, as predicted last ed, "not too shabby": dense inky colour, enticing black/blueberry perfumes woven with pencil lead and ethereal cigar scents. Hallmark tapered tannins frown on overt fruity exuberance, penetrating persistence in finish. Pvs. **91**, **90**, both VG.

✿ **Buiten Keur** ❦ When the lineage is wine that didn't quite make the stringent Christine selection cut, breeding is without question. Kirschbaum may call it an "alternative, not second-tier" blend (of merlot, cab s/f), but he can't restrain himself from muttering "give-away" when thinking about the price. Deliberately serious — few other producers release a 5 yr old 'entry level' red. But a metamorphosis imminent: dashes gamay/pinot to be culled, release time will 'shorten' to 4 yrs (very little **96**) name change in the offing (international focus demands something less parochial). Current **95** oozes sophisticated asphalt/choc/sweet red berries, but in understated Buitenverwachting way. Grippy palate 'purchase', long aftertaste. 18 mths small wood.

✿ **Sauvignon Blanc** ❦ While competitors strain for up-front fruit, this less flagrantly fragrant individual takes its time to gather speed. Released well after counterparts, it grows in bottle (flinty, gunsmoke steeliness, chalky depth) for about 2 yrs and once established, the momentum is irresistible. **00** product of drought which resisted by vine health. Tank sample reveals grassy, green fig hints, fine mouthful, still unyielding, closed. Rapier finish, excellent length bodes well for future. 13,6% alc. 10 000 cases. **99** straw colour still flecked with green; wild heather fragrance and emerging 'oiliness'; steely, white riverstone palate, remarkable length — this from a supposedly 'bad' year. Much fuller than when tasted last ed. **Selection Alexander van Essen** New (exclusive for German buyer) **00** under cover of Cecil Skotnes artwork; understated waxy nose but arresting pebbly grip in mouth. Ripe fruit cut by crisp structure.

✿ **Chardonnay** ❦ Another stayer, short on precocity, long on deferred power. Best 3–4 yrs post-harvest, when svelte citric ripeness matches oak vanilla in retreat. **99** 'tarry' aroma from wood-char, invigorating lemon/line riposte to creamy, chalky dominance of buttery wood. Rich tail. **98** reflects golden patina, developed earthy bouquet but palate offers beautifully integrated apple pie creaminess with grapefruit restorative. Bold 13,5% alc. Substantial oak 33/33 new/used barrels, rest tank; full malo. **97** *Wine* ✿ more 'classic', Chablis-like; ready.

✿ **Rhine Riesling** ❦ Confounding sceptics who believe riesling in SA lacks character, **00** breaks usual reserved mould and quicksteps into Mosel racy exuberance: billowing tropical fruit salad, intense fragrant spice. Focused, rich mouthful, petals and chalk. Bracing, utterly delicious. Uncommon intensity result of pitiful 1 t/ha yield ("Crop failure", is Kirschbaum's typically forthright assessment — others might have said "low yield"), inspired cellar tinkering. If reproducible, an 'experiment' which could usher in an exciting new direction…

7,1 g/ℓ acid, 7,2 g/ℓ acid. 1 500 cases. Pvs **99** scented, Belgian lace-like fine-ness to perfumed palate. **98** SAA closer than most to a European style.

🍂**Buiten Blanc** ✔ Hats off to a team that juggles highly contested, on-allocation boutique offerings above with this ubiquitous, enduring white blend. **00** hits new high in production (40 000 cases), quality. Understated but satisfying med-bodied mouthful; quiet grassy tension on nose, hints green fig. 3,6 g/ℓ sugar, so less austere than bone-dry; length of finish beyond its station. Sauvignon (60%), chenin, dashes riesling, pinot gris. Grapes ex-Durbanville/Darling. **98** SAA.

🍂**Brut MCC** Traditionally bottle-fermented **NV** sparkle, 50% pinot noir, with chardonnay, pinot gris. Languid bead, soft, fruity, puffs of biscuit/yeast rich-ness, grippy mousse. Current multi-vintage 97/98/99 degorged as required. (11,7 g/ℓ sugar) **00** to be bottled as single vintage — "the year deserves preservation on its own".

'Natural Sweet' New **00** from barrel fermented Dbnville sauvignon, registered as both sauvignon and NLH but marketing depends on final quality. Intense dried apricot, penetrating sugar (140 g/ℓ) cut by bold acid, equally big 14% alc.

Cabernet Company see Claridge

Cabrière Estate

Franschhoek (see Franschhoek map) • Tasting Mon—Fri 11 & 3 Tour & tasting Sat 11 Fee R15 p/p (R20 Sat and public holidays) Sales Mon—Fri 9—1, 2—4.30 Sat 11—1 • Cellar tours by Achim von Arnim every Sat 11 or by appointment Fee R20 p/p • Haute Cabrière Cellar Restaurant (see Eat-out section) • Owner Clos Cabrière (Pty) Ltd • Winegrower Achim von Arnim (since 1984) • Viticulturist Renier Theron (since 1998) Production 420 tons 30 000 cases • PO Box 245 Franschhoek 7690 • Tel (021) 876-2630 • Fax (021) 876-3390 • E-mail cabriere@iafrica.com • Website www.cabriere.co.za

"BUDDY, this must be the only vineyard in the world where you need to install drainage *and* irrigation!" laughs Achim von Arnim, nodding to the infant pinot and chardonnay vineyards clinging grimly to Franschhoek Mountain. The glint in Baron von Arnim's eye tells you he's on a crusade — again — and these struggling young vines — so densely planted, their Old World counterparts would feel positively agoraphobic — are his foot soldiers. Actually it's a continuation of the campaign the winegrowing philosopher began during his Geisenheim days, then at Boschen-dal down the valley and latterly in his own expanding vineyards, which now include this rock strewn eyrie — irrigated *and* drained — beside Franschhoek's ancient elephant trail. You could call it "the quest for the ultimate Cape pinot/chardonnay terroir", but von Arnim's homespun mantra — "Sun, soil, vine, man" — makes it sound vastly more poetic, exciting and fun. Which of course it is: an infectious pleasure principle informs everything here, including the vintner's personal Satur-day morning cellar tours featuring showy displays of sabrage, and the vaulted Haute Cabrière Restaurant, with views down to the barrel maturation hall (which doubles, rather dramatically, as a wedding chapel).

Haute Cabrière range

🍂**Pinot Noir** Always tells the story of the vintage in elegant yet powerful prose. Limpid ruby **99** still a closed book mid-2000, but future complexity already ap-parent in intriguing gamey, bouillon notes, subtle, sweet and toasty oak, juicy yet dry-finishing cherry fruit. **98** finely structured, light coloured but not evanes-cent; gaining mocha, undergrowth tones. **96** now coming into its own; meaty whiffs and silky finish. Taste from **00** barrel shows huge promise — possible heir to remarkable **94** (which rated 🌟 in this guide on release). These from new Burgundian clones, ultra-densely planted. Kid glove cellar regime includes gentle, almost whole bunch pressing; fermentation in closed tanks; 8 mths ageing in hand-picked Tronçais cooperage.

Chardonnay-Pinot Noir ✿ Characterful, early drinking just-dry white, blended from juice not required for the sparkling range below; so effectively a 'still' cap classique. Same whole bunch pressing, not oaked. Spice, herb and citrus aromas in **00**, 51/49 blend, firm, limey, juicy palate with 4 g/ℓ residual sugar for extra suppleness in the finish.

Pierre Jourdan range

Honouring the French Huguenot who founded the estate in 1694.

✿ **Cuvée Belle Rose** Wonderfully fine, blush coloured cap classique with delicate yet long, generous flavours. Raspberry crispness, bone-dry finish outstanding with Atlantic salmon, crayfish or duck. Latest release from 98 harvest (though **NV**), as always whole bunch pressed, early picked pinot noir; berries macerated 3 days for palest pink hue. Negligible 5,5 g/ℓ sugar. Like most of von Arnim's bubbles, rewards cellaring for a good few years. Salmon pink label.

✿ **Blanc de Blancs** Dark blue label. From first fraction of whole bunch pressed chardonnay. Pale greenish straw, some aromatic complexity: toasted bread, herbal whiffs; creamy citrus texture with elegant eddy of vanilla from partial oak maturation (40% champagne barrels). To be kept 3 yrs on lees in future. Finds ultimate food partner in a good crème brûlée. 4,5 g/ℓ sugar, black label, **NV** (latest is 97).

Brut ✿ Turquoise label. 60/40 chardonnay/pinot with former's elegance and cut, latter's more assertive thrust. Shy herbal whiffs, leesy, brioche undertones; all carry into full, tapering palate to bracingly dry farewell. Minimal 3,8 g/ℓ sugar. Excellent with perlemoen (abalone), Parma ham. Latest **NV** from 97 harvest. **Pierre Jourdan Brut Savage** ✿ Blue label. House austerity reaches its apogee in this arresting, austere, ultra-brut Cap Classique, with as many devotees as detractors. Negligible 1 g/ℓ sugar brings chardonnay/pinot interplay (60/40) — here expressed in pronounced yeasty, baked apple tones — into riveting focus. Really needs food, preferably fine fresh salty oysters. 98 just released (**NV** on label); sold mainly 'on consumption' in fine restaurants. **Petit Pierre Ratafia** Squares the chardonnay circle; unfermented sweet chardonnay juice, fortified with chardonnay potstill brandy, rather like an exotic muscadel. Traditional old champenoise tipple, with bright grapey fruit, warming 20% alc. Super winter aperitif, or partner to duck confit spring rolls, or a decadent dessert.

- -

Calitzdorp Winery ♟ ♟

Calitzdorp (see Klein Karoo map) • Tasting & sales Mon—Fri 8—5 Sat 8—12 Cellar tours during tasting hours • Terrace with panoramic views • Owners 66 members • Winemaker Alwyn Burger (since 1990) • Consulting viticulturists Stephan Joubert, Briaan Stipp (VinPro) • Vineyards 150 ha • Production 3 000 tons (38 tons, 3 000 cases own label) 93% white 7% red • PO Box 193 Calitzdorp 6660 • Tel (044) 213-3301 • Fax (044) 213-3328

FASHIONABLE SHIRAZ is the latest addition to the 150 ha vineyards grown for this co-op cellar, which roosts scenically on a hill overlooking the rural town of Calitzdorp, and surveyed with dismay, too, the damage to many of its 66 members' farms as floods swept through the (normally ultra-dry) valley during the harvest. But there are more pleasant liquid memoirs of 2000 too: Alwyn Burger notched up a decade of winemaking here, marking this with a new millennium vintage of Cabernet and a delicious LBV version of the speciality of the neighbourhood, Cape port.

✿ **LBV Port** New ▼ Alwyn Burger's growing assuredness with the region's distinctive style reflected in super **97**; 50/50 tinta b/touriga blend (as are Vintage, Ruby below), 3 yrs in large casks. Stewed prune, smoked meat mingle with choc and hints of ripe raisin in sweet tasting (though in analysis fairly dry — 80 g/ℓ) palate. 19% alc. 200 cases.

❖ **Ruby Port** One of SA's best 'true' rubies, inexpensively priced and hugely drinkable (try lightly chilled). Douro authenticity from traditional vinification, 'correct' varieties, low level 85 g/ℓ sugar. Good dusty whiffs, prunes, hint of tar in latest **NV** bottling. Yr Fr casks. 17% alc. 250 cases.

❖ **Soet Hanepoot** ▼ Textbook example of this under-appreciated fortified dessert style. Arresting yellow-gold **99** billows pineapple, orange, passionfruit and tangerine; viscous grapey flavour braced by spirity freshness. Perfect nightcap. 200 cases.

❖ **White Muscadel** ▼ Fattest, sleekest of these fortified 'stickies'. **99** growing in bottle; intense, almost 'oily' muscat aromatics repeat in honeyed, silky palate against seamless spirit backdrop. 200 cases.

Gamka Cabernet Sauvignon ‡ Millennium wine celebrating overflow of the Gamkakloof Dam ('gamka' San word for lion) in 2000 — rare occurrence in parched Little Karoo. **99** needs bit of time for oak edges to soften and meld with fruit core. 250 cases. **Merlot** ‡ Chianti-like savoury acidity, food-friendly tannins in unwooded **99**, notch up on pvs. Try lightly chilled. Lowish 11% alc. **Grand Vin Rouge** ‡ Uncomplicated wors-on-the-fire wine, med-bodied, oak-chipped. Tinta b in latest **NV** (99), hence pleasant tarry whiffs, with 50% merlot. 200 cases. **Blanc de Noir** ‡ Pretty salmon pink semi-sweet **NV** (99); soft winegum/treacle tones which somehow lack the usual charming juiciness. Tinta b. 11% alc. **Chardonnay** ‡ Bright, lemony **00** offers gentle peach/pear flavours and mere suggestion of oak. Med-bodied. 250 cases. **Sauvignon Blanc** ‡ Diffident **00** reveals only modest jasmine, mown grass hints; palate livelier with quince/rhubarb tang. Lowish 11,5% alc. 250 cases. **Vin Blanc** ★ Organic/herbal whiffs in **NV** dry sauvignon/hanepoot blend. 250 cases. **Goue Jerepiko** ❖ **New** Soft, luscious **NV** (99) fortified dessert from muscadel/hanepoot (50/50); fragrant orange peel, beeswax in sweet yet non-cloying palate. **Vintage Port** ❖ In the now classic Calitzdorp mould: dry, spirity, ageworthy. Latest **98** fuller, drier than pvs; some woodsmoke, fennel aromas with tobacco hints; choc and fresh earth in 50/50 tinta b/touriga palate. 2 yrs. 500 ℓ barrels. 18% alc. **96** SAYWS gold.

. . . .

Camberley Wines ▼ ▣

Stellenbosch (see Stellenbosch map) • Tasting, sales, cellar tours Mon—Sat 9–5 Sun by appointment • B&B guest cottages • Tourgroups • Views • Owners John & Gaël Nel • Winemaker John Nel • Viticulturists John Nel, with consultant • Vineyards 2,4 ha • Production 16–17 tons 2 000 cases (500 ml) 100% red • PO Box 6120 Uniedal 7612 • Tel/fax (021) 885-1176 • E-mail camberleywines@hotmail.com

JOHN AND GAËL NEL have leased 5 ha on a neighbouring farm, planted both cabernets, merlot and shiraz, and from 2002 will be able to broaden the fan-base for this limited edition label. Since 96 it's featured just the one wine — a distinctively minty-fruity Cabernet produced from their own 2,5 ha up the dramatic Helshoogte Pass. But apart from satisfying the local thirst for such elegant handcraftsmanship, the Nels number devotees in the UK, USA and Finland, and — after a recent visit to the Food & Hotel Asia 2000 exhibition — have got tastebuds going in Singapore. More Camberley is definitely needed, though they aren't about to give up their day-jobs (he's a Cape Town quantity surveyor, she a caterer who also runs the delightful guest cottages on the property). John Nel is adamant that the winery should remain "my relaxation", though he has to admit to being rather more driven about this than his other after-hours pastimes (stamp-collecting, cricket). "Ultimately I would like to make one great wine in my lifetime!"

❖ **Cabernet Sauvignon-Merlot** **New** Impact debut with this elegant Médoc style **99**, blend 79% cab, 21% merlot, sensitively Fr oaked (13 mths, 40% new) to showcase — not dominate — abundant ripe fruit. Opens with spicy stewed fruit, intriguing 'baked earth', savoury nuances; good dry finish with rather expensive-tasting oak-spicy aftertaste. 13,5% alc. Versatile food partner. ±875 cases.

✿✿Merlot New This surging Banhoek appellation gets a new benchmark in this exceptional first release, quantities severely limited (125 cases) so certain to be hotly fought over. **99** entirely new Fr cask aged, 13 mths, yet oak seamlessly enveloped by plush, velvety cloak of cassis. Ripe, layered flavours already soft, accessible, but there's plenty of flesh and backbone for further ageing. 13,5% alc.

Pvs **Cabernet Sauvignon 98** ✿✿, **97** ✿✿, first release **96** (not rated in this guide) *Wine* ✿✿. All above in 500 ml.

. . . .

Cape Bay Wines

VALUE QUAFFING negociant range by Cape Wine Master (and gastronome) Dave Johnson. Wines sourced from mainly Breede River cellars and blended, with winemaker son Gordon, at the Johnsons' Hemel-en-Aarde property to their own food-friendly specs. See also Newton Johnson and Sandown Bay.

✿✿Pinotage ▽ Unwooded version ("stainless steel cooperage") about as good as these get. Bright fresh, and so symbiotic with food, it almost drags you to table and makes you sit. **00** pre 'smoked' and sloshed with juicy tannin for instant pairing with spicy BBQ ribs. 13,3% alc.

Cabernet Sauvignon-Merlot ✿✿ Some frisky tannins in latest bottling (**NV**), also firmness and some pepper tones, so when Dave Johnson snaps his fingers for some hearty Yorkshire pud and roast lamb, feel free to follow his lead. Med-bodied 60/40 blend, not oaked. **Mellow Red** ✿✿ **NV** — here meaning 'No Vorries' quaffing, with trauma free price tag to match. Disparate flavours (green bean, coffee, tomato) meld pleasingly in juicy palate to balanced dry finish. Usual ruby cab/cinsaut affair, with dash cab f for extra interest. **Chardonnay** ✿✿ Action replay of pvs in **00**'s peach/citrus double-hander with papaya/melon among supporting cast. Arrestingly dry finish demands something rich or buttery on your plate. **Chenin Blanc** ✿✿ "Fish & chips wine," says Dave Johnson about zesty dry, lightish **00**, with lemons/limes thoughtfully built in so no time's wasted drizzling the day's catch with the real thing. **Sauvignon Blanc** ✿✿ Maintains gutsy stance adopted by pvs. **00** leads with sauvignon's aromatic guns blazing (cat's pee, nettle, green pepper, green fig), follows — more gently — with almost sweet sappy fruit, finishing satisfyingly crisp. **Bouquet Blanc** ✿✿ Different fragrances to pvs waft from off-dry lightish **00**, thanks to fresh varietal mix chenin/muscadel/gewürz. Honeysuckle, guava and some spice from last-named grape. Fresh sweet-sour finish levitates this eastward, culinarily speaking, towards curries and other spicy Oriental dishes.

. . . .

Cape Chamonix Wine Farm   ⛉ ⛉ ⛉ ⛉ ⛉

Franschhoek (see Franschhoek map) • Tasting & sales daily 9.30—4 Tasting fee R10 p/p for 5 wines. Also tasting & sales of farm-distilled spirits (bitters, grappa, etc.) and mountain spring Eau de Chamonix • Cellar tours 9—4 by appointment • La Maison de Chamonix Restaurant (see Eat-out section) • Picnic baskets • Spit barbecues in summer by arrangement • Fully equipped self-catering cottages Tel (021) 876-2494 • Weddings by arrangement (tables outside if weather permits) Tel (021) 876 2393 • Children's playroom • Gifts • Views • Tourgroups • Wheelchair-friendly • Owner Chris Hellinger • Winemaker/viticulturist Peter Arnold (since 1992) • Vineyards 50 ha • Production 240 tons (180 tons, 15 000—20 000 cases own label) 60% red 38% white 2% experimental MCC • PO Box 28 Franschhoek 7690 • Tel (021) 876-2494/8 office (021) 876-3241 tasting/sales • Fax (021) 876-3237/65 • E-mail office@chamonix.co.za • Website www.chamonix.co.za

THERE are so many wine competitions all over the place, and so mysterious can their judgments be, that it's tempting to ignore such side-shows. You can't drink a medal, and anyway, shouldn't a wine's performance with food and friends, not in an endless line-up in some stark hall, be the consumer's criterion? Yes and no. Here

. . . .

is one award you should take seriously: the Chardonnay du Monde competition, held in Burgundy, with 822 entries from 31 countries, judged over 3 days. It's the Olympic event for this grape, and for the Chamonix 97 Chardonnay Reserve to win a gold medal here in 1999 (one of only 16, and the only South African entrant to do so) is indeed a coup. Winemaker Peter Arnold's French-accented chardonnay style regularly wows international palates, but, rather strangely, elicits mostly silvers and bronzes from Veritas judges. Of course, all this may be beside the point if you're a member of the who-cares-about-medals club. But we have good news for you, too. The wines from this Franschhoek mountainside property also hold their own in the conviviality-and-cuisine arena. Nowhere more so than at Bom-Bom resort on the island of Principe, off the west coast of Africa. Chamonix owner Chris Hellinger is also the proprietor of this tropical retreat (and much else besides here and on sister-island São Tome).

✿ **Cabernet Sauvignon** Continues to improve. Latest **97**, featuring fruit bought in from Rbtson, Stbosch while young own vyds mature, 'sweet' strawberries, smoky/spicy oak. Some firm tannins in tangy liquorice finish. Med-bodied, 26 mths in oak, $^2/_3$ new. 4 000 cases.

✿ **Chardonnay Reserve** Prestigious gold medal at Chardonnay du Monde for sophisticated, showy **97**, gaining rich butterscotch/honeycomb overtones as it matures. Smooth, full flavoured; enough acidity to balance fairly forward honeyed bottle-age in finish. Entirely barrel fermented, new med-heavy toast casks, 14 mths; malo. 12,5% alc. 2 000 cases. Follow-up **98** very similar but fresher, marginally bigger at 13,% alc. Regular **Chardonnay** ✿ Punchy, chunky mouthful in **98**, some grapefruit, pineapple tang and bit of acidity which very good with food (grilled wahu?). Air France–Preteux Bourgeois laureate. 13% alc. 1 400 cases.

✿ **Sauvignon Blanc 00** subdued when tasted mid-2000, some passionfruit/pear/corn-on-the-cob whiffs. Zingy tropical tastes, suggestion of sweetness (though analytically dry) in the conclusion. 13,5% alc. 740 cases.

Pinot Noir New Consider the ✿ rating provisional: this first **99**, from own vyds, could step up scale when pronounced oak overtones (from 14 mths in small casks, 50% new) meld with undeveloped but ripe, mushroom/cherry flavours. 12,5% alc. 200 cases. **Chenin Blanc Oak Matured** Sampled pre-bottling, newest **98** rated ✿ but may become starrier with time. Assertive leesy/creamy flavours, fine smoky oak, good fruit/acid balance. Big 14% alc. 300 cases. Note: at press time a **Méthode Cap Classique** New, from own vyds, was still under wraps (so untasted) but likely to be released for the festive season. The **Sauvignon Blanc Reserve 00** was not ready for tasting; this for 2001 release.

. . . .

Cape Gables New

AFFORDABLE easy drinking range made for Ocean Traders International by Franschhoek Vineyards. Tel (021) 557-3799 • Fax (021) 557-3742 • E-mail craigoti@mweb.co.za • Website www.oti-africa.com

Cabernet Sauvignon ✦ Unwooded, med-bodied **00**'s blackberry fruits served with some strident tannins, so team with winter stews or something BBQed. **Merlot** ✿ Winemakers' note — "Young with upfront fruit" — says it all. Unoaked, med/full bodied **00** probably best within yr of harvest. **Pinotage** ✿ Light bodied **99** unoaked, aromatic and spicy, undemanding. **Grand Vin Rouge** ✦ Light, almost rosé **NV** natural table partner for pizza/pasta; uncomplicated, quaffable. **Rosé** ✦ Jazzy pink **NV** with tropical/floral wafts, gentle sweetness in lightish crisp palate. **Blanc de Blanc** ✦ Dry, lightish **NV** with green fig, cut grass zest. Chenin, colombard, semillon. **Sauvignon Blanc** ✦ Full, firm yet friendly sauvignon grassiness, dry finishing **00**. 13,4% alc. **Chenin Blanc** ✿ Guava toned light off-dry **00** with exotic passionfruit extras; fresh, easy; early drinking. **Venestia Blanc** ✦ Honeyed,

. . . .

med-bodied semi-sweet **00**, equal hanepoot, chenin partnership styled for curries, spicy food. Above 1 000 cases each.

Cape Indaba see Natural Corporation

Capelands

BUDGET priced, quality driven range by Winecorp.

Merlot ☆★ **00** unready for tasting; but should follow swish, sweet-fruitiness of **99**. 40% barrelled, mostly Fr. **Ruby Cabernet** ☆★ Uncomplicated fruity mouthful; low tannins; for early drinking. Mainly exported. **00** not ready for tasting. **98** SAA. **Classic Cape Red** ☆ **00** with cinsaut/cab's familiar sweet, juicy berry fruit; extra dimension/spice from splash merlot. Uncomplicated, ready to drink. Among first SA reds released in 1 000 ml botte. **Chardonnay** ☆★ Cellar chief Ben Radford's claim that there's a shortage of good quality chardonnay in Stbosch will possibly see no **00** bottling of this ready to enjoy dry white. **99** supple, satisfying but not too demanding. **Classic Cape White** ☆★ 'Classic' not an over-hopeful description if consistency, attribute of first 3 bottlings, plays role in such a claim. Currently **NV** (though shortly to be vintaged, varieties listed); preview of **00** shows all usual fruity charm cajoled from mix chenin/sauvignon/chardonnay/colombard. Meadowbloom fresh, bouncily bright, dash invisible sugar for extra-comfortable but not sweet landing. Sized to suit every occasion: 1 000 ml, 750 ml, 187 ml, bag-in-box and wine-by-glass dispenser. **98** SAA first class!

Cape Levant see Sonop
Capell's Court see Linton Park Wines

Capenheimer

SA'S ORIGINAL perlé, launched 1962. Based on the Italian lambrusco style, with a light, crisp sparkle. From Monis.

NV ☆ ☺ Colombard/chenin in super-frisky mode. Wafts of tropical ripeness, bracing effervescence in palate, clean and remarkably long.

Cape Point Vineyards

Cape Point • Tasting by appointment • Owner Sybrand van der Spuy • Winemaker Emmanuel Bolliger (since Jun 1996) • Viticulturist/farm manager Japie Bron (since 1999), with R du Plessis • Vineyards 35 ha Production 50 tons 60% red 40% white • PO Box 37700 Valyland 7978 • Tel (021) 785-7660 • Fax (021) 785-7661 • E-mail cpvines@mweb.co.za

MANY Cape vineyards claim maritime influences, sea breezes and various models of coastal air-conditioners. Few are as close to the ocean as this new venture based on three separate, authentically peninsular sites. French/Aussie-experienced winemaker Emmanuel Bolliger could practically surf Long Beach and the radical Outer Kom break from the Noordhoek vineyards (mostly whites and pinot noir) below Chapman's Peak; he could almost launch a Corvette from the cabernet (sauvignon/franc) and shiraz rows on Redhill, near the Simon's Town naval base; and at Fish Hoek, where the first phase of the cellar has been built, beach umbrellas would not be out of place amid the merlot and cabernet vineyards which are reclaiming land previously ravaged by kaolin mining. Well, we exaggerate — but not by much. When this property names its second label Scarborough, after a Cape Point beach, it's sound geography, not marketing deception. 35 ha of vineyards will rise to a total of 50 ha once all planting is completed — the wines below were made in

2000 from infant, 3 year old vines. Too young to rate conclusively, they reflect the excellent potential of these unique sites.

Sauvignon Blanc Headlining debut for this young label, with a nod from 2000 Young Wine Show judges as grand champion wine (mirroring feat accomplished pvs yr by Vergelegen's André van Rensburg with his Schaapenberg Sauvignon). Tasted in infancy (ahead of the show), this **00** bouquet subdued, merely hinting at some 'green' fruits/herbs. Palate more forthcoming with cut grass/green fig preserve and brisk acidity cascading into clear limey finish. Promising, should rate min ✿ on release. 13,5% alc. **Chardonnay** Not ready for tasting. 13% alc. Release date Feb 2001. **Semillon Noble Late Harvest** Attention-grabbing tussle between exotic tropical sweetness/penetrating acidity the most immediately striking feature of this promising oak-fermented botrytised dessert, glowing with ✿ potential. Pineapple/mango fruit and light layers of botrytis/vanilla hint at future intricacy. 14,5% alc, 104 g/ℓ sugar.

Scarborough range

Sauvignon Blanc Sampled immediately post-bottling (not rated), some mango and, intriguingly, nectarine barely peeping through; sweet-sour palate, short, bracing finish. 13,5% alc.

Cape Reflections see Vinfruco
Cape Safari see Cape Wine Cellars
Cape Salute see Coppoolse Finlayson-Sentinel
Cape Soleil see Sonop
Cape Table see Riebeek
Cape View see Kaapzicht, International Wine Services

Cape Vineyards

Rawsonville • General manager Henriette Jacobs • Marketing manager Dirk Conradie • Production 67% white 30% red 3% rosé • PO Box 106 Rawsonville 6845 • Tel (023) 349-1585 • Fax (023) 349-1592 • E-mail cape.vineyards@xpoint.co.za

EXPORTING to six countries in Europe, the United States and Canada, this joint venture among several progressive Breede River wineries handles mainly bulk wine but bottles small quantities under its own labels. One of these recalls the Scot Andrew Geddes Bain, pioneer road engineer, explorer, geologist (and writer of popular verse) whose projects include the pass which links the Breede and Berg river valleys and bears his name. The range, not available for tasting (pvs ratings in brackets), includes: **Andrew Bain Cabernet Sauvignon-Merlot 98** (✿), **Rawson's Ruby Cabernet-Merlot 00** (✿✿), **Andrew Bain Chardonnay 98** (✿✿), **Rawson's Chardonnay 98** (✿✿).

Cape Wine Cellars

Wellington • Sales from wheelchair-friendly SA Dried Fruit shop, Wellington (no tasting) Mon—Fri 9—1; 2—5 Sat 9—12.30 • Owners Boland Wine Cellar, Bovlei Winery, S.A.D. Group, Wamakersvallei Winery, Wellington Co-op • Team leader/master blender Jeff Wedgwood (since 1995), with cellarmasters from above wineries • Production 250 000 cases (rising to 400 000) 50% white 40% red 10% rosé • PO Box 508 Wellington 7654 • Tel (021) 873-1101 • Fax (021) 873-3112 • E-mail info@sadgroup.co.za • Website www.wine.co.za

THIS JOINT-VENTURE among S.A.D. Holdings, virtually synonymous with dried fruit in SA, and four Paarl/Wellington co-ops is on a serious roll. Freshly penned export contracts are poised to send annual output soaring to some 400 000 cases. Affable Jeff Wedgwood, officially "team leader and master blender", works with the cellar chiefs of Wamakersvallei, Bovlei, Boland and Wellington wineries to style the in-house Kleinbosch and Cape Safari ranges, as well as in-house labels for clients in

6 European countries and China, Japan and the US. Recent developments include one of SA's first cork-closed 1 000 ml reds, Kleinbosch Rouge. In the works are a Kleinbosch Reserve collection, to be launched in 2001, and cold storage facilities for about 40 000 cases in Pietermaritzburg. And if you can't make the shopping trip to S.A.D.'s famous store in Wellington, where the range is for sale (but not, unfortunately, for tasting), you can pop into CMC's new outlet on the Internet for on-line orders and information. It seems S.A.D.'s signature — a stylised image of the sun — is smiling on this team. The range, not tasted for this ed, includes (pvs ratings in brackets): Kleinbosch range: **Cabernet Sauvignon 99, Shiraz 98 (⚛), Merlot 99, Pinotage 99, Rouge 99 New, Chardonnay 99, Sauvignon Blanc 00, Chenin Blanc 99 (⚛), Special Late Harvest 99**; Cape Safari range (all **NV**): **Late Sun Red (⚛), Blush (⚛), Stardust (⚛), Late Harvest (⚛)**.

- -

Cape Wine Exports

Walker Bay • Not open to the public • Tasting for overseas guests by appointment • Cellar tours by appointment • Directors Riaan Pieters, Ben Chowney, Des Dall, KM Chowney • Production 7 000—8 000 cases 60% red 40% white • PO Box 898 Hermanus 7200 • Tel (028) 313-0137/8 • Fax (028) 313-0139 • E-mail cwe@itec.co.za • Website www.cwe.co.za

IT'S BEEN a year of personal growth for high-flying MD Riaan Pieters, who got his private pilot's licence — he flies a Cessna light aircraft — and also wrote the prestigious CM (SA) (Chartered Marketer) exam. From its Hermanus headquarters, CWE is in the process of creating a top-of-the-range brand for sale in the Benelux countries, as well as a first joint-venture brand in conjunction with a company abroad. They have also orbited into cyberspace with their own website. A big grounding influence in Riaan Pieters life was close friend DWR Hertzog, one of the founding members of the Rembrandt Group, from whom he learnt about 'brand building' in the liquor industry. He tries to implement these invaluable lessons, learnt by Hertzog and Dr Anton Rupert over many years, in his own business. Now if only he could get his photographs published in SA *Getaway* magazine…

Fernkloof range

⚛**Chardonnay** ▼ Rung above the stablemates below (though **00** refreshingly unpretentious and quaffable); light oak lifts zesty citrus fruit; provides underlying buttered toast richness. 13,5% alc.

Cabernet Sauvignon ⚛ Gently dry-finishing **98** good for get-togethers with friends, as Riaan Pieters suggests. Quite intense cherry/smoked meat attractions. **Merlot** ⚛ Savoury green olive tones, some dry tannins and light brush of oak in **98**. **Pinotage** ⚛ Ripe, juicy **98** with smoky mulberries and plums. Lingering flavours. 13% alc. **Chenin Blanc** ⚛ **00** very different to pvs. Exotic, heady, waxy flavours with cinnamon hints, peachy finish. Good early drinking. Unwooded. **Sauvignon Blanc** ⚛ Characterful and just a bit exotic: smoky melon, grapefruit tastes in **00**, crisply satisfying.

- -

Carisbrooke

Stellenbosch (see Stellenbosch map) • Tasting & sales Mon—Fri 9—5 • Owner Willem Pretorius • Winemaker/viticulturist Kowie du Toit (Vlottenburg Winery) • Vineyards 6 ha • Production 40 tons 1 500 cases 100% red • PO Box 25 Vlottenburg 7604 • Tel (021) 881-3034

SENIOR COUNSEL Willem Pretorius taps the considerable experience of Vlottenburg winemaker Kowie du Toit to make this single wine, a Cabernet Sauvignon, from 6 ha on Pretorius' Carisbrooke farm in Stellenboschkloof (Overgaauw, Uiterwyk among the splashy neighbours). The current release is **98** which rated ⚛ in pvs ed.

- -

Carneby Liggle

POLY-CULTURAL/REGIONAL venture between SA wine author/entrepreneur Graham Knox and German-owned Blaauwklippen, for export to UK. Portion made by Frenchman Etienne Charrier at Havana Hills cellar, Durbanville, remainder by seasoned local Hein Hesebeck at Blaauwklippen, Stellenbosch. To date a single ready-on-release cinsaut/zinfandel/shiraz blend; described, colourfully, by a British buyer as "black berry juice with balls". Not available for tasting. PO Box 54 Stellenbosch 7599 • Tel (021) 880-0135 • E-mail doolhof@mweb.co.za

Carnival

THESE are the Spar chain of convenience stores' boxed wines, available in 1, 3 and 5 ℓ packs. See also Country Cellars and Spar.

Classic Red ✳✳ **NV** Very soft and drinkable, with just a suggestion of tannin. Unwooded pinotage/merlot/ruby cab blend. Light/med-bodied. **Rosé** ✳ **NV** Now technically dry, though still a suggestion of sweetness in finish; formula remains pinotage/chenin. (4 g/ℓ sugar). **Grand Cru** ✳ Somewhat neutral but non-aggressive, clean, fresh and very dry. **NV**. From chenin. **Stein** ✳ **NV** Unpretentious semi-sweet quaff, pleasantly honeyed. **Late Harvest** ✳ **NV** Non-cloying light semi-sweet; good and fruity.

Cathedral Cellar

THIS IS THE RANGE that has conclusively banished the fusty, dusty image of KWV wines. Launched in 1990 as a single flagship label, with a Bordeaux-style red blend, it's grown into an export fleet that sails the world, and is admired wherever it docks. Locals must just hope that it keeps winning SAA awards (among countless others) and flying on the national carrier's wine list: you won't (at present) get it on the ground at home. Lavish new oak is part of the secret (KWV digging deep into pockets here) with cellar chief Kosie Möller's maturation policy favouring the lengthy lie-in. The range is named after the KWV's vast, domed cellar built in 1930 and now a tourist attraction — it's lined with avenues of massive vats featuring in carved form the history of winemaking in South Africa. For cellar tours, see KWV International.

✳✳ **Cabernet Sauvignon** This **Paarl 97** and following Stbosch version part of a terroir experiment: two cabs from neighbouring appellations vinified identically (regime included 26 mths 100% new Fr oak). This version more open, approachable (typical of Paarl cabs), well balanced with generous choc/mulberry tastes. Striking blueish/black colour. The 'control' **Stellenbosch 97** demonstrably tighter, more 'serious': colour deeper, more intense, nose less welcoming/developed; tannins firmer — overall, full yr behind Paarl cab in development. One for long-term cellaring. Cathedral Cellar cabs heaped with praise: **96** SAA, **95** VVG, SAA trophy, Concours Mondial gold, best wine at 1998 Sélections Mondiales, Canada. **94** VVG, overall champion red Ljubljana, Slovenia etc.

✳✳ **Merlot** Vivid contrast between **96** and **97** ✳✳ vintages; former silky, luscious in youth, latest **97** SAA tauter, more needful of further maturation. All necessary components present: potentially rich choc-plum, the usual minty scent, firm acids/ tannins, sturdy oak platform (26 mths 100% new Fr casks). Given time, could approach (or better?) standout **95** VG, SAA, best merlot at 1998 IWSC, Air France–Preteux Bourgeois trophy.

✳✳ **Pinotage** "This variety," Kosie Möller contends, "will not become one of the great wines of the world." Time (10–15 yrs?) might very well prove him wrong about **97** ✳✳, an enormous wine which could have been made in Bdx. Möller-favoured 'sur bois' supercharge (26 mths Fr oak, 100% new) imparts formidable, front-of-mouth-coating tannin structure to blackcurrant fruit density. This and pungent, high toned intensity give new meaning to the phrase 'long-term wine'. Contrast with pvs **96**, altogether more accessible, lighter — and virtually chained to the podium: VVG, SAA, ABSA Top Ten, golds at Michelangelo /International Wine Challenge etc. **95** SAA, Michelangelo gold. **94** VG, SAA Top 10.

✿ **Shiraz** Second release **97** ✿✿ VVG, SAA, like pvs, in house's pedal-to-the-floor mode, the now standard full throttle oak (26 mths 100% new casks) adding extra horse- (and staying) power to the design. Still idling mid-2000: nose subdued; palate grippy, earth, spice, diverse black berries present but undeveloped. Min 5 yrs needed for tight-sprung tannins to unwind. 50/50 Fr/Am barriques. Much tauter initially than first **96** VVG, from generally lighter yr, SAA runner-up red wine of 1998, International Wine Challenge gold.

✿ **Triptych** Kosie Möller wearing his lab coat in **97** ✿✿ SAA as formula changes from Bdx blend to 'Cape red': cab (60%, ex-Stbosch), equal portions merlot, shiraz, latter perhaps accounting for earthier notes in still shy mélange of black fruits, spice and vanilla. Firm cab backbone finely polished by merlot's sleekness. Very smooth, complex; excellent potential for development in bottle. 'Standard' oaking (100% new Fr casks, 26 mths). Tighter than **96**, whose history gallery stretches from VVG, SAA Top Ten, Michelangelo gold to listing on KLM. **95** VVG, gold at 1998 Sélections Mondiales, Canada, Michelangelo double-gold. **94** VG, SAA.

✿ **Chardonnay** Fine tuning here, too? Minimal malo sees pvs butterscotch/cream textural richness shift into somewhat crisper, zingier mode with lemon/lime fruit in **99** sharper focus. (Light vanilla overlay fits very well with Thai food — suggest lots of coconut milk). Gold on 2000 Vinalies. 100% new Fr oak, 7 mths.

✿ **Sauvignon Blanc 98** VG flew with KLM; **99** ✿ changes course (not totally convincingly) into herbaceous, grassy territory. Good green pepper tones, but these end abruptly.

✿✿ **Port** Cross-over style: not old Cape sweet/porty, nor modern 'Portuguese' dryness (though see Maatskappywordings Vintage Port under KWV for another take), high alc. Rich prune/vanilla flavours in **95**, gentle eucalyptus, sprinkling of pepper. Lowish alc (17%) for easier drinking. Medium dry finish. From tinta b.

Note: **Cabernet Franc 97** made but not released. Pvsly tasted **96** (first under this label) rated ✿✿.

· ·

Cederberg Wine 🍷 🍷 🍷 🍷 🍷

Cederberg (see Olifants River map) • Tasting & sales Mon—Sat 8—12.30; 2—5 • Bring your own picnic • Fully equipped self-catering cottages • Gifts • Walks/hikes • Views • Proclaimed conservation area • 4X4 trail • Mountain biking • Private observatory nearby tel (027) 482-2825 • Owners Nieuwoudt family • Winemaker David Nieuwoudt (since 1996) • Viticulturist Ernst Nieuwoudt • Vineyards 23 ha • Production 140 tons (7 000 cases own label) 70% red 30% white • PO Box 84 Clanwilliam 8135 • Tel (027) 482-2827 • Fax (027) 482-1188 • E-mail cederwyn@iafrica.com

THE NIEUWOUDTS have owned their Cederberg eyrie since 1835, grown table grapes there since 1965, and wine varieties since the early 1970s. But it's taken Elsenburg trained, Lievland seasoned son David to really make the vineyards fly. Tucked into a valley in the spectacularly rugged Cederberg wilderness area between Citrusdal and Clanwilliam, these are the highest parcels in the Cape (1 100 m above sea level) — so isolated and unique, they have their own appellation ("so don't lump us with Olifants River"). With show judges enthusing (double gold Veritas, runner-up SA Wine Chenin Challenge among recent credits) and consumers queuing, growth is in the rarefied air: 15 ha of mainly merlot and shiraz are being established, to join 23 ha of 'noble' varieties and pinotage. The cottages on this remote farm have long been a haunt for serious hikers, amateur astronomers and adventurous wine drinkers. Now 4 × 4 trailers and mountain bikers can put them on their itinerary too.

♣ **Cabernet Sauvignon** Much improved since cool-vintage **97** announced it as serious Cape cab. **98** ♣, warmer, more generous yr, showier, more concentrated. Current **99**, again warmer vintage, sees new (Fr) oak quota raised to 60%, which well absorbed. Thumbprint mulberry/black cherry, ripe tannins, broad fruity finish which needs more time to develop than pvs. Should attain similar rating if properly cellared. 14 mths in cask. 13,5% alc. 1 200 cases.

♣ **Chardonnay** First release **99** set cracking pace for this serious, full-bodied, 100% barrel fermented chardonnay. Next-up **00** ♣ not as immediately showy, more understated version. Though again oak well integrated with complex citrus/melon/yellow peach fruit. 80% aged extra 4 mths post-fermentation. 14% alc. 250 cases.

♣ **Sauvignon Blanc** Improves by the vintage. **00** textbook Cape sauvignon aromatics (grass/capsicum/gooseberry), plus more exotic pear. High 8 g/ℓ acid rescued from tartness by mouthfilling flavour, partly from extended lie-in on lees. 12,5% alc. 1 200 cases.

♣ **Chenin Blanc Barrel Fermented** Cleverly oaked **00** manages to enhance, not dominate, the delicate yellow-peach fruit with subtle vanilla undertones. Food wine. 40% Fr cask fermented/aged 4 mths. 13,5% alc. 600 cases.

Pinotage ♣ Maiden **97**, ABSA Top 10 finalist, set the pace. **98** ♣, tasted in youth last ed, has developed light bitterness which detracts from good gamey/cherry fruit. Sharpness also apparent in current **99**. Fr/Am oak, 60% new. 13,8% alc. 800 cases. **Cederberger** ♣ Chic, easy everyday red with winning formulation: ripe, succulent berries freshened/energised by brisk acidity, silky tannins, lightly oaked. Ruby cab/pinotage/merlot. 13,5% alc. 800 cases. **97** VVG. **Chenin Blanc Unwooded** ♣ Charming semi-dry **00** quaffer, ripe pears animated by nips of acid. 13% alc. 400 cases. **97** VG, SAA. **Bukettraube** ♣ Zingiest in Cape; generous scoop sugar freshened by bright acidity. Med-bodied **00** delightful ripe peach/apple tone just right for picnics, Oriental food. 1 100 cases. **98**, **97** VG.

. . . .

Cellar Cask

BOXED/screwcap range by SA Wine Cellars. These all NV.

Premier Claret Dry Red, not available for tasting. **Select Johannisberger** Semi-sweet version of above red. Not ready for tasting. **Premier Grand Cru** ♣ Fruity, crisp and dry. Lowish alc (11,5%). **Premier Semi-Sweet** ⚡ Basically PGC blend above tweaked with sugar. Some tropical tones, honeyed notes in finish. **Premier Late Harvest** Ripe, honeyed, touch tropical. Lowish 11% alc. **Select Johannisberger** Not ready for tasting.

. . . .

Chamonix see Cape Chamonix Wine Farm

. . . .

Château Libertas

SA'S BIGGEST SELLING CORK-CLOSED RED, blended, matured and bottled at Stellenbosch Farmers' Winery since 1932 (when it retailed for a shilling a bottle). Widely respected, unpretentiously priced. Retains French 'château' appellation by special dispensation.

Overall quality improvement at SFW reflected in this popular favourite, invariably unobtrusively oaked, medium-weight (though not lacking substance). Current **98** ♣ has more presence, dimension than pvs (partly from stout 13% alc). Plenty of ripe berry fruit, some red cherries for extra interest, well managed oak and unexpectedly lively tannin, needing food or a bit of time. Mainly cab, with merlot, some cinsaut.

. . . .

Cheetah Valley see Winecorp

Chiwara see International Wine Services
Cilmor Winery see Sonop

Cinzano

POPULAR, festive, lower alcohol range of carbonated sparklers. African Wines & Spirits is SA agent for this famous Italian brand. These all NV.

Spumanté ✿ Still huge consumer hit, good example of this light-bodied style. Smilingly fresh muscat nose; sweet softness livened by pert bubble. **Tiziano** ♣ Rose coloured, strawberry/cherry toned sweet fizz; lightweight (10% alc), lively mouth-expanding mousse.

Clairvaux Co-op

Robertson (see Robertson map) • Tasting & sales Mon—Fri 8—5.30 Sat 9—1 • Cellar tours: see intro below • Gifts • Walks • Wheelchair-friendly • Owners 23 members Winemaker • Kobus van der Merwe (since 1975) • GM/viticulturist De Witt LaGrange • Vineyards 80 ha • Production 1 200 tons (5 000 cases own label) 97% white 1% red 2% rosé • PO Box 179 Robertson 6705 • Tel (023) 626-3842 • Fax (023) 626-1925 • E-mail clairvaux@boland.lia.net

"WE SOUTH AFRICANS are very conservative," states Kobus van der Merwe, iconoclast and famously mischievous wit (the person he'd most like to meet is long-time Nederburg auctioneer and Master of Wine Patrick Grubb, "so he (Grubb) will have someone smart to talk to about wine.") "We're followers, not leaders," vdM continues, "when it comes to international wine trends." The seasoned winemaker (25 years at this cellar) doesn't say it, so we'll do it for him: some exceptions to the rule are to be found among the 23 members of this co-operative, right on the rural doorstep of Robertson, who are thinking about creating a range of healthcare products and a "muti (medicinal) house remedy aperitif". For more about these plans, may we suggest you visit this relaxed winery, where you'll be taken on a cellar tour "whenever you want to".

✿**Golden Muscadel Jerepiko** Consistently among the top traditional Cape sweet fortified desserts. **98**, like pvs, billows 'oily' orange rind/candle wax fragrances; these ring in very sweet, grapey palate with mellow spi9rity tang. White muscadel. 1 000 cases. Also in 250 ml.

Red Muscadel Jerepiko ✿ Vivid russet/topaz colour in **98** full-sweet fortified dessert, honeysuckle scents, quite elegant rose-flavoured palate with hint of tea leaves in finish. 1 000 cases. Also in 250 ml. **Vin Rouge** ♣ Kobus vd Merwe suggests you try this pleasant, light unwooded ruby cab/cinsaut **99** quaffer with, of all things, giraffe. Can he be serious? 500 cases. **Sauvignon Blanc ★ 99** assertively tart and dry. Better young. 1 000 cases. **Rhine Riesling** ♣ Off-dry **98** quite evolved, some marmalade/stewed pineapple in honeyed, blousy finish. 13% alc. **Soleil** ✿ Very ripe chenin/white muscadel (including some raisins) in light, sweet but not unctuous **99**. 1 000 cases. Also in 250 ml.

African Sunset range

2 ℓ bag in boxes. All NV, all New.

> **Rosé** ♣ 😊 Alluring jasmine, ripe grape aromas in succulently fruity party wine; instant infusion of sugar (25 g/ℓ) will keep you dancing through the night. Light bodied (10,5% alc). **Blanc de Blanc** ✿ 😊 Bright guava/lime fruit; juicy, gently dry finish. Lightish 11,5% alc. **Late Harvest** ✿ 😊 Floral/talcum whiffs in friendly, lightweight semi-sweet, nicely freshened with tingly acidity. Chenin/white muscadel.

Ruby Red ★ Similar varietal make-up to Vin Rouge above (ruby cab/cinsaut), but not as vibey. Austere; some porty tastes.

Claridge Wines

Wellington (see Wellington map) • Tasting & sales, cellar/distillery tours by appointment • Private luncheons for 6—60 guests by appointment • Owners Roger & Maria Jorgensen, with Michael Loubser • Winemaker/viticulturist Roger Jorgensen (since 1991) • Production 10 000 cases 90% red 10% white • PO Box 407 Wellington 7654 • Tel (021) 864-1241 • Fax (021) 864-3620 • E-mail claridge@dockside.co.za

HERE in once-sleepy Wellington, and in the unlikely shape of a former Kent strawberry farmer and (in holiday-time) diamond prospector, you'll find one of the most creative thinkers — and more crucially, doers — in the winelands. Roger Jorgensen doesn't know what convention is — unless it's there to be broken. He dreams up these extraordinary ideas — like registering for himself not just wine-names but wine-varieties — and goes ahead and makes them real. Imagine the chagrin of those in the Cape wine business long before Jorgensen (his first, personality-packed Claridge vintage was 91) when this outsider nips into the gap and grabs the brands of The Pinotage/Chardonnay/Cabernet/Pudding Wine Company! It is brilliant and cheeky and in no time at all he has supplied 40 000 cases of Pinotage to 2 350 retail outlets in the UK, and has firm orders for 120 000 cases of his 2000 vintage, sourced from Malmesbury and Paarl's Perdeberg area. (Not Stellenbosch: "too jammy" in 2000, he judges.)

✿ Red Wellington "Impressive hi-athletic assemblage," reads back label of this individual Bdx blend, current **96** release evidently jock with admirable stamina: no sign of premature ageing, still-fresh berry/cherry tones, soft tannins panting for another few circuits. Cab/merlot/cab f (60/30/10), 12—18 mths mixed cooperage. 13% alc. No **97**. **98**, **99** not tasted.

✿ Chardonnay Gutsy, individual style, combination Old World structure, New World fruit forwardness. **96** powerfully smoky, weighty, lashed by oak. No **97**. Current **98** another burly number (over 14% alc), packed with tropical fruit, nuts, earth, some leesy undertones. Old vines, mix Davis/Burgundy/Swiss clones, whole bunch pressed, barrel fermented. **99** not ready for tasting ("perennial problem of certification by Wine & Spirit Board").

Pinot Noir ✿ Klein Opten Horst label. **97** delicate cold tea colour, red fruits bouquet; distinctly Burgundian tones of farmyard, earth, mushroom; plus ripe red berries. Burgundian clones, yr oaked, mixed cooperage. Grapes from neighbour Naas Ferreira's farm, crop managed by Jorgensen. No **98**. **99** bottled but not tasted. **The Pinotage Company Bush Vine** ✿ Made to order for UK supermarket chains. **99** "a concept wine" for early drinking. Vivid purple colour, upfront ripe cherries/mulberries, soft tannins. Fr oak staved. Free from pinotage features UK consumers find objectionable. Bought-in grapes/finished wine from West Coast, Paarl. **The Cabernet Company** New **00** blend of Muldersvlei/Perdeberg cabs. Mid-2000 still to be "chipped up", but unrated preview reveals ample fruit/tannin, thumbprint Muldersvlei herbaceousness.

Clos du Ciel

Stellenbosch (see Helderberg map) • Tasting, sales, cellar tours by appointment • Guest lodgings planned — phone for details • Meals/refreshments by appointment or bring your own picnic • Play area for children • Small tourgroups by arrangement • Conferencing for small groups by arrangement • Views • Wheelchair-friendly • Owner Peter Aschke • Winemaker André Morgenthal (since 1999) • Vineyard 1,53 ha • Production 8 tons 80% white 20% red • PO Box 12830 Die Boord 7613 • Tel/fax (021) 855-2573 • E-mail wynsacci@hotmail.com

LAST YEAR, wine was made on Clos du Ciel, once John and Erica Platter's Helderberg wine farm, for the first time in several years. Brand-new winemaker André Morgenthal studied philosophy and drama, not winemaking. His interest began when he joined the Wine Culture Society at Stellenbosch University. Then, two years ago, he visited Australia — "mind-blowing" — and envisaged making his own wine.

Mutual friends introduced him to ex-advertising and fashion exec Peter Aschke, the new owner of Clos du Ciel, who lives a life of perpetual summers, in SA and the south of France. "It's a bit crazy, only the two of us with no real winemaking experience — but both with a passion for the stuff," says Morgenthal. Morgenthal's immediate aim is to bottle the current maiden vintage safely, and in the long-term equip the small cellar with "fine kit". He's had loads of advice and support from fellow wine folk, including globe trotters Phil Freese and Zelma Long, who "really liked" the **00** wines. These, owing to early deadlines, were incubating mid-2000 and impossible to rate.

· ·

Clos Malverne Estate

Stellenbosch (see Stellenbosch map) • Tasting & sales Monday to Friday 10—1, 2—4.30 and Saturday 10—1 during peak times • Owner Seymour Pritchard • Winemaker/viticulturist Isak 'Ippie' Smit (since Nov 1997) • Production 350 tons 23 000 cases 92% red 8% white • PO Box 187 Stellenbosch 7599 • Tel (021) 882-2022 • Fax (021) 882-2518 • E-mail closma@mweb.co.za

Two densely spaced pages of "International Comments" which form part of Clos Malverne's marketing handout tell you as much about the wines as about the personalities behind this quietly determined Devon Valley operation. "Simply wonderful." "Very impressive." "Stunning." "Classy." Few locals can boast such amplitude of offshore acclaim (a measure of Seymour Pritchard's early cultivation of global markets). But there's no puff-chested strutting here, and certainly no laurel resting. There simply isn't time. Visitors are flocking now that the farm is back on the Stellenbosch Wine Route (personal attention, splendid vistas among the charms); Pritchard's 25 year old son Llewellyn, ex-computer jock, has stepped into a new full time portfolio of local market development — the goal to grow domestic sales from the current 10% to 30–40% over the next few years. Daughter Belinda now manages the finances, giving Pritchard some elbow room to continue his fiercely enthusiastic advocacy of the local red grape: "The future of pinotage is incredibly bright," he thunders, and if you look in the least dubious he reminds that more than 60% of Clos Malverne's ±23 000 annual cases are 100% pinotage or include a good splash.

❀ **Auret** Stylish, approachable Cape blend of cab, local hero pinotage, merlot (60/25/15). **97**, as anticipated in pvs ed, has gained substance, complexity (and new rating) with extra time in bottle. Now better weighted, balanced, yet with vintage's more refined allures. Heaped with awards: VVG, SAA, 1999 Diners Club shortlist etc etc. 13% alc. Yr small casks, Fr/Am (75/25). Preview of **98**, superior red wine yr, very promising. **96** ❀ in modern approachable style, first announced with **95**.

❀ **Pinotage Reserve** Showy, muscular example, regular ABSA Top Ten honouree. Premium priced, deep flavoured barrel selection which needs time (±3 yrs) to soften. Possible exception is current **98**, which *deserves* rather than demands further maturation: already accessible, big but not overpowering, 'sweet' strawberry/banana spread the welcoming carpet. Gold at Mondial, Brussels. **97** VG, 89/100 in *Wine Spectator*, very tightly wound initially; don't rush to uncork. **96** ABSA Top Ten. Regular **Pinotage** ❦ Lighter oaking (4 mths Fr casks) for earlier/easier drinking; preferred to Reserve by UK and US customers (and 1999 ABSA Top Ten judges). **98** VG, best pinotage on SAYWS. Strapping but unintimidating — ripe fruit, melting choc, violet wafts, silk texture all add to approachability. 13,5% alc, comfortable 5,3 g/ℓ acid. 10 000 cases.

❀ **Cabernet Sauvignon** Steadily improving label, now showing purer, more emphatic varietal character, succulence, where some pvs offered more sinewy profile. Latest **98** SAA good plummy, strawberry flavours, well managed oak. 14% alc. ±1 000 cases. Tempo increased with **97** ❀, fragrant, with excellent oak-fruit balance.

✿ **Cabernet Sauvignon-Merlot** Chic, lightly wooded, highly drinkable blend. Current **98** SAA developing in bottle (hence brighter star power), some unheralded liquorice/toast sniffs add complexity; good firm, dry finish. (4 mths Fr oak). 13,5% alc.

✿ **Cabernet Sauvignon-Shiraz** ▼ Second-vintage **98** VG continues attractive earthy/savoury style of pvs. Spicy blackcurrants, well weighted palate and some grippy character-building tannins. 13% alc. 6 000 cases. **97** smoky green olive whiffs, toasty dry finish. These lightly wooded 4 mths Fr oak. *Wine* ✿.

✿ **Cabernet Sauvignon-Pinotage** New "A gamble which paid off," laughs Seymour Pritchard, who sold off all 3 000 cases of **98** in only 2 lots to UK customers. Punchy New World style, loads of personality but not overweening. Sweetly ripe berries, big soft palate and seamless tannin surround. 14% alc. *Wine* ✿.

Sauvignon Blanc ✿ Ippie Smit's vyd tinkerings (canopy management a key concern) have turned out a bright, fresh sauvignon in notoriously hot **00**. Lime cordial aroma, some apricot, passionfruit richness, zesty finish. Good value. 13,5% alc.

. . . .

Cold Duck (5th Avenue)

POPULAR LOW ALCOHOL pink sparkle with origins in Germany, where leftover wine in the pubs ('kalte ente') was poured into jugs and sold at reduced prices. At around 8% alcohol, can be flung back with more than usual gusto. By Stellenbosch Farmers' Winery.

NV ✿ Heady pineapple fragrance from Ferdinand de Lesseps grapes combine with candyfloss scent (and rosé colour) from pinotage in charming, gently sweet carbonated sparkle. Hyperactive bubbles.

. . . .

Coleraine Wines

Paarl (see Paarl map) • Tasting & sales by appointment • Views • Owners Kerr family • Winemaker Clive Kerr (since 1999, with consultant Loftie Ellis (since 1998) • Viticulturist Clive Kerr (since 1980) • Vineyards 30 ha • Production 127 tons (50 tons, ±4 000 cases own label) 100% red • PO Box 579, Suider-Paarl 7624 • Tel (021) 863-3443/2073 • Fax (021) 863-3443 • E-mail colerain@mweb.co.za

THE INSPIRATION for its name and the Celtic imagery of the Shiraz label come from ancestral Ireland, but Coleraine's aim is to express its Paarl terroir. Before 1998, when the modern cellar was built, grapes went to the local co-op. Now old-planted vines offer grapes along with new vineyards: recent plantings include cabernet franc and petit verdot (so watch for developments with their Bordeaux-style blend), and more shiraz to swell supplies for a wine which has already received critical acclaim. On the evidence offered by barrel samples of the 2000 Shiraz, owner Clive Kerr is settling well into his role, as winemaker Graham Weerts, who saw in the 1999 vintage, has now moved on.

✿ **Shiraz 99**, tasted for pvs ed, still in turbocharged mode, with youthful intensity which impresses widely: *Wine* ✿✿, SAYWS gold. Georgeously deep mulberry colour. Chocolatey, nutty, dusty notes to the ripe plummy fruit. Densely textured palate with choc-cherry flavours and juicy, savoury acidity. Deserves some time. Fr/Am oak, 35% new; 14,1% alc. 1 000 cases. Barrel samples of **00** (including a Reserve) wonderfully promising; slightly lighter, better balanced than pvs.

✿ **Cabernet Sauvignon-Merlot** New (Components tasted separately from barrel in pvs ed — 60/40%.) Blockbuster style **99**: big, powerful (14% alc) and woody. Ripe baked fruity aromas, wafted with sweet smoky vanilla, evidencing the Fr/Am oaking (40% new). Thickly muscled palate with matching tannins. 1 000 cases.

Fire Engine Red ✿✿ **99** combo of half ruby cab plus merlot, cinsaut; the name in tribute to the 1940s workhorse of the local fire brigade. Earthy, baked, tarry aro-

. . . .

mas/flavours; dense, ripe and rustic — and appropriately fiery from 14.5% alc. 2 000 cases.

. . . .

Constantia Uitsig

Constantia (see Constantia map) • Tasting & sales Mon—Sat 9—5 Tasting fee discretionary • Cellar tours by appointment • Constantia-Uitsig & La Colombe restaurants, Spaanschemat River Café (see Restaurant section) • Luxury Constantia Uitsig Country Lodge • Tourgroups • Gifts • Conference facilities • Views • Wheelchair-friendly • Owners Dave & Marlene McCay • Winemaker Nicky Versfeld, at Steenberg (since 1996) • Wine director André Badenhorst (since 1988) • Viticulturist André Rossouw (since 1997) • Vineyards 35 ha • Production 280 tons 22 000 cases 60% white 40% red • PO Box 402 Constantia 7848 • Tel (021) 794-1810 • Fax (021) 794-1812 • E-mail wine@icon.co.za • Website www.constantiauitsig.co.za

ANDRÉ BADENHORST, born and bred in this historic valley of vines, and current chairman of the small (but very select) Constantia Wine Route, is the guiding wine spirit behind David and Marlene McCay's beautiful 3 centuries old farm, a 60 ha oasis so tranquil it's almost inconceivable that the centre of Cape Town is only 20 minutes away, and suburbia creeps up to its gates. Fortunately it's very upper-crust, countrified suburbia which does not lower the tone set in this green space (35 ha of vines, a bucolic cricket oval, lovely gardens). The most exacting hedonist has to admit that Constantia Uitsig is a choice mouthful. The ingredients include a country hotel, two of the very finest restaurants in the Cape, a café so chic that trendoids turn over its tables four times a day, and of course, appropriately stylish wines. These are still made at nearby Steenberg (an own-cellar is on track for the vintage of 2002) but since the maiden harvest of 94, have quickly established their own, terroir driven character, and the farm's early ripening, Californian-clone chardonnay, in particular, has been a major success story: it's won strings of awards, has flown First Class on SAA and Business on KLM, and was chosen for the Nederburg Auction.

✿ **Merlot** Steadily delivering on potential as best in this cool valley. Projections from sample of **99** suggest a savoury, almost black olive core surrounded by spice from unstressed vineyards. Vibrant ruby colour, aromatic violets, creamy sheep's wool softness a more refined palate than bigger **98** which, while spicy, plummier, Christmas cake finish. Avoids jamminess. Flecked with bitter chocolate, mouthcoating flavours. **96** developed, lighter. Concentration from low 5–6 t/ha crop. No **97** under this label although an unwooded version (not tasted) available cellar door.

✿ **Chardonnay Reserve** ✓ Pvs high water mark set by late-blooming **97** ✿: sole SA chardonnay to garner both 1999 VVG and London Wine Challenge gold; also SAA listing. Current **98** SAA bounds ahead — albeit with appropriate restraint — delightful interplay of pink grapefruit tang, deep creaminess, demure oak. Succulent fruit, wood, weight (13,5% alc) all honed by good acid, tannin. Next **99** (essentially sold out pre-release, on strict allocation) bolder, in mould of **97** *Wine* ✿, without sacrificing finesse. Long, dry finish. These versatile with food. Fermented, yr lees-aged in barrel, all new from **00** vintage. **Chardonnay Barrel Select** New **99** a further blending of only the best barrels, 100 cases for property's restaurants/cellar door. Exceptionally beautiful structure: soft finesse balanced by acute focus of fruit intensity. Worth the detour.

✿ **Sauvignon Blanc** Leapfrogs out of pond into different class in **00**, first from new block in loamy soil. Gooseberry pith, tapered length, hugely promising for young vines. **99** ✿ grassy nose has faded, leaving pungent bluegum/asparagus, short green pepper finish.

✿ **Semillon Reserve** ✓ "We could sell four times the quantity," says André Badenhorst of variety he's convinced has natural home here. (Maybe C-U's success will spark revival for the grape most battle to sell.) Next **99** extrapolates the theme: stunningly scented nose, interwoven bees wax, fresh thatch and new cream, counterpoint to bracing limey freshness. **98** *Wine* ✿, bristles with limey fruit, wood flavours, unequivocal 14% alc. Massive, begs food. Flew SAA 1st class before being selected for the Queen's Commonwealth Heads of State banquet in Durban, Oct 1999 (Badenhorst muses over asking for a Royal Warrant). 100% oak, 80% new Fr. Sample **00** in same league but with added juicy kumquat freshness, all new wood. Unwooded version discontinued.

✿ **Semillon Noble Late Harvest** New Riveting botrytis dessert with immediate claim to excellence with maiden **00**. Clouds of tropical fruit scud out of the glass, an equatorial island melange arrests the palate but masterful acid spring-cleans. Only three barriques, which André Badenhorst not eager to show to owner Dave McCay: "He'll give it to all of his mates!" Harvested at 39 °B, gently pressed into barrel where fermented. Release planned.

Cabernet Sauvignon ✿ **99** (from barrel) something to look forward to. Dense colour, refined cedar, tobacco leaf, graphite core for soft sweet berry fruit, pacier than minty **98** with green finish. **Cabernet Sauvignon-Merlot** ✿ **97** Earthy tints to light colour, soft, oaked easy-drinker. **Chardonnay Unwooded** ✿ latest **00** packed with freshness: clean zesty nose, bracing melon, refreshing lime palate. Edge of breadth, chalky hints but faithful to chablis style that has won it UK followers. **Uitsig Blanc** ✿ Grape Packaging Award winner. **99** unwooded sauvignon/chardonnay (sadly sans pvs' semillon creamy, waxy breadth). Fresh, grassy, river-reed style, crisp truncated finish.

Coppoolse Finlayson-Sentinel Winery

Stellenbosch (see Stellenbosch map) • Visits by appointment. • Owners Rob Coppoolse, Walter Finlayson, Viv Grater • Cellarmaster Walter Finlayson (since 1992) • Winemakers Adele Dunbar & Riaan Möller (since 1998) • Production: 500 tons, 400 000 cases (20 000 cases own label) 60% red, 20% rosé, 20% white • PO Box 4028 Old Oak 7537 • Tel (021) 982-6175 • Fax (021) 982-6296 • E-mail wine@sentinel.co.za • Website www.coppoolse-finlayson.co.za

ELEVEN COUNTRIES, INCLUDING AUSTRALIA (something of a coup here, surely) import this livewire negociant company's broad range of wines, all tailored to clients' specs under the benevolent but beady eye of vastly experienced cellarmaster Walter Finlayson (of Glen Carlou repute) and winemakers Adele Dunbar and Riaan Möller. Soaring orders — from 65000 cases in 1997 to 400 000 in 1999 — prompted their move to a convenient (if not scenic) industrial park in Brackenfell and huge expansion of the production premises, which stretch over 13 warehouses, and will soon cover an entire block. Asked if there are any exceptional views from the property, co-owner Rob Coppoolse, a former civil engineer, ironically replies: "Bottle store and bakery (lovely pies!) right in front of us."

Sentinel range

✿ **Shiraz** Beautifully structured **98**'s spicy prune-and-fennel array difficult act to follow, though early preview of **99** ✿ shows simple cherry fruit, soft tannic flesh to which some backbone (and another star in the guide?) will likely be added prior to blend finalisation. **98** VVG, *Wine* ✿. Air France-Preteux Bourgeois laureate.

Cabernet Sauvignon ✿ Smoky mulberries laced with warm stewed fruit, fine oaky finish in **97**. 12 mths Fr oak-barrelled. **Merlot** ✿ New **97** Clean mocha fruit, tannic coat for cherry fruit, undemanding. **Pinotage** ✿ Lacy red fruit aromas carry through to sappy **98** palate; which ends dry. Barrel aged yr., 2nd/3rd fill. Not averse to light chilling. **Chardonnay** ✦ **99** ex-Stellenbosch, disjointed oxidative character, best enjoyed soon. **Sauvignon Blanc** ✦ **00** crisp grassy fruit, heather undertones. Tight acid cuts mid-palate. Drink young.

Cape Salute range

Not available for tasting for this ed. Includes **Cabernet Sauvignon** (pvs rating ✿✿), **Pinotage** (✿✿) ☺, **Chenin Blanc-Chardonnay** New, **Chenin Blanc** (✦).

Mount Disa range

Not available for tasting for this ed (pvs rating in brackets). Includes **Shiraz 98** (✿), **Cabernet Sauvignon** (★★), **Pinotage** (★★), **Cape Salute** (☆), **Chardonnay** (☆), **Sauvignon Blanc** (☆).

Kaapse Vreugd/Kaaps Genoegen range

Single biggest SA wine brand in Holland. **Kaapse Vreugd Cinsaut-Pinotage** ★★ Unassertive, soft and easy **99**, like pvs, light ruby colour, delightful strawberry aroma, supple 'sweet' jammy flavour ending briskly dry. Unwooded. **Kaaps Genoegen Chenin Blanc-Chardonnay** New ☆ **99** Fruity chenin character fleshed out with waxy texture. Dash oaked chardonnay adds to mid-palate.

Kaapse Pracht range   New

For the Netherlands market. **Cinsaut-Pinotage** ★★ Unwooded **99**, docile tannins; soft, easy stewed strawberry, baked jam flavour, ends briskly dry. **Droë Steen** ☆ Palate-clucking freshness in **00**, fruity chenin with wafts guava. Crisp thirst quencher.

· ·

Cordoba

Stellenbosch (see Helderberg map) • Tasting & cellar tours by appointment Mon—Fri 8.30—5 Sales Mon—Fri 8.30—5 • Owner Jannie Jooste • Winemaker/viticulturist Christopher Keet (since 1993) • Vineyards 31 ha • Production 100 tons, 7 000 cases 70% red, 30% white • PO Box 5609 Helderberg 7135 • Tel (021) 855-3744 • Fax (021) 855-1690 • E-mail cordoba@adept.co.za

CHRIS KEET'S dream is to develop this sensationally-sited farm, its cool 31 ha vineyards mountaineering up the face of the Helderberg, into "one of South Africa's First Growths". And if it's not yet — by his own admission — quite there (such clubs not always open to members of a mere 7 vintages-standing), the summit's in sight. Particularly now that he's playing all-out to this property's strengths. Cabernet franc, underplanted and underrated in the Cape, has been a revelation here, the secret of Cordoba Crescendo's stunning success. Merlot has proved exceptionally rewarding too. Frustrated fans of these wines, who cannot get enough of them, will be cheered by the plans to boost these varieties to 60% of the Cordoba crop. New plantings are underway — some on virgin soil, all minutely researched, each clone, rootstock and site painstakingly selected. You must have a certain attitude (plus physical fitness) to tackle such a project on vertigo-inducing inclines accessible only to the bravest men and machines. And Keet does. When asked what overseas travel he's recently undertaken, he can answer literally. No namby-pamby cellar tours for him lately. Just the inaugural Robben Island Challenge: over the sea indeed, by surf-ski, paddling from Cape Town, round the notorious former prison island and back (mind the sharks!).

★★**Crescendo** The force continues to mount — a Cape touchstone aiming to compete with St Emilion's best. Individual, powerful cab f fleshed out by merlot (20%), 10% cab s. Never loud, the extended growing season of measured **97** confirms previous no flash in the pan. Penetrating nose of herbaceous nettles, deep mineral flavours with blackcurrant echoes knitted into lavender-scented, velvety tannins; tapered, classy finish. Higher 13,7% alc, electric frisson of freshness — "too acidic", some would say, but made for deferred pleasure, no immediate fruit gratification here. Should rest for inversely as long as it rapidly sells out; likely to yield earthy, herbaceous richness with age. Latest match for starperforming maiden **95** ★★, *Wine* ★★, winner of Air France–Preteux Bourgeois Classic Wine Challenge. Refined **96** marginally lighter, reflecting lesser vintage: tobacco leaf aromas; dusty tannins enhance sappy fruit. More approachable, open earlier than pioneering **95** (70/20/10 cab f/cab s/merlot), **97**, both of which need 10 years. Infant **98** cab f/merlot (80/20) as in **96**. 13% alc. Expensively Fr oaked 18 mths; tastes it.

✿✿**Merlot** Understudy to Crescendo fanfare, but could easily top the bill else-where. Next **97** utterly delicious plummy/cherry aromas, choc/mocha lashings reined in by acid/tannin balance. Piercing finish. Finding niche on better restau-rant wine lists; to fill the time (luxuriously) waiting for big brother to mature. 17 mths Fr oak. 13,5% alc. Last **96** extraordinary concentration for generally lighter harvest, great elegance. 10 mths Fr oak. **95** gutsy, more outspoken; ripe pulpy fruit more concentrated than **94**.

✿**Shiraz Barrel Reserve 97** first since 400-bottle **94**, output now doubled! Fruity rather than spicy nose, fleshy red berries, hints tobacco leaf jostle with soft, ripe tannins. Succulent fruit, powerful mouthful. Touch more 'obvious' in style than flagships, gets same oak treatment. Will be popular.

✿**Cabernet Sauvignon 97** mirrors vintage, variety, cellar philosophy: cool, classy, understated restraint. Cigarbox, cedar wood and sharpened pencil dom-inate herbaceous palate; both minerally fruit and tannins less aggressive than deep, near-black **95**, resplendent in rich, plump fruit, puckering tannic tail. Both better than more austere **96,** leaner **94**. 12,5% alcs 14–16 mths Fr oak.

✿**Chardonnay** Latest **99** cements stylistic modification, attains target set for next ten years: altogether fuller, riper, more buttery with more generous mid-palate fruit and viscosity in finish. Breadth of palate gently cut by grapefruit citrus twists. Whole-bunch pressed, slow natural yeast fermentation in 60% Burgun-dian (Mercurey) oak, 50% new (and will rise) full malo, 12,5% alc. Grapefruity **98** tingly, tangy lemon-lime, short of breadth as in slender **97**, **96**.

Sauvignon Blanc ✿ Steely, flinty style, river-stone briskness of **99** softening with bottle age. Will be last; no **00**.

Mount Claire range

Mountain Red ✿ Now **NV** (bureaucratic vagaries) plummy, pepper-and-spice interest in firm, friendly 58% merlot, 28% shiraz, rest cab. s. mix, from 98 vintage; light, for drinking now. **Mountain White** ✿ Waxy breadth of **99** (now also labelled Pinot Blanc) lifted by tropical fruit, fresh acid, just off-dry finish. Splash sauvignon adds zip.

Count Agusta see Agusta Wines

Country Cellars

THESE are the Spar chain of convenience stores' cork-closed wines. See Carnival for the boxed range.

✿**Merlot Narrabos 98** has improved since last tasted: ripe and rich in palate, soft tannins and almost sweet plummy flavours; light tone (despite 13% alc) with some delicate floral scents.

✿**Shiraz Bayete** NEW Robust style with expansive plummy/herby flavours, earthy/toasty undertones. Easy feel from 'sweet' fruit and lenient tannins; clean finish. 13% alc. Above limited edition oak matured wines.

Cabernet Sauvignon Nyathi ✿ NEW ☺ Here's a good value cork popper with plenty of cab character and ripe fruit; med-bodied **99** very easy to drink; soundly backed by fragrant oak and just enough tannin to stand up to a rich rack of ribs.

Chardonnay Narina ✿ Solid, well made easy drinker; brush of honeyed bottle age gives soft, gentle feel in **99**. Fresh ripe-melon and smoky oak in background.

Varietal wines, mainly unwooded: **Cabernet Sauvignon** Too unformed to rate, but potentially ✿, **00** offers good solid quaffing with extra pizzazz from deep fruit flavour, good oaky vanilla backing, long supple tannins. Satisfying, though high

13,7% alc needs watching. **98** VG. **Merlot** Latest **00** sampled very young, so unrated, but already strikes the right varietal notes with ripe plum/sweet-violets, soft choc tones. Some quite harsh tannins still, but these should ease into comfortable ⚶ quaffing mode. Massive 14,9% alc. **Pinotage** Lightly oak matured, med/full-bodied **99** untasted. **Chardonnay** Latest **00** tasted pre-bottling (and not rated) but showed better than pvs. 'Sweet' pears, bits of peach in smooth palate with warming alcoholic glow (though 13% alc not particularly high). Potential ⚶. **Chenin Blanc 00** tasted from tank (and too young to rate) zestily dry, mouthfilling tropical flavours. **Sauvignon Blanc** Latest **00** too unformed to rate mid-2000. Fresh, fruity; cut grass/bell pepper tones; solid swigging style — potential ⚶. **Special Late Harvest** ⚑ From chenin, med-bodied. Clean, well made **99** still has enough acidity to balance sweetness; some good honeyed flavour. West Coast origin.

Generic NV range: **Claret** ⚑ No-pretensions barbeque sort of wine; merlot with shiraz/pinotage, lightly cask-matured. **Classic Red** Earthy dry blend. **Rosé** ⚑ Sound dry tippling at picnics and other alfresco occasions. Some delicate plums. Chenin/pinotage, med-bodied. **Dry White** ★ Uncomplicated honeyed tones; very dry finish. **Low Alcohol Dry White** ⚑ Some honeyed, bottle age tones. Simple; dry finish. 9,5% alc. **Stein** ⚑ Plain and simple but easy, med-bodied; good ripe tropical fruit. **Late Harvest** ★ No-frills semi-sweet quaffing; some muted honeyed flavour.

Sparkling wines: **Brut** ⚶ Fresh, energetic **NV** carbonated bubbles from West Coast chenin/sauvignon. Light, undemanding. "For drinking at every possible opportunity," says winemaker. **Doux** ⚑ Soft, sweet and very lightly carbonated fizz from chenin with splash muscadel. **NV**. Light and easy.

. . . .

Craighall

Reliable, popular value for money range from African Wines & Spirits. Styled for early/easy drinking. Remarkably classy considering large scale production.

Cabernet Sauvignon-Merlot ⚶ Brambles and fresh blackcurrants perform on ripe plummy platform. **97** just enough tannin to go well with food. No need to wait. Easy 12% alc. **Chardonnay-Sauvignon Blanc** ⚶ Drink-now **98** not like zingy predecessors: laid-back, attractively honeyed, with freshening citrus undertones and hints of vanilla to whet the appetite.

. . . .

Culemborg

GOOD value range from DGB in 2 ℓ screwtop glass jugs. All NV.

> **Dry Red** ⚶ 😊 Scarlet colour; bouncy strawberry fruit, soft and sappy with supple tannin for extra-easy quaffing. Med-bodied.

Blanc de Noir ⚶ Coral-hued blush style wine. Fresh, clean, lighter bodied for relaxed summery occasions. Zippy finish. **Grand Cru** ⚑ Tropical fruit tones in this med-bodied no-frills glugger, very dry across the palate. **Blanc de Blanc** ⚑ Light/med-bodied Caribbean fruits; good fruit/acid/sugar balance makes satisfying dry casual quaffing. **Light** ⚑ Delivers a lot of flavour considering the low alc. Light toned tropical fruit, agreeably dry and light. Coastal market only. 9,8% alc. **Stein** ⚑ Soft, delicate tropical essences, sweetish impression but enough acid to prevent cloy. Lightish 11% alc. **Late Harvest** ⚶ Smooth muscatty texture plumped by sweetness and ripe tropical fruit. Lightweight, easy. 1 000 ml, Port Elizabeth/East London only. **Diamanté Crystal** Perlé style easy drinker with big but soft, lively mousse, clean dryish finish.

Cullinan View

EXPORT range for Matthew Clark, UK, by Vinimark. The line-up (untasted) includes **Cabernet Sauvignon, Pinotage, Chardonnay, Chenin Blanc, Colombard, Sauvignon Blanc.**

Darling Cellars

Groenekloof (see Swartland map) • Tasting & sales Mon—Thu 8—5 Fri 8—4 Sat 8—12 Tasting fee R5 p/p • Cellar tours by appointment • Bring your own picnic • Seasonal wildflowers • 4 × 4 Trail on Oude Post farm • Wheelchair-friendly • Owners 22 shareholders • Managing director Chris Rabie • Winemakers Abé Beukes (since 1997) & Johan Nesenberend (since 1996) • Viticulturists Abé Beukes (since Dec 1997), with Nelius van Huyssteen (VinPro) • Bottling Jacques van Niekerk • Quality control Marius Botha • Sales Richard Hilton • Vineyards 1 500 ha • Production 8 000 tons 500 000 cases (4 800 tons 350 000 own label) 55% white 45% red • PO Box 114 Darling 7345 • Tel (022) 492-2276 • Fax (022) 492-2647 • E-mail rhilton@darlingcellars.co.za

THE PLAN is coming together rather nicely for this West Coast winery, remodelling itself from a small-town collective into a dynamic international presence. The early phases saw talented winemaker Abé Beukes return to home turf to help spearhead a drive into premium wines made from in-demand, classic varieties. The range was revamped, packaging face-lifted and a new top-of-the-line Groenekloof label launched to instant, rapturous acclaim (SAA Selections, ABSA Top Ten et al). And millions lavished on stainless steel, new crushers, state-of-the-art bottling lines—the whole gleaming number. Plus, tucked into the space where ancient concrete vessels used to glower, a dramatic barrelling hall with sail-like wall fittings bathing the oak casks in an ethereal glow. Setting the seal on the rebirth is a new top line, Onyx — "the semi-precious jewel in our crown," says Richard Hilton, the UK-born sales/marketing influence here (Onyx — "unlike 'Groenekloof', a name foreigners like me can pronounce!" and the new Flamingo Bay range among his ideas). At the helm is irrepressible MD Chris Rabie, whose persuasive charms have boosted exports to 90% of bottled production (most goes to Britain, the Benelux countries and Sweden).

Onyx range

- 🌟 **'Red Blend'** (To be named) **99** jewel in this crown, already opulent — appropriately — with splendid maturation potential over 4–6 yrs. Pinotage/shiraz blend; former's black cherry/ripe banana/plum in ascendance, shiraz's liquorice/black olive and sprinkle cinnamon in backdrop; all in soft, complex package which seductive now, irresistible in 4–6 yrs.

- 🌟 **Pinotage** (pvsly under Groenekloof label) Debut **98** showered with accolades (*Wine* 🌟, ABSA Top Ten, runner up SAA red wine trophy etc etc). Follow-up **99** potentially better, more densely packed with ripe berry fruit; 'summer pudding' textured palate broadens to firm, dry tannic finish which needs bit of time to settle.

Groenekloof range

- 🌟 **Cabernet Sauvignon** Opulence envisaged in pvs ed some way off. **98** still taut, some dry tannins, fragrant blackcurrants/mulberries dominated by high toned herbs/lavender. 6–8 yrs needed to reach peak ("Meanwhile, drink shiraz below," ventures Abé Beukes). 13,5% alc. **97** *Wine* 🌟.

- 🌟 **Shiraz 99**, from 2 hillside vyd sites, dense minerally, smoky black olive, spread with choc in broad, full palate. Though deeply layered, already approachable, firm dry finish. Very good now, sensational in 4–6 yrs. 14% alc.

- 🌟 **Sauvignon Blanc ▼ 00**, **99** vintages 'declassified' ("quality not there"), so fans should bide time dipping into **98** SAA. 'Green'/herbaceous attack of youth replaced with satisfying long, ripe gooseberry/fig tones. 13,1% alc.

✿ **Chardonnay** ⩗ **98** developing beautifully, initial vanilla/barley sugar flavours joined by lees/wheat/lime, all melded into weighty palate with silk texture. 14%. 9 mths new Fr oak, through malo. **99** similar but better lift of acidity; probably finer development potential.

DC range

✿ **Cabernet Sauvignon** ⩗ Soft, ripe instant drinkability; cherries/walnuts/tobacco in **99** ✿ full, 'sweet' palate. Generous, ready, but will hold couple of years. Flies off shelves in Sweden. Combo Fr oak barrels/staves. 13,5% alc. **98** sold out. **97** SAA.

✿ **Merlot** ⩗ **98** appreciating in bottle. Plums and some good savoury beetroot/green bean tones; full, smooth across the palate. Oak staved 4 mths. 13% alc.

✿ **Pinotage** ⩗ Benefit of mature vines felt even in this mid-tier range. Unoaked **98** mouthfilling (ripe cherry, leathery whiffs); pleasantly tart impression, like biting into slightly green banana. **97** SAA.

✿ **Shiraz** ⩗ The Rhône's St Joseph beckons in **99**, warm, easy spread of animal/herbaceous/spice tones with deep Ribena fruit. Well managed oak (±60% staves, rest casks). **98** VG, **97** SAA.

✿ **Sauvignon Blanc** No top-of-line Groenekloof sauvignon in 2000, so best fruit went into this **00**, with nettly/flinty tang, brisk dry wild-herbs finish. Unwooded. Drink in yr of harvest. 12,5% alc.

Chardonnay ✿ Oaking toned down for accessibility (future will feature greater portion unoaked). Ripe peach/grapefruit in med-bodied **99**, lemon zesty finish with light buttery hint.

Flamingo Bay range   New

Cinsaut-Cabernet Sauvignon ✿ Cinsaut ace Abé Beukes (his 'quaffing' Lievlander blend featuring this variety, made while at Lievland once aced a 5-star rating in *Decanter*) has tweaked **00** for supreme swiggability, soft pulpy fruit with aromatic wafts of clove. **Lagoon Rosé** ✿ Instant consumer hit in see-through 1 000 ml lipped bottle, revealing flamingo pink **99** inside. Really gulpable tropical fruit, some strawberries. Fresh, not oversweet. Suggest follow label's advice: "Consume with 12 mths". Med-bodied cinsaut/chenin.

> **Chenin Blanc-Sauvignon Blanc** ✿ ☺ Could be subtitled 'Abé's Baby' — Abé Beukes on arrival especially keen on the local chenin which, zapped with sauvignon, appears in this charming no-worries quaffer. Tropical guava, grass in soft, low-priced **00**.

Daschbosch see Louwshoek-Voorsorg
DC Wines see Darling Cellars

Deetlefs Estate   ⩗ ⩗ ⩗

Worcester (see Worcester map) • Tasting & sales by appointment • Traditional 'lapa' entertainment area for functions • Wheelchair-friendly • Owner/winemaker Kobus Deetlefs • Cellar manager Johan Lotz (since 2000) • PO Box 36 Rawsonville 6845 • Tel (023) 349-1260 • Fax (023) 349-1951 • E-mail deetlefs@wine.co.za • Website www.wine.co.za/deetlefs

KOBUS DEETLEFS travels almost as widely as his wines — he "four or five times a year — it puts everything into perspective" — and they to 7 countries, including the US and Japan. His aim has been to establish this small estate near Rawsonville "in the top 10% of the world market". Secret of the wines' sales success is (in Deetlefs' own capital letters) their DEFINITE and INDIVIDUAL style — "a combination of old-world elegance and new-world fruit". And the extra-long lie-in on the lees which he gives to both whites and reds for optimum MOUTHFEEL. While others rush their wines to early release, he's content to wait, and consumers should be too — knowing these are later-bloomers. Even the whites are best kept for at least a year after the vintage, though not perhaps for as long as the 74 Muscat d'Alexandrie fortified he released in 2000 (the end-result of a bet his late father took with another winemaker who insisted such wines were not long-haulers). The next release will be in 25 years' time!

✿ Pinotage Sets house style with assertive flavour, ample body from high 13,5% alc. Ripe plums/mulberries feature in **99** SAYWS gold, which gaining complexity with age. Initial sturdy tannins still mouthcoating, could go another few years. 50% oaked. **00** (sample), as with stablemates from this vintage below, distinct improvement. **98** SAYWS reserve champ, flew BA Business Class.

✿ Semillon 99 SAYWS gold, "best vintage ever" per Kobus Deetlefs, growing in bottle. Good light honey tones mingle with ripe peach/apricot and tangy lemon/herb. Finishes briskly with suggestion of smoky vanilla contrasting well with the 'sweet' flavours. New Aussie clone/±50 yr old bushvines. 50% aged in barrels, remainder unoaked, 8 mths on lees. 13,2% alc. 4 500 cases. Foretaste of **00** suggests _this_ best vintage ever; packed with peachy/lemony fruit, thumbprint lees creaminess. ✿ winking.

Merlot **00** "from unique plot where direct sunlight is minimal"; 100% oaked, malo in barrel; sample too young to rate, as is **Shiraz** New aromatic leathery/scrubby example. Cask matured. **Chardonnay** ✿ Full leesy style, supple and full-flavoured. **99** has evolved light ripe-melon/peach/honey tones to initial lime/lees tones, oak seamlessly integrated with light vanilla. Good now but should hold yr/2. Portion barrel aged, remainder sur lie in tank. 13,5% alc. **00**, even as unfinished sample, distinct all-round improvement. Could rate ✿ on release. **Chenin Blanc** ✿ Full, serious dry chenin, unwooded, 90 days sur lie for creamier mouthfeel; **99** evolving fruitfully with potential for further ageing. Complexity in ripe/dried peach, lemonade and honey/bottle-age nuances. 13% alc. 10 000 cases. **00** (sample), similar vinification, immediately more striking: likely ✿ on release. **Sauvignon Blanc** ✿ New **00**, tasted sur lie, highlights estate's signature fullness/body (13,2% alc). Differential picking gives spread of ripe gooseberry, green cut-grass/herbal tones. **Philippus Petrus Deetlefs Muscat d'Alexandrie** New Striking, modern packaging for a venerable oak-aged fortified dessert, designed to showcase ageability of hanepoot. Occasional label: first is **74**, released end 2000; next will be 2024! Preview reveals highly individual style, very evolved; for more specialised palates.

Stonecross range   New

Pinotage ✿ Modern, juicy style, lightly oaked to showcase generous sweet plummy fruit. **00** soft and ready to pour with food. 13% alc. Portion of sales from all Deetlefs wines donated to International Campaign to Ban Land Mines.

....

De Forellen see Lanzerac Farm &Cellar
....

De Heuvel Estate   ⛉ ⛉ ⛉

Tulbagh (see Tulbagh map) • Tasting, sales & cellar tours Mon–Fri 9.30–12.30 1.30–5 Sat 10–1 • Olive oil/olive products produced/sold ex-cellar • Facilities for children • Proclaimed conservation area • Owners Leonardo Antonio Bianco & Sons • Winemaker Antonio Bianco, with Mark Carmichael-Greene • Viticulturist Craig Bianco • Vineyards 15 ha • Production 50 tons 2 500 cases 100% red • PO Box 103 Tulbagh 6820 • Tel (023) 231-0350 • Fax (023) 231-0938 • E-mail bianco@lando.co.za

THE CABERNET SAUVIGNON from this cellar won Veritas plaudits for the maiden 1997 and follow-up 1998 vintages — a "terrific incentive" for the wine and olive growing Bianco family who, despite having deep vinous roots in the hills of Piedmont in Italy, are relative newcomers to the local scene. Winemaker Toni, wife Magda and sons Craig and Tony (all keenly involved) aren't about to indulge in laurel-resting, however. They've added barrelling facilities and tweaked the vinification process to get closer to their goal of fine Italian style reds. And though the Biancos' eyes are on the old country, their hands are full of authentically New World grapes: some pinotage was made for the first time in 2000, along with a splash of shiraz. After the crush, they headed for some northern exposure at Vinordic in Sweden and paid their EU customers a visit. Softer medium-bodied reds are the future for this property, reveals Toni Bianco, adding with a Latin flourish: "We'll continue to improve the range until all are superb without end!"

✿ **Bianco Cabernet Sauvignon** ▼ Individual, fleshy, aromatic; styled for early accessibility — and getting better by the vintage. Latest **99**, dedicated to Toni Bianco's father Rinaldo, hardly out of barrel and already soft and plump, succulence nicely tweaked with ripe tannin. Usual spicerack/herbgarden/hedgerow fragrances, but slightly drier than pvs (an Italian style the winemakers' ultimate aim). Yr Fr/Am casks. **98**, more conventional than extra-exotic **97** (both ✿✿), firmer too; needs further yr or 2 to soften.

. . . .

Dekkersvlei see Mellasat

. . . .

Delaire Winery

Stellenbosch (see Stellenbosch map) • Tasting & sales Mon—Sun 10—5 Tasting fee R10 p/p plus R12 glass deposit which is refundable • Cellar tours by appointment • Green Door Restaurant (see Eat-out section); picnics Oct—Apr (booking essential) • Two self-catering mountain lodges • Views • Owner Agrifarm International (Pty) Ltd, headed by Masoud Alikhani • Winemaker/marketing Bruwer Raats (since 1997) • Vineyard manager Jaco van der Westhuizen (since 1997) • Consulting viticulturist Paul Wallace, VineWise • Production 150 tons 10 000 cases 60 % white 40% red • PO Box 3058 Stellenbosch 7602 • Tel (021) 885-1756 • Fax (021) 885-1270 • E-mail delaire@iafrica.com • Website www.delaire.co.za

CATCH BRUWER RAATS on the run and he has the look of an out-of-breath rugby forward — thinking and pondering where the next challenge lies. The burly winemaker swopped electronic engineering for Elsenburg, and consequently racked up vintages in Bordeaux and California before fulfilling a dream in 2000 to be sole winemaker for a Tuscan harvest. Since taking over at Delaire in 1997 he hasn't stopped running: isolating single vineyard blocks, planting cabernets sauvignon and franc (for a future varietal wine) as well as merlot on virgin slopes around 380 m above sea level, replanting out-of-favour and lesser-quality blocks. Delaire rocked a few boats in 2000 with maiden Merlot 97 priced at R105 a bottle. Could the price justify the contents? Raats believes an 87 point rating by US wine guru Robert Parker, and a Veritas gold didn't hurt, but selling out in 7 weeks was the most persuasive proof. "Look at how Grange and its high prices elevated the Australian wine image — even if you don't think it's their best wine." Expect an even higher price for the new Botmaskop Cabernet which Raats, freshly returned from the Orient, no doubt hopes will be big in Japan.

✿ **Botmaskop Cabernet Sauvignon 98** New Not the flagship but an explosive statement wine from carefully selected grapes bought in from a meticulous grower. Named after the mountain peak behind the farm. Squid-ink black, oozing mulberry and sweet cherry fruit, dense palate packed with savoury spice and blackcurrant. Huge mouthful shored up with stacked tannins, classic dry finish lingers. Needs time to be 'broken in' before release June 2001. "This was not planned," says Raats, "it happened." The wine "made itself" with help from 50% new Russian oak, 10% new Am, the rest 2nd fill Fr. The label will be reserved for emphatic wines of exceptional years; no **99** but **00** rests in cellar.

✿ **Merlot** Delaire's flagship red, notable for its exuberance and limit-nudging price over R100 ex-cellar (and sold out!). Next **98** due on the market mid-2001 reflects massive style set by previous. Striking spearmint/mocha flavours set in matrix of loads of ripe tannins, bracing acidity sparks freshness. Austere and inaccessible mid-2000, demands patience. Raats reckons it will go 15 yrs. Grapes from single site with easterly aspect, shielded by trees, only 4 hrs daily sun in height of summer. 18 mths new Taransaud, Saury Fr oak barrels. 13,5% alc. **97** VG melange violets, fleshy plums woven with mint/cedary oak. A multi-tiered layered ensemble of mocha/chocolate/vanilla spice, now-relaxed tannins. 200 cases. No **99**.

⚜ **Cabernet-Merlot** 'Declassification' of straight cab and merlot above into this blend for **99** (pushing ⚜) sees second consecutive 'cracker' after last **98** ⚜. Latest dense vermilion hues, concentrated cassis sparked by choc-mint flash of merlot, ripe berry maturity on solid acid/tannin platform. 14% alc does no harm to the arrangement. 14 mths mostly Fr oak, 1/3 new, touch Am. **98** SAA opulently ripe, juicy, summer pudding puree of berries cosseted in vanilla, tangy mineral core. Tarry/charry oak does the farewell. 13 mths new Fr oak. **97** VG, SAA rich tea-leaf, forest-floor, mocha resonances; to peak in 2 yrs.

⚜ **Chardonnay** Green shards to **99** gold colour, wood-char on nose heralds soft peaches, ripe pears. Full buttery length of flavour cut by citric tang, gravelly finish endures. Super successor to **98**, Michelangelo gold, in same mould: fresh-picked peaches-and-pears in, broad citrus, butterscotch, vanilla pod and malty/caramel palate, leesy finish. **97** *Wine* ⚜, highly rated by UK *Decanter*. Latest 80% 9 mths Fr oak (mixed age), 20% stainless steel-fermented for freshness. 13,5% alc.

⚜ **Sauvignon Blanc** Barrel-matured. Vanilla sweetness jostles with full-frontal fruit in **99**, concentrated gooseberry, thatchy grass flavours sharing stage with wood that will soften over 1–2 yrs. 30% new Fr oak 6 mths. Similar style to **98** boasting gooseberries, cut-grass, nettles in punchy, big yet well balanced composite. 50% in Fr oak for 3 mths. 120 cases only for Blue Train. 13,5% alc. From highest sauvignon vyd in Stbosch (350 m+); bush vines.

⚜ **Sauvignon Blanc** Unwooded. **00** graduated power from differentially harvested parcels — all showing their wares. Tropical pineapple, green melon bolstered by green pepper piquancy, held together by crisp acid, 13% alc. Intense ripe gooseberry **99** seems 'sweet', but finishes bone-dry. Excellent structure; category heading for ⚜. **98** not as big, pungent cut-grass/nettle array.

Green Door range

For restaurant on the property and alternative bottlings until farm revamp takes form.

⚜ **Merlot Alternative** — not second-rate label — for merlot grapes (this vineyard now grubbed up), bolstered by 21% pinotage from old, low-yielding (2–3 t/ha) bushvines. 99 quiet savoury spice, hints of Marmite/meat stock usher in tasty but restrained palate, subtle rather than 'big'. 12 mths seasoned barrels. 13,5% alc. 98 subtle, leafy, cedary whiffs, violets bloom in nose; plummy flavours woven with mint, understated oak/tannins. Enjoy now. Yr new/used Fr oak. 13% alc. Popular good value choice of Wine-of-the-Month Club.

⚜ **Sauvignon Blanc** Winery's best seller. 99 ripe gooseberry, smidgeon vanilla; mouthfilling, soft tropical fruit in palate, leesy dimension plus green pepper spice. Squeeze of lemon in finish. Enjoy now.

Grand Vin Blanc ⚜ **New 00** blend sauvignon (60%) with chardonnay, left off-dry for versatility in restaurant/functions and what Raats politely calls "the national visitors", referring to summer holiday patrons. Fully fruity with round sweetness to match, late acid cleanup refreshes. **Chenin Blanc** ⚜ **New** Most promising impetus for nascent Cape chenin revival in **00**, bought in from Kuils River. Cool climate and 32 yr old bushvine concentration shows in flavourful palate. Off-dry 7 g/ℓ sugar and 7% wood treatment add breadth. **Weisser Riesling** ⚜ **New** First for range but swansong for farm — parcel removed to make way for black grapes. Green apple wafts, spicy nose, hints of green olive in palate. Off-dry 7,8g/ℓ sugar in tail.

Bubbly ✿✿ Foxy packaging sets tone for frivolous carbonated **NV** (99) brut spar-kler, vehicle for riesling (80%), bukettraube (both now removed) and 10% sauvig-non. Fresh, tart and undemanding.

. . . .

De Leuwen Jagt see Seidelberg

. . . .

Delheim Wines

Stellenbosch (see Stellenbosch map) • Tasting & sales Mon—Fri 9—5 Sat 9—3 Sun 11—3.30 (Oct-Apr) Tasting fee R10 Closed 1 Jan, Good Fri, Easter Sun, 25 & 26 Dec • Cellar tours Mon—Fri 2.30 Sat 10.30 • Formal tastings for groups of 15—50 in cask cellar by appointment • Vintner's platters (Oct-Apr) in Garden Restaurant Mon—Sat 12.00—2.30 Sun 12.00—2.30 Oct—Apr Tel (021) 882-2297 • Owners Hans Hoheisen & MH 'Spatz' Sperling • Winemaker Conrad Vlok (since Aug 2000) • Viticulturist Victor Sperling (since 1993) • Vineyards 150 ha • Production 1 000 tons 60 000 cases 60% red 40% white • PO Box 10 Koelenhof 7605 • Tel (021) 882-2033 • Fax (021) 882-2036 • E-mail delheim=@delheim.com • Website www.delheim.com

AT AN AGE when others might think of slowing down, Spatz Sperling remains in customary hyperdrive: the still vigorous eminence behind this resurgent Simons-berg property celebrated his 70th birthday up-country on a Delheim promotional roadshow. Yet the influence of his two children, Nora (Thiel) — in charge of mar-keting — and Victor — deeply entrenched in the vineyards — is obvious: with Philip Costandius (before he left for Neethlingshof after 16 years in this cellar), they drew a roadmap to take Delheim beyond 2000. Visiting the farm in the aftermath of "one of the oddest vintages ever", it's obvious they can't get beyond 2000 fast enough. Intense, unrelenting heat and devastating fires which will cost an estimat-ed R1-million over the next two years (7,5 ha of white grapes incinerated, not to mention Spatz Sperling's beloved pine plantations — and he'd just replanted 80 000 trees). No wonder the Sperlings feel they've been there, hated that. The upside — there is one — is that the remaining 140 hectares or so are beginning to perform like champions under Victor Sperling's increasingly practised eye. A 'grape-tasting' in the midst of the 2000 harvest demonstrated to invited experts just how the fruit and wines meshed. This was so successful, the whole performance was repeated in Johannesburg.

✿ **Grand Reserve** Longtime flagship shows results of Victor Sperling's attention to crop/moisture management, selective picking. **97** *Wine* ✿ dense liquorice, plum, fruitcake aromas lead to solidly structured, intensely fruity palate (es-sence of cassis coats tongue for ages after last swallow). 18 mths in 225 ℓ Fr barriques, half new, leaves sweet-oak impression; provides foundation for long keeping (some of these still impress after 15 yrs). **96** 92/100 in UK *Wine*.

✿ **Cabernet Sauvignon** ▼ Continues impressive run of fine value/quality, part-ly through increased attention to water management in vyd. Latest **99** with hallmark blackcurrant, raspberry notes, spicy plum pud whiffs. Smooth grained yet assertive 'sweet' wood tannins reflect 9 mths ageing in Fr barriques and indicate considerable maturation potential (some of these have cellared well for more than a decade). 10% merlot softens firm cab muscle. 13% alc. **98** VVG, Michelangelo gold, *Wine* ✿. **97** ✿✿.

✿ **Merlot 98** VG flew out the cellar. Next-up **99** trademark leafy, plum, choc aromas; some Pomerol lushness with lovely 'sweet' impression in palate though bone dry (1,5 g/ℓ sugar); rich fruitcake, cigarbox flavours. 11 mths in big upright Fr oak vats infuses just enough spice.

✿ **Pinotage** Latest **99** textbook example of new SA style. Bright raspberry notes, long mulberry flavours in lively, juicy palate, neat vanilla twist in finish. 9 mths Fr/Am oak enhances, doesn't dominate fruit: 13,4% alc. **98** ABSA Pinotage Top 10, VG, harking back to older style: more jammy, with plum/varnish notes.

✿ **Shiraz** ▼ All manner of intriguing opening notes in **99**: gamey fennel whiffs, some dark choc, ripe mulberries. Taut, still shy Rhônish style, palate beautifully poised, trails of ripe sappy red berries in farewell. Body improved by bleeding off some juice pre-fermentation. Minimal wood influence from 11 mths in upright 8 500 ℓ Fr oak vats. 13,5 % alc. Multi-awarded **98** ❀ VG, Michelangelo gold, *Wine* ❀, 89/100 *Wine Spectator*.

❀**Rhine Riesling Natural Sweet 00** slightly oily, smoky (that bushfire again?) terpene aromas; then hints of jasmine, rose petals. Gorgeously juicy, full-sweet and crisp; harmonious finish elevates a notch above maiden **99** ❀.

❀**Chardonnay** Notch up scale in **00**, brilliant pale lime green, refreshing fruit salad wafts — melon, pear, passion fruit; restrained oaking (only half barrel fermented, aged 4 mths, 60% malo). Bracing yet juicy flavours, wrapped in fine vanilla/butterscotch cloak. **99** ❀ with dash chenin, similarly lightly wooded; this the style since grapefruity **98**.

❀**Edelspatz Noble Late Harvest 00** from Chenin, ripe 128 g/ℓ sugar; intriguing lime/grapefruit whiffs, lusciously sweet, decadent palate, with botrytis honey notes. Most elegant — definitely not a sickly sticky. **98** in similar style, but from riesling, bukketraube.

Dry Red ❀ ☺ **00** blend of just about every red in the cellar (mostly pinotage, merlot). Leafy, strawberry jam notes and lively youthful palate. Unwooded except for small **99** component; lovely supple quaffer. Inconspicuous 3,5 g/ℓ sugar smoothes the juicy finish. **Pinotage Rose** ❀ ☺ **00** winks with bright rosy pink glints, wafts of Turkish delight, stewed plums and cherries; 15% muscat de frontignan adds spice. Juicy acidity (6 g/ℓ) and 15 g/ℓ sugar execute a high-wire balancing act in this honest, totally quaffable off-dry summer splasher.

Spatzendreck ❀ Spatz Sperling's signature wine, mostly bukettraube, muscat, dash chenin in **00**. Jasmine scents, ripe melon, papaya flavours, drizzled with touch lemon. Sweet yet refreshing. **Goldspatz Stein** ❀ **00** Another semi-sweet melange, this time mostly colombard, with SA riesling, soupçon muscat, splash chenin. Classic 'brown bottle' wine: shy talc aromas, fresh, crisp honeysuckle notes and some ripe limes adding zing to finish. **Chenin Blanc 00** not tasted; available in only limited quantity from cellar. Majority of first release **99** ❀ snaffled by one export customer. **Sauvignon Blanc** ❀ **00** sports delicate pear/floral whiffs, hints of green pea, grapefruit. Juicy, sweetish entry (4 g/ℓ sugar), trailing herbal and gooseberry flavours into palate; zesty acid in finish. **Heerenwijn** ❀ Another crowd pleaser. **NV** (00) ultra-crisp chenin/sauvignon blend, lemongrass and guava notes, plenty of limey zest zinging in substantial, bone-dry palate **Pinot Blanc Brut** ❀ NEW **99** charmat bubbly with fine, brisk bead; bracing pear and lemon-grass aromas, nutty flavours, grapefruit and rhubarb fruit add some complexity. 11 g/ℓ sugar just enough to add suppleness. Also **Three Springs White** and **Bianca Light**, for Woolworths (see that entry).

Dellrust Wines ♟ ♟ ♟ ♟

Stellenbosch (see Stellenbosch map) • Tasting & sales Mon—Fri 8—5 Tasting R5 for 6 wines R8 for whole range • Coffees, teas, light lunches Mon—Fri 9—5, also by appointment for birthdays and other functions (closed June holidays) • Cellar tours during tasting hours by appointment • Play area for children • Tourgroups by arrangement • Walks by arrangement • Gift shop • Wheelchair-friendly • Owner/winemaker Albert Bredell • Viticulturist Gerjo Ben van der Merwe (since 1996) • Vineyards 100 ha • Production 800—900 tons (80 tons own label) 65% red 35% white • PO Box 5666 Helderberg 7135 • Tel (021) 842-2752 • Fax (021) 842-2456 • E-mail dellrust@cybertrade.co.za

THE INSTANT, popular hit of the first public releases from this old family farm was Albert Bredell's quirky, unpretentious Cinsaut-Tinta Barocca blend. The 'noble' varieties did predictably well — these 100 ha vineyards in Firgrove, near False Bay, have long been a source of the KWV's prime fruit, and he's been planting a lot more merlot and shiraz. But it was the humbler blend, from grapes many other farmers have abandoned, that consumers here and abroad pounced upon. In this era of commercial, homogenised, formula wines, it's a relief to find that the charms of something altogether more rustic have not been forgotten. Elmarie Bredell's delightful little cafe under trees and a traditional reed roof, super child-friendly, everything fragrantly home-made, is in the same sort of spirit. Big brother Anton Bredell, the port specialist, now has some sibling competition in the big-personality wine stakes.

Merlot Swashbuckling style splashed with mouthfilling fruit, copious tannin. Ripe plum/mocha in **99** layered with minerals, suggestion of eucalyptus. Puckering still, so better now with food (try traditional Karoo lamb and sweet potato) or 2–3 yrs in bottle. 14 mths 500 ℓ Fr casks. SAYWS gold. 13,5% alc. 400 cases.

Chardonnay Unusually, pear flavours were evident in **99** berries pre-harvest, reports Albert Bredell, though these appear to have been transformed into more usual tropical/citrus in the finished wine. Big, broad, partly from off-dry styling — dictated by export market — and strapping 14% alc. 400 cases.

Chenin Blanc Seriously slurpable despite very liberal 14% alc. Offdry **00** uninhibited by oak; long zesty lemon mingles with passionfruit, guava, bits of pear. For early drinking. 1 600 cases. **Pinotage** Forceful, bordering on stern **99** not an easy drink mid-2000; should come round in yr or 2 but meanwhile needs cushion of rich cuisine. 300 ℓ Fr oak 14 mths. 13% alc. 450 cases. **Cinsaut-Tinta Barocca** Unusual French/Portuguese varietal combo a hit with consumers, especially foreigners, since maiden **99**. Aromatic, peppery, almost porty tones in follow-up **00**, individual and rather tasty. 4 mths oak staves. 2 700 cases. **Sauvignon Blanc** Bracing freshness headlines **99**, green grass/nettle joined by scoops melon in ultracrisp palate. Grilled crayfish's on winemaker's — and our — suggested menu. 550 cases.

De Meye Wines

Stellenbosch (but see Paarl map) • Tasting & sales Mon—Fri 9—4.30 Sat 9—1 • Owner Jan Myburgh Family Trust • Winemaker Marcus Milner (since 1999) • Vineyard manager Philip Myburgh • Vineyards 65 ha • Production 12 000 cases 90% red 10% white • PO Box 20 Muldersvlei 7607 • Tel (021) 884-4131 • Fax (021) 884-4154 • E-mail demeye@cybertrade.co.za

MARCUS MILNER'S long-distance cycling exploits, on various continents, are formidable. But when it comes to work, he's not into travelling too far. After five years at Stan and Norma Ratcliffe's Warwick cellar, he pedalled just over the hill to join Jan and Philip Myburgh (the latter an old schoolfriend) on their family farm. It's named after a river in Holland, origin of the first Myburghs to emigrate to the Cape around 1660. De Meye's 65 ha vineyards, in turn, are but a short sprint away from Natte Vallei, the Milners' own family estate. An attractive new-to-the-range Chardonnay will remain the only white wine; the Sauvignon Blanc has been culled so as not to distract from the main (red) items on the agenda. Red wines are this Muldersvlei area's speciality, and Philip Myburgh has recently planted cabernet franc and merlot, selecting specific sites from the farm's nine different soil-types. Easy-going fruity drinkability appears to come naturally here, but Milner's first full season at the controls has seen the wines move into higher gear.

Cabernet Sauvignon Winemaker reckons latest will go 5–10 yrs; we wager **99** will fly straight from liquor store shelf to your glass. Soft, appealing mulberry/leafy sappiness, extra interest from light dusting cinnamon/cloves from 12 mths Fr oak. 13% alc. 2 300 cases. More presence than **98**, easy, savoury, most drinkable but lower keyed.

✿ **Shiraz** New clones may be all the rage, but **99** shows there's charm in the gnarly old-timers. Savoury smoked meat, raspberry, dollops earth/tar mingle in fully fleshed palate, still firmly wrapped in tannin. Give yr/2 or team with sturdy cuisine. 20 yr old vines. 10 mths Fr oak. 13% alc. 1 400 cases.

✿ **Chardonnay** New Super **00** debut, shows dexterity in the barrelling department. Warm toasted hazelnut/vanilla invite you in, lead you along a lime scented path to a buttery, smooth, flavoursome conclusion. Don't keep this hanging about: enjoy in vividness of youth. 12,5% alc. 350 cases.

Pinotage ✿✿ New 'Old Cape' number, earthy and quite compact, though there's enough juiciness in **99** to make it a charming, nostalgic quaff. Fr oak aged. 25 yr old bushvines. 750 cases.

. . . .

De Toren

Stellenbosch (see Stellenbosch map) • Tasting, sales & cellar tours by appointment. • Views • Wheelchair-friendly • Owner Edenhall Trust/Emil den Dulk • Winemaker Albie Koch (since 1999) • Viticulturists Emil den Dulk, Albie Koch (since 1999) • Viticultural consultant Johan Pienaar (since 1994) • Vineyards 19,9 ha • Production 100 tons (60 tons, 2 000 cases own label) 100% red • PO Box 48 Vlottenburg 7604 • Tel (021) 881-3119 • Fax (021) 881-3335 • E-mail info@de-toren.com • Website www.de-toren.com

JUST -another new cellar, awash in new money, trumpeting its 'uniqueness'? Should you yawn and switch channels? No way. Here, on this prime perch on the Polkadraai Hills overlooking False Bay, is a new player of genuinely unusual promise, its big ideas grounded in minute detail, its whole approach, from vineyard to bottle to labour philosophy, thoughtful and individual. Owners Emil and Sonette den Dulk, refugees from the Johannesburg business world, "stumbled upon this little piece of heaven" in 1991, but were wary about plunging into a crowded field. They consulted the experts on the varieties best for their seven different soil types, and then held fire until they found their matching market niche. It's simple but ingenious (the inspiration of a top Cape winemaker, who must remain nameless.) De Toren has been dedicated to the Big Five Bordeaux-blend varieties, and will produce just the one "super-wine". To amplify the complexity quotient, 13 different clones were planted. To raise the quality bar, pumps ("instruments of torture," say winemaker and owners) were banned from the gravity-driven winery. Instead juice flows into a 4 000 ℓ pressure tank ingeniously fitted into a lift shaft; this "hoisting tower" (unique in South Africa) transports the wine between tanks. Young and serious, winemaker Albie Koch (via Perdeberg, Bellingham, Ch Capion in France and Quail Ridge in California) has now turned out an impressive first vintage. The end has indeed justified the means.

✿ **Fusion V** Splendid debut for this **99** Bdx red, combining complexity and controlled power. Rich, sweet wild berries layered with mint and fragrant cedary spice; warm, baked fruit appears in palate with good dusty oak and fine dry tannins — attractive counterpoints to the densely textured flavours. Very good now but even better in 3–5 yrs. Quintet of Bdx red varieties: cabs s/f, merlot, malbec, petit verdot (56/20/10/10/4), own vyds (60%) plus Stbosch, some Wellington; yr new tight grained Fr/Am casks. 13,5% alc. ±2 000 cases.

. . . .

De Trafford Wines

Stellenbosch (See Stellenbosch map) • Tasting, sales, cellar tours Fri & Sat 10–1, otherwise by appointment • Home made (by Rita Trafford, a professional cook) lunch for groups of 10–24 Booking essential • 'Serious' buyers (min 1 case) may bring own picnic lunch by appointment • Owner/winemaker David Trafford • Vineyard manager Mavis Trafford • Production 45 tons 3 000 cases 90% red 10% white • PO Box 495 Stellenbosch 7599 • Tel (021) 880-1611 • Fax (021) 880-1611

IF ICONOCLASM in Cape wine has a home, it's here and secure at Mont Fleur in a clump of oaks at the end of a very windy, very uphill narrow alley in the mountains south of Stellenbosch. Not excitable, tortured iconoclasm, mind. And only a small home — 3 000 cases a year. David Trafford the wineman, like Trafford the architect, goes his own way quietly. In a response to our questionnaire asking winemakers to choose a 1st XV team of Cape wine from among their peers, his was perhaps the most (wine) politically acute of all. But Trafford has now arrived at a point — 16 years after his father made a first home-brew in the cold store of the Bird Street butchery in town — where he can list many of the essentials of today's ultra-chic artisanal wine approach as his own. He arrived before the crowds started to form — unfiltered wines, fermented by the yeasts indigenous to his vineyards in the mountain fynbos, bottled by hand and vinified in presses and by processes in vogue 200 years ago. A walk into his small, below-ground *cave* is a very French or Italian experience — an unordered mix of differently shaped and sized barrels and tanks to manage nature's similarly disordered vintages of varied grapes and types and quantities. No serried rows of symmetry, nor uniform, polished tanks. An invisible sign seems to read — 'This is not a zone of commerce'. That's why, to be sure, along the way he's produced some fumbling, flat wines — for he wasn't going by the book. Now he's evolved a small, hand-crafted range of his and his vineyards' personality that quietly speaks clearly — and really isn't contrived; and each wine, excepting perhaps the Pinot Noir where one senses he wants to fumble just a while longer — has instantly discernible individuality and fine quality.

🌺 **Cabernet Sauvignon** Serious, boutique style — and quantities, 500 cases. Firm (but not mean), completely authoritative hand-crafted feel, with layers of flavours. **99** probably finest, most intense yet, with great persistence in finish. Low-yield Stbosch vyds, 60%/40% bought in/home grown. The packed cassis-plum fruit and spice matches the (unnecessarily majestic?) alcohols — 14% plus. A collectible stayer — 12 yrs, say. **98** burly, attractive too but shade gruffer, more disjointed tannins. **97** 🌺 ripe black fruit aromas, sumptuous palate. Air France–Preteux Bourgeois plaudit. Oaked ± 20 mths, almost half in new barrels.

🌺 **Merlot** From **97** on, convincing cherry-choc flavours mark this wine. But an extra depth and intensity single out **99**, where tannins are ripe, integrated — very warm ripening season. A smooth big wine (as in **98** too, at 14,5% alc.). Oaked some 17 mths, about one-third new. Seasoned with a lifting touch cab. Small quantities — 500 cases.

🌺 **Pinot Noir 99** (following pattern in all this cellar's reds from that vintage) a leap forward on previous. Delicious, fragrant — organic-savoury-sweet nose and palate. Ruby hues. Coats the mouth softly. "This **99** came from nowhere — just happened, but that's pinot for you," says De Trafford. (Preview **00**: showier, more deeply tinted colours, spicier, more flamboyant bouquet.) Pvs, specially, **96** firm, less yielding with light barnyard hints.

🌺 **Shiraz** Launched with **98**, which scooped top honours at *Wine* Magazine tasting of Cape shiraz. Not bad. But just a single barrel! May lack peppery Rhône individuality but scores with flaunting New Worldish juicy, toffee-raspberry flavours, which trail on and on in finish. (**99** not labelled separately, a constituent of Reserve below.)

🌺 **Reserve** Bdx-style blend (mainly — but includes shiraz) selection of best few barrels of vintage, also in magnums. **98** powerful, plenty of grip, plenty of spice — and complexity; earnest red for long keeping — 10–12 yrs. (cab 44%, merlot 37%, cab f, 6%, shiraz 13%); in oak for 21 mths, 85% new — hence spiciness; 14,7% alc. Oddly, for the varietal make-up, a shiraz nose seemed to prevail in 2000.) But **99** takes the cake again. Oozing ripe fruit, nutty-mocha flavours; inky-mineral look and feel for backbone and length, also for long keeping, should mature grandly, with its already grown-up, mouthfilling tannins. Cab 51%, merlot 26%, shiraz 23%: in barrel 20 mths, most new; unfined, so expect a deposit.

✿ **De Trafford Chenin Blanc 99** ✿ voted *the* top Cape Chenin in 2000 by *Wine* magazine, vindicating Trafford's persistent, individual approach (ripe picking, long skin contact, barrel- and indigenous yeast-fermentation, all contributing to his signature style); dry, firm, full, serious food partner. As far as it's possible to get from the more common, fruity, light, evanescent, sugary styles. Oak barrel (7 mths) treatment has vanilla-spice combining with some apricot/lime notes. Similar to quite reined-in **97**, showing some honeyed fullness. 6 mths oak, 25% new. From De Trafford vyds. "Although the most successful, **99** not necessarily our best year in my view" says David Trafford. Some tasters have found a dusty-straw character. He has high hopes for **00**. Back-tasting to **97** reveals sound — greenish hints surviving — attractive wines, retaining a firm palate freshness (**98** with oak still quite prominent).

✿ **Keerweder Chenin Blanc** Both **98**, **97** rated in top 6 of *Wine* Chenin Challenge **99** ✿ — a single vyd wine — in rare style, firm, dry and for keeping, herbal-haystack notes combining with sweet-marzipan tangs; rich, mouth-filling. From neighbour's 27 yr old vyds. Barrel- and natural yeast-fermented; consistently substantial palate-feel — 14% alc plus.

✿ **Vin De Paille** Complex, rack-dried in sun — for 3 wks — chenin. People danced and raved over **98** Air France–Preteux Bourgeois plaudit (with a sweet, metallic tang) and **97** as departure, discovery wines, but **99** is finer, sleeker and more balanced; less sugary (175 g/ℓ versus 222). A year in oak does its edge-polishing bit for sumptuous, aromatic, multi-layered — honeyed apricot, pineapple, marzipan — finish.

. . . .

Destiny see Ruitersvlei

. . . .

De Villiers Wines

Paarl (see Paarl map) • Tasting Mon—Fri 9—5 • Sales Mon—Fri 8—5 • Bring your own picnic • Views • Wheelchair-friendly • Owner/viticulturist Villiers de Villiers • Winemaker Dominique Waso (since 1999) • Vineyards 75 ha • Production 30 000 cases 60% red 40% white • PO Box 714 Noorder-Paarl 7623 • Tel (021) 863-8480 • Fax (021) 863-8755 • E-mail devwines@mweb.co.za

VILLIERS DE VILLIERS has been ringing the changes at this historic family estate in Paarl's Nantes Valley. Freshly renovated and open for tasting/sales is a century-old Cape Dutch farmhouse with its original rietdak, inviting fireplace, warm yellow-wood — the tasting counter is made from original pieces found in the house — and a stoep overlooking sprawling lawns and a dam. The new Nantes Valley trio (a range of white wines) joins the existing compact range. Winemaker Dominique Waso has just completed his second harvest here and pronounced it "exceptionally good". The Sauvignon Blanc was made by Marthinus Broodryk at Bovlei Cellar in Wellington as a limited release, also under the De Villiers label. The range was not available for tasting for this ed, but includes (pvs ratings in brackets, where applicable): **Cabernet Sauvignon 99**, **Merlot 99**, **Pinotage 99**, **Cabernet Franc-Merlot Reserve 97** (✿✿), **Cabernet Sauvignon-Merlot 98**, **Blanc de Noir 99**, **Chardonnay Reserve 99**, **Chardonnay 98** (✿) and **99**, **Sauvignon Blanc 00**.

. . . .

Devon Hill Estate

Stellenbosch (see Stellenbosch map) • Tasting by appointment • Olive oil from farm groves • Views • Owner Capamis (Pty) Ltd • Managing director Bernard Fontannaz • Winemaker Graham Weerts • Viticulturists Johan Carinus & Graham Weerts • Production 350 tons 80% red, 20% white (target) • PO Box 1142 Stellenbosch 7599 • Tel (021) 882-2453 • Fax (021) 882-2444 • E-mail devon@sonop.co.za • Website www.savisa.co.za

"AIMING for the top!" says newly appointed winemaker Graham Weerts at this modern winery perched on the crest of the Bottelary Hills above Devon Valley. Starting in January, 2000, after several vintages at Mulderbosch and Coleraine —

and an enviable stint as part of the premium red wine programme at Kendall-Jackson in California — he has set his sights high. The winery is undergoing a transition under the SAVISA management and no expense is being spared. The 99 vintage has all been sold overseas between the last edition and this one, so all the wines available for tasting are from the 2000 vintage, far too young to assess in the case of serious reds which were either still to start their sojourn in oak or else had had a mere six weeks in cask at the time of tasting (the NLH was still quietly fermenting!) Assessments should be regarded as 'sneak previews', as the wines were embryonic — the one exception being the Sauvignon Blanc.

Cabernet Sauvignon Clean cedar and rich mulberry fruit, sweet warm vintage written all over it. Full bodied, still tight and unyielding, fine-grained tannins. Destined for serious oaking, all new, Fr. 4-star material. **Merlot** Burgeoning cassis/choc with subtle violet/fennel and all balsamic notes of fine oak. Red velvet smoothness from very rich fruit, fine-grained tannins; well into its slumber in all new Seguin Moreau casks. Fine future ahead, 4-star material. **Pinotage** Huge waft of show-off sweet redcurrant/raspberry fruit very typical of the variety. Intense concentration, almost cordial-like, beautifully balanced by ripe tannins. Tank sample headed for oaking in combination Am/Fr oak, 40% new. One to watch, 4-star material. **Noble Late Harvest** 100% sauvignon still fermenting in barrel mid-2000. Gorgeous fragrance of pineapples/ginger biscuits/lime marmalade, constantly changing and evolving. Should be great.

✤ **Sauvignon Blanc** Terrific. Full blast of sauvignon capsicum/cut-grass/wild herbs with tropical passionfruit and sweet gooseberry. Aggressive sauvignon attack, explosive flavours which fill the mouth and expand; a real extrovert and a special achievement in a difficult year for sauvignon. Three pickings for perfect ripeness.

De Wet Co-op

Worcester (see Worcester map) • Tasting & sales Mon—Fri 8—5 Sat 9—12 Tasting fee 50c/wine • Cellar tours appointment • Wheelchair-friendly • Owners 60 members • Winemakers Piet le Roux (since 1995), André van Dyk (since 2000) • Vineyards 900 ha • Production 15 500 tons 95% white 5% red • PO Box 16 De Wet 6853 • Tel (023) 349-2710 • Fax (023) 349-2762

THIS FRIENDLY Breede River valley co-op with its snappy range of wines may be the oldest cellar in the Worcester area but it's firmly in the fast lane. Talented winemaker Zakkie Bester (here since 1989) has flown this co-op to take up a new challenge at Riebeek Cellars in the Swartland. Piet le Roux has been promoted to manager-winemaker. Reds are getting the green light as he believes that's way to go, with planned plantings of premium varieties. André van Dyk (ex Ashton Co-op) with his consumer friendly style of winemaking has joined him in the cellar.

✤ **Ruby Port** ▼ 99 from touriga naçional, commendable advance on pvs. Modern, Douro-inspired, firm spirity punch contrasts well with malty/toffee/choc. Good now, but deserves ±2 yrs. ±18% alc, 90 g/ℓ sugar. 500 cases.

✤ **Red Muscadel** ▼ 97 fortified dessert a standout, muscat intensity, honeysuckle/freesia fragrance. Follow-up to 98 ✤ more workmanlike, some cherry/raisins in uncloying sweet palate. 17% alc. 1 200 cases.

Cabernet Sauvignon ✤ 99 made with dollop merlot which shows up in pleasing charry/coffee taste; some weight (13,3% alc) but not too heavy. Unoaked. 750 cases. **Dry Red** ✿ Recipe for this instantly gulpable dry red changes every year, usually features dash of pvs vintage for extra smoothness (slug 99 blend joins 00 cab f/ruby cab in latest **00**). Spicy bell pepper/black berry/cherry in fullish, gently firm long finish. Lightly oaked. **Blanc de Noir** ✿ Striking orange-pink **00**, charming semi-sweet strawberry/cherry flavours. Lightly chill for summer parties. From pinotage. 650 cases. **Chardonnay** Oak-chipped **00** too embryonic to rate. 13% alc.

277 cases. **Clairette Blanche** ✿ Usually shows a bit of personality here (elsewhere very bland). Pear aroma in **00**, bright clean dry finish. Lowish 11% alc. Screwtop. 1 100 cases. **Riesling** ✿ (Cape riesling) Always swiggably light, tasty. **00** usual thatched roof nose, fruity-dry. 500 cases. **Bouquet Blanc** ✿ Easy apple tones in lightish off-dry **00** registering, like pvs, high on the quaff-o-meter. Chenin/gewürz/white muscadel 500 cases. **Petillant Fronté** ✿ Lightly spritzy, extra-low alc (8,3%) charmer gallops out of the cellar. **00** muscat-fruity, crisply sweet. 100% muscat de frontignan. SA Heart Foundation approved. 6 000 cases. **Special Late Harvest** ✿✿ Usual firm acidity lifts/freshens lightish **99**, gewürz in full petally flight. Super aperitif or with spicy food. Bargain priced. 1 100 cases **Hanepoot** ✿ **97** fortified dessert with delicate honeysuckle fragrance; needs to be drunk soon before it lapses into decadence. 17% alc.

. . . .

De Wetshof Estate   🍷 🍷 🍷

Robertson (see Robertson map) • Tasting & sales Mon—Fri 8.30–4.30 Sat 9.30–12.30 • Cellar tours by appointment • Mountain/vineyard views • Owner Danie de Wet • Winemaker Danie de Wet with John Loubser • Viticulturist George Thom (since 1996) • Vineyards 140 ha • Production 1 800 tons • PO Box 31 Robertson 6705 • Tel (023) 615-1853/7 • Fax (023) 615-1915 • E-mail info@dewetshof.co.za • Website www.dewetshof.co.za

THAT GIANT of a winemaker Danie de Wet can stand even taller: his Edeloes Noble Late Harvest 1998 shone as best botrytis dessert worldwide at the IWSC 2000 in London; his Chardonnay d'Honneur 1999 wowed the palates at the worldwide Chardonnay du Monde. And the follow-up 2000 Edeloes earns a high five in this guide — see below. All these accolades have meant leaving his beautiful mountains for some serious travel, including Belgium, the UK, Germany, Japan and Italy — De Wetshof was also among the first local wineries to go on show at the annual VinItaly in Verona. Adding to the bustle is the Danie de Wet range, an off-the-shelf white collection for supermarkets which is new to SA (though available in UK supermarkets for several years). Then he's had so many requests to turn his talents to reds that a small portion of black grapes was harvested for the first time in 2000 from newer, better sited plots. New plantings include merlot and cabernet, with semillon representing the whites. Die-hard De Wetshof fans need not fret: this pioneer of chardonnay in SA will still be "concentrating 99%" on his whites.

✿✿**Bateleur Chardonnay** The estate's flagship, always a personal Danie de Wet barrel selection — finesse, complexity the aims. These brilliantly achieved in **98**, with whiffs of Burgundy in rich toasted nut/smoky citrus array. Delicate peach/apricot fragrances — De Wetshof trademarks — carry into well oaked, classically dry palate. Premium priced. 8–10 mths mixed Fr cooperage. 13% alc.

✿✿**Chardonnay d'Honneur** Bold, flamboyant member of the De Wetshof chardonnay quartet. Still in rehearsal when tasted mid-2000, but chunky oak, lime-chalky zip suggest **99** will be a future star performer. Barrel fermented/aged 8–10 mths. Big 14% alc.

✿✿**Chardonnay Finesse** ✅ Most elegant of trio of barrel fermented chardonnays. Latest **00**, in contrast to stablemate below, virtually popping with vitality. Peach/apricot/cinnamon spice spill into peaches-and-cream palate, finish with luscious, sweet tasting flourish. **99** ✿✿ more delicate, citrus-toned. **98** SAA.

✿✿**Bon Vallon Chardonnay** ✅ Unwooded version, maiden **91** first in this style in SA. **98** first ever VVG in category; **99** leesy, juicy, powerful. Latest **00**, sampled young, rated ✿✿, usual upbeat citrus/peach flavours unexpectedly low key. However, no reason to suppose it won't grow in bottle to pvs heights.

✿✿**Blanc Fumé** ✅ Lightly wooded **00** particularly successful: brisk limey/chalky fruit broadened by seamless oaking. Usual bone-dry finish, parting vanilla twist. 13,5% alc.

✿✿**Rhine Riesling** ✅ Rhine comes to Robertson in exceptional **00**, here off-dry (**98** ✿✿ of pvs ed steely dry) but with gripping sugar-acid interplay, intense spicy

. . . .

lemon-lime bouquet, enduring finish. Should go couple of yrs in bottle, but why wait? 7,2 g/ℓ acid, 7,8 g/ℓ sugar.

⚜**Edeloes** Gorgeous, full-blown botrytis dessert from riesling, now with plausible claim to Cape premiership. IWSC gold medal and trophy for best NLH style wine, VG, *Wine* ⚜ for stunning **98** (portion being held back for later release). This extraordinary performance topped by follow-up **00** ⚜, opulent crushed pineapple, wild honey intensity checked by riveting nervous acidity. Luscious yet wonderfully fresh, elegant despite sturdy weight of alc. A triumph. 13,9% alc, 11,5 g/ℓ acid, 129 g/ℓ sugar. Chic 50 cl 'flint' bottle. 968 cases.

Sauvignon Blanc ⚜ "De Wetshof produced first sauvignon in SA," reminds Lesca de Wet. This experience reflected in handling of troubled **00** vintage: vivid tropical bouquet, crisp melon flavour. **Blanc Dewet** ⚜ Fresh, no-pretensions sauvignon/chardonnay/Cape riesling blend, drink-young **00** with bright floral/fried peaches sniffs, bone-dry finish. **Mine d'Or** ⚜ **93** and pvs labelled Rhine Riesling Moselle — clue to light-bodied/toned style of this delicate, extra-low alc, botrytis-brushed riesling dessert. Name translation of Goudmyn, the original farm (then-owner's rueful comment on astronomic purchase price). Initial arresting sweet-sour tension starting to fade in **98**, terpene notes becoming stronger; consider drinking up. 7,7% alc, 83 g/ℓ sugar. **Gewürztraminer** ⚜ Delicate, exotically-scented Natural Sweet dessert. **99**, follow up to **98** ⚜ VG, unexpectedly ephemeral in palate after billowing rose-petal bouquet. 8% alc.

De Zoete Inval Estate

Paarl (see Paarl map) • Tasting & sales Mon—Sat 9—5 • Bring your own picnic • Wheelchair-friendly • Owner Adrian Frater • Winemakers/viticulturists Gerard & John Robert Frater • Production ± 2 500 tons 50/50 red/white • PO Box 591 Suider-Paarl 7624 • Tel (021) 863-2375 • Fax (021) 863-2817 • E-mail dezoeteinval@wine.co.za • Website www.dezoeteinval.co.za

THE BERG RIVER runs right through this Paarl property, which has been in the Frater family since the late 1800s. The head of this close knit clan, Adrian, passed away recently and will be missed by his wife Suna and children. Fifth generation Gerard, who concentrates his energies mainly in the vineyards, was joined by younger brother John Robert, who now takes care of the winemaking. Eldest daughter Yogi still runs the tasting room although, she says, "everybody here does everything". The next generation is represented by Gerard's son William, who is only a few months old but bound to learn about wine at his father's knee.

Cabernet Sauvignon Vintages **80**, **81**, **84** all still available. "Traditional old-style cabs." Lowish alcs (±11%) Unwooded. **Chloë NV** Cab, lightly wooded. **Grand Rouge NV** 75/25 cinsaut/cab, unwooded. **Rosé Sec NV** (87) From cab. First released 1988. **Yvette 99** unwooded sauvignon blanc. Untasted. **Blanc de Blanc** ✷ **New** Steely dry white, bracingly fresh. **Capri ✷ 99** 100% chardonnay, unwooded. Full bodied (14% alc), soft, some almost 'old Italian' almond tones. **Late Harvest** ✷ Not unattractive sweet/sour effect in **00**, delicate hay/honey aromas. From sauvignon. **Port 98** untasted. "Mixture of old port varieties" fortified with 3 yr old brandy.

Die Krans

Calitzdorp (see Klein Karoo map) • Tasting & sales Mon—Fri 8—5 Sat 9—1 (9—4 during holidays) Private tasting for tour groups by arrangement • Cellar tours by appointment (December school holiday every hour on the hour) • Vintners platters 12—2 Sat & Wed during Feb (pick your own hanepoot); rest of year for groups of more than 10 by arrangement • Bring your own picnic • Extra virgin olive oil sold • Self-guided vineyard walks year round • Views • Owners/winemakers/viticulturists Boets Nel (since 1982) & Stroebel Nel (since 1988) • Vineyards 40 ha • Production 500—600 tons, 15 000— 20 000 cases 40% red 20% white 40% port & fortified desserts • PO Box 28 Calitzdorp 6660 • Tel (044) 213-3314 • Fax (044) 213-3562 • E-mail diekrans@mweb.co.za

BOETS AND STROEBEL NEL could well have thought their unfair share of natural retribution had been taken care of last millennium: a December 1999 hailstorm took out 30% of the port grapes which are the standard bearers in their 40 ha vineyards. But the heavens opened again, in March 2000, delivering the worst floods in living memory. Here in the arid Little Karoo, annual rainfall is normally measured in millimetres rather than hectolitres. At Die Krans, 6 ha of vineyards and orchards were swept away. On the other hand, the gods are also smiling on this, the Cape's answer to the Douro region, and on the affable Nel brothers in particular, whose ambition remains "to be/become" South Africa's top port-style producers. On current evidence, they're hard to beat. The Vintage Reserve is a cracker; the Cape Ruby an absolute jewel. And according to Boets Nel — and shouldn't a Cape Wine Master know? — such wines don't lead to hangovers. "The trouble," in his opinion, "has always begun with the bubbly!" See also under Masters' Port.

✿**White Muscadel Jerepigo** ✔ Benchmark of this fortified dessert style in Cape: concentrated, sweet and long lived (**88** sold at 1999 Nederburg Auction). Nel's aim to lower sugar/alc levels "to more accessible levels" without sacrificing complexity. This reflected in **99**, unctuous but uncloying, honey-macerated pineapple richness cut by fresh acidity. Regional show gold. 17% alc, 190 g/ℓ sugar.

✿**White Muscadel Reserve** ✔ Per Muscadel Jerepigo below, alcs/sugars being reduced in this fortified dessert for brighter/lighter feel. **99** ✿, like pvs in elegant flint half-bottle, full-blown muscat, barley sugar perfume; tug of acidity just rescues palate from syrupy decadence. **98** _Wine_ ✿, SAYWS gold. 16% alc, 195 g/ℓ sugar.

✿**Vintage Reserve Port** Flagship of this range and, since inaugural **90**, among the Cape's standard bearers. 'Declared' only in outstanding vintages. Portugal's the model here, though fine tuning, C'dorp terroir leave own fingerprints in minerally taut coffee/prune/nut array. Recent comprehensive vertical tasting topped by latest **97** ✿, VVG, _Wine_ ✿, Schulz/SAPPA trophy, featuring silky but powerful fruit, exceptional harmony and grip. Still a juvenile, potential for decade or more. Oaked 16 mths, half in large vats, remainder 500 ℓ barrels, all old. 90% tinta b from low yielding 24 yr old vyds, plus younger souzão, roriz, touriga. 19,2% alc, 88 g/ℓ sugar. "Best wine made so far at Die Krans but watch out for **99**!" No **98**. Youthfully purple **95** _Wine_ ✿ currently more opulent than **97**, softening but still quite spirity; needs time. Again 19,2 % alc., 88 g/ℓ sugar. **94** browning; grippy, dry, least luscious of these; time needed to round the edges (Boets Nel reckons 5 yrs). 82 g/ℓ sugar, 19% alc. **91** developing very well; spirity prune/nut combo slicked with creamy dark choc; sweeter than any above yet firm, pleasant nibble of tannin. 2–3 yrs to peak. 95 g/ℓ sugar, 18,3% alc. **90** brown edge; more recognisably Cape, sweetish, lots of soft vanilla oak. Ready. 105 g/ℓ sugar, 17,5% alc.

✿**Cape Vintage Port** Made annually, one of SA's soundest standard vintage 'ports'. Latest **99** ✿ reflects power, generosity of yr. Brooding, almost inky colour mirrored in intense black cherry fruit concentration, mouthcoating ripe tannin. This longer term wine than pvs, needs min 5 yrs. **98** ✿ shade lighter, good weight/structure but not as concentrated as **97**, from excellent vintage. 14 mths old 500 ℓ oak barrels.

✿**Cape Tawny Port** New Fiery garnet colour introduces this promising **NV** dessert, mainly tinta b with touriga, souzão, roriz and dash cinsaut. Dense, complex array of malt, Christmas cake, mocha and nuts, the richness balanced by gentle acidity and spirity tang; quite a dry finish. Ready now, though Boets Nel envisages long future (10 yrs). 19,5% alc, 105 g/ℓ sugar. Not overpriced.

✿**Cape Ruby Port** ✔ Never a second fiddle to the Cape Vintages above, this Portuguese styled dessert gets a standing ovation for its latest **NV** performance, boosted by 40% injection of star Port variety touriga. Immediately hits high note with a whole orchestra of plum, toasted nut and woodsmoke aromas, layered in palate with silkily lush fruit. As pvsly, there's enough amplitude for a vintage port, yet overall the tone is light, even delicate. Incredibly modestly priced at under R20 ex cellar. Regional show gold, best value selection by wine mail order club. 50% tinta b with souzão and roriz. 18,5% alc, 95 g/ℓ sugar. Also in 250 ml screwtops. ±4 000 cases.

Cabernet Sauvignon ⚘ Traditional Cape cab with gamey, green olive, bell pepper whiffs, discreetly oaked. **99** unusually tannic mid-2000, don't rush to uncork. Gold on regional show. 13,5% alc. **Pinotage** ⚘ Klein Karoo sunshine suffuses partially oaked **99**, fruitcake, 'sweet' crushed red berry richness lifted by good thread of acidity. Could age rewardingly. 26 yr old vines. Regional show reserve champ. **Tinta Barocca** ⚘ Nascent satsuma plums-and-cream nose previewed in last ed now fully fledged; no creaminess in palate, however, which robust, earthy, big. So team with sturdy cuisine (and watch that 14,5% alc). Class winner on regional young wine show. **Chenin Blanc** ⚘ New wave Cape chenin, dry, partially oaked "for better ageing". Exotic melon/spice ensemble in latest **99**, fair weight, nicely judged oak. Well priced. 13% alc. **Chardonnay (unwooded)** ⚘ Afrikaans label ("Very popular in Belgium, Netherlands"). No pretensions **99**, simple but not artless. Good fruit-acid balance, some dried peach flavour. 13,5% alc. **Chardonnay (wooded)** ⚘ English label. Uncomplicated quaffer. Mere suggestion of oak from **99** partial barrel fermentation; similar muted dried peach tones to above. Reserve champ on regional show. 13,8% alc. **Golden Harvest** ★ Sweet, lightish **99**, late harvested gewürz, hanepoot. **Spumanté** 𝄢 Feathery light **NV** semi-sweet fizz, carbonated version of Golden Harvest. **Heritage Collection White Jerepigo** ⚘ Immensely rich chenin dessert with botrytis whiff. Distinctive 'eco' label; profits to nature conservation. Barley sugar, raisins in **98**, delicate acidity overwhelmed by penetrating sweetness.

Diemersdal Estate

Durbanville (see Durbanville map) • Tasting & sales Mon—Fri 9—5 Sat 9—3 • Cellar tours by appointment • Meals for groups of up to 35 by arrangement • Conferences • Walks • Mountain biking • Wheelchair-friendly • Owner/winemaker Tienie Louw • Viticulturist Div van Niekerk (since 1980) • Vineyards 180 ha • Production 1 800 tons 80% red 20% white • PO Box 27 Durbanville 7551 • Tel (021) 976-3361 • Fax (021) 976-1810 • E-mail joelouw@iafrica.com

TIENIE LOUW be low profile, but he's got the whole wine business sussed. While in the immediate post-apartheid years others flirted with international markets, the moustachioed "born-to-be-winemaker" jumped into bed with Swiss-based Jacques Germanier Group and swept onto some of Europe's most prominent High Street store shelves. With Germanier's local offshoot, SAVISA, taking care of exports (which now represent the bulk of production), Louw's savouring the prospect of eldest son Thys, a champion speed skier, taking over the controls of the winery and letting dad live his ultimate lifestyle: game fishing on his well-seasoned launch.

⚘ **Shiraz** Estate's standard bearer, in these cooler maritime hills showing aromatic side of the grape. Expansive pepper/wild scrub/prune flavours in **98**, and vintage's fullness, weight in smooth generous palate, though nip of acidity probably better with food. 13,9% alc. 1 500 cases.

⚘ **Pinotage** The 'other' flagship here, in modern, fruity but not overblown style. Smoky, aromatic fruit in latest **98** *Wine* ⚘, SAA, lighter toned (though high 13,5% alc) with polished tannins and crisp acidity; twirl of woodsmoke again in tapering finish. This and above traditionally open-tank fermented, yr 1st/2nd fill oak. 13,5% alc. 1 500 cases.

⚘ **Cabernet Sauvignon** Latest **98** SAA glows with extra star quality thanks to transfusion of densely packed flavour from virus cleaned clones, coupled with brilliantly managed oak which allows the black cherry/dark berry fruit to thrust into foreground. Ripe tannin/acidity should carry this good few yrs. 13,7% alc. 1 500 cases.

✿**Private Collection** Invariably characterful cab-led blend with, in current **98** SAA, 25% merlot and 5% cab f. Bold, deep flavoured, as expected of vintage, though savoury green pepper/blackcurrant tones appear much lighter, fresher than strapping 13,8% alc would suggest. Quite oaky finish detracts. 1 500 cases.

Sauvignon Blanc ✿ NEW In an area renowned for 'sauvage' varietal character, **00** launches full-frontal sauvignon attack with nettle/green pepper punch and racy acidity. Potential for ageing, though good now, too, with the day's catch. 13,2% alc. 1 000 cases.

- -

Die Poort   ⛴ ⛴ ⛴

Herbertsdale (see Klein Karoo map) • Tasting & sales Mon—Fri 9—5 • Cellar tours by appointment • Hannelie Jonker's traditional meals, picnic baskets by appointment • Views • Wheelchair-friendly • Owner JPW Jonker • Winemaker/viticulturist Jannie Jonker • PO Box 99 Herbertsdale 6505 • Tel (028) 735-2406 • Fax (028) 735-2347

A 40-MINUTE detour inland from Mossel Bay will land you up at the only winery on the Garden Route. At the foot of the Outeniqua mountains near Herbertsdale, the farm has been in the Jonker family for two generations. You're guaranteed a warm welcome with home-grown wines and country cuisine in the satisfying traditional boerekos mode. Daughter Lissa, who has been dabbling with her favoured hanepoot for a while now, looked all set for a degree in oenology but at the last minute opted for a computer course in nearby George. Die Poort has its own potstill and produces brandy (which rocks the socks off holidaymakers), apple brandy and unmatured witblits.

The current range, unavailable for tasting, includes: red: **Cabernet Sauvignon**, **Pinotage**, **Hemelrood**; dry white: **Premier Grand Cru**, **Blanc de Blanc**, **Cape St Blaize**; semi-sweet white: **Late Harvest**, **Frölich Stein**, **Camilla** (perlé); sparkling: **Vin Doux**; desserts: **Selected Red Jerepigo**, **Red Jerepigo**, **Sweet Jerepigo**, **Selected White Jerepigo**, **White Jerepigo**, **Lissa Jonker Hanepoot**, **Golden Jerepigo**, **Raisin Jerepigo**, **Port Pinotage**, **White Port**.

- -

Dieu Donné Vineyards   ⛴ ⛴ ⛴ ⛴

Franschhoek (see Franschhoek map) • Tasting & sales Mon—Fri 8.30—4.30 • Cellar tours by arrangement • Bring your own picnic • Views • Owner Robert Maingard • Winemaker Stephan du Toit (since 1996) • Vineyards 40 ha • Production 16 500 cases 60% red 35% white 3% rosé 2% sparkling • PO Box 94 Franschhoek 7690 • Tel (021) 876-2493 • Fax (021) 876-2102 • E-mail dieudonne@zsd.co.za

A 99 PINOTAGE and an upcoming 2000 Shiraz are the latest indications of this mountainside winery's response to the global thirst for reds. Formerly a majority white wine property, it's rapidly reaching winemaker Stephan du Toit's projected ideal — a 70–30 red-white ratio — with lower lying land purchased specifically for this purpose, pushing the vineyard total up to 40 ha. Du Toit does not swoop down to these Franschhoek Valley floor plantings by air, but he could — paragliding is among his action-man pastimes; he's also an ace white-water kyaker and spearfisherman. Japan and Norway are the latest additions to Dieu Donné's export list which also features Mauritius — owner Robert Maingard has family roots on the island.

✿**Merlot** Invariably characterful, satisfying and in **98**, undisputedly the star of this show: rich, choc-mint complexity with hint of violets, properly dry finish. 16 mths Fr barrelling seamlessly absorbed, as is sturdy 14,5% alc. Late-blooming **97** ✿ elegant, fresh-finishing.

❋ **Noble Late Harvest** Luscious botrytised dessert from chenin, developing extra complexities (and star wattage) in bottle. Rich fruit salad in **97**, layered with marmalade, barley sugar. Brisk finish. 7,8 g/ℓ acid, 124 g/ℓ sugar.

Cabernet Sauvignon ⚜ 🙂 Comfortable, lightish toned, cuisine friendly cab (though not insubstantial at 13,5% alc). Fragrant violets, mulberries and smidgeon oak spill into gentle dry finish. Fr casks 18 mths. **Pinotage** ⚜ New 🙂 Full-blown pinotage tones in cask-aged **99**: banana, strawberry, savoury hints of chestnut and tar. Fat and ready. Should be especially good with venison. 14% alc. **Rosé** ⚜ 🙂 Casual semi-sweet quaffer for fun occasions. Not too sugary **98**, balanced strawberry flavours and decorative salmon-pink blush. Wine mail order club selection. Cab/chardonnay. **Sauvignon Blanc** ⚜ 🙂 Showy, appealing, drink-soon **00** is a table mate deluxe: lots of grassy/tropical fruit flavour, bright, crisp, figgy finish. Asparagus wrapped in shaved ham is vintner's foodie inspiration.

Cabernet Sauvignon-Merlot ⚜ Gold at International Wine Challenge for late-blooming, barrique-aged **97**, smoky chocolate sniffs, plump berry fruit still tightly swathed in tannin. Give another yr/2. 13,7% alc. **Chardonnay** (unwooded) ‡ Perky, uncomplicated quaffer, delicate fresh-peeled mango tone in clean dry finish. Try with cold chicken salad, winemaker recommends. 13,1% alc. **Chardonnay** (wooded) ⚜ Expensively oaked **98** not quite as luminous as pvs. Lees and honeyed, plus some butterscotch and more than a splinter of oak. 13,4% alc. Stand-out **92** gold in International Wine Challenge. **Chenin Blanc** ‡ Barrel-fermented/aged **99** now distinctly honeyed; for early drinking. 13,7% alc. **Special Late Harvest** ‡ **98** has filled out in bottle, gained some tropical richness. Generous dollops sugar not oversweet. Chenin. 13% alc. **Méthode Cap Classique** Blanc de blancs style **NV** brut from chardonnay. Untasted. **Dieu Donné Sparkling Wine** ‡ New No-frills **98** showing some muted chenin character.

Distillers Corporation

A LEADING PRODUCER of spirits and wines in SA. See also SA Wine Cellars. • PO Box 184 Stellenbosch 7599 • Tel (021) 888-3200 • Fax (021) 887-0728

Domein Doornkraal

De Rust (see Klein Karoo map) • Tasting & sales Mon—Fri 9—5 (8—6 during school holidays) Sat 8—1 • Cellar tours by appointment • Meals for groups of 10 or more by arrangement • Tourgroups • Gifts • Owners Swepie & Piet le Roux • Winemaker Piet le Roux (since 1992) • Vineyards ±38 ha • Production 250 tons (3 000 cases own label) 45% white 25% red 10% rosé 20% sparkling/desserts • PO Box 14 De Rust 6650 • Tel/fax (044) 251-6715 • E-mail doornkraal@pixie.co.za

AN EVENTFUL YEAR for the Le Rouxs. Flamboyant patriarch Swepie has been rounding up winemaking colleagues to form a Muscadel Association (between swapping notes with marsala producers in Italy); two of his six daughters are cooking up a cultural storm in their Oudtshoorn restaurant, Jemima's ("enchanting boerekos matched with selected Klein Karoo wines"); and winemaker son, Piet, quietly driving some quality improvements in the cellar, especially among the reds. The 2000 harvest was the smallest in 30 years, but the intention remains to "further refine our Semillon and concentrate on crafting some really good Merlot blends".

❋ **Semillon Reserve** New ✔ Good gear up on pvs 'standard' version: **99** full flavoured, ripe, almost sweet tasting yet smoothly dry. Bright lemony, herbal flavour undimmed by oak. 600 cases.

🌸 **Pinta** ✅ Latest bottling of this **NV** sweet jerepigo style dessert particularly good. Signature earthy/porty tones with deep chocolatey smoothness. Pinotage, tinta b. 500 cases.

🌸 **Diep Tanige Port** ✅ Very nice tawny port with plum/toasted hazelnuts bouquet; hints of woodsmoke, prune and some gamey notes (so perhaps good, as Swepie le R asserts, with smoked springbok or ostrich carpaccio). Blend **92**, **94**, **98** vintages, large Fr cask aged. 200 cases.

Cabernet Sauvignon 🌸 These **97** tannins have relaxed somewhat (though still mouthcoating, so Swepie le R's rustic culinary tip — lamb's neck in Provençal sauce — not a bad call). 450 cases. Doornkraal reds fined only with ostrich eggwhite. **Kannaland** 🌸 New Tasty dry red, **00** deep mulberry colour, plummy merlot flavour, smooth. Splash pinotage. Low priced. 500 cases. **Kuierwyn Effe-droog** ✸ No-pretensions semi-dry sipper, **NV**, muted tropical flavours. 13% alc. 500 cases. **Tinta Bianca Effe-droog** 🌸 Rosé style off-dry alfresco wine from chenin, merlot, pinotage, latter adding strawberry/earth in smooth, juicy palate. **NV** (99). 500 cases. **Tinta Bianca Soet Natuurlik** ✸ **99** identical to semi-dry version above but richer, sweeter, yet curiously dry finishing. Individual style. 500 cases. **Tickled Pink** 🌸 **NV** Friskily foamy, blush pink carbonated bubbly, gently sweet; lightish (11,5% alc). "Sets the spirit soaring". Shocking pink ostrich bijou duster optional extra. 600 cases **Majoor** ✸ Sweet, luscious fortified dessert returns to the guide still in **NV** uniform. 'Liquid sultana' says it all. 200 cases. **Kaptein** 🌸 Lusciously sweet raisiny fortified dessert with fruitcake flavours, high spirited finish. Try over ice with lemon twist. **NV**. 400 cases. **Luitenant** 🌸 Individual sweet fortified dessert, from zanté currants, partially fermented. Intense raisin/earthy flavours. This **NV** will be last: vyd has been grubbed up. 150 cases.

Douglas Green 🔻

Wellington • Not open to the public • Owner DGB (Pty) Ltd • Winemaker Cassie du Plessis • Wine buyer Arend Adriaanse • Oenologist Jaco Potgieter • Production 100 000 cases • PO Box 79 Groot Drakenstein 7680 • Tel (021) 874-1011 • Fax (021) 874-1690 • E-mail exports@dgb.co.za

"Douglas Green and the New World Team" has been the 2000 theme song at DGB, which now produces some of its ranges in its own cellars at Wellington. New oenologist, Jaco Potgieter, joined winemaker Cassie Carstens and wine buyer Arend Adriaanse to help drive the DGB objectives: "to establish the Douglas Green label as an international wine of top quality and value". Bringing in high powered business acumen is John Worontchak, who takes an advisory role in growing the range to New World heights.

Douglas Green range

🌸 **Chardonnay** "Not a formal style," says the DGB team, but partially oaked **00**'s not just a jolly quaffer: good lime/lees qualities with woodsmoke, hint of vanilla and bright zesty dry finish. Full bodied (13,4% alc). Portion through malo for extra smoothness.

🌸 **Ruby Port** More traditional style ruby with tawny colour, warm 'porty' scents and some pleasing nut/choc/bitter coffee flavours; very long dry finish. 5 yrs in oak. **NV**.

Cabernet Sauvignon 🌸 💬 Surging blackcurrant/raspberry followed by light smokiness, 'sweetness' from ripe fruit and savoury impressions in 99 which further enhance versatility at table. 13% alc.

Pinotage 🌸 Fragrant start to **99**, sappy red berry aromas/tastes and abundant smooth tannins which deftly cut the sweetness of the ripe fruit and ensure a clean dry finish. Well made wine, full bodied. 13,2% alc **98** SAA, gold on Concours Mondial. **St Augustine** Traditional old favourite in SA, first produced as 'Burgundy' in

1940s; given a make-over from **98**, though still mainly cab, and still full bodied (±13% alc). Untasted for this ed. **96** VVG. **Sauvignon Blanc** ⚖ Offers good spread of varietal tastes — ripe gooseberry, cut-grass, brush of nettle. Juicy **00**'s tangy tones probably best in flush of youth. Med/light-bodied. Try with chicken breast and basil pesto. **Blanc de Blanc** ⚖ Lightish **00** meets you with a big fruit salady bouquet, departs on a cheerful, crisply dry, satisfying note.

The Saints by Douglas Green

This range rejuvenated, renamed and garbed in award winning livery. All NV.

St Raphael ⚖ 🙂 Versatile no-ceremonies dry red quaffer with fruity/savoury tone and mildly grippy tannins which lend themselves to pizza/pasta/BBQ food/occasions. Cinsaut in lightish guise, unwooded. 12% alc. **St Claire** ⚖ 🙂 Natural Sweet low alc (8%) rosé with floral/honeysuckle fragrance and soft, grapey taste. Sweet but balanced, and very pretty in its blush-pink robes. Chenin/gewürz/pinotage.

St Vincent ⚖ After the patron of winemakers. Just-dry white sauvignon/chenin/colombard blend; subdued nose; some tropical fruit in lightish palate, bracing clean finish. **St Morand** ⚖ Label describes this as "fruit white", which it is, in semi-sweet mode (15 g/ℓ sugar) with lightly perfumed bouquet from muscat d'alexandrie (here teamed with chenin). Lightish tropical tastes and nippy finish. **St Anna** ☥ Though labelled "Natural Sweet", this tropical toned low alc (8,15%) sipper features some delightfully crisp acid which cuts the sweetness for a dryish feel. Chenin/gewürz. Also: range of 'sherries' Dry Fino No 1, Medium Cream No 2, Full Cream No 3.

Douglas Winery 🍷

Northern Cape (see Orange River map) • Tasting & sales Mon—Fri 8—1; 2—5 • Owner GWK Ltd (2 000 shareholders) • Winemakers WH 'Pou' le Roux (since 1978) & Danie Kershoff (since 1992) • Viticulturist Danie Kershoff • Vineyards 533 ha • Production 6 700 tons (8 000—10 000 cases own label) • PO Box 47 Douglas 8730 • Tel (053) 298-8200 • Fax (053) 298-1845 • E-mail wilmarie@gwk.co.za

"WE'RE NOT THAT BIG," says Danie Kershoff, referring to the relatively diminutive team looking after the outsize contingent of shareholders — 2 000 in all — growing not only wine and some raisins but also maize, olives, peanuts and cotton. Only a fraction of the grape crop is bottled as wine under the own label ("We'd like to increase that a bit"); most is sold as concentrate or distilling-wine. Ruby cab is the star here, though new merlot and shiraz are "looking fairly good, considering the difficult vintage". In the budget are fresh labels and additional red-wine-making facilities. And replacement 13 mm spanners for the ones Danie Kershoff keeps losing.

Pinotage ★ **99**'s gruff pinotage tannins need a fatty barbequed chop or hearty casserole. Unwooded. 13,7% alc. 902 cases. **Ruby Cabernet** ⚖ Earthy/spicy **99**, good plummy fruit, savoury dry finish. Unwooded. Lightly chill for summer quaffing. (40 t/ha yield!) 549 cases. **Dry Red** ☥ Honest lightweight **99** red, dusty dry savoury tastes. 50/50 ruby cab/pinotage, unwooded. 599 cases. **Mustique** ⚖ Sweetish rose-coloured blanc de noir from muscadel; good winey tastes in **00**. Not cloying. 492 cases. **Chardonnay** ⚖ New Attractive first showing, **00** with yellow peach and fragrant muscat hints, gently dry. 555 cases. **Colombard** ☥ Lightish, firmly dry **00**, with delicate ripe peach tones. 555 cases. **Grand Cru** ☥ Recipe changes to 100% chardonnay in lighter-bodied **99**, featuring some cool 'green' notes; balanced dryness. 563 cases. **Gewürztraminer** ⚖ Dainty litchi scents, technically semi-sweet but light-bodied **99** tastes dryish. Natural partner for spicy curries, asserts Danie Kershoff. 511 cases. **Stein** ☥ Gently sweet, lighter-bodied **NV**, chenin with dash colombard. 215 cases. **Late Vintage** ★ **NV** Light (10,5% alc) semi-sweet dessert, colombard/chenin/hanepoot. 340 cases. **Red Muskadel** ⚖ Sweet yet lively **NV** dessert, grapey/curranty tastes. Chill well in summer, winemakers suggest. 633 cases. **Red Jerepiko** ⚥ **NV** Unctuous fortified dessert, from ruby cab. Past its best. 480 cases. **Sweet Hanepoot** ⚘ Honeyed, sweet fortified dessert; full, quite luscious pineapple tones and bright, ringing acidity. **NV**. 603 cases. **Port** ⚥ Sweet, concentrated **N V**, some medicinal, dusty overtones. Ruby cab. 763 cases. In 230 ml 'Vino-Paks': **Dry White**, **Semi Sweet**. Also, under Oak Valley label, NV 5 ℓ bag in boxes: **Dry Red**, **Grand Cru**, **Late Harvest**. These all untasted.

. . . .

Drostdy Wines ⚐

Tulbagh (see Tulbagh map) • Tasting & sales Mon—Fri 8—12; 1.30—5 Sat 9—12.30 • Cellar tours Mon—Fri 11, 3; Sat 11 • Owner SA Wine Cellars • Winemaker Frans du Toit (since 1968) • PO Box 9 Tulbagh 6820 • Tel (023) 230-1086 Fax (023) 230-0510

A LOW ALCOHOL EXTRA LIGHT, ideal for weight watching vinophiles, is one of this venerable winery's top sellers. Less dainty, but just as evergreen, are the Drostdy Hof Cape Red and Chardonnay — both lunchtime favourites with a very wide appeal. The range is named after Tulbagh's old magistracy, now a national monument, and created under the very seasoned eye of Frans du Toit, keen believer in the two cornerstones: "selection and blending". Also made here are Two Oceans (see entry) and African Sky (export range, not tasted), all marketed by SA Wine Cellars.

Drostdy Hof range

Cape Red ⚘ 😊 Unwooded **00** blend of half-a-dozen varieties, with smoky berry fruit; honest rustic stuff. 4,2-million litres of it await your pleasure! **Chardonnay** ⚘ 😊 **99** should be as big a seller as previous, with citrusy, toasty aromas/flavours leading to a crisp lemon finish. **Adelpracht Special Reserve** ⚘ 😊 Lightish **99** mostly from chenin. Sweet SLH style (44 g/ℓ sugar), but balanced by acidity to make a fruity, light parcel of uncomplicated and undeniable pleasure, with a fresh honey/lemon finish.

Cabernet Sauvignon ⚘ Deep colour in **97**, notes of strawberry and cassis. Gently wooded and flavoursome. **Pinotage** ⚘ Ripe plums and bananas in **97**; soft and easy to drink. **Ruby Cabernet** ⚘ Baked spiciness in **98** with mulberry depths; soft and fruity. **Claret Select** ⚘ Lightly oaked **NV** blend; structured for unproblematic pleasure; dry finish. **Sauvignon Blanc** ⚘ **00** has bubblegum and grassy scents; well-balanced light and lively drinking. **Extra Light** ⚥ Nicely pungent aromas in this **NV** soft and dry best seller — all at low level 9% alc! **Steen/Chenin Blanc** ⚘ Tropical fruit notes in **00**; soft and round, but dry, with crispness gathering at finish. **Premier Grand Cru** ⚥ **NV** with particularly pleasant aromas and an uncompromising dry finish. **Stein Select** ⚥ **NV** Uncomplicated and easy-going, with gently acidic backbone. **Late Harvest** ⚥ **NV** Simple, sweetish, mango scents and flavours.

. . . .

Du Plessis see Havana Hills

Du Preez Estate

Rawsonville (see Worcester map) • Tasting & sales Mon—Fri 8—5 Fee R5 p/p • Cellar tours by appointment • Bring your own picnic • Play area for children • Tourgroups • Walks • 4x4 trail • Wheelchair-friendly • Owner HL du Preez • Winemaker/viticulturist Hennie du Preez • Vineyards 130 ha • Production 1 700 tons 65% white 35% red • PO Box 12 Rawsonville 6845 • Tel/fax (023) 349-1642 E-mail dupreezestate@intekom.co.za

"I GREW UP watching dad enjoy the challenges of every season," replies Hennie du Preez to our question, why did you choose a career in wine? It seems the young farmer has been having just as much fun as his father, also named Hennie, since junior took over the running of the Rawsonville family spread in 1995. In his hands the vineyards have blossomed — they've been among the top three in the local block competition three years running — and the wines haven't fared shabbily either, earning 4 medals at the 1999 Veritas show. New in the cellar on the 150 ha property are a bottling line and extra tanks for red wine production, which currently accounts for about 35% of the total. A bustling export business — customers in the UK, Belgium, Netherlands and Hong Kong — saw Hennie du Preez in London during 2000 looking over the International Wine Trade Fair. Declaring himself "very impressed", he's now on a mission "to raise the quality of our wines to match the best in the world".

Sauvignon Blanc 🔆 😊 **99**'s cut-grass tones are gentle and charming but need to be enjoyed soon while still quaffable and not too honeyed. 2 500 cases.

Polla's Red 🔆 'Polla' must be a strapping fellow, to judge from his **99** namesake with 15,4% alc! Beyond the spirity punch, some complexity and good minerally fruit. Blend shiraz/pinotage/petit verdot/ruby cab. 550 cases. **Pinotage 98**, first from this estate, past its best. 1 000 cases. **Hanepoot** 🔆 Attractive floral example of this traditional sweet Cape fortified dessert; generous, warming, with ethereal honeysuckle/muscat scents in **99**. 494 cases.

....

Du Preez Wine

Stellenbosch • Owner/winemaker Jan du Preez • Production 20 000 cases 70% red 30% white • PO Box 204 Stellenbosch 7599 • Tel (021) 887-9937 • Fax (021) 887-0566 • E-mail dupwine@intekom.co.za

"TOUGH" is how Jan du Preez describes the wine-competition he encountered on a recent tour of Europe. But the Stellenbosch-based negociant/winemaker is undeterred. His Migration brand ('Born in Africa, migrating to all wine lovers, worldwide' per the front label) "has really taken off from a packaging and wine quality point of view," du Preez reports. And now he's ready to go global. An excellent millennium harvest ("the wines made themselves") should provide an extra fillip for the brand's that's wowing consumers in Germany, Holland, France, the US and Switzerland, and a favourite of local Wine of the Month Club judges, who have selected it for their members.

Migration range

🔆 **Shiraz** N̲e̲w̲ Old World restraint the hallmark of this range, here well expressed in lightish but full flavoured strawberry/cherry tones with fragrant spice and oak char. "Looking for a Côtes-du-Rhône style". 350 magnums (1,5 ℓ).

Cabernet Sauvignon 🔆 Chic 'slimline' bottle with evocative front label. **98** has opened up since pvsly tasted: easy, accessible, ample red berry fruit. Lightly oaked. 13% alc. 3 000 cases

Twin Oaks range

Current range, not available for tasting, includes: **Ruby Cabernet 99, Sauvignon Blanc 00, Chenin Blanc 00.**

....

Dumisani   N̲e̲w̲

THESE are quaffing wines with a Xhosa flavour — from the name (Dumisani: praise) to the labels, which feature translations from Xhosa praise songs. Doubtless "the southern wind that paints the sky with vivid poetry ..." did not originally describe a ruby cabernet–merlot blend, but wine and poetic licence are age-old partners.

This is a joint-venture between Winecorp and UK agent Private Liquor Brands, listed in three major chains.

> **Ruby Cabernet-Merlot** ✿ 😊 Easy drinking 50/50 blend lively but not too wild; plums, bitter chocolate and grass in **99**; juicy flow tempered by gentle tannin squeeze. Satisfyingly dry.

Cabernet Sauvignon Reserve ✿ Robust **98**; modern-style blackberry/brambly gush toned down with touches cedary oak, some mellow development. Full bodied, good fruit, filling; gutsy tannins will benefit from ±12/18 mths further maturation. Fr oak matured. **Pinotage Reserve** ✿ **98** in bright, non-combative style. Pure, straightforward red berries, 'sweetened' with hints Am oak. Very soft, light textured — though full bodied (13,6% alc) — finishing with touch tongue-tingling bitterness. Fr/Am oaked. **Chenin-Chardonnay** ✿ Lightly oaked **99** happy, pleasing 70/30 mix. Honeyed/tropical roundness freshened by medium body, gentle oaky sweetness.

- -

Duncan's Creek see Rickety Bridge

- -

Durbanville Hills ⚑ ⚐ ⚑

Durbanville (see Durbanville map) • Tasting & sales Mon—Fri 9—5 Sat 10—2 • Light lunches/wine bar mid-Nov — mid-Jan (phone for details • Owner Distillers Corp with 7 local growers • Winemaker Martin Moore (since 1999) with Riaan Oosthuizen • Vineyards 300 ha initially, rising to 540 • Production 8 000 tons (total capacity) 70% white 30% red (ultimately 60/40) • PO Box 3276 Durbanville 7551 • Tel (021) 558-1300 • Fax (021) 558-9658 • E-mail DHills@dist.co.za

DON'T even think of calling this spanking-new, R70-million winery 'co-operative'. Yes, it's a joint venture — among 7 leading vineyard-owners in this prime area and Distillers Corporation. But no, there isn't a trace (some curiously archaic, tongue-tying wine names aside) of the lumbering, quantity-driven ox-wagon about this classy, modern re-invention of the winelands' traditional group-vehicle. It's simply a case of the locals striking back. Growers here had for too long seen their vineyards raided by sensation-seekers from other parts — who proudly trumpeted "Durbanville fruit" and "cool breezes from Table Bay" and "from one of the finest viticulture areas in the Cape" as the keynote components of the wines they fashioned elsewhere. Now cellar chief Martin Moore, ex-Groot Constantia, is keeping the pearls — for example, the extraordinary grapefruity Sauvignon below — back where they belong, right here at home. Here's regional identity at its accessible best — mere minutes from Cape Town.

✿ **Cabernet** New Exciting newcomer which showcases cabernet potential of this appellation. Big structure, intense flavours in **99**. Parsley bouquet; minerals/tomato cocktail in palate (Moore/Oosthuizen nodding to the Old World, St Emilion in particular), no hint of greenness. Serious cab for keeping min 5 yrs. 13,5% alc. 100% Fr oak, 70% new.

✿ **Merlot** Big, fleshy **99**, intense varietal choc-cherry plus hint of mint, generous tannins and ultra-dry finish. Yr Fr oak, ⅞ new. 13,8% alc. Flagship merlot planned for Mar 2001 under Rhinofields label, after fynbos ('renosterveld') reserve above cellar. This, from barrel, similar to version above with extra intensity; 18 mths all-new Fr oak.

✿ **Pinotage** "Very friendly, accessible wine" the intention, convincingly realised in **99**, with bright (yet not facile) strawberry, cherry, banana fruits. Big (13,8% alc), picked super-ripe (24—27 °B), but with firm harnessing tannins and savoury Dutch licorice aftertaste. 50/50 new/2nd fill oak, 6—7 mths.

✿ **Shiraz** New Exciting new-style shiraz: not an odorous farmyard or sweaty saddle in sight. Generous blackberry fruit, whiffs of clove, seasoning spice (pepper *and* salt) in easy drinking (though not unserious) **99**. Very ripe picked grapes ex 16–17 yr old vyd on Hooggelegen farm. Good food wine. 70% first fill oak (10% Am, 90% Fr).

✿ **Chardonnay** Slow starting **00** needs at least yr in bottle, drink optimally for further 5. Intense, almost decadent orange peel aroma, hints of tropical fruit, nuts and butter. Complex fruit/oak interplay. Back blended with dollop **99**. 5 mths wood (40% oak staves, 60% barrel). Single vyd (Hillcrest farm) version to be released 2001 under Rhinofields label. 17 mths all-new Fr oak barrels which had been "broiled" (long, slow toasted). 'Cheese curls' aromas (and much more) in this **99**; wood/fruit in passionate embrace — "exactly the sort of wine I'm trying to make," says Martin Moore.

✿ **Sauvignon Blanc 00**, like pvs, will get going only after ±yr. Uncommunicative mid-2000; some shy green fruits in palate, grapefruity aftertaste. **99** now has broad, enveloping mouthfeel with wide screen khaki bush/green pepper/capsicum flavours. Pvs (at press time still available from cellar; may also be available in retail): **Elsjes Corael Chardonnay 99**, **Biesjes Craal Sauvignon Blanc 99**.

Du Toitskloof Winery

Worcester (see Worcester map) • Tasting & sales Mon—Fri 8—5 Sat 8.30—12 • Cellar tours by arrangement • Formal tasting for groups max 40 • Views • Owners 12 members • Winemakers Philip Jordaan (since 1983), Shawn Thomson (since 1999), Jaco Brand (since 1999), Derick Cupido • Consulting viticulturists Schalk du Toit & Willem Botha (VinPro) • Production 11 000 tons • PO Box 55 Rawsonville 6845 • Tel (023) 349-1601 • Fax (023) 349-1581 • E-mail dutoitcellar@intekom.co.za

DON'T make the usual bulk wine assumptions about these 12 growers and their unsleepy winery below the Du Toitskloof mountains. They're young and dynamic, and they keep focused on the business of wine (as opposed to brandy, which was the centre of their parents' farming lives) by reading, tasting and travelling widely. Setting the pace and direction is the seasoned cellar captain, Philip Jordaan (who switched from Physical Education to Oenology at Stellenbosch University after his 'hobby', swigging Tassenberg at Tollies bar, "got the upper hand"). A new presence is Shawn Thomson, dux student from Elsenburg College who's bringing his youthful enthusiasm to the "exciting prospect" of replanting the prime sites, currently given to muscat varieties, with more fashionable reds. This might elicit grumblings from the numerous fans of the decadent Muscadel and Hanepoot fortified desserts, but Jordaan assures the cellar's aim "will always be to keep consumers smiling with quality wines at reasonable prices".

✿ **Red Muscadel** ✅ This and white version below among the Cape's top muscats: opulent, elegant and an unbelievable bargain at ±R14 ex-cellar. **99** in the usual sparkly form after **98**'s ✿ unexpectedly subdued showing. The later vintage glows fluorescent pale pink, billows heady rose petal and honeysuckle fragrances; in palate, luscious litchi/mango tastes and a good fiery tang at the end. Low (for this style) 15,3% alc.

✿ **Hanepoot Jerepigo** ✅ Needs its own trophy hall: **95** VG, Michelangelo gold; **97** VG, *Wine* ✿, SAYWS champion ("once in a lifetime achievement") among the recent accolades. Latest release didn't show well initially, though winemakers presciently assured: "Given time, will reach heights of predecessors." Yr on, **99** ✿ has grown beyond all recognition. (and scooped *Wine* ✿, Michelangelo gold). Shimmering brassy-gold colour, intriguing botrytis hints turning almost vegetal in absolutely silky, 'choc-orange liqueur' palate with limpid spirity warmth. Low-cropping bushvines from Swastika farm, owned by TC Botha. Astounding ±R14 ex-cellar price as above. These 16–17% alc, ±4 g/ℓ acid, 200–230 g/ℓ sugar.

Chardonnay ✦✦ 😊 Wood fermented **00**, big (13,8% alc) but balanced, some fairly rich butterscotch/vanilla lifted by clean citrus grip. Good with smoked salmon, report winemakers. **Special Late Harvest** ✦✦ 😊 Rose petals and some honey with botrytis tones, ripe fruit salady tastes in gentle, lightish semi-sweet **99**, still with pleasingly zingy finish. **00** similar but fresher, if less complex. Chenin/hanepoot. **Sparkles Brut** ✦✦ 😊 Light, undemanding carbonated **NV** with bracing muscat/lemon tones, huge fizz and crisp dry finish.

Cabernet Sauvignon ✦✦ Savoury berry/cherry fruits in **99**, supple 'sweet' fruity flavour, soft tannin. This and varietal reds below oak influenced, well priced at under R20 ex-cellar. **Shiraz** ✦✦ One of the new-generation stars of this cellar, **99** bright Ribena fruit mixed with spice/peppercorns, long tangy finish. **Merlot** ✦✦ Spice/mint/woodsmoke plus smoky bacon whiffs in highly aromatic **99**, plenty of soft tannins; easy drinking. 50% carbonic maceration. ±13 alc. **Pinotage** Sweet ripe plums/berries in value quaffing **99**, good fruity mouthful with supple tannins. ±14% alc. **Dry Red** ⚹ "Braaivleis wine," says Philip Jordaan. Fleshy strawberries, smoky notes, soft, gluggable **NV** (500 ml screwcap) from ruby cab/cinsaut; unwooded. **Blanc de Noir** ⚹ Snazzy coral-blue colour; stemmy nose, strident dryish finish with some juice in palate. Easy 11,9% alc. **Chenin Blanc** ✦✦ Chic med-bodied lunchtime sipper; light, honeyed, with mouthfilling dash sugar though technically dry. **Colombard** ✦✦ New "All day drinking wine," say winemakers. **00** with green apple scents, fruity tastes, clean dry finish. **Sauvignon Blanc** ⚹ Reductively handled, lightish **00** with uncomplicated fresh hay tones. Might fill out with bit of time. Good foil for crispy duck with lemon sauce, recommends Philip Jordaan. **Riesling** ★ Lightish dry **00** quaffer from Cape riesling; demure green apple tones. **Blanc de Blanc** ⚹ Unwooded, light, dry **NV** chenin swigger in 500 ml screwtop bottle; delicate floral/pear scents. **Semillon-Chardonnay** ⚹ New Attractive tropical toned dry **00** with balanced fruit/acid and moderate alc. **Bukettraube** ✦✦ Gentle, light floral semi-sweet **00**. 11,5% alc. Single vyd on winery chairperson Johan de Wet's farm. **Late Vintage** ★ Light-bodied, honeyed **NV** semi-sweet from chenin/white muscadel. 500 ml screwtop. **Port** ✦✦ Interesting Cape style port from pinotage; **98** with smoky prune aromas with whiffs of herbs; long peppery finish. Yr oaked, 18% alc.

· ·

EagleVlei

Stellenbosch • Not open to the public Tasting & sales for trade by appointment • Owners Steve & Jean Weir, André & Tess van Helsdingen • Winemaker André van Helsdingen • Viticulturist Tess van Helsdingen • Consulting viticulturist Paul Wallace (VineWise) • Vineyards 7 ha • Production 1 500 cases 100% red • PO Box 969 Stellenbosch 7599 • Tel/fax (021) 880-1846 • E-mail Avanhels@adept.co.za • Website www.eaglevlei.co.za

THE 7 HA of merlot, cabernet and pinotage on this 50 ha farm in the classy red-wine precinct of Muldersvlei have been boosted with another 3 ha of cabernet, but while these vines are growing up, grapes have been bought from a neighbour. The first releases — with high-chic packaging — garnered appreciative reviews and export orders from the UK, Germany and Switzerland. But partner André van Helsdingen, builder of the winery and now looking after the winemaking too, would ideally drink the Cabernet below nearer home — with his wife (whose portfolio is the vineyards) and mates "on a bush trip deep in Africa".

✦✦**Pinotage** (Eaglet in pvs ed) After a soaring debut in **98**, follow-up **99** ✦✦, tasted soon after bottling, appears to cruise at a slightly reduced height (or may be in shock). Flavours are plentiful and satisfying but less intense, glossy. Plums, some ripe banana the main attractions, toasty/smoky oak properly in background. Good wrapping of tannin approachable now and promising some shorter term development. 13,4% alc. 500 cases.

✿ Cabernet Sauvignon Announced itself in dramatic fashion with stylish looking and -tasting **97**, brilliantly showcasing the elegance of that cooler yr. **98** richer, more concentrated, in line with warmer vintage. Latest **99 ✿**, tasted in same stage of development, not as impressive. Green, quick tannins and overt sweet-oak not yet melded with cherry/strawberry fruit-core. May improve with time. Fr oak, 12 mths. Lowish 11,9% alc. 500 cases.

Eersterivier Cellar

Stellenbosch (see Stellenbosch map) • Tasting Mon—Fri 9—5 Sat 9—2.30 Sales Mon—Fri 9—5.30 Sat 9—3 • Cellar tours by appointment • PO Box 465 Stellenbosch 7599 • Tel (021) 881-3886 or 881-3870 • Fax (021) 881-3888 or 881-3102

THIS cellar, offering consistently individual, affordable wines from a prime area, is now part of the Stellenbosch Vineyards group (see that entry for more details).

> **Muscat d'Alexandrie ✿ ☺** Consistency keeps this, one of Cape's few dry hanepoots, in popularity charts. **00** tamer than some pvs. Delicate grapiness complemented by medium body; clean, refreshing. Good partner to range of spiced dishes.

Cabernet Sauvignon ✿ 98 disappointing showing from this usually reliable quaffing cab. Quite sullen, overripe nose, roughish tannins with more than dash bitterness in tail. Barrel-matured. **Cabernet Sauvignon-Merlot ✿** (pvsly Grand Reserve) Plummy **99**, short-lived fruit on palate, best consumed while still fresh. Unwooded. **Pinotage ★** Full, soft **99** with rather too persistent 'burnt rubber' character. Unwooded. **Sauvignon Blanc ✿** Undemanding **00**; grassy/gooseberry hints set off by few grams sugar; unassertively fresh. **Chenin Blanc ✿ 00** with gentle fruit salad spread; juicy flavours enhanced/firm acid downplayed by dollop sugar.

Hanseret range

Popular, tamely priced anytime range. Mainly NV.

> **Special Late Harvest ✿ ☺** Pleasantly ripe-smelling **00** (though little indication of chardonnay origin); med-bodied with zesty acid balancing the ample sweetness.

Claret ✿ Ready to drink cinsaut/cab/shiraz blend; soft, light-textured with gentle red berry juiciness. Will happily take light chilling. **Edelblanc ✿** Uncomplicated, anytime gewürz/sauvignon/chenin, lightish, whispers of spice. **Bouquet Blanc** No decision at deadline on future of this semi-sweet blend. Possibly will be discontinued.

Eikehof

Franschhoek (see Franschhoek map) • Tasting, sales, cellar tours by appointment • Owner F Malherbe • Winemaker Francois Malherbe (since 1992) • Vineyards 40 ha • Production 70 tons 4 000 cases 60% red 40% white • PO Box 222 Franschhoek 7690 • Tel/fax (021) 876-2469

A VIRTUAL viticultural museum, Eikehof nurtures some of the oldest vineyards in the Cape — parcels of nearly century-old bush vines, established by Francois Malherbe's great-grandfather around 1903, after clearing a portion of his then oak-shady Franschhoek farm. Semillon remains Francois Malherbe's speciality, but he has brought in some reds — shiraz being the most recent addition. The strong, silent type (white-water kayaking and marathon running his fortes), when pressed he describes the 2000 harvest simply as "dry" and "good".

✿Cabernet Sauvignon Since debut **93**, densely packed, showy, sturdy tannin build for long keeping. Latest **00** cast in this mould: rich, full, smoky cherries/mulberries in profusion. Tannins astringent still, need time. 13,5% alc. Earlier peaking **99** ✿ has lost its youthful asperity, open red fruit now most quaffable.

✿Bush Vine Semillon Deep-flavoured dry white, with distinction of springing, with admirable verve and freshness, from low cropped 98 yr old bushvines, among most venerable in Cape. **00** ripe peach, mango, melon, vanilla-oak bouquet already quite developed; palate less so: light youthful finishing astringency needs bit of time to soften. Should develop interestingly. Routine vinification: whole bunch pressed, 50% oak fermented/aged 6 mths. Tank-fermented portion sur lie. ±13,5% alc. 600 cases. Regular **Semillon** ✿ Mix ancient/young, bush/trellised vines, briefly oaked, similar smells/tastes but notch less intense, earlier peaking. **99** drinks well now, clean limey freshness, some buttery oak complexity. 13,5% alc. **00** too young to rate. 500 cases.

✿Chardonnay Since maiden **93**, habitually more accessible than semillons above, ready on release. **99** with appealing melon/lemon aromas; full, creamy mouth, tapered citrus zesty finish. **00**, clearly in bottle shock, not rated. Whole bunch pressed, cask-fermented 50/50 Fr/Am but not matured. ±13% alc. 800 cases.

Merlot ✿ **98** set the tone with lively, med-bodied plumminess. After more subdued **99** ✿, return to form in **00**: velvety, rich, promising well. 700 cases. **Shiraz** **New** **00** being raised in 225 ℓ Nevers casks when sampled mid-2000 so not rated. Showed some complexity, fine shiraz smokiness, ripe cherry fruit. Own vyds. 100 cases.

- -

Eikendal Vineyards

Stellenbosch (see Helderberg map) Tasting & sales Mon—Fri 9—5 Sat 9—4 (Oct-Apr); 9—1 (May-Sept) Sun 10—4 Tasting fee R5 p/p • Cellar tours Dec—Feb 11.30 & 2.30 • Summer light lunches (Oct-Apr); winter soup, musselpot, bockwürst, fondue (May-Sept) Sun lunch mid Nov-mid Apr • Famous Fri evening Swiss cheese fondues Jun—Sep (book ahead) • Eikendal Lodge B&B • Reception facilities • Owners AG Für Planatagen (Switzerland) • General manager/winemaker Josef Krammer (since 1987) • Cellar chief/winemaker Anneke Burger (since 1991) • Production 500 tons 30 000 cases • PO Box 2261 Dennesig Stellenbosch 7601 • Tel (021) 855-1422 • Fax (021) 855-1027 • E-mail eikendal@netactive.co.za • Website www.eikendal.com

"WE'VE just discovered this amazing winery! You can't believe its Chardonnay! And the Merlot! And the Rouge — such a brilliant little quaffer!" And so on and on — we hear this sort of excitable babble about this cellar all the time, despite the fact that it's been bottling since 84, and has won umpteen local and international awards. But we understand, and share the incredulity. Not about the consistent quality of the wines, but about the studiously low-key publicity policy. This Swiss-owned property could yodel deafeningly about all its attributes — including vineyards on the prime slopes of the Helderberg, fine home-grown olive oil, jolly fondue-and-music evenings, and a luxury B&B lodge. But winemakers Josef Krammer and Anneke Burger, and chef-de-tasting room Mandy Lutz, a ✿ in own right, are more of the soft-whispering sort, as is another star of the cellar, their assistant Leonard O'Rein, winner of the 2000 Patrick Grubb scholarship, which whisked him off to premium US producer Stimson Lane Vineyards, to pick up extra know-how. One of Eikendal's greatest charms is precisely that they do not batter your ears with all that every-wine-a-masterpiece sort of stuff. They rely on quiet word-of-mouth for their loyal (local and foreign) fan-base, and retain a freshness, almost an innocence, in an age of hard-sell and hype.

- -

✿**Cabernet Sauvignon Reserve** Only made in exceptional years and then only released when up to demanding scratch; previously only from cellar door, next **99** will be for CWG Auction. Dense ruby colour, aromatic cedar oak betrays classic blackcurrant/cassis fruit heavily shielded by tannic armour mid-2000. Fragrant spices, firmly structured, minerally-flinty notes all in restrained rather than flagrant display. Latest features 15% merlot to soften cab. 14,5% alc. Only 100 cases. Pvs **96** 100% cab, 2 yr in cask, 4 barrel selection. No **95**. **94** ready.

✿**Merlot** ▼ Eikendal has led Cape merlot direction since first 91. Latest **99** less luxuriant than previous, still irresistibly charming. Ethereal perfumed nose loaded with cherry fruit, creamy texture. More tannic than before, ends touch bitter. Ripe **98** blackberry flesh, venison/roast coffee scents plump up mineral flavours. Bigger 13,5% alc but no less stylish. **95** reticent, light. **94** *Wine* ✿. Mix new/yr-old Fr oak, 10 mths.

✿**Cabernet Sauvignon-Merlot** New **99** limited bottling (100 cases) of "Anneke Burger's special blend". Seductive soft fragrances, berries/meat with vanilla cleanness, luscious mouthful pulpy cherry fruit braced by sturdy ripe tannins. Full, firm and very good. Cellar door only.

✿**Chardonnay** Vaulting intentions signalled from first **92** (SA champion white wine of yr), delivered from **94**, **96** both *Wine* ✿, then **97** VVG; **98** SAA, 4th slot Tri Nations Chardonnay Challenge. Current **99** sweet butterscotch aromas cut by limey fruit; big, arresting, still very chic. Barrel sample **00** maintains the excitement: grapefruit pith in mid-palate, super length. Barrel-fermented, now 100% new wood, most through malo. **Reserve 99** on sale cellar door only, released late 2000, better still: flinty orange zest nose, buttery palate underpinned by wonderful chalky complexity. Fantastic finish.

Rouge ⚥ ☺ Best seller with bearing. **99** tarry char bouquet; dusty, clean strawberry Cape melange of mainly cinsaut, dashes cabernet/merlot/pinot. 6 mths old large wood. **Chenin Blanc** ✿ ☺ **00** continues generosity of style set by pvs. Billowing tropical/guava, ripe 13% alc, off-dry (7 g/ℓ sugar). Brush of Am oak colours in the spaces. **Special Late Harvest** ✿ ☺ **00** boisterous tangerine/pink grapefruit packed with peachy fruit-salad medley. Refreshing late grip, cleansing acid. From chenin, less sweet-tasting than most (but around 40 g/ℓ sugar), voluptuous round palate from botrytis hint. These develop richness over 2 yrs; full, delicious; even determined dry white drinkers can't resist.

Classique ✿ **98** sees merlot portion upped to 45% to soften cab, 10% cab f making this a triangular Bdx blend. Quiet nose, classic understatement in youth, puckering tannins cosset black fruits mid-2000. Needs time in bottle to soften. 20 mths new/2nd fill Fr barrels. **Cabernet Sauvignon** ✿ Eikendal's motto of understatement gets welcome boost from forest-floor fruits in next **98** — toasty wood/chewy tannins resist the slide to frivolity. ±2 yrs used oak, some Am for spice. **Pinot Noir** ✿ Sample **00** reflects influence of French cellar assistant, Christian Cardet: incredible colour extraction from unfashionable BK5 clone; wafting cherry scents and big, firm mouthfeel — tannins with deportment! **Sauvignon Blanc** ✿ **00** somewhat neutral nose, quiet fruit in mouth elevated by late grassy grip. Not for keeping. **Blanc Fumé** ✿ Individually irreverent; maintains style/name being deserted by other producers pandering to market confused by difficult barrel-fermented sauvignon arena. Good wine too. **00** intriguing mix thatch/oak/tropical fruit bursting out from under cover. Creamy oak vanilla adds 3rd dimension to standard label above. **Blanc de Blanc** ⚥ Invariably fresh, undemanding drink young dry white chenin (55%)/sauvignon blend. **00** ripe melons, roundness beyond price level. Stein ⚥ Amiable chenin juiciness, semi-sweet, fruit-salad finish. **Sauvignon Blanc Brut** ⚥ Carbonated bubbly bearing Anneke Burger's own label design, grassy nose, refreshing finish. **Chenin Blanc-Sauvignon Blanc Demi-Sec** ★ Unwieldy name for simple, floral sparkler, sweetness will appeal to many.

. . . .

Eikestad see Vinfruco
Elements see Hartswater

Elephant Pass Vineyards

Franschhoek • Closed to the public. • Self-catering guest cottage Tel (021) 876-3280/082-937-3789 • Owners Peter & Ann Wrighton • Consulting winemaker Jean Daneel (since 1998) • Viticulturist Steve Smith (since 1998) • Vineyards 5 ha • Production ±800 cases 50/50 red/white • PO Box 415 Franschhoek 7690 • Tel (021) 876-3666 • Fax (021) 876-2219

SEEMS every window here comes with a heavenly aspect. The charming Owl Cottage B&B in the vineyard has "arguably the best view in SA" according to owners Peter and Ann Wrighton, and from the kitchen you can still see the pass which the elephants — they once rocked and roamed the valley — trod over the Franschhoek mountain. The wines which take their name from this ancient route are vinified from grapes grown on the Wrighton's Oude Kelder farm at the small cellar on adjoining farm Guldenheuvel by Jean Daneel, here in a consulting role (he also flies solo under his Jean Daneel Wines banner). The Wrightons are focusing on merlot as their flagship wine. Having scaled the heights of most of the mountains, it's retired executive Peter Wrighton's dearest wish to produce a five-star wine.

✿✿ **Merlot** New Young vines, in their first public performance, brilliantly rise to the occasion in **98**, showcasing pure merlot fruit — plums/coffee/bitter choc — and good charry oak. Still in formative stage; give min 2 yrs to gain richness. 20 mths Fr oak, 40% new. 13,5% alc. 200 cases.

Celebration ✿✿ Toasts this property's miraculous escape from 1999 raging forest fire. Bold, forthright **NV** blend (oaked 98 chardonnay/unwooded 99 chenin) needs time to realise its potential. 13% alc. 156 cases. **Chardonnay Reserve** New **99** not ready for tasting. Fr oak matured, 40% new. 12,5% alc. 75 cases.

. . . .

Emerald Glen Vineyards

Stellenbosch • Not open to the public • Owner Dave Lello • Winemaker Peet le Roux (since 1998) with Beyers Truter • Viticultural consultant Eben Archer • Vineyards 11 ha • Production 59 tons 100% red • PO Box 12426 Die Boord 7613 • Tel/fax (021) 880-1200

THE FIRST WINES from this 110 ha Stellenbosch Mountain farm should be ready for sale in March 2001; they were hand-made ("old-style, minimum machinery, fermented in wood") by owner Brian Lello and winemaker/farmer Peet le Roux in a lean-to adjoining an old barn; a cellar and tasting room will be built as production rises — their recent visit to Italy suggests in Tuscan style. Currently there are 11 ha of vineyards — mainly merlot, ruby cabernet and pinotage; all new plantings will be red-wine varieties. Kanonkop's Beyers Truter, and University of Stellenbosch guru Eben Archer are consulting. The aim is "wines which are soft, fruity and pleasant for the majority of drinkers".

. . . .

Equus see Zandvliet

Excelsior Estate

Robertson • Not open to the public • Cellar tours by appointment • Owners/viticulturists Stephen & Freddie de Wet • Winemaker Jaco Marais (since 1996) • Vineyards 250 ha • Production 3 800 tons 60% red 40% white • PO Excelsior Estate Ashton 6715 • Tel (023) 615-2050/1980 • Fax (023) 615-2019 • E-mail stephendewet@hotmail.com

"BELIEVE it or not, we had a shortage of white wine last year," marvels Jaco Marais. "So sauvignon blanc and chardonnay plantings are in the pipeline," he continues, swimming against current SA trends. Reds cracked a nod with new plantings of shiraz last year on this Ashton estate, which belongs to brothers Stephen and Freddie de Wet (branches of that extended high-profile De Wet family tree, which includes Zandvliet's Paul and De Wetshof's Danie). It's the aim here to market more and, eventually, all their wines under the Excelsior label (they currently make a wide variety of private labels for supermarkets, including Tesco in the UK). Their whole range of labels has been given a more upmarket packaging treatment. The 2000 harvest was pronounced very wet and very 'rotten' but promising quality-wise. "I learn every day," says Marais, "and I stay happiest among the tanks."

✿ **Special Reserve** ✅ Unquestionably cream of this crop — flavour-packed but not profligate, oak well judged, ripe plums and mulberries in good dry finish. 100% cab, yr Fr/Am casks, 20% unwooded. 14% alc. 2 400 cases.

Cabernet Sauvignon ✿ Sunripe fruity succulence in **99**, some plummy baked fruit freshened by good acidity. 14% alc. 60 000 cases. **Chardonnay** �“ Same no-pretensions style of pvs in **00**, "for those who are *gatvol* (fed up) with oaked chardonnays," says Jaco Marais, colourfully. 14% alc. 4 000 cases. **Sauvignon Blanc** ✿ Ascorbic acid, dry ice — the full oenological monty to protect flavour/freshness in **00**, though only modest dusty capsicum detectable mid-2000. Track record suggests this should perk up with bit of time. 13,5% alc. 20 000 cases.

. . . .

Fairseat Cellars

Not open to the public • Owner Dick Davidson • PO Box 53058 Kenilworth 7745 • Tel (021) 797-1951 • Fax (021) 762-9656 • E-mail fairseat@mweb.co.za

NEGOCIANT and Cape Wine Master Dick Davidson sources wines locally for export to Belgium, Netherlands and Germany. The range, WO Western Cape, features a widely praised label with original oil by well known Cape artist James Yates. The collection, not tasted for this ed, includes **Ruby Cabernet 99**, with splash cab; selected by two wine mail order clubs; and **Chardonnay 00**.

. . . .

Fair Valley

Not open to the public • Wines mainly for export, but may be available ex-Fairview (see that entry). • Owner Fair Valley Workers Association • Winemaker Awie Adolph • Production 1 500 cases • PO Box 583 Suider Paarl 7624 • Tel (021) 863-2450 • Fax (021) 863-2591

NOT JUST a cosmetic, politically correct gesture — the seven officers of the Fair Valley Workers Association (duly elected by fellow Fairview cellar staff) take their responsibilities very seriously. "Fair Valley is one of the first farm worker empowerment initiatives in the Western Cape. It has taken some time to get started, mostly due to bureaucratic and permitting problems," they state frankly. Despite these hiccups, development of the 17 ha farm next to Fairview, purchased with Department of Land Affairs assistance, is on track. Committee member Ann Gouws, who helps run the cheese/wine tasting locale at Fairview, envisages: "Eight homes for the longest serving staff will be underway soon." Goats milk production is on the cards, and though the proposed winery and first vineyards may be a year or two off, this hasn't stopped Awie Adolph from making his third Chenin from grapes bought at cost from Fairview's Charles Back. And the Pinotage 2000 is a first. UK retailer OddBins is now firmly established as a customer; a further revenue stream will come from conversion of old cottages on Fairview to holiday units for winelands tourists.

Chenin Blanc ✿ Fine guava/peach/sweet talcum whiffs in **00**, from low yielding (5 t/ha) Malmesbury bushvines on Charles Back's Klein Amoskuil holding. Though almost bone dry, suggests sweetness in full (13,3% alc) citrus/fruit salad palate.

. . . .

Fairview

Paarl (see Paarl map) • Tasting & sales Mon—Fri 8.30-5 Sat 8.30-1 Closed Good Friday, Christmas, New Year's Day • Groups by appointment • Cheese tasting/sales Fee R10p/p • Play area for children • Views • Wheelchair-friendly • Owner Charles Back • Winemakers Anthony de Jager (since 1996) & Charles Back • Viticulturist Johan Botha • Marketing Jeremy Borg • PO Box 583 Suider-Paarl 7624 • Tel (021) 863-2450 • Fax (021) 863-2591 • E-mail fairback@iafrica.com • Website www.fairview.co.za

'GOATS DO COOK' Trust this team of talented nonconformists to create a suitably offbeat banner for their latest PR inspiration: tapas evenings starring Fairview's wines and the considerable culinary gifts of Jeremy Borg, the San Francisco and London (River Café) seasoned chef who now keeps the marketing department of this highly successful wine and cheese business on a very brisk boil. Ingredients for these Backanalian cook-ins (sample menu item: bunyols of salt snoek potato with romesco sauce) might come from "the earth and oceans of our [Cape] region", but the winemaking inspiration increasingly comes from offshore — the Rhône and California, to be precise. Believing that "our national grape mix is a disaster", Charles Back has put his money into red grapes — in Paarl, Malmesbury and contracted vineyards scattered around the Swartland. Not just the regular Big Mac varieties, either: Back's opted for the exotic and trendy — mourvèdre, grenache, carignan and, among the whites, globally swooned-over viognier. "We now have the most comprehensive range of Rhône varieties in SA," he states. But the mercurial Back's already ranging beyond the Rhône: his latest flame is zinfandel. "If we had more of this, we could take the Californians to the cleaners..." Which is no idle threat: Fairview's Cyril Back Zinfandel 97 won a hot-fought gold medal at the 2000 International Wine Challenge — one of 24 awards gained at this benchmark competition, out of 24 wines entered. "A clean sweep!" beams Jeremy Borg. Having conquered the UK market ("...one of the best winemakers in the New World," gushes British journalist Tim Atkin), the rest of Europe is already mapped out for attack. Now the US is receiving the usual analytical and thorough Background check ...

✿✿ **Shiraz** This winery's signature and Cape bellwether since benchmark **74**. Recent vintages mark change from more traditional sinewy style to fruitier opulence à la Rhône. As in **98**, developing complex smoked meat/fennel/black pepper aromas, oak (14 mths mostly Fr, some Am) adding toasty dryness to concentrated red berry finish. 14,3% alc. Follow-up **99** stylistically still in southern France (perhaps more so) with bigger sloshes choc, same hallmark toasty oak, hillside scrub, packed with redcurrant fruit. **93** IWSC Dave Hughes Trophy winner, a Cape classic.

✿✿ **Cyril Back Shiraz** A salute to Charles Back's late father, shiraz pioneer; fittingly in more modern, expressive style as above. **98** glows blackish plum; inky, almost tarry nose but same watermark pepper-and-blackcurrant, with creamy vanilla finish. Similar oak regime to standard blend. Yr Am/Fr casks. 14,3% alc.

✿✿ **Merlot** More accessible than most SA merlots, reflecting benefits of 'repositioning' vyd from bottom of farm to more favourable top; **99** also supercharged with portion purchased fruit from aptly named Primo vyd. Plush choc-plum flavour, lovely soft texture, long sappy finish. 13,7% alc.

✿✿ **Goats do Roam** ✔ Sounds/tastes like a fruity young French Côtes du Rhône — which it's meant to: "A celebration of all things Rhôney," says Jeremy Borg, whose canny promotional blitz for this Franco-SA varietal cocktail generated an unheard-of number of raves in the UK press. Blend (carignan, grenache, cinsaut, mourvèdre, pinotage, shiraz, gamay noir) "personal selection by the rampant Fairview Goats as they Roam the vineyards for the ripest fruit", according to the Back label. Technicolor wild berry flavours, earthy notes, supple yet solid enough to carry off extravagant **00**, which more concentrated than **99** ✿. Exceptional with — what else? — Fairview's goats milk cheese. 13,5% alc.

✿ **Chardonnay** ▼ **99** from Anthony de Jager's favourite s-w sloping vyd: "Consistent thread of citrus from this block." Lime-grapefruit juiciness wrapped in vanilla from Fr/Am oak (equal new/2nd fill); firm, muscular finish with butterscotch twist. 13,8% alc.

✿ **Akkerbos Chardonnay** New ▼ Toasting the numerous English oaks shading the property (acorns pvsly tasty snacks for the farm pigs). Top drawer Cape chardonnay. Rich, burnished gold **99**, ripe pineapple/passionfruit, wonderful firm, concentrated citrus; big, lingering toasty finish. Single vyd cuvée given full Fr oak treatment (sur lie 14 mths new Burgundian 300 ℓ barrels). 13,7% alc.

Anthony's Chardonnay Winemaker proudly gave his name to **98**, which now gaining some authentic Burgundian marzipan/toast overtones, less overt fruit. No fining/filtration — for the purists.

✿ **Viognier** Now a signature wine for this cellar; hailed as among the finest in the New World from this delicate Rhône grape, the new challenge to winemakers from Australia to California. Maiden **98** *Wine* ✿, IWSC gold, praised by wine eminence Jancis Robinson ("a triumph of world class"); follow-up **99** more concentrated, richer. Latest **00** still a pup, not yet revealing hallmark floral oiliness (increasingly late bloom to be expected as vines mature). Sturdy 14% alc and healthy acidity will support some yrs' bottle development, allowing peach-pip/lime/almond and delicate oak to expose their inherent beauty.

Gamay Noir ✿ ☺ **00** refreshes with green-pea, tart cherry zestiness. Luminous ruby/crimson glints, exotic tropical, banana whiffs. Drink chilled — and soon.

Cabernet Sauvignon ✿ **98** maturing into elegant cassis mouthful, savoury green olive aromas with hints tobacco/eucalyptus. 15 mths 2nd/3rd fill oak. 13,7% alc. **Malbec** ✿ Massive wafts of damson, prune, warm earth signal another **99** French style glow-inducer. Real 'bistro wine': gutsy sweet fruit/tannins, long food-friendly finish. **Carignan** ✿ Another — more demure — corner of the Rhône, sprouting fennel and redcurrant, some strawberry coulis. **99** lighter style oak-aged quaffer from old Swartland vyd; splash shiraz. Sensational with Jeremy Borg's empenada of duck, choc, prunes and chili (see intro above). **Zinfandel-Cinsault** ✿ Another bit of creative Back blending, eagerly snaffled in quantity by canny UK retail chains. **99** super example of New and Old world fruit pairing — grapes fermented together on oak staves, then wooded further 6 mths. Ripe (14,3% alc), sweet strawberry jam/stewed prune flavours. **Goats do Roam Rosé** ✿ New Natural companion to red billy above; in juicy-dry Provençal style. **00** shimmering pink colour, fleshy cherries/strawberries and bits of warm earth. Firm finish which good with food. Super youthful fruit, selected by "in-house cheese making family goatherd from best pinotage, grenache, gamay, shiraz and cinsaut vines". Partly oak fermented. **'Straw Wine'** ✿ New (To be named) Red version, from cinsaut; medium garnet-ruby hue, much shyer nose than white version below. **00** hints of dusty raspberries, drier palate (122 g/ℓ), more berry-like flavours. **Chenin Blanc** ✿ New-oak fermented **99** still showing fine yet muscular lime/peach notes, wood now integrated since last tasted. 14% alc. **Sauvignon Blanc** ✠ Exceptionally fresh for warm **00** vintage; wafts of warm stewed guavas/green nettles lead on to frisky citrus/pineapple flavours. Bright fruity acids run all over the tongue. From Malmesbury bush vines. **Special Late Harvest** ✠ "This bottle is crammed with fully ripe grapes" enthuses the back label, though we found **99** nose rather quiet (some talcum/floral fragrance); palate livelier: fruit cocktail in otherwise ordinary but well balanced sweet chenin. **La Beryl** ✿ Riesling 'straw wine', one of the new-breed Cape desserts (ripe grapes given extra oomph by allowing to air-dry on straw mats). **99** rich yellow-gold; shy, creamy fruit salad aromas and touch spice; succulent lime, honeysuckle, jasmine palate, soft, supple juicy-sweet finish. *Wine* ✿. 13,4% alc, 122 g/ℓ sugar, smooth 7,3 g/ℓ acid. Peek into barrel reveals really spectacular **00**, from chenin, exotic dried peach/apricot carrying through to rapier-sharp sweet/sour palate of massive concentration (250 g/ℓ sugar, balanced by 9 g/ℓ acid). Not the final blend, but potentially ✿.

Hanepoot ✿ Elegant **99** with exotic grapey profile, slightly more alcoholic, drier than some (17,5%, 160 g/ℓ). Sweet, juicy peach and nut tones. Also available (not tasted for this ed): **Cabernet Franc 99**, **The Amos Pinotage 98** (pvs rating ✿). **Oom Pagal Semillon 99** .

- -

Fat Bastard

Enquiries: Richard Kelley MW at Vinimark (see that entry).

NOW HERE'S something larger than life to bring to the table — SA's very own Fat Bastard, destined to be anything but a demure dinner guest. After a long afternoon's blending by F-B's creators, Thierry Boudinaud and Guy Anderson, one blend stood out as being truly exceptional and Anderson commented that it was reminiscent of a good Bâtard-Montrachet; Boudinaud retorted that it was more of a "fat bastard of a chardonnay" and the name stuck. In 1995, some 1 800 cases were produced and soon snapped up; by 1998 production was upped to 26 000 cases (it's already available in the USA, Canada, Hong Kong and Australia). The wine for SA's inaugural FB below was sourced from the Roberston valley. Fat Bastard, with its label featuring a heavyweight hippo, has its tongue firmly in its cheek.

✿ **Fat Bastard Chardonnay** Bastard, perhaps, but not (yet) Fat. Present citrus/acid verve needs yr/2 to calm down, whereupon **99**'s toasty vanilla will take over and the whole should slide into rich tubbiness. Meanwhile, it's zesty and rather nice. 13,5% alc. Partly barrel fermented. 500 cases.

- -

Fernkloof see Cape Wine Exports

- -

Flagstone Winery & Vineyards

Cape Town • Tasting, sales, cellar tours by appointment • Owners Jack family • Winemaker Bruce Jack (since 1999) with Dudley Wilson (since 2000), Jon Berlin (2000 crush) • Viticulturist Bruce Jack • Production 300 tons 20 000 cases 44% red 50% white 6% blanc de noir • 14 Glendarrach Road Rondebosch Cape Town 7700 • Tel (021) 685-2080/425-7430 • Fax (021) 686-9080 • E-mail terraceroad@icon.co.za • Website www.flagstonewines.com

THOSE DUTCH SETTLERS struggling with Cape viticulture would have grown vines handily close to the Jacks' winery in Cape Town's Waterfront, but Flagstone has to source its grapes more widely, reaching out to vineyards from Darling to Elim. The maritime address is not for the sake of tourism, though: it's mostly to do with the cold storage facilities alongside for the fishing industry. Chilling grapes overnight allows Bruce Jack (ever searching for ways of avoiding additives) to get away with using less sulphur at the crusher. This concern for naturalness (which includes avoiding acidification wherever possible, and using wild yeasts rather than ones from a packet) goes with an enthusiasm for ripeness, for experimentation, for expanding the range, for building the capacity of the cellar workers. In fact, enthusiasm is clearly built into the Jack set-up. Now they're moving underground at the Waterfront, into a recently rediscovered tunnel, with ideal storage conditions and space for a gravity-flow winery at the entrance. All wines below have synthetic closures; all **99** except where indicated.

✿ **Cabernet Sauvignon** All-new, mostly-Am wood and very ripe fruit the dominant notes in this showy but soft, friendly wine. Still fairly closed, restrained (tasted very young), but good balance, firm but undaunting tannins, long savoury finish suggest a rewarding future — though it's already pretty tasty. 275 cases.

❦ **Chapman's Chance Pinotage** New Mostly exported; locally available only at Blues Restaurant, Camps Bay. Ripe smells of dark chocolate, plums, boiled sweets. Dense, powerful, rich, showing abundant Am oak, and satisfactory grip of acid, tannin. 500 cases.

❦ **The Dragon Tree Cabernet Sauvignon-Pinotage** New Gorgeous plush ruby-velvet colour (recalling sap of the dragon tree, planted directly above cellar?); the local variety (about 30%) adds sweetish raspberry luxe to good structure of cab. As with Cab above, tasted before bottling — should develop with a few years, perhaps absorbing some of the obvious oak (here 40% Am, 60% Fr barriques, all new). 1 200 cases.

❦ **Two Roads Chardonnay** Has developed nicely in yr since last tasted, now has some complexity — no doubt helped by fermentation with naturally-occurring yeast (unusualness, in Cape, of approach hinted at in name, after Robert Frost poem *The Road Not Taken*). Bread, citrus scents lead on to rich, creamy, leesy palate, fruit supported by well-judged oak (Fr/Am for ferment/maturation). 800 cases.

Noon Gun ❦ New 😊 'Crisp, fruity and refreshing' claims the label, and it's right. But this med-bodied, dry white blend of equal parts sauvignon, chardonnay, chenin, riesling is a little more interesting than just those things. Very lightly oaked. 600 cases.

BK5 Pinot Noir ❦ Cherry-coloured, and cherries to smell, along with tobacco, strawberry and vanilla. Pleasant, with lingering, baked flavours. Jack has faith in the unfashionable BK5 clone, though pinot character less obvious here than the Oz-inflected style: very ripe fruit, large dollops Fr oak, sturdy alcohol (14%). Blue Gold medal at Sydney 100 show. 400 cases. **Resolute 166 Chardonnay** ❦ New '166' refers to the rather muscat-scented clone used. Flowers and citrus to sniff at, well rounded and easy to taste (gentle on pocket, too). Mostly fermented in equal lots Fr/Am casks, which don't announce their presence more than they should. 450 cases. **Sauvignon Blanc** ❦ Muted tropical fruit, honeysuckle in 00 nose, but more intense to taste; youthfully zesty with crisp acidity and mouthwatering green-apple finish. Due to extra-gentle winemaking regime, might throw harmless deposit. 700 cases. **Heywood House Barrel Fermented Sauvignon Blanc** ❦ Reference to the home of Elsie Fraser Munn, Bruce Jack's grandmother, "an African legend". Pleasantly pungent, with butterscotch and spice. Try not to overchill, Jack suggests. Another year might reveal the fruit lurking in the soft and creamy oak-dominated texture. 500 cases.

Flamingo Bay see Darling Cellars
Fleermuisklip see Lutzville

Fleur du Cap

Tasting & sales at the Bergkelder (see that entry)

ALWAYS A GOOD BET when confronted with a limited wine list — or wine shelf — and generally improving. The 'unfiltered' range (introduced with the 96 vintage) is aiming at the highest level, with less manipulated wines, and reveals the Bergkelder's desire to shed its conservative image. More leeway is being given to winemakers (as opposed to technicians) to decide treatments — hence the reduction in flavour stripping fining and filtering, and the winemakers getting more involved in the vineyards and in selection of grapes for ambitious wines. Joining red-winemaker Coenie Snyman, newly appointed Karl Lambour — responsible for the whites in the range — brings youthful enthusiasm and energy, plus a vital awareness of international wines. Ambitions are high, and the wines generally getting even better, with some excitement injected into the reliability.

'Unfiltered' collection

✿ **Cabernet Sauvignon** Still youthful, deeply coloured **97**, with toasty, choc notes along with plum and cassis. Well fleshed with fruit over good tannic bones, supported by 100% new oak (20% Am, rest Fr), but rather tart finish. **96** ✿ revealed intentions for a modern, sophisticated cab to lead this unfiltered, unstabilised range — which may throw harmless deposits if given the few yrs it deserves.

✿ **Merlot** Deep, dark **97** showing herby, spicy, cedary, chocolate flourishes among the blackcurrants, and a coconut quality from plentiful oak (80% new, 20% Am, rest Fr). Richly powerful herby, mocha palate, high acid, good tannin structure. Will reward few yrs' bottle age. **96** ✿ first in this range, starring exotic ginger spice, violets, herbs.

✿ **Sauvignon Blanc 00** intriguing pungent nose, with notes of green beans, nutmeg and pepper. Rich, full in mouth, big flavours, big acid, big alc (14,3%) — a convincing entrant in the blockbuster stakes.

Standard range

✿ **Cabernet Sauvignon** Deep colour in **96**, despite generally light yr. Cassis, green pepper, coconutty wood notes from 70% new oak, mostly Fr, 20% Am. Tasty, savoury palate, lightish in middle, slightly tart to end; probably readier for drinking than previous few vintages.

✿ **Merlot** Impressive tradition started with **95** VVG, continuing with **96** SAA Top Ten selection, **97** VVG. Latest **98** ✿ invites with whiffs of cherry, mocha, caramel. Mouthfilling, good soft tannins and plenty of dark fruit unintimidated by high alc (13,5%), and 40% new oak (10% Am, rest Fr).

✿ **Pinotage 97** has puffs of smoke and dried banana over plummy/raspberry fruit. Approachable but somewhat tart, with dry tannic finish. Matured in older Fr oak. **92**, **90** VG; **91** VVG.

✿ **Shiraz** Blackberry, herbs and boiled sweets in **98** ✿, quite firmly structured, with dominating acidity. **97** ✿ richer, more intense. **96** soft, mouthfilling, succulent. **94** VG.

✿ **Chardonnay 99** Toast, beeswax, hazelnuts add complexity to citrus nose. Rich, limey palate, well balanced with crisp finish. Wood-fermented (30% new), 90% through malo. **98** ✿ low-keyed, elegant yet rich. **97** big, full-flavoured, citruspacked.

✿ **Sauvignon Blanc** Gooseberry, figgy notes dominate **00**. Forceful flavours, packed with ripe fruit, supported by good acidity, leading to crisp, lingering conclusion. Probably at best after yr in bottle.

✿ **Noble Late Harvest 96** ever better as it develops: marmalade, old honey and pineapple jostling amicably for attention. 109 g/ℓ sugar ably supported by crisp acidity and moderate 11,5% alc, making for fresh, lingering finish. Still yrs to enjoy this in.

Riesling ✿ Tinned pears and peaches in pleasant ready-to-go **00**. Well balanced palate, softened and rounded by a little sugar but crisp dry finish. Cape riesling.

Natural Light ✿ **00** has forthcoming tropical fruity, dusty nose. Round and soft, not insubstantial despite low 9,5% alc. Mostly from chenin.

. . . .

Fontein see International Wine Services

. . . .

Fort Simon Estate   🍷 🍷 🍷 🍷

Stellenbosch (see Stellenbosch map) • Tasting & sales Mon—Fri 9.30—5 Sat & public holidays 10—2 Tasting fee R5 for 5 wines • Cellar tours by arrangement • Light meals for up to 50 by appointment • Locale for receptions for 40—50 guests by arrangement • Views • Wheelchair-friendly • Owners Renier & Petrus Uys • Winemaker Marinus Bredell (since 1997) • Viticulturist Renier Uys (since 1983) • Vineyards 61 ha • Production 20 000 cases 60% red 40% white • PO Box 43 Sanlamhof 7532 • Tel (021) 906-0304 • Fax (021) 906-2549 • E-mail fortsim@iafrica.com

IN THE MOST whimsical, fantasy-winery in Stellenbosch — all mod cons within a moated, turreted, drawbridged fort, authentic handsome knights and damsels in distress territory — Marinus Bredell is turning out some fine wines for Renier and Petrus Uys. Their success — for example, the first, 98 Merlot won Veritas double-gold; the Merlot-Pinotage blend made the Diners Club top 10 — is rooted in a combination of Bredell's experience and this property's 61 ha vineyards. Their Bottelary Hills neighbours all shine on the red front in particular, and malbec, pinotage and merlot are recent recruits to Fort Simon's red brigade. In 1998 the red-white variety ratio was 40–60; it's now the other way around. Exports travel to 8 countries, including Estonia.

Shiraz Evolving elegantly in bottle, **98**'s ripe berry flavours filling out pleasurably. Expansive palate features peppery Karoo bush/smoky whiffs around an appealing sweetish fruit core. Yr 2nd fill 300 ℓ Nevers barrels. More moderate alc than reds below at 13,4%. Room for further development. 550 cases.

Pinotage Complexity promised by first-release **98** when tasted last yr realised in richer taste/complexity. Nose-to-palate raspberry/plum joined by banana, cinnamon, brush tar. Relaxed tannins appear sweetish — an effect underlined by thumping 14% alc. 9 mths Fr oak, 2nd fill. 600 cases. Follow-up **99** lighter with some distinct up-tight tannins which will need plenty of time.

Merlot 98 first release growing pleasingly soft, rich in bottle. Blackcurrant/violet bouquet and flavours, with house's distinctive sweetish impression emphasised by smidgeon sugar (2,5 g/ℓ) and strapping alc (14%). Stretches out lengthily to attractive mocha conclusion. 9 mths 300 ℓ Fr oak, 2nd fill.

Anna Simon Merlot-Pinotage Terrific fruity jumble in bouquet of newest **99**: ripe cherries, plums, blackberries — even whiff tomato. All echo in big (13,8% alc), broad palate with spicy oak. Distinctive sweetness cut short by drying tannins. Promise of 6–8 yrs' development. Combo oak chips/barrels 4 mths. 2 880 cases. **98** VVG, Diners Club shortlisted.

Chardonnay Marinus Bredell's affinity with this grape again demonstrated in **99**, leading with floral scents, then passionfruit/barley sugar and some bready warmth, all brushed with sweet vanilla and a woodsmoke swish. Full lees/lime mouthful. 2 000 cases. **98** VG, *Wine*. These fermented/aged 8 mths new 300 ℓ French oak. ± 13,5% alc. Aussie smoothing trick — touch of imperceptible sugar (± 3,5 g/ℓ) — used. Particularly good with food.

Wooded Chenin Blanc Deftly oaked to highlight rich melon/hay/tropical tones which, in latest **00**, also feature some piquant lemon tingles layered with smoky oak. 14% alc. Fermented/aged oak ± 4 mths. ± 1 750 cases. **99** wine mail order club selection. **98** SAA.

Sauvignon Blanc Reductively subdued **99** features light grass/hay tones and palate-clucking freshness. Could do with bit of time to flesh out, though Marinus Bredell "aiming for racy Sancerre style." 13,4% alc. **Restelle Sauvignon Blanc-Chardonnay-Chenin Blanc** New Anytime refreshment from spicy citrus, ripe pears and some richer mealy tones ex-chardonnay. **99** brushed with oak to round chenin's bracing freshness. 13,3% alc. 550 cases.

Fraai Uitzicht 1798

Robertson (see Robertson map) • Sales at Fraai Uitzicht restaurant daily 11am–10pm (also see Eat-out section) • Cellar tours during restaurant hours • B&B/self-catering cottages • Gifts • Walks • Views • Birding • 4x4 trail • Mountain biking • Owners Axel Spanholtz & Mario Motti • Winemaker Pieter Ferreira (consulted in pvt capacity for 2000 harvest only) • Viticulturist Laing Vermeulen • Vineyards 9 ha • Production 60 tons 500 cases • PO Box 97 Robertson, 6705 • Tel/fax (023) 626-6156 • E-mail fraai.uitzicht@lando.co.za • Website www.lando.co.za/fraaiuitzicht

THE ROMANCE of a ramshackle wine cellar circa 1798 had former pharmaceutical specialist Axel Spanholtz hooked a full two centuries later. In 1998 Spanholtz, in search of the "positive, enjoyable way of life which wine brings", swopped Sweden and Germany for the Klaas Voogds valley between Robertson and Montagu. He found his Valhalla on the 175 ha historic property of Fraai Uitzicht, complete with wonderful valley and mountain views, rich birdlife, rose, vegetable and herb gardens … and vines. Nine ha of mainly merlot, shiraz and cabernet (a smattering of chenin and colombard was formerly delivered to Ashton Co-op) will now be vinified and bottled here. Though slickly re-equipped, the red-wine-dedicated cellar retains its romance. The grapes for the 500 cases of maiden Merlot 2000 were hand-sorted, basket-pressed (in an Italian, wood-staved traditional press) and fermented/matured in new American and French oak. Share this wine — the first to carry the Klaas Voogds wine of origin designation — with Spanholtz and partner Mario Motti in their cosy guesthouse, self-catering cottages and cosmopolitan-country restaurant.

Franschhoek Vineyards

Franschhoek (see Franschhoek map) • Sales Mon—Fri 9.30—5 Sat 10—3 Sun 11—2 Tasting as above, doors close 15 mins earlier Tasting fee R5 p/p, groups R10 p/p (includes 20 min audio-visual presentation) • Traditional SA breakfasts, lunches, coffees/teas Tue—Sun 10—4 (alfresco, weather permitting) Or bring your own picnic • Conferencing for ±100 • Gift shop • Audio-visual 'A Tour of the Franschhoek Valley' • Videos for children • Terrace with vineyard/mountain views • Wheelchair-friendly • Owners 85 shareholders • Winemakers Deon Truter (since 1980) & Driaan van der Merwe (since 1984) • Consulting viticulturist Andrew Teubes (VinPro) • Vineyards ±500 ha • Production 4 200 tons 80 000 cases (70 000 cases own label) • PO Box 52 Franschhoek 7690 • Tel (021) 876-2086/7 • Fax (021) 876-3440 • E-mail fhoekvin@mweb.co.za • Website www.franschhoekwines.co.za

THERE'S AN EXPANSIVE MOOD at Franschhoek Cellars. Despite the early drought, they had an excellent harvest in this self-contained valley and are extending the red wine facilities (traditionally they concentrated more on white) and upgrading the white ones. This comprehensive cellar, wine centre and restaurant, housed in a neo-classical stone building on the outskirts of the Cape's 'gourmet capital', focuses its energies on a variety of easy drinking wines under the La Cotte and Franschhoek Vineyards labels. According to winemaker and keen angler Driaan van der Merwe, who has had a sparkle in his eye since hooking some Veritas medals, the aim is to epitomise the Franschhoek style by producing "award-winning white and red wines at affordable prices".

Franschhoek Vineyards range

Cabernet Sauvignon ✻ Lightly-wooded **98** smoothing into easy-drinker we foresaw in pvs ed. Gentle choc-mulberry tastes, but flick of tannin won't be overwhelmed by richer cuisine. 2 400 cases. **Pinotage** ✻ No shortage of tannin in oak-aged **99** (nor raspberries, plums, herby/minty accents), so pair with equally robust cuisine or keep 2–3 yrs. 13,5% alc. 2 000 cases. **Chenin Blanc Barrel Fermented** ✖ Don't hesitate to pop this **98** cork. Vanilla/peach aromas, fresh hay/dried fruit tastes are at their peak. 13% alc. 2 000 cases. **Sauvignon Blanc** ★ Unlike pvs, which almost aggressively grassy/nettly, latest **00** reveals almost nothing about itself. May develop. 13,5% alc. 1 000 cases. **Semillon Barrel Fermented 97** very tired now. Best young and fresh. 13% alc. 1 000 cases.

La Cotte range

Cabernet Sauvignon Special Reserve ✻ Ruby-hued **97** still freshly herbaceous in nose, choc-cherry flavoured, but tenacious tannins need sturdy cuisine. Small Fr oak aged 9 mths. **Merlot** ✖ Again light coloured/toned in unwooded **99**, raspberry hints reprised, with distinct bite of tannin in very dry finish. 7,4 g/ℓ acid. 1 700 cases. **Grand Rouge** ‡ Well-made gulpable red. **99** very light coloured/toned, some earthy/strawberry interests. From cinsaut; unoaked. 7 000 cases. **Rosé** ♣♣ New Uncloying sweet pink prettiness. **99** richer than most of this style (though alc is relatively light at 11,5%), raspberry/plum palate smooth rather than sugary. 2 000 cases. **Chardonnay Unwooded** ‡ Doesn't shout chardonnay, but **00** clean, fresh, mouthwateringly dry. 13% alc. 3 000 cases. **Chenin Blanc** ‡ Undemanding tipple, less complex **00** than pvs, but pleasant enough. Off-dry peach/tropical flavours finish with acidic nibble. 5 000 cases. **Sauvignon Blanc 00** Untasted. 5 000 cases. **Blanc de Blanc** ‡ **NV** Sociable swigging, youthfully floral with peachy sniffs, lemon zest in crisp dry, med-bodied palate. Semillon, chenin, colombard. 10 000 cases. **Light** ‡ ✔ What else but … light? **00** also soft and gently fruity. Will please many. Chill and drink soon. 9,3% alc. 2 000 cases. **Semi-Sweet** ‡ Curries, heat-generating dishes generally on winemakers' minds when making this dainty, lightly grapey semi-sweet **NV**. Equal proportions chenin/hanepoot. 4 000 cases.

The following sparkles all carbonated: **Chardonnay Brut** ♣♣ Characterful, lively, gently dry bubbles, **99** with more substance than some ambitiously priced MCCs. 2 000 cases. **Sauvignon Blanc Brut** ‡ Enough oomph in **00** to please speed-ace Michael Schumacher, with whom Truter/vd Merwe would like to pop this just off-dry cork. Hugely fizzy, mouthfilling, distinct sauvignon character. 2 000 cases. **Demi Sec** ‡ Expansive, decidedly sweet **NV** fizz, broad foamy mouthful. Chenin/hanepoot. 1 000 cases.

Port ♣♣ Light, likeable ruby style, from pinotage. Unoaked **98** features plummy/berry fruit, bright, dry spirity finish. 18,5% alc, 78 sugar. Screw cap. 1 000 cases. **95**, **94**, **92** VG.

. . . .

Forrester Vineyards see Ken Forrester
Frasers Bay see International Wine Services
Fredericksburg see R&R
Freedom Road see Backsberg
Friesland see Kaapzicht
Gecko Ridge see Long Mountain
Genesis see Stellenbosch Vineyards

. . . .

Gilga

Owner/winemaker Chris Joubert • Production 300 cases 100% red • PO Box 28746 Danhof 9310 • Tel (051) 436-9029 • Fax (051) 446-4615

RATHER appropriate, this, a shiraz named after a character in a Persian legend. Gilga was the shy young maiden in the Caliph's harem who discovered the pleasures of fermented grape juice. Although quite how such a discovery would be regarded in Iran today is a moot point. Made 'after hours' by Overgaauw cellar chief Chris Joubert, this wine immediately attracted a cult following. No tasting/sales at Overgaauw. Enquiries: Eugene Viljoen at above numbers.

♣♣ **Shiraz 98** *Wine* ♣♣ same barrel selection as Overgaauw CWG Auction Reserve, with shot cab. Deep, bright purple colour; penetrating, powerful bouquet packed with cherry, milled pepper, spicy oak. Mouthfilling, succulent palate gently firmed by ripe tannin. Long, warm finish. Fr/Am (50/50) oak: yr new, 6 mths 2nd fill. 13,5% alc. No **99**. Preview of **00** very impressive; bigger tannins hint at longer maturation horizon than **98**'s ±5 yrs.

. . . .

Glen Carlou Vineyards   ♟ ♟ ♟

Paarl (see Paarl map) Tasting & sales Mon—Fri 8.45—4.45 Sat 9—12.30 Tasting fee R5 p/p • Tasting/sale of home-made cheese • Cellar tours by appointment • Wheelchair-friendly • Owners Walter & David Finlayson/Hess Holdings, Switzerland • Winemaker David Finlayson (since 1994) with Arco Laarman (since 2000) • Viticulturist Marius Cloete (since 2000) • Vineyards 65 ha • Production 25 000 cases 60% white 40% red • PO Box 23 Klapmuts 7625 • Tel (021) 875-5528 • Fax (021) 875-5314 • E-mail glencarl@mweb.co.za • Website www.glencarlou.co.za

SOMEONE once said the Cape wasn't chardonnay country. Someone was clearly not American. David Finlayson's version is so sought-after in the States that it's SA's single biggest premium wine export to the US. It's been rated a 90-pointer 5 times in a row by *Wine Spectator*. It was a major wow at the splashiest show in the wine world, the New York Wine Experience — winemakers practically kill for an invitation to this A-list do. No sign of chardonnay-fatigue there — or here. This variety heads the pack soon to come on-stream: 20 ha of chardonnay, plus zinfandel, shiraz and a smattering of petit verdot and tempranillo. Latest plantings (Worcester lad Marius Cloete now assists on the ground) are mourvèdre, merlot, cabernet and more pinot noir — Glen Carlou's Pinot has been getting glowing UK reviews. Richard Camerrer, viticulture consultant to California's Hess Collection winery (owned by the Finlaysons' cosmopolitan partner Donald Hess) also lends his expertise here — David Finlayson believes "the Americans are still light years ahead of SA". Glen Carlou's Simonsberg slopes are a great deal gentler than another of his projects for Donald Hess — planting the world's highest vineyard in the Argentinean Andes. Father Walter Finlayson, who started the honours roll here, is now far too busy to interfere (much) in son's winemaking activities — he cellarmasters for the export Coppoolse-Finlayson wines, and looks after his dairy herds and gourmet cheeses (he's chairman of the SA Farm Cheesemakers' Association, and helped organise its inaugural, sell-out festival in 2000). But with David F already vice-chairman of the Cape Winemakers' Guild, fatherly footsteps are being followed — and Arco Laarman (ex-Kaapzicht), after a season at Hess Collection, has slotted neatly into the cellar.

✿ **Grand Classique** 'Classic' claret ('Grand' now correctly sans 'e' thanks to a French consultant!), dominated by cab. s. with 40% merlot, 5% seasoning cab f. Petit verdot comes online from **00** with malbec to follow. Bold **98** (13,5% alc), scented, stony mineral core lifted by dark roast coffee richness. "A firm nod to Bordeaux," says David F, with cellar experience at Ch Margaux (whose *regisseur* Paul Pontallier rated **96** VVG, SAA, *Wine* ✿ best Paarl cab blend). 3 500 cases. Médoc restraint obvious in **97**, Air France–Preteux Bourgeois laureate: wafts of blackcurrant/cedar/vanilla. Remains reserved; spine of ripe tannins still holding back plush fruit. 24 mths mainly new, some 2nd fill barriques.

✿ **Pinot Noir** David F quietly dismissive of competitors trumpeting the coolness of their vineyards, indirectly implying quality pinot can't be made in warmer climes — he claims a "continental climate" in his terroir. String of top-rank releases add fuel to his argument, including latest **99**: ripe cherry kept taut by waxy richness, delicate tannin structure. 13% alc. 2 500 cases. Similar perfumed cherry-tobacco, forest floor mélange of **98**, which offered vibrant youngberry fruit framed by non-intrusive grape/oak tannins. Oak regime now ratcheted up to yr new Dargaud & Jaegle Fr oak. **96** *Wine* ✿. **Pinot Noir Reserve** ✿ New **99** bottled for CWG Auction a stunner! Compact ruby hue; minted cherry aromas, exhilarating gravelly texture, lengthy elegant flourish. From oldest newclone (113, 115) plantings in Cape — now 15 yrs old. Will develop beautifully over next 5 yrs. 13,5% alc. 50 cases.

✿ **Tortoise Hill Red** Started life as Les Trois then Cellar Select; now 'THR' firmly establishing itself as Finlayson's 'other red'. His experience with Peter Lehmann in South Australia (young winemakers get around nowadays) will come into play in styling this "spicy flavourful Mediterranean-style red": zinfandel, shiraz and other piquant varieties will dominate blend in time. Latest **99** even has splash touriga dizzying up cab/merlot base. Fun, tasty wine egging on the party but dense enough tannins to be taken seriously. 13% alc. 600 cases. **98** more Fr than local despite 36% pinotage infusion: compôte warm red berries, tobacco, eucalyptus notes. Name suggests tortoise shape of hill dominating the farm (perhaps also hard-shelled visitors?). ±Yr mainly 2nd fill Fr/new Am oak.

✿**Chardonnay Reserve** New Cape benchmark, making waves in USA where this punchy style highly sought after. **99** rich, undulating layers of citrus fruit, swathes of oak vanilla, superb chalky palate density. From best fruit (paradoxically "worst looking" site — mix quartz/clay), natural yeast fermentation; yr new Fr oak, 100% malo — all add breadth/width to creamy finish. Best 18 mths after bottling, can last 10 yrs. Only 20 barrels. 13,5% alc. Intensely creamy/melony **98** fleshed out by toasty aromas/flavours. Oak, often prominent in youth, softens with time. **97** fetched highest price (R95/bottle) of any white at 1999 Nederburg Auction. Standard **Chardonnay** More readily accessible (and available); led by lemon/lime fruit as in next **99**; toasty wood currently ascendant but melange citrus fruit won't be held back. Fantastic chalky, pebbly backdrop separates it from other tutti-frutti pretenders. 13,5% alc. Serious quantity: 14 000 cases. **98** SAA, *Wine* ✿ leaves serious dry Burgundian impression after initial melon/butterscotch impact. Partial natural yeast ferment. 8 mths mix 1st–3rd fill Fr cooperage.

✿**Devereux** ▼▼ ▼ Double value marker for this benchmark Cape chenin, now in drier-tasting mode than pvs. Own vineyards grubbed up, but label saved by Finlayson snr whose wisdom prevailed — good quality fruit bought in (from Delheim's Vera Cruz property, among others). **00**, with splash chardonnay, more concentrated chenin flavours than before; vanilla oak patina to the floral richness (fermented in casks pvsly used for chardonnay; some Am barrels as extra capacity needed "and they were at hand"). 13% alc. 400 cases. **99** again with touch chardonnay, citrus/juicy quince aromas/flavours spill into bone-dry, long finish. **98** ✿ perceptibly sweeter, creamy, supple, wafts toasted nuts. Fruity **97** *Wine* ✿ honeyed nuances from bottle maturation. 4 mths sur lie; natural yeasts, barrel-fermented (30% new).

✿**Cape Vintage** Correctly labelled (the word 'port' does not appear) for both export/domestic markets. **98** pungent spiced berry bouquet reminiscent of mulled wine, serious tobacco pouch aromas precede dry (90 g/ℓ sugar — pvs even less), tense but plump prune finish. Classic (Portuguese) 'vintage' formula: 'correct' varieties — touriga, tintas b/r, cornifesto; solid 19% alc. 2 yrs seasoned Fr oak. 700 cases. **97** dusty prune whiffs, hints cinnamon, delicious ripe, juicy plum/choc, twist liquorice in tail. **96** ✿ (though *Wine* ✿) more evolved, slightly volatile raisin nose, softer, mature prune flavours, hints of fennel and leather.

Goede Hoop Estate   ♈ ♈ ♈ ♈

Stellenbosch (see Stellenbosch) • Tasting, sales, cellar tours by appointment • Self catering facilities by arrangement • Bring your own picnic • Conferencing for small groups (10–15 people) • Wheelchair-friendly • Owner Pieter Bestbier • Winemakers Pieter Bestbier (since 1988), with Willie Malherbe (since 2000) • Viticulturist Johan de Beer (since 2000) • Vineyards 80 ha • Production 700 tons (345 tons 12 000 cases own label) 56% white 44% red • PO Box 25 Kuils River 7579 • Tel (021) 903-6286 • Fax (021) 906-1553 • E-mail goede@adept.co.za • Website www.goedehoop.co.za

"WINES of a high standard at reasonable prices": winemaker-owner (and former teacher) Pieter Bestbier says these are his future goals from these 80 ha vineyards in the excellent Bottelary area. We'd say that he scored these long ago, only he's far too modest to say so. Don't be deceived; don't think that where there is little sound of trumpets there's no music. Here are (and have been for years) some most delicious wines, in demand in 5 foreign countries and ungreedily-priced. If you're seeking the antithesis of today's over-hyped wine world, it's right here at this tranquil, very personally-run estate.

✿ Cabernet Sauvignon ✔ **97** first cab release from this property since **91**. Quite sophisticated, fine layering of mulberry, cassis, black cherry fruit, supple tannins hold it all gently in place. Alc just right at 12,8%. Should peak in about 3 yrs, though already accessible. *Wine* ✿. Yr new Fr oak. 1 000 cases.

✿ Shiraz ✔ Track record over past few vintages places this Fr-toned shiraz in the Cape's upper crust. **98**, wine mail order club selection, evolving in bottle, fine layered intensity, some classy whiffs of truffle, smoky oak. Follow-up **99** smoke/spice again, plus fine dusty oak, mouthfilling flavour (though moderate alc: 12,6%). Mix new/old clones; ±6 mths Fr casks, none new. 1 500 cases.

✿ Vintage Rouge Now a Bdx blend (merlot/cab 60/40 — pvs were variations on cab, shiraz, pinotage) but in New rather than Old World idiom. Full-bore black-berries/cherries in **98** ✿, 'sweet' fruit supported by good tannins, though lacking mid-palate vim of pvs. 4 mths 2nd/3rd fill casks. 14,2% alc. **97** VG.

✿ Pinotage ✔ These Bottelary vyds are alive with brilliant pinotages, so expect this first **99** and follow-ups to grow into something special (pvsly went into Vintage Rouge above). Already some warm richness, unusually polished tannins which should become even glossier with time. Lightly oaked (6 mths 2nd/3rd fill). 13% alc. 1 000 cases.

Sauvignon Blanc ✿ Pungent grassy/herbaceous **00**, some green-fruit tones, bracing acidity so best with food. Light/med-bodied. 500 cases. Note: **Chardonnay 00** not available for tasting. Pvs **99** rated ✿; sold out on release.

- -

Goedgeloof see Kanu

- -

Goedvertrouw Estate

Walker Bay (see Elgin/Walker Bay map) • Tasting, sales, cellar tours "all hours by appointment" • Elreda Pillmann's home-cooked meals by prior arrangement. • Play area for children • Small conferences • Walks • Views • Proclaimed conservation area • Wheelchair-friendly • Owners Arthur & Elreda Pillmann • Winemaker Arthur Pillmann • Vineyards 8 ha • Production 25 tons 70% red 30% white • PO Box 37 Bot River 7185 • Tel (028) 284-9769 • Fax (028) 284-9443

APPROPRIATELY for a farm whose name means 'Trustworthy', a vintage has been made here every year since 1990 (except in 1997, when Arthur and Elreda Pillmann were "just too busy building"). But not in 2000: a freak pre-Christmas hailstorm all but annihilated the crop, and though Arthur Pillmann tried to harvest what was over, there was nothing worth picking. "You can't fight nature," he sighs pragmatically. Weathered but not beaten, the 83 year old engineer turned organic wine grower and wife Elreda (who makes her own butter and delicious morale boosting cuisine) are working "terribly hard" in the vineyards. Due to hail damage, no **00**. Pvs releases: **Pinot Noir 99** ✿, **Cabernet Sauvignon 99** ✿, **Pinotage 'Sarita' 99** ✿, **Chardonnay 98** ✿ (no **99**), **Sauvignon Blanc 99** ✿.

- -

Goedverwacht Estate

Robertson (see Robertson map) • Tasting & sales Mon—Fri 9.30—4 Sat 10—1 • Cellar tours by appointment • Bring your own picnic • Tourgroups • Owner/winemaker Jan du Toit • Viticulturist Danie Visser (since 1990) • Vineyards 110 ha Production 1 600 tons 80% white 20% red • PO Box 128 Bonnievale 6730 • Tel/fax (023) 616-3430 • E-mail goedverwachtestate@lando.co.za

COLOMBARD may not be the international flavour du jour, but Jan du Toit's not losing his taste for one of the most populous vines on his Bonnievale estate. Why should he, when local and overseas buyers are flocking, and critical accolades are rolling in — Best Imported White under DM15 in German *Alles über Wein* among the recent eclats. But the market's also clamouring for reds and du Toit, whose other life-passion is hunting in the Karoo, is on target with a new Cabernet-Merlot launched in Germany and the Netherlands in October ("The Dutch are into SA wines in a big way," he reports). Back home he's opened a visitor centre offering tastings/

sales of the range, which helps fund research into the conservation of SA's avian emblem, the blue crane.

Sauvignon Blanc ✱✱ Bright gooseberry/guava in med-bodied **00**, reductively made to preserve the delicate fruit flavours; crisp, bone dry. 3 000 cases.

Cabernet Sauvignon-Merlot Too young to rate conclusively, **00** hints at ✱ potential. Blackberries/cherries wafting with violets in toasty, sweet-oak background. Own very young vyds. 10% new Fr oak. **Wooded Chardonnay 00** sample with tropical fruit and toasty oak enriched by leesy fullness; ripe pear/peach/citrus impart pleasing departing tang. Should rate ✱ on release. ±13% alc. 3 000 cases. **Chardonnay Sur Lie** Unwooded version rides the spectrum from tropical pineapple/papaya through yeasty lees to piquant lemon in **00** (sample). Brisk agreeable quaffer should rate ✱✱ on release. 3 000 cases. **Colombard** ✿ This estate's critically acclaimed signature, always with arresting 'brut' finish. 25 yr old vyd apparently frazzled by **00**'s heat: only muted guava tones, lightish flavour/body; initially not as sparky as **98** VG, though might perk up. Lowish alc 11,9%. These best young and fresh. 6 000 cases.

. . . .

Golden Alibama

BIG-VOLUME WINE BRAND of Stellenbosch Farmers' Winery, sold in 250 ml, 2 ℓ and 4,5 ℓ packs. A new 5 ℓ plastic container was recently added to range. Untasted.

. . . .

Goudini Winery   ♈ ♈ ♈

Worcester (see Worcester map) • Tasting & sales Mon—Fri 8—5 Sat 10—1 Tasting fee R2 p/p • Cellar tours by appointment • Closed religious public holidays • Light meals for larger groups (20-plus) by appointment • Reception facilities for functions/conferences • Tourgroups • Wheelchair-friendly • Owners 42 members • Winemakers Hennie Hugo (since1985) & Pieter Breugem (since 1999) • Viticulturist Pierre Snyman • Vineyards 1 018 ha • Production 20 000 tons (8 000 cases own label) 93% white 7% red • PO Box 132 Rawsonville 6845 • Tel (023) 349-1090 • Fax (023) 349-1095 • E-mail cellar@goudiniwine.co.za • Website www.goudiniwine.co.za

FROM GOUDINI, 'place of bitter honey' (a Khoisan expression), comes an increasing choice of reds (with growers taking a much more active role and interest in producing quality grapes). And a fresh presence in the cellar: assistant winemaker Pieter Breugem, whose passion for wine started as a 10 year old rummaging through his father's cellar. The Stellenbosch-trained rookie and old-hand Hennie Hugo (1999 Worcester Winemaker of the Year) plan to market an increasing portion of production under their own label.

Chardonnay ✱✱ Easy/early quaffing style; the usual peach joined by dry hay/butterscotch in **00**. Yielding palate carries a big punch (13,8% alc), so proceed with caution. 270 cases.

✱ **Ruby Cabernet Reserve 98** First oak-matured reserve from this cellar — and it's a promising one. Big, warming (13,7% alc), deep-flavoured with ripe mulberry leading and variety's green pepper tang not far behind. Karoo bush, clove, herb aromatics fill out the rich composition, which ends satisfyingly dry. Approachable now but probably better left few yrs for current oaky edge to smooth. Packaging consistent with limited release status. 11 mths oaked.

✱ **Port** New ✔ **99** winery's first 'port', from cinsaut, here showing unusually powerful extract/flavour. Floral/herby notes contrast well with more resonant mulberry/strawberry; well judged spirit highlights fairly dry tone (though sugar's not low at 116 g/ℓ). Altogether good first attempt. 17,4% alc. 280 cases.

Pinotage ✱✱ 'Textbook' pinotage with bright sunny flavour of ripe plum, **99**'s alc refreshingly moderate at 12,4%. 540 cases. **Ruby Cabernet-Merlot** ✱✱ Diners Club shortlisted **99** expands your palate (and consciousness) with waves of gutsy plum/mulberry flavour and surging alc (14,7%). The whole, including brush of oak, quite balanced however, with lively, attractive tannins for now or for 2–3 yrs. 540 cases. **Chenin Blanc** ‡ Invariably a smoothie, licensed to quaff. Med-bodied off-dry **00** with guava/mango and gentle sweetness, ready to party/BBQ. Multiple wine mail order club pick. 270 cases. **Clairette Blanche** ‡ **00** delicate, soft and light, as always, distinct dry freshness needs food. Screwcap. Frequent local classwinner. 270 cases. **Riesling** ‡ Traditional Cape riesling, often spotted on platforms at local shows. White-peach, clean lemon in med-bodied **00** with lively dry finish. Enjoy in fruity youth. 270 cases. **Sauvignon Blanc** ‡ **New** Lightweight **00** simple, easy drinking; very dry finish. 540 cases. **Umfiki** ⚶ ('Newcomer') Early-release semillon/chardonnay blend, unwooded, lightish and quaffable. Tropical/citrus in just-dry **00**, with bright acidity. 270 cases. **Late Harvest Steen** ‡ **99** getting a bit tired, some redeeming honey tones. Better young. Screwcap. 540 cases. **Special Late Harvest** ⚶ **00** fresh guava nose mirrored in palate with tropical fruit salad and bits of apple. Attractive, lightish and not oversweet. Enjoy soon. 270 cases. **Sauvignon Blanc Vonkelwyn** ‡ Frenetically fizzy carbonated bubbly with easy, semi-sweet drinkability. NV. Lowish 11,1% alc. **Hanepoot** ⚶ Regular award winning full-sweet fortified dessert, with intricate honeysuckle/muscat/herb/mint and jasmine fragrance in latest **99**. Warming and nice. 17% alc. 270 cases.

Goudveld Estate

Orange Free State • Tasting & sales Mon—Sat 8—6 • Cellar tours by appointment • Light refreshments by arrangement • Conference/reception locale for 100—120 guests • Barbecue area • Owner Jan Alers • Winemaker/viticulturist Merkil Alers (since 1985) • Vineyards 18 ha • Production 174 tons (2 000 cases own label) 75% red 25% white • PO Box 1091 Welkom 9460 • Tel (057) 352-8650 • Fax (057) 353-2140

IRREPRESSIBLE, INNOVATIVE Merkil Alers is delighted to report an addition to the range — Chardonnay — which, he beams, has the distinction of being the first varietal bottling of this grape in the Free State. This newcomer follows hot on the heels of the province's first Pinot Noir and Ruby Cabernet which Alers proudly unveiled in 1999. Also new in the portfolio are a sweet colombard Kellertrots, a Port and a semi-dry red from red muscadel and pinotage. More venerable is Alers' collection of some 600 cycads — the largest in SA. Some of the specimens are believed to be more than 2000 years old. Beyond the above-mentioned wines, the range, untasted for this ed, includes: **Cabernet Sauvignon**, **Pinotage**, semi-sweet **Rosé**, **Late Harvest** and **Golden Nectar Hanepoot**.

Goue Vallei Wines

Olifants River (see Olifants River map) • Tasting & sales Mon—Fri 8—5 Sat 9—12.30 • Cellar tours by appointment • Wheelchair-friendly • Bring your own picnic • Proclaimed conservation area • Owner Goue Vallei Wines (Pty) Ltd • Winemaker Bennie Wannenburg (since 1996) • Consulting viticulturists VinPro • Vineyards ± 1 300 ha • Production 8 000 tons 85% white 15% red • PO Box 41 Citrusdal 7340 • Tel (022) 921-2233 • Fax (022) 921-3937 • E-mail gouwin@yebo.co.za

MORE THAN 100 growers contribute to this 'Golden Valley' brand, now exported to six European countries and Japan. And while their produce is increasingly raved about locally and overseas, the farmers aren't about to put their feet up and enjoy the splendid views. "Market focus and the very best service have made us successful," says Bennie Wannenburg, "we're pushing ourselves to step up the pace." Which means grubbing up yesterday's heroes and replanting with tomorrow's stars (35 ha of shiraz coming on-stream in 2001 harvest), tweaking the packaging with new labels across the board, and taking advantage of cool-climate plots owned by about 15 growers in the Piekenierskloof, some 480–750 m above sea level. These eyrie vineyards are considered so distinct, they have their own Wine of Origin appellation.

Cardouw range

Premium range for export; named after Cardouw ('Shortcut') farm, well known in the Olifants River area.

❖ **Cabernet Sauvignon** ✅ These perhaps slow starters, judging from **98** which only now beginning to show its potential. Ripe dark-berried fruit, hints of prunes; good concentration and balance in more compact, discreet style. 13,3% alc. 3 000 cases.

Pinotage ❖❖ **98**'s warm spicy plums don't shout pinotage, but don't disappoint either. Fleshy, rounded with good dry tannins. Med-bodied, 8 mths oaked. 13,2% alc. Chardonnay ❖❖ New 99 relaxed tones for easy quaffing, peachy fruit with hints of roasted nuts (though unwooded) carry through to soft dry finish. Med/full-bodied. 2 000 cases.

Goue Vallei range

Cabernet Sauvignon 99 ❖❖ offers warm mulberry succulence, some good ripe tannins for now or for 2–3 yrs. 12,5% alc. 3 000 cases. **Pinotage** ☀ Uncharacteristically reserved and astringent in oak-aged **99**, so probably a table partner rather than standalone drink. 13,5% alc. **Chianti** ☀ Characterful **99** swigger (**NV** on label) reviewed for pvs ed now tastes very lean. Better in flush of youth. Lightly oaked. 13% alc. 1 500 cases. **Classique Rouge** ❖❖ Charming everyday red which sprints out of the cellar. Latest is 99 (though label **NV**), lively, tangy, juicy basket of ripe fruit through to dry finish. Fuller than pvs at 13%. Cab/tinta b/ruby cab/cinsaut. Unwooded. 15 000 cases. **Blanc de Noir** ❖❖ Different, rather pleasant semi-sweet blush with exotic shell-pink colour in **00**, delicate talcum powder fragrance, soft med-bodied palate. **Chardonnay** ❖❖ Untaxing med-bodied **00** with some dried peach attractions and firmly dry finish. 1 500 cases. **Chenin Blanc** ❖❖ Understated example, well priced (still below than R10 from cellar). Mouthwateringly zingy in **00**, plenty of dry chenin flavour. 13% alc. 2 000 cases. **98** flew with SAA. **Sauvignon Blanc** ☀ **00**, like pvs, lightish-toned/bodied, refreshing, grassily dry. 1 500 cases. **Blanc de Blanc** ❖❖ These alternate between dry and off-dry. It's the former in latest **00**, unwooded med-bodied chenin/colombard in tropical/herbaceous mood. Tangily dry. 2 000 cases. **Bukettraube** ☀ Unpretentious semi-sweet white with pretty powder-puff fragrance in **00**. Soft, light 10,5% alc. 4 000 cases. Classique Rouge, Blanc de Blanc also in 187 ml. **Special Late Harvest** ❖❖ **00** tasted in extreme youth, not as zingy as pvs but has potential to grow into ❖❖ adulthood. Ripe, soft chenin with fresh honey tastes; lowish 11,5% alc. 1 500 cases. **Hanepoot Jeripiko** ❖❖ **NV** VG. Powerfully muscatty fortified dessert with raisins and some honey in very sweet palate. 2 000 cases. **White Muskadel** ❖❖ Honeyed sweet fortified **NV** dessert, not much varietal character but pleasant enough. 2 000 cases.

Also available, not tasted, is the Sonnigdal range in 1, 2 and 5 ℓ packs: **Dry Red**, **Grand Cru**, **Stein**, **Late Harvest**.

· ·

Graça

VINHO VERDE INSPIRED PETILLANT QUAFFER, at 3,5-million litres a year SA's top selling cork-closed wine (Portuguese-looking bottle and livery part of carefully cultivated brand persona). Ubiquitous on local wine lists. Now also a Rosé. Both NV. By Stellenbosch Farmers' Winery.

> **Graça** ❖❖ 😊 Latest bottlings, featuring tweak of chenin to sauvignon, semillon, Cape riesling combo, sparkier than pvs. Stronger fruit intensity — mainly guava, lemon — with trademark effortless, off-dry, light-bodied potability. These also in pot-bellied 375 ml 'dinkies'.

Graça Rosé ✱ New Blend as above with pinkly prettifying pinotage. Ripe plum and nectarine in sweetish palate; light spritz, tickle of acid keeps the tone airy, refreshing. Lowish 11% alc for nonwoozy lunchtime tippling.

Graceland Vineyards

Stellenbosch (see Stellenbosch map) • Tasting, sales & cellar tours by appointment • Two-room B&B with many amenities and expansive views • Owners Graceland (Pty) Ltd • Consulting winemaker Rod Easthope (since 1999) Consulting viticulturist Johan Pienaar (since 1996) • Vineyards 9 ha • Production 25 tons 1 500 cases 100% red • PO Box 7066 Stellenbosch 7599 • Tel (021) 881-3121 • Fax (021) 881-3341 • E-mail pmcn@iafrica.com • Website www.gracelandvineyards.com

KIWI TRANSPLANT Rod Easthope is the new (consultant) winemaking force behind Paul and Susan McNaughton's reds. He follows Martin Meinert — a guiding inspiration after the McNaughtons decamped from Johannesburg to the Helderberg, planted citrus trees ("a disaster"), and about-turned to cabernet, merlot and shiraz. Meinert (with another New Zealander, James Graham) made the first **98** releases, rave-reviewed not only for their opulent flavours and texture, but also for their stand-out label. It features the suitably voluptuous Three Graces entwined (gracefully of course) round the neck of the elegant bottle. Experienced consultant Johan Pienaar oversees the 9 ha vineyards with Susan McNaughton; the vintage is quick (if not painless) due to Vino the dalmatian's penchant for encouraging pickers by nipping at their heels.

✿ Cabernet Sauvignon ▼ This expansive, classically styled Helderberg cab made a splashy debut in **98**, from exceptional red wine yr. Big yet elegant (13,5% alc), some classic claret whiffs of strawberry, damp earth, fruitcake, good minerally flavour; now beginning to soften though tannins still quite tight. Follow up **99 ✿** bigger alc (13,8%) but less immediately striking, quieter; red berry fruit currently dominated by savoury tones; some astringent tannins, forceful oak need time to settle. Own vyds; open tank fermented; 18 mths Fr oak, 30% new. 600 cases.

✿ Merlot ▼ 99 very fine follow-up to first release **98**, which marked this as a first rate Cape example. Latest not as instantly voluptuous — oak-fragrant dark cassis still tightly wrapped in youthfully taut tannins; but these are ripe and should soften, allowing good earthy, chocolatey, savoury fruit to show. 13,5% alc. 18 mths 2nd fill Fr casks.

Graham Beck Wines

Robertson cellar

See Robertson map • Tasting & sales Mon—Fri 9—5 Sat 10—3 • Cellar tours by appointment • Bring your own picnic • Gifts • Views • Private game park • Owner Graham Beck • Cellarmaster Pieter Ferreira (since 1990) • Winemaker John Loubser (since 2000) • Consulting viticulturist Johan Wiese • Vineyards 185 ha • Production 152 000 cases 45% white 30% red 25% MCC • PO Box 724 Robertson 6705 • Tel (023) 626-1214 • Fax (023) 626-5164 • E-mail cellar@grahambeckwines.co.za • Website www.grahambeckwines.co.za

Coastal Cellar (Franschhoek)

Not open to the public • Cellar tours by appointment • Owner Graham Beck • Winemaker Charles Hopkins • Consulting viticulturist Johan Wiese • Vineyards 159 ha • Production 90 000 cases • PO Box 134 Franschhoek 7690 • Tel (021) 874-1258 • Fax (021) 874-1712 • E-mail coastal@grahambeckwines.co.za • Website www.grahambeckwines.co.za

ONE CORPORATE BODY, two beating hearts: the report on the recent restructuring of mining tycoon Graham Beck's wine interests shows them to be in good health. Trimmed of excess weight (his majority shares in DGB sold to management), vitamin supplemented via fruit from two Helderberg area farms, Beck's Robertson cellar (on Madeba farm) and his Coastal cellar (on Bellingham, Franschhoek) now operate in tandem, dual pacemakers for the company's new-millennium, international image building strategy. In Pieter ("Bubbles") Ferreira and Charles ("Cabernet Franc") Hopkins, respective cellar chiefs, Beck has two of the Cape's standout talents — and, just as crucially, greatest wine enthusiasts. Hopkins went into winemaking "because it suits my personality. I am absolutely passionate about viticulture, vinification, wine and the fun of the process ... permanently experimenting in search of the ultimate". Ferreira says wine is "a never ending, pleasurable learning experience".

'Coastal' range

🔱 **Cabernet Sauvignon** Sampled in gawky adolescence for pvs ed, **98** has grown into handsome young adult. Strapping, dense, firmly structured for the long haul. Expensive cigarbox whiffs from 21 mths Fr oak, cassis ripeness. 13,5% alc. 800 cases. Follow-up **99** more accessible, choc-cassis in aromatic bouquet. ±Yr Fr barrels. 13% alc. 5 600 cases.

🔱 **The Old Road Pinotage** 🆕 This newcomer has an instant pedigree: grapes pvsly went to Southern Right, Grangehurst. Single vyd at Firgrove consisting of dryland bushvines planted 1963, owned by Graham Beck since 1998. **99** statement wine, generously oaked (14 mths new Am casks), yet with elegance, purity, not big or jammy. Intense colour, high-toned bouquet with cinnamon spice. 12% alc. 1 600 cases. Tighter than starry **98** SAA, ABSA Top 10, *Wine* ⭐⭐, with mint/eucalyptus whiffs, bold red/black cherries. 13% alc. 800 cases.

🔱 **Pinotage** Larger quantities than above (4 000 cases), lighter oaking (±yr Am oak, 30% new). "Potjie braai on patio" sort of wine, says Charles Hopkins. Inky **99**, compact and tight still; sniffs of spice, eucalyptus, mint, red cherry tastes and firm ripe tannins. 12,5% alc.

🔱 **Shiraz** Northern Rhône style — shiraz power in a velvet glove. Grapes ex-Firgrove, F'hoek. Leather, spicy white pepper in **99** 🔱. ±13 mths Am oak, 80% new. 5 000 cases. More accessible, lighter (13,6% alc.) than massive but elegant **98** VVG, SAA, which needed couple of yrs to soften. 14,5% alc.

Merlot 🔱 🆕 Assertive, concentrated style; big bodied (13,5% alc) **99** with choc, red cherries; quite tight still, tannins firm, so give bit of time. Yr Fr Fr oak, some new. 4 000 cases.

Sauvignon Blanc 🔱 Lighter style for early drinking. Firgrove fruit powers **00**, with youthful green tinge, tropical fruit palate, bone-dry finish.

Robertson range

🔱 **The Ridge Shiraz** Standout in increasingly crowded field of serious Cape examples. **98** heaped with praise — VG, SAA, *Wine* ⭐⭐: excitement continues in **99**, more Fr style than pvs, more spice/white pepper, less bustling fruit yet fine intensity, balance; very dry finish. Single vyd (opposite *avant garde* tasting room); rich red limestone soils (Rob'son version of Coonawarra's famous *terra rossa*). All new oak, 80/20 Am/Fr; partial barrel fermentation. 13,5% alc. 3 200 cases. **97** 🔱 gold on Concours Mondial.

🔱 **Merlot** (New to the guide, though **98** was first) **99** huge alcohol (15+% — "grapes picked at full phenolic ripeness") yet balanced. Luminous purple colour; savoury nose, spice and bacon in palate, with well integrated aromatic oak. (2nd/3rd fill barrels, 60% Am, 40% Fr).

🔱 **Chardonnay** Elegant Fr toned chardonnay, **99** with honeyed bouquet, spicy minerals and fruit, seamless oak. Delicate lemons/limes in absolutely dry finish. 100% whole bunch pressed, 10 mths oak, 50% new. 13% alc. 7 000 cases. Note: Lonehill Chardonnay reviewed in pvs ed destined to become single vyd release.

🔱 **Waterside White** 🔻 Generic Rob'son 'happy wine', inspired by success of Craighall Chardonnay-Sauvignon (sourced from Rob'son). Goal accomplished:

Waterside volumes now top 30 000 cases a yr. 50/50 chardonnay/colombard, latter's tropical tones out front for first 6 mths, then former takes over, supplying mouthfeel. Med-bodied **00**, SAYWS class winner, with fresh colombard acidity for satisfying patio sipping. Bargain priced.

☆☆Cuvée 2000 ▽ Closer to a French champagne than the MCCs below (and proof that sometimes non-vintage fizz is superior to vintaged variety). Gorgeous 'partridge eye' blush; beautiful pinot noir fruit: rich red berries, fine creamy mousse, good dry finish. Will develop for couple more yrs; present sherbet character will mutate into biscuity richness. Multi-vintage brut (95, 96, 97), pinot/chardonnay (90/10), grapes ex-Firgrove. 2 yrs on lees, 10 g/ℓ sugar, 12% alc. 6 000 cases.

☆Blanc de Blancs Vintaged all-chardonnay brut MCC, regularly among Cape's classiest. Signature toasty character from barrel fermentation of 50% of base wine in traditional champagne oak. Newest **96**, 5 yrs on cork, speaks with definite French accent: lemon/citrus character, creamy but still fresh with lots of complex flavour. 4 000 cases. **93** now full of good secondary characteristics. 6 yrs on lees.

☆Brut ▽ MCC which maintains consistently sparkly quality despite stellar quantities (22 000 cases). SAA trophy winner in 1999. Latest **NV** (97) bottling wonderfully balanced equal chardonnay/pinot noir partnership, 24 mths on lees; delicate pale lemon colour, creamy/fruity elegance and fine, fresh mouse. Clean-cut commercial style with panache.

☆Rhona Muscadel ▽ New wave muscat de frontignan fortified dessert: concentrated without being cloying. First **96** *Wine* ☆ well received by critics, consumers. Follow-up **97** forward muscat nose, menthol/spearmint in palate, fresh mouthfeel. Aperitif or dessert wine (chill, then dip your biscotti into it). Now in more conservative, squatter bottle (all sorts of problems inserting cork into pvs elegant, swan like neck). 2 500 cases. **96** developing well: grapefruit-honeysuckle aromas, hint of bottle-aged complexity; sleek marmalade, coconut flavours enhanced by balanced sugar.

Railroad Red ☆ Volume quaffer (30 000 cases) on a somewhat higher quality track in **99**, yet still friendly, accessible. Juicy plum fruit, solid mid-palate from touch of oak, dry/sour finish. Cab, shiraz. 13,5% alc. **Cap Classique Sparkling Red** ☆ Champagne-style pinotage, "a world first" — which Pieter Ferreira would like to celebrate by sharing a glass with "the Queen". Second release features gutsy pinotage fruit; a little oak balancing out the tannins. At 13,5% alc, a sit-down-fizz. Should get the Sacred Palates spluttering into their Krug. **Fleury Cabernet Sauvignon-Merlot** Not available for tasting this ed. Pvsly rated **98** ☆. Destined to become a certified organic wine.

Grand Mousseux

SINCE 1929, SA's affordable, dependable sparkler for all occasions. Clairette blanche/colombard blends carbonated, sweetened according to style. By Stellenbosch Farmers' Winery.

Vin Sec ☆ Least sweet of these; fresh clean bubbles, mouthfilling, tropical aromas echo in finish. **Vin Doux** ☼ Big, creamy fizz; brisk acidity, fine carbonation prevent this ubiquitous toast from sliding into decadent sweetness. **Spumante** ☆ Clean muscat, tropical, floral tones; lowish 10,5% alc nicely fleshed by fruity sweetness. **Grand Rouge** Not tasted for this ed. Pvs rating ☆.

Grangehurst

Stellenbosch (see Helderberg map) • Sales Mon—Fri 9—5 • Owner/winemaker Jeremy Walker • Grapes from 4 Stbosch areas • Production 85 tons 5 500 cases rising to 135 tons/9 000 cases by 2001 100% red • PO Box 206 Stellenbosch 7599 • Tel (021) 855-3625 • Fax (021) 855-2143 • E-mail winery@grangehurst.co.za

AT SOME STAGE it was inevitable that Jeremy Walker's compact little wine business, one of the success stories of the decade, would acquire its own vineyards. The modest start began in the family's squash court, then barrels spread into the guest quarters; even aviaries and tennis courts yielded — to the expanding business and its offices. The work-in-progress, the carefree bootstraps air, of course didn't conceal the intrinsics in the bottle — which showed Walker's very formal Stellenbosch University training (though he says the wines have improved as his intuition and confidence have grown, the less chemically formulaic he's become. "I've developed my own sense of grape ripeness beyond the pH meter.") A new dedicated maturation cellar and winery finally have been built — to manage the grapes from several Stellenbosch vineyards and give Walker some elbow room. The specialist focus on a handful of reds will remain at Grangehurst's new 15 ha piece of prime Stellenbosch land, just south-west of the town abutting L'Avenir. "So there's nothing wrong with the terroir! The problem is rootstock and plant material — we'd like to wait for the very best material, obviously, but we don't want to lose time," says Walker, who always seems in a hurry. He'd be a shoo-in choice for the top ten Cape producers of both pinotage and cabernet — and he's garnered 3 (so far unmatched) 5 stars from *Wine* magazine (for the Hidden Valley Pinotage 97, Grangehurst Cab Merlot 93 and the Grangehurst CWG Cab 95). But many will be bowled over by a new star in the range: the Nikela. Walker wanted to make a wine in honour of his late parents and chose the name Tribute. It was already registered — though unused. The Xhosa equivalent, however, was free! Walker says: "To honour my folks I wanted to include in the wine something of everything we do here, all the varieties. And at the same time I wanted to conceptualise a genuine harmony of distinctive grapes, including pinotage, to make real Cape blend." Asked to describe some of the flavours and tastes, he replies: "Ag, I'm not much good at wine descriptions."

⭐⭐**Nikela** NEW **97** cab, pinotage, merlot merger, (46/45/9) 1999 Diners Club shortlist. Grangehurst's answer to the great Cape red blend debate and intended as a regular small flagship — about 5 000 bottles including magnum — each year. Seriously dark-hued and luscious, in both nose and palate (pinotage playing subservient role to cab) but displaying unusual minty-spicy complexity, which sets it apart. Needs time — 10 yrs or so. **98**, similarly proportioned but perhaps even more of a headline-grabber, thick, dense, dark, tightly layered flavours (including mulberry), a collectible (& tradeable?) wine that could quickly achieve icon status if it builds up a longer track record. Grapes from Stbosch, Devon Valley; new oak matured.

⭐⭐**Cabernet Sauvignon-Merlot 98** untasted. **97** (71/29 blend) has some of the complexity and confident style of **95** ⭐⭐ (which confirmed Grangehurst on serious Cape wine map after brilliant debuts in **92**, **93**); wafts of mulberry, coffee, mint swirl about on tense, compact palate which promises rewarding development in bottle. **96** ⭐ leaner, lighter. **94** SAA earned top 4-star UK *Decanter* rating. French feel to it, dry finish.

⭐**Pinotage** Has become a marker for Cape pinotage, since **95** (all round, Jeremy Walker's anno mirabilis so far — "If I could have that vintage again, I'd never ask for more.") Leavened with splash (8–14%) cab since **92**, has turned a difficult grape into a wine with some elegance — easier tannins, acids, especially in more recent vintages since vyd ripeness has become a Grangehurst obsession. Latest release **98** ⭐⭐ shows relatively subdued bouquet but pleasant palate flavours — lush cherry/cloves and some mushroom whiffs. Lighter **96** more herbaceous, savoury farmyard style. Charmer for many remains **95** *Wine* ✿. All barrel-aged, about 25% new, 65% Fr, 35% Am oak. **97** *Wine* ✿.

✿ **CWG Auction Reserve Cabernet Sauvignon** (the only unblended cab from this cellar) **98** (barrel sample) three-vyd (all Stbosch) selection for 2001 Auction in just 5 new oak barrels: for those with taste for packed, intense, grippy wines, this is a top Cape one — flaunting some classic fine cab violet scents. **97** also luxury version, cigarbox wafts with cassis flesh, similar at early stage to **95** which swept boards as sole *Wine* ✿ from that star vintage. **93** SAA.

✿ **CWG Auction Pinotage** (CWG Auction Grangehurst/Hidden Valley Pinotage in pvs ed) Collaboration with Dave Hidden, owner of excellent Devon Valley pinotage vyd. **00** due on 2001 Auction, untasted. Last was **97**, a statement wine, 18 mths new wood. Also, like regular above, with dash cab. No **96**. **95** fetched remarkable (in 1996) R100/bottle.

Granite Creek see Laborie

Green Peak see Linton Park

Groblershoop see Oranjerivier Wynkelders

Groene Cloof Estate

Swartland (see Swartland map) • Tasting & sales Mon—Fri 10—4 Sat 10—1 • Cellar tours by appointment • Views • Proclaimed conservation area • Owner Johan van der Berg • Winemaker Frikkie Botes (since 1998) • Consulting viticulturist Paul Wallace (VineWise) • Vineyard manager Derrick van Graan • Vineyards ± 200 ha • Production 20 000 cases (10 000 cases own label) 60% red 40% white • PO Box 125 Darling 7345 • Tel (022) 492-2839 • Fax (022) 492-326 • E-mail adv.se.vanderberg@mweb.co.za • Website http://home.intekom.com/groenecloofwine

WAY BACK in 1975, Frikkie Botes' matric teacher suggested a career in wine. She was obviously on the right track. Now he's part of the new generation of winemakers heading up a quiet renaissance on the West Coast (in the Groenekloof Valley on the outskirts of Darling and only a waft from the Atlantic, to be precise). Between hunting and hiking in his beloved Karoo hills, he also headed north for his first French harvest. Fresh plantings of chardonnay and cabernet franc are due to be harvested, with new merlot, shiraz and cinsaut to follow (he feels that the quintessential South African style of wine should encompass 'old Cape' cinsaut and pinotage). Groene Cloof, the fruition of a vision by ex-legal eagle Johan van der Berg, who bought the farm in 94 and completed the cellar in 97, is certainly going places.

✿ **Cabernet Sauvignon** Modern, well-made cab with considerable presence and weight. Current release shade more elegant than pvs **98** (which not available for tasting for last ed — nor were any below), though **99** has higher alc (14% vs 13,5). Sophisticated strawberries-and-cream texture, fine dry tannins, leafy cassis intensity complete an attractive picture. Milestone **98**, first wine bottled in new cellar, chunkier, almost Australian fruit concentration. Bushvines, aged 9–12 mths in barriques .

✿ **Pinotage** First release **98** garnered 4 star accolade in *Decanter* pinotage tasting, but we prefer follow-up **99** ✿, plush-piled, softly tannic with sleek allspice/mulberry aromatics. Super wine, not nearly as strapping as 14,5% alc suggests. 4 200 cases. **98** slighter, more savoury yet good fruity presence. Bushvines, oaking as above.

Bush Vine NEW **99** unwooded, full-bodied (13,5% alc) red blend mainly cinsaut (34 yr old vines), equal pinotage, cab. Untasted. 2 100 cases. **Chenin Blanc** ✿ Gentle melon tones with chenin dry-haystack hints. Attractive creaminess in **99** dry, med-weight palate from extended ageing on lees. Unwooded. Well priced at R18 ex-cellar. 500 cases.

Groenekloof see Darling Cellars

Groot Constantia Estate

Constantia (see Constantia map) • Tasting & sales daily except Christmas Day, Good Friday. Tasting 9—5.30 Dec-Apr; 10—5 May—Nov Fee R12 for 5 wines (includes glass) Sales 9—6 Dec-Apr; 10—5 May—Nov • Cellar tours on the hour 10—4 summer; 11, 3 & 4 winter Booking essential R10 p/p, includes AV presentation Large groups can book times to suit. • Jonkershuis Restaurant and Tavern • Picnic baskets by arrangement • Playground for children • Gifts • Conference facilities • Walking trail • Museum • Managed by Groot Constantia Trust • General manager Jean du Toit • Winemaker Bob de Villiers with Roger Arendse (both since 1999) • Vineyard manager Callie Bröcker • Vineyards 100 ha • Production 600 tons 45 000 cases 51% white 49% red • Private Bag X1 Constantia 7848 • Tel (021) 794-5128 • Fax (021) 794-1999 • E-mail gct@mweb.co.za

"IT DOESN'T get much prettier than this." In the short 18 months since Bob de Villiers exchanged Barrydale co-op and the sinuous Tradouw valley for historic Groot Constantia, he has learned to love what must be some of the most breathtaking views on the planet. Scenery which, in the millennium fires which struck the Cape peninsula, came close to being laid waste. De Villiers points to the spot, 400 m up Constantiaberg, where a new sauvignon vineyard was threatened by flames sweeping over the mountain crest from Hout Bay. "We were so lucky!" Meanwhile, in the cellar below, forests of new French oak are being transferred into the cellar: R1,2-million's worth of 300 ℓ casks in 2000 alone. "I need to boost the proportion of new wood from under 5% to nearer 50%." Far from oak obsessed, de Villiers is pushing hard for more fruit flavours from the extensively replanted vineyards.

✿ Gouverneurs Reserve Since inception as estate's standard bearing red, always from best performing blocks, as judged by cellarmaster, who decides varietal makeup. **99** retains Bdx profile: cabs s/f (cab from still immaculate 1992 KWV vineyard block competition winner); complex, warm plum whiffs, spicy tobacco from all-new 300 ℓ Fr barrels. No hint of old style green/vegetal flavours; only plush, modern lingering mulberry fruit.

✿ Merlot-Shiraz ▼ Pvsly Heerenrood. For early drinking, thoroughly modern quaffable style. **99** less grassy than pvs. Fleshy choc/mulberry notes carry to velvet palate; sweetish, tobacco laced finish.

✿ Shiraz ▼ From selected block of an ancient vineyard (this variety long a talisman of the cellar). **99** deep plum; wonderful, earthy choc/wild berry aromas; supple, beautifully balanced flavours; sprinkle of peppery Rhône spice; deft use of new Am (75%), Fr oak to frame vibrant new SA shiraz style. Solid structure (14% alc) in deceptively velvet garb.

✿ Pinotage ▼ Latest **99** several steps up on pvs (**97**); now in modern idiom with plush tannins, sweet, rich vanilla. Blackish plum, royal purple rim. Already complex smoky plum/earthy aromas, De Villiers' deftness keeps negative esters/jamminess at bay.

✿ Chardonnay ▼ Deeply flavoured barrel fermented chardonnay. **99** rich yellow-gold; orange marmalade on toast, butterscotch in substantial yet silky-dry, creamy palate. Conservative oak trim. 13,5% alc. Barrel fermented/aged 3 mths new Fr oak. **00** barrel sample, from low yield (2,7 t/ha) vyds, pungent toast/cinnamon, hints of ginger. Low (5,6 g/ℓ) acid, broad, creamy texture.

✿ Sauvignon Blanc ▼ **99** classic Constantia grass/fig profile, developing complex herbal notes. Nearly 14% alc aids development, palate roundness, perky 'sweetness' in finish from ripe fruit. Hot-year **00**, with touch semillon, sampled from tank more tropical, less vegetal. Should show more elegance, with lower alc (13,2%), softer finish. Potential ✿.

✿ Weisser Riesling ▼ One of the Cape's best and most consistent. Powerfully botrytised (50%) **99**, ✿ on release, impressed with fragrant crushed pineapple/honey/muscat spiciness; vibrant flavour with burst of fresh acidity. Back-tasted mid-2000 still remarkable, and still in good condition though bit advanced for its tender years. Lots of complexity — botrytis, riesling terpene and honey. Should last while longer. 28 g/ℓ sugar. No **00** ("quality's not there"). **98** similarly bold, much lower sugar (18 g/ℓ). These can age well; as botrytis intensifies, palate-weight mounts. Great match for spicy Cape-Malay cuisine.

Bouquet Blanc ✿ 🍷 Jasmine perfume from morio muscat in semi-sweet **99**, framed with sauvignon nettle and fig. Pretty, supple; popular seller from estate.

Cabernet Sauvignon ✿ Elegant, well behaved version, with soft yet dry, minerally red berry flavours, dusty finish in **98**; some warm, dusty stewed plum aromas, hints of cocoa. **99** more in claret style, fuller, with more new wood. **00** (potential ✿) more of everything, juicy farewell shows de Villiers' fresh touch. 300 ℓ Fr oak, 80% new. **Merlot** ✿ NEW Creditable debut in **98** with fleshy berries/smoky plum/cocoa. Yr new/older wood. **99** barrel sample touch riper, good varietal choc, shy grassy whiffs over ripe cassis. Gently extracted tannins neatly sidestep unacceptable green flavours of too many SA merlots. 8 mths oak, some new. **Constantia Rood** ✿ From 'left-over' reds once more cultivar-driven needs are met (though not an afterthought); blend varies with vintage. Good value. Cab/shiraz **98**, smoky, mulberry aromas and supple, sweet redcurrant taste, with bare hint vanilla. Small oak, none new. **Constantia Blanc** ✿ **00** unwooded dry chardonnay/sauvignon/morio muscat crowd pleaser; delicately floral, finishes with juicy twist. **Ruby Port** ✿ To be replaced by more serious ruby style, featuring touriga naçional. Current **NV** shiraz/pinotage/tinta b; multi-vintage blend with bright fruit, good peppery attack. Large old vats.

· ·

Grootdrink see Oranjerivier Wynkelders

Groot Eiland Winery　🍷 🍷

Worcester (see Worcester map) • Tasting & sales Mon—Fri 8.30—12.30; 1.30—5 Sat by appointment • Cellar tours during tasting hours • Walks • Views • Owners 17 members • Winemaker Erik Schlünz (since 2000) with Marthinus Joubert (since 1965) • Consultant viticulturist Schalk du Toit (VinPro) • Vineyards 600 ha • Production 10 600 tons 90% white 10% red • PO Box 93 Rawsonville 6845 • Tel (023) 349-1140 • Fax (023) 349-1801

IT'S ALL SYSTEMS GO at this Goudini cellar with its rolling lawns. The reception area is being spruced up to be more tourist friendly, and new red varieties are being planted (which figures, in light of the fact that new — since January 2000 — winemaker Erik Schlünz bagged some Veritas golds for his reds while at Spruitdrift Winery on the Olifants River). New label and bottles for the popular grape juice follow hot on the heels of the new wine label. And the Groot Eiland range, which has been extended, is being actively marketed both domestically and overseas. Sports-mad Schlünz, who loves "bundu bashing in southern Africa", says he owes a lot to Distillers Corporation, where he "gained experience in all facets of the wine process, as well as in the vineyards and laboratory".

Rosé ✿ NEW 🍷 Schlünz & Co leaping confidently aboard rosé bandwagon with candiflossy semi-dry **NV** (00), with funky pink lights and juicy, drier than expected finish. Well made, light chenin/pinotage combo. **Chenin Blanc** ✿ NEW 🍷 Super, unpretentious **00** cork-popper, zippily fresh with peach/guava and hints of pear in firm dry finish. Med-bodied. These ungreedily priced R11 ex-cellar.

Cabernet Sauvignon ✿ Sound everyday quaffing, well priced. Med-bodied **98** plump, plummy, warmly satisfying and smooth. **Pinotage** ✿ Dependable and full flavoured; good summer drinking (chill lightly). Savoury **99** with plum/woodsmoke hints, developing well in bottle. Broadened by 13,8% alc. **Shiraz** ✹✹ New Quite sophisticated strawberry/cherry aromas in med-weight **00**, good juicy mouthfeel and dry finish. Unwooded. **Chardonnay** ✹✹ Spicy buterscotchy **00** pleasantly creamy from well managed oak; satisfying, weighty (13,7% alc) vanilla toned finish. **Sauvignon Blanc** ✹ New Lightish pleasant, if somewhat simple dry white, not bradcasting varietal character but wafting some dusty green nettles. **Meander** ✹✹ Cellar's most popular drops (reference to sinuous Breede River nearby). Just off-dry, lightish **00** chenin-driven, high-acid sauvignon adds zing to delicate fruit salad tastes. **Hönigtraube** ✹ "Poolside quaffing" semi-sweet **NV**, spicy dried apricot, raisin, fresh grape flavours; light, bright not oversweet finish. Colombard/hanepoot. Screwtop. **98** VG. All above 270 cases.

Groote Post Vineyards

Darling (see Swartland map) • Tasting & sales Mon—Fri 8—12, 2—5 Sat 8—12 • Wheelchair-friendly • Owners Peter & Nicholas Pentz • Winemaker to be appointed • Viticulturist Johan Pienaar (VinPro) • Vineyard manager Jannie de Klerk (since 1996) • Vineyards 70 ha • Production 270 tons 12 000 cases 52% red 48% white • Private Bag X1 Bloubergrant 7441 • Tel (021) 557-0606 (office) (022) 492-2825 (winery) • Fax (021) 557-8280 (office) (022) 492-2693 (winery) • E-mail gpwines@iafrica.com

SAUVIGNON BLANC has blazed out of the starting blocks here, on a dairy and vineyard spread so eco-sensitively managed that owner Peter Pentz became the first individual to win South Africa's top, state-conferred, conservation award. Its first 99 Sauvignon picked up 4 stars in *Wine's* across-the-board tasting (one of only four of that "vintage from hell") and it leads the 70 ha dryland plantings here in the Darling Hills, just 7 km from the Atlantic Ocean. But there's an up-and-coming red brigade too — merlot at 16 ha is the next-biggest block, pinot noir and cabernet are flourishing, and cabernet franc was planted in 2000 under the expert eye of consultant Johan Pienaar. The West Coast is a new-discovery area of modern Cape wine, and these vineyards are adding to its growing reputation. End-goal of the Pentzes (son Nick is a co-owner and director) is 120 ha by 2002, but right-of-admission to the cellar will be reserved for only the best 350 tons of grapes. The property may be huge — 5 300 ha in total — but the wine philosophy is of the small-is-beautiful sort.

✹✹**Sauvignon Blanc** Sea-breezy Groenekloof established among top Cape sauvignon terroirs, reflected in first release **99**, which struck all right notes with well rounded, grassy/tropical performance. **00** ✹✹ more polished act yet full of verve, intensity. Fruit salad again, plus cut grass and whiff fig in deliciously crisp, clean finish. No rush to uncork; this better after yr. 13% alc. 5 700 cases.

Merlot ✹✹ New Firm, currently quite wiry **99** youngster should be given yr or 2 to gain some flesh. Good handfuls choc, mulberry, black cherry suggest patience will be rewarded. Small Fr oak 10 mths. 13,5% alc. 400 cases. **Pinot Noir** New **99** not available for tasting. **Chardonnay Unwooded** ✹✹ You might find sushi, grilled linefish or butternut soup on winemaker's table when he uncorks **00**, as these among his favourite food matches for this reductively made wine, which deserves a few mths' character building in bottle. Lively, crisp; promises well. Med-bodied; well priced. 180 cases. **Chardonnay Wooded** New Tasted from barrel, **00** too unformed to rate, but plentiful lime, tropical fruit and vanilla oak, all elegantly presented. 8 mths 300 ℓ Fr oak. 1 000 cases. **Chenin Blanc** ✹✹ New **00** med/light bodied, delicately tropical, very pleasant but not initially reflecting intensity promised by 18 yr old bushvines. So give bit of time to develop. Inexpensive. 1 287 cases.

Groot Geluk see Vinfruco

Grünberger

POPULAR BERGKELDER RANGE with a Germanic inspiration that extends to the Frankish flagon type 'bocksbeutel' bottle used for the non-spritzy wines. NV except where indicated.

Rosenlese ✿ Pale coral, offering soft sweet berries; from sauvignon and ruby cab; this and Freudenlese below 7,5% alc. **Freudenlese** ✿ Sauvignon and gewürz — the latter flaunting rose petals and honey. Like Rosenlese, made in Natural Sweet style. **Stein** ✿✿ **99** has charming floral fragrance and yet more rose petals in soft, off-dry palate; 11,5% alc. **Spritzenlese** ✿✿ New In tall 'tower' screw-topped bottle; **00** Natural Sweet-style ushers in gentle waves of tropical fruits with happy gush of bubbles; sauvignon/chenin blend. 8% alc. **Spritziger** ✿✿ **00** packaged and carbonated similarly to above, an easygoing off-dry fruit salad of bubbles, 11,5% alc.

Grundheim Wines   🍷 🍷 🍷

Oudtshoorn (see Klein Karoo map) • Tasting & sales Mon—Fri 8—5 Sat 8—1 • Cellar tours on request • Distilling demonstrations Mar—Apr • Owner Danie Grundling • Winemaker Dys Grundling • Vineyards 20 ha • Production 300 tons 50/50 red/white • PO Box 400 Oudtshoorn 6620 • Tel/fax (044) 272-6927

A BRANDY maturation cellar is taking shape on this captivating Klein Karoo farm, better known for its home-distilled spirits and fortified desserts — and Susan Grundling's excellent preserves and folk remedies. A fresh presence in the cellar is Dys Grundling, unapologetic admirer of Australian muscats. Whether this appreciation signals a departure from the winning Grundheim formula remains to be seen. For now the heroes below, made by Danie Grundling, should keep the fans in good spirits.

✿✿ **Red Muscadel** This traditional fortified dessert (and white version below), speciality of the house, vinified the 'old Cape' way: fermented in open cement *kuipe*, basket pressed, Bright, coppery **94** has lost its initial spirity punch, gained honeyed smoothness, fragrant pepper/cinnamon spice. Gold on local show. **95** ✿ past its best.

Wit Muscadel ✿✿ Shimmering gold **94**, complex muscat/honeysuckle/beeswax perfume, some nutty/cashew tastes in viscous palate. Appears more spirity than when last tasted, so suggest drink up to catch at peak. This and above 18% alc. **Cape Ruby Port NV** (95) Blend of cinsaut/pinotage/cab.

Guardian Peak see Rust & Vrede
Guess see Winecorp

Hamilton Russell Vineyards   🍷 🍷 🍷

Walker Bay (see Walker Bay map) • Tasting & sales Mon—Fri 9—5 Sat 9—1 • Cellar & vineyard tours by arrangement • Tasting & sales of cold pressed extra virgin olive oil, estate matured cheese • Works by artist Arabella Caccia, who lives/works on property, viewed by appointment • Views • Owner Anthony Hamilton Russell • Winemaker Kevin Grant (since 1994) • Viticulturist Stephen Roche (since 1998) • Vineyards 51,33 ha • Production 200 tons, 15 000 cases 60% white 40% red • PO Box 158 Hermanus 7200 • Tel (028) 312-3595 • Fax (028) 312-1797 • E-mail hrv@hermanus.co.za

"A WINEMAKING milestone, quite possibly our best yet," says Anthony Hamilton Russell of the 2000 vintage of pinot noir — the variety this property practically patented locally, 20 years ago, when it was considered the height of madness — or presumption — for an upstart from the Cape (and from its outer fringes on the eastern seaboard nogal) to dare launch a bid for an international reputation based on Burgundy's most demanding grape. Even with its first, not altogether satisfactory clone, the BK5 from Champagne, HRV proved the doubters and obstructionists wrong; since replanting with new Dijon clones 9 years ago, it has entrenched its position on the world pinot noir map. And has shown a masterly grasp of that other Burgundian speciality, chardonnay (which will be in short supply from 2000; a hailstorm took out 27% of the already low-yield crop in just half an hour). But this is not Burgundy-by-the-sea (or the Atlantic Ocean or even Walker Bay). It is not even the Hemel-en-Aarde valley or this property in general. It is very specifically the individual sites chosen for each variety, their micro-terroirs, which infuse the HRV wines with the 'otherness' which distinguishes them from the crowd. Anthony HR is almost alarmingly fanatical about this: he now refers to himself as a "soil farmer", and speaks of "those extra spikes of individuality, unique to a certain place and not common to technique or variety … the extra mile a variety will walk only in a certain soil in a certain site". In the 5 years since the farm was mapped into 16 different soil types, winemaker (and fellow-obsessive) Kevin Grant has been studying the impact of these soils on wine style — for example, via the characteristics of each of the 18 separately vinified chardonnay blocks. And the earth-mother of them all turns out be to what AHR calls "serendipitous deposits" of stony, clay-rich Bokkeveld shale, a dream-home for pinot noir and chardonnay in the classic, complex, more understated older-world mould. A major house-moving exercise is underway: any sauvignon blanc (see under Southern Right) that has been squatting in these areas is being transferred to the lighter Table Mountain sandstone areas on the farm; HRV's two keynote varieties are seizing possession of the prime plots. "The most extensive replanting programme in the vineyards' history," says AHR. See also Ashbourne.

⚜️**Pinot Noir** Featuring all new (Dijon) clones (777, 115, 113 and 667) for the first time, **99** luminous strawberry colour, fragrant black cherry bouquet which echoes in palate with raspberry, wild berry seductions. Finely structured; as always understated, elegant. Easily confused with young Grand Cru Burgundy — a Musigny, perhaps? 9 mths small Fr oak. 5 100 cases. Touch lighter (13,6% alc.) than big, open **98** *Wine* ⚜️, vivid maroon colour to match the rich red-berry, medicinal scents; fleshy black cherries and generously ripe tannins. Fast-forward to **00** (20th vintage, still in barrel) discloses fine structure, great concentration from small crop, ripe fruit. "Shaping up to be a winemaking milestone for HRV," notes Kevin Grant confidently. **97** ⚜️ HRV triumph of the decade, tighter initially, some earthy tones to grippy tannin structure. **96** *Wine* ⚜️, with 80% new clone infusion, smoky liquorice/fennel hints, some tight tannins.

⚜️**Chardonnay** We noted of pvs HRV chardonnays that yearly variations ("the drama of vintage") are reflected and magnified in these wines. Yet a 2000 vertical (the first ever) uncovered a set of constants amid the variety: a wonderful tight, pebbly, citrus quality, sometimes with fresh-herb (mainly liquorice) embellishment. This present in first **82** (labelled Premier Vin Blanc), very much alive still with curious brandy like whiffs from Limousin casking. Thread follows through vintages **83–90**, most by Peter Finlayson, picked slightly early, with fine acidic lift to honey-butterscotch richness; **91–94** by Storm Kreusch, cropped marginally riper, with corresponding higher 13%-plus alcs; and **95** to present **00**, by incumbent Kevin Grant, perhaps the most classically, meticulously structured of all, with fine varietal definition, fruit/oak interplay. This very evident in current **99**, harking to restrained, almost austere **97**. Tasted mid-2000, **99** still closed, tight, but exceptionally long. That riverstone/mineral quality reprised, and familiar lemons, limes; occasional licorice puts in appearance, as does less familiar smoked meat. This deserves 2–3 yrs' keeping; optimal drinking until 2006 at least. 12,8% alc. Barrel fermented/aged 8 mths, malo. 6 900 cases. **00** barrel sample revisits tightness, length of **99** with viscous mouthfeel of **98** ⚜️, which more New World style (and much prized in US). Standout **97** with intricate weave of restrained butterscotch, pebbly, mineral tones, lingering chalky length.

Hanseret see Eersterivier

Hartenberg Estate

Stellenbosch (see Stellenbosch map) • Tasting & sales Mon—Fri 9—5 Sat 9—3 Closed Sun, religious holidays, New Year's Day Nominal tasting fee for groups, refundable with purchases • Vintners lunches (alfresco, weather permitting) 12—2 daily except Sun: picnic platters in summer; soup, vetkoek in winter Booking advisable • Views • "Great bird life including fish eagles" • Owners Fiona Mackenzie, Tanya Browne • Winemaker Carl Schultz (since 1994) • Viticulturist Frans Snyman (since 1996) • Vineyards 105 ha • Production 650 tons, 35 000 cases 60% red, 40% white • PO Box 69 Koelenhof 7605 • Tel (021) 882-2541 • Fax (021) 882-2153 • E-mail hartenberg@cybertrade.co.za

"THE HOME of unhurried wine" they say at this classy example of a new-generation Cape estate in the excellent Bottelary Hills area of Stellenbosch. Well fine, we concede; they don't let their headline reds loose until they've shown signs of grown-up gravitas; their varietal whites are often late (and lovely) bloomers; they don't tear off in hot pursuit of every trend. Others may ladle "blatantly sexy" American oak all over their shiraz, but here — where it's been the signature grape for decades — they go for the more "subtly seductive" charms of the Rhône. Across the board, it's modern Cape versions of the classics which play here, not disco novelties. But if "unhurried" signifies a slow, pottering-along-in-low-gear sort of place, we're simply not swallowing the notion. Hartenberg has not moved from old, lumbering campaigner to the front row of Cape estates without putting foot. Hectic! That's more like the pace here. Loads of red-wine varieties are revving up in the 105 ha vineyards, including the farm's first pinotage (this on a small scale, intended to "show solidarity" for our national grape); new-clone sauvignon blanc is swinging into action; and viticulturist Frans Snyman's latest foreign dash was to California, where he focused on zinfandel — Hartenberg, one of the very few in the Cape growing this variety, is determined to unlock its secrets. Carl Schultz (chair of the Cape Winemakers' Guild 1998—2000) took off for Milan with Maya Diniso, head of bottling and labelling ops, to source new machinery. Diniso, a fine example of Hartenberg's "empowerment without fanfare" policy for employees, flew back to Italy for an intensive course in driving the new acquisition, quite unperturbed by possible communication problems (his home-tongue is Xhosa).

✿ Cabernet Sauvignon 1997 vintage, long, cool ripening period, often alluded to as most 'European' in recent years. Translates into much brighter fruit, more elegant structure; youthful sternish profile not so apparent, though no shortage of backbone. Interwoven into this **97** cassis/mint/warm tea leaves, fresh-shelled walnuts, underpinned with mocha richness. Initially flows with un-cab-like, un-fettered silkiness over tongue, fine, dry tannins kicking in much later. A slow developer, Schultz believes, so don't be deceived by apparent accessibility. Effortlessly absorbs 20 mths Fr oak, 40% new. 2 483 cases. **96** harmonious, good example from ambiguous year. 16 mths Fr casks, 45% new. 95 VVG a stunner, unfined. All built to last good 7—9 yrs.

✿✿ Merlot Most accessible of premium 1997 reds. **97 ✿** billows bitter chocolate, plum intensity gives way to mouth-coating velvety texture, melt-in-mouth tannins; fruity substance rather than broadness of **96/95** provides staying power. Should unfold with time. 17 mths Fr oak, 40% new. 13,5% alc. 2 500 cases. **96** features sweetest Hartenberg fruit of vintage, finely calibrated oak. *Wine* **✿✿**. Not as impenetrable as massive **95** VVG, SAA, Air France–Preteux Bourgeois trophy; but should have good 5—7 yrs' staying power. 14 mths Fr 225 ℓ oak, 40% new.

✿✿ Shiraz Schultz's favoured variety, on Hartenberg and in Cape; here shows stylistic versatility with quality, discreetly exercised power with thumbprint heady snatches of scrub, fresh earth, roasted spices. Cooler conditions in **97 ✿** added violets to list, though overall profile remains shy; savoury tannins presently most delicious feature. Tasted mid-2000, obvious that patience will be required. Yet even tightly swaddled, convincing, potentially very fine. 18 mths Fr oak, 45% new; malo in barrel. 2 880 cases. **96** intense, deep, sensuous. **95** VVG; **93–96** SAA.

Zinfandel 97 reviewed in pvs ed, only released spring 2000; extra year mellowed edges without dimming rhubarb/raspberries/cherry pip and bitter chocolate distinction; melange now integrated, smoothed by 19 mths 100% Am oak, 50% new. Elegantly fresh (10% cab adds extra oomph); sweet-fruited landing. Tasting room stats reveal this popular with 25–35 age group. 13% alc. 1 416 cases.

Cabernet Sauvignon-Merlot Release of **95**, resembling top-class Bdx in build, again postponed. In no hurry to loosen up, parade its finely layered tannins, creamy chocolate, savoury rich filling. Watch this space. 60/40 blend, 22 mths oak. None since.

Chardonnay Reserve No **99**. Pvs **98** with spicy oak, subtle roasted nuts. Rich flavours, ripe, dry finish; lengthened by firm but nonintrusive acid. Not as concentrated as **97** SAA. Fermented/matured 15 mths Fr oak, all new.

Pontac ✿ Only Cape bottling of this firm, dry, rustic red. Released sporadically: **97**, **96**, **95** never bottled individually; next is **98**, make-up not finalised in time for tasting. **93** avg R124/btl at 1999 Nederburg Auction. **Cabernet Sauvignon-Shiraz** ✿ 🏆 Lip-smackin' good red, versatile, well priced. Though fans will have to look sharpish for latest lightly oaked **98**: quantity of all reds sliced in half through vintage conditions. 55/45 blend features all warmth, robustness of yr; spice, red fruits, thick spread of tasty savouriness in palate. Usual friendly tannins. 13% alc. 4 500 cases. **Chardonnay** ✿ "Very popular overseas," confirms Tanya Browne, "people say it's very un-South African." **99** *does* ring with more Burgundian nuts, lees, smoky bacon tones, and glimpses of well toasted oak. Creamy but not heavy (despite 13,7% alc.), fresh citrus lift though caramelly tail less flattering. Barrel fermented/matured 15 mths Fr oak, 20% new. 1 333 cases. **Sauvignon Blanc** ✿ "Like chalk and cheese," grins Carl Schultz. **00**, maiden crop from new clone, much livelier, more immediately appealing than pvs. Fresh tropical gooseberry wafts, mouthwatering ripe acidity (all natural), extra bounce/richness from lees contact. Probably best before mid-2001. 13,6% alc. 2 500 cases. **Chatillon** ✿ 🏆 Lovely drinking, great value **00**, to carry semillon/chenin origin on label (also contains splash sauvignon/pinot blanc). More expressive than usual: luscious melon honeycomb ripeness, lingering 'sweet' fruity finish (though technically dry). Portion semillon oaked. 13,5% alc. 44 000 cases. **Weisser Riesling** ✿ **00** in much lighter, though no less charming guise than pvs. Invigorating limey, spicy tones, floral freshness, though soupçon 10% botrytis should introduce new complexities with time. Piquancy, raciness accentuated by lowish 10,4% alc, 7 g/ℓ acid. non-cloying 22 g/ℓ sugar. 900 cases. **L'Estreux** ✿ One of the less unctuous SLHs, its official designation. With departure of gewürz (vines being uprooted), **00** becomes first 100% schönberger released locally. More German-accented, dainty floral spice, 'cooler', more delicate feel (despite 13% alc.); nicely offset by 20 g/ℓ sugar. Named after original Huguenot farmer. 4 200 cases.

Following **NV** housewines thoroughly good value, food-friendly.

Bin 6 ✿ 😊 Gentle canned-pineapple fragrance, juicily sweet, but cleansing acidity ensures only fruit lingers. Latest 100% morio muscat.

Bin 9 🍷 Youthfully gluggable cab; uncomplicated dark berry, green walnut aromas; light-textured, zesty. Could take chilling. **Bin 3** ✿ Next will be semillon/chenin, not blended in time for tasting. Will follow usual route: mouthfilling, softly dry. All-round food partner.

Hartswater Wine Cellar

Northern Cape • Tasting & sales Mon—Fri 8.30—5 Sat tasting by appointment, sales from outlet in Hartswater town • Phone ahead for cellar tours • Fully licensed restaurant with barbecue • Conference facilities • Owner Senwes • Winemaker Roelof Maree (since 1978) • Production 4 800 tons • PO Box 2335 Hartswater 8570 • Tel (053) 474-0700 • Fax (053) 474-0975

THE PHRASE 'hall of stainless steel' takes on a new meaning at this northernmost Cape cellar, part of the Senwes group of companies. Manoeuvred — gingerly — into position in 2000 were eight enormous vertical stainless steel tanks, each with a capacity of more than 90 000 ℓ and weighing 90 t. The behemoths required some fancy footwork by the consulting engineers, who constructed a soil float to ensure the surface storage facilities won't unexpectedly turn subterranean. All in a day's work for veteran winemaker Roelof Maree and his team, who are preparing a new Master Plan to guide the cellar into the 21st century.

Hinterland range

✿ Jerepigo Lively, fresh fortified dessert, raisins/honey from nose to tail, prickle of acidity keeps the tone light. Hanepoot/colombard. NV. 17% alc.

Ruby Cabernet ✿ Fresh-turned earth in **99**, unusual herby finish. Light, flavourful; to sip while TV-channel surfing, says Roelof Maree. Unwooded. **Chardonnay** ✿ **99** undemanding light, dry quaffer. Not for keeping. **Chenin Blanc** ✿ Light, uncomplicated off-dry **99**, some slight dried apricot tones.

Elements range

New

Rouge ★ Highly individual tangy/earthy ruby cab/pinotage blend. **White** ✿ Winemaker's comment — "wine for the moment" — captures this delicate, easy blend of colombard/chenin/fernão pirez. **Rosenfreude** ✿ Natural Sweet rosé with good red-wine flavours (from ruby cab, with colombard/therona), despite elaborate sweetness. These **NV**, 5 000 cases each.

Haute Provence see Agusta Wines

Havana Hills

New

Tygerberg • Not open to the public • Owner Kobus du Plessis & Nico Vermeulen • Winemaker Nico Vermeulen (since 1999) with Joseph Gertse (since 2000) • Viticulturist Andries van der Spuy (since 1999) • Vineyards 43 ha • Production 80 tons 6 000 cases 90% red 10% white • PO Box 36770 Chempet 7441 • Tel (021) 972-1106 • Fax (021) 972-1105

A DREAM of 25 years has finally, wonderfully, scenically come to life for Nico Vermeulen, ex-L'Ormarins, Savanha, now in seventh heaven in his own winery between Melkbosstrand and Philadelphia on the West Coast (his partner here is Kobus du Plessis, a Cape entrepreneur and businessman who made the Cabernet and Merlot below himself, finishing touches by Vermeulen). From his spanking new workplace Vermeulen has "the world's most beautiful view" of Table mountain and the Atlantic, whose breezes air condition the 43 hectares of young cabernet, merlot, shiraz and sauvignon blanc. While these mature Vermeulen and du Plessis buy in fruit from mainly Malmesbury and Durbanville. With their maiden 99 wines below in bottle and ready to pour, the partners' aim is to "grow Havana Hills into one of the top wineries in SA and world-wide".

✿ **Havana Hills Cabernet Sauvignon-Merlot** Slated for release ahead of its stablemates, this **99** sets the new-Cape tone with fashionable extra-ripe fruit (picked at 25 °B), full-throated alc (13,5%), mouthfilling 'sweet' flavour and melt-in-mouth tannins. Broadened with gamey/savoury notes and hints of woodsmoke. Malmesbury fruit. 11 mths small oak. 2 000 cases.

✿ **Havana Hills Shiraz** Savoury/prune aromas introduce full-flavoured/bodied **99**, with peppermill grinds over wild red berries. It would be a pity to let this extra-ripe charmer turn porty, so suggest drink fairly soon. Dbnville fruit. 13% alc. 400 cases.

✿ **Havana Hills Sauvignon Blanc** Powerfully aromatic spectrum of 'Durbanville dust', capsicum, fig and gooseberry covered in expansive, full-bodied **99**, with crisp palate finishing lip-smackingly dry. Nico Vermeulen would want to wash this down with freshly caught grilled galjoen linefish — and so would we. 13% alc. 400 cases.

✿ **Du Plessis Cabernet Sauvignon** Soft smoky plums and cassis lead this super **99** full-bodied procession of cassis and aromatic liquorice to gentle dry finish. Understated oak-spice/choc nuances add interest. Malmesbury fruit. 13,5% alc. 14 mths new oak. 250 cases.

✿ **Du Plessis Merlot** One of the more supple, chocolatey, sweet-flavoured examples in Cape; **99** without green coarseness which afflicts some of this variety. Complexity from smoked meat/green pepper/undergrowth sniffs, wafting from dramatic crimson-black depths. Pleasing style that should fly off the shelves (if the meagre 250 cases aren't intercepted en route). Malmesbury grapes. 13,5% alc. Yr Fr oak.

✿ **Du Plessis Shiraz** Here's one of those swashbuckling Am-oaked numbers everyone is talking/raving about. If you like that style, place your order now because **99** is about as good as it gets (extra incentive: only 500 cases made): great scented waves of tar/choc/fennel roar into mulberry jam, charry palate rippling with alc; blast of oak needs to settle and meld with fruit, which it should do given time. Malmesbury fruit. Yr oaked. 13,5% alc.

· ·

Hazendal Estate

Stellenbosch (see Stellenbosch map) • Tasting & sales Mon—Fri 9—4.30 Sat/Sun 10—3.30 Tasting fee R10 p/p for groups of more than 10 • Cellar tours weekdays at 11 & 3 R10 p/p (includes tasting) • Full à la carte restaurant (see Eat-out section) • Conferences • Tourgroups by appointment • Museum of Russian Art & Culture • Gift shop • Play area for children • Views • 4x4 trailing by appointment • Wheelchair-friendly • Owner Mark Voloshin • Winemaker Ronell Wiid (since 1998) • Viticultural consultants VinPro • Vineyards 66 ha • Production 400 tons, 20 000 cases 85% white 15% red • PO Box 336 Stellenbosch 7599 • Tel (021) 903-5112 • Fax (021) 903-0057 • E-mail info@hazendal.co.za • Website www.wineroute.co.za

IT'S EASY to be blinded by all the glittery trimmings at this estate: its exotic Moscow-born owner Mark Voloshin, chairman of the international Marvol Group; its in-house Marvol Museum of Russian Art and Culture; its Fabergé showroom (more than mere eggs); its "fashion extravaganza" and classical music evenings; its "corporate entertainment and team-building" facilities (4x4 driver training, clay shoots, quad biking); its swish restaurant; the dramatic contrast between its old, national monument facade and its super-chic modern interior ... Voloshin has pulled off a dazzling makeover of this three-centuries-old property. But don't let all this obscure the message here: what it really shows off is a commitment to quality, rather than flash, and in modest winemaker Ronell Wiid you find the perfect illustration of that. Winner of South Africa's loftiest Diners Club's 1999 Winemaker of the Year award (Jancis Robinson the imported judge), for the 98 Hazendal Estate Shiraz Cabernet (made while lugging 3-month-old Harry around the cellar, nursing him between barrels), she's first astounded, then delighted, finally worried. "I have to prove that this wasn't a flash in the pan! Prove that Hazendal wines are worthy winners." Those who know these 66 ha vineyards in the quality Bottelary neighbourhood and those who remember her flair from the Boschendal cellar (the Shiraz she made there currently wowing the crowds) will also know that Ronell Wiid has little to prove.

Hazendal Estate range

✿ **Shiraz-Cabernet Sauvignon** Controversial — and close — winner of Diners Club award for Ronell Wiid. Upset many that a wine *sans* home-grown pinotage could win a Cape Blend category, but proof's in this **98** bottle, which now opening to reveal full charms: intense spicy fruit dominated by smoky shiraz (55%) with bushvine cab blackcurrant refinement, cigar box subtlety, firm tannic support. 15% 2nd fill Nadalie Am oak gives extra zest. **99** (correctly Cabernet Sauvignon-Shiraz — cab leads here) delicious; richer, sumptuous blackberry fruits shielding shiraz spice. No green tannins/excess wood (both anathema to Wiid). "Cab and shiraz better together than alone," states winemaker.

✿Merlot 🆕 Will be regular "but not big" feature of range as quantities are small. Second crop **99** (barrel sample) peppery/spicy rather than opulent merlot fruit; soft tannins reflect Wiid's preference (although it got "the whole wood treatment and all of that"). Trifle short at present, this has potential once young vines mature.

✿Chardonnay Promising **99**, fermented/aged in Burgundian barrels, oozing wood vanilla at present, ripe peach/toasted hazelnut aromas lead to creamy mouthful. 1st release **98** from young vines, flew out of cellar (some into Blue Train's wine list).

✿White Nights Brut Cap Classique 98 Expansively and strikingly packaged MCC, released as Cuvée de l'An 2000 for millennium festivities. Active bead enhances desire, yeasty marzipan weight to otherwise light and very refreshing mouthful. Cleansing/enervating despite low acid. 1st crop 50/50 pinot noir/chardonnay, 15 mths on lees, likely to gain gravitas as vineyards develop.

Sauvignon Blanc ✿ Tank sample of **00** shows ripe, fresh tropical fruit, extra dimension from extended skin contact; crisp and dry. Unfussy, best so far. "Vineyard work paying off," explains Wiid. **Chenin Blanc** (wooded) ✿ More serious than non-oaked version below. **99** broadened by year in bottle: honeyed nose but fresh sweet-sour fruit lingers in mouth, resists any oak dominance. 13,5% alc. Super food/restaurant wine. (**00** not tasted as blend incomplete). 50% gets full (fermented/aged) Fr/Am oak treatment, rest stainless steel.

Kleine Hazen range

'Little Hares', allusion to farm's German founder (1699), Christoffel Hazenwinkel, literally "hares' corner". Does not carry estate name as includes bought in grapes.

✿Reserve Red Not a serious wine needing prolonged ageing, but a delightful, available, unwooded blend shiraz/merlot/cab. Latest **99** peppered with warm spice, plump ripe fruit, trademark soft tannins. Quality above its station; a great drink if the intellectual focus is elsewhere. Good quality Dbnville grape source.

Pinotage ✿ 🆕 For UK market only, response to demand. **99** unequivocal unwooded pinotage; candyfloss nose, packed with ripe bananas/clove/cinnamon. Easy tannins, for drinking without too much thinking. **Chenin Blanc** ✿ Unwooded **00** best yet, from 30 yr old bushvines yielding paltry 3 t/ha. Concentration shows in billowing honeyed tropical melange (melon/guava/pear/pineapple), ends full and dry. Drink young. **Konynwijn** ✿ Another play on the hare theme. **99** semi-sweet unwooded chenin, made for own restaurant. Still bristling with guava/melon/spice. 13,5% alc adds body.

....

Heerenhof

POPULAR budget-priced 5 ℓ vat range from DGB. All NV.

Dry Red ✣ Good vinous character, bit of tannin balanced by almost fresh-grapey red fruit. Clean, dry, med-bodied. **Grand Cru** ✣ Straightforward dry white from chenin. Med-bodied. **Stein** ✣ Equatorial fruits samba in soft, pleasing palate. Good lightish casual quaff. **Late Harvest** ✣ Plain and simple honeyed semi-sweet.

....

Helderberg Winery

Stellenbosch (see Helderberg map) • Tasting Mon—Fri 9—5 Sat 9—4.30 Closed Sun Sales Mon—Fri 9—5.30 Sat 9—3 • Cellar tours by appointment • Country lunches daily except Sun Book ahead Tel (021) 842-2012 • Owner Stellenbosch Vineyards • Head winemaker Chris Kelly • Winemaker Elizabeth Augustyn • PO Box 465 Stellenbosch 7599 • Tel (021) 842-2371 or 881-3870 • Fax (021) 842-2373 or 881-3102

EXCELLENT maritime/mountain-influenced vineyards supply this winery, part of the Stellenbosch Vineyards operation (see that entry). Helderberg's own labels are easy on palates/pockets.

Merlot-Cabernet Sauvignon ✲✲ Bright spicy plums in oaked-aged quaffable **99**, extra interest from soft choc undertones. Tannins non-interfering yet sufficient to stand up to most rustic meat dishes. **Cinsaut-Cabernet Sauvignon** ✷ Very smooth, soft **99**; welcomingly unjammy, long fruity tail. Oak-influenced. **Chenin Blanc-Sauvignon Blanc** ✷ **00** follows fresh figs and honey tones of **99** plus hint of leesy richness; fresh, cool feel, despite sturdy 13,5% alc. Soupçon residual sugar adds to all-round drinkability.

Cabernet Sauvignon ✲✲ **99** displays vintage's appealing elegance in refined blackberry/sweet mulberry/cassis fragrance; very fresh, mouthcoating though not heavy, satisfyingly dry. 30% Fr oak, none new. **Pinotage** ✷ Instantly recognisable redcurrants softened with touch flattering oak. Light textured, pleasant fruity bite, less alluring sweet/roughish finish. **Chardonnay** ✲✲ Delightful **00**; just enough oatmealy warmth, oak spice to lift out of vin ordinaire category; more spry citrusy palate but nothing brash. "Quintessential café wine — one can drink bottle after bottle," Chris Kelly assures. 25% barrel-fermented. **Chenin Blanc Reserve** ✲✲ Fairly serious new-wave oaked example, usually most civilised but **00** quite a whopper (14% alc), unyielding when tasted mid-2000; oak nicely judged but still bit apart. So give time to settle into itself. 30% barrel-fermented. **Chenin Blanc** ✷ Characteristic tropical generosity of ripe chenin in semi-dry **00**; full bodied with harmonising dash sugar; more food than aperitif style. **Sauvignon Blanc** ✲✲ Hints of gooseberry and asparagus in juicily upbeat **00**; good persistence, varietal bite but nothing over-assertive. **Port** ✷ Very fruity, sweetish **97** with agreeably surprising spicy kick. 18,6% alc.

Helderkruin Wine Cellar

Stellenbosch (see Stellenbosch map) • Tasting, sales, cellar tours Mon—Fri 9—5 Sat 9—1 • Light meals mid-Dec to mid-Jan • Tourgroups • Gifts • Views • Wheelchair-friendly • Owner Neil du Toit • Winemaker Koos Bosman (since 1998) • Viticulturist Pietie Goosen • Vineyards 80 ha • Production 800 tons (200 tons 10 000 cases own label) 85% red 15% white • PO Box 91 Stellenbosch 7599 • Tel (021) 881-3899 • Fax (021) 881-3898 • E-mail helkruin@iafrica.com • Website www.helderbergwineroute.co.za

KOOS BOSMAN, who makes the wines at this sunny yellow cellar, looks for innovative tastes in both his wine and food (he's very taken with Australian fusion cuisine and tunes into the Carlton food channel for inspiration). He's following his love of painting (oils are his medium) at art classes and has already participated in several group exhibitions in Stellenbosch. He still finds time to craft his wines, in particular a new reserve pinotage honouring ex-Springbok Ben du Toit, who in 68 bought Helderkruin (originally part of the Groenerivier farm, one of the earliest land grants in this area in the 1700s), who passed it on to his son Niel. The Workers Cape Port led to channels being opened for an 'empowerment' wine (from the workers' trust's own label) for a university in the UK. The profits from these wines — "just a beginning" — will fund projects chosen by the workers.

Helderkruin range

Ben du Toit Special Reserve Pinotage N̲e̲w̲ Champion red wine on 1999 SAY-WS. Previewed from (specially made Am/Fr oak) barrels, **99** tightly shut, oaky, unyielding. Some mulberry/minty notes. Unrated. 250 cases. **Cabernet Sauvignon** ⚡ Oak aged **99** starts with sweet-ripe plums but turns very dry, tannic in finish. **Merlot** ⚡ Interesting peppery presence in **99**'s plummy background, soft tannins and hint of oak, finish bone dry. 13% alc. 1 000 cases. **Shiraz** Latest **99** (sample) showed similar ⚡ form to pvs when tasted mid-2000. Shiraz woodsmoke, wild scrub , cinnamon, all tapering to dry finish. Very low-yielding (3 t/ha) vyd. 16 mths Fr/Am oak. 13% alc. 1 000 cases. **Chardonnay** ★ Light-bodied **98** very honeyed, past its best. 11,5% alc. **Sauvignon Blanc 00** (sample) with sherbety/lemony tones, light hint of sweetness, should rate ⚡ on release. 450 cases. **Forté** ⚡ Individual unwooded sauvignon. Some light papaya/mango tones in full-bodied **98**, but finishes austerely dry. Food wine. 13% alc. **Semillon 98** past its prime. 13% alc. **Phyllis Hands Cap Classique** ⚡ Tribute to Cape wine educator, writer and, lately, -grower, Phyllis Hands. Pleasingly spartan, biscuity **98**, intensely active bubbles race to bracingly fresh finish. 100% chardonnay, 10 mths on lees. ±11% alc. 500 cases. **Workers Vintage** ★ This **98** 'port' crushed the traditional way by farmhands. Some oaky, liquorice tastes. 19,5% alc.

Yellow Cellar range

Dry Red ⚡ Cinsaut in unsophisticated quaffing mode, with some gentle strawberry 'sweetness' in **99**. 13% alc. **Dry White** ⚡ Soft, simple **98** with resin/spice hints. 11,62% alc.

. . . .

Hercules Paragon see Simonsvlei

. . . .

Here XVII

WELL ESTABLISHED and reliable NV sparkler from the Bergkelder cellars.
Souverein ⚡ Latest with dollop of muscat — though the move is to 100% sauvignon. Clean, pleasant carbonated bubbly, with touch of sweetness.

. . . .

Hermanus Heritage Collection

"A LIBRARY of South African wine", is how Paul du Toit describes his Wine Village shop at the entrance to Hemel-en-Aarde valley. Not that the comparison in any way suggests a wide-eyed and whispering wine audience. The separate white/red 'streets' of the Village are frequently filled with all kinds of visitors — sampling the daily selection or debating their way through the sections. And invariably lingering over the Hermanus Heritage Collection ▼, six wines selected from Walker Bay cellars featuring striking front labels by artist David Errington. Funds from sales go to a local shelter for homeless children and adults. PO Box 465 Hermanus 7200 • Tel (028) 316-3988 • Fax (028) 316-3989 • E-mail wine@hermanus.co.za • Website www.wine-village.co.za

Shiraz ⚡ Swashbuckling **99** all the shiraz you need (farmyardy smoke, pepper etc) for good solo tippling or with a good hearty casserole (cassoulet?). By Bartho Eksteen. **Merlot** ⚡ **97**, from WhaleHaven (next door to Wine Villlage), maturing well; cool-climate class and compactness. **Cabernet Franc-Merlot** ⚡ Unready **98** redolent of wild scrub, fennel, capsicum; puckering tannins need 2–3 yrs. **Chardonnay** ⚡ Partially barrel fermented **98** from Newton Johnson; Chablis-style restraint; chalky citrus and some Old World 'damp cellar' character. **Crispy White** ⚡ **99** Partly barrel fermented blend chardonnay/chenin/colombar ex-Wildekrans. Toasty limes/lemons, soft (not crispy!), balanced. **Chenin Blanc** ⚡ Here's the 'crispy white'! **97**, from Beaumont, lively with drop of honey, quite rich, refined. These all 13–13,5% alc. 500 cases.

Hex see Overhex
Hexagon see Overhex

Hidden Valley Wines

Stellenbosch • Sales Mon–Fri 9–5 • Owner Dave Hidden • Winemakers Jeremy Walker (from 1997) with Guy Webber (1997/8) • Viticulturist Johan Grobbelaar (since 1999) • Vineyards 16 ha (rising to 36) • Production 45 tons 100% red • PO Box 12577 Die Boord Stellenbosch 7613 • Tel (021) 855-0296 • Fax (021) 855-0297 • E-mail hiddenvalley@mweb.co.za • Website www.hiddenvalleywines.com

JOHANNESBURG-BASED Dave and Margie Hidden are a very bio-tuned couple and they've now begun to implement their ideals in their two prime Stellenbosch vineyards (23 ha in Devon Valley, already planted, 28 ha on the Helderberg to be planted); no plastic covers, but natural mulch, for example. And it's work *with* the bugs, not against them. Only a few minimalist sulphur sprays. This is all still orchestrated from Gauteng (they run an ozone-friendly aerosol business) but they plan to build a home on the Helderberg and probably, eventually, a winery too. Ex-Nietvoorbij scientist Johan Grobbelaar is the enthusiastic vineyardist cajoling *with* nature. Grangehurst for the time being will be the home of Hidden Valley wines. Jeremy Walker and Hidden — who is a qualified wine-maker too — both studied at Stellenbosch University, then did MBAs together and went on to work for BP. Walker responded first to the call of the vineyards, but the Hiddens have followed. Their stunning wines — on a small scale so far, and confined to pinotage and now a new cabernet — from Walker's Helderberg cellar herald a major new Cape label. The focus will remain entirely on reds: pinotage, the two cabernets, merlot and shiraz.

Pinotage Standout, with a lengthening pedigree (from **96** debut) and **99** again offering an unusually fine supple-and-structured combination; perfumed, with ripe sweet juiciness and some drying rhubarb, tannin twists in finish — for keeping. All from prime Devon Valley vyd, made by Jeremy Walker at Grangehurst, a pinotage boffin who believes the grape absorbs plenty of oak well — sometimes in these Hidden Valley labels giving them a long, almost claret-like, spicy length. **97** remains in class of its own, *Wine* ✸, 1999 ABSA Top Ten; inky, concentrated violets/cinnamon with plummy, mouthfilling succulence. (All new oak). **98** continues quality and depth of pvs, marginally drier, perhaps less persistent finish — given about 15 mths in 1st–3rd fill oak, about one-third Am. 13,8% alc. 1 400 cases. **96** ABSA Top Ten, even more appeal than its excellent Grangehurst stablemates. **CWG Auction Pinotage 98** striking collector's pinotage, more of the above, plus trimmings (more new oak): a riper, more perfumed intensity, richer array of spices; darkly juicy and luscious; greater persistence in finish.

Cabernet Sauvignon New **99** barrel sample but should join big league, perhaps even cult potential: showing youthful purple depths, outstanding ripe mulberry/cassis and minerally spiciness in palate with *drinkable* tannins already. From purchased grapes, two vyds, Helderberg/Firgrove.

High Constantia

Constantia (see Constantia map) • Tasting, sales, cellar tours by appointment • Owners/winemakers/viticulturists Bob de Villiers & David van Niekerk • Vineyards 14 ha (owned/leased) • Production 25 tons (rising to 125 tons) 88% red 12% white • Puck's Glen Groot Constantia Road Constantia 7800 • Tel (021) 794-7971/082-494-5671 • E-mail davidvn@mweb.co.za

A NEW CELLAR on the very old, very established Constantia block with its handful of wineries has just opened its sales (and, soon, tasting) doors to the public. It's a joint venture between Groot Constantia winemaker Bob de Villiers, growing serious roots in this valley since his transplant from the Klein Karoo, and financier David van Niekerk. "Two years ago we made a few barrels of wine from the small vineyard at van Niekerk's home (Puck's Glen) on part of what was the original farm High Constantia. We subsequently found one or two untapped parcels in the area, from which we can buy grapes in return for managing them," says De Villiers, who will initially act as advisor, with Van Niekerk doing the lion's share of the work ("He has much more time on his hands than I," de Villiers quips.) These well-travelled partners have just completed the cellar and it's been a time of "decisions, decisions", with many final ones still to be made. What's for sure is that they will only be using grapes from Constantia, despite the very real challenge of urban creep. Wines below all **00** barrel samples, too young to rate.

Cabernet Franc Even in formative stage, undoubtedly the star of this show. Ripe mulberry, minerally tones, sweet violets and hints of choc, good grip. Low cropped vyds (4 t/ha). New 300 ℓ Vicard barrels. 400 cases. **Cabernet Sauvignon** Good backbone of fruit/tannin. Promising. 300 ℓ Fr oak, some new. 1 000 cases. **Chardonnay** Toasty butterscotch introduction; still acidic, oak dominant, but potentially very good. Barrel fermented/aged 300 ℓ Fr casks. 100 cases.

. . . .

Hildenbrand Estate

Wellington (see Wellington map) • Tasting, sales, cellar tours daily 10—6 Tasting R5 p/p if no wine purchased • Light Mediterranean meals daily, served in weinstübe or on terrace • Klein Rhebokskloof Guest & Country House, offering many amenities • Tourgroups up to 15 people • Small conferences • Walks • Views • Wheelchair-friendly • Owner Reni Hildenbrand • Winemaker Reni Hildenbrand, with Benoit Roque • Viticulturist Reni Hildenbrand • Vineyards 14 ha • Production 100 tons (2 000 cases own label) 50/50 red/white • PO Box 270 Wellington 7655 • Tel/fax (021) 873-4115 • E-mail info@wine-estate-hildenbrand.co.za • Website www.wine-estate-hildenbrand.co.za

WHEN RENI HILDENBRAND'S husband's life was cut short, the former Gauteng-based interior architect lived out his dream of running a wine and olive farm in the Boland. She took over the historic Rhebokskloof property in 1991, renovated the manor house and now, with Lore Rohmer and Antje Purbhoo, runs a luxury guesthouse and restaurant. A local co-op still gets a portion of the grapes — mainly cabernet sauvignon, chardonnay and chenin, with unharvested shiraz and semillon pointing to the future — but most of the crop now travels no further than the 1853 cellar, which has been revamped to Reni Hildenbrand's specifications (former owners, seventh generation Cillies, are so impressed they bring friends to see the changes!). Flying in for the crush is Bordelaise eminence Benoit Roque, whose fine tuning is aimed at "a non-copycat South African style". The super-palates at Vinitaly, who tasted the maiden unwooded Chardonnay felt it sufficiently distinctive to pin a Gran Menzione ribbon.

❀ **Cabernet Sauvignon** (wooded) "International wine guru Robert Parker might appreciate this great wine," states Reni Hildenbrand, tongue only partially in cheek (?). Certainly *we* appreciated **99**'s sappy cassis, vanilla oak richness, concentration and length — narrowly missed ❀. Very light bitterness in finish only blemish in otherwise commendable debut. Yr Fr oak. 13,5% alc. 570 cases.

Cabernet Sauvignon (Unwooded) ❀ **99** features mouthwatering freshness, keen tannins which anchor — dont'd overwhelm — juicy cab fruit. Good now, especially with food, or over 2–4 yrs. 13,5% alc. 360 cases. **Chardonnay** (unwooded) ☘ Several 'un-s' here: *un*pretentious, *un*fettered by oak, *un*usually compact and dry for SA chardonnay — which partly explains Vinitaly judges' enthusiasm for **99**, which gastronome Reni Hildenbrand pours with Tuscan bean soup or roast pheasant with polenta. 13% alc. 250 cases. **Chardonnay** (wooded) ❀ Slenderness the main feature of this oaked **99** version, too. 7 mths Fr barrelling adds length rather than breadth. 13% alc. 250 cases. **Chenin Blanc** ❀ Like first release **99** ☘, latest **00** (sampled from tank) in sinewy mode, very fresh, very dry, some finishing green apple tartness. 375 cases.

Hilltop

CERTIFIED, VINTAGE DATED BAG IN THE BOX WINE offering remarkable value. Launched 1999, the original unwooded Ruby Cabernet and Chardonnay in 2 ℓ boxes still available. By Stellenbosch Farmers' Winery.

> **Ruby Cabernet** ✦ 😊 Flashy headline of mulberries, green peppers, light smoky/toasty sidebars, gentle tannins in spirited farewell. **Chardonnay** ✦ 😊 'Sweet' butterscotch toasty creaminess freshened by twist of lime. Bright clean finish. Both **99**, med-bodied.

Hinterland see Hartswater

Hippo Creek

VALUE range for Picardi-Rebel liquor chain. Not available for tasting (pvs ratings in brackets).

Cabernet Sauvignon (✦) **98** Stbosch fruit 50% yr Fr oak. **Pinotage** (✦) **99** blend Worcester/Stbosch grapes, unoaked. **Chardonnay** (✦) **00** 40% oak matured, ex-Rawsonville.

Honey Blossom

INTRODUCED IN 1965, this Stellenbosch Farmers' Winery brand was taken off the market and re-launched some 20 years later. Semi-sweet white of consistent quality; available in 750 ml as well as 2, 4 ℓ and 5 ℓ packs; 5 ℓ plastic containers were introduced in 1999. Untasted.

Hoopenburg

Stellenbosch (but see Paarl map) • Tasting & sales Mon—Fri 9—5 Sat & public holidays 9.30—1 Fee R10 p/p refundable with purchases of 6 bottles or more • Cellar tours by appointment • Views • Owner/winemaker/viticulturist Ernst Gouws • Vineyards 35 ha • Production 20 000 cases 70% red 30% white • PO Box 1233 Stellenbosch 7599 • Tel (021) 884-4221/2 • Fax (021) 884-4904 • E-mail hoopen@new.co.za • Website www.hoopenburgwines.co.za

IF THERE'S ONE winemaker whose 'selection' you could blindly trust, it's Ernst Gouws'. So when Hoopenburg's all-in-one dynamo (he's the owner, winemaker, viticulturist and, in the words of wife and staunch supporter Gwenda, "charismatic marketer") launches a Winemaker's Selection reserve range, you're virtually assured it will not only taste great, but offer good value too. "Serious effort" went into this new line-up, which currently features a Cabernet Sauvignon and a Chardonnay (he hopes to include a Merlot soon). Gouws' wines have won raves in Ireland, England and Germany, which he ascribes to "quality, service and price". Relentless in his search for quality, Gouws did not hesitate to strip his pinot vineyards of nearly half their bunches during the growing season to create a more concentrated wine.

✦ **Winemaker's Selection Cabernet Sauvignon** 🏅 Great charm and personality in **98**, with Bdx-like feel (which possibly why chosen for KLM Business Class — also flew with SAA). Warm core of cassis wrapped in stylish oak; good light savoury fruitcake whiffs, moderate 12,5% alc. Yr new Fr casks (pvs releases unwooded). Grapes ex-Muldersvlei, Bottelary, Malmesbury. Crop thinned to 6 t/ha for extra intensity. 1 300 cases.

✦ **Merlot** 🏅 Tighter grained, more compact version of this habitually approachable wine, **99** deserves time to unveil its considerable charms. Plush red-velvet texture with mulberries, cut-grass, whiffs of best fresh thatch; some tobacco in soft, 'sweet' redcurrant finish. 5 mths new Fr/Am oak. 13% alc. 1 000 cases.

98 more approachable at same age, fleshy with trademark ripe wraparound tannins.

✿**Pinot Noir** Deep ruby colour hints at much improved quality in this elegant **99**; more intense, fragrant, flavoursome than any pvs. Wild cherry/raspberry, some smoky/gamey whiffs — all in balance. Own fruit, aged 5 mths 2nd fill Fr casks. Ernst Gouws suggests you try with escargot, porcini risotto or turkey roast. 12,6% alc. 720 cases.

✿**Winemaker's Selection Chardonnay** ▼ **98**, under 'regular' label, gold on France's Vinalies 2000 competition. **99** ✿ features usual fine oak/fruit balance, flavoursome marmalade toast flavours, manageable alc (12,8%), lovely creamy finish. Yet mid-2000 not quite as lusciously mouthfilling as pvs, though might simply be slow starter. Barrel fermented/aged yr new Fr oak. 500 cases.

✿**Sauvignon Blanc** ▼ Unwooded, non-aggressive example, properly dry; good standalone sip and versatile at table. **99** big, power-packed yet friendly. Med-bodied **00** ✿ uncharacteristically steely, sharp when tasted mid-2000. Give bit of time to settle. 2 000 cases.

Huguenot Wine Farmers

Wellington • Not open to the public • Owner Kosie Botha • Cellarmaster Bill Matthee (since 1984) • Trade enquiries Gert Brynard • PO Box 275 Wellington 7654 • Tel (021) 864-1293 • Fax (021) 873-2075

PRIVATELY-OWNED WHOLESALER which blends, markets and distributes table and dessert wines, liqueurs and spirits. The range (not assessed) includes: **Cabernet Sauvignon**, **Pinotage**, **Smooth Red** (cinsaut, splash pinotage), **Premier Grand Cru**, (chenin/Cape riesling), **Stein** (semi-sweet chenin), **Late Harvest** and **Special Late Harvest** (both chenin), **Hanepoot**, **White Muscadel**, **Red Jeripico** and **White Jeripico** (red/white muscadel), **Invalid Port**, **Tawny Port**, **Nagmaalwyn**, and carbonated bubblies **Valentine Cerise** (pinot noir semi-sweet pink), **Valentine Vin Doux** (chenin, clairette blanche).

Hutton Ridge see Arlington
Inglewood see Neil Ellis

Ingwe   New

Helderberg • Not open to the public • Owner Alain Mouiex • Winemaker Etienne Charrier (since 2000) • Viticulturist Francois Baard (since 1999) • 3 ha producing in 2000 (8 ha coming into production 2001) • Production 13 tons • Château Mazeyres 56 Avenue Georges Pompidou 33500 Libourne France • Tel 0933-55-757-0048 • Fax 0933-55-725-2256 • E-mail MAZEYRES@wanadoo.fr

A BIG BORDEAUX name brings considerable cachet and savoir faire to this sea-breezy vineyard near Somerset West. While Alain Mouiex leaves his Pomerol base at Ch Mazeyres four times a year to consult in the Cape — for his joint-venture with Winecorp, the premium Naledi and Sejana labels — here at Ingwe is his own stake in South African soil. Sauvignon blanc and chardonnay vineyards were in place when he invested in this 40 ha farm, and his years in New Zealand should impact here. But the future focus is firmly on reds — no prizes for detecting a French accent — with 20 ha already planted by viticulturist-manager Francois Baard. Ch Angelus-trained winemaker Etienne Charrier has up to now flown around France under the Moueix consultancy banner; now he's re-locating to South Africa for Ingwe and Siyabonga (partner Graham Knox's Wellington farm). Alain Moueix weighs in during the 6–8 weeks which he annually spends at this, his Cape home-from-home. Predictably, the first fruits are full of élan, and because this is a vine-yard-only property were handled at Havana Hills winery.

✿**Chardonnay** Potential of the maritime Schaapenberg terroir amply reflected in this entirely barrel fermented debut **00**, which impresses with soft citrus/tropical fruit amplitude, butterscotch richness and seamlessly absorbed oak. Positive firmness, crispness in finish hint at good development — and possible ✿ luminosity — over 2–3 yrs. Single vyd on Ingwe property. Fr oak, mix new/2nd/3rd fill. 13,5% alc.

Sauvignon Blanc ✿ Quieter style: doesn't trumpet or jump about, yet not lacking personality. Fresh acidity balanced by tropical fruit with fragrant hints of mango. Embryonic when sampled mid-2000; could grow into more extrovert individual.

Inkawu see Laibach
Interlude see Verdun

International Wine Services—Pacific Wines

Production 700 000 cases 60% white 40% red • 5 Baring Road Beaconsfield Buckinghamshire HP9 2NB United Kingdom • Tel (1494) 68-0857 • Fax (1494) 68-0382 • 21 Pison Street Eden Stellenbosch 7600 South Africa • Tel/fax (021) 880-1282 • E-mail iwsinsa@new.co.za • Website www.wine-info.co.uk

UK-BASED FLYING winemakers Kym Milne and Alistair Maling, with SA-based, Barossa Valley-born John Weeks, work with cellars in Stellenbosch, Wellington, Worcester and Robertson, producing an annual 700 000 cases targeted at the British market. The millennium was marked with the launch of an IWS website, the release of the new Apostles Falls range, and Weeks's 20th vintage — which he rates as delivering the highest quality overall in the 3 years this group, with projects spread around the winemaking world, has operated in the Cape.

Apostles Falls range   New

✿ **Cabernet Sauvignon** Good varietal character with cedar spice from 10 mths Fr oak over cassis/mulberry fruit; mid-2000 fair amount of **99** tannin which needs further maturation or sturdy cuisine. 13% alc.

Merlot Big, chunky style with sweet-violets and minerals; severe tannins in this preview **99** sample (unrated).

✿ **Chardonnay 99** Assertive, oaked style with unusual spread of well defined citrus — lemon/lime/orange and some marmalade — plus light brush of vanilla in bright, brisk palate with peach-pip in the conclusion. 13% alc. 50% barrel fermented, 8 mths aged.

Also available, not tasted: River/Fontein range: **Cinsaut-Merlot, Merlot, Chardonnay**; Kleinbosch range: **Cabernet Sauvignon Reserve, Young Vatted Pinotage, Bush Vine Muscat, Chenin Blanc/Sauvignon Blanc**; Plantation range: **Ruby Cabernet, Semillon**; Cape View/Winelands range: **Cabernet Sauvignon, Merlot, Pinotage, Cinsaut-Shiraz, Cinsaut-Tinta Barocca, Shiraz-Cabernet Sauvignon, Chardonnay, Chenin Blanc-Sauvignon Blanc, Chenin Blanc-Muscat**; Rylands Grove range: **Cinsaut-Tinta Barocca**, Barrel-fermented **Chenin Blanc; Chenin Blanc-Colombard, Muscat, Sauvignon Blanc**; Chiwara range New: **Pinotage, Cinsaut-Ruby Cabernet, Colombard-Sauvignon Blanc**; Frasers Bay New: **Cabernet Sauvignon, Pinotage, Chardonnay, Chenin Blanc**.

Jacaranda Estate   ▼ ♈ 🍴 ▼

Wellington (see Wellington map) • Tasting, sales, cellar tours Mon—Fri 10—5 Sat 10—1 (but phone ahead). • Self-catering guest house/B&B • Cheese made, olives grown on property • 1-km "leg stretch" • Views • Owners Jan & Trish Tromp • Winemaker/viticulturist Jan Tromp • Vineyards 2,8 ha • Production 25 tons (300 cases own label) PO Box 121 Wellington 7654 • Tel (021) 864-1235

THE RUSTIC CHARMS of Jan and Trish Tromp's tiny estate — vineyards just 2,8 ha, total area just over 4 ha — now also include home-made cheese and home-grown olives ("subject to cow and crop co-operation"). And a little Cape Dutch cottage in the vineyards — scones, farm butter and serene mountain views on its bed-and-breakfast menu. The Jacaranda wines are real rarities — only 300 cases are produced — and as individual as the cellar in which they're produced, Jan Tromp's inventive make-over of an old, circular reservoir.

Merlot ✲ Unwooded **99** combines winegum and smoky mulberry tastes in big (14% alc) soft, ripe glassful, with alluring plum/purple colour. **Chenin Blanc** ★ Returns to guide in **99** with usual totally idiosyncratic (French?) style: organic smells, jab of alc (14%), Karoo scrubby whiffs and bone-dry finish. **Jerepigo** ✲ Individual and good, **96** fortified dessert from chenin scented with bees-wax, honey, rooibos tea; sweetness balanced by fine thrill of acid. 18% alc. Also available (but not ready to taste), two chenins, both dry: **Golden Oldie 99** and **Schuss 95**.

. . . .

Jacobsdal Estate

Stellenbosch • Tasting & sales at Bergkelder (see that entry) • Owner C H Dumas Trust • Winemakers/viticulturists Cornelis & Hannes Dumas • Vineyards 105 ha • Production 150—200 tons (7 000—10 000 cases own label) 100% red • PO Box 11 Kuils River 7579 • Tel/fax (021) 905-1360 • E-mail dumas@iafrica.com

PINOTAGE PIONEER Cornelis Dumas, having specialised in the local grape since he took over the family farm from his father Hansie in 1966, says he's now ready to try a "Cabernet Sauvignon with just a touch of merlot and cabernet franc". No doubt his many fans, some as far away as Norway, Sweden and the Benelux nations, will loudly applaud. Yet while Dumas' vision is of the Médoc, his soul is rooted in Burgundy, where he recently travelled and marvelled anew at the "widespread use of traditional methods including natural yeast fermentation" — the very philosophies he's always advocated and practised. A resolutely low-profile man of the soil, Dumas credits his father with instilling the belief that "only absolute dedication and the pursuit of quality can ensure success in the wine business".

✲**Pinotage** One of the originals and still among best. Since **94** ABSA Top Ten, Vinexpo gold, more modern, approachable, brighter, with still firm tannin structure for development. **95** VVG, SAA, twice-in-a-row ABSA Top Ten. **96** another individual; broad, smoky with restraining tannins needing couple of yrs to soften. Latest **97** ✲, in a cooler, 'European' vintage, spreads more rustic charms with Jacobsdal's signature restraint. Farmyard whiffs and tar, earthy stone-fruit and smoky plums carry into very dry palate. Despite big alc (13,8%) and some subliminal sugar (3,4 g/ℓ), effect is sinewy, almost austere, something like traditional Barolo. Highly individual, not conventional pinotagey at all (so will have its own appeal). These from 25–33 yr old unirrigated bushvines. Natural yeasts, fermented in open kuipe, freerun juice only, 12–18 mths small Fr oak, 13% alc. 7 600 cases.

. . . .

Jacques Pinard

INTERNATIONAL SELECTION of wines from the greater wine producing regions of the world, sold under the name of wine négociant Jacques Pinard. Varieties/styles chosen to appeal to local consumers; the wines vary from year to year, with a red and white released annually in 1 000 ml bottles.

Sauvignon Blanc-Semillon ✲ **99** still bright and quaffable, lemon/lime, cut grass lift; invigorating dry finish. **Merlot** under this label is not from SA, it's from the Languedoc in France.

. . . .

JC le Roux

Stellenbosch (see Stellenbosch map) • Tasting & sales Mon—Fri 8.30—4.30 Sat 8.30—1 Closed Sun & public holidays Tasting fee R7.50 • Cellar tours, preceded by AV show, Mon—Fri 10, 11, 3 Also self-guided tours • Sparkling breakfasts, light lunches Mon—Fri 11—3. • Conferences • Tourgroups • Gifts • Views • Wheelchair-friendly • Owner SA Distilleries & Wine • Winemaker Melanie van der Merwe (since 1994) • Farm manager/viticulturist Willem Laubsche

• Vineyards 25 ha • Production 620 000 cases 40% white sparkling, 22% red sparkling, 38% MCC • PO Box 184 Stellenbosch 7599 • Tel (021) 882-2590 • Fax (021) 882-2585 • E-mail jclr@dist.co.za

DEDICATED TO SPARKLING wine only, the House of JC le Roux — its resounding official name — is a one-stop cellar for bubbles enthusiasts. The choice runs from elegantly dry to pop-palate sweet; the methods from classic bottle fermentation — à la Champagne — to carbonation; the fan-club from Soweto (La Chanson red fizz is the toast of the townships) to London. Bubbly brunches and lunches are a feature, plus self-guided tours through the (super-stylish) cellar, set in the vineyards of pretty Devon Valley. Chef de cave, steering 620 000 cases annually, is energetic (scuba-diving) Melanie van der Merwe, whose personal wine inspiration is Madame Clicquot — "she made remuage so much easier!"

Pinot Noir One of the Cape's top cap classiques, exceptionally well priced. **89** VVG, *Wine* evolving steadily, wonderfully in bottle. Alluring lemon-straw colour; big, foamy mouthful; delicious, still fresh apple/strawberry/biscuit flavours, fine length and complexity through to satisfying dry finish. Amazing vitality for its age. 12% alc, 7,5 g/ℓ sugar. 10 000 cases.

Chardonnay Consistently excellent blanc de blancs MCC, 100% chardonnay. Still-stunning **91**, the current release, offers classic yeasty/citrus tones; terrific, austere flavours and long, elegant crisp-dry finish. 12% alc, 7,5 g/ℓ sugar. 1 000 cases. **90** *Wine* , **89** , *Wine* . These classically long matured — 5–9 yrs on lees. Malo complete, bottled without sulphur additions.

Pongrácz Excellent, consistent non-greedily priced **NV** MCC, winner of numerous local/international awards (including VVG, *Wine*). Pinot/chardonnay (60/40), min 2 yrs on lees. Signature apple/brioche tones, layered with toast and ripe fruit; firm, almost chewy dry mousse. Very satisfying anytime bubble. Named after late Desiderius Pongrácz (pronounce Pon-*grats*), aristocratic Hungarian army officer who became a controversial but much-loved Bergkelder viticulturist. 12% alc, 11 g/ℓ sugar. 40 000 cases.

Le Domaine Huge selling (245 000 cases) **NV** white carbonated fizz with crowd pleasing Asti-style floral/peachy/muscat tones, fiercely energetic bubbles, and low 7,5% alc for non-stop party fun. Sauvignon/muscadel. 76 g/ℓ sugar.

Sauvignon Blanc Extra-refreshing charmat fizz with 'sweet' candyfloss aromas in **00**, followed by bone-dry varietal green-pea/fig flavours. Bright crisp finish. 12,5% alc, 6,3 g/ℓ sugar. 38 000 cases.

La Chanson **NV** Hugely popular sweet red carbonated fizz from pinotage, with splash shiraz. Features extra-low alc (7,5%). Massive creamy mousse, delightful sweet strawberry fruit with some light tannins which make it appear less sweet than 78 g/ℓ sugar would suggest. Maintains fine standard despite being made in large quantities (120 000 cases). **La Vallée** Mould-breaking semi-dry MCC, with ± 30 g/ℓ sugar which gives impression of smoothness rather than sweetness. Very popular and a good introduction to the MCC style. Delicate earthy/organic tones in **98**, nutty/fruit salad flavours, very lively mousse. Well made, not as complex as house mates above, but satisfying. From pinot gris. 12,5% alc. 22 000 cases.

Jean Daneel Wines

Franschhoek • Tasting, sales, cellar tours by appointment • Owner/winemaker Jean Daneel • Production 2 800 cases • PO Box 1329 Stellenbosch 7599 • Tel 082-553-2101 • Fax (021) 887-8072/876 4914

"GOOD fruit, German precision and the temperament of the French" is the signature of this model family business — vastly experienced Jean Daneel (past Diners Club Winemaker of the Year), wife Rene and sons Jean-Pierre and Marchand — up to their elbows growing "natural and honest wines to be enjoyed with good food and good company." Jean Daneel, having made his reputation at Buitenverwachting and more recently in the cellars of Morgenhof, is enjoying the challenge of controlling his own destiny. Future plans, he says succinctly, are "to expand" — by which he means the 40 ton crush through his little converted stable in the Franschhoek valley. That's just for openers. Committed to grow the young Jean Daneel Wines *vigneron-negoce* business, this expert archer has taken aim — and knows how to hit his target.

❀ **Cabernet Sauvignon-Merlot** In classically elegant mould, neither French nor conventional Cape, an own style. **98**, exotic dark choc/spice, hints of mocha and ripe cassis — both varieties strutting their stuff. Finely tuned, firm structure supports 20 mths in 40% new Fr oak with aplomb; long creamy blackcurrant lingers in dry finish. Selected Stbosch grapes. 14% alc. 800 cases.

❀ **Chenin Blanc-Sauvignon Blanc 99** fragrant jasmine/talcum fragrance opens further to peaches-and-cream; bold, lemony dry palate shows no dominance of either variety in this balanced, flinty food wine. Should continue to develop in bottle couple of yrs. Stbosch/F'hoek fruit. 13,5% alc. 2 000 cases.

. . . .

Jean le Riche

POPULAR PAIR of NV carbonated sparklers from Simonsig, pioneers of cap classique. These show fine blending mastery of some of the estate's many grape varieties.

Vin Sec ☆ With pin-point bubble, well balanced semi-sweet aromatic blend of clairette blanche, chenin, riesling. **Vin Doux** ☆ More richness, sweetness in grapey palate; full-sweet, morio muscat and bukettraube complement each other well.

. . . .

John Faure see Ruitersvlei

. . . .

Jonkheer

🍷 🍷 🍷

Robertson (see Robertson map) • Tasting by appointment • Sales Mon–Fri 8–5 • Cellar tours by appointment • Views • Proclaimed conservation area • Owners Nicholas Jonker & Sons • Cellarmaster Erhard Roothman (since 1970) • Winemaker Dirk Jonker (since 1992) • Viticulturists Nicholas & Andries Jonker • Farm managers Gideon van Niekerk (since 1983), André Coetzee (since 1996) • Vineyards 150 ha • Production 2 000 tons 75% white 15% red 5% rosé 5% fortified • PO Box 13 Bonnievale 6730 • Tel (023) 616-2137/8 • Fax (023) 616-3146 • E-mail info@jonkheer.co.za • Website www.jonkheer.co.za

THE 'ULTRA-REVAMP' on NL Jonker Estate, Bonnievale home of the Bakenskop and premium Jonkheer ranges, continued throughout 2000 and ensured director/winemaker Dirk Jonker and his industrious family continued to have an impressively proportioned to-do list (Mon: prepare rocky slopes for red grapes; Tue: renovate cellar; Wed: plant first semillon & bottle first Chardonnay Reserve; Thu: finalise contract with French cooper to supply new barrels yearly; Fri: install new cooling plant for cold stabilisation). Somehow they found the time to open supply channels to the Movenpick hotel group in Switzerland as part of their aim to "establish Jonkheer as a premium range worldwide".

Jonkheer range

❀ **Pinotage** Most of **98** exported to Switzerland, where this lighter, more elegant, spicy/cherry style (with no off-putting acetone) won adherents. Full, accessible but firmish tannin probably mellower in yr or 2. 12,3% alc. No **99**.

❀ **Cabernet Sauvignon-Merlot** Somewhat forceful style with long chewy tannins, fair palate weight (12,8% alc). **98** violets/minty scents to cassis/black cherry, creamy oak. **99**'s youthful exuberance still trammelled by tannins, so give bit of time to settle.

❊**Chardonnay Reserve** New Serious, classically styled **00**, well fleshed with pineapple/mango/oak vanilla; very good flinty-dry finish. 100% new oak fermented.

Chardonnay ❊ Unwooded, full-bodied version leads with intensely ripe, almost sweet pear/citrus in **99**; ends properly dry with melon/apple. Lie-in on lees plumps palate. ±13% alc. **Muscatheer** ❊ Individual new-wave fortified dessert targeting European taste for lower alcs/sugars. **NV**. Super honeysuckle/spring flower fragrance, fine acid 'lift', dryish finish. 15% alc, 120 g/ℓ sugar; muscat de frontignan, splash gewürz.

Bakenskop range

❊**Red Muscadel** Where Dirk Jonker makes the New Age euro-muscat above, Erhard Roothman created this this ultra-traditional, ravishingly sweet number (and counterpart below). Mouth-warming, gloss-textured **98** oozes muscat, yet lacks the white version's exhilarating acidity.

❊**White Muscadel** No mistaking the grape variety in this billowing raisiny fortified dessert; **98** virtually drips sweet muscat/caramel/marmalade, but tangy spirit invigorates the palate. **91** *Wine* ❊.

Colombard ❊ New ☺ Up-tempo style, plenty of tropical zing in lighter-bodied **00**, fruity-dry finish.

Cape Riesling ⚘ New Characterful quaffer with variety's pleasing honey/hay tone; fullish, firmly dry, satisfying **00**. **Chardonnay** ❊ Recipe change to unoaked in full-bodied **00**, citrus/pears which start sweet but end briskly dry. 13,5% alc. **Chenin Blanc** ⚘ New Extra-ripe 'sunburnt guava' aroma, **00** quite full, long punchy finish which probably better with food. **Sauvignon Blanc** ⚘ Some tropical fruit in full, bone-dry **00**, not an easy sauvignon vintage.

Joostenberg Wines

Paarl (see Paarl map) • Tasting & sales Mon- Fri 9—5 Sat & Sun 9—3 (Oct-March) Tue—Fri 10—5 Sat & Sun 9—1 (Apr-Sep) Closed public holidays • Cellar tours by appointment • Light meals/refreshments on property coming soon (phone for details); meanwhile at nearby Muldersvlei Market (where gifts also available) • Home grown cutflowers for sale • Tourgroups • Owner Myburgh Winery Pty (Ltd) (Philip Myburgh snr/jnr, Tyrrel Myburgh) • Winemaker Tyrrel Myburgh (since 1999) • Viticulturist Philip Myburgh (since 1999) • Vineyards 40 ha • Production 200 tons 3 000 cases 75% white, 25% red • PO Box 82 Elsenburg 7607 • Tel (021) 884-4932 • Fax (021) 884-4052 • E-mail joostenberg@mweb.co.za

OF THE 2000 HARVEST, philosophy graduate turned winemaker Tyrrel Myburgh smiles: "New winery, new winemaker, new vineyard manager, hot and dry in the vineyards … we all learnt a hell of a lot, to say the least!" This fallen-by-the-wayside triathlete's running shoes haven't touched ground lately. Before he joined the family wine business he worked harvests at nearby Villiera and De Meye, then off to St Emilion and the Languedoc, and on to Sonoma, California. The Myburghs have farmed this glossy Muldersvlei property for over 120 years, and the old Cape Dutch homestead and yard, where the winery is situated, are historical monuments. The family always intended to start making wine here again (they haven't since 1947). Philip Myburgh snr shares in the overall wine responsibilities and continues to run the popular Muldersvlei Market. Philip jnr, an escaped advocate and now vineyard manager, is doing his Masters in wine technology and marketing through Monash University in Australia. They have just planted two trendy varieties, viognier and shiraz, which fit right into their future plans: "To produce a white and a red blend in the Rhône tradition but with a distinct Muldersvlei character."

❊**Cabernet Sauvignon** Hardly out of the starting blocks, this (bought-in, ex-Stbosch) label's form is improving already. **99** more balanced than pvs; dense raspberry/mulberry/black cherry fruit wrapped with ripe tannin. 13% alc. 100

cases. Unwooded, unlike **98** , which new Fr oak matured. Lighter, tighter than the later vintage, but should relax in next yr/2.

Pinotage Unusual and interesting example of the local grape. **00** barrel sample reveals Xmas pud spiciness, soft plummy richness and finely layered fruit. Fruit ex-Stbosch. 13% alc. 425 cases. **Chardonnay Wooded 00** too young to rate conclusively, still lashed by oak mid-2000, citrus fruit barely peeping through. 100% barrel fermented, 25% new Fr oak, remainder 2nd fill. 13% alc. 280 cases. **Chardonnay Unwooded** **00** (sample) limpid, light, lovely even in extreme youth. Tyrrel Myburgh's comment bears repeating: "Perfect for drinking on a summer evening with the smell of seafood on the nose, the sound of waves breaking and the sun setting in the distance." 13% alc. 266 cases. **Sauvignon Blanc** Looking for a partner for Thai green curry? This med-bodied tropical/figgy **00**, with freshness and enough stuffing to be unintimidated by a chilli, could be the answer. 266 cases. **Chenin Blanc Noble Late Harvest** Tasted in extreme youth this **00** still undeveloped, botrytis character barely discernible though flavours already long, balanced. Potential to bloom into something special.

Jordan Vineyards

Stellenbosch (see Stellenbosch map) • Tasting & sales Mon—Fri 10—4.30 Sat 9.30—2.30 (Nov-Apr); 9.30—12.30 (May-Oct) Tasting fee R7.50 p/p, refundable with purchases • Cellar tours by appointment • Bring your own picnic during tasting hours • Owners Ted & Gary Jordan • Winemakers Gary & Kathy Jordan (since 1993), with Rudi Schultz (since Nov 1998) • Viticulturists Ted & Gary Jordan (since 1982) • Production 650 tons 45 000 cases 50/50 red/white • PO Box 12592 Die Boord 7613 • Tel (021) 881-3441 • Fax (021) 881-3426 • E-mail jordanw@cybertrade.co.za

IF COMPLIMENTS really could turn the head, Gary and Kathy Jordan would be terminally dizzy. The world's most influential wine writers simply love all the stuff this high energy young couple produces from these 146 ha vineyards, air-conditioned by both False and Table Bays. But let's focus just on the Chardonnay. Jancis Robinson picks Jordan's version as one of her best buys for Christmas 1999 and the new millennium (*Financial Times*); Tim Atkin, for *Life* magazine, places it on a level with "some of the world's greatest whites", which he lists thus: "Burgundies from Montrachet, Corton-Charlemagne and Meursault, not to mention the wonderful Chardonnays made by Kistler, Saintsbury and Au Bon Climat in California, Leeuwin and Piper's Brook in Australia, Jordan in South Africa and Kumeu River in New Zealand … " These are songs of praise to the 98; watch for the opera dedicated to 99. Because that's the way it's gone ever since the Jordans, he a geologist, she an economist, after a wine and vine crash-course in California, returned to the family farm in Stellenbosch and tackled their first vintage. Instantly, remarkably, they shone. And in just 7 years they've simply got better and better, with the recent assistance of Sonoma-polished Rudi Schultz, and, of course, the root of all good wines, fine vineyards. Gary Jordan's soil science has kicked in here; his latest recruit is French-clone shiraz. Have they now reached cruising altitude? No way. The vintage of 2000 was good enough to have them adjusting their altimeters. "If this is how the 21st century has started, we look forward to the next 99 vintages!" the Jordans say.

 Cabernet Sauvignon Whatever the vintage, Gary & Kathy Jordan create a wine of refinement, balance, without losing vintage individuality. Latest **98** lively tobacco, cassis aromatic intensity matched by equally energetic mouthfilling flavours. Altogether bigger wine than pvs (14% alc vs 13% in **97**); requires yr/2 to settle, come round. Should improve for further 4—7 yrs. Effortlessly absorbs 19 mths in 60% new Fr oak. **97** model of understated elegance, streamlined length.

 Cobblers Hill (Merlot Reserve in last ed) Designed to be ultimate expression of best vyd of vintage; while varieties remain same, proportions will vary according to conditions. **98** expansive, bold, generously oaked, yet as always reflects Jordans thumbprint of New World elegance. Success has much to do with balance;

as in the vibrant mix-'n-match of cedary oak with rich choc/cassis acquired during 18 mths in 100% new Taransaud Fr oak barrels. No fining/filtration. 14,5% alc. Substantially different composition to maiden **97** SAA: 53/47 cab/merlot vs 89/11 merlot/cab, but exudes similar class.

✿ **Merlot** Older vineyards, strength of fruit guide **99** into ranks of SA's best. Variety's voluptuous charm rings deep within generous, ripe tannin frame; sense of richness, silky texture rather than overt fruit. Quality oak influence also part and parcel of whole. Completed malo, yr mix new/used Fr oak. **98** ✿ ripe, generous vintage, 14% alc.

✿ **Chameleon Cabernet Sauvignon-Merlot** Jordans, like many consumers, believe biggest market gap lies at this quality/price bracket. **99** admirably fills hole; also good stylistic stepping stone between Bradgate, Cobblers Hill. Pleasantly firm but not intrusive tannin; bit more flesh than pvs, extends spicy, cassis flavours. Complementary sweet oak topping. All composed for present drinking but in no danger of collapse over next 3–4 yrs. 51/34 cab/ merlot with 15% cab f. Fr oak- 7–12 mths.

✿ **Chardonnay** Gary & Cathy Jordan keep an on-going record of their wines' awards; the longest, most comprehensive list belongs to this wine. Seemingly permanent SAA berth, also frequently flies with other airlines, *Wine* ✿, other starry accolades too numerous to mention. However, **99** ✿✿ tops all seven vintages released to date. Gorgeous hazelnut/oatmeal/citrus peel and leesy complexity; bold, powerful but never flashy — the fruity abundance, dense chewy texture harnessed by spicy oak tannins, freshness imparted by 20% tank-fermented portion and reductive use of vanilla (rolled to mix in lees, rather than oxidatively stirring lees through bung-hole). Epitomises grace achievable in unequivocal New World style. Mix clones (including Davis, Burgundian), coopers, yeasts; malo. 13,7% alc.

✿ **Sauvignon Blanc 00** quietly authoritative (typical of these sauvignons when young); cool, slightly chalky undertones to asparagus freshness. Broader more vivid flavours, full of energy with tongue tingling though not rasping 7,6 g/ℓ acid.

✿ **Blanc Fumé** If above wine slow starter, this is the extrovert (though never at expense of honest varietal character, balanced oaking). **99** in usual exuberant mode; wafts ripe figs, gooseberries, tropical fruits 'sweetened'/expanded by gentle oak vanilla. Big, juicy but also, thanks to fresh acid spine, digestibly moreish. 56% Fr barrel fermented, 52% new; 7 mths on lees. Quality confirmed by frequent SAA listings, *Wine* ✿.

Chenin Blanc ✿ Modern, stylish version of Cape's workhorse white variety. **99** all barrel-fermented, adds leesy interest without damping down warm honeyed chenin fruit. Mouthfilling flavours, supple, roundly dry with balanced fresh acid extending trademark ripe citrus/naartjie peel finish. 14% alc. **Chameleon Sauvignon Blanc-Chardonnay** ✿ One of few in genre to have survived/thrived long after fashion for this combo faded. Justifiably: partnership always carefully matched to maintain strong showing on multitude of restaurant wine lists, therefore complement food rather than varietal sparring contest. **00** (untasted, undergoing stabilisation) blend follows footsteps of **99** SAA where sauvignon leads; slightly lower proportion (55% vs 60% in **99**); injects freshness, lively fruit to broader, lees-enriched chardonnay portion. Technically dry 3,5 g/ℓ sugar, pvs with smoothing 5 g/ℓ. Named after Cape dwarf chameleons found throughout the vineyards. **Rhine Riesling** ✿ Spicy/limey aromatics in **00**, intensity aided in palate by tangy ripe acidity. Eased into all-round popularity by just on 11 g/ℓ fruit enhancing residual sugar, moderate 12% alc. Everything in place to mature well over next 2–3 yrs. Excellent partner to anything from seafood to Thai dishes.

Bradgate range

Well priced, easy drinking, developed mainly for Dutch market, but also available locally.

> **Cabernet Sauvignon-Merlot-Cabernet Franc** ✿ 😊 Light-texture, pliant tannins highlight ripe blackberry juiciness in **99**. Lingering finish perfects the easy drinking/thoroughly satisfying formula the Jordans seek. Rounded in Fr oak.

Chenin Blanc-Sauvignon Blanc ☆ **00** similar 60/40 partnership as pvs; quietly vinous nose; more zingy sauvignon flavours, unassertively dry.

Joubert-Tradauw Winery

Barrydale • Tasting & sales Mon—Sat 9-5 • Cellar tours by appointment • Local cuisine prepared by Beate Joubert (tel 028-572-1619/082-420-6180) and served in the garden, weather permitting. Also picnic baskets R30 p/p • Op-de-Tradauw self-catering guesthouse (tel Beate Joubert as above) Also Lentelus B&B tel (028) 572-1636 • Large play area for children • Tourgroups • Tractor rides • Gifts • 4×4 Trailing • Mountain biking • Walks • Views • Proclaimed conservation area • Wheelchair-friendly • Owner JA Joubert Family Trust • Winemaker/viticulturist Meyer Joubert (since 1995) • Vineyards 30 ha • Production 300 tons 80% red 20% white • PO Box 15 Barrydale 6750 • Tel/fax (028) 572-1619/082-420-6180

FOLLOW THE CURVES of the Langeberg along Route 62 and you'll come to landmark Vleiplaas, one of the oldest farms in the Klein Karoo. An old building on the property has been restored into a maturation cellar and a fermentation hall was built out of local stone. Slow-ripening grapes (a fresh southeaster rolls into the valley every evening) are selected from the four family farms: Vleiplaas, Lentelus, Sandrivier and Op-de-Tradauw (grapes previously delivered to Barrydale co-op). Fruit orchards and a dairy are part of the mix on this bustling farm. The dairy even plays a role in production: grape skins, stalks and pips are mixed with sawdust in the kraal, where the cows add their ample contribution, and voila! — a potent organic mixture which is worked into the vineyards twice a year. Meyer Joubert (who inherited his love of good wines from his KWV chairman father) came back from California (stints at Cakebread and Quail Ridge in Napa Valley, Quail Creek in Green Valley) totally motivated to make wines. He's passionate about his home turf and would like to see it stand up and be counted as a wine-producing region: so much so that the merlot/cabernet blend is named R62. Note: Four hundred cases of the first chardonnay were released at the end of 2000. These not ready for tasting.

✿ **R62** Creditable debut for this good looking (Grape Top Ten packaging award) dry red blend, recalling the splendidly scenic byway linking Worcester and Oudtshoorn. Nothing backwaterish about **99** merlot/cab (52/48), evoking California in strapping 14% alc, mouthfilling smoky cherry/greenpepper flavour with spicy vanilla undertone. 1 200 cases.

JP Bredell Wines

Stellenbosch (see Helderberg map) • Tasting & sales Mon—Fri 8.30—5 Tasting fee R2 • Cellar tours by appointment • Wheelchair-friendly • Owner/winemaker/viticulturist Anton Bredell • Vineyards 95 ha • Production 950 tons 66,5% red, 22% white, 11,5% port • PO Box 5266 Helderberg 7135 • Tel (021) 842-2478 • Fax (021) 842-3124

ANTON BREDELL relaxes, out of his vineyards and cellar, underwater — spear fishing — or on his Little Karoo game farm. "NB!" he stresses. "My game farm, not my port farm!" He's underlining his conviction that South African port-country is right here in these Helderberg vineyards, close to False Bay — nowhere near the area of the Little Karoo, which its residents like to dub the Douro of the Cape. But so friendly is the rivalry that Bredell and Calitzdorp's Carel Nel have collaborated in an inter-regional blended port, and beam about it as broadly as their fans, who are thrilled with the notion (and the flavour) of two giants squeezed into one bottle (see Bredell & Nel). 2000 is the year ports will be the focus of the judges in Diners Club's Winemaker of the Year competition, and though Bredell says he never makes his wines with shows in mind, the clever money is on his splendid Cape Vintage Reserve as the one to beat. It's been a sensation since the first 91 release introduced after-dinner aficionados to the fruits of these 95 ha vineyards, which had previously disappeared into the bowels of the KWV. A lot of the crop still heads that way, but happily for consumers, Bredell now siphons off a bit here and there (5 000 cases in total) to offer not only the glamorous ports but also some boomingly good reds.

✿✿Merlot Maiden **98** still on the up. Peppermint/violets bouquet with some herbaceous notes. Complex array of plums, cinnamon, aniseed, vanilla flavours. Dash sugar (5,2 g/ℓ) hardly visible. Yr new, tight grained Fr oak. Classically elegant label. 13% alc. 565 cases.

✿✿Pinotage Big, fruity **98** *Wine* ✿✿ more complex, clove-spicier than pvs; ripe bananas, blackberries framed by supple tannins. Touch vanilla in quite a salty finish. ± Yr Fr/Am oak. 13% alc. 780 cases. No **97**. **96** *Wine* ✿✿.

✿✿Shiraz 98, with concentrated, distinctive bouquet, still 5 yrs from ideal (though long tannins already silky). Spicy berry/cherry, some exotic rose petal fragrances and whiffs vanilla. Am oak, mostly new, 8–9 mths. 13% alc. 850 cases. **97** ✿ (though *Wine* ✿✿).

✿✿Chardonnay Naturally fermented, new Fr oak matured **99** first chardonnay from this cellar (**98** made but not released). Inviting butterscotch/vanilla with hints ripe white-peach transferring to big, generous palate. Optimal drinking mid-2001. 13% alc.

✿✿Cape Vintage Reserve Splendid Cape benchmark 'port' since first vintage **91**. Aims to "fill not only mouth but whole body with flavour", which latest **98** does totally convincingly, deliciously. Fruit expression, greater complexity hallmarks of excellent vintage, new dash touriga f adds extra dimension to touriga n's flesh, tinta b's now standard backbone. Somewhat oaky, subdued mid-2000, but will gain balance, disciplined opulence with time. 2 yrs Fr oak; 20% alc; quite dry at 92,6 g/ℓ sugar but still above Bredell's 90 g/ℓ cut-off to maintain balance. 1 255 cases. Notch up (but it's all relative!) on **97**, with 10% touriga n, 65/25 tinta b/souzão, latter featuring for first time. dense, black, viscous, aromatic waves of ripe plums, Xmas pud; big, muscular in palate, smooth and supple with good grippy finish, lashings of spice. Holds even greater promise than glittering **95** *Wine* ✿✿, but needs more time — these deserve 5 yrs at least. No **96** — released as LBV below. **94** *Wine* ✿✿, **93** *Wine* ✿✿ (rarely accorded rating).

✿✿Late Bottled Vintage Lighter **96** VVG did not, Anton Bredell believed, justify a Vintage Reserve, so this an LBV — but not a poor relation: trademark power/refinement here in amplitude: ripe silky package with plums, blackberries and attractive dry finish. Smooth but lively; for now or keeping 5 yrs or longer. 70/30 tinta b/souzão. 2 yrs Fr oak. 19,7% alc, 98 g/ℓ sugar. Also in 500 ml. 920 cases. *Wine* ✿✿.

. . . .

Kaapse Hoop see Vinfruco
Kaapse Pracht see Coppoolse Finlayson-Sentinel
Kaapse Vreugd see Coppoolse Finlayson-Sentinel
Kaaps Genoegen see Coppoolse Finlayson-Sentinel

. . . .

Kaapzicht Estate ⚲ ⚲ ⚲ ⚲

Stellenbosch (see Stellenbosch map) • Tasting & sales Mon—Thu 9—12.30; 1.30—5 Fri 9—12.30; 1.30—4 Sat & public holidays 9—12 Tasting fee for larger groups (new bottles opened may be taken away) • Cellar tours by appointment • Restaurant/kitchen/barbecue facilities ("soon also dance floor") for up to 200 people • Bring your own picnic (tables/chairs available) • Walks • Views • Wheelchair-friendly • Owner Steytdal Farms • Winemaker Danie Steytler •

Viticulturist George Steytler • Vineyards 136 ha • Production 1 250 tons (20 000 cases own label) 60% white 40% red • PO Box 5 Sanlamhof 7532 • Tel (021) 906-1620/1 • Fax (021) 906-1622 • E-mail kaapzicht@mweb.co.za

THEY'VE been shouting it from the Bottelary Hills for ages, producers here, as they frustratedly hear praise-songs to the vineyard pre-eminence of every 'prime' area, 'golden triangle', mountainside and coastline other than their own hills and dales. Now it really is time to listen. Treasures are buried here, and Kaapzicht's 98 Steytler is a great example. Winner of the ABSA and *Wine* magazine Pinotage Champion 2000 award, trouncing 70 other versions of our national grape, it's a stunning tribute to the neighbourhood. Winemaker Danie Steytler is the first to acknowledge his debt to the terroir. There's also his dedicated team, not least his viticulturist brother. But ever modest, Danie Steytler downplays his own role. We shall have to blow the trumpets for him. Carefully and steadily — that's how he's approached 4 Two Oceans and 3 Comrades marathons too — he has ratcheted the quality of this once little-known label upwards, while keeping prices as down-to-earth as he. Kaapzicht has become one of the Cape's least pretentious, most charming pin-ups in 13 countries, its export drive assisted by his German wife Yngvild, who recently took the wines to their first international trade fair in Düsseldorf.

Steytler range

Honours the late George Steytler, who farmed Kaapzicht from 1946–1984.

✿✿**Pinotage** Danie Steytler decided to keep back selected barrels of his best and hike the over-friendly standard price to stem demand — the reverse was true! Second **99** only 20 barrels (2 kept back for CWG Auction), similar dense dark colour but even better fruit/acid balance (despite bottle shock when tasted) than stunning maiden **98** VG, ABSA Top 10, *Wine* ✿✿ (Pinotage Champion), fitting super-reserve pinotage from this estate. Deeply perfumed, intense mulberry/raspberry/dark cherry, opulent banana; massive initial palate yielding wonderful finesse, exceptionally long finish. Supple, mouthcoating tannin for next decade. Fine wine in any language. George Steytler would have been delighted. 17 mths new Fr oak.

Kaapzicht range

✿✿**Cabernet Sauvignon** (Reserve in pvs ed) **97** shows Steytler's skills beyond his favourite grape. Heady perfumes tobacco/cedar/spice prelude subtle cassis fruit, good length of flavour, gentle tannins from older oak. Next **98** bigger, more arresting still, ripe succulent blackberries endowed with 50% new wood, well managed. Ripe and gutsy, 13,5% alc in balance. Will offer even more in 4 yrs. **96** *Wine* ✿ initially forward, full of red berries, drying out, drink now. 'Standard' **95** Air France–Preteux Bourgeois trophy.

✿✿**Merlot** (Reserve in pvs ed) **98** reflects vintage: full, wild, muscular and meaty, big enough for both 50% new Fr oak (17 mths) and 14% alc. Huge frame belies elegant inner structure. Mocha flavours will be winner with venison. **97** also ripe, plums, lively sweet-sour tang, good whack of tannin but slighter than rampant sibling. 13% alc. 6 mths 3rd fill then 3 mths new Fr oak.

✿✿**Pinotage** The best barrels may have moved on to Steytler range above from **98**, but no threat to estate's position in the Cape premier pinotage league. Deep ruby red, plush bouquet of juicy cherries, ripe plums against smoked oak highlights; luxurious fruity texture, piquant sweet-sour effect offsets sturdy tannic launch pad. Masterfully avoids bitterness that can mar pinotage. *Wine* ✿. Sample upcoming **99** in even better form: gently structured acid balance, excellent. Now 50% each new, 2nd fill Fr oak. **97** (pre-Steytler flagship, labelled Reserve), 100% new wood, VVG; **97/98** ABSA Top 10 trophies. **96**, **97** *Wine* ✿.

✿✿**Shiraz** (Reserve in pvs ed) **98** yet another arrow in the Steytlers' quiver. Compact fruit heightened by compellingly pungent spice — milled black pepper, tints lemon grass — with palate managing excellent balancing act of fruit/tannin ripeness with refined finish. Prior **97** VG (300 cases) earthy, wild scrub/buchu nose, quieter berries back big, tannic mouthfeel. Palate shortening when tasted mid-2000. Oaking similar to merlot above: 6 mths 3rd fill Fr barrels then all-new 3 mths.

* **Hanepoot Jerepigo 98** VVG deliciously decadent, either as an aperitif over lemon-zested crushed ice or a winter's digestif, both severely chilled. Golden shot with green, muscat essence ensconced in honeysuckle, lemon and fresh honey. **92** VG in 1992/5.

Bin 3 ♣ Equal portions cab/merlot blend, lightly wooded (older oak). Named on spur of moment as was the 3rd blend made! **99** marginally lighter (13% alc) more 'delicate' than previous but doesn't lack fruit complexity. **Kaaproodt** ♣ More substance than many reds from light **96** vintage, now moderate ruby, plummy fruit gaining wild edge, tannins still take centre stage — calls for a hearty plate. Cab/merlot/pinotage (50/25/25). **98** 'declassified'; next release undecided. 16 mths 3rd fill Fr oak. **Chenin Blanc** ⚓ **97** partly barrel-fermented, oakiness lines palate with tropical fruit but now tiring. **Sauvignon Blanc** ⚓ **99** unwooded, fine effort for difficult year, flinty/grass notes parallel melon fruit, 13% alc. Best in bloom of youth. No match yet for **97** VG, *Wine* ♣.

Cape View range

Mainly for export.

Cabernet Sauvignon ♣ Fresh purple **99** brimming with red berry/cherry fruit, ripe tannins, decent 13,3% alc. 3 mths Fr oak staves. **98**, **96** bottled as **Cabernet Sauvignon Wooded** ⚓ **98** suffering bottle shock when tasted mid-2000, hard and tannic. **96** has developed fresh blackcurrant fruit, nicely built, good length. 17 mths seasoned Fr oak. **95** VVG. **Merlot** ♣ For everyday drinking. Balanced **98**, easy; baked plums, straightforward red berries, touches spice, lick charry wood. Lightly oaked 3 mths small Fr. **96** VG. **Rouge de Kaap** ⚓ Undemanding **99**, dusty berries, pepper/spice, soft tannins. equal cinsaut/shiraz/cab, unwooded. **Dry Red** ⚓ Don't stand on ceremony. **99** light ruby, pulpy ripe strawberries, injection of chenin adds fruit and freshness. **Chenin Blanc** ♣ **00** snappy reductive style, oozing tropical fruit, lees contact brings breadth, satisfying mouthful. **97** still alive. **Special Late Harvest Chenin Blanc** ⚓ Sweet, light-and-fluffy **97**, chill and drink up. **Brut** ⚓ **99** sauvignon sparkler; racy, peachy, refreshing. **Demi Sec** ⚓ **99** fizzy 50/50 sauvignon/chenin. Sweetness dampens fruit.

Friesland range

For export to Netherlands.

Bin 3 ♣ 50/50 cab/merlot, lightly wooded older oak. **98** VG wild, raspberry fruit, smoky merlot gaminess. Plum/blueberry flesh in mouth, oak reserves, 13,5% alc. **Merlot** ♣ Easy **98** labelled Wooded; baked plums, simple red berries, touch of spice, for everyday drinking. Lightly oaked 3 mths small Fr. **96** VG. **Cabernet Sauvignon** ♣ **97** pale ruby, grassy, bit stalky, green pepper zip. Enjoy now. 3 mths Fr oak staves. **Dry Red** ⚓ **99** Light ruby, sappy ripe strawberries, burst of chenin adds fruit/freshness to cinsaut/shiraz/cab. **Chenin Blanc** ⚓ **98** unwooded, off-dry (6 g/ℓ sugar), drink up.

Kakamas see Oranjerivier Wynkelders

Kanonkop Estate ⚑ ⚑ ⚑

Stellenbosch (see Stellenbosch map) • Tasting & sales Mon—Fri 8.30—5.30 Sat 8.30—12.30 Closed New Year's/Christmas days, Good Friday • Traditional snoek barbecue by appointment (15 guests or more) • Owners Johann & Paul Krige • Winemaker Beyers Truter (since 1981) • Vineyards 100 ha • Production 400 tons 25 000 cases 100% red • PO Box 19 Elsenburg 7607 • Tel (021) 884-4656 • Fax (021) 884-4719 • E-mail wine@kanonkop.co.za

THIS is not so much an estate but an empire, with a red army conquering palates all over the world. Kanonkop, the long service senior field marshall, currently occupies 37 countries; Beyerskloof and Bouwland, the more recent recruits, campaign in 30 and 20 foreign fields respectively. It's all part of a remarkable, modern battle plan drawn up by Kanonkop heirs Johann and Paul Krige and winemaker Beyers Truter. With hindsight, the choice seems clear: either risk the first-Cape-growth reputation of the estate by enlarging its range to cater for diverse tastes and budgets — or branch out and beyond, using Kanonkop expertise and muscle to launch second and third strike forces. The strategy has been a resounding success; they've split, then sewn up the market place; Kanonkop's top-echelon niche is secure. Beyers Truter can pamper his beloved Pinotage and his aristocratic Bordeaux blend to distraction, and keep coaching them to trophy after international trophy. Some of the 100 ha vineyards took a knock during the runaway fires which ravaged the slopes of Simonsberg during the harvest of 2000, but premature reports of a wholescale incineration (fans from all over the globe rang and e-mailed to commiserate) were fortunately highly exaggerated. As the trio reassured anxious followers: "The Kanonkop ship is sailing, and the Western Cape is still the most beautiful place on earth!"

Paul Sauer Twice winner of prestigious Pichon-Longueville Comtesse de Lalande trophy for best blended red wine at IWSC — in 1994 for **91** and 1999 for **95**. Latest **97** embroidered with class, far more elegant than pvs, more refined, but as flavoursome as big, bold 'statement' reds of past three decades. Luscious cassis, hints of spearmint stitched into palate with beautifully ripe tannins. Upholstered velvet finish lingers. 14% alc in synch. Refined breeding will take time to release all its charms; too easy to drink now, a crime to plunder in its youth. 80% cab, 10% each cab f/merlot. **96** VVG, *Wine* ✻, bucked vintage trend with powerful stunner from low-yielding (4,5 t/ha), 30 yr old vines. Focused bouquet of concentrated blackberry, sensuously fragrant Fr oak. Silky blackcurrant, hints of choc, textured tannins and excellent fruity persistence. 23 mths 225 ℓ Nevers oak, 100% new, Seguin Moreau cooperage. 12,5% alc. **95** VVG, *Wine* ✻✻.

✻ **Cabernet Sauvignon** Paul Krige believes new clones coming to fruition will show less vintage fluctuation as they ripen earlier and so miss potential late summer heatwaves. Latest **97** classic combination of ripe fruit (and 13,5% alc.) with demurely elegant, knitted tannic structure. Perfumed lanolin nose, clean creamy wood, pebbly mineral core hem in cassis fruit. A far cry from sinuous, dusty, leafy styles of the past. **96** crossover Old/New World symphony of exuberant fruit-penetration with restraint: dark cherry/red berry fruits resonate on harmonious palate accented by fragrant, understated oak. Not as much stamina as pvs yet good for 4–6 yrs. ± 30 yr old vines. 12,5% alc. **95** *Wine* ✻, deep textured; US *Wine Spectator* 91 points. 22 mths 225 ℓ Nevers, third each 1st/2nd /3rd fill. 13,5% alc.

Pinotage Barrel samples of **99** shaping to have power of rampant **98** ✻ (full house of awards: VVG, SAA, *Wine* ✻, ABSA Top Ten, Michelangelo gold); magenta purple colour, piercing aromas of ripe damson/plum, sweet banana, gutsy mineral fabric; massive, complex palate layered with seriously delicious ripe choc-cherry, cinnamon and clove, opulent creaminess. Firm but fine tannin for good 10 yrs' keeping. **97** VVG, SAA, *Wine* ✻, IWSC gold, huge, ripe; potential for bottle development over 8–10 yrs.

✻ **CWG Auction Reserve Pinotage** Unexpectedly low-key **98**, both more restrained and accessible than sibling above; open and succulent where the regular version is less yielding.

✻ **Kadette** ▼ Cleverly packaged, exceptional dry red, rated by US *Wine Spectator* among "50 great red wine values" — from producers who understand the advantages of delivering more than expected at entry level. **98**, 1999 Diners Club shortlist, waxy nose without obvious tropical aromas from pinotage base (55%), solid gravity to palate freshened with ripe cherries. Serious finish. **97** a gentle beauty: ripe mulberry, cedar aromas, sprig of mint. Ditto palate with soft tannins, fresh bounce. Subtle oak throughout. 2–4 yrs to peak. Classy food wine.

. . . .

Kanu Wines

Stellenbosch (see Stellenbosch map) Tasting & sales Mon—Fri 10—5 Sat 9—1 (Dec-Mar) Fee R1/wine • Owner Hydro Holdings • Sales & marketing manager Sean Griffiths • Winemaker Teddy Hall (since 1998) with Theo Brink jnr (since 1999) • Viticulturist Johann Schloms • Vineyards 45 ha (additional 40 ha leased) • Production 30 000 cases • PO Box 548 Stellenbosch 7599 • Tel (021) 881-3808 • Fax (021) 881-3514 • Kanu: E-mail info@kanu.co.za • Website www.kanu.co.za • Spier Estate: E-mail info@spierwines.co.za • Website www.spierwines.co.za

WE REACHED Teddy Hall, the Kanu winemaker, on his mobile phone on the road, on holiday, and he dispensed with the pleasantries immediately in favour of the "vital importance" of even spacing between the vine's spurs and bearers and how that has a direct bearing on even ripening of berries. The traffic roars in the background but he's into his favourite subject. "It's overall vineyard management that counts, it's about getting sunlight into the canopy, cutting out the suckers, not just once but throughout the growing season." A recent trip to Australia obviously fired him up. "But in fact all the knowledge is available here, it's even in my (Stellenbosch University) lecture notes; but if, like me, you didn't listen properly at the time, then you have to hire your Prof as your consultant!" Which is exactly what he's done. Prof Eben Archer guides Teddy Hall and his team here. And chenin blanc is a particular obsession. Hall heads the viticultural research sub-committee of the Chenin Blanc Association and it won't be long before they develop, in the manner of the French and others, criteria for quality classifications for chenin blanc and apply them to specific Cape regions and vineyards. That would be a viticultural first — grower-driven (as opposed to government) vineyard quality specifications that consumers can relate to individual sites and labels.

Kanu range

Reference to bounty-bestowing bird of southern African folklore.

✿ **Keystone Limited Release** New ▼ Flagship red, "keystone of all other Kanu reds". Near-equal partnership cab/merlot in debut **98**, from Vlottenburg/Koelenhof vyds managed by Kanu team. Plenty of excitement in varietal interplay among cassis, sweet-violets, ripe plums, spiced with almond and nougat; cab slightly in the lead, its tannins featuring in firm but ripe structure which should give pleasure for min 3–5 yrs. 18 mths Fr barriques, some new. 2 500 cases.

✿ **Cabernet Sauvignon Limited Release** New Voluptuous choc-coated raspberries, plums and cassis are the main attractions of first release **98**, fragrant with cedar and sweet spice; some fruitcake hints contrast pleasingly with savoury, chewy tannins which should see the wine through 4–6 yrs. 100% new Fr barriques, 18 mths. 13% alc. Gourmet Teddy Hall offers a detailed menu of food partners for this wine; we'll settle for springbok fillet sizzled over hot coals or traditional ostrich neck potjie. 950 cases.

✿ **Merlot** Gutsy, widely lauded **98**, Air France–Preteux Bourgeois Top 10, 87 rating in *Wine Spectator,* developing well in bottle; initial tannins smoother now, ripe cherry fruit stretched on rich canvas of choc/mocha and mint with scents of violets. 14,5% alc. 15 mths Fr barrels. 650 cases.

✿ **Shiraz** Just 14 rows of venerable vines on the home farm are the source of this wine, which sees style change from oak-lashed **98** to more aromatic **99**, with wild scrub/white pepper and clove/nutmeg spices wafting over soft ripe berries and dark cherries. Tannins are firm but ripe and undaunting, and though good now, will give much more pleasure in 4–6 yrs' time. 14 mths Fr oak. 13,5% alc. 300 cases. **98** *Wine* ✿.

✿ **Chardonnay** ▼ **98** ✿ got this label off to cracking start: *Wine* ✿, SAA First Class (runner-up White Wine of Year), runner-up 1999 Tri-Nations Chardonnay

Challenge. Follow-up **99** to us the better wine, more focused and coherent, more concentrated ripe peach flavour against fragrant oak-backing of spice and vanilla. Beautifully smooth and dry. Oak well managed/integrated. Good now and for 2–4 yrs. Barrel fermented/matured: Yr 225 ℓ Fr oak, 70% new; 20% natural ferment. 1 100 cases.

❀ **Chenin Blanc Limited Release** New "The future is chenin," believes Teddy Hall, so this deluxe 100% barrel fermented version now officially the cellar's white flagship. Richness from ultra-ripe tropical fruit and muscled 14% alc; melon/banana tones more than ample for quite obvious vanilla-oak. **00** (sample) bigger in every way, potentially excellent. Fruit ex-elevated Koelenhof bushvines, in-house managed. 7 mths 225 ℓ Fr barriques, 70% new, balance 2nd fill, portion through malo. 200 cases.

❀ **Bulkamp Sauvignon Blanc** New Stunning first release, much fuller, more robust than standard version below; opens with fragrant nettle/white pepper attack relenting to soft tropical pineapple/melon in broad palate; extraordinary aromatic finale of marjoram and rosemary which lingers for ages. Single Koelenhof vyd, limited quantities (200 cases). 'Bull camp' in name alludes to pvs use of vyd site. 13% alc.

❀ **Noble Late Harvest** New Gorgeous **99** from hárslevelü, 100% new-oak fermented/aged, which brilliantly absorbed in intense riesling-like bouquet layered with pear/peach/marzipan and toasted hazelnuts in palate. Sumptuous, sweet and interminably long, but bracing 9 g/ℓ acid reels in richness to thrilling, clean conclusion. Raisined/botrytised grapes fermented 100% new Fr oak barriques, aged 15 mths. 375 ml. 500 cases.

Red 😊 Delightful, juicy **99** ruby cab/cinsaut equal blend with abundant strawberry/cherry fruit for quaffability and smoky/toasty add-ons for instant BBQ compatibility. Good value. Moderate 12,5% alc. 5 000 cases. **Chenin Blanc** ❀ 😊 Cheerful unwooded easy drinker packed with fresh lemons and limes; ripe fruit gives sweetish impression but finish is gently dry. 13% alc. 1 300 cases.

Sauvignon Blanc ❀ Early-drinking **00** shows better varietal definition/fruit expression than pvs. Bright gooseberry/guava in foreground, green pepper behind with sprig rosemary in finish. Best over next 12–18 moths. 1 200 cases.

Spier Wine Estate label

❀ Chardonnay 98's initial oaky flush has subsided, revealing rich grapefruit/cashew/bready flavours and oak spice. Ready, should hold 2–3 yrs.

. . . .

Keimoes see Oranjerivier Wynkelders

. . . .

Kellerprinz

Some pruning by Stellenbosch Farmers' Winery sees this top selling range reduced to a pair of wines, both NV, in returnable glass or boxes.

Stein ❀ Tropical attractions in this soft, fruity semi-sweet swigger, freshened by good zip of acid. Now only in 2 ℓ. **Late Harvest** ❀ Tropical fruits as above, but richer, honeyed, some muscat scents. Same uncloying finish.

. . . .

Ken Forrester Wines   🍷 🍷 🏠 🍷

Stellenbosch (see Helderberg map) • Tasting & sales at 96 Winery Road Restaurant (see Eat-out section) • Cellar tours by appointment • Luxury guesthouse • Conferences • Facilities for children • Gifts • Views • Wheelchair-friendly • Owners Ken & Teresa Forrester • Winemakers Ken Forrester & Martin Meinert (since 1998) • Viticulturists Hannes Bredell & Johan Pienaar • Vineyards 28 ha • Production 24 000 cases 70% white 30% red • PO Box 1253 Stellenbosch

. . . .

7599 • Tel (021) 855-2374 • Fax (021) 855-2373 • E-mail ken@forresterwines.co.za • Website www.forresterwines.co.za

WHEN Ken and Teresa Forrester decamped from Johannesburg to a three centuries old farm below the Helderberg in 1993 their first motivation was "to have the luxury of space to raise a family" (they have two knock-out daughters). The vines on 28 ha Scholtzenhof would be handy for their string of restaurants, including the one they opened just over the road — 96 Winery Road, that is, for many, the most sympa eat-outery in wine country. (Forrester is hotel school-trained, the former head of South Africa's hotel and restaurant association and an inspirational cook.) And of course they would enjoy "the privilege of partnering nature" to home-grow their own wines. The idea was a quiet rural life. But Ken Forrester is too large, energetic and passionate a personality to sit about ruminating. In no time he's become one of the most effective movers-and-shakers in the winelands, challenging the establishment, driving changes — and with partner Martin Meinert, producing arrestingly avant-garde, food-cordial wines which have flown to fame far beyond local restaurants. His Sauvignon Blanc and Grenache-Syrah were served at the opening gala dinner of the new Scottish Parliament. New plantings of merlot and shiraz are bound to deliver more originality — 'orthodox' and 'conventional' are not in Forrester's vocabulary. But chenin blanc is his most serious addiction, and while there had been cheeps about rescuing the reputation of this ubiquitous grape in the Cape, when he lent his formidable weight and eloquence to the cause, it really began to roll.

✿ **Grenache-Syrah** True individual: you either love the aromatic fireworks, the mouth expanding 14% alc, the European dryness — or you leave. **98** improving in bottle (and promise of further growth). Showing an astonshing array of scents/tastes: lavendar, turpentine, old leather shoes (!), cloves, cinnamon, black pepper, eucalyptus, forest leaves, sappy berries and — whew! — not quite ripe mulberries. Unwooded Devon Valley grenache (two-thirds) teamed with Forrester-grown shiraz, oaked 9 mths. Limited quantities. **99** (from barrel) all above but warmer, more intense.

✿ **Merlot-Cabernet Sauvignon** New Where the Grenache-Syrah above is individual and uncompromisingly 'sauvage', this fresh face in line-up, featuring dollop cab f, is friendly, inviting. Welcomes you with booming smoky, ripe cherry/violets bouquet, with background notes of clove/cedar spice from 14 mths oak. Ripe, fine tannins carry all to long, balanced conclusion. 13% alc. 1 400 cases.

✿ **Chenin Blanc** ✔ "Grande Chenin" as Ken Forrester calls it, from over 25 yr old Helderberg bushvines, pruned for low yields. Big but balanced, just-dry, serious in intent; wood/bottle-aged to develop breadth to match cuisine. **97** firmly established the new-generation, weightier style (without detracting from grape's intrinsic delicacy). **98**, with forward 13,5% alc, evolving brilliantly: full, enveloping body softened by licks of honey; flavours/aromas richer, more 'available'. Current **99** ripe tropical fruit and honeysuckle fragrance, rolling mouthful of fruit layered with oak and exotic papaya/melon extensions concludes with velvety dryness. Mid-2000 probably closer to ✿, with potential to grow into **98**'s terrirfic shoes.

✿ **Sauvignon Blanc** Flying high once more after **99** ✿✿ had stuffing knocked out of it by harvest heatwave. **00** "picked to ensure a range of flavours", which there is: from extra-ripe gooseberry/passionfruit to green grass to dry hay. Impression of sunshiny ripeness, yet no hint of sweetness in bright zesty finish. 13% alc. Unwooded. 5 000 cases.

✿ **'T' Noble Late Harvest Chenin Blanc** Tribute to Teresa, Mrs Forrester; barrel fermented, Sauternes-style, after cold maceration. Magical **98** with peach pip, tropical melon decadence cut with zesty lemon lift, immense, lubricated drumroll on the tongue. Drier style: 84 g/ℓ sugar, 12,5% alc, acid 7,7. **99**'s (sample) wide-angle spectrum extended furteher by kumquat fragrance; flavours/aromas all buoyed with subtle oak and botrytis, silky smoothness cleansed by lemon zest finish.

Petit Chenin ✿ This the 'quaffing' version of chenin above, for consumption within yr of harvest. Usually loaded with flavour, though **00** tasted immediately postbottling somewhat muted: only delicate floral wafts of lilac plus ripe guava. In full lime/lees palate, dusty firm dryness which will be very good with food. 2000 the "very best yr for chenin in the past 5 or 6", so expect the ensemble to quickly gain the usual high speed. 100% chenin, unwooded, extended lees lie-in for extra richnes. 13,5% alc. 15 000 cases. **Blanc Fumé** ✿ 99 has improved with bit of bottle age; creamier now, more lees-limey with ripe fruit and some vanilla; attractive smokines in firm, quite zesty finish. 13% alc. 50/50 tank/ barrel fermented, Am oak.

- -
Kersfontein see Sonop
Kevin Arnold see Waterford

· ·

Khanya Wines

Durbanville • Not open to the public • Owner/winemaker Nico Vermeulen • Production 500 cases • 3 Pieter Hugo Street Courtrai Suider-Paarl 7624 • Tel/fax (021) 863-2048

AFTER making his first wines in the Bloemendal cellar, Nico Vermeulen followed his wine star westwards to his and Kobus du Plessis' new spread, Havana Hills, near Melkbosstrand, where the 2000 harvest was crushed (Vermeulen's fascination with a star-themed Californian label, first glimpsed in 1995, was the inspiration for Khanya — 'shine' in Xhosa). The original Sauvignon and Cabernet-Merlot have been joined by a promising 2000 Shiraz-Cabernet, made from Durbanville fruit.

✿ **Cabernet Sauvignon-Merlot** First 99 introduced a serious, big yet elegant claret with ageing potential, full-blown blackcurrant/mint/green pepper complexity with new-oak vanilla, dryish tannins not instantly accessible. These characters return, in extra-concentrated form, in infant **00**, way ftoo young to rate but potentially bigger, better, longer lived. Five stars winking here? 13,5% alc. 150 cases.

✿ **Sauvignon Blanc** Subtitled Izelle's Choice. 99 classic, assertive cat's pee/nettles bouquet, yet quite slow in mid-palate until crisp acidity takes the baton and races to brisk flourish. 13,6% alc. Preview of **00**, from single vyd on Bloemendal, reveals a late starter. Subdued, very fresh, needs time to gather itself. 13,5% alc. 150 cases.

Shiraz-Cabernet Sauvignon New Plucked from its (small Fr oak) cradle, **00** glows with potential. Packed with ripe mulberry/green pepper, swirling with smoke. For release Sep 2001. 80/20 ratio. 13,5% alc. 150 cases.

· ·

Klawervlei Estate

Stellenbosch (see Stellenbosch map) • Tasting & sales Mon—Fri 10—5 Sat 10—2 • Cellar tours by appointment • Wheelchair-friendly • Proprietors Hermann & Inge Feichtenschlager • Winemaker Hermann Feichtenschlager • Vineyards 35 ha • Production 2 500—7 000 cases • PO Box 144 Koelenhof 7605 • Tel (021) 882-2746 • Fax (021) 882-2415

"NEW WAY to fight peronospera biologically." Hermann Feichtenschlager's reply to our question, what's fresh in your vineyard? brings this 114 ha Koelenhof estate (35 ha under vines) into focus: wine growing here is done organically, as nature intended. Which explains Feichtenschlager's and wife Inge's quiet delight about discovering a natural way to combat downy mildew, a fungal blight which has destroyed a number of their crops. What's not been lost is brimming enthusiasm,

(Hermann Feichtenschlager now back in his earlier winemaker role), and the couple remain among the Cape's foremost eco-gladiators.

Cabernet Sauvignon Latest **00**, sampled in angular youth, arguably the best yet from this organic farm: super-intense colour, long ripe tannins, sturdy platform of fruit. Good 🍷 potential, though probably will need few yrs' keeping. 12,5% alc. 475 cases. **Merlot** ✻ New to this ed, full-bodied **98** not an easy wine. Feral aromas, almost impenetrable tannins. 13,5% alc. 750 cases. This steeliness returns in latest **00** (sample), with some ruby cab-like tones. **Chenin Blanc Reserve** ✿ Appears slighter than 14% alc suggests. Some oaky/caramel tastes (though not barrelled), sharp bite of acid. 430 cases. **Chenin Blanc Late Harvest 00** too young to rate. 200 cases.

. . . .

Klawer Winery

Olifants River (see Olifants River map) • Tasting & sales Mon—Fri 8—5 Sat 9—12 • Cellar tours by appointment • Bring your own picnic • Tourgroups • Conferences • Views • Wheelchair-friendly • Owners 80 members • Winemaker Johan Delport • Production 27 000 tons • PO Box 8 Klawer 8145 • Tel (027) 216-1530 • Fax (027) 216-1561 • E-mail klawerwyn@kingsley.co.za

JOHAN Delport is well into his second year in the driver's seat at this Olifants River co-op, named after the wild clover that thrives here alongside myriad indigenous plants which explode into riotous colour in spring, the West Coast's famous flower season. He's stepping up the red cultivars and fine-tuning for fruitier whites. Foreign markets — mainly Holland, Britain and Sweden — are still an emphasis.

Klawer range

> **Merlot** ✿ 😊 "BBQ wine," says Johan Delport unequivocally, and we agree. **99** lightish, tasty choc/black cherry fruit. 1 000 cases. **98** flew with British Airways/Comair. **Grenache Blanc de Noir** ✿ 😊 Only BdN entirely from this grape in SA. **00** coppery blush, pleasing red-wine meatiness; dollop sugar tastes smooth rather than sweet. Lightish 11,5% alc. 1 200 cases.

Pinotage ✿ New Strapping, almost porty **00**, 'sweet' character from 14% alc. Not for the fainthearted. Unoaked. 12 000 cases. Also in 1,5 ℓ magnums. **Colombard** ✿ **00** something of a celebrity: first 2000 vintage wine (from anywhere) on Swedish liquor shelves. Lightish, but good dusty green-guava attack, bone dry. Best in youth. 1 300 cases. **Late Harvest** ✻ **NV** (00) semi-sweet chenin/colombard, simple, not too sugary. 750 cases. **Special Late Harvest** ✿ Pleasantly uncloying sweet dessert from chenin. **00**'s light honeyed richness balanced by acid. 13,5% alc. 1 200 cases. **Best Wishes Cuvée Brut** ★ Despite feel-good name, this not an easy toast. Heavy in palate, lacks zip. **NV** carbonated sparkle from sauvignon. 7 000 cases. **Michelle Doux** ✿ Charming, very sweet carbonated sparkler from red muscadel. Pretty pale coral lights; frisky mousse; billowing muscat. Lowish 11,5% alc. 2 000 cases. **Red Muscadel** ✿ Regular show-winner. **00** very sweet but not unctuous; quite spirity still so give bit of time before sipping solo, or pour now over crushed ice. 18,5% alc. 700 cases. **White Muscadel** ✿ **98** VG showing bit of age in honeyed 'oiliness' in bouquet, though tropical fruits still balanced in palate by good acidity, spirity bounce. 16,5% alc. 1 500 cases. **Hanepoot** ✿ Sweet, spirity **99**, some medicinal tones but good acidity. 19% alc. 1 000 cases. Also available (not tasted): In 750 ml: **Dry Red, Chardonnay, Chenin Blanc**; in 5 ℓ 'barrel bags': **Grand Cru, Late Harvest**.

Birdfield range

Export range, striking packaging suitably avian themed.

> **Merlot** ⚘ 🙂 Super little quaffer, choc-cherries smoothed to suaveness by supple tannins. High 13,5% alc needs watching. 1 200 cases.

Shiraz ‡ Full-bodied **99**'s varietal smoke/red cherry generosity marred by bracing acidity. 13% alc. Not oaked. 660 cases.

. . . .

Kleinbosch see International Wine Services, Cape Wine Cellars

Klein Constantia Estate   ⟰ ⟰ ⟰

Constantia (see Constantia map) • Tasting & sales Mon–Fri 9–5 Sat 9–1 Tasting fee R10 p/p for groups • Cellar tours as above by appointment • Views • Owners Duggie & Lowell Jooste • Winemaker Ross Gower (since 1984) • Viticulturist Kobus Jordaan (since 1980) • Vineyards 73 ha • Production 600 tons 45 000 cases • PO Box 375 Constantia 7848 • Tel (021) 794-5188 • Fax (021) 794-2464 • E-mail kleincon@global.co.za • Website www.kleinconstantia.com

LE MONDE recently sent one of its foreign correspondents to South Africa on a special 3-day assignment. He had a serious issue to investigate. Not post-Mandela society, not our Aids crisis, not World Cup football blues or other matters of state; his brief was solely to probe the only Cape representative the French newspaper had targeted for a major feature on "great wines of the world". It's instructive that a news journalist rather than a wine-writer was dispatched to uncover the secrets of Klein Constantia Vin de Constance's success. Because while rhapsodies can be and are written about its flavours, Constance most strikingly tells the story, both ancient and modern, of the South African wine industry — its early glories and new struggle to re-captivate the world. In fact, perhaps this replica of the 18th century Constantia desserts — 'vin de Napoleon' the French call it, after a famous fan — does qualify as a State affair after all: luscious lubrication for the Mbkeian concept of the African Renaissance? Such is the clamour for Constance that muscat de frontignan plantings (from the same clones imported to the Cape in 1656) have grown to 7,5 ha. The vineyards — all replanted since the Jooste family began the rescue operation of this more than 3 centuries old estate in 1980 — now total 73 ha. Happily they escaped the fires which rampaged over the Constantia mountains during the harvest of 2000, destroying the surrounding forests — though some sauvignon blanc was sandblasted as blaze-fighting helicopters scooped up water from the KC dam. It's white wines in general but this variety in particular which affable winemaker Ross Gower sees as the estate's "kingpin". After 16 years in this post (and still prone to wickedly teenage antics given half a chance) it's clear he's still having fun, and with young owner Lowell Jooste, epitomises the relaxed, friendly, unpretentious but well-informed team-spirit which gives this modern Cape showpiece its notable visitability.

✿**Cabernet Sauvignon** Consistent performer, in crossover style; mix of 'new' fruitier clone (about 40%), some dusty 'old' clone notes (60%). More echoes of former in **97**; spicy, mint/cedary fragrance toned down by some traditional cab undertones. Med-weight, sweet-fruited length presently trimmed by minerally tannin grip; good potential to develop more interesting complexity; one of nicest of recent vintages. Pvs more understated. **96** ⚘ stylish, oaky-fruit nose, hints of mint, firm tannins. Oaked 2 yrs. **Cabernet Sauvignon Reserve** Single vyd, all new, fruity/mint clone. **97** two bottlings, one for CWG auction, barrel selection; second ✿ sold from farm; much bigger, richer than above; oaky cigar box tones adds gravitas to fresh, minerally, cassis outpouring. Dense, very intense flavours, ripe tannin infusion. All suggests will grow in complexity over next 2–4 yrs. Oaking as above.

. . . .

✦ Marlbrook Bdx-style blend distinguished from Cabernet above by more classic cab green walnut/cassis character. Latest **97** one of best since maiden **88**. **97** with fresh, pure-toned fruit from cool vintage, unfolding ripeness paced by expensive cedary oak scents. Very sleek, with fine-tannined elegance; belies its 13,8% alc. 3 700 cases. **96** and most pvs ✦✦. From **94** cab-dominated, typically 55% with 40% merlot, 5% cab f. Fr oak polished, small portion new.

✦ Chardonnay Released around 18 mths after vintage, "when French 'stink' has blown off," chortles Ross Gower. **99** (due Jun 2001, by when might have improved on present ✦✦ rating) amply illustrates his point; he assures an evolution similar — though on lighter scale — to **98**, itself showing benefit of extra year's mellowing. Drier, more contained; even touch of Burgundian ripeness (an occasional trait in these chardonnays), induced by roasted hazelnut/oatmeal complexity, greater harmony between palate's lemony grip, leesy richness. Still has some way to go to reach unified whole. Fermented classically in 500 ℓ Fr oak, 45% new (usually closer to 30%) 13,5% alc. 4 500/6 000 cases.

✦ Sauvignon Blanc ▼ Blazed trail for variety and Constantia valley since **86**; probably most frequent SAA listing of all wines entered over period of these awards; often multi-vintage/older selections (eg **97** on 2000 list). These (all unwooded) are stayers, witness **86**'s top rating in a 14-vintage vertical tasting mid-2000. Since **95**, includes 10% semillon booster, which broadens sweeping gooseberry/fig purity, fruity 'sweetness' of current **00**. Full of youthful bravado, though less typically 'thrusting' (acid 6 g/ℓ — gram lower than usual). Preferred by Gower over **99** for its "better fruit". All machine-harvested to achieve ±13,5% alc. 17 000 cases.

✦ Rhine Riesling ▼ "The poor man's Klein Constantia," sighs Gower. Whereas price hikes on the Sauvignon and Chardonnay see them rush out of the cellar even faster, this — with proven track record — merely trickles out at real value R24. New vintage introduced only when pvs sold out, coincidentally big advantage, as these best after 3–4 yrs — in some yrs even longer. Secondary toastiness creeping into **98**, deepening the limey/spicy keenness; honeyed botrytis tones expand resonating tail. **99** still bears straightforward fruity mantle; floral simplicity a giveaway to its youth, as is still-obvious sweetness — with age these become mellow, apparently drier. Extremely versatile food partner throughout meal, not only spicy Eastern dishes. 5 400/2 400 cases.

✦ Sauvignon Blanc Noble Late Harvest This and Constance below, much admired in France (where most of this opulent, gorgeous dessert is sold). Indeed, reflects some French Sauternes influence, though generally weighing in somewhat sweeter (latest **98** 120 g/ℓ sugar; Sauternes usually below 100 g/ℓ); similar oak polish intensifying spicy-sweet botrytis dimension. Deep orange peel/ toffee brittle resonance, the steelier edge of sauvignon for grip in finish. Very small quantities (800 cases) — and in 500 ml bottles — intermittently part of KC's range, at least for auctions. 14,5% alc. Yr new 500 ℓ oak.

✦ Vin de Constance One of the Cape's few cult wines — justified as much by its inherent individuality as its icon status with the British — UK visitors to the Cape can be identified by the number of cases of Constance in their luggage. "They're buying a legend" says Ross Gower. Indeed, this delicious white dessert harks back to — and echoes — the original Constantias (whose reputation the British helped establish). Made from the same variety, muscat de frontignan; vyd propagated from the very clones imported by Dutch Governor of the Cape, Jan van Riebeeck, in 1656. Not botrytised — this is not a pseudo-Sauternes. And while Constance may not tower over full-blown 'noble rot' stunners, it has its own riveting, complex minty, sweet lemon-honey impact, the muscat flavours (absent in most 'noble rot' wines) a restrained part of a larger, complex ensemble. The world's most famous near-teetotaller, former President Nelson Mandela, has been known to sample this tipple — now on celebrated restaurant lists from Paris to Singapore. Latest **96** as always brilliantly presented (acknowledged by Grape's Packaging Award judges). Burnished gold perhaps only indication of more than usual raisined percentage, otherwise characteristic mint/toffee/lime aromas, true to the style; a bold structure (14,7% alc.) ensures keepability, promises a long, operatic unfurling in bottle. On the sweet side of many desserts, at about 120 g/ℓ sugar. Picked ultra-ripe — 40 °B — with berries at all stages of dehydration (yield: 4 t/ha); requires Herculean effort from fermenting yeasts, which stumble to defeat; then 18 mths rounding-off in seasoned 500 ℓ oak casks. 1 500 cases. **94** *Wine* ✿✿, **95** *Wine* ✿, **93** *Wine* ✿.

✿ **Brut Triple Zero** Those who hold that the millennium begins on 1st Jan 2001 will benefit from extra yr afforded this one-off **NV** MCC millennium sparkler; limited magnums still available for this second celebration; should be even better than first time around. 100% chardonnay, acknowledged slow developer; tantalising warm biscuit, doughy bouquet mellowed by **92–95** vintage span, some barrel-ferment enrichment. Stunningly dry; no sugar addition. An all-night party animal; could mix unnoticed with many Champagne counterparts. Ex-estate only, about R120. 4 700 (1,5 ℓ)magnums.

Pinot Noir ✿ **98** dark plummy patina, light-texture/structure, but sufficient guts to absorb yr's maturation in 50% new Fr oak, not lose agreeable ripe cherry/truffle nuances. New clone 113. Fermented, unusually, by natural yeast. Barrelled, 50% new, in Burgundian-favoured Allier/Vosges from single cooper. 280 cases. **Shiraz** ✿ Dramatic, deliberate New World style; identified in **98** by vivid blood-red hue, familiar pushy Am oak spicy sweetness. Lightish texture, though not body; some gamey savouriness will beneficially emerge as oak fades. 800 cases. **97** Air France–Preteux Bourgeois trophy, *Wine* ✿✿.

Kleindal

VINIMARK owned easy drinking range made in conjunction with local growers mainly for export to the UK, Netherlands and Germany.

✿ **Cabernet Sauvignon** Good few rungs above pvs. **00**, sampled young, most promising: long, savoury tannins and touch vanilla from light oaking. 13% alc.

Sauvignon Blanc ✿ ☺ Reductive handling from vyd to cellar delivers fruity vibrancy in **00**, super minerally texture.13,2% alc.

Pinotage 00 tank sample too unformed to rate, but hints at ✿ potential. Some acetone/ester overtones, earthy resonance. 13% alc. **Rosé 00** untasted. **Chardonnay** ✿ **00** buttery tropical fruit toned with vanilla, clean dry citrus finish. Well wooded. 13,3% alc. **Chenin Blanc** ✡ Lightish gentle **00**, undemanding just-dry; some quaffable lemonade tones.

Kleine Draken 🍷 🍷

Paarl (see Paarl map) • Tasting & sales Mon–Fri 8–12h30, 1.30–5 Closed Jewish & public holidays • Owner Cape Gate (Pty) Ltd • Vineyards 12 ha • Production ± 10 000 cases • Tel (021) 863-2368 • Fax (021) 863-1884 • E-mail zandwijk@capegate.co.za

"IT'S JUST NOT KOSHER" are words that you won't ever hear at this Paarl cellar, where wine is made under the supervision of the Cape Beth Din to super-strict Kosher and Kosher le Pesach standards. Initially, winemaker Neil Schnoor did not find the requirement that he 'cook' his wines very … well, kosher. "Flash pasteurisation is integral to the process," explains the ex-industrial chemist, who, despite himself, was drawn into the challenge of preserving the grape's delicate aromas and flavours into the bottle. He's certainly got the hang of it: his first vintage — "surprisingly easy" — is the first from this property in several years to be certified. Schnoor intends to maintain an even keel, which bodes well for the future of these unique wines, previously marketed under the Zandwijk label. The range, unrated, in the winemaker's own words includes: **Cabernet Sauvignon New 99** Full bodied, rich, dry red with prominent wood. **Dry Red** A fruity cab/merlot **NV** blend that needs no ageing. **Sauvignon Blanc New 00** very crisp dry white with subtle background fruit. **Dry White** A lovely, fruity, blended **NV**. **Kiddush** The traditional sacramental beverage used for Shabat etc. **NV** from cinsaut. 100 g/ℓ residual sugar.

. . . .

Kleine Zalze Wines

Stellenbosch (see Stellenbosch map) • Tasting & sales Mon—Fri 9—5 Sat 9—2 Tasting fee R10 p/p refundable with purchases exceeding R50 • Cellar tours by appointment • Light meals by arrangement • Proclaimed conservation area • Function venue • Owners Kobus Basson & Jan Malan • Winemaker Willem Loots (since 1999) • Viticulturist: Schalk du Toit & Jan Malan • Vineyards 280 ha • Production ±1 800 tons, 80 000 cases total (± 1 600 tons, 70 000 cases own label) 75% red 25% white • PO Box 12837 Die Boord Stellenbosch 7613 • Tel (021) 880-0717 • Fax (021) 880-0716 • E-mail quality@kleinezalze.co.za • Website www.kleinezalze.com

BIG THINGS are happening at this medium-sized Stellenbosch winery, a family partnership between Wellington grape grower Jan Malan and Stellenbosch ex-lawyer Kobus Basson. The pair has agreed to link their planned golf course/residential estate along Blaauwklippen river to the glitzy downstream Spier/Ritz-Carlton development. They also plan to open a country-style restaurant on the historic Kleine Zalze property, first planted with vines in 1683 by Nicolaas Cleef, a German from the village of Gross Salze. Property development of a different kind is taking place near the old mission village of Elim, where some 20 ha of sauvignon, semillon, merlot and chardonnay, as well as pinot and gamay noir have taken root very near Cape Agulhas in a joint-venture with the van Niekerk brothers of Knorhoek. On Kleine Zalze itself, merlot, pinotage and shiraz lead the red vine focus, while Jan Malan's Wellington's parcels include mature bushvines and some new-clone plots. Though Europe remains the chief foreign market, some less traditional markets such as Poland and China now feature on transport waybills — and Kleine Zalze is the only SA name on Shangri-La wine lists in Malaysia.

Vineyard Selection range

✿ **Cabernet Sauvignon Barrel Matured** ✔ **98** reviewed in pvs ed still long way from peak, needs 5–7 yrs to give its best. Deep, concentrated, ripe; silky texture with fragrant minty, oak-spicy overlay. Clanks with show awards — VG, golds at SAYWS/Monde Selection/Singapore International Challenge. Kleine Zalze vyd, ±30 yrs old, Fr barrique aged, some new, 14 mths. 12,5% alc. 500 ml. 1 700 cases. **97** ✿ also good but lighter, not as much pizzazz. For drinking now.

✿ **Shiraz Barrel Matured** ✔ Spicy, aromatic **98** pounced on by wine mail order club. Still developing though already some bottle-age roundness/richness. Attractive savoury/'wild' character balanced by ripe plummy fruit, supple, long tannins. 14 mths oaked, 90% Fr, remainder Am casks. 13% alc. 1 100 cases. Newest **99**, from barrel, too young to realistically rate but in similar 'untamed' mould. Promising.

✿ **Chardonnay Barrel Fermented** ✔ Robust and big (14% alc), **99** packs a powerful fruity punch — almost sweet citrus backed by vanilla oak. Appears some way to go still, so no need to rush to uncork. Partly barrel fermented/aged 4 mths Fr barriques. 500 ml. 3 100 cases.

Merlot Barrel Fermented ✿ **98** has shed some of its initial oakiness, but plummy fruit needs bit more time to assert itself. SAYWS gold. Yr Fr oak. 13% alc. 1 500 cases. **Chenin Blanc Barrel Fermented** ✿ **00** newest release of this Fr oak fermented/aged vyd block selection not as immediately convincing as pvs, which flew with SAA. Understated lemonade/guava tones, powerful oakiness all need time to develop/settle.

✿**Pinotage** Trademark green banana/redcurrant in latest **00**, sampled straight from barrel and too unformed to rate. First release **98**, yr Fr oaked.

Kleine Zalze range

Gamay Noir ✿ 🍷 Wellington grapes, unornamented by oak, star in this bright cherry-red number. Probably more super-sipper than quaffer (14,5% alc), **00**'s light-toned, raspberry/banana mouthful is wonderfully moreish, as is the R18/bottle cellar price. 800 cases.

✿**Cabernet Sauvignon** Oak-brushed **98**, featured in pvs guide, continues to charm: soft, almost sweetly ripe fruit, gentle yet quite full, some coconut/liquorice fascinations in finish. 9 000 cases. SAYWS gold. Mail order club pick, as was **97** SAA.

Merlot ✿ New Easy, non-challenging; plenty of varietal character — plums and whiffs of violets/pepper — light and satisfying. Winemaker's food match sounds intriguing: "pork belly-wrapped kudu fillet with lemon herb mozzarella dressing, grilled to perfection". 1 750 cases. **Chardonnay** ▼ Latest unwooded **00** youthfully gawky when tasted mid-2000, difficult to rate conclusively but showed ✿ potential. **98** still available at press time, mail order club selection, as was **99** ☆ SAYWS gold, prematurely tired. **Chenin Blanc Bush Vines** ✿ Straightforward everyday **00**, with crushed sugar cane/barley sugar hints, some tobacco whiffs, strident acidity which would cut the richness of, say, paella or lightly chilled seafood. Strapping 13,7% alc needs watching. 850 cases. **Sauvignon Blanc** ✿ Medbodied **99** no longer leaps friskily out of the glass. Now gently lopes through nettle/gooseberry/green pepper patches. 1 300 cases. Latest **00** ☆ slow out of the starting blocks. Perhaps needs time to energise.

Klein Gustrouw Estate

Stellenbosch • Tasting, sales, cellar tours by appointment • Bring your own picnic • Facilities for children • Tourgroups • Walks • Views • Proclaimed conservation area • Wheelchair-friendly • Owners Chris & Athalie McDonald • Winemaker/ viticulturist Chris McDonald • Vineyards 16 ha • Production 103 tons (23 tons, ±1 500 cases own label) 100% red • PO Box 6064 Stellenbosch 7612 • Tel/fax (021) 887-4556

"HOW MANY WINERIES can claim, as can we, that the winemaker has eyeballed every single bunch of grapes in every vintage to date?" challenges the proud owner of those eyeballs, Chris McDonald. And long may he continue to do so — the grapes seem to respond well to the scrutiny, although there are no plans to expand the single label range. This guide has played a happy role in the household wellbeing — a UK reader has secured for Chris and Athalie McDonald the long- sought replacement for Hamish, the Scottish Deerhound who died in 1998 (but soulfully lopes across the wine label, in front of the entrance to the 1817 Cape Dutch homestead). The new resident is named Henry.

✿**Cabernet Sauvignon-Merlot 98** reflects good hot vintage in deep colour, ripe berry aromas, along with notes of vanilla and chocolate. Ripe, soft tannins support cherry accented fruit; slight medicinal twist in finish. Typically blend includes some 63% cab; Nevers oak barriques, one-third new. 13,8% alc. 1 300 cases. **97**, with green pepper mingling with the cherries and dusty charry oak, shows that this wine has capacity to develop with a few years in bottle. **96** VG.

Klein Simonsvlei see Niel Joubert Wines

Kloofzicht Estate

Tulbagh (see Tulbagh map) • Tasting & sales daily 9—6 • Cellar tours by appointment • B&B/ self-catering guest cottage • Play area for children • Walks • Views • Owner/winemaker/viticulturist Roger Fehlmann • Vineyards 1,5 ha • Production 8 tons 600 cases 100% red • PO Box 101 Tulbagh 6820 • Tel/fax (023) 230-0658 • E-mail thesunqueen@lando.co.za

THIS QUIRKY TULBAGH property is up for grabs: maverick winemaker-owner Roger Fehlmann is heading for the hills of Piedmont in northern Italy. In search of a new environment and stimulation, he discovered "Le Langhe, the kingdom of Nebbiolo and Barbera, King and Queen among vines" and waxes lyrical about ancient hilltop villages that slumber away, a canvas-like landscape where truffles grow and wild boars roam the forests. What clinched it for him was when some local Dionysian character proposed a membership to the 'Guild of the Knights of the Truffle and Good Wines' and offered an opportunity to play a major hand in the collaboration to raise the local winemaking tradition to new heights. But all this means that Fehlmann and his partner Sharon are moving in the direction of lessening their engagement on the SA front. "Our beautiful farm and winery is for sale. We hope to find a party who is prepared to uphold the Kloofzicht tradition in the same loving and sincere manner!"

✿**Alter Ego** Releases of this highly individual merlot/cabernet blend sporadic/ spontaneous. Pvs was **94**, featuring ripe, soft fruit and quite grippy tannins for unusual firm and sappy effect. Now it's the turn of **92** ✿, which peacenik Roger Fehlmann would like to share with Saddam Hussein and "anyone who'd would rather talk love rather than war". Hungarian/French oak. 13% alc. 1 000 cases. For old time's sake, and because it's his 50th birthday, we'll let the winemaker describe his creation in his own words: "Probably the pinnacle of my winemaking career in SA. Initially an enfant terrible — harsh, tart, acidic, intent on resisting any taming effort. Ultimately morphed into a bigger, deeper and more expressive wine than usual. I could not have chosen a more ponderous occasion than my 50th birthday to release the wine (Demi-Centenary Edition) to the public."

Kloovenburg

Riebeek Berg (see Swartland map) • Tasting & sales Mon—Fri 9—4.30 Sat 9—2 • Owner Pieter du Toit • Winemaker Pieter du Toit • Vineyard manager Bennie Liebenberg (since 1998) • Vineyards 130 ha • Production 2 600 cases 70% red 30% white • PO Box 2 Riebeek Kasteel 7307 Tel (022) 448-1635 • Fax (022) 448-1035 • E-mail kloovenburg@mbury.new.co.za

"SHIRAZ is the star of the valley," says an enthusiastic Pieter du Toit from the newest winery in the Riebeek Valley, whose own Shiraz is something of a stunner. Wines were last made on this old family farm, where the steeply terraced vineyards bring to mind the home of shiraz in the northern Rhône, in the 50s. Until four years ago, when Du Toit and his son jumped in feet first and made some 200 bottles of foot stomping wine (it was matured at the University of Stellenbosch), a rehearsal for the 98 debut. Wines were originally made at Riebeek Cellars with the assistance of winemaker Eric Saayman but the restored cellar on the farm is now in use. The 2000 harvest featured some exceptionally hot weather (fortunately cooled by the West Coast breeze) and Du Toit is surprised at how soft the red wines are. Shiraz may be the star but new players include a full bodied pinotage and a lightly wooded chardonnay, with a deserving role for Kloovenburg's olive oil, the first pressed in the valley.

✿**Shiraz** ✔ Unlike so many current Cape shirazes, showing restraint in **98** yet with no lack of fruit (new clones) or varietal character: sweet spice/ woodsmoke/grind of pepper; long supple tannins; apparent sweetness in finish from a few grains sugar (3,2 g/ℓ). Accessible now with promise of good development over 3–5 yrs. Yr new Am oak. 1 000 cases. 13% alc.

✿ **Chardonnay** Barrel fermented, assertive **00** with bold 14% alc, yet delicate floral introduction plus tropical whiffs of papaya, ripe banana and understated oak; new Fr barrelling more apparent in palate: sweet vanilla/peach tones; mouthfilling, good firm finish. 333 cases.

Pinotage ✿ Relaxed plummy style, fragrant oak and some attractive walnut hints in med-bodied **98**; some edgy tannins need yr/2 to smooth (which should add extra star luminance). From 30 yr old vyd, among first Swartland pinotage lots. 6 mths new Am oak. 1 300 cases.

. . . .

Knorhoek

Stellenbosch (see Stellenbosch map) • Tasting & sales Mon—Fri 10—4 Sat 10—1 • Cellar tours by appointment • Meals/refreshments for groups by arrangement • Guest house (accommodates 16) with small conference/function/entertainment area • Facilities for children Tel (021) 882-2114 • Tourgroups • Views • Wheelchair-friendly • Owners Hansie & James van Niekerk • Winemaker Hansie van Niekerk with the Kleine Zalze team • Viticulturist James van Niekerk, with Morne Kruger • Vineyards ± 100 ha • Production ± 800 tons (60 tons, ± 5 000 cases own label) 50/50 red/white • PO Box 2 Koelenhof 7605 • Tel/fax (021) 882-2627 • E-mail hansie@knorhoek.co.za • Website www.knorhoek.co.za

SCHOOL TIES go a long way for Knorhoek co-owner Hansie van Niekerk and Kleine Zalze's Kobus Basson. The latter, on hearing his old chum wanted to launch his own wine label, provided cellar space, modern winemaking technology and marketing know-how. Now that Knorhoek is up and flying (locally and to the UK, Netherlands and Switzerland), van Niekerk and brother James aim to secure more permanent cellar space in the next two years (the facilities on their Simonsberg eyrie are outdated). Meanwhile they've consolidated their assets, selling off most of the fruit orchards and some 30 ha of vines to businessman David King, who has built a house and cellar of his own. About 130 ha of top-notch vineyards remain, and major replantings and greenfields development over the next 3 years will focus on cabernets sauvignon and franc, merlot, shiraz and pinotage. Meanwhile southerly parcels established near Cape Agulhas in a joint-venture with Kleine Zalze will come into fruit in 2001.

✿✿ **Cabernet Sauvignon** ⛤ In its first outing, this excellent Simonsberg cab vaulted over the heads of many to steal the limelight locally (raves in *Wine* ✿✿, among others) and overseas with New World style **97** VVG. Follow-up **98** in more linear 'Cape' mode: mulberry/cassis disciplined by fine-grained tannins, clean cedar spice from 18 mths Fr barriques, half new; suggestion of pencil shavings in satisfying dry finish. Like pvs, approachable now, though probably best in 3–5 yrs. 12,9% alc. 1 600 cases.

✿ **Pinotage** With super-dense, almost viscous fruit/tannins, this a pinotage for stronger constitutions, at least in strapping youth. **98** ✿✿, like **97** *Wine* ✿✿, needs several yrs, but patience should be rewarded. Good black cherry fruit, fragrant vanilla oak. Yr small oak, 50/50 new/used. 13,4% alc. 1 200 cases.

Sauvignon Blanc ✿ Uncompromising, individual **99**, austere almost stark with light gravelly tones (though far from insubstantial at almost 13,5% alc), fiercely dry. 1 200 cases.

. . . .

Koelenhof Winery

Stellenbosch (see Stellenbosch map) • Tasting & sales Mon—Thu 8.30—1; 2—5 Fri 8.30—1; 2—4.30 Sat 8.30—12.30 • Self-catering picnics (deli nearby) • Owners 75 shareholders • Manager Helmie de Vries (since 1969) • Winemakers Louw Engelbrecht (since 1997), Andrew de Vries (since 1997) • Production 12 000 tons (4 000—5 000 cases own label) 83% white 16% red 1% rosé • PO Box 1 Koelenhof 7605 • Tel (021) 882-2020/1 • Fax (021) 882-2796 • E-mail koelwyn@mweb.co.za

. . . .

THE "TERRIFYINGLY HOT" 2000 harvest put the previous three years' upgrade of this Stellenbosch cellar to the ultimate test. "All previous volume-records were broken — per day, per week and harvest average," reports winemaker Louw Engelbrecht. To top it all, the heat caused one of the cellar's main fuses to melt, setting fire to the vegetation around an electrical transformer in the garden. A hastily assembled, occasionally angst-ridden crew of volunteer firefighters, including local farmers, the landscape architects and some truck drivers gamely beat the flames until the fire department arrived. "Not much fun-time this harvest," remarks Engelbrecht dryly. As if in celebration of surviving the crush, the range has spouted fresh labels featuring an attractive reinterpretation of the winery's arum lily motif.

✿ **Merlot First release 98 Wine** ✿ developing fruitfully in bottle; velvety colour to match smooth blackberry/cherry fruit, with mocha/oak-spice nuances. Smidgeon cab for extra complexity. 9 mths 2nd fill Fr/Am barriques (50/50). **00** preview similar quality; plummier, attractive mineral tones.

> **Koelnektar** ✿ ☺ Natural Sweet style 'Cool Nectar'; **00** again 100% gewürz, 100% charming: textbook rose-petal bouquet, sweet, smooth. Lowish 10,2% alc. Louw Engelbrecht recommends Indian cuisine. 210 cases. **Sec Sparkling** ✿ ☺ NV Delicate melon/mango flavours in bright, gently dry-finishing carbonated sauvignon/chenin. Lowish 10,8% alc.

Cabernet Sauvignon-Merlot ✿ **98**'s initially frisky tannins have relaxed, revealing ripe blackberry/cassis, firm dry finish. 70/30 blend. Still a bit of tannin, which can be matched with richer cuisines or kept another yr/2. 9 mths 2nd fill barriques, 50/50 Fr/Am. 13,2% alc. 223 cases. Preview of **99** (labelled Koelenberg), 80/20 blend, full flavoured, easy to drink yet quite refined. **Pinotage** ✿ **99** (new label) vivid cerise colour; some plummy fruit and emphatic charry wood. Oak-chipped. 13,5% alc. **Cabernet Sauvignon** Full-bodied **00** tasted from barrel promises deep blackberry fruit with oak-spice backing, lingering flavours and ripe tannins. Should crack ✿ on current form. **Cinsaut-Shiraz** NEW 80/20 blend, **00** (sample, not rated) reveals well defined fruit, firm structure. Potential ✿ on release. **Pinotage Rosé** ✿ This cellar's calling card, and "the wine we're most complimented on". Pale cherry red with bright pink sheen. Cherries again in **00** palate, with raspberries and lots of (natural) sweetness. Usual lowish alc: 10,6%. 625 cases. **Koelenhoffer** ✿ Cellar's perennial top seller, semi-dry blend sauvignon/chenin. Tasted soon after bottling, not quite as zingy as pvs; should perk up, however, and beguile with its usual lemon/cut-grass flavours. Also 1 000 ml screwcap. Good beach party fare. **Bukettraube** ✿ Passionfruit and some minerally aromas in **00**, easy drinking with delicate sweetness and smooth finish, moderate 12% alc. Enjoy young and fresh. 240 cases. **Hanepoot** ✿ Gentle, sweet fortified dessert, **99** with delicate quince flavours and soft finish. 15,8% alc. ± 400 cases. **00** sample much more intense, powerful raisin/fig tones. Traditional style.

Kupferberger Auslese

POPULAR lightish semi-sweet by Bergkelder.

NV ✿ Little connection with German 'auslese' wines, but pleasant blend of chenin with dollop riesling, for early, easy drinking. 12% alc.

KWV International

Paarl (see Paarl map) • Cellar tours by arrangement tel 807-3007/8 • Kelkiewyn bistro for light meals/coffees 9—4 tel (021) 863-2500 • Tours of brandy cellar at Worcester by arrangement tel (023) 342-0255 • Gifts • Tourgroups by arrangement • Owner KWV • Chief cellarmaster Kosie Möller (since 1993) • Viticulturist Chris Albertyn (since 1993) • PO Box 528 Suider-Paarl 7624 • Tel (021) 807-3911 • Fax (021) 807-3000 • E-mail customers@kwv.co.za • Website www.kwv.co.za

THE NEW-MILLENNIUM KWV — a group of companies carved out of the monolithic co-operative block which was previously both referee and team captain in the South African wine game — remains a major force. But just as Springbok rugby is changing its style to meet the demands of a faster, more open, dynamic tactical game — on an increasingly crowded global playing field — so too KWV has re-invented itself to tackle the challenges of the modern marketplace. Spirits are still an important element — over 50% of local brandy emanates from this organisation; its Worcester distillery is the largest in the world; its fortified wines, sherries, liqueurs etc remain big business. But it's the starched-tablecloth and gourmet-picnic drinker whom KWV International targets in 28 countries. (It has a subsidiary, Edward Cavendish & Sons, in the UK; majority shares in Eggers & Franke in Germany; and a "full share" in La Concorde wines — named after its gracious Paarl HQ — in the Netherlands.) Leading its winemaking team is Kosie Möller, who was only 25 when he was hired in 1993. With all the confidence and cheek of youth, he sent the establishment to the bench and initiated an attacking new approach. Squads of new barrels (3 000 a year) were drafted in; lumbering passengers in the side were dropped (previously, producer and co-op members of KWV had made their own wines which were lumped into vast blends). He said this co-op system was "absolute stupidity". And so on. To the credit of the powers-that-were, they listened. Möller's new-era wines have been a revelation. From the chosen leader of the pack, the $100, single vineyard Perold (a Shiraz in its first incarnation, though named after the man who invented pinotage), to the front-row Cathedral Cellar (see under separate entry), to New World-styled Robert's Rock and the regular KWV range, there's been a revolution in the ranks. Even old warhorses like Roodeberg have a fresh set of legs. See also separate entries for Cathedral Cellar, Robert's Rock.

KWV natural wines

✿ Cabernet Sauvignon Continues livelier, more modern pace set by **94**. Latest **98** best of the nineties, in Kosie Möller's estimation, after standout **95**. We agree, though current version, curiously, in more traditional mode with forward herbaceous/vegetal character, no hint of new clone mint. But good and round, berry fruit and nuts in palate held firmly in position by ripe tannins. Should peak around 2005. 13% alc. More accessible than **97**, which more elegant, vinous. **96** gold at 1998 Concours International des Vins, Portugal. **95** Vinexpo gold.

✿ Merlot Pacy **98** several laps ahead of **97 ✿**, which hamstrung by some tough tannins. Latest showcases full blown merlot plumminess, firm but ripe tannins, sound structure. Full, classically — thrillingly — dry. Yr mostly second fill barrels. **96** SAA.

✿ Shiraz 98, as anticipated in pvs ed, open and doing brisk business in the aromatics department: dark-roast coffee, woodsmoke, tobacco all milling about rather sensuously. And again in **99**, here with a pleasant mid-palate 'sweetness' from 8 mths mainly Am oak, velvet finish. Full bodied (13% alc).

Pinotage ✿ Past few vintages not as starry as pvs (**97 ✿**, **94** VG; **92** SAA and VG). **99** metallic, acetone whiffs redeemed by some rich berry fruits and attractive volatility. Finishes short.

✿ Roodeberg This stalwart set to lose even more 'old Roodeberg' fans as Kosie Möller exercises his love of wood. (And there's more to come.) Transformation from clunky pickup truck to sleek coupé reflected in **98** 🌺 with shiraz spice, merlot flesh to cab tannic skeleton and ruby cab's ruddy colour (20/20/45/15 respectively). Some mushrooms, forest floor interests (which good with food). 8–12 mths oak, none new. Dramatic improvement already obvious in **97** (though some dry tannins here call for cellaring or robust cuisine). **96** Concours International gold.

🌺 **Chardonnay** Oak volume gets turned down in **00** (Kosie Möller "not happy" with untasted 99, hence decibel reduction). Allows some lovely 'green' citrus fruit (predominantly lime) to step up to podium. What oak there is (cf bright golden lights, hint of well balanced vanilla) is well judged.

Steen 🌺 'Old Cape' name for chenin blanc used for this bone-dry version (grain sugar distinguishes rendition below, also 100% varietal) **99** still fresh yr out, some tropical fruit with crisp, lemon finish. Good value, easy drinking. **Chenin Blanc** 🌺 Semi-dry version; **00** dash sugar (6,5 g/ℓ) gives nice rich mouthfeel to ripe guava. SA's biggest selling cork-closed export white wine. **Sauvignon Blanc** ⚘ **99**'s initial nettle, cut-grass tang only a memory.

KWV Fortified wines

⚘⚘ **KWV Maatskappywordings Vintage Port 97** N̲e̲w̲ When KWV converted from co-op to company, Kosie Möller was so glad he "wanted to bake a cake". He made this instead (and went on to win 1999 SAA 'port' trophy). Hugely theatrical looks: a black pool of dense, tense, tannic fruit, already fairly developed but demanding much more time — 10–15 yrs? Full (18% alc), grippy, relatively dry in the modern Cape manner (100 g/ℓ sugar). Rises to the occasion.

🌺 **Millennium Vintage Port** N̲e̲w̲ LBV style fortified dessert making a serious statement on its first **99** outing (and speaking in a Portuguese-accented tones: varieties à la Douro (tinta b, souzão, splash touriga); good dollop alc (19,5%), lower-range sugar (99 g/ℓ), strapping tannin structure for keeping. All very convincing and rather nice, but distinctly spirity mid-2000 so give plenty of time.

🌺 **Full Ruby Port** 🏅 Cape-wide trend to Portuguese style evident even here. This **NV** (mostly 95) quite dry, big, mouthfilling, generous ripe berry flavours 19,5% alc, 105 g/ℓ sugar; 2 yrs large wood. Give-away price.

Full Tawny Port 🌺 🏅 Cinsaut's flagrant sweetness takes the dry edge off this gentle, appealing facebrick-coloured wine with some ruddy hints. Tinta b and slosh souzão provide a little extra nuts-and-raisins flavour but no real complexity. 7 yrs old oak, 19,5% alc, 125 g/ℓ sugar.

· ·

Laborie Estate ⚘ ⚘ ⚘

Paarl (see Paarl map) • Tasting & sales Mon—Fri 9—5 Sat 9—1 (winter) Sat/Sun 9—5 (summer) Tasting fee R5 p/p • Cellar tours by appointment • Laborie Restaurant & Wine House (see Eat-out section) • Picnic baskets (24 hours' notice required) • Scenic walks • Owner KWV International • Winemaker Gideon Theron (since 1994) • Viticulturist Henri van Rheenen (since 1998 • Production 35 000 cases 70% red 30% white • PO Box 528 Suider-Paarl 7624 • Tel (021) 807-3390 • Fax (021) 863-1955 • E-mail therongi@kwv.co.za • Website www.kwv-international.co.za

THIS IS KWV'S model estate, just below the pearly granite boulders that give Paarl its name, and equipped with all the requisite winelands accessories — a gracious 200 year old Cape-Dutch manor house, modern tasting room and a restaurant serving authentic regional dishes, all in a working vineyard setting. The valley views from the walking trail that winds through these vines are brilliant, and many visitors book picnic basket at the tasting room to enjoy at designated spots on this micro-wine route.

🌺 **Cabernet Sauvignon** Open, generous Paarl cab, firm but accessible tannins, touch of mint, juicy 'sweet' fruit and nuts, velvet finish. Latest **98** SAA continues upward path broken by **96**, **97** *Wine* 🌺 with few-found oomph. **98** intense purple red, coffee and chocolate in nose. Yr Fr oak. 14% alc.

❀ **Merlot** Attractively grippy, properly dry **98** garbed in brilliant ruby red, intense cherry nose, berries and spice in palate, some firm upfront tannins which perhaps better with grilled fillet. 13% alc.

❀ **Chardonnay** Fat, flavoursome **98** with wraparound mouth appeal: lemon butter in palate, broad citrus and butterscotch to end. 13,5% alc. 4 mths small oak. Upscale from **97** ❀.

❀ **MCC** Highly rated méthode traditionelle sparkle, always a blend of chardonnay, pinot noir, plenty of character from ±3 yrs on lees. Latest **95** led by chardonnay with pinot's ripe fruit apparent in back palate; smooth entry, fine mousse, touch fizzy in mouth, some yeast/ice-cream flavours. More accessible than **94**, which more ageworthy; good mousse and acidic green apple finish. Alcs around 12%.

❀ **Pineau de Laborie** Luxurious, rich dessert in Cognac tradition (grape juice fortified with spirit) — here unabashedly, uniquely South African: made with pinotage (single vyd selection, lightly oaked) with spirity backbone of KWV potstill brandy (17% alc). Gorgeous sweet-prune, marzipan, chocolate array; just the right dollop sugar (90 g/ℓ) for solo sipping of after dinner with dessert or even cheese. **97** in trademark long-necked 375 ml bottle with pinotage purple label.

Pinotage ❀ Firmer, not ungenerous style. **98** touch of rubber in nose, strawberry/raspberry flavours, some resolute tannins but more pliable in palate, 'sweet' finish, good length. 8 mths in oak. 13% alc. **Merlot-Cabernet Sauvignon Bin 88** ❀ Plummy, violet scented merlot has upper hand in undemanding **98**, small Fr oak aged 12 mths. Earthy, dusty introduction; then cherry and some firm but well balanced tannins. 13% alc. **Sauvignon Blanc** ❀ **99** deep-coloured but lacks matching fruity depths. Some shy asparagus/gooseberry tones, crisp finish. **Blanc de Noir** ✣ Bottle fermented sparkler from pinotage, pinots gris/noir. Roses in **97** nose, vigorous bubble though, unusually, lacks balance; sweet aftertaste. Lightish 11,5% alc.

Granite Creek range

Export only collection (untasted), includes Merlot-Cabernet Sauvignon, Chardonnay, Sauvignon Blanc.

. . . .

La Bri

Franschhoek • Tasting & sales at Franschhoek Vineyards (see that entry) • Owner Robin Hamilton • Winemaker Driaan van der Merwe (Franschhoek Vineyards) • Vineyards 18 ha • Production 130 tons 60% white 40% red • PO Box 180 Franschhoek 7690 • Tel (021) 876-2593 • Fax (021) 876-3197 • E-mail info@la-bri.co.za • Website www.la-bri.co.za

FORMER proprietor Michael Trull, ex-advertising agency chief who helped energise this once sleepy valley, died in 2000. He and wife Cheryl co-founded the Vignerons de Franschhoek, pioneered the practice of individual vineyard wines being made by co-ops for members and, though keenly involved with the Denbies vineyard operation in Surrey, England, found time to put the national award winning Quartier Francais restaurant on the Cape culinary map. La Bri continues to bloom, however, in the hands of Rob Hamilton, who bought the beautiful gabled property from the Trulls in 1997. Extensive replanting has seen the vineyard balance shift redwards, with cabernet sauvignon and merlot now the main varieties. A recent milestone was the clinching of a deal with a major local wine mail order club to bottle the new Semillon, grown from venerable century-old vines, exclusively for its members.

❀ **Chardonnay-Semillon** ▼ **98** has improved in bottle beyond all recognition. Partial barrel fermentation now shows as spicy buttered toast richness with chardonnay's citrus tang, semillon's waxy perfume making a fine, modern dry blend.

Cabernet Sauvignon-Merlot Reserve ✦ **98** fuller than pvs yet characteristically restrained, cassis/plum/vanilla spice with good nutty conclusion. 13,5% alc. 3 000 cases. ±Yr small Fr/Am oak. **96** VG. **Chardonnay** Small Fr oak aged **99** not ready for tasting. 450 cases. **Sauvage la Bri** ‡ Unoaked sauvignon, versatile with food. Med/full-bodied **99** in non-assertive mode: supple green apple mouthful, pleasing dry finish. Try with fresh grilled kabeljou or prawns, ventures Driaan van der Merwe. 1 500 cases. **Semillon** ✦ **New** Oak-brushed **99** tastes almost sweet initially, but tangy grapefruit turns briskly dry in lightly waxy finish. SAYWS classwinner. Ancient bushvines. 1 000 cases.

La Cotte see Franschhoek Vineyards

La Couronne

Franschhoek (see Franschhoek map) • Tasting & sales daily 10—3 • Cellar tours by appointment • Continental restaurant (see Eat-out section) Picnics Nov—Apr • Luxury hotel • Tourgroups • Gifts • Conferences • Walks • Mountain biking • Views • Winemaker Velten Tiemann • Viticulturist Sakkie Daniels • Vineyards 15 ha • Production 80 tons 6 000 cases 80% red 20% white • PO Box 448 Franschhoek 7690 • Tel (021) 876-2770 • Fax (021) 876-3788 • E-mail bookings@lacouronnehotel.co.za • Website www.lacouronnehotel.co.za

IT's been a year of highs and lows at this young Franschhoek cellar. Talented 27-year-old winemaker Spike Russell tragically died in a car accident. Passionate about life — and wine — "he was just coming into his element," says owner Miles Oates. "The wines Spike made in 99 are exceptional." Two of these, a Cabernet Sauvignon and a Bordeaux style blend, were released in August 2000. The 2001 crush will be handled by German winemaker Velten Tiemann. On the same property in the Franschhoek valley are lavish lodgings (with 9 new bedrooms), gourmet cuisine (kitchen presided over by high profile chef Peter Goffe-Wood) and a paragliding launch site, with new additions a wine bar and cigar lounge. The wines below were not ready for tasting last year, so all are **New** to this ed.

✦**Ménage à Trois** Refined Bdx blend with excellent borderless fruit/oak structure. Blackberry perfume turns into long, deep, minty-cassis flavour which, despite low acidity (4,6 g/ℓ), is really bright and refreshing. 13,8% alc not noticeable. Cabs s/f, merlot cohabitation; 17 mths Fr oak, none new. 1 000 cases.

✦**Cabernet Sauvignon 99** weighty, deep coloured statement of cassis/black fruits, vanilla oak perfume and long, well woven tannins. Yr new Fr oak. 13,7% alc. 1 500 cases.

✦**Merlot** Less demanding than many Cape examples, but not without interest; **99** lighter toned/bodied, lightly oaked; accessible red cherry in soft dry palate. 13% alc. 700 cases.

✦**Chardonnay** Restrained oaking, says Velten Tiemann, means this "an excellent transition from our crisp cold sauvignon on a hot summer day to our easy drinking merlot with dinner". Taste **99** and you get his point: soft, sweet vanilla oak melds seamlessly with ripe pineapple/mango for effortless drinkability (though strapping 14% alc needs watching). 700 cases.

Sauvignon Blanc ✦ **00** youthful gooseberry/grassy sauvignon bounce, though med/full fresh dry palate ends quite abruptly. **Sauvignon Blanc-Chardonnay** ✦ Aperitif/sundown style **99** not too breathtakingly fresh; gooseberry/pear/citrus smoothed into quaffability by granule sugar. 13% alc. 1 500 cases.

Ladismith Co-op

Klein Karoo (see Klein Karoo map) • Tasting & sales Mon—Fri 9-1; 2-5 • Owners 95 members • Winemaker André Simonis (since 1992) • Production 9 000 tones • PO Box 56 Ladismith 6655 • Tel (028) 551-1042 • Fax (021) 551-1930

MAJOR investments in spirits distilling facilities are the headlines news from this Little Karoo co-op below the 'cloven' Towerkop peak, which gives its name to the small range made by André Simonis. Untasted for this ed, the line-up includes **Ruby Cabernet**, **Chardonnay** (wooded and unwooded), **Chenin Blanc**, **Colombard** New, **Riesling** (Cape), **Stein**.

. . . .

La Fontaine see Long Mountain

. . . .

Laibach Vineyards   ⚐ ⚐ ⚐ ⚐

Stellenbosch (see Stellenbosch map) • Tasting & sales Mon—Fri 9—5 Sat 9—1 Tasting fee R5 p/p • Cellar tours by appointment • Picnic baskets during season by arrangement (24 hours' notice required) • Views • Owners Laibach family • Winemakers Stefan Dorst (since 1997), with Francois van Zyl (since 2000) • Viticulturist Michael Malherbe (since 1994) • Vineyards 40 ha • Production 230 tons (224 tons 17 400 cases own label) 75% red 25% white • PO Box 7109 Stellenbosch 7599 • Tel (021) 884-4511 • Fax (021) 884-4848 • E-mail info@laibach.co.za • Website www.laibach.co.za

COSMOPOLITAN — that's the quality that emerges strongly from these 40 ha vineyards and avant-garde winery in the toney Muldersvlei bowl, within spitting distance of Warwick and Kanonkop, and with similar top red wine ambitions — replanting has been going on at a furious pace. It's a family affair. The owners are Friederich and Loni Laibach, retired from their German business (manufacturing labour safety equipment), who commute regularly between their homes here and on the shores of Lake Lugano in Italy; and daughters Karin (teacher and toyshop owner), Petra (a doctor specialising in cancer research) and her husband Rudolf Kuenst, whose field is broadcast law and who is "a dedicated winelover like all the members of the Laibach family". The winemaking consultant, Stefan Dorst, is a frequent-flyer too. A graduate of Weinsberg in Germany, he's worked all over the place (Australia, Argentina, in Chile for the Jacques Lurton team) and also consults in Spain, at Venta d'Aubert in the Aragon area. Wherever, his winemaking nonnegotiable is ultra-ripe grapes. His new assistant, Francois van Zyl, has rather closer origins — he's from Robertson — but he looks far north for inspiration. The winemaker of Ch Petrus is the person he'd most like to meet.

✿ **Laibach** Impressive new flagship, merlot-powered in **98** with dash cab for complexity (blend makeup to vary with vintage); softer, 'sweeter' than other reds in this company, more initially approachable underfelt of tannin; fragrant cherry, oakspice, plum and some chocolatey richness; good dry finish. 13,6% alc. 2 yrs small oak "individually selected by winemaker". 425 cases.

✿ **Merlot** Firm, sinewy house style reflected in latest **99** ✿, with mulberry, choccherry fruit, light minty wafts. Some strident tannin in need of mellowing age, but good platform of fruit should carry the wine through to maturity. 13,5% alc. 1 500 cases. **98** bit more open, luxurious. These 14 mths in oak.

✿ **Pinotage** Speciality of the house, always brash, broad-shouldered. **97** ABSA Top Ten finalist. **98** plummy, initial oak prominence in palate calling for patience. Plums again in latest **99** ✿ with mulberries and generous slug of oak; undeveloped, so don't rush to uncork. Yr small casks, ±20% new. 1 250 cases.

✿ **Cabernet Sauvignon-Merlot 97** made splashy début with Air France—Preteux Bourgeois competition laurel. This now followed by darker toned, massive **98** ✿ (14% alc). Inky plum colour, dark/bitter choc tastes, some stalkiness, thrusting tannins need time. 2 yrs Fr/Am oak. 2 000 cases. **Cabernet Sauvignon-Merlot Unfiltered 97** not tasted for this ed. Pvs rating ✿.

Cape Classic Dry Red ✿ New ☺ Quaffable, soft, lightly oaked cinsaut/ cab/merlot trio with savoury undertone, spiced with tobacco leaf and sweet strawberry. "Versatile with any cuisine, from poultry to sosaties." 12% alc.

. . . .

Cabernet Sauvignon These definitely not early maturers: **98** ⚘ still very firm, needs good few yrs to relax. Distinct oakiness apparent in latest **99** ⚘ when sampled mid-2000, needs time to meld with good core of fruit. 14 mths Fr/Am oak. More than 13% alc. 1 250 cases. **Chardonnay** ⚘ Partially barrelled (in new Fr oak) **99** quieter than pvs, some tropical, sweet-oaky tones, firmly dry. Try with Christmas turkey roast, suggests the Laibach team. 13,5% alc. 500 cases. **Chenin Blanc** (unwooded) ✲ **00** tasted young, so uncharacteristic quietness perhaps temporary. Lick of sweetness should smooth current acidic bite. Grapes from Saxenburg neighbour farm, Skoonheid. 13,3% alc. 1 250 cases. Also under Inkawu label for export. **Sauvignon Blanc** ⚘ **00** returns to quieter, lighter, grass toned mode (**99** uncharacteristically forward). Latest off-dry, some extra tropical whiffs, clean acidic mouthful. 13% alc. 1 500 cases. **Sweet Natural** ⚘ Unusual (in Cape) blend of riesling, chardonnay (50/50), with intriguing — attractive — melange of toffee apple, menthol and cashew nut. Fruit still holding, but suggest enjoy soon ("with baked dessert lashed with custard"). 375 ml. Will make way for Noble Late Harvest in botrytis years. 425 cases.

. . . .

La Motte Estate 🍷 🍷 🍷

Franschhoek (see Franschhoek map) • Tasting & sales Mon—Fri 9—4.30 Sat 9—12 Fee R5 p/p (groups larger than 10 by arrangement) • Tourgroups by arrangement • Views • Wheelchair-friendly • Owner Hanneli Koegelenberg • Winemaker Jacques Borman (since 1984) • Viticulturist Pietie le Roux (since 1987) • Vineyards 104 ha • Production 800 tons 30 000 cases (375 tons 25 000 cases own label) 70% red 30% white • PO Box 94 Paarl 7622 • Tel (021) 876-3119 • Fax (021) 876-3446 • E-mail cellar@la-motte.co.za • Website www.la-motte.com

RED WINE? From Franschhoek? Well, what can you expect from a youngster whose best school subject was art? Who originally wanted to be an architect? Jacques Borman happily didn't waste time answering such sceptical questions from oldtimers in the wine industry. He started at this prestigious, historic Huguenot estate owned by mezzo-soprano Hanneli Koegelenberg — daughter of Dr Anton Rupert — in 1984, and quickly established not only red wine vineyards (including then-underrated shiraz) but himself as one of the outstanding winemakers of his generation. On intimate terms with every vine, he's unashamedly French-influenced, citing Emile Peynaud and Romanée-Conti's *regisseur* as his wine-idols. And while he admires New World styles (and has turned out some of the nicest for Woolworths), here at La Motte he remains heart and soul a classicist. But never an old-fashioned one. He and his staff come back from France every year bursting with new ideas, all geared towards capturing what Borman calls "the holy grail" — richness and finesse in the same bottle. And those creative talents are fully stretched — he's acknowledged by peers to be a local maestro of the fine art of blending. La Motte's range is no longer being distributed via Bergkelder, but by a new company, Historic Wines of the Cape, headed by the estate's MD, Hein Koegelenberg. Soon to contribute new fruit to the spectrum is La Motte's long-distance vineyard in Bot River. "Fantastic," says Borman.

⚘ **Cabernet Sauvignon** Difficult vintage conditions reflected in **96**'s ⚘ lighter tones (though alc generous 13%); but fine complexity from gamey/spicy hints among the cassis/blackberries fruit. Still with cellar's signature restraint. **95** stylish, steely on release, multifaceted flavours deserving few years to unfold fully.

✲ **Shiraz** A single old mountain vyd yields this longtime Cape benchmark. **97** ⚘ with lip-smacking savoury tannins, layered prosciutto/pepper and gamey wafts over ripe mulberries/plums. Tannins tight still, so give min 2—3 yrs for the pleasure level to rise. 13% alc. As always, superb food wine in drier style. **96** intensely spicy with pepper/smoky aromas. **95** VG.

✲ **Millennium** Finesse typifies this blend of cab s/merlot/cab f, with Borman's Bdx sojourns evident in the styling. **97** ⚘ maintains hallmark minerally richness-with-restraint, complexity. Cassis/red cherries against peppery/oaky backdrop with sweet-violet perfume. Needs time to reach potential. 13% alc. **96** generous build in troubled yr. **95** VG.

✿ **Chardonnay** Individually crafted, irregular release, only when vintage yields a corker. **97** rich, creamy with almond-nutty flavours, superbly lengthy finish. **98** ✿ not as showy; some tropical melons, whiffs of peach; oak integrated but, overall, lower keyed. Limited release, available from estate only. Balance for export etc.

✿ **Sauvignon Blanc** Since maiden **91**, consistently classy table companion, usually longer-lasting than many Cape examples. **99**, with fine counterweight of fruit. **98** more steely structure. Warmer-vintage **00** ✿ good range of fruity/herbaceous flavours, impression of sweetness polishes as it smoothes. Savoury crisp finish. 13% alc.

Blanc Fumé ✿ Oaked and, when young, usually big, bold. Very good food wine. Wood understated in **00** ✿, generally light-toned (though full 13% alc); some subtle gooseberry/green pear fruitiness which concludes with dry acid tang.

. . . .

Landau Du Val

Franschhoek (see Franschhoek map) • Tasting by appointment • Sales Mon—Fri 9—5 • Views • Wheelchair-friendly • Owner Basil Landau • Winemaker Jean Daneel (sauvignon blanc), Karl Lambour (semillon) • Viticulturist Jaco Schwenke (since 1992) • Vineyards 17 ha • Production 200 tons (500 cases own label) • PO Box 104 Franschhoek 7690 • Tel (021) 876-2317 • Fax (021) 876-3369 • E-mail landau@mweb.co.za

This tiny range — a Semillon and a Sauvignon and, new in 2000, a limited release Sauvignon Reserve — must be one of the most pampered in the entire winelands. It's waited on and fussed over by two high-powered winemakers, Jean Daneel, Diners Club laureate, here in one of his guru roles, and Karl Lambour, whose day job is making the white wines at Bergkelder. The vines, on Franschhoek's La Brie property, have their own long-time wellness consultant, Jaco Schwenke, who knows their every need (some rows, more than 90 years old, may require more attention than others). Coddler-in-chief is the owner, retired industrialist Basil Landau, who bought the farm in 1986 and realised a dream in 1995 when he released the first Sauvignon. The range, owing to early deadlines, not available for tasting. Previous ratings: Sauvignon Blanc **99** ✿, Semillon **98** ✿.

. . . .

Landsdowne see Arlington

. . . .

Land's End Wines

Not open to the public • Winemaker Hein Koegelenberg • Viticulturist Tienie Wentzel • Vineyards 35 ha • Production 45 tons 60% white 40% red • PO Box 94 Paarl 7622 • Tel (021) 876-3119 • Fax (021) 876-3446

PUSHING THE SOUTHERN FRONTIER of Cape wine to its extreme is this ground-breaking venture into the misty, rolling hills around the old mission village of Elim; Cape Agulhas, where the Indian and Atlantic Oceans meet, is a sea breeze away. Here, 35 ha of vineyards — sauvignon blanc, semillon, merlot and cabernet — have been established on three properties. The wine below represents not only the first fruits of these young vines but also introduces a new, cool climate area to the South African wine map (Elim has been designated an official 'ward'). Seven "wine-lovers and pioneers" are involved, fronted by experienced cellarmaster Hein Koegelenberg (MD of La Motte where the wine was made).

Sauvignon Blanc ✿ If you're tired of megaphoning New World sauvignons you'll appreciate this non-shouting individual. Delicacy the hallmark, yet no lack of complexity in floral, gooseberry, tropical assembly with unusual apricot scents. Good tingle of acidity reminds these are cool climate vyds, though vines' relative youth evident in overall lighter impression. 13,3% alc. Not overpriced. 2 000 cases.

Landskroon Estate

Paarl (see Paarl map) • Tasting & sales Mon—Fri 8.30—5 Sat 9—1 • Cellar tours by appointment • Light lunches/
coffees/teas on terrace 1 Nov—30 Apr, Mon—Fri 8.30- 2.30 • Self-catering cottage • Play area for children • Gifts •
Views • Permanent display of Stone Age artefacts • Owners Paul & Hugo de Villiers • Winemaker Paul de Villiers jnr
(since 1980), with Kobie Viljoen (since 1999) • Vineyard manager Hugo de Villiers jnr (since 1995) • Vineyards 275 ha
• Production 80% red 20% white • PO Box 519 Suider-Paarl 7624 • Tel (021) 863-1039 • Fax (021) 863-2810 •
E-mail landskroon@mweb.co.za • Website www.landskroonwines.co.za

IT'S MORE MYTH than legend that the Huguenots brought a great array of winemaking
skills to the Cape in the 17th century — many learned on the job when they arrived
to find vineyards established by the Dutch colonists. An exception, however, was
one Jacques de Villiers, a French winemaker by profession. It's in his footsteps that
direct descendant Paul de Villiers jnr is following, on this 9th generation family
estate. And very sure steps those are, at all times, it seems. When asked for his
pet cure for a hangover, this winemaker replies: "Never had one yet." Assuming
he consumes, like most in his position, a fair share of his own produce, this is
certainly a good health testimonial — in fact he and brother Hugo de Villiers jnr,
(whose portfolio is the 275 ha vineyards) make a point of minimum chemical dosing
in and out of the cellar. Also contributing to the no-headaches effect is Landskroon's admirable price policy. These wines win loads of prizes and are sought
after in 13 countries, but the short- and long-term goals here are distinctly unop-
portunistic: just to "provide value-for-money" Paul de Villiers says.

✿ **Cabernet Sauvignon** Steadily improving label, buoyed by first-class fruit and
infusions of expensive new oak. **99** (sample), 30% aged in new casks, terrific
culmination of improvement begun with **97** SAA, with suppler tannins, bigger
fruit than pvs. **98** denser, riper, some minty new-clone whiffs, rich vanilla oak
backing. Good now and over 3–6 yrs. **99**, most satisfying of these, hints at ✿
potential in classic minerally/lead bouquet, sweetly ripe berry fruit, big soft tannins. **Cabernet Sauvignon Reserve** The elevator sweeping above Cabernet
into Cape's top echelon reaches its final destination with this penthouse version,
98 ✿ oozing sophistication and style from all new small Fr oak ageing, 10 mths.
Concentrated mulberry/red berry fruit, minerally/lead pencil bouquet, hints of
mint choc and almost sweet tasting toasty oak; obvious but soft tannins. You
could dive in right now, but another 6–8 yrs will multiply the pleasure. 13% alc.
Peek into **99** casks, mostly cleaned-up clones, reveals massive concentration;
crackles with potential.

✿ **Merlot** ▼ Everything about **99** ✿, upscale from pvs. Riper, fleshier, better
defined plum/cherry fruit, very nicely backed by sweet violets, sweetish/charry
oak. **98**, itself step beyond pvs, ready; could go few more yrs.

✿ **Shiraz** This label really going places from **00** (sample). More bountiful, purer
fruit (mulberries/blackberries/black cherries), powerful varietal aromatics of
woodsmoke/toast/fresh earth. Potential ✿. ±14% alc. No **99**. **98** *Wine* ✿
developing well, could still go 4–6 yrs. **97** ✿ SAA.

✿ **Morio Muscat Jerepico** ▼ Yr in bottle has begun to release **99**'s potential.
Fortifying spirit now more integrated; flavour, though still fresh, richer, more
velvety; swirling jasmine/honeysuckle/muscat perfumes. Non-cloying, almost
brisk finish. 17,5% alc.

✿ **Port** With their third prestigious SAYWS championship for non-muscat fortified
preening in the trophy cabinet, Paul & Hugo de Villiers (cocking a snook at colleagues in Calitzdorp) have declared Klapmuts 'Port Kapital of SA'. Which should
please the admiring multitudes who snap up this amazing bargain (spiralling
demand places strain on the dVs' policy of having 2 vintages available concur-
rently). **96/97** will be last to feature triumvirate tintas b/r, souzão (future to
include transfusions of touriga, Rolls-Royce of port varieties). Inky dark, almost

opaque; fragrant, rich as the most opulent Christmas cake, spicy; yet for all the luxe, dry finishing. Next **00** (sample), with 25% touriga turbocharge, set to sweep the boards. **96** VVG, Paarl show champ, runner up SAA trophy. **95** VVG, Wine ✿, SAA port trophy.

Cinsaut ✿ 😊 This variety so at home, might well have been born here. **00** usual super-drinkable self: sappy strawberries, smoky/toasty tones from oak chips, lightish feel (though full 13,5% alc). **Cinsaut-Shiraz** ✿ 😊 Very jolly unwooded quaffer, **99** with added allure from shiraz's wild scrub/herbs, good savoury notes. 13% alc. Flies off shelves of UK chain Safeway. **Blanc de Noir Pinot Noir** ✿ New 😊 Charming, velvet-textured **00** pops with raspberry/cherry fruit; dash of sugar glides smoothly rather than sweetly across the palate. Med/full bodied. **Chenin Blanc Dry** ✿ 😊 **00** zippy, refreshing as always, clear lemon/lime/peach tones, zesty dry palate. Med/full bodied. **Sauvignon Blanc** ✿ 😊 Drink-young **00**, like pvs, not a shouter but compensates with good, food-friendly mouthfeel; gentle gooseberry/cut-grass and hints of khaki bush in bone-dry finish. 13% alc.

Cabernet Franc ✿ Bottle age has smoothed **98**, brought forth ripe plum, black/green pepper, fragrant tobacco sniffs. Very dry finish. No **99** (future more likely to go into blends). **Pinotage** ✿ These usually need bit of time to bring out the bright plum/banana flavours, relax still chewy tannins. **99**, like pvs, quite full, densely fruity. 6 mths small Fr oak. **Chardonnay** ✿ New Unwooded (as are all latest whites from this cellar — these also whole bunch pressed "to better capture fruit"). First crop **00** surprisingly generous tropical flavour tapering to fresh figgy conclusion. 13% alc. **Chenin Blanc Semi-sweet** ✿ Lemonadey **00** trips lightly on tongue with no hint of cloy. Real tropical fruit salad tastes. Prickle of acidity freshens, brings you back for more.

. . . .

Landzicht Winery　　　🍷 🍷 🍷 🍷

Jacobsdal, Free State • Tasting, sales, cellar tours Mon—Fri 8.30—1; 2—5 Sat 8.30—12 • Fee dependant on meal, available on request • Bring your own picnic • Tourgroups • Views • Owners 45 members & Min Patrick Lekota • Winemakers Ian Sieg (since 1984) & Johan Stemmet (since 2000) • Viticulturist Dirk Malan • Vineyards 325 ha • Production 3 000 tons 231 000 cases (30 000 cases own label) 60% white 15% red 15% rosé 10% fortified • PO Box 94 Jacobsdal 8710 • Tel (053) 591—0164 • Fax (053) 591-0145 • E-mail landzicht@inext.co.za

"I GUESS WE now have to say 'Cape winelands and Ian Sieg'," a winewriter was heard to say at a tasting. Armed with a brand-new, extra-gentle Bucher press, this highly individual winemaker is launching a global attack from the northerly Free State because he strongly feels "SA's wines are neglected! We must produce, for example, a true chenin". After a difficult 2000 harvest, Sieg and newcomer Johan Stemmet "somehow" still made good chardonnay, sauvignon, cabernet, merlot and white muscadel. "We have to work smarter, not harder. Winemaking is like a marriage, for better or for worse…" he says ruefully. A lovely tree-lined venue in striking distance of some historically significant battlefields, Landzicht is worth visiting for its renowned 'all-SA tastings' accompanied by a traditional barbecue. And if these prove too convivial, the Veenwouden guesthouse up the road is a comfortable stay-over.

Cabernet Sauvignon ✿ Lightly oaked **00** offers stewed plum aromas and uncompromising tannins which need few yrs to relax. 13% alc. 1 300 cases. **Chardonnay** ✺ New Unwooded nutty **00** features spicy aromas (though unwooded), full bodied with taut dry finish. Power alc of 14%. 1 000 cases. **Red Jerepigo** ✿ Fortified dessert from pinotage/ruby cab emitting powerful strawberry/cinnamon gusts over grippy/zesty fruit; long sweet finish. 650 cases. 17,5% alc.

Red Muscadel ✿✿ Well made sweet fortified dessert with evocative rose garden/spring jasmine perfumes; full-sweet grapey palate ends on refreshing, almost tart note from high (for this style) 6 g/ℓ acid. Ian Sieg's quirky food suggestion: crocodile. 17,5% alc. 1 000 cases. **White Muscadel** ✿✿ This traditional sweet fortified dessert is the cellar's medal-festooned signature. **97** *Wine* ✿✿, mail-order club selection; **98** VG, Michelangelo gold. Latest **00** penetratingly sweet with spirity herbal/earthy tones; endless length. 17,5% alc. 1 000 cases.

Blanc de Blanc (Grand Cru being phased out in favour of this more modern label). **00** showcases cellar's first crop of young-vine sauvignon (here with chardonnay); crisp and zesty, assertive citrus fruit in full dry palate. 13% alc. 600 cases. **Rein Blüm** ✿ Fresh, lightish and uncomplicated semi-sweet from colombard/chenin/muscadel. **NV** (00). 11,5% alc. 650 cases. Also available, not ready for tasting (pvs rating in brackets) **Special Harvest 00** (✿✿), **Hanepoot 00** (✿✿).

Merlot ✿✿ New ☺ Ian Sieg says: "These are 3 yr old vines; imagine how well they'll perform when they mature." Plenty of satisfaction now in unwooded **00**, with bright cassis and soft choc. Light toned despite heavy 13,5% alc. 600 cases. **Pinotage** ✿✿ ☺ Latest **00** registers high on the quaffing graph without needing to shout: understated savoury/strawberry tastes, juicy fruit, lightish tone though not insubstantial at 13,5% alc. **99** flew with SA Express. Lightly oaked. 6 700 cases. **Gewürztraminer** ✿✿ ☺ Sweet and delicate **00**; talcum/jasmine whiffs carry into limey palate which nicely freshened by gentle acid. Rose petals, spicy tones and clean ringing finish. Lowish 11% alc.

Rosenblümchen ✿✿ ☺ Semi-sweet low-alc rosé with plenty of character. **00** sappy, perfumed tastes from pinotage/chenin/white muscadel blend; attractive deep pink shade. Ian Sieg would pour this for guests at a "tropical drinking party". 7,5% alc. 3 000 cases. **Blümchen** ✿✿ ☺ Low alc (8%) sweet summery drink with balanced acidity and plenty of soft muscat flavour. Noncloying. Colombard/chenin/white muscadel blend. **Vin Doux** ✿✿ New ☺ Bright yellow-straw lights wink from this super **00** semi-sweet carbonated sparkle; refreshing lemony tastes for effortless poolside/party sipping. Light 10% alc. 500 cases.

Langverwacht Co-op ⚐

Robertson (see Robertson map) • Tasting & sales Mon–Fri 8–12.30; 1.30–5 • Cellar tours by appointment • Owners 30 members • Manager/winemaker Johan Gerber (since 1986) • Viticultural consultants VinPro • Production ±10 500 tons (±1 500 tons own label) 85% white 15% red • PO Box 87 Bonnievale 6730 • Tel (023) 616-2815 • Fax (023) 616-3059

"OUR new red wine cellar must be fully operational for the 2001 harvest," says Johan Gerber, manager-winemaker at this Bonnievale co-op, which is poised to bring in the first crops of shiraz and cabernet sauvignon. Although Gerber is hesitant in these early days as to whether or not the new reds will be bottled under the own-label — the bulk of production goes to local merchants — the long-term aim is to have a top red or two. To date, the only 'wine of colour' in the in-house range is ruby cab, with whites represented by the cellar's trademark colombard and chardonnay.

Ruby Cabernet ✿ ☺ **99** first bottled red from this cellar eminently gluggable. Woodsmoke/mulberry/gamey sniffs; obvious juicy fruit; extra-soft tannin. All just R10/bottle ex cellar. 13% alc.

Colombard ✿ Drink-soon **00** picnic partner, pungently floral, lemon grass/guava tang complemented by sparky dry acid. 12,3% alc. **Chardonnay** ★ Unwooded **99** past its best. **Colombard-Chardonnay** ✿✿ Same herby tones as pvs in med/full-bodied **00**, appetising peaches-and-cream aroma, crisp dry lemony finish. These 280 cases each.

....

Lanzerac

UNDER a gentleman's agreement, the wines below are made by SFW while the Cabernet Sauvignon, Merlot and Chardonnay are grown on the historic Lanzerac property on the fringe of Stellenbosch town, now owned by tycoon Christo Wiese. SFW holds the Lanzerac trademark, however, and distributes both ranges bearing this famous marque. Tasting & sales at Oude Libertas (see Stellenbosch Farmers' Winery). See also next entry: Lanzerac Farm & Cellar.

✿ Pinotage World's first pinotage, 59 released 1961, and still a benchmark of this local-hero variety. Luxe black and gold packaging reflects modern, sumptuous wine within (pvs dumpy 'skittle' bottle, impossible to lay down, now a rustic memory). Blue-tinged **98** different in appearance to pvs, also in taste: riper, toastier, more 'modern'; underwritten by sweet long tannins, velvety plum/cherry/banana assembly that ends in nutty dryness. 14% alc. Pour now or wait (older vintages have proved very long lived). Upcoming **99** shows benefit of renewed focus on quality, made possible by premium pricing. One to watch.

Rosé ✿ Hugely popular semi-sweet **NV**, sniffed at by Noses but consistently charming and satisfying — though the pleasure rating does depend on how fresh the bottling is. Latest appeared newly harvested — bright, zippy — as it should. Usual strawberry/cherry joined by raspberry, plum in smooth fruity roundabout. Serve well chilled.

....

Lanzerac Farm & Cellar

Stellenbosch (see Stellenbosch map) • Tasting & sales Mon—Fri 10—6 Sat 10—1 Service fee R15 p/p refundable on purchase • Cellar tours Mon—Fri 11.30, 2.30 • Five-star Lanzerac Hotel for stay-overs Tel (021) 887-1132 • Governor's Hall Restaurant and Craven Lounge • Bring your own picnic or order in advance from hotel or tasting centre • Conference facilities • Tasting & cellar tours for tour groups Tel (021) 886-5641 Meals & accommodation for groups Tel (021) 887-1132 • Jonkershoek Valley Views • Walks • Wheelchair-friendly • Owner Christo Wiese • Winemakers Wynand Hamman (since 1993) & Hazel Hamman (since 1997) • Viticulturist Truter Prins (since 1997) • Vineyards 50 ha • Production 350 tons 25 000 cases 90% red 10% white • PO Box 6233 Uniedal 7612 • Tel (021) 886-5641 • Fax (021) 887-6998 • E-mail wine@lanzerac.co.za • Website www.lanzeracwines.co.za

FILLED with Cape history, the 300 year old Lanzerac property is owned by well-known Cape businessman Christo Wiese, who has spent an impressive amount of money restoring this national monument and adding a few sybaritic touches to what is now a five-star establishment placed at the start of the very beautiful Jonkershoek Valley. Improvements have extended to the ultra-modern winery, where they've been busy experimenting with micro-oxygenation and creating a new Bordeaux blend. In the vineyard, they're planting shiraz and making full use of futuristic weather stations (data from the Australian Deviner system already populating the spreadsheets pored over by cellar duo Wynand and Hazel Hamman and viticulturist Truter Prins). A popular choice here is the full-bodied Cabernet Sauvignon 96, which swept the boards with the Grand Diplome d' Honneur at Vino Ljubljana in Slovenia, with a follow-up performance gold medal at the Cidado Do Porto in Lisbon.

✿ Merlot Jonkershoek's signature gamey/barnyard/charry scents combine with merlot's more familiar coffee/choc in **98**, in different league to pvs. Complex (extra dimension from dash 98 cab f), rich, elegant, long; comfortable tannins for now or next few yrs. 14 mths 300 ℓ Fr oak, one-third new. 12% alc. 4 200 cases.

✿ Cabernet Sauvignon That Jonkershoek farmyard again in **97**, here paired with red/black berries, some black cherries, spicy oak. Good grip of tannin. Like Merlot above, understated, invites you in rather than yells at you from a distance. Moderate 12,5% alc. 9 000 cases. **96** showered with show awards (see intro), selected for Westin wine lists (Sheraton/Hilton and Pacific hotels), flew with Emirates etc. These blends 6 clones, Bdx yeast strain, 18 mths Fr oak, some new.

Chardonnay ✿ Individual style; sweet-oaky/vanilla/ toasted hazelnuts contribute to soft, almost honeyed tone which carries through into enduring finish. Barrel-fermented, 11 mths sur lie in small Fr oak. Through malo. 12% alc. 3 500 cases.

De Forellen range

Alternative label. De Forellen (trout) tribute to Angus Buchanan, owner of Lanzerac in the 1940s and angler extraordinaire. Features the names of present Lanzerac owner Christo Wiese's daughters.

Clare ✿ Elegant, lighter Bdx blend of cabs s/f, for earlier drinking. **97** reprises ripe blackberries of pvs, plus above intriguing organic whiffs. Super drinking now and over 2–3 yrs. 12 mths oaked. 3 000 cases. **Chardonnay** ✿ New Unwooded, uncomplicated **00** sipper with delicate peachy fragrance. Full flavoured/bodied, balanced. 13% alc. 500 cases. **Christina** ✿ Exotic cantaloupe perfume in latest **99**, unwooded pinot blanc (unusual variety in Cape). Fuller, riper than pvs. Roundness enhanced by malo in tank. 13% alc. 900 cases. **Thanya** ✿ New The Tswana label says "Wake up!", the flavours say " … and go picnic". Dry **00** pinot blanc/chardonnay in youthfully fresh, outdoorsy mode. Unwooded; low acidity for extra smoothness. 13% alc. **Lerato** ✿ New Natural Sweet rosé, charming and sweet from its delicate blush colour to its Tswana name, which means 'love'. Soft cherries, light 10% alc. All red grapes: merlot/cabs s/f. 850 cases.

La Petite Ferme Winery

Franschhoek (see Franschhoek map) • Tasting by appointment Sales daily 12—4 • Winery tours by appointment • La Petite Ferme Restaurant (see Eat-out section) Wines below available in the restaurant or direct • 3 luxury guest suites with many amenities • Views • Mountain biking • Wheelchair-friendly • Owners Dendy Young family • Winemaker Mark Dendy Young (since 1996) • Vineyard manager John Dendy Young • Vineyards 8 ha • Production 50 tons 3 500 cases 70% white 30% red • PO Box 55 Franschhoek 7690 • Tel (021) 876-3016 • Fax (021) 876-3624 • E-mail lapetite@iafrica.com

TRUE to its name, 'The Little Farm' is maintaining its small winery status, despite an extension to the existing cellar and the increased range (semillon and an unwooded chardonnay). A 50-case export order is a huge one and could just blow them right out the water, laughs self-taught winemaker and keen fly fisherman Mark Dendy Young. Though it's a "wonderful problem, not having enough stock. We service the restaurant first, then the cellar door, then our regular clients." Though every last drop is locally bought and consumed, export buyers are circling. Fresh accessible white wines and softer, more fruit-driven reds are what they are aiming at as a part of really establishing their own identity. New plantings of merlot and sauvignon blanc mark the birth of son Timothy as the next generation winemaker, while grandfather John Dendy Young still tends the vineyards of this relaxed, friendly family restaurant-cum-winery, famous for its stunning situation up the Franschhoek Pass.

✿ **Chardonnay** Foodie-styled, barrel fermented (mostly new oak) chardonnay; makes lasting impression at table in the Petite Ferme restaurant or, even mellower, alfresco on the immaculate lawns with sensational views. **00** ✿barrel sample youthfully gangly; on release (Dec 2000) should have reached heights of **99**, with buttery melon/pear tones. 13% alc.

✿ **Blanc Fumé** Softer, broader version of unwooded sauvignon below. **99** with long guava/quince flavours. **00** ✿ more understated. Partly barrel fermented. Favourite with a restaurant speciality: home-smoked trout. **96** VVG.

Shiraz ✦ From vyd in front of restaurant. **99** with Rhône-like complexity, highly rated by SA *Wine*. Follow-up **00** similar, lighter bodied (12% alc) with sappy raspberry, mouthwatering savoury-dry finish. **Chardonnay Unwooded** ✦ **New** Lightish, delicate **00**; fragrant peach/citrus wafts, good dry finish with cellar's signature firm, food-cordial acidity. **Sauvignon Blanc** ✦ Shades of Bordeaux in **00**, with assertive earthy/hay character and gravelly raciness. Individual and rather good. Unoaked, dry. 13,5% alc. **Semillon** ✦ **New** Variety's lanolin/lemon flavours subtly expressed in light, fragrant, pleasantly dry **00**.

. . . .

Laughing Waters see Le Grand Chasseur

. . . .

L'Avenir Estate 🍷 🍷 🍷 🍴 🍷

Stellenbosch (see Stellenbosch map) • Tastings & sales Mon—Fri 10—5 Sat 10—4 Tasting fee R10 • Group cellar tours, tasting, barbeques by appointment • Luxury 9-bedroom guest lodge with pool • Own preserved/dried olives/olive oil for sale • Owner Marc Wiehe • Winemaker Francois Naudé (since 1992) • Vineyards 53,5 ha • Production 22 000 cases 320 tons 50% red 48% white 2% rosé • PO Box 1135 Stellenbosch 7599 • Tel (021) 889-5001 • Fax (021) 889-5258 • E-mail lavenir@adept.co.za • Website www.adept.co.za/lavenir

BIG, EXPRESSIVE, RED WINE-STAINED HANDS chop the air and thump the table: "I will never harvest grapes that are not absolutely ripe. Never." Winemaker Francois Naudé is stating what should be an obvious *sine qua non* to fine wine — but it's a revealing remark. Certainly in the past, too many Cape wines showed hasty harvesting, sloppy handling — and disjointed acidities, mean tannins. For nearly a decade, Naudé has kept L'Avenir well away from such amateurishness but the subject — leaving grapes to ripen fully — has its dangers too: almighty alcohols. It's prompted this thoughtful wineman, with a scientific bent (he was a chemist in another, Transvaal-based life, an *inkruiper* to the Cape) to ask questions rather sooner than many peers. Most will try to steer this conversation in another direction. Here, intellectual curiosity has focused Naudé: "We need to look at our yeasts, perhaps the little buggers are now too efficient; maybe rootstocks could be tweaked, and vineyard techniques refined to achieve physiological ripeness at lower sugars. But don't ask me to pick unripe grapes." Another hobby horse: the relative importance of taste and bouquet. Modern wine making is sophisticated enough to manipulate these. "But," says Naudé, "my consumers taste the wine, they hardly sniff: that's for the professionals." L'Avenir shows Naudé's perfectionism off well in a focused, hand crafted range. He's now congenitally incapable of making a clumsy wine. And his best are quite terrific.

✦ **Cabernet Sauvignon** A first rate and consistent Cape cabernet, specially since **95** VG, and including **96** — a poorer year for many — but the real lift-off, staking a claim in the Cape A team, begins with **97** SAA, *Wine* ✦ — and hasn't stopped. That and following 2 brilliant vintages (grapes left to hang on vine until fruit-rich and very ripe) show off this winemaker's passion for classic deep colours, super-ripe fruit but still firm textures — and finer tannins than in early 1990s. **99** perhaps has the edge; gorgeous, expensive smell of violets. Expansively (one third new) oaked, sitting on 14% alc, (highish but keepworthy) and, since **95**, with touch of merlot — 12–14%. **94** VVG.

✦ **Pinotage 99** a stunner (though the outstanding vintage offered winemakers no excuses) from this leading grower of Cape's home-bred red variety. Almost antithesis of loud and hectic pinotage stereotype; this significantly juicier, broader, finer in the mouth. As good as **96** *Wine* ✦ — pvsly cellar's best. Plenty of oak, helps fine down assertive primary (banana, plum, green fig) flavours nicely. Small 5 t/ha yields help, so too that fruit is mostly (80%) from non-virus vyds. L'Avenir's pinotages bedecked in laurels: **97** *Wine* ✦; this and **96** both VVG, ABSA Pinotage Top Ten trophies; **95** VG; **96**, **94** Perold trophies at London's IWSC for best Pinotage. **98** splendid too. These latest also distinguished by an absence of green, acid bitterness in finish, which mars many pinotages. **CWG Auction Reserve Pinotage 99** ✿ extra oak and proportion of 35 yr old vyd fruit for backbone: super-concentrated collector's piece — very tight, dense for long (10–12 yr?) ageing; should unfurl into a pinotage masterpiece. **96** *Wine* ✿.

✿ **L'Ami Simon** Softer-structured merlot/cabernet for good early drinking: easy tannins, with good 'give' and 'yield' in palate. Appetising, healthy dark colours and some minerally, plum fragrances in **98**, 56% merlot, 44% cab blend, rounded out with yr used Fr oak. **97** ✿; **96** VVG, SAA

✿ **Chardonnay** Not a fence-sitting style; it's plump, oaky, peachy, rich and weighty; the crisp, citrusy, lean, non-oaky minimalist approach is for others; and winemaker Naudé says he's aiming for "Burgundy — but of course we're South African; I make what I like to drink, and this is it." **99** was first year in which all wine was in barrel — 10 mths — with long yeast-lees enrichment — accounting for characteristic oatmeal notes. Consistent with pvs — but slightly drier in finish. **97, 96** topped SA entries on 1997/1998 French Chardonnay du Monde competitions with silver, gold medals. **Chardonnay Special Cuvée** ✿ **98** CWG Auction bottling. 100% barrel-fermented, 40% new. Less ready than above chardonnay, also stronger New World tones.

✿ **Chenin Blanc** A repeated Cape chenin winner — and so is **00** but with significant change of emphasis: for first time it's dry where pvsly off-dry (some years stirred into exceptional chenin complexity with botrytis). Latest has silky, rich but less razzmatazz mouthfeel, yet with fair fruit salad mix of flavours. Naudé's response to a low-acid vintage was to lower the sweetness marginally to retain balance on palate for what ultimately may be a more classical dry food wine; but he did apply some vintage-compensating devices, including a barrage of 3 competing yeasts during fermentation to tease out flavours. As usual, unwooded, 100% varietal. **99** broad-shouldered too (13,8% alc.) concluding with trademark mango tang. **97** VG, *Wine* ✿ and Chenin Blanc Challenge award.

✿ **Sauvignon Blanc 00** best, by far, to date from this winery, ironically in a so-so, too-hot sauvignon year; quietish nose but very forward, full on palate with fresh, dry finish, flaunting ripe melon and some varietal gooseberry flavours — more on palate than nose. A super, serious but weighty (sit-up-and-pay-attention 13,8% alc) drink. **99** SAA.

✿ **Vin de Meurveur Noble Late Harvest** A weighty low-sugar version of these golden desserts in **00** from colombard/Cape riesling (77/23%) assisted to some spicy complexity by Fr oak barrelling. Sugar at 83 g/ℓ compares with showy **97** ✿, winner of inaugural Air France–Preteux Bourgeois trophy, SAA, *Wine* ✿, at 144,5 g/ℓ. Both around 13,5% but the former is easier to drink!

✿ **Rosé Maison 00** an 80% clairette blanche (with 20% cinsaut) might not drop the jaw, but here's a delightful light pink all-rounder, fruitier — strawberries, dry heather — than usual; off-dry at 10 g/ℓ sugar. (Visiting French winemaker was given his head by Naudé to improve the style.)

Vin d'Erstelle ✿ **00** a riesling-colombard (50/50) all-occasions, well above average quaffer, off-dry (6,8 g/ℓ sugar) with some keeping qualities — riesling asserting itself with some complexity after a yr or so. **98** SAA.

Le Bonheur Estate ♈ ♈

Stellenbosch (see Stellenbosch map) • Tasting & sales Mon–Fri 9–5 Sat 9–12.30 Closed Sun • Special tastings on request • Light meals by arrangement • Owner Lusan Holdings • Winemaker Sakkie Kotzé (since 1993) • Production 435 tons 31 473 cases • PO Box 56 Klapmuts 7625 Tel (021) 875 5478 Fax (021) 875 5624

THIS UPPER-CRUST FARM in the tony Simonsberg neighbourhood had its already fawned-over vineyards manicured once again in 2000 (soils having been completely remodelled under fanatical ex-cellarmaster Michael Woodhead, and more recently analysed and remapped at the behest of equally methodical incumbent

Sakkie Kotzé). It's all part of Kotzé's business-as-usual approach to the millennium, and his unwavering belief in "my four wines" — chardonnay, sauvignon blanc, cabernet and merlot — which are the building blocks of this small, highly rated range. The estate itself has a dramatic driveway, splashed with torch-lilies and roses. Exclusive catered-for dinners are spread — only by special arrangement — in the dark wood interior of the old manor house, which, with its rich parquet floors, is the very essence of the old Cape.

✿ **Prima** Always classy, yet deliciously unintimidating. **98** no exception: well-ripened cassis, dark chocolate, cedary oak lead to an elegantly structured (12,5% alc) yet richly mouthfilling palate with good spicy fruitcake flavours. 75% merlot, rest cab. Mix new (40%), 2nd fill Fr oak, 18 mths. **97** equally well balanced, touch more refined. In difficult year, **96** VVG, SAA, *Wine* ✿ evidenced adroit handling. **95** VG, SAA, *Wine* ✿. No **94**.

✿ **Cabernet Sauvignon** Great track-record through 1980s for this wine, and still very fine. Cherries, mulberries, cassis in **98**. Ripe, powerful tannins still dominating tight well balanced structure, though there's fruit aplenty. Dark, brooding **97** ✿ VVG even more youthful, also needs — and deserves — time. Cedar, spice and berries lead to elegant palate showing power of fruit rather than alcohol (12,5%). These small Fr oak ±18 mths, 60% new, rest 2nd fill. **96** VG, *Wine* ✿ reflects benefits of new clones. **95** VVG, SAA, *Wine* ✿. **94** *Wine* ✿.

✿ **Chardonnay** Aromas of apricot and peach interweaving buttery toastiness in **99**. Round, understated palate, a touch chalky; good dry finish. 40% fermented in new Fr oak. 13% alc. After juicy, rich **97**, **98** unexpectedly dry in mouth.

Sauvignon Blanc ✿ Pleasant tropical fruit aromas/flavours in **00**, complemented by green, gooseberry tones. **99** trifle less focused and crisp. Lowish 12% alc in both. **97** ✿.

- -

Leef op Hoop see Le Riche

- -

Le Grand Chasseur Estate   ⛋ ⛋ ⛋ ⛋

Robertson (see Robertson map) • Tasting & sales Mon—Fri 8–5 • Cellar tours by appointment • Bring your own picnic • Walks • Views • Wheelchair-friendly • Owner/winemaker Albertus de Wet (since 1979) • Viticulturists Francois Viljoen, Jurie Blanché, Freddie de Jager • Vineyards 240 ha • Production ± 3 000 tons 60% white 37% red 3% rosé • PO Box 439 Robertson 6705 • Tel/fax (023) 626—1048 • E-mail lgc@intekom.co.za • Website http://home.intekom.co.za/legrand

A VISIT to Russia was an eye-opener for Albertus de Wet, owner of this 1 400 ha property below the Sandberg mountain near Robertson. "They have poor-quality wines," is his frank report, "and the export potential is excellent." Which should suit this widely read sail-boarding enthusiast very well. He's on a mission to "upgrade the cellar and vineyards to boost quality", and new vineyards of shiraz, cabernet sauvignon and merlot should help him attain his goal. There's plenty of room for any further expansion he might contemplate: only about 20% of Le Grand Chasseur is developed — the remainder is home to a variety of wildlife, including the splendid African Fish Eagle — the great hunter alluded to in the farm's name.

The range, untasted for this ed, includes: **Shiraz 00** and **Pinotage 00** both single-vineyard limited releases, both **New**; **Ruby Cabernet**, **Chardonnay**, **Chardonnay-Colombard**.

- -

Leidersburg Vineyard

Paarl • Winemakers Jan du Preez & Willie Malherbe (since 1996) • Viticulturist Jan du Preez (since 1996) • Vineyard 6 ha • Production 45 tons (1 000 cases own label) 100% red • PO Box 204 Stellenbosch 7599 • Tel (021) 887-9937 • Fax (021) 887-0566 • E-mail dupwine@intekom.co.za

"WE WANT to build Leidersburg to be the top Cabernet Sauvignon producer in South Africa," says high-powered winemaking entrepreneur Jan du Preez, anchor of this compact property near Elsenburg College with fan clubs in Germany, Holland and Switzerland. The present 6 ha are poised to multiply to 18 as nearby virgin land is primed and planted with cabernet and some parcels of shiraz and merlot. The wines, made at Goede Hoop in the Bottelary hills, have been instant hits with local wine mail order clubs as well as cabernet fans overseas. The new dab hand in the cellar, Willie Malherbe, aims to stoke these flames of popularity. Adding to the allure will be a tasting venue scheduled to open in 2001.

Vintner's Reserve Cabernet Sauvignon ✿ Open, accessible style with fairly intense red/blackberry tastes in **98** and some gently firming tannin. 13,5% alc. 1 000 cases. Suggest drink young as pvs **97** (14% alc), back-tasted mid-2000, showed some baked/porty tones.

Lemberg Estate

Tulbagh (see Tulbagh map) • Tasting, sales, cellar tours daily 9—5 and by appointment. Tasting fee R5 p/p • Gourmet meals/picnics by arrangement (1—2 days' notice required) • Light lunches/cellar tours for groups Book ahead • Luxury B&B/self catering rondavel for 2—4 guests • Birding • Walks • Views • Wheelchair-friendly • Owner/winemaker/viticulturist Klaus Schindler • Vineyards 4 ha • Production ± 1 000 cases 85% white 15% red • PO Box 317 Tulbagh 6820 • Tel (023) 230-0659 • Fax (023) 230-0661 • E-mail schindler@lando.co.za • Website www.kapstadt.de/lemberg

THIS RUSTIC PROPERTY, neatly tucked below the Witzenberg range, has become a sought-after winelands destination, with a very private lakeside guesthouse set in lush gardens, excellent meals and ample picnic baskets, mountain views, country walks, bird watching, and a laid-back ambience. And if you're not completely chilled-out by all the above, the European-style wines on this working wine farm will do the rest. The range, not available for tasting for this ed, includes: **Sensual Red 99** cab/merlot, oak-matured. **Lipovina 99/00** hárslevelü, unwooded. **The Laughing Duck 00** sauvignon, unwooded.

L'Émigré Wines

Stellenbosch (see Stellenbosch map) • Tasting Sat 9.30—5 and during December holiday Mon—Sat • Four self-catering guest cottages with fine views • Scenic walks • Owner FV Gentis Trust • Winemakers Emile Gentis (since 1990) & Frans Gentis (since 1992) • Viticulturist Victor Gentis (since 1998) • Vineyards 55 ha • Production 500 tons (2 000 cases own label) • PO Box14 Vlottenburg 7604 • Tel (021) 881-3702 • Fax (021) 881-3030

"I WANT TO TRAVEL AND WORK in all the world's wine countries," confides young Emile Gentis, fired-up co-winemaker (with father Frans, ex-chair of Welmoed) on this family farm in the viticulturally lustrous Stellenboschkloof (Jordan's right next door, Uiterwyk down the road). "In the long run that's the only way to really put our cellar on the map." Clearly, Elsenburg trained Emile Gentis is inspired by L'Emigré's resonant motto — "From the land of the scimitar to the western world and beyond" — an allusion to the diaspora of both the vine and the Dutch Gentis family who settled in the Cape early in the last century. On the farm itself, the clan are planting 5 ha of cabernet franc and putting the finishing touches to a hand-built (like everything here) restaurant. And, in cyberspace, a website will open soon.

✿ **Muscat d'Alexandrie** ◤ Rewind to **96** (pvsly rated vintage was **98**) for an instantly mature, extra-smooth treat. Lovely golden amber glow, tangy marmalade through to finish, sweet-smelling honeysuckle afterthoughts. Non-cloying, some yrs to go. 17% alc. 200 cases.

Shiraz ✿ Made-for-keeping **97**, good varietal spice/pepper seasoning, med/light-bodied cherry fruit (11,8% alc) which is undeveloped, needs time. Spanish-oak-aged 2 yrs. ± 100 cases. **Azure Chardonnay** ✿ Chablis style **99**, leaner/flintier than pvs; vanilla/oak spice still quite obvious, so give bit of time. Vosges oak, 7 mths. **00** not tasted. **Azure Sauvignon Blanc** ‡ Unusual riesling-like sensations in **00**: terpene/lime aromas, viscous impression on tongue; dry citrus finish. 13% alc. These in distinctive tall azure bottles. ± 250 cases. **Glorieux Special Late Harvest ★ 98** past its best. **Port** ✿✿ Lighter ruby style (though vintaged — **98**), some engaging black-choc tastes. Tinta b/cab. Yr Spanish oak. 17,4% alc. 400 cases.

....

Le Pavillon see Boschendal

....

Le Riche Wines

Stellenbosch (see Stellenbosch map) Tasting & sales Mon—Fri 8—5 • Guest house/B&B • Views • Owner/winemaker Etienne le Riche • Production 5 000 cases 100% red • PO Box 6295 Stellenbosch 7612 • Tel/fax (021) 887-0789 • E-mail lerichewines@adept.co.za

A REVEALING, uplifting story — in this new-glitz age of Cape wines: Nietvoorbij oenological research institute scientist turned winemaker Etienne le Riche, who was at Rustenberg for more than 20 years, went solo in 1997 and has watched, bemused, as R20-million, R30-million, R40-million new wineries mushroom all around — in the idiom of California 'chic'. Many of these are marketing statements — and more, a number perhaps intended as returns on ego more than equity. "I and my assistant bottle about 50 cases a day," says Le Riche, standing before a hand-held, home-crafted labeller. The bottling and packaging take care of about three winter months. Almost all the equipment for this 5 000 case a year winery has been assembled from others' expansion and upgrade castoffs. It is a model of ingenuity, thrift and functionality. The old Rustenberg Wilmes press Le Riche uses here was commissioned in the 1950s and produced his fabled Rustenberg 82. "Barrels and grapes are my only expense really — and I won't stint there, but the machinery and refurbishing of this rented historic old building (a restored winery in disuse for more than 30 years). It all cost me much less than R1-million. Thank God wines are not made by machines but by nature in the vineyard," says Le Riche. Next, Le Riche is planning a single vineyard Cabernet, from his old friend and now supplier on an adjoining Jonkershoek vineyard, Stellenbosch attorney Roger Chennells, a longtime civil rights campaigner on behalf of the San people. After several years of working with the grapes, le Riche is convinced the site's grapes are worthy of standing apart.

Le Riche range

✿✿ **Cabernet Sauvignon Reserve** Has established itself as a leading Cape cult wine (from the least cult-conscious of winemakers) in the first 3 released vintages since **97**. The array of flavours — violets, minerals, sweet cinnamon spiciness in **99** — is accommodated in a supple frame where the fruit engulfs the tannins. The effect is one of calm elegance. Were it a touch drier and firmer, it would be more Old World than New; as it is, it hovers between the two very nicely. The sound, ripe-fruit/tannin balance is key and promises 10 yrs of smooth ageing. Receives extended oaking, in 80% new Fr barrels, 13% alc, about two-thirds grapes from Jonkershoek, rest from maritime-swept Firgrove. **97** VVG, SAA, *Wine* ✿✿, Air France-Preteux Bourgeois trophy, huge critical acclaim. **98** ✿✿, *Wine* ✿✿ initially tighter; similar vinification/oaking, 13,3% alc, Stellenbosch grapes. (A two-barrel lot is 'stolen' from this to make the annual CWG Auction wine (in magnums); in 1999, the **98** fetched R500 a magnum, the 2nd highest price overall. Standard **Cabernet Sauvignon 99** ✿✿ A dark plum/ruby colour signifies quality from the start; sweet toffee/coffee smells lead to luscious, limpid mouthcoating pleasure. Where the brooding, assertive Reserve compels more attention, there's already a seamless elegance, easier drinkability in this well modulated, understated wine. A downside? It will not last as long, nor perhaps develop the complexity of the Reserve. Partial new oaking. **97** ✿✿, recognisably from same hand. Pushing over 13% alc; fruit from Stbosch, Firgrove.

* **Merlot-Cabernet Sauvignon 99** healthy plum/maroon colours, matching mulberry/cherry aromas preface creamily-textured (merlot-tweaked?) sleekness and fruity delicacy in palate; from old, low yielding Jonkershoek vyds. Very lightly, almost imperceptibly (old, large) wooded; 60% merlot to 40% cab. Delicious. **98**, similarly styled, touch weightier but with ripe tannins, was Cab-Merlot 60/40, proportions which Le Riche will revert to for **00**.

Leef op Hoop range

Mainly for export to UK and Netherlands.

* **Cabernet Sauvignon** A second label to outclass some 1sts, and showing more of winemaker Le Riche's subtle side; soft, ripe-sweet black cherry tones in **99** make for quiet-toned charm; at 12,5% alc a touch more quaffable than **98**. The quickish finish might diminish its formal wine show chances but confirms a friendly informality. Unblended cab, briefly oaked in older wood, not for long ageing.

. . . .

Libertas

BOTTLED FOR THE EXPORT MARKET, this widely distributed brand fills a modestly priced slot in the Stellenbosch Farmers' Winery portfolio.

> **Cabernet Sauvignon** ☘ ☺ Much to like about charming **98** quaff: clean varietal fruit, sleek tannin, savoury tail-end tang. Med-bodied for non-challenging palatability.

Pinotage ☘ Totally different personality to pvs. **98** ripe, open, welcoming, ready when you are. Bit of tannin, so won't be overwhelmed by food. Med-bodied. **Chardonnay** ☘ **99** with some authentic (if unexpected, at this price point) oak-char; good tropical/citrus briskness. Barrel-matured, med-bodied. **Chenin Blanc** ☘ Zingy, dry, med-bodied. Drink-young **00** with well defined guava/green apple relish; crisp, well made refreshment.

. . . .

Lieberstein

SEMINAL SEMI-SWEET table wine; revolutionised SA's wine drinking habits at launch in 1959. An instant success, by 1964 the largest selling bottled wine in the world (over 31-million litres). Still a model of reliable, unpretentious quaffing. By Stellenbosch Farmers' Winery.

Fresh, tropical **NV** ☘, hints of honey and guava; charming everyday tipple.

. . . .

Lievland Estate   ♟ ♟ ♟ ♟

Stellenbosch (see Stellenbosch map) Tasting & sales Mon—Fri 9—5 Sat 9-1 • Cellar tours by appointment • Bring your own picnic • Walks • Views • Owner Paul Benadé • Winemaker/viticulturist James Farquharson (since 1997) • Vineyards 60 ha • Production 350 tons 50/50 white/red • PO Box 66 Klapmuts 7625 • Tel: (021) 875-5226 • Fax (021) 875-5213

JAMES FARQUHARSON gives new meaning to the phrase 'flying winemaker'. When the genial Scot's not back home visiting relatives, he's at the London Wine Trade Fair casting beady eyes on the global opposition ("SA could learn some serious lessons") or, off-duty and further-flung, catching some exotic waves in Indonesia ("Awesome!"). And during the local harvest he flies down the road to the Polkadraai Hills farm Uitzicht, where he makes a small range after hours with his mate (and fellow cool surfer dude) Johan Reyneke. Noting the effects of global warming, Farquharson deplores the three hot vintages in a row (2000's already high heat worsened by horrifying Simonsberg bushfires which scorched 20% of the crop, especially shiraz and cinsaut). But, more positively, the blistering climate gives Farquharson the opportunity to practice one of his favourite cellar crafts — blending — to make up for what the climate did not deliver.

✿ **Shiraz** One of the Cape's top-drawer examples, capable of good ageing. **98** VVG, *Wine* ✿ astonishingly dense and broad (15,2% alc), black berry fruits with gamey/wild herb scents in intense profusion. Despite richness, good dry finish with sufficient ripe tannins for the long haul. Needs 3-5 yrs after which should unfold brilliantly. **97** hints at how well these mature; where **98** is opulent, this is silky smooth with burgeoning complexity. Rounded dark-berried fruits now showing, dusting black pepper in finish. Fr oak-matured, 40% new (before **95** portion Am wood); some fermentation finished in barrel. Preview of **99** freeze-frame of a different shiraz persona: roasty/toasty, aromas dry as coffee, good savoury finish.

✿ **DVB** Serious Bdx-style blend and, unusually in Cape, mainly cabernet franc — in hot-vintage **98** 50%, with merlot (30%) and splash cab s. Big wine but elegant. Terrific ripeness the first impression, with sweet black cherry/berry aromas, then layers of luscious ripe fruit, almost caricatured in their intensity; yet the almost sweet flavours end satisfyingly dry. Oak mainly Allier, 40% new. **97** lighter vintage, no less flavour; serious oaking to back more finely drawn fruit, some austerity. Also cab f-dominated. **96** 🌡 lighter year, rather oxidative, touch of greenness in tail.

✿ **Weisser Riesling** 🏷 No new vintages in **99/00**: "Too hot." Pvs **98** now more giving; minerally stones quality; exciting racy acidity, which presently gives impression of leanness, needs perhaps another yr to soften further. Opens/broadens in the mid-palate to a fine minerally flourish. 8 g/ℓ sugar. No **97**.

Lievlander ✿ 😊 Winery's best seller and good value at ±R24 ex-tasting room. **99** no slouch. Plummy ripe fruit, good density, initially smooth but some good tannin comeback in finish. Despite difficult, hot vintage "I'm happy with the way it came out," says Farquharson. Blend of all farm's reds, combination staves/barrels. **Chéandrie NV** ✿ 😊 Pretty, light summer quaffer with pleasing sweetness. Dew-fresh, pristine fruit, lively but easy. Equal chenin/sauvignon/riesling blend. Also available (not tasted).

Chardonnay ✿ NEW Unwooded version in **2000**, high-toned estery fruit, mainly floral with fresh peachy aromas. Light bodied with fresh acidity, clean, longish finish. Cool fermented.

Linton Park Wines 🏆

Wellington (see Wellington map) • Tasting, sales, cellar tours by appointment • Owner Linton Park plc • MD Malcolm Perkins • Winemaker Ian Naudé (since 1998) • Vineyard manager T C Botha • Production 500 tons 15 000 cases 60% white 40% red • PO Box 533 Wellington 7654 • Tel/fax (021) 873-1625 • E-mail iannaude@iafrica.com

IAN NAUDÉ now has a throw-away wine-line many of his peers would die for: "As I was saying to Jancis Robinson the other day, over a few bowls of caviar … " The international wine-writing queen has long been the person this winemaker would most like to meet in the wine world, and he got to do exactly that at a caviar tasting which she hosted at her London home. These celestial fish-eggs are among Linton Park's multiple food and drink (tea, coffee, wine) interests all over the globe; they're the biggest importers of caviar (12 tons per year) into the UK. Is Naudé on a good wicket here, or what? Not that he doesn't contribute to the company's luxurious image. The knockout Capell's Court Shiraz from this 285 ha Wellington farm flew straight onto Concorde, and 1st Class on British Airways; it touched ground only to glide along locally with the Blue Train. Naudé says that two hours after a BA flight landed in Cape Town, the calls would start coming in from seduced passengers panting after more. The pace continues to build: a website has been launched, as well as two new ranges — Snake River (after the farm's name, Slangrivier) and Green Peak (after its position on the slopes of the Groenberg) — both made exclusively for UK supermarkets.

⚜️ **Shiraz** Ⓝⓔⓦ This cellar's flagship from single vyd named, appropriately, Summer Hill: real Wellington sunshine intensity in first release **99**. Confident red/black colour tells you this is shiraz; spice, gamey plums and blackberries, plus some strong but ripe tannins remind this not a fruit-juicy style: there's structure, longevity here (though crowds clamouring for 5 times current production of 1 000 cases probably looking for instant, not delayed gratification!). Yr oaked, 70/30 Fr/Am casks, none new. 12,5% alc.

⚜️ **Cabernet Sauvignon** 1 300 cases of power-packed, black-fruited lushness gliding statuesquely across the palate to a huge, full throated finish (14,5% alc). **98** ⚜️ is jammy, in the nicest way; it's over the top and, with 4 g/ℓ sugar (*just* the right side of technical dryness), guaranteed to stick in the craw of those who judge wines with the aid of pocket calculators. But it's nice, smart looking, and trendy. And, with a winemaker whose idea of a made-in-heaven culinary marriage for this wine is "something lavished with black truffles", can you go wrong? From single vyd Bush Vine Hill. Yr 100% new Fr oak. **99** same provenance but more compact, reserved, quieter alc (12,5%), 'properly' dry. Mid-2000 not as flamboyant. But who knows what pleasures lurk ...?

⚜️ **Chardonnay** 🏆 From top vineyard, Claire Division **98** ⚜️ full throttle oaking (100% new Fr oak 10 mths) well absorbed. Quite soft buttery texture (through malo), lemon/lime and charry butterscotch lead into big, smooth palate; Meursault style, balanced. 13% alc. 1 500 cases. **99** creamy and almost sweet, some vanilla from new oak. Needs time for components to meld. 13% alc.

Capell's Court range

⚜️ **Shiraz** Out with those abaci and slide rules, folks. Here's another of those Linton Park sweetish reds — and yes, it's another consumer smash. **98** picked super-ripe at 29 °B, failed to ferment dry. Saved from the drain by nosy UK supermarket buyer who tasted, loved, ordered. 14,5% alc, 6 g/ℓ sugar. **99** anorexic by comparison (12,5% alc) but again flaunting that sweet succulence, effortless drinkability. 3 mths oaked, Fr/Am.

⚜️ **Chardonnay** 🏆 Perceptibly sweet **98** shunned by SA consumers, so entire **99**, **00** production shipped to UK in whose cooler clime **00**'s "summer wine" styling (full blown fruit, deep scoop of alc) should find instant favour. Unwooded, dry (really!). 14% alc. 4 000 cases.

Cabernet Sauvignon ⚜️ Upfront fruity, soft, everyday drinking; unwooded **99** lighter than pvs (11,5% alc), but more fun. **Sauvignon Blanc** ⚜️ New World exuberance (gusts of grass, asparagus), fatness; Old World tight-knit structure in **00**; long, crisply dry finishing. 13,5% alc. 4 000 cases. **Snake River Sauvignon Blanc-Chardonnay** ⚜️ Ⓝⓔⓦ **99** specially for UK chain ASDA. Highly quaffable, deep draughts of different sorts of bright fruit: citrus, gooseberry, peach and lemon, all with a peppery twist. 13% alc. **Merlot 00** Ⓝⓔⓦ, maiden vintage tasted from barrel, too young to rate; ultimate positioning within range undecided at press time.

· ·

Long Mountain Wine Company

Stellenbosch • Owner Pernod Ricard SA • Group wine development director Robin Day • Managing Winemaker Jacques Kruger (since 1998) • Production 270 000 cases 57% white 43% red • PO Box 1324 Stellenbosch 7599 • Tel (021) 880-1688 • Fax (021) 880-1691 • E-mail jacques@prsa.co.za

THIS CONTEMPORARY wine company is not afraid to stick its neck out — in fact, Long Mountain is sponsoring giraffes at both the London and Belfast zoos. The SA subsidiary of international group Pernod Ricard, ensconced in its new Tuscan-style headquarters in Stellenbosch, is flaunting its New World style, an unqualified success both on the domestic and export markets (28 countries in total and now the top-selling SA wine in Republic of Ireland and Northern Ireland). Managing winemaker Jacques Kruger and group wine development director Robin Day work closely with viticulturists employed by partner wineries they are involved with. With pinotage added to the range and a difficult harvest — with positive end results — behind them, the aim is to "expand and grow our business in core markets," according to Kruger.

Long Mountain range

🌸 Merlot-Shiraz Shiraz dominates initially in latest 99: vibrant redcurrants draw you into the glass where chocolatey merlot takes over and plumps the palate to a balanced, dry conclusion. ± 13% alc.

> **Ruby Cabernet** 🌸 😊 Typically effusive smoky/wild berry whiffs; succulent, ripe 'sweet-sour' fruit with plummy nuances, long sappy farewell. Lightly oaked for early drinking. Stock up now for your next BBQ.

Cabernet Sauvignon 🌸 Made for early drinking or keeping yr/2 without losing varietal character. **99** savoury/green olive and taut cherry-stone character; light 'green oak' hints in finish. Partly oak-fermented/matured. **Pinotage** 🌸 **New** Here's a well-crafted example of the local yokel grape; **99** with smoky berry, soft plummy fruit, sweetish touch of oak in firm dry palate. Not excessively alcoholic at 12,8%. Partly oak-fermented/matured. **Dry Red** 🍷 **New** Ruby cab and cinsaut cavort in this **99** light, cherry-toned swigger with mulberry whiffs. Simple but good juicy flavour, dry finish. Manageable 12,8% alc. **Chardonnay** 🌸 **99** will appeal cream/butterscotch fans. Richness, now accentuated by light bottle age, managed by brisk acid and fragrant tropical/peachy fruit. **Chenin Blanc** 🌸 Bottle ageing has added rich beeswax/herbal aromas to **99**'s initial lime/lemon tastes; creaminess in palate gives way to very dry finish for quite a European tone. 12,6% alc. **Sauvignon Blanc** 🌸 **00** features assertive sauvignon character and a fine spread of bright flavours, from nettles to figs and even pineapple. In palate, juicy crispness finishing on a flinty note. Restrained 12,2% alc. **Semillon-Chardonnay** 🌸 **99** developing attractive creamy/honeyed overtones as it ages. Extra smoothness from extended lie-in on lees. 75/25 blend, lightish 11,8% alc. **00** sample with supple pineapple/floral/talcum array. Sure to be a crowd pleaser.

Gecko Ridge range

> **Chardonnay Brut Sparkling** 🌸 **New** 😊 Lively NV carbonated bubbles, med-bodied, with lime/hay aromas and satisfying just-dry tastes.

Rosé 🍷 **New** Lovely pale salmon shade anticipating supple candyfloss sweetness in bouquet and palate. Finishes surprisingly dry with light cherry nuance. **Chardonnay** 🌸 Unoaked **99** carefree quaffer with citrus zest smoothed by a broad creamy texture. Rather nice. ± 13% alc. **Chenin Blanc** 🍷 **99** has lost its youthful bounce; now features shy herbal tones. Better in youth. **Sauvignon Blanc** 🌸 Pleasing **99**'s acquired some good bottle age, and with it grapefruit/capsicum attractions which should be versatile at table; crisp, balanced and still fresh. Moderate 12% alc. Preview of **00** tastes faintly spicy with a fruit salad background; crisp, limey on tongue with a sherbety finish. Med-bodied. **Dry White** 🍷 Sophisticated jasmine perfume carries through from bouquet to palate in this unpretentious just-dry **NV**.

La Fontaine range

Rosé ✿✿ New ☺ **NV** Chic quaffer with sunset-pink complexion, exotic spice, honeysuckle and stewed plum aromas. Supple and not oversweet.

✿ **Chardonnay** Partly oak-fermented/matured **98** ageing gracefully; forthcoming butterscotch/toast and some tropical aromas changing to lemon/lime in palate with fairly prominent toasty tones, needing flavoursome food. 12,9% alc.

Sauvignon Blanc ✿ Its initial freshness diminished, **99** shows earthy/pear tones and austere, bone-dry palate with lemon/lime finish. 11,1% alc.

Longridge Winery

Stellenbosch (see Helderberg map) • Tasting & sales Mon–Fri 9–5 Sat 9–1 Tel (021) 855-2004 • Owner Winecorp • Winemaker Ben Radford • Production Longridge 16 000 cases Bay View 80 000 cases • PO Box 99 Lynedoch 7603 • Tel (021) 881-3690 • Fax (021) 881-3699 • E-mail winecorp@iafrica.com

THIS WINERY on the slopes of the Helderberg is part of the Winecorp group, producing the prestige Longridge and jolly-with-style Bay View ranges. It's also an illustration of the dramatically shifting Cape wine scene. The new, internationally-focused vision; the new labels rising from stagnant wine pools; the more intimate relationships between growers and cellar; the policy of buying grapes not by the ton but by the block; the willingness to tap into outside expertise. Burgundian Martin Prieur's imprint on the award-winning Chardonnay here is instructive; the 2000 vintage had the input of Phil Lehmann, from a famous Australian winemaking family. Longridge has presented a fresh image ever since it burst onto the market in 1995, the big wine company (though the actual cellar is manageably human) with the quality criteria and close-to-the-ground approach of a small estate. Personifying all this is group winemaking chief Ben Radford. He's from the Barossa Valley in Australia (scion of another leading wine dynasty), via Nuits-Saint-Georges, Ontario and many other likely and unlikely vineyards; and his training is in all-important soils and viticulture, though he's clearly naturally talented in the cellar. In little more than five years, this gate-crasher has become a leading light of the party, setting new-Cape standards and trends.

Longridge range

✿✿ **Cabernet Sauvignon** Moves up to same quality level as rest of range in **99**, reveals similar vintage fruit purity, elegance in modern Cape style. Minerally cassis with warm, ripe brambleberries, background whiffs of cedary oak, fine, dry tannin. Needs time to shake off youthful edges, though wait will be worth it. **98** SAA flavoursome, rich, grows in mouth. 100% cab from single Helderberg vyd. Small Fr oak, portion new, 15 mths. Unfiltered

✿ **Merlot** Like others in range, building up impressive track record. Vintage elegance immediately apparent in **99** fragrant swirls of pure minty, spiced plum ripeness. Creamy yet still tight knit core, sweeping fantail finish. Very fresh profile. Beautifully finished with fine, polished tannins. Less new wood than pvs: 40% fermented/matured Fr/Am (80/20) oak. **98** SAA.

✿ **Pinotage** Radford's favourite; his goal to cloak the home-boy in more Rhône-like garb. Current (and pvs) show more than passing glimpses of France: **99** ✿✿ brooding with dense smoky richness, whole spice rack in palate — clove, cinnamon, ginger, sprinkling liquorice, nutmeg. Creamy, viscous palate, finishes with opulent savouriness. Yet all harmoniously structured for grand maturity in 8–10 yrs. 300 ℓ Fr barrels, none new. **98** vividly spicy: fresh ginger, cinnamon, intensified by mineral tones of macerated plums. Partly cask fermented, oak aged 14 mths. No **97**. **96** ✿✿. SAA. Single Helderberg vyd.

✿ **Chardonnay** ▼ One of the most consistent, individual in Cape, blazing trail of excellence since **96**, picking up armfuls of accolades along the way including approval by many members of ABC (anything but chardonnay) brigade. Intricate minerals, baked cinnamon apples, warm toasted oats are its thumbprint, plus delicacy, depth and ripe citrusy zest in palate. Within these constants are necessary vintage variations. **99** lighter-textured, tauter than **98**, brighter lime/baked-apple tones. Very fine, dry, long-finishing. Perhaps better keepability than **98**, which now beginning to reveals yr's broader, fuller nature (though shows no sign of flagging). 13,5% alc. Single Helderberg vyd. 100% Fr oak-fermented/matured 13 mths, 45% new. 30% through malo. **99** gold Challenge International du Vin; **98** VG, _Wine_ ✿✿, Le Civart trophy Vinexpo. **97** SAA; **97, 96** Virgin Atlantic 1st class. **96** Michelangelo gold.

Brut MCC Reliable, well-priced méthode champenoise sparkle, classic chardonnay/pinot varietal make-up. Next release (untasted) by Spier's Frans Smit, under either Longridge or Spier labels. Available from tasting room only. 2 yrs on lees. Pvs 94 ✿by MCC specialist, TJ's Nicky Krone. Sold out.

Bay View range

Most attractive quality-value range; 95% own production.

✿**Cabernet Sauvignon** ▼ With merlot below, most successful in range. **99** well up to pace. Forthcoming, harmonious mix of sweet blackberry/cassis with soft, cedary oak. Bright, intense flavours, dense, juicy texture providing aimed-for accessibility but sufficient structure to improve over 4–5 yrs. Oak matured, portion new, 11 mths. As with other Bay View reds, neither cold-stabilised nor filtered, so sediment may form with bottle maturation. **97** SAA.

✿**Merlot** ▼ Irresistible plummy succulence in **99**, inviting ruby brilliance too. Full body balanced by fruity concentration; well judged oak reins in more voluptuous elements, adds touch spicy zest. Give few mths' for extra pleasure. Partly cask-fermented/matured 11 mths used Fr oak. 13,67% alc. **97** SAA.

Shiraz ✿✿ Sensuous, warm **98** SAA followed by more elegant **99** ✿✿. Light-textured but flavoursome; best over next yr–18 mths. Lightly oaked. **97** SAA. **Pinotage** ✿✿ Here's a thoroughly modern but still recognisable example. Partly Fr oaked **99** familiar deep, dark purple colour; warm smoky, dried fig nuances more modish, as are the well-tamed tannins. **97** SAA. **Chardonnay** ✿✿ ✿ Plenty of chardonnay fruit without variety's sometimes overblown richness in lightly-wooded **00**, freshened by intense lemon/lime, firm acid backbone and hints of toasty oak. Early, balanced drinking, with 2–3 yrs growth in bottle. **Chenin Blanc** ✿✿ ▼ **00** redolent of honeysuckle/flowers; fuller, bouncy texture from long lees contact, suggestion of toasty oak. Grain of sugar provides balanced length. **99** golds on Concours Mondial, Challenge International du Vin (Bdx). **Sauvignon Blanc** ✿✿ ✿ Pure grassy/tropical notes on easy-to-enjoy **00**. Ripe without being heavy; clean, lingering finish. **Chenin-Chardonnay** ✿✿ A favourite on German market. Ample fruity richness in **00**, more chenin's tropical fruit salad on nose, chardonnay citrusy crispness livening up weighty palate. 70/30 blend, partly wooded. **Ridge Red** ✿✿ Dry, modestly fruity **NV** blend of SA pinot, ruby cab and 30% cab, syrah from France. Unobtrusive wild, spicy strawberries, gentle springy feel, rounded for current pleasurable drinking. Next bottling 100% SA fruit. **Bay Blanc** Aromatic, lively, med-bodied dry quaffing. Regular colombard, chenin, sauvignon mix. **00** untasted. **Bouquet Blanc** Off-dry, gently fruity bukettraube, chenin/colombard blend. **00** not blended at press time.

L'Ormarins Estate ❦ ❦

Franschhoek • Tasting by appointment • Cellar tours Mon—Fri 10 11.30 & 3 • Wheelchair-friendly • Owner & managing director Anthonij Rupert plus three directors • Winemaker Wrensch Roux (since 1997) • Viticulturist Danie Botha (since 1998) • Vineyards 210 ha • Production 1 300 tons 50 000 cases (800 tons own labels) 60% white 40 red • Private Bag X6001 Suider-Paarl 7624 • Tel (021) 874-1026 • Fax (021) 874-1361 • E-mail sales@lormarins.co.za

FOR MORE THAN three centuries vines have flourished on this 500 ha property founded by Huguenot refugee Jean Roi — his family crest, and those of other pioneer French settlers are recorded on the barrels in the historic cellar at L'Ormarins. Now owned by Anthonij Rupert, youngest son of global mogul Dr Anton Rupert, these vineyards stretch for 210 ha, with sauvignon, chardonnay, merlot and cabernet the main varieties; less fashionable SA and weisser riesling blocks are being replaced. A tasting visit here (now by appointment only) offers liquid inspiration over and above the wines made by young Wrensch Roux, presented in super-swish surroundings. But you must go during winter: this is when a spectacular waterfall on the farm cascades down the Groot Drakenstein mountainside.

✿ Optima ▼ Chic, dependable merlot-dominated Bdx-blend, very well priced for this quality. Cabs s/f in supporting roles in beautifully elegant **97**, the cooler vintage here very well handled with balanced fruit/oak, ripe tannin and finely etched flavours of cassis and vanilla woven with light eucalyptus and camphor. Merlot brilliantly used to flesh out cabs' spicy austerity. Not yet at its best — give ± 2 yrs for extra pleasure. 18 mths oak, 60% new. 12,8% alc. 5 800 cases. **96** something of a triumph in difficult vintage: elegant, satisfying. **95**, warmer vintage, supple, minty.

✿ Shiraz (La Maison du Roi) This sticking to its own course: neither traditional nor new-Cape style. Cooler **97** vintage brings out its signature white pepper, plus eucalyptus and redcurrants. While acid's quite low (5,2 g/ℓ), tastes tart — though this somewhat offset by berry fruit 'sweetness'. Oak matured 18 mths, 50% new. 12,9% alc. 1 050 cases.

✿ Cabernet Sauvignon (La Maison du Roi) Cooler vintage leaves its imprint in more sinewy **97 ✿**, some dry, dusty tones in very compact package. Tasted mid-2000 perhaps at an awkward stage, fruit in hibernation. 4 644 cases. **96** herby, cedary on release. Neither reach gorgeous heights of **95✿**.

Merlot ✿✿ Ripe-vintage **98** generously flavoured, more vinous than fruity with savoury/warm hay tones and med-weight (though 13,2% alc); fragrant lead pencils in dry finish. 15 mths oaked, 70% new. 5 070 cases. **Chardonnay ✿✿** Partially barrel fermented, full-bodied **99** still quite oaky mid-2000, subtle citrus somewhat overshadowed by (good) toast/caramel. On form of pvs should meld, given bit of time, and acquire attractive smoky/creamy palate with hints of lemon-curd. 13,3% alc. 5 000 cases. **98** SAA. **Sauvignon Blanc ✿✿** Quality progression from 97 (more stringent fruit selection) continues in newest **00**, med-bodied with wide-angle tastes of tropical fruit/capsicum/nettles; rounded palate tapers to very dry, almost austere finish, which naturally gravitates towards food. 4 800 cases. **Blanc Fumé ✿** Oak-matured sauvignon in understated, food-cordial mode. Med/full-bodied **99** offers subtle grassy hints, some quiet smoky tones in crisp dry palate. 6 500 cases. **Grand Vin Blanc ✿✿** Divergent melange of flavours in **00**, ranging from leafy/'green' tobacco to citrus/caramel from lightly oaked chardonnay portion (rest unwooded sauvignon); pleasing fullness (though alc's not high at 12,4%) makes this a good food style. 4 700 cases. **Rhine Riesling ✿✿** Invariably redolent of an attractive off-dry style. **00** with delicate almond blossoms and honey perfumes and smooth, mouthfilling taste. 12,6 alc. 2 800 cases. **96** *Wine* ✿✿. **Pinot Gris ✿✿** Food-friendly easy-drinking soft dry white. **00**, freshly bottled when tasted, bit *sotto voce*; should perk up and reveal usual generous lemon/lime/floral attractions, juicy dry finish. Unwooded. 14–18 yr-old vyds. Lightish 11,8% alc. 3 400 cases.

Lost Horizons Wines

Tasting & sales at Simonsvlei International (see that entry) Tasting fee R5 for 6 wines • Owner Norton Cooper • General manager Jacques Jordaan • Consulting viticulturist Schalk du Toit (VinPro) • Production ± 550 tons 150 000 cases 60% white 40% red • PO Box 568 Paarl 7624 • Tel (021) 863-3848 • Fax (021) 863-3850 • E-mail horizons=@global.co.za • Website www.global.co.za/~horizons/

THIS ICON of new Cape winedom — a US-European-SA joint venture tapping the considerable local resources of Du Toitskloof, Koelenhof, Franschhoek Vineyards and Simonsvlei — now ships upwards of 150 000 cases of its distinctive, chicly packaged produce to more than a dozen countries including the Caribbean, Mexico and Poland. Actually a 'virtual winery', Lost Horizons buys in wine from Worcester, Paarl and Stellenbosch vineyards, but also crushes 550 tons of purchased grapes at two of its partners' cellars. Bottling and storage are done at yet other premises. Foreign customers are lapping it all up, especially in Germany where the export-only Guardian label has been embraced with a full-throated prost! (so much so a local release is being contemplated). Good news for fashion-conscious local imbibers who've made the popular Quantum white spritz their tipple of choice: a rosé version, still being blushed and stylishly outfitted at press time, is on the cards.

> **Classic Ruby Red** ♣ ☺ Most of these 20 000 cases go to the UK, Canada, which means grill-a-holics in those countries needn't miss out on this **99** deluxe BBQ partner, smoothed with invisible sugar, slicked with ripe smoky cherries and blackberry jam. Ruby cab/cab/merlot. **Sauvignon Blanc** ♣ ☺ High altitude Bottelary vyds impart zesty, sweet-sour flavours of apricot, whiffs of sweet flowers in long, clean dry finishing **00**. 13,4% alc. 4 500 cases. **Quantum** ♣ ☺ Cool party animal in 1 000 ml blue bottle, chenin-sauvignon with refreshing carbonated tingle. Cool tastes, too: peaches and limes in **99**. Made off-dry for even easier celebrating. 40 000 cases.

♣ **Cabernet Sauvignon** ▽ Oodles of 'sweet' fruit in unwooded **98** (mulberry, blackcurrant jam, stewed fruit in finish), plus actual smidgeon residual sugar (5,1 g/ℓ) for extra-smooth sipping. 8 000 cases.

♣ **Chardonnay** Ongoing tinkering sees change to unwooded (pvs oak-chipped) in **00** ♣♣; some bright pineapple fruit and big body (14% alc). 4 000 cases. **99** improving in bottle; butterscotch, passionfruit and citrus in creamy full palate. 7 000 cases.

Cabernet Sauvignon-Merlot ♣ Jacques Jordaan & team would like to share **98** strawberry toned easy drinker with "all restaurant owners". Draw your own conclusion as you sniff the cassis, taste the unoaked food-friendly fruit. 1 000 cases.
Chenin Blanc ♣ Zingy fruit bowl of pvs now filled with guavas/pears; clean dry flavours, gutsy finish suggest this won't be cowed by rich or spicy cuisine. 5 000 cases. **Classic White** ♣ "Though dry, big seller in Gauteng Province," say winemakers. Actually, there _are_ a few grains of sugar (4,5 g/ℓ) in **99**, but these impart suppleness, don't sweeten. Lowish 11,7 alc enhances lunchtime tippleability. 10 000 cases.

Louiesenhof Wines

Stellenbosch (see Stellenbosch map) • Tasting & sales Mon—Fri 9—5 Sat 9—1 (Easter-Sep), otherwise Mon—Sat 9—5 Sun 11—5 Tasting fee R5 p/p • Light meals served on terrace Nov-Mar. Booking essential • Views • Owner/winemaker Stefan Smit • Viticulturist Casper Burger (since 1995) • Vineyards 169 ha • Production ± 1 300 tons • PO Box 2013 Dennesig 7601 • Tel (021) 882-2632 • Fax (021) 882-2613 • E-mail lhofwine@iafrica.com • Website www.louiesenhof.com

WHEN VISITING this Koelenhof locale, don't expect to be taken on the usual tour of gleaming fermentation cellars or dark barrelling halls: the business end of Stefan Smit's wine growing operation is folded away in a workmanlike cellar a short distance from the visitor centre, which is immaculately lodged on a smallholding looking out over Simonsberg mountain. Here you can taste the range made by Smit from his recently augmented holdings (he bought about 20 ha of cabernet on a farm next to the Smit family farm, Koopmanskloof, in the Bottelary hills). Also new are parcels of cabernet franc, merlot and, soon, shiraz. Rubernet, a new ruby cab/

cabernet cross which produces "amazing colour", is earmarked for a future 'port'. Packaging is a particular focus here, and Smit has drawn on two diverse talents for his front label artwork: Cape Town artist Francina Greenblatt adorns the premier reds, while the premier whites have miniature masterpieces by Smit's nine year old daughter Louie.

Sauvignon Blanc ⚜ 🟢 Splash chardonnay smoothes any sharper edges in 99, imparting extra drinkability to sauvignon's grassy, somewhat sweet-toned fig flavours. Crisp flinty finish not too acidic, though big 13,6% alc needs noting. 5 600 cases.

Premier Collection Cabernet Sauvignon-Cabernet Franc ‡ Another idiosyncratic style from this cellar: scents of eucalyptus/molasses and some caramelised notes in 97, soft tarry/creosote hints in palate. 70/30 blend. Elegant tall Italian bottle. **Chardonnay Sur Lie Limited Release** ⚜ Minerals and tropical fruit in latest 99, plenty of leesy character in palate with light oak nuances in dry finish, which a tad short. 13% alc. Fr oak, on lees 12 mths. 2 500 cases. **Chardonnay** ‡ Understated version; 99 with light tropical tastes and hints of oak, quick finishing dry palate. Fr barrels, 7 mths. 5 000 cases. **Louiesenhof Red Muscadel** ⚜ Individual sweet fortified dessert with powerful muscat/honeysuckle aroma and viscous texture in 99, concluding with unusual whiskey-like aftertaste. 92 SA Reserve champion. 17% alc. **Perroquet Cape Tawny** ⚜ NV In stylish ceramic carafe. Low yielding tinta b, blend of 93–95 vintages. One of the Cape's driest at 85 g/ℓ sugar; muscular 20% alc (Stefan Smit long-time port enthusiast and a pioneer of more 'Portuguese' style.) Fortified with 100% aged brandy. Individual (agreeable) sun-dried tomato/raisin/prune tastes; distinct warming glow as it goes down.

Louisvale Wines

Stellenbosch (see Stellenbosch map) • Tasting & sales Mon–Fri 10–5 Sat 10–1 Fee R8 p/p • Bring your own picnic • Upmarket self-catering guest house • Gifts • Views • Wheelchair-friendly • Owners Hans Froehling & Leon Stemmet • Winemaker/viticulturist Simon Smith (since 1997) • Vineyards 13 ha • Production 300 tons 50/50 red/white • PO Box 542 Stellenbosch 7599 • Tel (021) 882-2422 • Fax (021) 882-2633 • E-mail louisval@iafrica.com

THIS charmer of a farm — delightful owners, wines and 26 dogs — celebrated a decade in the marketplace in 2000, and Hans Froehling and Leon Stemmet can look back with satisfaction. And forward, too. They've grown Louisvale from Chardonnay-only to a cellar known for both whites and reds here and in 10 different export destinations, grooming its image as carefully as their champion Great Danes and miniature Schnauzers. Harrods Cabernet and Chardonnay are Louisvale under another, distinguished label, and their first Pinotages — two versions of this local hero from winemaker Simon Smith — might be next on this exclusive shopping list. While the consistently excellent chardonnay comes from the farm's own 13 ha Devon Valley vineyards, the red grapes are bought in.

⚜ **Dominique** Flagship red, pvsly labelled Cabernet Sauvignon-Merlot, in 97 ⚜ switched to honour owners' champion miniature Schnauzer. This first 'canine' now outgrowing youthful gawkiness, acquiring softness, harmony. Follow-up 98 emphatically back in 4-star pack: taut, sweet-violets/spice intensity augurs good development over 4–5 yrs. Cab/merlot 65/35, 12 mths small oak, 13,4% alc. 3 300 cases. 96 VVG, 94 *Wine* ⚜.

⚜ **LV Cabernet Sauvignon** "Everyday-drinking red, to share with friends," says Hans Froehling, yet newest 99 more serious than pvs, potential to improve over 2–4 yrs. Med-full bodied, lightly oaked. 2 000 cases.

⚜ **Louisvale Chardonnay** Since maiden 89, among most consistent and best Cape chardonnays. Invariably features on Nederburg Auction. Current 99, like pvs, barrel fermented, then on lees 8 mths. Distinct European impression —

feature of the vintage at this property; good citrus and toasty oak intensity. Substantial 13,6% alc seamlessly absorbed. Drink within 5 yrs, Hans Froehling advises, though excellent track record hints at greater longevity. 3 000 cases. **Louisvale Cabernet Sauvignon** ♣ Comfortable, nicely-padded food wine (as are all these reds), featuring compote of berries/green pepper/spice in second-vintage **97**. For now and next 2–3 yrs. Lightly-oaked. 13% alc. 750 cases. **Louisvale Merlot** ♣ Light-toned (but not -flavoured) example, from single vyd in Stbosch area. **98** fleshier, more extrovert than pvs; firm but not lean, good piquant finish. 500 cases. **96**, **94** VG. **Louisvale Chavant Chardonnay** ♣ Begun with **91** as lightly oaked option to Louisvale Chardonnay. Racier style continues in **99**, Burgundian hint of mushroom, lemon/grapefruit tang. 4 000 cases. Very popular restaurant wine. **LV Chardonnay Unwooded** ♣ Not a poor relation to above oaked versions. Second-vintage **99** up the scale, richer, more mouth-filling. Tropical mangoes, melons, plus twist of lemon. 1 000 cases.

- -

Lourens River Valley see Morgenster

- -

Louwshoek-Voorsorg Winery

Worcester (see Worcester map) • Tastings & sales Mon—Fri 8—1, 1.30—5 • Cellar tours by appointment • Guest cottages on Dwarsberg farm Tel (023) 349-1919 • Walks • 4x4 trail • Owners 32 members • Manager Gerrit van Zyl (since 2000) • Winemaker Anton Nel (since 1996) • Consulting viticulturists VinPro • Vineyards 840 ha • 13 500 tons (± 2 750 cases own label) • PO Box 174 Rawsonville 6845 • Tel (023) 349-1110 • Fax (023) 349-1980 • E-mail louwshoek@xpoint.co.za

ANTON NEL is aiming to join the super-stringent Master of Wine programme, an inveterate reader, considered in his opinions. While this cellar is doing great export business — making labels for Rylands Grove and Sea of Serenity for overseas clients — and scooping Young Wine Show and Veritas medals, and many winemakers would be quite happy with this status quo, he thinks beyond the comfort zone. "There is still lots of place for improvement." But not at an incautious pace. "We are upgrading systematically." With a recent harvest season in the Languedoc doubtless in mind: there he picked up, over and above French wine techniques, new ways of combining "manpower and machines in the cellar". In the 32 co-op members' vineyards (12 different varieties grown) "we are working together to ensure that it's not just grapes which are delivered to the cellar, but quality grapes."

Daschbosch range

> **Rosé** ♣ 😋 Generous boiled sweet cinsaut flavour in this discernibly sweet yet balanced quick quaff. 13% alc.

Cabernet Sauvignon ♣ Deep, plummy **00** fruit needs just a bit of time to develop. The good mulberry undertones should emerge and meld with soft, slightly green tannins. 13,3% alc. This unwooded version currently a step up from **Limited Release 99** ♣, sinewy style which presently closed, needing 1–2 yrs to develop. Some richness from vanilla oak. 12 mths Fr/Am casks, none new. **Merlot** ♣ Light, raspberry toned **00** for early enjoyment. 13,3% alc. **Pinotage** Limited quantities of **99** available but not tasted. **Shiraz** ♣ New Gentle, no-demands **00** offers mulberry/savoury flavours, very light tannins and expansive mouthfeel from 14%-plus alc. **Chardonnay** ♣ Lingering tropical fruit, orange peel in **00**, with 3 mths' rounding on lees with Fr oak chips. Light, breezy feel throughout though certainly not insubstantial at over 14% alc. **Sauvignon Blanc** ★ **00** no-frills dry white. **Nectar de Provision** ‡ First local version of Cognac's classic aperitif, Pineau des Charentes; follows French methods: colombard, fortified with 5/3 yr old brandy, matured in brandy vats. Now in modern slimline bottle. Latest is **99**. Develops rich, highly individual choc/liqueur-brandy tastes as it ages. "The longer you keep it, the better," says Anton Nel. **Cape Vintage Port ✖ New** Accommodating style; light, soft, ready on release. **98** shows ruby cab's high toned fruit, good winter warming stuff. Not oversweet at 90 g/ℓ sugar. Also: **Louwshoek-Voorsorg Sweet Hanepoot ✿✿ 99** very sweet yet clean finishing.

· ·

Luddite

Walker Bay • Tasting & sales by appointment • Owners Niels Verburg & Hillie Meyer • Production 7 tons 500 cases, doubling annually 100% red • PO Box 3 Bot River 7185 • Tel (028) 284-9450 • Fax (028) 284-9617

"ALL THIS FANDANGLED EQUIPMENT and machinery is making wine grey, uniform," booms assured Niels Verburg, who's vocal when it comes to winemaking (and, he'll be first to admit, not just winemaking!). Getting back to basics, seasoned Verburg (he's worked in France, New Zealand, Western Australia, Chile and, since 1995, at boutique Beaumont Winery at Bot River) is resolute about creating "real wine for real people". Hence the succinct Luddite own-label (which harks back to the early 19th century British anti-progress lobby), reflecting Verburg's strong feelings: "There are a few machines that should be banned before they make winemakers redundant." He's chosen shiraz as his flagship ("If you focus on a variety, you can get to truly master it"), and the first release below was made in Beaumont's cellar from selected Stellenbosch grapes. Verburg plans, however, to grow his own shiraz rows. "I truly believe in Bot River as red wine country. Now I've got my foot in the door with my first 500 cases."

✿✿ **Shiraz** Scrubby Rhône hills click into focus when you sniff **00**, glowing purple/black in a pool of smoky cassis. Toasty oak backdrop dramatises intense, spicy red fruit which, though youthful, already tastes creamily lush. Velvet gloved power (14% alc) for long keeping (up to 20 yrs, Niels Verburg ventures). Low cropped vyd (5 t/ha), 13 mths oak, 80/20 Fr/Am. 500 cases for release May 2001.

· ·

Lusan Premium Wines

Enquiries Garth Whaits • Tel (021) 883-8988

COLLECTIVE operations/marketing umbrella for Alto, Le Bonheur, Neethlingshof, Stellenzicht and Uitkyk. Wines from these farms, totalling some 800 ha of vineyards, marketed exclusively by SA Wine Cellars. See individual entries.

· ·

Lushof Estate

Stellenbosch (see Helderberg map) • Tasting/sales/cellar tour hours not available at press time. Phone for details • Owners Steyn family • Consulting winemakers Rod Easthope & Emma Williams • Viticulturist Schalk Keyser • Vineyards 12,5 ha • Production 100 tons (2 000 cases own label, rising to 7 000 by 2003) 70% red 30% white • PO Box 899 Stellenbosch 7599 • Tel (021) 855-3134 • Fax (021) 855-3623 • E-mail henni@icon.co.za

"A LIFE-LONG ambition to combine my technical skills with the art of making good wine" brought chemical industry businessman Hennie Steyn and family to this 14 ha property on the Helderberg in 1999 — a first-class neighbourhood: Longridge, Grangehurst and Clos du Ciel are just down the road. He has wasted neither time nor ground. A compact boutique cellar was up and running by the end of the year; the process of replanting 12,5 ha of vineyards with the latest clones of sauvignon, chardonnay, merlot, cabernet and shiraz is well underway, and export outlets in the UK and the Netherlands are already lined up. With Kiwi Rod Easthope and Emma Williams consulting in the cellar, Schalk Keyser in the vineyards, and Hennie Steyn's own impetus ("we need to speed up, not get further behind in our technology") this new estate is humming.

Sauvignon Blanc ✹ Gentle start to this estate's journey into wine in **00**, with classic cut-grass/nettle/tropical freshness without sauvignon's sometimes shrill acidity. 13,6% alc.

. . . .

Lutzville Vineyards

Olifants River (see Olifants River map) • Tasting & sales Mon—Fri 8—1; 2—5 Sat 9.30—12 • Cellar tours by appointment • Bring your own picnic • Function/conference venue • Tourgroups • 4x4 trail • Owners 106 shareholders • Winemakers Jacques du Toit (since 1997) & Albie Rust (since 1989) • Viticulturist Jan Kotzé • Production 42 000 tons 95,6% white 4,4% red • PO Box 50 Lutzville 8165 • Tel (027) 217-1516 • Fax (027) 217-1435 • E-mail lutzville@kingsley.co.za

FROM THEIR progressive cellar on the Olifants River, this energetic pack have been sending emissaries around the globe (to the UK for the London Trade Fair, to Italy and Japan) and stepping up exports to the United Arab Emirates. At the last crush they found themselves in a bit of a squeeze with a bigger intake of grapes, so there's expansion of the current cellar underway and a whole new red wine cellar to be built, all to cope with the pumped-up volumes. They're also installing a mass cooler and practising strict vineyard selection to improve quality. The Fleermuisklip brand derives its name locally from a massive rock, once a shelter for bats and early explorers, now a national monument.

Colombard ✹ New ☺ Lively, smooth, easy **00** with variety's guava, fresh tropical fruit. Under R10/bottle ex-cellar.

Cabernet Sauvignon ✹ First release **98** holding in bottle (though not improving). Leafy/stemmy tones, tannic grip, bit of fruit appears in finish. **Pinotage** ✹ Juicy style **99** with firming tannin and charry mulberry/plum. Should go yr/2. **Chardonnay Unwooded** ✹ **00** doesn't shout chardonnay, but it's clean, crisp, dry. Medbodied. **Chenin Blanc** ✹ **00** frisky off-dry with light lemonade tones. **Semillon** ✹ **00** very brisk dry white; not much fruit. **Diamant Vonkel** ✹ Nearby diamond-rich West Coast is allusion in name of this lightish **NV** (99) carbonated bubbly, energetically fizzy, fruity, surprisingly dry. Also available, untasted for this ed (pvs ratings in brackets): **Ruby Cabernet 99** (✹), **Chardonnay Wooded 98** (✹), **Sauvignon Blanc 99** (✹).

Fleermuisklip range

Robyn ✹ ☺ **99** carnivore's delight glows blood red; ripe berries with pepper seasoning, some fresh tomato on the side. Needs nothing more than a carving knife. Ruby cab/cab/merlot. 12,5% alc.

Bukettraube ✹ Off-dry **99** very delicate floral aroma, hint of dry straw; bracing fresh finish. **Misty Morning** ✹ Comfortable dry tropical tastes in **00**, fresh, lightish blend chenin/colombard/semillon. 500 ml screwtop. **Sunny Day** ✹ **00** a sweet Misty Morning with extra serving bananas. From colombard. **Somersoet** ★ **00** literally 'Summer Sweet', which it is. Colombard. **Late Harvest 98** past its best. **Hanepoot Jerepico** ✹ New **99** starts with mint julep brightness but ends in dull 'murky' tones. 18,5% alc.

. . . .

Lyngrove

Stellenbosch (see Stellenbosch map) • Tasting by appointment • Restaurant/kitchen facilities by arrangement • Luxury guest house • Walks • Baarsma SA (Pty) Ltd • Winemaker/viticulturist Danie Zeeman (since Nov 1998) • Vineyards 76 ha • Production 550 tons (5 000 cases own label) • 80% red 20 • white • PO Box 7275 Stellenbosch 7599 • Tel (021) 842-2116 • Fax (021) 842-2118 • E-mail lyngrove@iafrica.com • Website www.lyngrove.co.za

. . . .

THIS is one of those delightful all-in-one winelands spots where you can taste (the in-house range is overseen by seasoned Danie Zeeman); eat (in — a fully equipped kitchen awaits your inspiration; or out — culinary hotspots 96 Winery Road and L'Auberge du Paysan just around the corner); stay over (at the stylish Lyngrove Country House on the property, with all the extravagances you'd expect), walk (± 80 ha on the doorstep to explore) or lounge beside the pool and marvel at the mountain views. All courtesy of Hennie van der Merwe, dynamo here and, through the Baarsma SA company, headquartered at Lyngrove, in the international wine market (10-million litres exported annually to the UK, France, Netherlands and Canada). All that's missing is a producing cellar on the property — and they're working on that.

Cabernet Sauvignon ✿ **99** Soft slightly sweet raspberry/mulberry flavours, easy, unpretentious with very soft tannins for comfortable sipping. **00** similar style but lighter, perhaps needs bit of time to fill out. **Chardonnay** ✿✿ **00** reflects warm vintage in fat, tropical palate which glides across the tongue. Quite rich leesy notes in warming finish. **Sauvignon Blanc** ✿✿ **00** plump, unintimidating with broad tropical fruit salad tones and fragrant melon/papaya; gentle acidity.

. . . .

Makro

In-store tasting Sat 10—2 • Sales Mon—Fri 9—6 Sat 8.30—4 • Enquiries Gary Barber • Tel (011) 797-0664 • Fax (011) 803-8695 • E-mail gbarber@makro.co.za • Website www.makro.co.za

THIS NATIONAL discount chain's big-time buying power gives Gary Barber and his team an edge which, coupled with real commitment and effort, has resulted in some exciting one-off special releases and quality custom-made wines, which they commission from various cellars for exclusive sale through Makro outlets nationwide. Adding extra prestige to the line are labels bought at top wine shows and auctions. Babbling Brook is an easy on the palate and pocket own-label which offers its own brand of excitement, as does the array of generous magnum-sized wines which make such great gifts.

Private Reserve range

These all exclusive to Makro, all **New**.

- ✿ **Overgaauw Touriga Naçional-Cabernet** Densely extracted blue/blackberry fruit in powerful, velvet palate with firm but not uncomfortable tannins. **99** (sample) highly unusual (in Cape) pairing of these varieties, and fine follow-up to pvs **97**, big, deep flavoured with excellent ageing potential. **99** 13,3% alc.
- ✿ **Porcupine Ridge Reserve** Pinotage **99** see Boekenhoutskloof.
- ✿ **Villiera Pinot Noir** Generous fruit and well-managed tannins add to the still unfolding pleasures of **98**; new-clone ripeness, generosity (and warmer vintage) evident in raspberry/strawberry forwardness and assertive alc (13,4%). Can be enjoyed now but deserves time to reach its potential.
- ✿ **Boplaas Private Reserve Bin 620 Vintage Port 97** Boplaas' generous, welcoming style evident in wonderful soft, enveloping fruitcake introduction leading to choc-earthy depths of dark, not-too-sweet fruit. Light stalky hints in finish. Appealing and still youthful, should develop very well in its magnum bottle. 18% alc.

Stellenzicht Malbec ✿✿ **99** fairly light-bodied with cherry/strawberry tastes and good grip of tannin. Youthfully exuberant — needs bit of time to develop. 11,5% alc. **Hartenberg Merlot** ✿✿ **97** Most enjoyable lighter style with savoury/spicy touches and hints of mint/eucalyptus; **97** could even be lightly chilled in summer for easy alfresco sipping. **Stellenzicht Private Reserve Bin 504 Cabernet Franc** ✿✿ **99** (sample) reveals flamboyant side of variety not all that frequently glimpsed in Cape. Great gulps of black fruit and choc, some 'green'/spicy sensations and charry aftertastes; chunky alc (14,4%) with dab invisible sugar (3,1 g/ℓ) amount to a real dinner table conversation-stopper. **Steenberg Private Reserve Bin 232 Sauvignon Blanc-Semillon** ✿ Sauvignon in the lead throughout **00**, with cut-grass/gooseberries immediately staking their claim to nose and surfacing again in finish. Mid-palate shows hint of semillon's flesh, and this should become more apparent with time. Good food wine. **Cellar Release Sauvignon Blanc** ✿ **99** from Rickety Bridge. Solid, well made example with gooseberry/grass ahead of passionfruit in crisp departure. 13,2% alc. **Cellar Release Sauvignon Blanc-Semillon** ✿ **98** (sample) another Rickety Bridge exclusive. This one will need time for the (gorgeous, fragrant) oak to meld with the yet undeveloped kernel of tropical fruit. Will be stunning in couple of yrs. 13% alc. **Cellar Reserve Chenin Blanc** ✿ Tasted as 'preview', **99** fairly subdued, straightforward though easy to drink. Some pears in bouquet, mingling with ripe guava in quaffable palate. Also available (not tasted): **Leef-op-Hoop Cabernet-Merlot 99**, **Misty Mountain Sauvignon Blanc 00**, **Babbling Brook Grand Vin Blanc 99**, **Babbling Brook Dry White 00**.

Malan Family Vintners

COLOURFULLY and simply attired range by the Malan brothers of Simonsig, including brands listed under Simonsig in previous editions. Mainly for offshore markets, though available from selected local outlets and as housewines in some restaurant chains.

> **Adelberg Cabernet Sauvignon-Merlot** ✿ ☺ 'Budget Bordeaux' **99** with smoky stewed plum aromas, savoury flavours, twist of fennel in finish. Chardonnay ✿ ☺ **99**, lightly oaked, with floral, herb and spice notes; supple, juicy finish from light brush of sweetness.

Pinotage ✿ Bright unwooded **99**'s cherry/mulberry fruit ends with almost Italian tartness, so slightly chill and pour with pasta. **Rouge du Cap ✦ 00** spicy cherry/strawberry arrangement carries through to dry, simple finish, which won't interfere with food. Ruby cab, pinotage, pinot noir. **Sauvignon Blanc** ✿ Briskly limey **99** maintains subtle cut grass and green pea whiffs of **98**. **Blanc du Cap ✦** Attractive **99** quaffing companion wafts talcum scents and firm dry finish. Clairette blanche, colombar, riesling, chenin. **Adelblanc ✦** Chenin, colombard bring you demure pear and honey whiffs, comfortable crispness in **99**.

Maskam see Vredendal

Masters Port

VERY distinguished Cape port: equal-parts blend of the best 500 ℓ barrels from Calitzdorp Cape port maestros, Carel Nel of Boplaas, Boets Nel of Die Krans, and Tony Mossop of Axe Hill, all three Cape Wine Masters. Enquiries: Boplaas Tel (044) 213-3326 • Die Krans Tel (044) 213-3314 • Axe Hill Tel (021) 780-1051 • Also see those entries for tasting/sales information.

✿ **Cape Vintage Reserve** A serious customer, reflecting some diverse talents. The question will be asked: does the **98** ✿✿ sum upstage all its pedigreed parts? Perhaps not quite. Garnet-plum hues — not as deeply intense as some of its peers — with complex, choc-coated nutty aromas. Warm, ripe fruity spread in palate, including dried figs, nuts and, in finish, some wild heathery/sweet herbs tastes to match the comforting alcohol. Touriga, tinta b, souzão. 18 mths 500 ℓ Portuguese oak. **97** smooth, soft, balanced. These accessible on release but probably best from 6–10 yrs after vintage. Both _Wine_ ✿✿. Alcs 19%, sugars 95 g/ℓ. Only ±2 000 numbered bottles.

McGregor Winery

Robertson (see Robertson map) • Tasting & sales Mon—Thu 8—12.30; 1.30—5 Fri 8—5 Sat 9—12.30 • Cellar tours by appointment • Owners 41 members • Winemaker Pieter Carstens (since 1999) with Gerhard Swart (since 2000) • Consulting viticulturist Briaan Stipp (since 1993) • Vineyards 680 ha • Production 9 754 tons 25 000 cases • Private Bag X619 McGregor 6708 • Tel (023) 625-1741 • Fax (023) 625-1829 • E-mail mcg@intekom.co.za

"LIFE'S FULL of surprises," muses ex-Groot Eiland winemaker Pieter Carstens, for whom opportunity knocked in the form of a residency in rural McGregor, where the unspoilt beauty and charm is soul-food for someone who chose a winemaking career "to be close to nature". His team mate in the cellar is newcomer Gerhard Swart, who arrived at the quieter end of a crush which doubled the previous red wine production. A trip to Poland impressed marathon-running Carstens with its "huge potential which has never been developed, because wine is not yet part of their culture". The range, not available for tasting, includes (**00**, dry, not oaked unless noted, pvs ratings in brackets where applicable): **Village Red (✿)** 99 ruby cab, oak-influenced. **Rosé** New Semi-sweet, from pinotage. **Sauvignon Blanc (✿)**. **Chenin Blanc (✿)** **Colombard (✿)** Off-dry. **Colombard-Chardonnay ✿ Brut** Carbonated sparkling. **NV**. **Vin Sec** Sweet carbonated sparkle. **NV**.

Meerendal Estate

Durbanville (see Durbanville map) • Tasting & sales Mon—Fri 8.30—5 Sat 9—12.30 Closed Sun Tasting fee R10 p/p • Function/conference facilities, call Francois Ferreira • Wheelchair-friendly • Owner JCF Starke Trust • Winemaker/viticulturist Soon Potgieter (since 1973) • Vineyard manager Fanie Rost (since 1996) • Vineyards 200 ha • PO Box 2 Durbanville 7551 • Tel (021) 975-1655 • Fax 975-1657 • E-mail meerendal@mweb.co.za

SOON POTGIETER'S conviction that Meerendal's future is in red blends has proved spot-on: the first of these, rather resoundingly named Cabochon, is a stunner. But the varietal Cabernet's no slouch either: in just 3 vintages, it's rehearsed, auditioned and landed a place in this guide's august ✿✿ company. On the sweeter side, golden gewürzes still feature strongly at this historic (1702) estate, with its landmark Cape-Dutch homestead and pastoral views over the Durbanville hills.

✿✿ **Cabernet Sauvignon** ✔ The warm, elegant, generous **98** vintage delivers an absolute corker in this intensely ripe, refined cab, with bountiful mulberry/blackberry fruit, subtly perfumed with cedar oak. Fine-grained tannins and some classic cassis aromas. 13,6% alc. Yr Fr small-oak.

✿ **Merlot** Good varietal character in **98**; tangy/minerally entry builds to slightly sweet cassis/dark choc mid-palate. Ripe fruit, ample 14,2% alc lend substance; firm dry tannins keep a rein on the richness. Should keep another 5 yrs. SAYWS gold. Yr Fr barriques. **97**, barrel-fermented, first release.

✿✿ **Cabochon** New ✔ Stunning debut for this **98** Bdx blend of cab and merlot (50/50), each contributing their full, weighty charm (14,2% alc) to the whole: merlot's fleshy opulence, cab's form-giving discipline. Aromatic intensity from swirling cassis with savoury Parma ham. Yr Fr small oak. This and above also in 1,5 ℓ magnums.

✿ **Pinotage** ✔ Latest **98**, in Bdx bottle, showcases only positive pinotage attributes. Absolutely packed with red crushed cherry/raspberry fruit, smoothed/spiced with fragrant vanilla oak through to crisp, properly dry end. Pvs **96** tiring a bit after good start. **95** juicy modern style.

✿ **Shiraz** ✔ Smooth, urbane **98** presently hiding its considerable allures, so be sure to give ample time for development. Everything's in place for future pleasure: blackberry fruit, eucalyptus top notes, even whiffs tar/sweet violets. Medium weight (though 13% alc), balanced, good dry finish. ±Yr Fr oak. Since **95** in more modern idiom. Pvs **96** massively, almost explosively flavoursome.

Liberte Blanc ⚘ **New** 😊 Gewürz, this estate's white signature, in bright, cheerful partnership with chardonnay. Rose-petal bouquet, sappy dry flavour make super summer sipping. Full 13,6% alc.

Blanc de Blanc ⚘ Dbnville's 'dusty' sauvignon fingerprint all over this satisfying dry med-full blend with chardonnay. **99** ripe, multi-layered food wine with asparagus tones. **Navette New** Semi-sweet style gewürz. Not tasted. **Natural Sweet** ⚘⚘ **98** VG, *Wine* ⚘ and champion sweet wine on SAYWS, first dessert from estate. Tasted mid-2000, promisingly/assertively gewürzy, yet oversweet in palate, lacking verve. 12,9% alc.

Meerlust Estate ⍢ ⍰

Stellenbosch (see Helderberg map) • Tasting by appointment Fee R45 p/p (includes cellar tour) • Sales Mon—Thu 9—5 Fri 9—4.30 • Cellar tours by appointment • Wheelchair-friendly • Owner Hannes Myburgh • Winemaker Giorgio Dalla Cia (since 1978) with Rudi de Wet (since 2000) • Viticulturist Cyril Ress (since 1994) • PO Box 15 Faure 7131 • Tel (021) 843-3587 • Fax (021) 843-3274 • E-mail meerlust@iafrica.com

MORE THAN THREE centuries of history echo in Meerlust's white-washed, swirly-gabled homestead, the family crypt, the winery and even the walled swimming pool — all Cape-Dutch architectural gems. The whole estate is a national monument. And you'll find the same sense of classic continuity in the wines, and a similar fusion of SA and Europe. Eighth-generation owner Hannes Myburgh is a Francophile; his father was a pioneer of the Bordeaux-style blend in the Cape. Giorgio Dalla Cia, winemaker for 21 years, hails from an old Italian wine family, and his annual wine pilgrimages are always to Bordeaux, Burgundy or Tuscany. Their double vision is Old, rather than New World, concertos rather than rap, and in a contemporary world of wild winemaking swerves in every brash new direction, you might think Meerlust had been caught in something of a time-warp. You would be utterly wrong. Elegance and excellence will never go out of fashion. Unmoved by the chardonnay feeding-frenzy, Dalla Cia experimented for 13 years before adding his considered, singular version of this white to Meerlust's red ranks. He was equally deliberate about tweaking the house Pinot Noir style, and boosting the power of the Merlot, determined not to lose the refinement that's the Meerlust hallmark. You may be sure there'll be no stampede to stream in new plantings of petit verdot and viognier. And Meerlust buyers should not rush either. These wines should carry a neck label warning against premature drinking.

⚘ **Rubicon** Standard bearer of the range and, for many, pre-eminent Cape 'claret' over its 20 yr history (with Welgemeend and Overgaauw, first to blend merlot with cabs s/f). Consistently stamped with fine blackberry fruit, restrained tannins yielding elegance with time. Needs bottle maturation to show its best. When the suggestion that too many pull the cork prematurely is put to Dalla Cia, his reply is: "A sin, actually". Upcoming **97** ⚘, from extended ripening season in cooler yr, closed-in nose but intense berry/black cherry concentration in palate; dense, latticed dry tannins finish with extraordinary length. No obvious cheery fruit here, Am oak conspicuous by absence; will grace refined cellars for yrs. Arresting extraction suggests this deserves keeping min 7 yrs, preferably longer. Such density needs forbearance and will bring its rewards. Par with **95**, **91** and greats of the 80s. **96** slighter (in context), from less ripe year. Cherries again, some cassis/spices including cloves but tannic gravitas has Dalla Cia expecting a 20-yr life span (though who could resist getting reacquainted from time to time?). **95** SAA, 90 rating in *Wine Spectator*, matches 3 finest years of the 80s — **89**, **87**, **86**. Blend settled at 70% cab, 20% merlot, rest cab f. Petit verdot set to join the palette when vines mature. New Nevers barrel matured ±18–24 mths.

✿ Merlot Associations with good bitter choc/well hung game get Dalla Cia going. Chocolate, he explains, shares some key flavour/aroma compounds with merlot. So, blueberry/magenta-cherry in nose of **97** with time will develop into truffly/game characters ("pheasant breast" are his actual words"). Palate still tight, somewhat spartan, but elegant minerally structure is compelling. **96**, from lighter yr, more immediately 'charming': sweet red berries, flesh to softening wood, fruit still bound up in sturdy palate. These age well: sample of **89** from magnum rich black truffle/chocolate/game birds. Tannins settled and integrated. Mature vyds (13–36 yrs), small 5–6 t/ha yields, 80% new Nevers oak (looser grain allows oxygen contact), mainly medium toasted — all for concentration and style desired. Always includes 10% cab. No local releases **90**, **91**, **92** though some exported.

✿ Pinot Noir Reserve Pivotal shift in style (from edgy to fuller-bodied), commenced **95**, gathers momentum with next **98**. Deeply coloured; effusive full-roast coffee aromas/ripe red cherries. Bigger than pvs, promise of earthy wild forest mushrooms as the fruitiness fades. **97** replete with wild strawberries/black cherry/clove spice; youthful fleshiness bridled by dry tannic grip. Superbly balanced, rich decadence beckons. First vintage with mix old/new clones for fruitier/plummier profile. **96** generous, full. This Reserve estate's sole Pinot label from **95**. Pre-**94** leaner, more savoury, less berry character, lighter texture, leafier quality. Cellar regime changed in **96** to new heavy-toast tight Alliers oak, non-standard full malo to "promote seamlessness".

✿ Chardonnay Definitively weighty SA chardonnay, built to mature, made for table. 13 yrs of experimentation preceded launch of **95** — nothing less than the best could be risked behind a Meerlust label. **98** dominated by ripe fruit in infancy, big palate tense with crisp acid. 13,5% alc. **97** more settled, roast almonds emerging, excellent length and balanced 13% alc. Approaching readiness with nougat/marzipan/candied chestnuts. Usually 18 mths wood (**96** had 22) full malo. 100% barrel fermented in heavy-toast, tight-grained Alliers oak, designed to reduce wood coarseness while giving powerful roasted almond/butterscotch characters. Then rest on fine lees 17 mths with lees stirring, reducing primary fruit and enhancing later flavour spectrum. "Meursault was our benchmark" says Dalla Cia.

Meinert Wines ▼

Stellenbosch (see Stellenbosch map) • Tasting & sales at 96 Winery Road Restaurant (see Eat-out section) • Owner/winemaker/viticulturist Martin Meinert • Vineyards 13 ha • Production 250 tons 17 000 cases (4 000 cases own label — all red) 54% white 40% red 6% NLH • PO Box 7221 Stellenbosch 7599 • Tel/fax (021) 882-2363 • E-mail meinert@netactive.co.za

HE's the most cerebral of Cape winemakers, Martin Meinert, congenitally unsuited to paddling about in the shallows; reading, music (jazz, classical, blues) and diving for crayfish are his relaxants of choice. Which means his simple answers to the simple questions we asked everyone for this edition are decidedly the most provocative. Who was the biggest influence on his winemaking? "Oh no, no! My own mistakes! Everything?" He offers an original theory (laced with the usual Meinert self-deprecation) and throws the question back. The debate could rage for ever. The same applies to whom he'd most like to meet in the wine world — our query. His reply: "Oh no, no, no!" (With all the commas correctly in place as befits a former sub-editor of the famous *Rand Daily Mail*). "Please guys!" he implores. "Everyone? They all have something to offer." Sounds flippant, until you think. As Meinert does, rigorously and — fans of the talents he showed at Vergelegen were beginning to believe — interminably. He kept postponing his personal comeback; kept — tantalisingly — turning out splendid wines for friends and neighbours. Now he's shed a couple of consultancies (Ken Forrester and Sylvanvale remain) and has at last concluded the internal agonies about the reds from his own 13 ha Devon Valley vineyards and winery. They are grown-up enough to be let out of their play-pen! His mates joke that he's been pregnant with these for 9 years. But hang on a minute (or a few more years): where is the Pinotage that we are reliably informed is still lurking? When will it be released? "Who knows?" Meinert answers.

✿ Merlot ▽ Elegant **97** still evolving — and as yet no drink-by date evident. Some fresh violet, green tea scents and classy, earthier cigar box notes. Cool, classic dry (but not over-extracted/tannic) finish. Used Fr oak. 13,5% alc, 8 yr old vines, 6 t/ha yield. **98** fleshier, flashier, fuller, though **97** probably longer maturing. The later vintage expensive-smelling with new leather, sweet-oak nuances; middle palate richness and some grippy but well controlled tannins.

✿ Cabernet Sauvignon-Merlot Nicely styled, well-spiced **97** with fine oak, enough ripe red fruit, tannin integration to carry many more yrs. 25% new Fr oak, rest 2nd fill. 13,3% alc. *Wine* ✿, **98** gorgeous claret intensity, from deep purple-plum colour to thrusting minty/leafy palate with finishing smoky swirl. Easy 6–10 yr life ahead. About 70%–30% cab to merlot. Very low-yield vines (5 t/ha), ±18 mths in cask, 35% new Fr.

. . . .

Mellasat　　　　　　　　　　　　　　　　　　　　　　　　🍷🍷 🍷

Paarl (see Paarl map) • Tasting, sales, cellar tours Dec—Mar (inclusive) Sat 9—1, otherwise by appointment • Sales also through www.cybercellar.co.za • Views • Wheelchair-friendly • Owners Stephen & Alison Richardson • Winemaker Stephen Richardson (since 1999) with Poena Malherbe • Viticulturist Poena Malherbe (since 1996) • Vineyards 8 ha • Production 1 000 cases 57% red 43% white • PO Box 7169 Paarl 7623 • Tel/fax (021) 862-4525 • E-mail mellasat@mweb.co.za

HOPPING BETWEEN two hemispheres, Stephen and Alison Richardson have gone a step beyond flying winemakers — they represent a young generation of truly global farmers. The sport-loving couple farms wheat, barley and sugar beet in Britain and wine grapes in SA. "UK winemaker, Rob Hemphill (from Shawsgate Vineyard) who is knowledgeable, thorough and unflappable in a crisis" has been the Richardsons' mentor since they bought a portion of Dekkersvlei farm in 1996. After replanting their 13 ha they now have nearly 60% of production dedicated to cabernet sauvignon, shiraz and pinotage. With renovation of the old homestead completed, all extra time is devoted to the new barrel maturation cellar. Poena Malherbe, "a forward-thinking kind of farmer", who has been the vineyard manager since 1996, has joined Stephen Richardson in the winemaking venture.

Cabernet Sauvignon Reserve ✿✿ 😊 Not too assertive savoury/green olive tastes ensure versatility, satisfaction at table. Plummy softness in **99** conclusion. **Dekkersvlei Chenin Blanc Reserve** ✿✿ 😊 Peaches and cream (from extended lounge on lees) and soft floral fragrances in med-bodied **00**; juicy dry finish refreshing on its own or with food. 12% alc. 270 cases. Also in 500 ml.

Dekkersvlei Pinotage Reserve ✿✿ Pleasing unpretentious style with gamey/smoky sniffs over sweet, just-not-jammy mulberries. **99** ends crisply dry. 135 cases. **Sauvignon Blanc** ☆ **New** Soft-finishing **00** aperitif with bright guava fruit and balanced acidity. 150 cases.

. . . .

Merry-go-Round

SPRUITDRIFT is the source of these cheerful-looking 1 ℓ NV value packs, also available on export shelves. All **New**.

. . . .

Grand Cru ✿ Fresh from top to tail, lightish (11,5% alc, as are all these), clean. Non- aggressively dry. **Stein** ✿ Smooth and light, easy quaffing; not overly sweet. **Late Harvest** ✿ Pleasant, undemanding sweet white.

· ·

Merwespont Winery

Robertson (see Robertson map) • Tasting & sales Mon—Fri 8—12.30; 1.30—5 • Cellar tours during harvest by appointment • Bring your own picnics • Nearby Merwenstein B&B Tel (023) 616-2806; Peet se Plek & Ou Waenhuis self catering Tel (023) 616-3151; Toy Cottage self catering Tel (023) 616-2735 • Conferences • Walks • Views • Tourgroups by arrangement • Wheelchair-friendly • Owners 50 members • Winemakers Dirk Cornelissen (since 1983) with Charles Stassen (since 1998) • Viticulturist Charles Stassen (since 2000) • Production 9 000 tons (10 000 cases own label) 50% white 50% red • PO Box 68 Bonnievale 6730 • Tel (023) 616-2800 • Fax (023) 616-2734 • E-mail merwespont@lando.co.za

WITH VINEYARDS from Bonnievale to Swellendam, this squad is among the co-op leaders in the race to replace high-cropping white varieties with in-demand reds and 'noble' whites. They're focusing on the Big Six: cabernet, merlot, shiraz, pinotage, sauvignon and chardonnay. Dirk Cornelissen, veteran of nearly 20 vintages here, brings experience to Charles Stassen's brimming enthusiasm. With the departure of viticulturist Hendrik Myburg, Stassen now also has the vineyards of the 35 growers in his portfolio. He worked a vintage in Bordeaux ("the milder climate means you can do more with the wine without messing it up"), but returned to a tricky, early 2000 crush which featured with some distinctly Bordeaux-like rain during picking.

Agulhas range

Cabernet Sauvignon ✳✳ 💊 Lightly oaked **98** with smoky redcurrants leading seamlessly into lightish palate; merest hint of oak in dry minerally finish. Unpretentious early enjoyment. 500 cases. **Red** ✳✳ **NV** 💊 Juicy everyday blend starring smoky mulberries, unadorned by oak. Versatile enough for summer heat (lightly chilled) or winter cold (by a roaring fire). Lightish 11,7% alc. 4 000 cases.

Chardonnay ✳✳ **97** showing bit of age in creamier, broader texture with apples and some honey. Still a satisfying drink (and standing test of time much better than many sniffy labels). **White** ✿ **NV** Casual quaff with dry herbal tones; lightish, undemanding chenin/colombard/sauvignon blend. 2 500 cases.

Merwespont range

Mainly for export and local restaurants.

Chardonnay ✳✳ 😊 Light lemony tones and marzipan hints in **99**, light oaking doesn't overpower fruit. Fairly moderate 12,7% alc for easy lunchtime sipping. 300 cases. **Cabernet Sauvignon** ✳✳ 💊 Nutty plum-cake and sappy cassis transform this 99 into a tasty, juicy drink. Extra allures of supple texture, lightish body. 500 cases.

· ·

Merwida Co-op

Worcester (see Worcester map) • Tasting & sales Mon—Fri 8—12.30; 1.30—5 Sat 9—1 • Cellar tours during tasting/sales hours • Merwida Country Lodge tel Diane Slabolepsky (023) 349-1435 • Gifts • Tourgroups • Conferences • Views • Wheelchair-friendly • Owners Schalk & Pierre van der Merwe • Winemakers J 'Wollie' Wolhuter, Sarel van Staden • Viticulturist CP le Roux • Vineyards 550 ha • Production 8 600 tons (10 000 cases own label) 75% white 25% red • PO Box 4 Rawsonville 6845 • Tel (023) 349-1144 • Fax (023) 349-1953 • E-mail wines@merwida.com • Website www.merwida.com

BACK IN THE GUIDE after a hiatus of several years, this collective winery just outside Rawsonville has maintained a remarkably even keel. Winemaker-manager 'Wollie' Wolhuter has been heading up the cellar since 1965, and fellow winemaker Sarel van Staden has been there for more than 15 years. The relatively small range of wines includes a diverse mix of styles. Following wines all to this ed.

> **Ruby Cabernet** ✳ 😊 **99**'s savoury dryness, light-toned crushed berry/plum texture could have been made in Italy (so virtually tailor-made for pizza, pasta). 13,5% alc.

Cabernet Sauvignon ✳ Vinous rather than fruity **98**, med-bodied, lightly oaked, good dry savoury finish. 13% alc. **Merwo Blanc** ⚥ **00** gentle dry white, pretty wildflower perfume. **Weisser Riesling** ★ **00** crisp, clean, dry white. **Cuvée Brut** ⚥ Lightish, gently dry **NV** bubbles with lick of honey.

··

Middelvlei Estate

Stellenbosch (see Stellenbosch map) • Tasting & sales Mon—Sat 10—4.30 Tasting fee R3 p/p • Cellar tours by appointment Jan—Apr • Small conference facility (15—20 guests) • Walks • Owners Jan (snr), Tinnie & Ben Momberg • Winemaker Tinnie Momberg (since 1992) • Viticulturist Ben Momberg (since 1992) • Vineyards 130 ha • Production 1 200 tons (±800 tons crushed in own cellar) 300 tons/21 000 cases own label 62% red 38% white • PO Box 66 Stellenbosch 7599 • Tel (021) 883-2565 • Fax (021) 883-9546 • E-mail info@middelvlei.co.za • Website www.middelvlei.co.za

"NOT JUST FRUIT, also backbone; somewhere between traditional French and New World styles": that's how Tinnie Momberg sees the ideal national profile, and his impressive wines fit it perfectly. It's a three-brothers-and-family show at this property fringing Stellenbosch, with Ben Momberg manicuring the 130 ha vineyards, his wife Jeanneret directing marketing, Jan jnr doing the business management bit, and Tinnie's wife Leana handling community development (Middelvlei's excellent workers' facilities include a clinic and a crèche). Father Stiljan Momberg, though officially retired, remains an inspirational presence. There is more than devotion to duty here. Tinnie Momberg is still enchanted that he can "drink a glass of wine at 9 in the morning with a new friend and call it work" and while others relax outside the winery, he goes into the new maturation cellar (opened in 1999, after the estate's amicable exit from the Bergkelder stable) to unwind. "When I close the door behind me, no-one knows where I am, no telephones ring (I hate phones) and I have tasted my 960 barrels at least twice each."

✳ **Shiraz** Hit the ground running with new-style **95** and hasn't looked back. Product of maturing virus-cleaned vines (50/50 old 1977 vyds, new 1990 plantings). Current **98** deep blue-black; bold ripe fruit aromatics, unusual tropical wafts (banana, pear); gutsy spice and choc-a-block tannins shore up sweet fruit. Barrel sample **99** still gaining more from wood, very savoury. 50/50 new/2nd fill Fr. 13,2% alc. 3 300 cases. Acclaimed **97**, SA champion young wine of yr, on higher Rhône-like plane, sold out, not tasted for this edition. **96** ✳ exceptionally concentrated, complex. No **92—94**.

✳ **Cabernet Sauvignon** Latest **98** ✳ leafy, green, touch stalky but lots of guts, fruit masked mid-2000. Lightish 12,2% alc. All cleaned-up clones, 50% each new/2nd fill Fr oak. 12,2% alc. 2 701 cases. No **97** due to stringent quality control. **96** penetrating mulberries, cassis folded with spice, huge wood (70% new) dominates but tannins will soften in bottle. 12,5% alc. 3 300 cases. Same mould as **95**, tobacco pouch, ripe cherries, blueberries/blackcurrant. Good balance.

✳ **Pinotage** Solid red wine rather than fashionable confection-cup of sweet bananas/vanilla. Upcoming **98** nose still muffled, gutsy grip in mouth plumped up with creamy vanilla, showy 47% new Am oak (rest new Fr). Length curtailed by green finish. 12% alc. 1 107 cases. **97** pick of this bunch, altogether more refined. Creamy, ripe berry fruit, flossy bonbons balanced by elegant tannic structure. 12,4% alc. 4 005 cases. **96** raspberry/mulberry keynotes dominated by smoky oak, soupçon pinotage ester; astringent tannic grip in firm style, full fruit in wings. 16 mths 2nd-fill Fr barrels. 12% alc. **95** soft, seductive.

✿ Pinotage-Merlot Open, forward fruit the added value in estate's biggest seller, popular in export markets (35% on foreign shelves). **98** medley of ripe banana skins/game bird wildness/cloves. Melodious pulpy pinotage (always at least 50% of blend) hunted down by merlot restraint, firm tannins to age. 13,5% alc. 11 138 cases. **97** more intense, perfumed, classy. Less obvious, less aggressive, lasting finish with notable creaminess. 12,5% alc. 3 600 cases. These yr small oak, ±1/3 new **96** ✿ VVG, *Wine* ✿.

✿ Chardonnay Pre-bottling sample **00** quiet nose but creamy fruit, citrus tang and assertive alcohol (14,5%) getting ready for the main event. Crisp, fresh. 30% fermented/matured 4 mths new small Fr oak, with malo; rest stainless steel. 2 000 cases. Popular **99** sold out rapidly. **98** Crisp citrus layered with creamy butterscotch/ripe peach/cinnamon, lees/lime extends flavour dimension. Restaurant favourite.

....

Middlepost Wines

Enquiries Nick Dymoke-Marr • Tel + 44 1858 57-0600 • Fax + 44 1858 57-0601 • E-mail nick@orbitalwines.co.uk.

A BIT of a United Nations, this export range: a collaboration between the UK's Orbital Wines, the Hanwood Group (with Eastern European experience), and the Cape's Winecorp; the wines fashioned by Aussies (Phil Lehmann, Ben Radford) and California-trained Scot Steve Donnelly — all with British supermarket customers and a price-point of under £5 in mind. Named after South African-born actor/writer Anthony Sher's novel, of the same title. Enquiries Nick Dymoke-Marr • Tel + 44 1858 57-0600 • Fax + 44 1858 57-0601 • E-mail nick@orbitalwines.co.uk.

Cabernet Sauvignon ✿ Fresh, clearly-defined mouthful brambleberries/blackcurrants in full-bodied, Fr-oaked **99**; well judged cedary wood lends more substance, form. Best over next 2-3 yrs. 13% alc. **Chardonnay** ✿ Full-bodied, wood-fermented **99** with complementary tropical/lime/spice bouquet, freshened by zesty acid, flavours extended by sweetish oak vanilla. Soupçon unoaked. 13,5% alc.

....

Migration see Du Preez Wine
Millbrook see Arlington

....

Mischa Estate   New ❖ ❖ ❖

Wellington (see Wellington map) • Tasting, sales, cellar tours by appointment • Refreshments/light meals on request or bring your own picnic • Tours of nursery's grafting sheds on request • Walks • Views • Wheelchair-friendly • Owners John & Andrew Barns • Winemaker/viticulturist Andrew Barns • Vineyards 40 ha • Production 312 tons (2 775 cases own label) 100% red • PO Box 163 Wellington 7654 • Tel (021) 864-1019/20 • Fax (021) 864-2312 • E-mail mischa@webmail.co.za

HIS FIRST VINTAGE gave self-taught new winemaker Andrew Barns minimal growing pains. After four years of working in the well-known Mischa wine nursery (on the same premises as this new wine estate) in Wellington, it was a natural leap for this 23 year old to make wines, with such fine stock and vineyards to hand. His grandfather bought the farm post-WW2. His father, John Barns, has been growing vines here for the past 25 years and says that he (with remarkable restraint) "followed a policy of non-interference when Andrew said he was ready to start making wine". Father and son share a passion for the vine and the former enthusiastically adds: "This gives another dimension to the operation. Visitors have the chance to see the whole process, right from the grafting sheds to the making of wines." They eagerly await the sale of their first wines, which have been greeted with "enthusiastic response" by their friends and colleagues-in-wine.

✿ **Shiraz** French or American oak? That's a question occupying many Cape winemakers, including those working with this trendy, chameleon-like grape. Andrew Barns may not yet have the answer (perhaps he does?), but this first **99**, offered in separate Fr and Am oaked versions, makes two fascinating cases in point. Both glimpsed mid-2000 as gawky (but strapping: 14%+ alc) teenagers, but even then American Oak had the edge: fruitily ripe; lashed by mouthcoating tannin but already supple, merely needing time. Plenty of soft, peppery/toasty berry fruit to carry into probable ✿ adulthood. 6 mths casked. **French Oaked** ✿ Stretches 'New World' to its juiciest, happy-fruitiest extreme; almost nonvinous in its cordial-like intensity, 9 mths oaking swallowed by waves of enveloping sweet blackcurrants. Though charming in own right, lacks complexity, structure.

Cabernet Sauvignon ✿ Single vyd cab; **99** first wine made on this farm. And it's a good one: familiar cassis/mulberry, some light vanilla touches; slight greenness in finish, which should disappear with time. 9 mths all-new oak. 14,2% alc. 300 cases.

. . . .

Misty Point see Barrydale
Mondial see Alphen Mondial

. . . .

Monis Wines

Paarl • Tasting & sales at Oude Libertas See Stellenbosch Farmers' Winery • Owner SFW • Winemaker Dirkie Christowitz • Production 24 000 cases • PO Box 266 Paarl 7626 • Tel (021) 872-1811 • Fax (021) 872-2790 E-mail dchristowitz@sfw.co.za

THE CAPE'S oldest (established 1906) and one of the most illustrious fortified wine ranges is master-crafted by seasoned (20 years at this cellar) Elsenburg graduate Dirkie Christowitz. Apart from turning out winning wines — since the inception of the Veritas awards, 65% of all Monis entrants have received gold or double-gold medals — he oversees production of ciders, spirits, liqueurs, aperitifs and even fruit juices at the Paarl cellar, a division of Stellenbosch Farmers' Winery.

✿ **Wooded Muscadel** New Once-off **92** fortified red dessert, only tiny quantity made and sure to be hotly fought over. Hedonistic and quite superb. Muscat de frontignan ex-Breede River, 6 yrs in oak. Powerfully sweet (228 g/ℓ sugar), concentrated, packed with spice and heady muscat scent, clean spirity tang. Expensively packaged.

✿ **Moscato Muscadel** From **99**, this sumptuous fortified dessert vintage dated. **99** lighter than pvs NVs, slightly younger with distinct freshness in nose; sweeter, too, though clean, zingy fortification prevents any cloy. Pvs featured billowing muscat nose with cinnamon spice, spirity brightness in clean long finish.

✿ **Very Old Tawny Port** ✓ Gorgeous example of this rare in Cape style; latest **NV** VVG blend features usual arresting mahogany sheen; suave toffee/honey/caramel textures with dark-roast coffee. Less sweet (±100 g/ℓ), in line with modern Cape trend, non-cloying. Cinsaut, mainly ancient untrellised bushvines in Paarl area. Blend of **87**, **90**, **91** (60/12/28). Clanks with competition medals: 3 VVGs, 5 VGs since 1993; SAA trophy.

. . . .

Mons Ruber Estate

Klein Karoo (see Klein Karoo map) • Tasting & sales Mon—Fri 9—5 Sat 9—1 • Cellar tours by arrangement • Self-catering guest area above the tasting room • Bring your own picnic • Gifts • Conferences • Walks • Miniature museum of artefacts from ostrich feather era • Hiking trail in proclaimed conservation area • Owners Radé & Erhard

Meyer • Winemaker/viticulturist Radé Meyer (since 1990) • Vineyards 38 ha • Production 500—700 tons (50 tons own label) 80% white 20% red • PO Box 1585 Oudtshoorn 6620 • Tel/fax (044) 251-6550 • E-mail monsr@lantic.net

"DOES ONE get a diploma for filling in your form?" enquires Radé Meyer. While we can and do sample the thousands of wines, the far-flung nature of the Cape's vineyards make it impossible to visit every winery individually; for glimpses beyond tasting notes we must rely on answers to our — yes — exhaustive questionnaire. And no-one responds more gamely, with an inimitable blend of irony and information, than the co-owner, winemaker, "and hundreds of other less imposing titles" — we hereby add our own honorary Doctorate — of this wine, brandy and ostrich farm (38 ha of vineyards; the rest of the 1 700 ha not only for the birds; the spectacular red hills of its Latin name are a South African Natural Heritage site and hiking trail). Our advice: don't just read about this gem of the Little Karoo, near Oudtshoorn; it merits your personal attention. Over-enthusiastic sampling of the after-dinner specialities and the Cabernet (which lured Radé Meyer away from lawyering and back to the farm) need not pose problems. The tasting room is in a restored 19th century mail-coach inn, now a National Monument; its upper-storey (splendid views) can be yours for rest and recovery.

❧ **Muscadel Elusivo**. 'Elusive' once-off **89** white muscat, decade tucked away in used sherry vats. Deep tawny hue with sherried dimension and mellow biscuity complexity; unexpectedly dry finish. 21,4% alc, 97 g/ℓ sugar.

Cabernet Sauvignon ☆ ☺ **98** lovely soft plummy mouthful, tucked with a bit of ripe tannin and vanilla-oak. Drink soon to catch at charming best. Lightish 12,2% alc. 167 cases.

Conari ☆ Uncertified cab from 1987 (!) vintage. Light, fragile old-timer, some dusty tobacco leaf. Released 1998. "Just a few bottles left …" 250 cases. **Red Muscadel Jerepigo** ❧ Fortified dessert with unusual thatchy tones and more conventional raisins; powerfully sweet **99** very young still, needs time. 15,8% alc. 156 cases. **White Muscadel Jerepigo** ❧ **98** burnished amber colour looks as densely sweet as it tastes; amazing concentration and almost syrupy texture (260+ g/ℓ sugar), which lacks freshening acidity. Alternative label: Regalis. **Hanepoot Jerepigo** ❧ Raisiny sweet aromas in **98**, rich, unctuous taste. 17,8% alc. Alternative label: Bonitas. **Cabernet Sauvignon Jerepigo** ❧ Individual powerfully sweet fortified dessert; **99** combines mature red-wine characters with intense curranty sweetness. 170 cases. Alternative name: Elegantia. **Sultana Jerepigo** ☆ **99** another individual Radé Meyer tinkering: fortified sultana juice. Tastes powerfully of dusty sweet raisins. 18,3% alc. 220 cases. **Port** ❧ Tawny style **93**, less sweet than most traditional Cape 'ports' at 87,5 g/ℓ sugar; nutty/caramel/woodsmoke wafts. Uncertified, from cabernet. 18,7% alc. 40 cases.

Montagu Winery ▼

Montagu (see Klein Karoo map) • Tasting & sales Mon—Fri 8—12.30; 1—5 Sat 9—12 • Cellar tours on request during harvest, else by appointment • Owners 70 members • Winemaker Sonnie Malan (since 1972) • Production ± 1 400 tons (± 4 000 cases own label) 97% white 3% red • PO Box 29 Montagu 6720 • Tel (023) 614-1125 • Fax (023) 614-1793 • E-mail mkwkelder@lando.co.za

THIS COMBINE on suddenly-trendy Route 62 is making the inevitable gear-change to red wine production, and a new pressing hall specifically built for this purpose will be fired up for the 2001 harvest. "We've made small quantities of red for several years, but now that we're getting into it seriously, we need bigger facilities," explains winemaker Sonnie Malan, who's seen his share of changes in almost 30 harvests here. Growers on the Cogmanskloof feeder farms have been planting mainly merlot, shiraz and pinotage, and these vines in future years will begin to even the grape balance, presently overwhelmingly skewed to white. A very low-key presence on local retail shelves means the wines below are the almost exclusive reward of those undertaking a trip to quaint Montagu town, renowned for its warming muscadel desserts.

Merlot-Ruby Cabernet ✿ Individual style **99**, nutty/wild-berry/herby tones, few smoothing grains sugar. Med-bodied, unoaked as pvsly. **Chardonnay ★ 00** unwooded full-bodied dry white. Simple and very fresh. 13,9% alc. **Chenin Blanc ★** Ethereal fruit flavours, big whoosh of acid in **00** tail. Med-bodied. **Mont Blanc** ✿ Foursquare med-weight unfortified semi-sweet white muscadel;. **NV** 500 ml screwtop. **Vin Doux** ⚘ Unpretentious lightish style; active tropical/muscat bubbles, sweet and smooth. **NV**. **White Muscadel** ⚘ New Well made fortified dessert; **00** refined muscat flavour, sweet and quite spirity. 16,1% alc. **Red Muscadel** ✿ Very little varietal character, **00** unctuous and bit burny. 16,6% alc.

. . . .

Mont Destin

Paarl (see Paarl map) • Tasting & sales by appointment Mon—Fri 8.30—4.30 • Self-catering loft apartments (breakfasts by arrangement) • Outdoor tasting area for functions max 30 people (catering can be arranged) • Private chapel for small weddings • Views • Owners Ernest & Samantha Bürgin • Consultant winemaker Stefan Dorst with Ernest Bürgin • Viticulturist André van den Berg (since 2000) • Vineyards 18 ha • Production 100 tons (7 000 cases own label) 70% red 30% white • PO Box 1237 Stellenbosch 7599 • Tel/fax (021) 875-5040 • E-mail destin@adept.co.za

ERNEST AND SAMANTHA BÜRGIN, now officially an item (it says so on the freshly inked marriage certificate), divide their time rather delightfully between a small olive spread in Provence and this wine farm below Simonsberg (stone's throw from Lievland, Le Bonheur). 'Under construction' since 1996, Mont Destin is taking its first firm wine steps in conjunction with German cellar whiz Stefan Dorst, here in flying winemaker mode (he also consults to down-the-road Laibach), and in-house vineyardist André van den Berg. They've harvested the first pinotage ("hand picked from bushvines — brilliant quality") and some chenin ("good potential"), reports Ernest Bürgin. And completed plans for a restaurant. Now they've "started discussing" the construction of their own cellar, to join the six spacious loft apartments with beautiful long-range views.

⚘ **Passioné** 🍷 Soft, sophisticated, ageworthy Bdx blend merlot/cab (80/20). Lithely muscular **98** developing splendidly: plum/blackberry depths now slicked with choc; some cracked pepper/mulberry add richness, extra interest. 16 mths Fr oak, half new. 13,8% alc. 300 cases.

⚘ **Chenin Blanc** New 🍷 Carefully crafted chenin of considerable character; **00** with the whole fresh-fruit basket (pineapple, guava etc etc) plus 'smoky vanilla' sensations (though unoaked); upbeat zesty finish. 13,4% alc. Very well priced; could age interestingly. 250 cases.

. . . .

Mont Du Toit

Wellington (see Wellington map) • Tasting & sales by appointment • Owner Mont du Toit Kelder (Pty) Ltd • Winemakers Bernd Philippi, Bernhard Breuer, Pieter-Niel Rossouw • Viticulturist Alwyn Myburgh (since 1999) • Vineyards ± 25 ha • Production ±100 tons 100% red • PO Box 704 Wellington 7654 • Tel/fax (021) 873-3222

MORE and more wine people have been whizzing around the planet, contributing their global ideas and expertise to joint ventures. Sandton-based senior counsel Stephan du Toit and wife Carolina have been spearheading one such intriguing collaboration: top German winemakers Bernhard Breuer and Bernd Philippi bring their international perspective to Wellington and this exclusively red wine range. Enthusiastic young Pieter-Niel Rossouw from Bonnievale, the newly appointed full time winemaker, certainly stands to benefit from this exchange of ideas. Du Toit is adamant that Wellington is much underrated as a red wine area. UK *Wine* magazine's palates seem to agree: they recently rated the flagship Mont du Toit blend

92 points out of 100 in an 'international joint ventures' tasting — par with the splashy Errazuriz-Mondavi collaboration, Seña.

⚜⚜**Mont du Toit Le Sommet NEW** "Eruptive fruit" (Bernd Philippi's phrase) makes a sweeping red wine statement in this **98** cracker, absolutely packed with cassis/mulberry/choc, sweet vanilla spice, palate-stretching 15% alc. For all the intensity the texture's velvety, the ample tannins supple enough to enjoy now — with food — or keep a while. Strict bunch/cask selection (varieties not disclosed), ±4 t/ha yield, harvested at more than 26 °B, aged ±2 yrs Fr barriques, unfiltered. Very limited quantity — only 150 cases.

⚜**Mont du Toit** First release **98** marked this as a bold, serious Cape red of intense concentration, richness. Follow-up **99**, tasted pre-final blending, probably better, longer maturing, though the long 'charry' tannins are already comfortably soft. Full bodied (14% alc), densely ripe cassis/mulberry/cherry with light minty perfume. Potential for eventual ⚜⚜ rating. Cab/merlot/shiraz, dash cab f. ±2 yrs Fr barriques. 1 500 cases.

⚜**Hawequas NEW** Stephan du Toit's "patio wine" — unpretentious, but with quite a sophisticated fruit/tannin structure which lifts **99** out of the quaffing class. Ripe mulberry/strawberry firmed by good charry oak. Named after the splendid mountain range which fills the views from above-mentioned veranda. 13% alc. ±600 cases.

Mont Rochelle Mountain Vineyards

Franschhoek (see Franschhoek map) • Tasting & sales Mon—Sat 11—5 Sun (Sep-May) 11—1 Tasting fee R5 p/p • Cellar tours 11, 12.30, 3 • Summer picnics/winter warming soups (bottle of wine included) Booking essential • Tourgroups • Walks • Views • Wheelchair-friendly • Owners Graham & Lyn de Villiers • Winemaker Justin Hoy (since 1999) • Viticulturist Alwyn Geldenhuys (since1993) • Vineyards 10 ha • Production 200 tons 18 000 cases (8 000 cases own label) • PO Box 334 Franschhoek 7690 • Tel (021) 876-3000 • Fax (021) 876-2362 • E-mail montrochelle@wine.co.za

SA WINE INDUSTRY eminence Graham de Villiers was an advertising high flier in his previous life, and it shows in inventive, market-tickling products like a unique Cabernet-Sauvignon Blanc blend (see Vignerons du Monde), and his well turned phrases when describing his 60 ha farm. "God has given us one of the most beautiful valleys in the world, nature gave us a variety of terroir capable of realising the full potential of all the noble cultivars, history gave us a direct lineage from the greatest winemaking nation on earth and providence has given us a collection of the country's most creative and energetic young winemakers." Add swelling music, pan slowly around mauve mountains and Mont Rochelle's 10 ha of green vineyards, throw in a horse — preferably white — from the De Villiers's equestrian centre, and their summer picnic baskets, and it's made for TV. The lineage bit refers to this family's 8th generation Huguenot descent; the contemporary creative artists to consultant Kiwi Rod Easthope (now influencing a string of the Cape's top wines), and new cellar presence Justin Hoy, a former vegetable farmer in the UK whose passion for wine led to studies at Elsenburg College in Stellenbosch, and taking over from Anna-Mareè Mostert (midwife of the outstanding Jacques de Villiers 97 Cabernet below). In fact, no air-brushing or image-enhancement are needed here: Mont Rochelle's increasingly impressive wines stand on their own merits.

Mont Rochelle range

⚜⚜**Jacques de Villiers NEW** This cellar's flagship, recognising the owner's Huguenot ancestor in a splashy new single-vyd cab, lavishly packaged — lavishly flavoured, too, in ripe, mouthfilling style. Minty/eucalyptus/liquorice perfumes to beautifully pure, ripe, almost essency blackberry fruit. Long, tapering, lightly tangy finish with touch tannin. Best 3 barrels from the **97** vintage, aged 2 yrs Fr oak. 13,2% alc. Minuscule quantity (50 cases), super-premium priced.

❀ **Cabernet Sauvignon** Since maiden **96** VVG, sophisticated deep-flavoured cab with signature mint/eucalyptus/black pepper fragrance. **98** full but somewhat restrained on release. Latest **99** ❀ more open, thrusting; spicy seasoning to ripe mulberry fruit; vibrant supple tannin poised to carry wine to maturity in 4–8 yrs. 18 mths Fr oak, some new. 13% alc. 600 cases.

❀ **Oak-Matured Chardonnay** Full, buttery, popular style with fresh-honey/ripe citrus tones in **98**, which reprise in step-up **99** ❀ ▼. Generous full-bodied flavours (14% alc), rounded texture with lemon/lime crispness which should continue to refresh as wine develops. Fermented/aged yr Fr casks. 2 000 cases. **96** VG.

Merlot ❀ Wide contrast between **99** soft, sweet-violets/vanilla bouquet and puckering dry tannins. These are ripe, however, and should soften with time. 15 mths Fr oak, none new. 14% alc. 300 cases. **Pinotage** ❀ New **99** an uptight number which needs plenty of time to mellow and grow. Good underlying plum/banana flavours augur well for development. 17 mths Fr oak, some new. 13,5% alc. 600 cases. **Natural Chardonnay** Creative winemaking is what deceives here: this unwooded individual tastes almost oaky, with a sumptuous nose, plush texture and buttery flavour — these courtesy of lees contact and malo. **00** (tasted from tank mid-2000 and too unformed to rate) strong lees character with pleasing green-apple zest. 13,8% alc. 750 cases. **98** ❀ travelled with the Blue Train. **97** developed very well. No **99**. **Blanc de Blancs** ❀ Bdx-style zippy dry white. Med/full bodied **00** sampled very young; still bit sharp but refreshing, sauvignon adding grass/green pepper bite to semillon's more tropical tones. 500 cases. **Sauvignon Blanc** ‡ These usually good table-mates with, in **00**, grassy/herbaceous flavours bolstered by invigorating dry acid. 13,5% alc. 2 000 cases.

Petit Rochelle range

Splendid Little Sauvignon Blanc ❀ 😊 **00** pleasant ripe gooseberry/herby tones, crisp dry finish. 13,2% alc. 2 500 cases.

. . . .

Mooiplaas Estate   ♈ ♉

Stellenbosch (see Stellenbosch map) • Tasting, sales, cellar tours by appointment • Owner Mooiplaas Trust • Wine-maker Louis Roos (since 1983) • Viticulturist Tielman Roos (since 1980) • Production 850 tons (5 000 cases own label) 95% red 5% white • PO Box 104 Koelenhof 7605 • Tel (021) 903-6273 • Fax (021) 903-3474

WHO took more strain in 2000's extra-hot, dry harvest, Louis Roos or his sauvignon? "Parched conditions put a lot of stress on the vines," he recounts, "but at 400 m above sea level it's too expensive to irrigate or pump water. Instead we harvested earlier — and I'm pleasantly surprised by the quality." It wasn't all pain and no gain, however: the reds are very promising with "good intensity and colour", says the Stellenbosch oenology graduate, with a passion for pinotage (he's a contributor to the Beyerskloof international runaway success). "Any true SA red blend must be based on the local variety," states he, still flushed with pride at clinching a prestigious ABSA Top Ten nomination for his own Pinotage, which he makes with viti-culturist brother Tielman. They have farmed the family's Bottelary Hills property since the early eighties.

❀ **Pinotage** Local/international applause for first **98** (VG, ABSA Top Ten etc), growing in bottle but probably never a match for follow-up **99** ❀, riper, richer, more forward; deeply layered with approachable mulberry/oak spice. Styled for accessibility," confirms Louis Roos. 25 yr old bushvines, partially small oak aged. 13,4% alc. 1 500/2 000 cases.

❀ **Sauvignon Blanc** ▼ Good bottle development in **99**, mellowing into pleasing asparagus/nettle plumpness. **00** tasted immediately post-bottling, so ‡ rating provisional. 'Sweet' gooseberry/asparagus entry, muted tropical aromatics. ±13% alc. From breezy hilltop vyd. 325 cases.

Cabernet Sauvignon ⚘ Later harvesting sees immediate **98** improvement on pvs: riper, fuller; chewy tannins but no longer green. Promise of some development. 15 mths small oak. 13,5% alc. 3 000 cases.

Mooiuitsig Wine Cellars

Robertson (see Robertson map) • Sales Mon—Thu 8—12.30; 1.30—5 Fri 8—11 • Group tasting & cellar tours by appointment • Catering for groups including traditional cuisine by arrangement • Two large guesthouses • Functions/conferences at in-house venue or Lure Anglers Lodge. Contact Linda Claassen linda@lure-anglers-lodge.co.za • Walks • Wheelchair-friendly • Owners Jonker & Claassen families • Winemaker Jacques Conradie (since 1999) • Viticulturists Adolph Jonker & Francois Claassen • Vineyards 250 ha • Production 4 500 tons • PO Box 15 Bonnievale 6730 • Tel (023) 616-2143 • Fax (023) 616-2675 • E-mail info@mooiuitsig.co.za

MOOIUITSIG'S ROOST on the quiet Breede riverside at Bonnievale gives no hint of the constant bustle within one of the largest independent liquor wholesaling businesses in SA (the Jonker and Claassen families have been trading for more than 50 years). Helping to keep these finely tuned wheels turning is new winemaker Jacques Conradie. With viticulturists Francois Claassen and Adolph Jonker, he's driving Mooiuitsig's extensive replanting with current international raves merlot, pinotage and cabernet. Not yet well known, perhaps, as a tourist destination, there are plenty of attractions and amenities to lure visitors including gardens, tinkling waterfalls and a characterful stay-over featuring yellowwood fittings from an antique church in Mossel Bay. The wines below were unavailable for tasting for this ed.

Mooiuitzicht range
Dry red including: **Mooiuitsig, Light/Dark, Stokkies, Partners Light**; certified table wines: **Cabernet Sauvignon, Pinotage, Blanc de Noir, Chardonnay, Sauvignon Blanc, Riesling**; also: **Clemence Creek Chardonnay, No 1 Late Harvest**; semi-sweets including: **Bonistein, Mooiuitsig, Hanepoot, Bonselect, Sweetheart**; fortified desserts including: **Bonwin Ruby, Marsala Nagmaalwyn** (sacramental wine), **Sweet Hanepoot, Overberg Hanepoot, Red/White Muskana, Red/White Jerepigo**. Also 'ports': **Tawny, Invalid, Old White**; sparkling wines: **Mooiuitzicht, Potjie Semi-Dry, Oulap se Rooi**; bag in boxes: **Overberger Late Harvest, 'Vat Ohio' Late Harvest/Grand Cru**; foil bags: **Sweetheart Late Harvest, Bonnibag, Dry Wine Dark, No 1 Late Harvest**.

Rusthof range
Cork-closed wines: **Dry Red, Premier Grand Cru, Late Harvest**.

Oude Rust range
Sweet fortified desserts including **Red Muscadel 98, Sweet Hanepoot 97, White Muscadel 98**.
Also range of brandies, white spirits, witblits, whiskeys, liqueurs and 'sherries'.

Môreson Soleil Du Matin

Franschhoek (see Franschhoek map) • Tasting & sales Tue—Sun 11-5 Dec-Apr, otherwise Wed—Sun 11-3 Tasting fee R5 p/p Open public holidays • Cellar tours by appointment • Môreson Bread & Wine Restaurant (see Restaurants section) • Views • Wheelchair-friendly • Owner Richard Friedman • General manager/viticulturist Anton Beukes (since 1995) • Sales & marketing manager Uschi van Zweel (since 1996) • Winemaker Pierre Wahl (since 1998) • Vineyards 17 ha • Production 16 000 cases 50% red 50% white • PO Box 114 Franschhoek 7690 • Tel (021) 876-3055 • Fax (021) 876-2348 • E-mail uschi@moreson.co.za • sales@moreson.co.za • sales@pinehurst.co.za

"Wine, wine, wine — is there life beyond creating the best wine?" responds Uschi van Zweel to the question of the Môreson crew's extra-winery activities. She's the livewire marketing manager of this Franschhoek valley property (its wines making their export mark all over Europe and the USA) and her portfolio is clearly a pleasure. Winemaker Pierre Wahl and viticulturalist Anton Beukes, who've recently visited Italy "to experience its passion for wine and food", are delivering the goods here, both from their own 17 ha vineyards and grapes sourced from Paarl and Stellenbosch. Môreson's haul of double-gold and gold medals at Veritas 1999 put it in the top 10% of the national show's entrants; and competing for the first time for a berth on SAA's wine list, second-label Pinehurst Cabernet made it onto international flights. Appropriately, the next birdie-label for this wine will feature a Crowned Eagle. Renovations to the Bread and Wine restaurant at Môreson are complete, and its in-and-outdoor charms can now be spread to 150 guests.

Môreson Soleil Du Matin range

✿ **Cabernet Sauvignon** Latest **97** brilliant follow up to **96** VG, Michelangelo gold; **95** VVG; **94** *Decanter* ✿. **97** expansive, 'sweet' mouthful (14,2% alc) of blackcurrant and green pepper fleshed out ripe black cherries; some savoury and good earthy hints, plus distinct but supple tannins ensure a properly dry conclusion. Excellent now but should develop well. Helderberg fruit. 2 yrs Fr oak, 80% new, remainder 2nd fill. 750 cases.

✿ **Merlot** Super-soft, chocolatey style has a touch of romance about it, which probably why Pierre Wahl would like to share **98** with "my very special girlfriend". Floral introduction with violet wafts; fresh-prune flavours which glide across the tongue with vanilla and embrace of soft tannin. Big 14% alc helps the smoothing effect. Deserves 2–3 yrs to realize its potential but will probably be opened long before then. Helderberg grapes. 18 mths Fr oak, 60% new. 750 cases. **97** VG. **95** VVG.

✿ **Premium Chardonnay** Slow starting **98** reviewed for pvs ed has evolved brilliantly in bottle: flavours have fanned out into expansive citrus/leesy mouthful with butterscotch and toasty oak aftertaste. Big gutsy mouthful (14% alc) which needs yr/2 more to fulfill its promise. Own grapes, 13 mths Fr oak, 60% new. 650 cases. Upcoming **99** with, interestingly, more evolved, softer profile at this early stage. **97** VVG.

✿ **Premium Chenin Blanc** ✅ Marked jump in quality from pvs to this just off-dry **00**, with hallmarks of a long, steady maturer. Youthful, attractive core of ripe papaya wrapped in racy acidity and long leesy dry aftertaste. Give bit of time to settle, then follow Uschi van Zweel's advice and share with someone special over lunch (and watch that 14% alc). Own grapes. 650 cases. **99** ✿ with bracing acidity, sweetish flicker in tail. **95** *Decanter* ✿.

✿ **Sauvignon Blanc** ✅ **00** spectacular fresh tropical nose, bursting with lemon/gooseberry vitality. Fruit/acid balance for easy/early drinking. Unwooded, reductively made. Selected block on own farm. **99** VG, **97** SAYWS gold.

✿ **Soleil du Matin** Brut **NV** Extrovert blanc de blancs style cap classique with explosive mousse, brisk lemony aromas and citrus/yeast tastes which linger endlessly; elegant bone-dry finish. Chardonnay from own farm, with splash chenin. 18 mths on lees. Lowish 11,5% alc. 250 cases.

Pinotage ✿ Sunshine-in-bottle unoaked style with cheery ripe plums/cherries and side-serving of redcurrant in **99**, juicy feel in mouth. A crowd pleaser. **Jerepigo** ✿ New Farm's own sauvignon features in this **NV** fortified dessert; very sweet and spirity.

Pinehurst range

With colourful 'postage stamp' labels depicting birds of nearby forest, now offered as collectibles.

✿ **Cabernet Sauvignon** ✅ Decorated **98** SAA, *Wine* ✿ gaining richness and complexity in bottle with potential for development for further 2–3 yrs. Balance, firm structure with savoury green pepper headlines and dark choc/liquorice/toasty oak nuances. Grapes from Helderberg. 14 mths Fr oak, 40% new. Brawny

14% alc. 2 000 cases. **97** ✿✿ (though Wine ✿) big, chunky, similar profile to above.

> **Chenin Blanc** ✿✿ **New** ☺ Bright, still-fresh **99** offers thirst slaking lemonade and sherbet, plus limes, lemons and zingy acidity for instant summer refreshment. Moderate 12,4% alc. Own grapes. 400 cases. **Sauvignon Blanc** ✿✿ ☺ Gusts of pear/guava in **99**, slightly tart rhubarb balances sweet-fruit introduction and leads into crisp dry finish. Needs to be enjoyed soon. Restrained 11,9% alc. Own grapes. 2 000 cases.

Pinotage ✿✿ **99** vibrant, juicy, generous strawberry whiffs, soft sappy fruit with dollop vanilla in finish. 6 mths Fr oak, 2nd fill. Fruit ex-Paarl. 13,3% alc. 2 000 cases.
Chardonnay ✿✿ Attractive, undemanding **99** with light citrus/ripe peach and creamy texture which concludes cleanly and softly. 15% barrel fermented. 13,2% alc. Own grapes. 3 500 cases.

. . . .

Morgan see Sonop

. . . .

Morgenhof Estate

Stellenbosch (see Stellenbosch map) • Tasting & sales: In season (Nov—Apr) Mon—Thu 9-5.30 Fri 9—5 Sat & Sun 10-5 Out of season: (May—Oct) Mon—Fri 9—4.30 Sat & Sun 10-3 Tasting fee R10 p/p Closed Christmas Day, Good Friday, New Year's Day • Light meals daily12-2.30 • Owner Anne Cointreau-Huchon (La Tour International Investments Pty Ltd) • Winemaker Rianie Strydom (since 1993) with Gunter Schultz • Vineyard manager Pieter Haasbroek • Vineyards 59 ha • Production 250 tons 25 000 cases • PO Box 365 Stellenbosch 7599 • Tel (021) 889-5510 • Fax (021) 889-5266 • E-mail info@morgenhof.com • Website www.morgenhof.com

THE FEMALE FORCE is with this glamorous, French owned estate. Owner Anne Cointreau-Huchon and winemaker Rianie Strydom are in every way *'femmes formidables'*. The former's philosophy draws on her heritage as a member of an illustrious French wine family: "no compromises over quality, good taste and attention to detail". She and her husband Alain have transformed a rustic old farm into a sophisticated Cape château. Rianie Strydom — who began working here as a student, nearly a decade ago — epitomises the passionate, ambitious, confident new talents who are making the older guard feel positively ancient. There wasn't a hiccup when former cellarmaster Jean Daneel ("always my teacher," says Strydom) hied off to do his own thing; she simply took over the controls and flew on. An intimate knowledge of the vineyards (approaching 80 ha and soon to deliver malbec to add to the Bordeaux blend) grounds her winemaking; seasons in St Émilion, Burgundy, the Languedoc and Italy gave it wings — the signature-style here is decidedly, elegantly European. Coolest moment of the "tricky, hot and compressed" harvest of 2000 was while runaway fires were raging in the neighbourhood. Morgenhof lost very few vines, but Strydom was thoroughly drenched in a direct hit from a fire-fighting helicopter.

✿✿**Merlot Reserve** **New** Staking its claim to Cape cult status (only 500 cases made), this Bdx-styled single-vyd selection turns up the heat on standard Merlot below. House elegance reflected in **98**, deep plum hues, sensuous smoky, gamey, mocha whiffs, minerally twist; substantial though well behaved 14,5% alc provides foundation for considerable fruit extract (10 day skin contact), 18 mths 50% new Fr barriques.

✿✿**Merlot** Cape standout since **93** first electrified the crowds (*Wine* ✿✿, SAA, golds at Vinexpo/IWSC); strong claim as estate's flagship (though see contenders above, below). Latest **98** ✿ taut still (winemaker suggests drink in another 5 yrs — we agree), muted, leafy cassis whiffs, firm tannin structure from 10 day skin maceration; 18 mths Fr oak, 40% new. **96** VVG.

⚒ Première Sélection Quintessential claret; taut; expensively — thoughtfully — oaked, held back extra yr before release but even then for not for instant gratification. **97** ⚒ in crested bottle, earthy farmyard whiffs over chocolatey, redcurrant flavours. 18 mths Fr oak, 65% cab, 25% merlot, 10% cab f. 13,5% alc. Juicy 6 g/ℓ acid promises fine maturation. **96** *Wine* ⚒. **95** ⚒.

⚒ Pinotage Burgundian traits (appropriately for Fr toned estate) of this homespun variety evident here (partly result of cool, elevated vyd). **98** thumbprint mulberry sweetness, intriguing smoky, dark choc aromas; juicy raspberry/vanilla farewell. 27 yr old vyd. 18 mths Fr oak. 13,6% alc. **96** ABSA Pinotage Top Ten.

⚒ Cabernet Sauvignon Reserve **New** Special barrel selection, all new oaked, massive (14,2% alc) yet reigned in; **98** (in same livery as Merlot Reserve) already spectacularly flavourful: black/garnet hue, complex tobacco, mint and ripe plum aromas. Finely tuned fruit, oak tannins still tense but obvious fruit quality balances, promises superb development on back of taut 6,3 g/ℓ acid. Standard **Cabernet Sauvignon** ⚒ Definite Old World restraint in **98**, shy cigarbox, green olive, cassis notes; restrained sweetish palate with fine-grained tannins; taut red berry fruit adds to compact feel. Needs yr or 2 in bottle to soften.

⚒ Chardonnay Has spread its wings since reviewed last yr (showing rare ability among Cape chardonnays to age gracefully). **98** fresh asparagus, coconut aromas, limey whiffs; yellow gold hue. Sleek, dry finish shows some Burgundian pedigree, with creamy, toasty brioche flavours, easily carrying 14% alc. 9 mths Fr oak, malo complete. **99** freshly bottled when tasted mid-2000, trademark leesy notes, ripe, punchy fruit; some gawky edges which will smooth with time. **97** VG.

⚒ Sauvignon Blanc Always sure seller from the farm. Typical flinty whiffs in **00**, nettle/fig undertones carry to firm, steely palate redolent of grapefruit. Firm acidity (7 g/ℓ) balance taut fruit structure. One of the best in hot, difficult vintage.

⚒ Chenin Blanc From venerable 32 yr old vyd, consistently excellent since maiden **96** won SA Wine's Chenin Challenge. Richly complex **99** offers cream-and-honey aromas, hints of lanolin, muscular 14,5% alc adding appearance of sweetness to wraparound palate which shifts a gear into juicy, tropical fruit salad overdrive. Touch of sugar (4,3 g) lends suppleness to finish, with just the right dollop oak from 8 mths oaking. Serious wine which will convert chenin sceptics. 1 200 cases.

⚒ LBV Port One of the Cape's most 'correct' late bottled styles: nearly 5 yrs oaked, tinta b, 18,9% alc and dryish 88 g/ℓ sugar. Current **95** deep plum; complex beeswax, smoky stewed fruit, prune aromas; silky medium-weight flavours; vanilla oak notes in finish from (newish?) small barrel maturation.

⚒ Vintage Port **New** Dramatically dark, almost black **98**, dusty woodsmoke, tobacco whiffs over rich dark fruitcake aromas. More fruit, extract than LBV, also sweeter (98 g/ℓ sugar), similar alc. Very satisfying, long, gutsy finish: Future addition of touriga will add to tinta b's more limited spectrum. 2 yrs used 225 ℓ barriques.

⚒ Merlot-Malbec **New** Fashionable malbec brings spice and zest to this promising first **99**, merlot contributes prominent leafiness and choc notes. 14 mths 2nd fill Fr oak. Release date uncertain. 1 200 cases.

L'Atrium Rouge d'M ⚒ **NV** (mostly **98**) Bdx trio of cab, merlot, malbec, plus Burgundian seasoning of pinot. Supple choc/cherry notes, bold berry-laced finish. **Sauvignon Blanc-Chenin Blanc** ⚒ (Pvsly L'Atrium Blanc de M) Attractive, supple **00**, fresh lemony twist in dry finish. 72/28% blend, unoaked, with dusty citrus/talcum whiffs. Bright and zesty. Also available: **Noble Late Harvest** Not tasted for this ed. **98** pvsly rated ⚒.

Reserve Centenaire range New

Chic 'crested' bottles in wooden presentation casket, for millennium; small quantities still available.

✿✿**Reserve 98** Bdx red blend (see also Première Sélection above), 62% cab, 26% cab f, 12% merlot, matured separately in new Fr oak, blended before bottling. Cab f adds spice plus violets; similar brooding long term cellaring style to other Centenaires. Miserly 6 t/ha, massively ripe 14,4% alc. 2 000 bottles made, mostly for this gift pack foursome.

✿**Chardonnay 98** complex baked apple and cream aromas, dusting of cinnamon; elegant lime, passion fruit; oak-ageing well integrated. 16 mths Fr oak (60% new). More Chablis-like than standard version above; crisper, with less oak influence.

✿**Brut** In showy '2000' moulded bottle. Leesy, lemony **97** MCC from pinot/chardonnay with firm red grape flavours — raspberry jam on toasty brioche. Elegant, fine mousse; lingering, zesty dry farewell. Some acidity promises cellaring potential. Watch for stunning **Rosé Brut**, tasted pre-degorging/final dosage and so unrated.

✿**Vintage Reserve Port 98** barrel selection of above 'port', less time in oak (18 mths), smoked meat whiff in similar rich nose. Ripe, almost raisiny flavours, choc twist in seemingly drier finish (though sugar, alc similar at 98 g/ℓ and 19%). *Wine* ✿.

Morgenster Estate

Stellenbosch (see Helderberg map) • Tasting & sales by appointment • Olives, olive oil & olive paste also grown/sold on property • Owner Giulio Bertrand • Winemaker Marius Lategan (since 1999) • Vineyards 38 ha • PO Box 1616 Somerset West 7129 • Tel (021) 852-1738 • Fax (021) 852-1141 • E-mail mail@morgenster.co.za

"YOU ARE MAD!" Perhaps it was the thought of clearing large tracts of indigenous *fynbos* for the olive groves, or carting in many tons of topsoil for the vineyards, or renovating the graceful but faded homestead. Whatever future obstacles Giulio Bertrand's famous Italian compatriot and wine-friend Angelo Gaja saw in 1992 have been swept aside in a remarkable redevelopment which has left, almost literally, no stone unturned on this 18th-century farm. Olive oil is flowing (and winning the extra-virgin equivalent of the Oscars, the first red has been released and a grand Revel Fox-designed winery is being built for the 2001 crush (the old cellar now houses an impressive computer-controlled olive press). Urbane winemaker Marius Lategan, ex Gilbeys, Eersterivier, Verdun, is at home here. A Bordeaux harvest at Cheval Blanc (its *president*, Pierre Lurton, is Bertrand's hand-picked consultant; local vineyard guru Eben Archer a further fount of expertise) has attuned Lategan to the intended Morgenster style, which is unabashedly, determinedly classic: "Marius must produce wine in the style that I like … and St-Émilion is my favourite wine".

✿**Lourens River Valley** New Most impressive debut, set to become collector's item on scarcity of supply, undoubted quality. **98** intense plummy colour, lively purple edge. Blackberry/raspberry, chocolate array in nose, vanilla whiffs from 13 mths Fr oak; lush berry fruit in palate, reined by firm tannins; good balance and long, smooth finish. Distinct Bdx feel, also in moderately full body (12,6% alc). Now to 2006. This cab-merlot blend (52/48), made at Lanzerac, under alternative Lourens River Valley label; flagship Morgenster marque reserved for future wines made on property (these to feature proportion cab f).

Motif see Steenberg
Mount Claire see Cordoba
Mount Disa see Coppoolse Finlayson-Sentinel

Mount Marble see Simonsvlei

Mount Rozier Wines

Stellenbosch (see Helderberg map) • Tasting by appointment • Sales Mon—Fri 9—5 • Views • Conservancy area • Wheelchair-friendly • Owners Michael Rubin, Peter Loebenberg, Dave Lyddell • Consulting winemaker Ernst Gouws (Hoopenburg) • Consulting viticulturist Johan Wiese • Vineyard manager Dave Lyddell • Vineyards 45 ha • Production 2 000 cases 40% red 60% white • PO Box 784 SomersetWest 7129 • Tel (021) 858-1130 • Fax (021) 858-1131 • E-mail wine@mountrozier.co.za • Website www.mountrozier.co.za

AFTER CUTTING their teeth on 10 ha in Franschhoek, partners Dave Lyddell, Peter Loebenberg and Michael Rubin couldn't resist the challenge of a 110 ha virgin property on Schaapenberg, the viticultural equivalent of Hollywood Hills near Sir Lowry's Pass. Now their own vineyards are in production (pvsly grapes were bought in from Stellenbosch and Malmesbury, among others) and, on advice from winemaking guru Ernst Gouws, off-duty from his Hoopenburg property in Stellenbosch, partial new-oaking is standard for the top reds. Merlot, cabernet and shiraz parcels have been extended, and a toe has been dipped into export waters in association with French negociant Ginestet.

✿ **Merlot** Vibrant carmine colour introduces **99**, several notches above pvs thanks to better fruit definition and serious oak ageing (11 mths Fr barriques, 50% new). Ripe plums, coffee/choc and Xmas pud, all gliding across full palate to fine, lingering mineral-tangy finish. 13,8% alc. 475 cases. **98** lighter, casual quaffing.

Cabernet Sauvignon ✿✿ **99** savoury plums and smoky oak, chunky tannins need plenty of time. Own vyds. ± 16 mths Fr oak, 50% new. 475 cases. **98** VG. **Pinotage** ✿✿ **99** heralds style change from earthy/plummy to perfumed vanilla (transfused by 11 mths new oak, 30/70 Am/Fr). Chewy tannins need time to relax. 300 cases. **Annie Rozier Red** ✿✿ **98** ripe, 'sweet' plumy fruit backing into very dry tannins. 100% merlot, lightly oaked. 13% alc. 2 200 cases. Next-up **99** sees addition of 40% cab, 20% pinotage to original merlot base.

Mouton-Excelsior Wines

Cape Town • Owner Mouton family-owned Universal Commodities & Communications • Production 15 000 cases 70% red 30% white • PO Box 251 Cape Town 8000 • Tel (021) 426-2684/5 • Fax (021) 426-2728 • E-mail ucc@winejoy.com • Website www.winejoy.com

"THINGS ARE GOING very well," is the upbeat report from Gerda Mouton, globe trotting Cape Town negociant (and aspirant Cape Wine Master) who exports a select range of local wines to markets in Europe, north America, the Orient and some Indian Ocean islands. The wines are styled to Mouton's specifications by partner winemakers in a variety of wine areas including Stellenbosch, Robertson, Swartland and, for the whites, some of the cooler climate production zones. New to this edition is the value-priced Cape Mouton collection, featuring a chirpy Cabernet Sauvignon for the UK market. The budget spectrum is covered by the Itakane portfolio, whose name hints at the family roots of this wine business — it's the Xhosa equivalent of lamb/mouton (Gerda Mouton acknowledges husband Benjamin and Vriesenhof stalwart Jan Boland Coetzee as the biggest influences on her career — "they threw me into the deep end of winemaking!"). At the premium end of the range, new labels and upmarket 'encrusted' bottles now add to the all-round allure.

Mouton-Excelsior Huguenot Reserve range

✿ **Shiraz** Seamless fruit/oak integration the standout feature of **98**, upscale from pvs with subtle aromas of leather/clove joined in palate by rich chocolatey tastes. Rounded and satisfyingly long. 13% alc. 18 mths Fr barriques.

✿ **Chardonnay** ▼ Hints of Burgundy in Fr oak fermented/aged **98**, with rich, plump, toasty flavours of marmalade and beeswax. You'll find Norwegian salmon drizzled with hollandaise sauce on the Mouton's table when they drink this full-bodied wine, which is at peak. 500 cases.

Pinotage ✿ New **98** attractive old style example, big and robust, with rustic farmyard/fennel/eucalyptus aromas and inky, almost black colour. 13,5% alc. 1 000 cases. **Sauvignon Blanc** ✿ High-altitude Stbosch grapes reflected in relative delicacy, light herbal tones in **99** (though 13% alc); good juicy flavours of fresh rhubarb and fig. 1 000 cases. Also available (not tasted for this ed — pvs ratings in brackets where applicable): **Huguenot Reserve 98** (✿) Bdx blend; **Cabernet Sauvignon 98**; **Merlot 99**.

Mouton-Excelsior range

✿ **Cabernet Sauvignon** Different wine to **97** of pvs ed. This claret style, ex-Stbosch, Fr barrique aged 18 mths, which reflected in fine oak-spicy overlay to blackcurrant fruit, long tannins and minerally finish. 13% alc. 1 000 cases.

✿ **Merlot** ▼ This grape something of a house speciality; usually soft and fleshy in more restrained mode. **98** with pretty violets and minty wafts; latest **99** ✿ not quite as striking as pvs, yet with pleasing sweet-tobacco fragrance, well ripened red berries, soft tannins. Elegantly oaked. Try with veal piccata or Greek lamb, recommends Gerda Mouton. 3 mths small oak. 13,5% alc. 1 000 cases.

✿ **Pinotage** ▼ Unwooded med-bodied **98** improving in bottle; shows some complexity in pinot noir-like aroma/flavour spectrum. Velvety redcurrants with hints of undergrowth. Grapes ex-Darling. 1 000 cases. **00** (sample) promising: creamy mulberry fruit, juicy texture, fine tannins.

Cabernet Sauvignon-Merlot ✿ New ☺ Savoury **99** greets you with mouthwatering smoked meat/berry aromas, then earthy/tar hints in smooth, full-bodied palate. Gerda Mouton likes to serve with pork kebabs or BBQ chicken. Partially Fr oaked. 13% alc. 1 000 cases. **Chardonnay** ✿ ☺Lightly oaked **99** features Aussie-style suggestion of sweetness, imparting beguiling smoothness to the broad toasted-pastry/green grass/vanilla flavours. Instant seafood partner.13,5% alc. 1 000 cases.

Chenin Blanc ✿ Unwooded, med-bodied **99** offers some gentle honey/bottle age tones with fragrant herbal nuances. New release. 16 000 cases. Preview of step-up **00** ✿: melon with hints of clove; creamy, harmonious dry finish. Also available (untasted): **Sauvignon Blanc 00**.

Cape Mouton range   New

Cabernet Sauvignon ✿ ☺ Perky New World cab with juicy redcurrants and green olives jostling pleasingly in big, gutsy unwooded **99** palate. 14% alc. 2 000 cases specially for UK retail chains.

Itakane range

Chardonnay ✿ ☺ Barrel-fermented **99** very easy to drink (so do note the high 13,5% alc). Light peaches-and-cream flavours with butterscotch, good toasty dry finish. Team with pasta salads or quiches. Specially for UK customers, who should love this generous, accessible style. 1 000 cases.

Pinotage ✿ New Demure berry aromas and understated 'green' sensations in **99**, med-bodied, partly oak-matured. 1 000 cases. **Cabernet Sauvignon-Merlot** New Perfumed **99** offers delicate potpourri wafts and sweet strawberry fruit; ready to drink, with soft tannin.

Mulderbosch Vineyards

Stellenbosch • Closed to the public • Tasting by appointment • Sales Mon—Fri 8—5 • Owner Hydro Holdings • Winemaker Mike Dobrovic (since 1991), with Desmond Hendricks & Edward Kershaw • Viticulturist Johann Schloms • Marketing/sales Sean Griffiths • Vineyards 27 ha • Production 275 tons 18 000 cases 70% white 30% red • PO Box 548 Stellenbosch 7599 • Tel (021) 882-2488 • Fax (021) 882-2351 • E-mail info@mulderbosch.co.za • Website www.mulderbosch.co.za

THE HANG-DOG, slightly bent gait (an unsteady Dustin Hoffman sort of shuffle down a crowded sidewalk) and the almost ceaseless emissions of bon mots and risqué jokes, belie winemaker Mike Dobrovic's entirely serious and gifted approach to wine. Dobrovic manages to imbue an urgent importance — or philosophical imperative — to the glass in front of him. He is Mr Mulderbosch, having planned and nurtured it virtually from scratch (sweaty and sawdust-coated for hours, weighed down by a chainsaw felling trees) in the late 1980s. For two successive owners of Mulderbosch, he's managed to project a once unknown label to international status — and keep it there, especially for the racy Sauvignon Blanc. But he has fans too for his Chardonnays and the original Steen-op-Hout as well as the cleverly named Faithful Hound. Among the most persuasive of Cape winemakers on the chemistry front (though don't ask him to spell methoxy-isobutyl pyrazines — " I can't even spell chardonnay on a good day") he's even happier on the subject of wine and music; "I play Mozart, lots of Mozart, specially during the harvest, and specially when nerves are frayed. I've seen glowering men on the verge of fisticuffs melt and smile at each other within a few minutes of Mozart booming around the cellar. If things get really dire, I have Kiri te Kanawa sing Ave Maria."

✿**Faithful Hound** ▼ Bdx blend — not wine show gobsmacker, more in juicy-limpid style. **97** is example: restrained red berry fragrance, finely structured, clean minerally flavours with sound tannin background. Effect is of claret-type lightness, direct clarity rather than thick, burly whammer. **98** has more to it, deeper colour, wider mouthfeel but retains characteristic limpid gluggability with tannins nicely covered by ripe fruit. Roughly equal parts merlot, cab with about 10% malbec; 12–18 mths. Fr oak, 25% new. Dobrovic reckons **94** stunning now.

✿**Alpha Centauri** Also Bdx blend (cab f/s 80/20). One-off bottling in just 1 500 magnums, from rich **98** vintage; spicy, elegant with grown-up dry finish, some wild berry/nutty cab f flavours in palate; 14 mths new Fr oak.

✿**Chardonnay** Reliable, sometimes understated. Ripe wheaty/lemon hue in **98** with hazelnut/oatmeal bouquet, also snatches of citrus zest. Rounded, with nutty savouriness in finish. Partly barrel (±60%) and tank fermented. (Back-tasting of **93** reveals fairly intact wine, excellent colours with some green hues surviving in the lemon-gold, but — like almost all Cape chardonnays — lacking the rich and delicate toasty mealiness of a ripe old Burgundy.)

✿**Barrel-Fermented Chardonnay** 97, 98 (also partly natural-yeast fermented) gives much more New World, forward richness and intrigue on palate; **98** *Wine* ✿ specially inviting, fleshed out for mouthfilling appeal. (Top Cape white, of 200, in Air France–Preteux Bourgeois taste-off.) **99** untasted. **97** multi-flavoured winner of AF–PB trophy, *Wine* ✿.

✿**Steen-op-Hout** ▼ Distinctive, popular new-wave chenin; concentrated fruit from dryland, old, low-crop vines, small proportion oaked (mainly Am, some Fr). Acacia, honey fragrance, full flavours; sweetish palate impression though bone-dry. Broad-shouldered **99** (with touch of sauvignon blanc) bit more lush, softer than pvs; mesmerising **98** *Wine* ✿ with heady, fresh wild honey scents probably remains benchmark. **97** *Wine* ✿, **96** SAA.

✿**Sauvignon Blanc** ▼ This cellar's — and one of the Cape's — showcase wines since early 1990s. Excruciatingly (for the grower!) light yields of 3–4 t/

ha in past few vintages, especially **99**, **00**, guarantee flavour focus. Misleadingly light colour/structure — nose, palate deliver proper sauvignon flinty-gooseberry spectrum. M'bosch aficionados may hark back to phenomenal crisp, delicious full but racy vintages — **93** and **97** — and find **00** doesn't match them, but nor does it disappoint. Unwooded. Untrellised bush vines. Showered with SAA, *Wine* ✿ accolades. **95** only SA gold medal at USA Intervin, also only SA selection in German Top 100 Wines of the World list for 1996

Barrel-fermented Sauvignon Blanc ✿ Shows its own charm; less racy, the gooseberry fruit flavours partly shut out by the oak, but some figgy-steely-spicy crisp edge retained in latest **NV** (99). Dobrovic believes these peak around 3–5 yrs. **95** *Wine* ✿, SAA; **94** SAA.

. . . .

Muldersvlei / Starke Wines

Stellenbosch (but see Paarl map) • Tasting & cellar tours by appointment Sales Mon—Fri 8.30—5 • Luxury B&B • Views • Owner/viticulturist Julian Starke • Winemakers Ian & Julian Starke • Vineyards 30 ha • Production 90 tons 3 500 cases 90% red 10% white • PO Box 66 Muldersvlei 7607 • Tel (021) 884-4433 • Fax (021) 884-4324 • E-mail wine@muldersvlei.co.za • Website www.muldersvlei.co.za

HERE'S another bright young recruit to the ranks: Ian Starke, assisted by father Julian and winemaker mate Marcus Milner, has taken this 311 ha family farm public with some cracking first-release wines. New vineyards are being planted — with trellising systems designed for effective canopy management and mechanical harvesting — to bump up the current 30 ha of pinotage, cabernet, shiraz and chenin. Ian Starke caught the winemaking bug in 1996, when he was a Std 8 schoolboy: "I picked up a book on winemaking in the library and have never put it down." It's become "a passion, I guess". The person he'd most like to meet in the wine world is "the guy who found out how to make wine, to congratulate him on his terrific discovery, which has made so many of us happy!" Enviably energetic, this young man relaxes, out of the cellar, by "working in my dad's dairy as well as in the fruit orchards".

✿**Pinotage** ▼ **99** impresses with harmonious, highly drinkable Old/New World styling: billowing (but not jammy) pinotage fruit — smoky plums/mulberries — well controlled by ripe tannin and oak. Super debut; value-priced. 13% alc. 13 mths oaked. 250 cases

Shiraz ✿ Lighter, sappy style, uncomplicated, quaffable. Charming ruby glow reflected in **99**'s strawberry hints, real 'sweaty saddle' aromas. 50 cases. Oaking as above. **Juliette** ✿ Firm, attractively dry **99** blend pinotage/shiraz with latter's smoke in bouquet, former's juicy mulberry softness on the tongue. Med/full-bodied. Oaked as above. 75 cases. **Chenin Blanc** Lightly oaked **00** not tasted. 100 cases.

. . . .

Muratie Estate

Stellenbosch (see Stellenbosch map) • Tasting & sales Mon—Fri 10—5 Sat 10—3 and Sun 11—3 (Nov-Mar) • Cellar tours by appointment • Meals by arrangement • B&B • Owner Melck Family Trust • Winemaker Mark Carmichael-Green (since 2000) • Viticulturist Paul Wallace (VineWise) • Vineyards 40 ha • Production 250 tons 10 000 cases 99% red 1% white • PO Box 133 Koelenhof 7605 • Tel (021) 882-2330/6 • Fax (021) 882-2790 • E-mail muratie@kingsley.co.za

A NEW WINEMAKER for the new millennium at this 300 year old estate beneath the Simonsberg: experienced Mark Carmichael-Green (some of SFW's leading labels formerly his charges) has joined the Melck brothers, who own the farm and, with viticultural consultant Paul Wallace, is applying some new maths. In the vineyards they're both adding — new plantings — and subtracting, reducing the crop to about 5 t/ha for more ripeness, better balance (this quite aside from the slash-and-burn effects of the runaway fires which naturally pruned many vineyards in the area early in 2000). In the 200 year old cellar there's been some multiplication — an array of new oak barrels, and a limited edition Shiraz 2000. But Rijk Melck stresses that Muratie will never grow bulky: only 40 ha of the estate's total 120 ha are vineyards, and that's more or less how things will remain. When the late SFW MD Ronnie Melck bought Muratie in 1988, he set about repolishing a family jewel — the farm came into the Melck family in 1763, and stayed for more than a century. The new generation at this specialist red and after-dinner wine estate is determined to keep the family flag flying high, producing what Rijk Melck targets as "terroir-bound wines of excellence".

✿ Pinot Noir SA's first pinot vines were planted in these vyds around 75 yrs ago. Nowadays low-yielding (3,5 t/ha) Dijon 113/115 clones feature here, reflecting in latest **99 ✿** luminous ruby colour and equally vivid cherry/banana aromas, mutating into strawberry juiciness in palate (carbonic maceration an influence here). Flavours are finely-drawn and light, with pleasing elegance and moderate alc (12,4%), though not as complex as 98, with earthy/mushroom aromas and spicy/plummy fruit. These made in traditional open fermenters, cask aged ± yr, malo in barrel.

✿ Ansela Van der Caab Stylish, well-oaked dry red blend named after a slave freed in 1695, who married the first owner of this farm and helped establish its vyds. **98** cab/merlot mix "from 4 special blocks", undeveloped mid-2000 but ripe with promise. Fine savoury aromas, some strawberry notes; fleshy flavours 'sweetened' by high 14% alc, gently firmed by ripe tannins. 5 000 cases. **97** 50/50 cab/merlot evolving very well, darker toned than above with merlot's earthy/mocha tones to cab's fragrant redcurrant. **97** medium weight (though 13% alc), yr 20% new, remainder 2nd fill Fr oak. **96** VG. All with lingering, firmly dry finish.

✿ Amber ▼ Fortified dessert from muscat d'alexandrie with loyal following since the George Paul Canitz era, circa 1925. Label harks back to this with Canitz painting of soft, voluptuous model. **98** ageing with distinction; profusion of nuances including pine nuts and eucalyptus in surprisingly dry citrus palate with bits of (top quality) thatch in finish. Unusual and deservedly popular. 18% alc.

Port ✿ Tasty ruby style **NV** with shyish smoky hints of prunes/orange zest and some savoury tones. Fairly dry, sinewy style, which should broaden with time. Traditional Portuguese varieties tintas b/r/f, souzão, yr oaked. 19% alc, 100 g/ℓ sugar. 1 750 cases.

. . . .

Mystery see Wine Warehouse

. . . .

Naked Truth

THE ULTIMATE no-frills range: budget-priced wines with the bare minimum of labelling, for extra cost saving. For the Picardi liquor store chain by Kempens of the Cape. Not available for tasting.

. . . .

Namaqua see Vredendal

. . . .

Natural Corporation

Stellenbosch • Owners Gary & André Shearer, with non-active shareholders • Winemaker Ansgar Flaaten (since 1999) • Production 60 000 cases 60% red 40% white • PO Box 5421 Cape Town 8000 • Tel (021) 881-3810 • Fax (021) 881-3814 • E-mail gary@natural.co.za • Website www.natural.co.za

CELEBRATING its 10th year in business, the Natural Corporation has pulled off a stunning hat trick: the powerful Metro group in Europe selected the Cape Indaba wines for inclusion in the portfolio; they achieved additional listings in the difficult Liquor Board-controlled Canadian market of Ontario; and, in the USA, where they have distribution of all of their products in almost 30 states country-wide, they have had the Indaba products re-listed in a leading supermarket chain this year (the first SA company to have achieved this in the USA), with several other chains wanting to follow suit. Then, to top it all, their US-based company Cape Classics has been appointed the sole consultant for all restaurants (including a $5–6m account) in the new 72 ha Disney African theme park. In the export market, the Shearers still represent most of the top SA properties they started out with. Their own brand, Cape Indaba, which reflects the quality of the 2000 vintage, is now achieving real success as a seriously rated brand with an eye-catching new label. Success of exports has meant meaningful quantities for the cellars that supply them. Employing winemaker Ansgar Flaaten (ex-Audacia) has further lifted overall quality. Ensuring the future, the Natural Corporation has two students at Stellenbosch University funded entirely by a portion of the profits from sales of Cape Indaba around the world.

Cape Indaba range

Pinotage You can drink this much-improved **00** now or in 2–6 yrs, its fruit/tannin structure is pleasingly supple yet robust enough to go the distance. Smoky/toasty oak, spicy touches from splash ruby cab impart complexity to primary plum/black cherry fruit. 40% Fr oaked. **99** old-style pinotage with estery character, mouth-coating tannins. 13% alc.

Cabernet Sauvignon Textbook cassis carries though from bouquet to 'sweet' fruity palate and long crisp finish. Satisfying, balanced. 50% Fr oaked. **99** lighter, uncomplicated. 13% alc.

Shiraz New Appealing style which showcases the peppery/smoky ripeness of the grape. Very smooth, dab of Am oak adds just a hint of vanilla spice in **00**.

Chardonnay ★ Quantum leap from **99** ★ to **00**, showing balance and restrained oak ("What the US market wants," says Gary Shearer, "is only a touch of oak and then only refined wood"). White peach, lime, lees and hint of spicy oak in full, curvaceous palate, protracted fresh finish. 13% alc. Am/Fr oaked.

Sauvignon Blanc Range's fastest mover world-wide. Bright green-apple zing, plus ripe passionfruit and cut-grass in **00**; acid and 'sweet' fruit harmonious, not overfresh; alc quite moderate at 12,7%. Best young .

Brut Sparkling NV These bubbles are calculated to bring you back for more. Tastes of lemon-cream biscuit and ripe peach, with some vanilla scents from 100% oaked base-wine, all chardonnay; extra-smooth almost double-cream palate with fine active mouse. Clean, bright finish.

Chenin Blanc ☺ Attention-seeking bouquet of lemon/lime jostling with pear/pineapple/lemonade in palate; smoothing but dry 3,5 g/ℓ sugar. Country-fresh and bouncy. Temperate 12,5% alc.

Merlot 00 not available for tasting. Pvs **99** competently-crafted, light everyday fare.

Rainbow Nation range

Currently two labels: **Pinotage-Cinsaut** (also known as African Red) and **Chenin-Chardonnay**, neither available for tasting.

Napier Winery

Wellington • Not open to the public • Owner GRT Farming & Financial (Pty) Ltd • Winemaker/viticulturist Leon Bester (since 2000) • Vineyards 21 ha • Production ±150 tons 4 500 cases 60% white 40% red • PO Box 638 Wellington 7654 • Tel (021) 864-1231 • Fax (021) 864-2728 • E-mail dock@iafrica.com

OWNER CHRIS KÜHN (neighbour of Claridge's Roger & Maria Jorgensen) exports 90% of his production through a wine shop in Amsterdam, so very little is left to spread around locally. However, a little truffling will turn up parcels on some exclusive winelists including The Upper Crust Restaurant, Western Province Cricket Club, Kelvin Grove Club and Swartberg Country Lodge. Range below untasted.

Red Medallion 96 Cab/merlot/cab f blend, 2 yrs small oak, 2 yrs bottle aged. **Cabernet Sauvignon 96** 100% cab, aged as above **Chardonnay 97** 100% barrel fermented, 7 mths min on lees, 2 yrs bottle matured. **Chenin Blanc 99** unwooded, dry.

Nederburg Wines 　　　　　🍷 🍷 🍷 🍷

Paarl (see Paarl map) • Tasting & sales Mon—Fri 8.30—5 Sat 9—1 (April—Oct) Sat 9—4 and Sun 11—3 (Nov—March) Public holidays (except religious holidays) 9—5 • Cellar tours Mon—Fri (none on Sat/Sun/public holidays) by appointment, in English, Afrikaans, German, French Fee R12.50 p/p • Picnic lunches Nov—Feb R55 per person (vegetarian baskets/ children's meals on request) • Banquet facilities in conjunction with Cape Sun Intercontinental Hotel • Video/slide shows • Owner SFW • Winemaker Newald Marais (since 1989), with Wilhelm Arnold (white wines), Hennie Huskisson (auction and red wines) • Farm managers/viticulturists Hannes van Rensburg, Dirk Bosman • Marketing Jeff Gradwell • Public relations Elsa van Dyk • Production 12 000 tons • 800 000 cases 55% white (including sparkling) 30% red 15% rosé • Private Bag X3006 Paarl 7620 • Tel (021) 862-3104 • Fax (021) 862-4887 • E-mail nedwines@sfw.co.za • Website www.nederburg.co.za

SINCE THE FIRST BOTTLING in 1937 (though the actual Nederburg farm dates back to 1792) this giant has raised Cape wine-consciousness like no other. It has fought the battle for wine, against the mighty forces of beer in this thirsty land, more doughtily than any compatriot. (And done yeoman overseas service too.) In the middle of the Kalahari, in just about every *platteland* hotel, in remote game reserves and village stores, in supermarkets and restaurants, you'll always find a Nederburg. And you'll always know it'll be good. Or even better. While sustained reliability is the brand's strong suit, you'll also find stars every bit as glittery as those in smaller constellations. The famous Edelkeur, for one, which brings us to Nederburg's sterling service to the industry via its annual Auction, the splashiest event on the SA wine calendar. There's no narrow-targeting of social responsibility here either. With auctioneer Patrick Grubb, Nederburg has established a scholarship open to applicants from all wineries which have participated in the Auction: aspiring winemakers and viticulturists from disadvantaged communities (black and coloured, to be precise) are sent abroad to travel and study. Is any more evidence needed of services to wine beyond the call of duty?

Standard range

🌸 **Edelrood** Classic blend cab/merlot, firm but unaggressive. **97** 🌸 precipitated more modern style via transfusion of new clone fruit from cooler regions. **98** notch higher: perfumed cedarwood; gently tannic mouthful shores up cassis fruit. 65% yr seasoned oak. 13,1% alc. 39 000 cases.

🌸 **Noble Late Harvest** Stylish, sumptuous sweet dessert, sometimes more interesting than super-scarce Edelkeur below, always better value: **99** shimmering golden hues; rich pineapple, tropical coconut, litchi with zesty acidity, good puff of botrytis. 75/25 chenin, riesling. 13,2% alc. 375 ml. 500 cases.

Paarl Cabernet Sauvignon 🌸 Undemanding, gently textured red. **98** quite tannic, some chewy blackcurrant reserves. Needs time or food. 50% old-oak aged. Splash merlot for extra fruit, drinkability. 13,2% alc. 107 000 cases. **Pinotage** 🌸 **98** savoury, 'wild' nose with sweet vanilla deflated by dusty, gum-numbing tannins (hopefully fruit currently resting). Yr Fr/Am oak. 41 000 cases. **Baronne** 🌸 Rustic, country-style red, with spicy twist. **98** reverts to usual cab/shiraz mix (60/40) after soupçon merlot dotted **97**. Smoky, savoury, generous, with dusty tannic end. 50% in big old barrels (through this deserves newer, smaller oak). 13,3% alc. 66 000 cases. **Rosé** ⚘ Has many adherents, and not just on 14th Feb — amazing 117 000 cases. Coppery tints start the allure, pulpy cherry/strawberry fruits maintain interest and 21g/ℓ sugar does the rest in lightish **00**. Cinsaut freshened with dash gamay.

Chardonnay 🌸 Improving by the vintage, but losing none of its trademark drinkability. **99** features some quite charry oak and appetising hot butter nose. 13,1%

alc. 45 000 cases. Portion new French oak fermented/matured. Regularly flies SAA economy class. Seldom needs to, but can go 4 yrs. **Paarl Chenin Blanc** ✦✦ Modern fuller style, toasty tropical fruit easing over to nutty roundness in med-bodied **99**. Partially oaked. 5 000 cases. **Sauvignon Blanc** ✦✦ Plenty of ripe, unoaked fruit in **00**, attractively fresh, succulent; fig/gooseberry flavours and flinty edge. Best within 18 mths of harvest. 25 000 cases. **Paarl Riesling** ☆ Looking for reliable, consistent quaffing? Join the throngs who snap up 32 000 cases annually, ensuring this remains one of SA's top-selling dry whites. Drink-young **00** (from Cape riesling) exactly like any other yr: inoffensive; crisp, light, unassertively fresh. 11,5% alc. **Rhine Riesling** ✦✦ Lightly chilled, this a fragrant, invigorating aperitif with presence. Exuberant potpourri/floral bouquet; gently sweet **99** palate. Follow-up **00** true to this aromatic style. 10 000 cases.

Prelude ✦✦ Undimmed popular acclaim (17 000 cases annually) for this pioneering sauvignon/chardonnay, lightly oaked for solo sipping or table accessorising. Gear up in full-bodied **99** with buttery fruit, citric tang, dry exit. 13,3% alc. Labelled Sauvignon Blanc-Chardonnay for export. **Premier Grand Cru** ☆ Anachronistic misnomer of a brand but brilliantly consistent, ever popular (23 000 cases). Lightish, bracingly dry **NV** ("contains no fermentable sugar"), wonderfully refreshing. Chenin plus colombar, dash semillon. **Lyric** ☆ Unpretentious, reliable lightish off-dry white, hugely popular (65 000 cases). Gentle **00** floral, fruity flavours. Sauvignon/Cape riesling/chardonnay. **Elegance** ✦✦ Lavish grapey energy from **99** trio muscats — morio, ottonel, frontignan — plus delicate rose petals. Freshened by fruity acid for overall easy drinkability. 6 000 cases. **Stein** ☆ Most wine ranges have an entry level; for many, this characterful lightish semi-sweet is an introduction to not just Nederburg but wine in general. **99** with plenty of uncloying personality. 47 000 cases. **Special Late Harvest** ✦✦ Three's not a crowd in medley of chenin, gewürz, riesling, touch of botrytis adding 4th dimension. Luscious rather than simply sweet, minerally tones add class in **99**, 10 000 cases.

Sparkling range

Blanquette ✦✦ Bottle-fermented dry MCC; pinpoint bead, golden yeasty roundness, pebbly fullness cut with delicious brisk zip. Lightish **95** ripe complexity from 4 yrs on lees; 25% barrel-fermented base wine. 100% chardonnay. 1 000 cases. **Premiere Cuvée Brut** ✦✦ SA's biggest brut, a stalwart which has survived many advances/pretenders; lightish, not too fruity, not too dry, crisp and utterly refreshing (refreshing lack of pretension too). Charmat method; **NV** (99) from chenin, Cape riesling, sauvignon. 55 000 cases. **Kap Sekt** ✦✦ Gently dry, floral bubbles which develop golden hues, ringing oiliness over time. Next lightish **97** still fresh, round, enticing. Mainly Rhine/Cape riesling with chardonnay. Charmat method, 9 mths on yeast lees. 5 000 cases. **Premiere Cuvée Doux** ☆ Light, sweeter version of Brut, same blend. Sugar balanced by fresh spiciness. Sold only from farm; exported to New Zealand. 5 000 cases.

Reserve range

❈**Cabernet Sauvignon** Balanced complexity in essentially supple, elegantly ripe **97**; perfumed oak, restrained violets, chocolatey whiffs. Fine tannins of cool vintage (esp in Elgin, source of 85% of fruit). Needs 2 yrs to unfold. Yr new/used Nevers casks. 13% alc. 3 000 cases. Rung above first **96** and potential vehicle with which to reclaim former Nederburg finesse.

❈**Chardonnay** Flagrant modern style which cries out for food. **99** warm bread nose heralds full tropical fruits, very limey with oak present but not obvious. 8 mths on lees in new Fr oak. 13,6% alc. 2 500 cases.

Sauvignon Blanc ✦✦ Much improved **00**, sweet hay, fresh cut grass, crisp finish. 13,5% alc. 2 000 cases. Much more elegant than **99**, piercing nettle, gooseberry out of harness and kilter.

Nederburg Auction wines

These made in small quantities, usually from special vyd blocks, offered in lots of ±500 cases. Originally labelled under meaningless Bin number, prefaced by letter (R indicates dry red, D dry white, S dessert and C Cap Classique); more recent vintages carry variety/blend. The Nederburg Auction, now in its 27th yr, is SA's biggest. It's open to any producer whose wine passes the selection process (Nederburg also subject to strenuous screening). Groot Constantia, Delheim and Nederburg have featured every year (other stalwarts include Simonsig and Overgaauw) under the gavel of Patrick Grubb MW, inaugural and still incumbent auctioneer. 2000 saw sales reach R5,86-million; 83% went to local buyers led by Spar and Makro.

✿ **Cabernet Sauvignon Private Bin R163** Traditionally old clone, very gradually shifting to new, brighter fruit. **93** retains huge, rustic, dusty tannic frame. Deeper than earlier vintages but not so dramatically as to disturb traditionalists. Yr mix small/large used oak. 500 cases.

✿ **Shiraz Private Bin R121** Dramatic strides away from old-style, unyielding pvs. Shimmering garnet **95** heightens ethereal violet, spice, delicious cinnamon spiked fruit woven into prune/plum palate which not aggressive. 500 cases. Preview of **97** (nudging ✿) confirms trend. Yr Fr barriques, 90% new.

✿ **Pinotage Private Bin R172** Latest **97** leaps over forebears with ripe fruit, new wood (which these wines need/deserve), soft tannins. Southern Rhône spiciness tames the banana, super density yet with fine tannins. 500 cases. Superior to **95** ✿✿, parsimonious with fruit, over-generous wood.

✿ **Cabernet Sauvignon-Merlot Private Bin R109** Now carries fresher, more modern standard; aromatic nose (lead pencil, tobacco leaf, dusty bottle age) laced with vanilla spice, minty ripe fruit, nicely balanced in **93** mouth. Now all it needs is new oak (whereas older 300 ℓ Fr casks actually used). 500 cases. **94** less dramatic, still numbingly tannic (so give plenty of time). These around 60/40 cab, merlot.

✿ **Chardonnay Private Bin D270** Latest **98** cut above **97** (slim, trim, though not insubstantial) and **96** (rich, Burgundian persistence) which held own at 2000 event. Complex bouquet of wood, candle wax, citric fruit. Heavy-char buttery oak supports still-fresh lime in interesting, bold palate. 7 mths new Fr oak. 14% alc. 500 cases.

✿ **Edelkeur** Grand dame of SA botrytis desserts; *raison d'être* of Nederburg auction (sales still exclusively via this fiesta) but sadly deserted by market in 2000 — first time ever parcels left unsold. Drier than pvs, less voluptuous perhaps, but mercifully less unctuous, more modern (so perhaps weakening of Asian markets to blame). Complete collection **76–96** (excluding never-released **94**, unusually dry at 84 g/ℓ) sold for R100 000 in charity slot of 25th auction. Current **98** glittering gold, shards of amber-green, distillate of dried apricots/peach pips with fleshier pineapples, robust acidity. 13,5% alc, 120 g/ℓ sugar. 375 ml. 500 cases. **97** very rich, full-bodied, evolving slower than many but built to last. **96** classic but bit short on excitement.

✿ **Sauvignon Blanc Private Bin D234** Unambiguous barrelled **99** sauvignon, pungent essence of nettles, fynbos, burnt wild scrub. Plus creamy oak ascendant in mouth. Match for **98**, bargain of 2000 auction. Carefully wooded (6 mths new Fr casks) to support rather than overwhelm. 13,6% alc. 250 cases.

✿ **Semillon Natural Sweet (Wooded)** New **99** less accessible, less botrytised, less intense than below, but full rev of wood (6 mths new small Fr casks) gives structure (and current retaining shroud). Same grapes ex-Dbnville as below, though jury's out as to whether or not it can handle the oak. 14,8% alc. 375 ml. 250 cases.

❖ **Semillon Noble Late Harvest** Modest debut but super buyers' value at around R25 for **97** at 2000 jamboree. Next-up **99** more concentrated, fleshier; thatchy nose quickly overtaken by intensely delicious tropical fruit in measured, full yet balanced palate. Lanolin richness will develop with age. High 144 g/ℓ sugar, 14% alc. Unoaked. 375 ml. 250 cases. No **98**.

❖ **Weisser Riesling Special Late Harvest Private Bin S306** SLH style which Nederburg has almost made its own: Milder 11,6% alc, softer 31,6 g/ℓ sugar in **97** put grape's delicacy in relief. Vital, fragrant rose-petal tension, extra honeyed veneer. Lime pickle, dried apricot and tangy pines, all brushed with botrytis, finishing beautifully clean. Effortless but not evanescent sipping. 250 cases. VG for **93**, **94**.

❖ **Weisser Riesling Noble Late Harvest Private Bin S316** Celestial performances at auction, often better value than Edelkeur. Epitome of poise, charm; superb **97** scintillating gold, intense botrytis nose, very ripe pineapple core cut by litchi, pickled lime tang. Youthfully sweet, robustly strong (14,4% alc) but will mellow with age. 375 ml. 250 cases. **92** VG; **90** *Wine* ❖.

❖ **Private Reserve Port 64** Masterly, venerable, truly rare. Really is 'private' (only 520 half-cases) and 'reserve', made by Günter Brözel in 1964, then stashed away until bottling in 1982 to rest until now. One-off sale at suitable prices (topped R400/bottle) in 2000. Remainder will stay firmly in Nederburg vinotèque. Old shiraz, fortified to just under 20% alc, ±160 g/ℓ sugar; with dated Wine of Origin Superior sticker.

❖ **Gewürztraminer-Weisser Riesling Special Late Harvest Private Bin S354** Exotic blend (65/35), unmistakable in **99**: veritable censer of heady rose petals; rich yet balanced palate far more finessed than somewhat ponderous pvs. Back to usual more genteel 12,4% alc, 34,5 g/ℓ sugar; return of light agility. 250 cases.

Merlot Private Bin R181 ❖ Yet to be released **97** promising modern minerally freshness; dense mocha texture lifted by cinnamon spice; firm dry tannins. 250 cases. 13,4% alc. Sample **98** riper still, fleshy berry softens austerity. **Petit Verdot Private Bin RXXX** Unfinished sample, not rated; shows what ripe fruit, new wood can do for the wines, especially **97**. Indigo colour intensity, fragrant damson, blue/blackberries, aromatic spice. Delicious. 13% alc. 250 cases. **Cabernet Sauvignon-Shiraz Private Bin R103** ❖ No need to further age these ±70/30 cab/shiraz blends: they're ready when they go under the gavel. **94** fresher, softer cassis fruit and viscous vanilla than **93**, but also some old-style dense tannic firmness. Portion small Fr oak matured, some new. 500 cases. **Shiraz-Cabernet Sauvignon Private Bin R115** ❖ Old style, sinuous lighter-bodied red ready for table. **94** smoky, thatchy, meaty aromas, mouthcoating dusty prunes, austere tannic corset. 500 cases.

Pinot Blanc Private Bin D250 ❖ Concentrated **99** up-front, modern. Waxy quince with spicy, sweet Am oak; chalky mineral depth to palate carrying boiled sweets; surprisingly restrained finish. More complexities should unfold over 1–2 yrs. 12,6% alc. 500 cases. **Semillon Private Bin D266** ❖ Returns to the guide with **99**, creamy caramelised vanilla pod nose offers much, palate defers with tight, still closed structure, crisp finish. Should open in time for 2001 release. Fermented/matured 6 mths mix Am/Fr oak. 13,2% alc. 500 cases. **Chardonnay-Sauvignon Blanc Private Bin D218** ❖ **99** developing golden gloss, thatchy whiffs to buttery nose, med-full hay fruit in palate; lacks complex development. 13,6% alc. 250 cases. 7 mths new Fr oak fermented/matured. **Muscadel-Steen Private Bin S333** ❖ **99** has fingers glued together with spun candyfloss, boiled bonbons. Minty, grapey tones simply too sweet for this league. 13% alc. 250 cases. **97**, **95**, **94** VVG. **Eminence** ❖ **99**, from muscadel, shows why so popular at Auction: strong golden yellow lights, clean billowing grapey muscat but lighter, easier, not as complex as currently more in-vogue Edelkeur above. 11,6% alc. 150 g/ℓ sugar. 375 ml. 500 cases. **98** altogether riper, bigger within grapey/floral paradigm. No **97**. **95**, **94** VVG. **Private Bin C92** ✿ MCC bubbly, **93** 5 yrs on lees and showing golden yeasty roundness, toasty lees development; dry but not aggressive. Firm, persistent mousse. Like Blanquette above, 100% chardonnay. 25% base wine barrel-fermented. 230 x 6 bottles.

. . . .

Neethlingshof Estate   ⚑ ⚑ ⚑ ⚑

Stellenbosch (see Stellenbosch map) • Tasting & sales Mon—Fri 9—7 Sat—Sun 10—6 (closes two hrs earlier in winter) Also tasting/sales of Stellenzicht wines. Tasting fee R20 p/p for 6 wines (includes glass) • Cellar tours by appointment • Lord Neethling Restaurant, Palm Terrace • Farm tour with barbeque • Owner Lusan Holdings • Winemaker Philip Costandius (since 2000) • Viticulturist Danie van Zyl • Production 923 tons 66 713 cases • Tel (021) 883-8988 • Fax (021) 883-8941 Email nee@mweb.co.za • Website www.neethlingshof.co.za

RESOUNDINGLY NAMED Marthinus Laurentius Neethling, a colourful 19th century owner of this glossy Stellenbosch estate, lends his signature to the crème of the range, which will include only "the very, very best" (predominantly red wine) the farm has to offer. Onetime mayor of Stellenbosch and, at the pinnacle of his career, senator of the Cape, the flamboyant farmer was known as 'Lord Neethling' because of his aristocratic mien. His name appears in the portfolio at the moment when another — oenological — blueblood, Philip Costandius, takes over as master of this high-profile cellar, part of the Lusan joint-venture among Le Bonheur, Uitkyk, Stellenzicht and Alto (where Neethlingshof's former winemaker, Schalk van der Westhuizen, now presides). Widely experienced Costandius, ex-Delheim, has proved himself more than capable of handling a variety of styles, from Bordeaux reds to sweet desserts, with skill and panache.

✿ **Lord Neethling Laurentius** New Splendid and serious **97** offers minted black berries, dark fruitiness and tealeaf notes in firm long finish, good savoury acidity. Palate copes effortlessly with 2 yrs in new Fr casks. Big all round (13,6% alc), but well balanced. Largely cab, with 10% merlot and dollop malbec.

✿ **Lord Neethling Cabernet Sauvignon** First release **97** with dusty cherry aromas, earthiness, spice and vanilla. Full-flavoured, dense blackcurrant and chocolate, well balanced. 13,4% alc; 2 yrs Fr oak. Like Laurentius above, deserves time to develop.

✿ **Lord Neethling Pinotage** Raspberry and cherry aromas/flavours, touched up with mocha and choc-mint in first release **97** VVG, *Wine* ✿. Elegant palate, with fairly restrained 12,7% alc, but powered by fruit. Supple dry tannins, with finish hinting at sweet Am oak (10%, remainder Fr).

✿ **Cabernet Sauvignon** Minerals, earth and green peppers in **97**, with berries and smoky dark chocolate. Balanced, and perhaps still to reveal its best. 13,4% alc; 2 yrs older Fr oak. **96** ✿ one of the finest from patchy yr.

✿ **Shiraz** Scattering of dry wild herbs (sage, thyme, lavender) over smoky fruit — **97** evokes Provence; Rhône-like in style, too. Fine firm tannins and acid well balanced with 13,7% alc for overall silky effect. Supportive but unobtrusive wooding (18 mths small Fr oak, new/older). Smoky, toasty **96** ✿ lighter (12,7% alc), quicker developing. Plums, milled pepper and smoky/wild scrub in **95** VG.

✿ **Merlot** Current **97** herby, green pepper bouquet, accented by cherry and strawberry. Weighty on tongue (13,5% alc), high toned with touch of eucalyptus. 18 mths new Fr oak. Pvs **96** ✿ less opulent (and, sensibly, less expansively oaked in response to troubled vintage). Soft tannins, warm palate but with some jarring burnt rubber notes. Past couple of vintages not quite as luminous as rich, mouthfilling **95**.

✿ **Chardonnay** Latest release affirms this label's claim to equal status with sibling Stellenzicht. Peach, apricot and buttery, toasty tones in **99**. More toasted wood and vanilla, from 9 mths new Fr oak, revealed in lemony finish. Should develop for few years. **98**, cut above pvs, continues happily: broad, soft butterbeans on fresh citrus background.

✿✿**Semillon** Reserve First release **98** a new benchmark for this variety in Cape: massive and rich, with long grippy finish. Follow up 99 ✿ tangy, herby, toasty, with extra tropical dimensions. Citrus and lanolin mark big, well-balanced palate. Continuing evolution of pvs indicates this deserves time to show its best. New Fr oak 9 mths.

✿ **Gewürztraminer 00** ✿ has expected rose-petal fragrance, but wears it with notable grace. Beautifully poised and elegant; occasion to abandon prejudice against non-dry wines: the 10,2 g/ℓ sugar softens rather than sweetens when well balanced by acidity as here. **99** headily perfumed with honeysuckle. **98**, **97** SAA.

✿ **Sauvignon Blanc** Fresh grass aromas mingle with tropical fruits in fragrant, almost pungent **00**. Powerful (13,3% alc) and crisp, with long-floating tail.

✿✿**Weisser Riesling Noble Late Harvest** Unbroken garland of awards stretching back to **90**, national champion NLH of yr, affirms this is the aristocrat of the Cape's botrytis desserts. Invariably unwooded, sumptuous, intensely sweet yet buoyed by waves of elegant citrus acidity. **98**, featured in pvs ed, most refined of the recent vintages. Flourishes of apricot, peach and honey herald rich, concentrated and complex palate, whose 133 g/ℓ sugar well balanced by acidity. *Wine* ✿. Those who admire this Günter Brözel masterminded wine will be devastated to learn there will be no **99** — grapes not considered good enough — or **00** — an unfortunate accident in the cellar made a commercial release impractical. All eyes, then on the 2001 vintage and incoming cellarmaster Philip Costandius …

Pinotage ✿ The full pinotage monty in **97**: strawberry, banana and boiled sweets, plus pleasant fruity flavours. 18 mths older wood. Medium 12.5% alc. **96** ✖ somewhat lighter, though defiantly brandishing strawberry 'sweetness'; notably dry finish, with bitter twist. **Neethlingsrood** ✿ This popular label returns in **97** from extended leave (pvs was **93**) completely transformed (now cab-merlot — 60/40) and evidently refreshed: nice smoky berry fruits, big 13,4% alc, soft but sufficiently structured by tannins. Ready for satisfying drinking.

Neil Ellis Wines   ♈ ♈ ♈

Stellenbosch (see Stellenbosch map) • Tasting & sales Mon—Fri 9.30—4.30 Sat 10—2 • Wheelchair-friendly • Views • Owner Neil Ellis Wines (Pty) Ltd • Chief winemaker Neil Ellis (since 1986) • Winemaker Louis Nel (since 1998) • Viticulturist Pieter Smit (since 1989) • Consulting viticulturists Eben Archer, Johan Pienaar • Vineyards 104 ha • Production 45 000 cases 50/50 red/white • PO Box 917 Stellenbosch 7599 • Tel (021) 887-0649 • Fax (021) 887-0647 • E-mail info@neilellis.com • Website www.neilellis.com

FROM REBEL UPSTART TO INDUSTRY PACEMAKER in the 1980s, Neil Ellis has kept a berth in the top, very serious order with some ease — the outstanding range below now an accepted Cape standard bearer combining breadth, imagination and focus. And often something else that's elusive in the Cape — and admired by his peers: wine elegance with richness and power. Ellis and his grape sources may be widely spread geographically — from Elgin to Stellenbosch to Darling — but he has stuck to the varieties and styles he knows best. And the ideas he pioneered in the Cape nearly 20 years ago: seeking out highly individual parcels of vineyards and coaxing — sometimes shaming — growers into modernization and improvement. "What we still lack is viticultural *thinkers*. With exceptions that I can count on one hand, winemakers are not great vineyardists. And the two disciplines are so specialized now — as in everything else — that one person can't really do both jobs in the old fashioned, jack of all trades way," he says. Where many in the industry are preoccupied with the New World competition — Australia, New Zealand, Chile — Ellis, predictably, has a more complex view: "I'm not so worried about our southern hemisphere rivals — it's what the Europeans are doing that impresses and worries me, specially Italy and France. We need to think big and radically — it's not going to be much use just buying a new broom to sweep the same old yard. And we have too many bulls in their own china shops here — meeting endlessly, just more and more meetings:" There isn't time, during the tasting for this guide, to elaborate, but he's clearly thinking futuristic technology and genetics. And Ellis clearly will let others have their meetings; he'll make his own decisions.

Neil Ellis Reserve Vineyard Selection

Single-vineyard wines for long maturation

✿✿ Cabernet Sauvignon Reserve Neil Ellis declares cab "the variety we'll saddle up with before all others" and it shows in this dark, brooding, sleek and pedigreed 100% varietal; from choice cool (relatively) s-w facing Oude Nektar vyds in Jonkershoek. 98, 97 VVG both fine vintages, excellent dark prune colours, very full bodied but elegant. For long — 10 yrs plus — keeping, unsparingly oaked to prepare for long haul.

✿ Shiraz Reserve His peers talk about Ellis' uncanny knack of producing powerful *and* elegant wines (too often, it's either/or) and this shiraz is an example, especially 98, which begins with a sweet-smoky harmony on nose and follows on to luxurious finish, punctuated by some varietal spicy pepperiness. Lovely mouth presence. Like 97, denser model of shiraz below. All new oak.

✿✿ Pinotage Reserve 98 judged among Top Ten ABSA pinotages of year, a swansong legacy from an ancient Oude Nektar vyd, since uprooted (attrition had made it financially unsustainable). Initially uncommunicative, this 98 is evolving into what could almost be called "an elegant petit Bourgogne" — assisted by 14 mths in new Fr barrels, tempering pinotage's summer pudding fruits and layering these with some sweet spiciness.

Neil Ellis Stellenbosch range

✿ Cabernet Sauvignon Consistency a hallmark here — fruit selection and immaculate cellar routines well established and rigorously applied since early 1990s. 98 will vie with 97 as recent standout yr (until 99 released around 2002, when it will become a three-horse race); these characterised by whiffs of cigar boxes, roasted coffee and clear, bright blackcurrant fruit, serious structure but also generous, fine finishes; latest should probably outclass pvs — which, however, now show good suppleness. Oaking less pronounced than in Reserves above, but 50% in new barrels. 96, 94 *Wine* ✿.

✿ Pinotage 99 ✿ trendily understated, with deep black cherry colour and unusually fine-toned bouquet of brambly fruit; a grown-up, dry finish; 98 also manages to sidestep much of pinotage's sometimes invasive sweetness and rambling tannins. Mostly new barrel matured, partly (about 15%) Am. Oak.

✿ Shiraz 99 latest, generous smokiness, fine all-rounder, with sweet 'soft underbelly' making it quaffable even at bottling. 97, 98 ✿ richer, rounder (from warmer yr); both show gentler face of variety. SAA red wine trophy. 97 featured cool yr's trademark, violet overtones, white pepper scents. Supple fruit intensity; matured partly (about 15%) Am oak.

✿ Cabernet Sauvignon-Merlot ▼ More sinuous 'give' in palate in this than any other 98 Ellis red; may not offer tight-grained intensity of grander ones above, but there's generosity and stylish ripe fruit, merlot obviously contributing to approachability. Once more, this cellar's techniques leave the tannins present but not disjointed. 97 also featured fine tannins, layers of ripe fruit; both vintages will repay some — about 5 yrs — cellaring.

✿ Chardonnay ▼ Latest 99, like most recent releases, has quietish nutty bouquet, muted but discernible lemon-grapefruit accents, but cleanly oaked — a sound, dependable wine — with deep straw hues. "It's well enough made, but there are 45 others out there that are also okay," says Ellis modestly. Quite burly, full on palate. From Oude Nektar vyds.

Neil Ellis Elgin range

⚡**Chardonnay** Unflamboyant chardonnay; **99** good example, making up with generous, crisp citric freshness in palate for what it may lack on (in this case its still youthful) nose. Several pvs vintages also gave lie to idea that Cape isn't chardonnay country; nonetheless best drunk within 2-4 yrs, though Elgin's slower grape-ripening climate generally gives these wines more keeping power. **98** achieves complexity, understated elegance. (Partial malo — winemaker believes these grapes not complex enough to carry 100% malo. Fermented, matured about yr Fr oak, mostly new.)

⚡**Sauvignon Blanc** An on-and-off label, now discontinued (no **00**). A trailblazer in its time, the first sauvignon — purchased grapes — from an Elgin apple farm, opened many eyes in the early 1980s and Ellis continued to produce one of the most consistently fine benchmark sauvignons for years. Last was **99** SAA with cutting, gooseberry edge, good, generous mouthfeel. For drinking young.

⚡**Pinot Noir 97** sole to date. Showed noticeable oak influence on release; variety's dark cherries, spice, macerated raspberries hovered in background. A one-off, not to be repeated.

Neil Ellis Groenekloof range

(West Coast, near Darling)

⚡**Sauvignon Blanc** **00** ⚡ a hot vintage which would have sapped fruit and substance (though not alc) from wine but for a coolish Feb; this retains some sinewy, grassy-fruity penetration — some characteristic crisp gooseberry too, but not in dazzling abundance of some pvs where you could imagine the cool, steel-flinty bite sweeping straight off Darling's windy Atlantic shores and into the wine. Usually a more austere, classic sauvignon — compared with tropical-fruity version ex-Elgin. **99, 98** *Wine* ⚡.

Neil Ellis Inglewood range

⚡**Cabernet Sauvignon-Merlot** **98, 99** from vyds chosen for soft fruit, gentle tannin/acid. Not too heavy; bright red/black berry fruits rounded by oaking; clean. A lunchtime red?

⚡**Pinotage** New **99** polished — smooth, friendly palate for so youthful a wine — with some oak touching up to make an attractive, quite complex, mouth satisfying, easy drinking red.

⚡**Shiraz** New **99** soft, smoky newcomer, from Stbosch vyds, showing warm, dry year's contribution to quite substantial core. Unblended.

Sauvignon Blanc ⚡ New **00** clean, fresh, straightforward dry white, with some tropical fruitiness livening it up.

- -

Nelson's Creek Estate

Paarl (see Paarl map) • Tasting & sales Mon—Fri 8—5 Sat 9—2 (sales also by arrangement) • Cellar tours by appointment • Restaurant meals/picnics by arrangement Or bring your own basket • Self-catering guest-house • Conference/lecture centre • Tourgroups • Gifts • Views • Mountain biking • Owner Alan Nelson • Winemaker/viticulturist Carl Allen (since 1995) • Vineyards 44 ha • Production 345 tons (15 000 cases own label) 60% red 40% white • PO Box 2009 Windmeul 7630 • Tel (021) 863-8453 • Fax (021) 863-8424 • E-mail nelsonscreek@wine.co.za

THERE'S SOMETHING for everyone at Cape Town senior counsel Alan Nelson's Paarl estate: for day trippers, light meals/picnics spread on the rolling lawns, with splendid mountain views; for business people and educators, a smart, fully equipped conference centre; for wine tasters, not one but *two* characterful ranges — one by in-house cellarmaster Carl Allen, who seems to lavish the same attention on his wines as his after hours passion, growing ornamental trees; the other by New Beginnings' Matthewis Thabo (see entry). There's even a point of note for scientific buffs: a 400 million year old geological fault which bisects the property and is responsible for the profusion of soil types in the vineyard. And if you're into feel-good family togetherness, you're in the right place too: the Nelson children, Lisha, Jo-anne and Danny are keenly involved, and help out in the tasting venue whenever they can.

❀ **Cabernet Sauvignon** Flagship label on an upward track, approaching quality of standout **95** VG. Current **98**, later picked for bigger, riper blackberry flavour, some herby sprigs plus wine's signature: green olives. Very smooth, generous tannin in dry finish, but non-aggressive. Yr Fr oak. 12,5% alc. 3 100 cases. Next **99** youthfully bright, potential ❀ but needs time.

❀ **Merlot** Another improving label. Current **99** lightish-bodied (11,8% alc) but not lacking plummy merlot fruit; extra interest from eucalyptus/violets and some mushroom hints; smooth, long dry exit. 1 900 cases. Next **99** better in every way; potential ❀. These small Fr oak aged, 13 mths, portion new. **97** SAYWS gold. **95** VG.

❀ **Pinotage** ✔ Unwooded for max fruit expression; **98** was first, introducing sappy, easy style with generous mulberry/smoky varietal character. **99** ❀ similar, not as intense but brightened by slightly tart redcurrant fruit. "Different, but good," believes Carl Allen. 12,8% alc%. 3 800 cases.

Albenet ❀ 😊 Juicy berries boom out of unwooded, med-bodied **98** sappy sipper. Added pleasure from savoury/leather tones, 'sweet' choc finish and lots of comfortable tannin. Shiraz/cinsaut.

Shiraz ❀ Gutsy style with black cherry/peppery sniffs. **98** crisper, fruitier than pvs; good soft tannin bite. 11 mths Fr oak, none new. 2 000 cases. Upcoming **99** glows with ❀ potential. **Chardonnay** ❀ Lower keyed but satisfying oak-matured style; attractive peach/honey tones in med-bodied **99**. 1 200 cases. Lemon/lime tang more prominent in follow-up **00** ❀, with 'sweet' spice from portion Am oak. **96** champion SA young wine of its year. **Chenin Blanc** ‡ New Estate's first varietal chenin, a med-bodied dry **98**. Good bottle development, some tropical fruit, ready. **99** similar, but not as honeyed. **Sauvignon Blanc** ❀ Maiden **99** lightish bodied, herby/tangy, dry. Much improved **00** ❀, fuller (13,8% alc), zingier; extra-soft tropical fruit for smooth quaffing. Well priced. **Chenin Blanc-Chardonnay** ‡ Light, pleasing **99** repeats pvs subtle sourdough/yeast character, clean dry finish. 2 100 cases. **Marguerite** ❀ Crowd pleasing light semi-sweet white, a toast to Alan Nelson's wife; **99** soft, smooth dry-hay/honey with honeysuckle scent, brisk lemony finish. Chenin/hanepoot.

New Beginnings Wines   🍷 🍷 🍶 🍶

Paarl (see Paarl map) • Tasting & sales Mon—Fri 9—5 Tasting fee R10 p/p for groups • Light meals/refreshments by arrangement • Vineyard tours by appointment • Visitors' centre (for details see Nelson's Creek Estate) • Owner Klein Begin Farming Association • Winemaker Matthewis Thabo (since Jan 1998), with viticulturists from VinPro • Production 13 000 cases 60% white 40% red • PO Box 2009 Windmeul 7630 • Tel (021) 863-8453 • Fax (021) 863-8424 • E-mail nelsonscreek@wine.co.za

"ON THIS LAND we do it like Frank Sinatra — our way". The 16 families who started this first black owned winery in SA are referring to the 11 ha given to them in 1997 by Alan Nelson, owner of next-door Nelson's Creek Estate, and the extra parcel which they bought with proceeds from their small, pioneering wine range, New Beginnings. These new-SA farmers (who are also employees of Nelson Creek) now own 20 ha, which they have partly replanted with cabernet and pinotage. The wines are made by Matthewis Thabo, an ex-casual labourer who used to look after the estate's beautiful lawns before spreading his wings in the Nelson's cellar, on loan to New Beginnings without charge. The wines are waltzing down supermarket isles, and onto restaurant tables — in the Netherlands, UK and, most recently Japan — with such speed, these New Beginners have to buy in finished wine for blending under their own brand. A British distributor is being sought, and a first order from Malaysia is an exciting possibility, reports Victor Titus, former schoolmaster and mentor. The international press continues to take a keen interest, and many journalists are delighted to echo the sentiments of Christine Austin, writer for the Yorkshire Post: "The wines taste good and they make you feel good, too."

Classic Dry Red 99 Not available for tasting. **Rosé** New ✱✱ Soft, gentle newcomer to this fast growing in Cape category. Delicate blush-pink **00**, strawberries and tropical fruit mingle in light palate to clean dry finish. **Dry White** ✿ Unpretentious, light **99**, some sweet-hay/tropical tones, not too dry finish. Uncomplicated quaffing.

. . . .

Newton Johnson Wines   🍷 🍷 🍷

Walker Bay (see Walker Bay map) • Tasting & sales Mon—Fri 9—4 Sat 9—12 • Cellar tours by appointment • Views • Wheelchair-friendly • Owners Dave & Felicity Johnson • Winemaker Gordon Johnson, advised by Bartho Eksteen • Vineyards 3,5 ha • Production 5 000 cases 55% white 45% red 5% • PO Box 225 Hermanus 7200 • Tel (028) 312-3862 • Fax (028) 312-3867 • E-mail capebay@netactive.co.za

THINGS ARE COOKING for the down-to-earth Johnson family, whose outdoor lifestyle and huge enjoyment of wines and food reflects on their label (is that Neptune's trident in the logo of their new negociant label, Sandown Bay, or a barbeque fork?). They've purchased an additional 40 ha, with 10 ha to be planted initially — this in the face of the 2000 hailstorm which destroyed almost the entire crop, with only enough for one barrel of pinot salvaged. Dave Johnson, Cape Wine Master and "custodian of the family overdraft", is a tad dismayed at the current obsession for wines to be varietally-identifiable. "Whatever happened to vinosity and just plain delicious?" he asks, pointedly. "To hell with showboat wines made to impress judges but exhaust your palate after a glass or two." So no neat little boxes at this splendid hilltop eyrie, from where you can see right down the Hemel-en-Aarde valley to a wedge of blue ocean in the distance (maritime conditions play a big role). "Anyway," continues Johnson, sometimes taster for this guide, "(wife) Felicity's unerring palate slices through technical jargon to cut out the dross." They've just celebrated 30 years of marriage (she even allowed him to buy a new boat; now he just wants to get sons Bevan and Gordon to take over entirely so that he can go fishing). Cape Bay is their popular negociant label of fresh, affordable and eminently drinkable wines to buy and enjoy straight away. The new Sandown Bay label is positioned between Cape Bay and the flagship, Newton Johnson (see separate entries). .

✿ **Cabernet Sauvignon** ▼ Splash shiraz adds its sultry tones to **99**, with cherry/plum succulence in backdrop of lightly charry oak. Distinct European feel from woodsmoke/pepper dimensions; big juicy tannins which won't be intimidated by more rustic cuisines (the Johnsons would opt for lamb shank casserole or cassoulet). Firgrove grapes; 11 mths Fr oak, some new. 13% alc. 1 200 cases. **98** with extra flavour injection of 14% merlot.

✿ **Pinotage** New ▼ New-wave pinotage with bright, bold splashes of fruit and oak which impressed competition judges (*Wine* ✱, ABSA Top Ten), and should be hit with consumers looking for instant drinkability with ageing potential. **98** gets off to fine minerally start, then extra-concentrated mulberry/blackberry/ripe banana fruit through to discernibly tannic but soft finish. Walker Bay grapes. 11 mths Fr/Am oak. 13,6% alc.

✿ **Felicité** ▼ (Pvsly Clairet — renamed after described as "a happy wine" in last ed of this book.) Rosé for grown-ups: unashamedly dry, but tweaked for comfortable pairing with food (Johnsons' swing past the fishmonger's would reel in Thai prawn and kingklip stir-fry). Or, lightly chilled, summer solo tippling.

Formula-change from merlot to **00** pinot helps ensure softness, accessibility with good cherry fruit backing, even-touch tannin for structure. Fruit from White-hall, Elgin. 13,5% alc. 400 cases.

♣ **Chardonnay** **99** continues pvs perkier style with zesty lemon-lime combo leading into quite full, leesy but not buttery palate (no malo), with marmalade/ripe peach/toast and barley-sugar hints in cleansing racy finish. 'Endorsed' by Thelema eminence (and fishing mate) Gyles Webb ("He said it wasn't bad," reports Dave Johnson). Kaaimansgat fruit (Villiersdorp area). 13,5% alc. 450 cases. Like **98**, oak-barrelled; super now, potential for development over 2–5 yrs.

♣ **Sauvignon Blanc** **00** back up to speed after slight dip in **99** ♣. The now usual gooseberry/passionfruit joined in **00** by nettle/pineapple and smoky oak from dollops barrel-fermented sauvignon/semillon. Latter's weight/textures help tone down 7,1 g/ℓ acid's steely edge, ensuring vibrant clean finish. Bot River fruit. ±12% alc. 1 600 cases.

. . . .

Nicholas L Jonker Estate see Jonkheer

. . . .

Niel Joubert Wines

Paarl (see Paarl map) • Tasting, sales, cellar tours by appointment • Walks • Views • Owner Niel Joubert • Winemaker Ernst Leicht (since 2000) • Viticulturist Daan Joubert (since 1982) • Vineyards 300 ha • Production 2 200 tons (220 tons own label) 60% red 40% white • PO Box 17 Klapmuts 7625 • Tel (021) 875-5419 • Fax (021) 875-5462 • E-mail neiljoub@iafrica.com

"REDS." Uncompromisingly and without hesitation, newly installed winemaker Ernst Leicht declares his speciality. He linked up with the Joubert family on their farm Klein Simonsvlei below the Simonsberg after a 3 year study stint at Weinberg in Germany. The Jouberts, still among SFW's grape and bulk wine suppliers, aim to bottle an increasing quantity of reds (merlot and shiraz in particular) under their own Niel Joubert label (current own labelling is about 10%). Sizeable new plantings probably are best viewed on foot or, if you have the stamina, on the trot: the annual Sanlam Niel Joubert footrace is held here. It's a delightful (and probably rather exhausting) 10-13 km jog among the vineyards on the 900 ha property.

Cabernet Sauvignon (oak aged) ♣ Thumbprint firmness offset in **98** by easy plum and cassis softness, layered with aromatic dusty oak. A cork to pop now or, for extra pleasure, keep 2–3 yrs. 12 mths small casks. 13% alc. 600 cases. **Cabernet Sauvignon** (lightly oaked) ♣ Above compactness again in this **98**, of which only a 15% portion aged in cask. Some light 'green' tones tempered by full cassis/blackberry fruit. Potential for short-term development. 13% alc. 2 400 cases. **Pinotage** ♣ Striking contrast in **98** between soft plummy/mulberry flavours and some austere tannins. As with pvs **97**, needs time or sturdy cuisine. 13% alc. 650 cases. **Sauvignon Blanc** ♣ Sound, easy drinking **00**, with fat figgy palate, gently crisp finish. Satisfying mouthful. Single vyd on own farm; reductive vinification. 13% alc. 1 800 cases.

. . . .

Nietvoorbij

New

Stellenbosch (see Stellenbosch map) • Sales by appointment • Owner ARC • Winemakers Kous Theart & Adéle Louw • Viticulturist WHL Laubscher • Vineyards 50 ha • Production 5 000 cases • Private Bag X5026 Stellenbosch 7599 • Tel (021) 809-3091 • Fax (021) 809-3002 • E-mail adele@nietvoor.agric.za

ASTONISHING BARGAINS are these wines, grown and made at the vineyards and cellar of the Nietvoorbij fruit, vine and wine research institute on the outskirts of Stellenbosch, and now available to the public for the first time. Except for the Port (at R13.50 a bottle) they're sold by the 6-pack, with individual bottle prices working out to between R14.95 and R8.15 for reds, and R7.50 for the costliest white, the

Chardonnay! Nietvoorbij farms 50 ha of experimental vineyards; the grapes are made into wine, both to check on the influences of various viticultural practices, and to probe a variety of cellar techniques. Experiments done, there's wine going begging, explains winemaker Adéle Louw, an Honours oenology graduate from Stellenbosch University, who previously worked at Clos Malverne.

⚜ Kwartet Name alludes to quartet of varieties (merlot/cab s/malbec/cab f) in this **98** Old World style Bdx blend. Dark berries unobtrusively oaked, med-weight despite ample 13,2% alc. Very drinkable now but could fruitfully age few yrs. Yr Fr barriques. 550 cases.

⚜ Pinotage Dare we say it? Some 'real-world' producers could take a leaf from this sophisticated **98** book, which should be subtitled 'Pinotage for grown-ups'. All necessaries are here — fruit ('sweet' red cherry/raspberry), oak (yr large/small casks), body (strapping 14,2% alc), length — but all in restrained, classically understated, cuisine-cordial form. Yr large/small oak. 1 000 cases.

⚜ Cabernet Sauvignon **98** 'correct', well made, but lacks sex appeal of above reds (reality check: this R12/bottle!); mulberries and winegummy hints, lightly brushed with oak. 13,2% alc. Yr large/small Fr oak. 1 400 cases.

⚜ Chardonnay **99** showcases fragrant ripe peaches unadulterated by oak (though some woodsmoke smoulders in background — cellar BBQ?). Good dry lingering finish with bit of a kick in tail, courtesy of 14,2% alc. 1 000 cases.

Merlot ⚜ 98's nutty cassis, choc/spice flavours still reined in by tannins; needs bit more time to give its best. Yr small Fr oak. 12,8% alc. 500 cases. **Ruby Port ⚜** Fortified dessert which, curiously, vintage-dated — **96** vs customary NV, though this not out of character with contents, which more vintage style than ruby. Nevertheless, a pleasant drink which deserves bit more time to show its best. 19,1% alc. Old oak aged. 750 cases. Above all 6 x 750 ml cases.

Nitida Cellars

Durbanville (see Durbanville map) • Tasting & sales Mon—Fri 9—5 Sat 9.30—1 Negotiated fee for tour groups • Pro-claimed conservation area • Cellar tours by appointment • Wheelchair-friendly • Owners Veller family • Winemaker/viticulturist Bernhard Veller • Vineyards 13 ha • Production 125 tons (5 000 cases own label) 60% red 40% white • PO Box 1423 Durbanville 7551 • Tel/fax (021) 976-1467 • E-mail nitida@ct.lia.net

BERNHARD AND PETA VELLER sum up the 2000 harvest with feeling: "The heat!!!! This is the year we have been most thankful, relieved and overjoyed when the mists came rolling in at sundowner time, ruining many a beautiful sunset, but bringing down temperatures and minimising transpiration water loss — a serious threat for dryland farmers like ourselves." And it went on and on, with an unprecedented 11 weeks between picking Nitida's acclaimed sauvignon blanc and ("giving us the usual stomach ulcers") the cabernet. Even the ever buoyant Vellers might have sunk a little low had there been no gain from this pain, but they were thankfully able to extract "knock you out" flavours and colours from their reds and believe Durbanville's whites in general this vintage are stunners — theirs assisted by a new ("small and humble") barrel cooling cellar, featuring Bernhard Veller's self-invented temperature control system. "No fancy equipment here," he says, "just extreme hands-on." Herein lies the charm of the wines from these well sited 13 ha vineyards not far from Table Bay, and the Vellers intend to "resist temptation and stay small and handcrafted".

⚜ Cabernet Sauvignon Forward style, with generous fruit padding, but good dry tannins for a more polished lasting impression. Latest **99**, labelled Reserve, gentler, more refined than pvs. Well managed oak, enough ripe tannin for 4–5 yrs' keeping. 14% alc. ±Yr Fr oak, 30% new. ±200 cases.

⚜ Shiraz Something of a lone ranger amid the Cape current stampede towards trumpeting behemoths. Cool climate aromatics in latest **99**, herbs, wild scrub and swirling woodsmoke; ripe plum and toasty oak all present but in quieter, non-broadcasting mode. 13% alc. Top rated by SA *Wine* magazine panels: **98** ✿, **97** ✿✿.

✿ **Calligraphy** (Merlot-Cabernet Franc in pvs ed) Attractive claret style red, jointly fronted by cab/cab f (35/35) with merlot striding forward with good tarry counterpoint to sweet violets, logan berries in pre-blending (unrated) **99** sample. ±500 cases. **98** VG intense, long, with some aromatic farmyard complexity.

✿ **Chardonnay** One of the Cape's more characterful examples since **98** VVG. Step-up **99** juicy, lively, very long zesty finish. Upcoming **00** too unformed to rate conclusively mid-2000. But ✿ wink in vivid citrus crispness broadened with oaky vanilla/butterscotch. 13,5% alc. 1 000 cases. These whole bunch pressed, partly barrel fermented. Around 13% alc.

✿ **Sauvignon Blanc** Comes with a track record stretching to **95** VVG, made by Bernhard Veller, which splashed the cellar's name in headlines on its very first competitive outing. Latest **00** ▼ clearly in that starry league, and though very youthful, radiating ✿ intensity. Piercing blasts of gooseberry, passion fruit, fresh cut grass, vibey clean fresh med-bodied palate. Should improve over 2–3 yrs. 1 250 cases. **99** brisk nettly tones, delicious bracing finish. VG, SAYWS gold.

Pinotage ✿ Latest **99** not ready for tasting. **98** well balanced, easy, good now and into 2002.

- -

Nordale Winery ℗

Bonnievale (see Robertson map) • Tasting & sales Mon—Thu 8—12.30; 1.30—5 Fri 7.30—12.30; 1.30—4 • Cellar tours by appointment • Owners 32 members • Manager Emile Schoch • Winemaker to be appointed • Consulting viticulturists VinPro • Vineyards 600 ha • Production 10 000 tons • PO Box 105 Bonnievale 6730 • Tel (023) 616-2050 • Fax (023) 616-2192 • E-mail nordalewines@yebo.co.za • Website www.nordale.co.za

TEMPORARILY without a winemaker at press time, Emile Schoch found himself unexpectedly hands-on in this Bonnievale co-op cellar, blending and fining and quite enjoying it ("I'm used to playing more of a consultant's role"). In conjunction with VinPro consultants, the 32 growers are implementing a quality programme encompassing canopy/water management and yield reduction. They're also focusing on transforming unfashionable white vineyards into red, mainly cabernet, shiraz, merlot and ruby cab. A highlight of 2000 was the delivery to French negociant Ginestet of some Nordale blended red. This, for better or worse, is unlikely to have the same restorative effect as a natural remedy from France which Schoch is thinking of importing. "It's amazing, but you can't sleep because it seems to have similar effects to viagra, if you see what I mean. It's also brilliant for reducing your blood-alcohol level, so you're a bit fresher the next day ..."

✿ **Red Muskadel Jerepigo** ▼ **96** fortified dessert; beautiful mahogany/topaz lights with complex, rich, developed flavours to match: sweet tomato jam, stewed fruit and, in palate, red berries/muscat and endless waves of honey. 17,5% alc. Follow-up **98** not tasted.

Vin Rouge ✿✿ ☺ Reverts to straight ruby cab in **99**, with variety's juicy plums, woodsmoke/earthy whiffs smoothed by light, well judged oaking. 13% alc. **Colombard-Chardonnay** ✿✿ ☺ Winery's fastest seller, bargain priced. Brushed with oak, **00**'s sweet floral/apple aromas translate into juicy, bright, full palate with fragrant guava and grain plumping sugar (3,9 g/ℓ). 13% alc. 1 150 cases.

Shiraz ✿✿ **New** First shiraz under cellar's banner a worthy addition to range. Varietal white pepper/fennel aromas recur in full-bodied palate with choc/coffee and concentrated red berry fruits. **99** accessible with potential to improve over yr/2. 13,7% alc. 250 cases.

Nuy Wine Cellar

Worcester (see Worcester map) • Tasting & sales Mon—Fri 8.30—4.30 Sat 8.30—12.30 (cases and 2-bottle packs only) Tasting fee for larger groups • Barbecue facilities • Owners 21 members • Winemaker Wilhelm Linde (since 1971) • Production 10 500 tons • PO Box 5225 Worcester • Tel (023) 347-0272 • Fax (023) 347-4994 • E-mail wines@nuywinery.co.za

"ENOUGH CHALLENGES for the next millennium!" says Wilhelm Linde of the harvest of 2000, but we've never seen this immensely capable winemaker ruffled. With more than a quarter of a century's experience at this cellar, a familial bond with his farmer-producers, and a deep-rooted knowledge of his mountain-ringed valley's soils and microclimate — Linde could probably run Nuy in his sleep. Which, of course, is a notion that would horrify this most conscientious and unassuming of men, whose bottom-lines are "strong discipline, hard work, ongoing efforts to improve quality even more". His short- and long-term ideals are the same: "Always to deliver the best for our cellar and farming community". It's difficult to imagine how much better he could possibly do: twice winner of South Africa's most prestigious award, the Diners Club Winemaker of the Year, plus a tanker of other medals (a raft would sink), he has given Nuy's range an image that belies its small size (only 3% is kept for own-label bottling, the rest is a secret behind the success of many SFW wines).

Red Muscadel Heady, exotic, satin-textured dessert, intensely sweet yet not over-rich. Newest **99** unusually muted when sampled mid-2000, usual billowing muscat/spicerack undeveloped. So give bit of time. No rush to uncork anyway: these age very well. **96** *Wine*.

White Muscadel Exemplary Karoo and Cape dessert, one of SA's best. Invariably manages difficult feat of delivering richness, flavour yet avoids blowsy, raisiny decadence. Latest **99** barley sugar, pineapple notes plus usual twist lime to freshen succulent honey-sweetness. Heaps of VVG, VG medals; **85** Diner's Club Award; regular at Nederburg auction. **96** rare *Wine*.

> **Chant de Nuit** Unique, Ferdinand de Lesseps table grape-containing white blend with legions of fans — though devotees looking for signature iced-pineapple-cake aroma in latest (**NV**) will find lemon pie, chamomile tea! Reassuringly, still a versatile super-quaffer; lighter bodied, bone dry. With chenin, colombard. **Riesling** Gluggable, light, outdoorsy wine, from Cape riesling. Sea-breeze/ozone, fresh hay in dryish **00**. Best young, but shouldn't come to harm over yr or 2. Diner's Club award in **91**.

Cabernet Sauvignon No-pretensions **00** quaffer with plenty of cassis flavour, ripe tannin for uncorking now. Appears med-bodied despite sturdy 13,6% alc. **Rouge de Nuy** ‡ **99**, unlike pvs, quite firm and robust, so partner with full-blooded, rustic cuisine. 13,5% alc. **Chardonnay** Seafood, cream-sauced cuisine spring to mind when sampling **00**, unwooded as usual, with delicate peaches and swirl of woodsmoke. 13,3% alc. **Colombard** Dry. Among most dependable in Cape. Racy, light, flavourful, as in frisky **00**, with light pétillance. Don't hold back: best in yr of vintage. **Sauvignon Blanc** Not much varietal character in **00** (yet another difficult sauvignon yr in Cape), but pleasantly zingy. Some muted green pepper/cut grass in smoothly dry finish. **Fernão Pires** Light, lemon-toned, semi-dry lunchtime sipping in **00**, not quite as springy as pvs but easy, refreshing. **Colombard Semi-Sweet** ‡ Lighter-bodied **NV** sipper, discernibly sweet but not unctuous. Delicate guava/citrus tones. **Sauvignon Blanc Sparkling** ‡ Gently dry beach/sundowner, now vintage-dated. **00** light, floral, palate-poppingly fizzy.

Oak Valley see Douglas
Oak Village see Vinfruco

OddBins see Shoprite Checkers

Old Bridge Wines

New

Franschhoek • Not open to the public • Owner Paulinas Dal Farm Holdings (Pty) Ltd • Production 50 000 cases 55% white 45% red • PO Box 101 Franschhoek 7690 • Tel/fax (021) 874-3959 • E-mail rickety@iafrica.com • Websites www.oldbridgewines.com, www.oldbridge.co.za

FRANSCHHOEK BASED, export focused producer, negociant and wholesaler sourcing wines from the Western Cape region for a variety of labels. These include Paulinas Drift International for export, and Old Bridge/Old Drift for the southern African market. Also a number of private labels for clients both locally and overseas. The wines, not available for tasting, include: Paulinas Drift International **Cape Classic Red**, **Cape Classic White**; under Paulinas Drift Premium label: **Cabernet Sauvignon**, **Merlot**, **Pinotage**, **Chardonnay**, **Chenin Blanc**, **Sauvignon Blanc**; under Paulinas Drift Reserve label: **Cabernet Sauvignon**, **Merlot**, **Shiraz**, **Pinotage**, **Chardonnay**, **Sauvignon Blanc**. Above, with exception of Reserves, also under **Old Bridge/Old Drift** marque.

Old Brown see Sedgwick's

Old Vines Cellars

Not open to the public • Owners Irina von Holdt & Françoise Botha • Winemaker Johan le Hanie • Production 12 000 cases 100% white • 50 Liesbeek Road Rosebank 7700 • Tel (021) 685-6428 • Fax (021) 685-6446 • E-mail oldvines@iafrica.com

"IF EVER there were a variety that needed a fairy godmother to wave a wand and transform her, it's South Africa's trusty chenin blanc," says Irina von Holdt. While this feisty Cape Wine Master (formerly a blood research scientist) and taster for this guide is impossible to picture in a frilly tulle tutu with tinsel in her hair, it's she who's done most to magic up a modern revival of this country's most ubiquitous grape. "Waving a wand" is far too floaty and languid to describe her campaign to dig chenin out of the sugar bowl and whip it into its rightful place — "on the table with the great white wines of the world". This is Joan of Arc, not Sugar Plum Fairy stuff, and she rides into battle as acting chair of the Cape's newly formed Chenin Blanc Association. Not solely a producers' body, it's involving all sectors of the industry, plus consumers. Viticulture, oenology and marketing research, and the training of a specialist tasting panel, narrow-focused on chenin, are underway. Simultaneously she keeps a beady stylist's eye on her contributions to the struggle (see below) launched with the famously blue-bottled 95 Blue White. Now there are four, with this mother and daughter (Françoise Botha) partnership turning out 12 000 cases, exported to 8 countries, including Japan — a recent visit there convincing IvH that chenin is the perfect match for Japanese cuisine with its "delicacy, freshness and subtle flavours".

* **Blue White** The original unwooded dry chenin in this range, still preferred by many, still in its eye-catching blue bottle. Latest is **98**, richest vintage to date; weighty (14% alc), deeply flavoured, cloaking itself in honey/melon as it develops. Finishes creamily dry (so should complement the sort of cuisine recommended by IvH: Thai chicken in coconut cream.) 10 000 cases. **97** *, with hint botrytis, complex, smooth.

* **Old Vines Chenin Blanc** Sister to above, in traditional green bottle. Light botrytis coating imparts extra richness in **98** which, though unwooded, is developing similar character to Barrel Reserve below. Weighty (13,9% alc), full flavoured, with enough substance to go few more yrs.

* **Old Vines Barrel Reserve Chenin Blanc** This is the oak-aged version (François Frères barriques, 5 mths), clearly more 'serious' and, judging from form

of first-release **98**, apparently able to age with some distinction. Ripe pear/vanilla/lees richness brushed with vanilla; bottle-age honey still properly in background. Deserves few more yrs to reach full potential. 13,5% alc. 750 cases. Foretaste of **99** reveals toast/pineapple tones, balanced fruit/acid.

Cheerful White ⚜ **New** The fresh presence in this range is — what else? — cheerful, lighthearted, fun, for early drinking. Especially good, reports IvH, with vegetarian meals eg spinach roulade. Med-bodied **NV**. 1 000 cases.

Onderkloof Vines & Wines

Sir Lowry's Pass (see Helderberg map) • Tasting, sales, cellar tours Mon—Fri by appointment • Private functions (max 20 people) Oct—Mar by arrangement • Self-catering cottages available from Jun 2001 • Views • Owners Danie Truter & Beat Musfeld • Winemaker/viticulturist Danie Truter (since 1998) • Vineyards 34 ha • Production 80 tons (3 750 cases own label) 60% white 40% red • PO Box 90 Sir Lowry's Pass 7133 • Tel/fax (021) 858-1538 • Fax (021) 858-1536 • E-mail wine@onderkloofwines.co.za

THE TIDE has certainly turned for onetime surfer-boy and keen sailor Danie Truter, who has been making wine for a quarter of a century. It was always his dream "one day to be able to produce wine from own grapes, grown close to the sea where I was born. This is where I am now." Truter and Swiss partner Beat Musfeld, who shares the seafaring bent, are keeping their eyes firmly on the distant horizon. Part of the plot they've charted is to put this area on the map. "Onderkloof's vineyards are on the south-facing slopes of the Schaapenberg and I'd like to see this premium area declared an official 'ward'," says Truter, who is actively involved in a tourism initiative for the Sir Lowry's Pass area. Plans are to replant shiraz, merlot and cabernet by the year 2010, retaining 2 ha of chardonnay as the only concession to whites.

⚜ **Cabernet Sauvignon** Assertive, intense **99** with just a hint of cab's 'sauvage' quality in bouquet; more conventional tastes of mulberry/green pepper/eucalyptus in palate with definite but supple tannin. At table, good foil for venison. 13% alc. 14 mths Fr oak. Unfiltered. 315 cases.

⚜ **Chardonnay 99** has lived up to its early starry promise and drinks very well now, with richness in reserve for 2–4 yrs. The tongue discovers all sorts of nuances in these fruit-oaky depths: milk choc/shortbread/pineapple/lime and creamy lees; all linger pleasingly to clean dry finish. Cuisine-cordial style. 9 mths new oak, Rousseau cooperage. 13,5% alc. 460 cases.

Young Vines Cabernet Sauvignon ⚜ **New** Attractive early drinker with more complexity than you'd expect from teen vyds. Ripe mulberries, herby/savoury tastes and lightish sappy tone. **99** unwooded/unfiltered. 550 cases. **Chenin Blanc** ⚜ Developed, multi-layered **99** rendered creamy from extended lees infusion, though finishes firm and steely-clean. 13,5% alc. 680 cases. Well priced. **Floreal** ⚜ **99** big sunny wine with just enough acid to balance the fragrant richness of fruit salad and honey. Danie Truter's culinary matches — Thai/Malay curries and traditional bobotie — will all work well with the semi-dry tone. Unwooded blend chenin/Cape riesling/sauvignon/muscat d'A. Value at R14 ex-cellar. 13,5% alc. 1 648 cases.

Onyx see Darling Cellars

Oom Tas

ONE OF SA'S TOP-SELLING BRANDS (2-million cases a year, all in returnable glass). Budget priced, has such a large, loyal following, it's produced 24 hours a day. Sometimes consumption beats supply: one December it went out to stores, was consumed and returned the same day — snappy turnaround in anyone's book. By Stellenbosch Farmers' Winery.

Deep amber colour looks 'sweet', but **NV** ✿ glugger finishes decidedly dry. Muscat fragrance, spicy hints of cardamom, cinnamon add interest. Available only in Western Cape, where it holds over one-third of the market.

. . . .

Opstal Estate

Worcester (see Worcester map) • Tasting, sales, cellar tours Mon—Fri 9–5 Sat 10—1 • Light picnic lunch by prior arrangement • Owner/winemaker Stanley Louw (since Jan 1980) • Viticulturist Kobus Theron (since Dec 1978) • Vineyards 100 ha • Production 1 470 tons (15 000 cases own label) 72% white 28% red • PO Box 27 Rawsonville 6845 • Tel (023) 349-3001 • Fax (023) 349-3002 • E-mail opstal@lando.co.za

IT'S BEEN all systems go at this mainly export-driven cellar since they recently opened their doors wide to the local wine-loving public. Opstal's wines are now available both on the estate and from specialised wine stores. A PR and a media consultant have also been appointed to keep them in the news. Winemaker Stanley Louw learnt the family's language of wine at his grandfather's knee. His family has been farming this land in the picture-perfect Slanghoek valley for six generations and the estate is suffused with a sense of community. Many of the farm workers' families have been there for generations. "I was born into the wine industry and I wouldn't swop it for anything. It's challenging and satisfying," says this keen golfer.

✿ **Cabernet Sauvignon** Steps into different league in latest **99**, with New World alc generosity (13,7%), smoothing grain sugar and rounded mulberry texture. Lightly oaked. 6 000 cases.

Hanepoot ✿ 😊 Lighter, less demandingly sweet **98** fortified dessert with variety's honeysuckle perfume and fresh, uncloying finish. 16,3% alc. 600 cases.

Carl Everson Classic Red Lightly oaked **99** cab; ruby cab, pinotage. Unpretentious. 2 500 cases. **Chardonnay** ★ Lightly wooded, full-bodied unwooded dry **99**. 13,7% alc. 3 000 cases. **Sauvignon Blanc** ✿ **00** ample grassy/figgy flavour, crisp finish. Lightish 11,5% alc. 2 000 cases.

. . . .

Oranjerivier Wynkelders

Orange River (see Orange River map for individual cellars) • Tasting & sales at Upington, Kakamas, Keimoes, Grootdrink and Groblershoop cellars. Tasting only during school holidays Mon—Fri 8–5 Sat 9—11.30 Sales year round Mon—Fri 8–5 Sat 8.30—12 • Cellar tours mid-Jan to March, Mon—Fri • Tourgroups up to 40 • River/vyd views from Kanoneiland • Owners ±750 members • General manager Noel Mouton • Winemakers Jannie Engelbrecht, Bolla Louw, Jurie de Kock, Chris Venter, Danie Volgraaff • Production ±100 000 tons • PO Box 544 Upington 8800 • Tel (054) 331-2186 (head office) • Fax (054) 332-4408 • E-mail marketing@owk.co.za • Website www.owk.co.za

THE KALAHARI DESERT might not spring instantly to mind as a wine area, but threading through its arid red soils is the Orange river, and strung out along its banks are both vineyards and this six-winery co-operative, the largest in the southern hemisphere, second largest in the world, with 750 members. They don't measure their vines by the hectare here, but by the square kilometre (about 300), producing around 100 000 tons of colombard, chenin, hanepoot, ruby cabernet and sultana varieties. New labels (lauded by judges of inaugural Grape Packaging Excellence awards), and a new boxed range (ideal for venturers into the nearby Kalahari Gemsbok and Augrabies Falls Parks) have been launched; exports go to five different countries.

Ruby Cabernet ★ Authentic bell-pepper aromatics in **98**; some chunky tannins call for time or robust cuisine. **Bonne Souvenir** Strong earthy tones in **98** ruby cab/pinotage blend. **Rosé** Ruby cab driven semi-sweet **NV**; some grapey, herbaceous notes and flick of tannin. **Blanc de Noir** Off-dry **99** blush from ruby cab. **95** SAYWS trophy winner. **Chardonnay** Freshness rather than varietal character the keynote in **99**, wood-maturation evident in honeyed palate. **Chenin Blanc** Extra-dry **99** not giving much away when tasted mid-2000. **Therona** 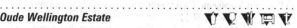 Clean, bone-dry, demandingly fresh **99**. Only varietal bottling of this grape in the guide. **Blanc de Blanc** Tight, somewhat metallic extra-dry **NV**; chardonnay fermented with oak chips. **Grand Cru** Arrestingly fresh **99** much loved by German customers "because it's so dry". **Colombard** Clean, fresh off-dry white **99**. **Nouveau Blanc** Chenin based semi-sweet "for young, sporty people". Latest **99** demandingly fresh. 9,5% alc. **Stein 99** semi-sweet chenin in fragrant, muscatty mood. **Late Harvest** Low-alc (9,5%), semi-sweet allsorts blend. **99** honeyed, earthy. **Special Late Harvest** Multivariety, light bodied fusion. Current **99** untasted. **Red Muscadel** ★ Spirity **98** dessert with unusual treacle-toffee nose. Very sweet. **Jerepico Red** ‡ Altogether more interesting than white housemate below. **98** redcurrants and fresh-ground spice; broad, penetrating sweetness. From ruby cab. 17,5% alc. **Soet Hanepoot** ‡ Deep-hued **98** dessert; tank/bottle age showing in gentle honeyed texture. Try with curry, say winemakers, "or share with your yachting mates". 17% alc. **White Muscadel** ⚜ Fresh, feel-good muscat de frontignan dessert. **98** VG with attractive 'burnt honey' aroma, bright, spirity mouthfeel. Winemakers, tongues firmly in cheeks, recommend sharing with "high class wine snob with a sweetish tooth" 17% alc. **Jerepico White** ★ Intensely sweet dessert from sultana. Extraordinary 'linseed oil', dried figs aromas in **98**. 17% alc.

. . . .

Oude Rust see Mooiuitsig

. . . .

Oude Wellington Estate

Wellington (see Wellington map) • Tasting & sales by appointment • Tasting fee R10 p/p for groups larger than 6 • Cellar tours by arrangement • River Café Restaurant • Guesthouse • Tourgroups • Views • Owner Rolf Schumacher • Winemaker Vanessa Simkiss (since 1995) • Viticulturists Vanessa Simkiss & Rolf Schumacher • Vineyards 15 ha • Production 80—120 tons (2 500 cases own label) 70% white (50% for estate brandy) 30% red • PO Box 622 Wellington 7654 • Tel (021) 873-2262 • Fax (021) 873-4639 • E-mail rrs@cis.co.za • Website www.kapwein.com

WHEN SHE NEEDS a tonic to boost her self-confidence, Vanessa Simkiss turns to winemaking mentor Roger Jorgensen of Claridge, "a great inspiration for winemakers like myself who do not come from formal wine education centres." She recently travelled to Singapore for the Asia 2000 Expo and found the people "positive, graceful and gentle, very wine-knowledgeable". She also had an encouraging trip to Germany where Oude Wellington's wines with their punchy purple-on-gold labels were well received. Grappa is now made on the estate by retired dentist Rolf Schumacher, who also distills the estate's brandy (the first five-year-old release is eagerly awaited in 2004). You can make a meal of it at the estate's River Café (the building dates back to 1785, has outdoor seating with great mountain and vineyard views, and indoors, a cosy fireplace in the working distillery) or even stay over in the historic Cape Dutch manor house.

⚜ **Cabernet Sauvignon** ⛛ Emphatic Wellington red: **98** full-bodied (14,5% alc), deep flavoured with ripe plums/cassis layered with vanilla and oak-spice from 14 mths Fr oaking, some new barrels. Long tapering finish.

Rubignon ⚜ **NV** Individual cross-vintage (96/97) ruby cab/cab s blend; dark toned with earthy/smoky undertones. Still angular, needs more time. 12,6% alc. **Ruby Cabernet** ⚜ Reflects a rarely glimpsed side of this grape, which more usually soft and accessible (and unoaked) in Cape. Bold, intensely peppery **98** with extra-dense tannins, arresting dryness. Needs plenty of time. 50% Fr barriques, 12 mths. **Currant Abbey** ⚜ (Ruby Cabernet in pvs ed) **99** huge friendly wine, extra-ripe berry flavours unadorned by oak and smoothed by brush of sweetness. 14% alc, 6,7 g/ℓ sugar. **Chenin Blanc** ⚜ Lightly oaked **99**, fresh citrus/apple, brisk dry palate, suggestion of vanilla in aftertaste. 12,7% alc.

. . . .

Oude Weltevreden see Weltevrede

Out of Africa see Sonop

. . . .

Overgaauw Estate   ▼ ▼ 🏠

Stellenbosch (see Stellenbosch map) • Tasting & sales Mon—Fri 9—12.30; 2—5 Sat 10—12.30 • Fully equipped self-catering cottage • Owner Braam van Velden • Winemaker Chris Joubert • Vineyards 75 ha • PO Box 3 Vlottenburg 7604 • Tel (021) 881-3815 • Fax (021) 881-3436

"I LOVE WEIGHT!" admits winemaker Chris Joubert, no 'lighty' himself. And a tasting of the past 3 vintages of the Tria Corda Bordeaux blend (95, 97 and 98) makes his point: the unashamedly big SA red is far from dead. Here's some serious competition for the tutti-frutti, instant-drinking school. But then Overgaauw, with wines made by father David van Velden, then by son Braam, stood out from the crowd even before Joubert joined up a decade ago. Appropriately for one of the First Families of Cape wine, the Van Veldens have made a habit of leading the pack. This was the estate that gave South Africa its first single varietal merlot in 1982; one of the first Cape Bordeaux-style blends; one of the pioneers of chardonnay; the only producer since 1971 of a fragrant and spicy sylvaner; first estate to break the R1 000/case barrier at the CIWG auction (in 1994); among the first to use small 225-litre French oak barrels for maturing cabernet sauvignon; first estate to plant the Portuguese port cultivars; first to bottle touriga naçional as a single varietal port; and first estate to drop the contentious name 'port' from its labels 5 years ago.

✿ Cabernet Sauvignon "A sin to open this wine for at least two more years," says Chris Joubert of **97** �★☆, a stunning, seriously complex cab with enough power and guts to go 18 mths in 100% new Fr oak in the wettest, coolest vintage of the decade. Fruit's so densely packed, in fact, it's not even begun to lift through the oak ceiling. Inky black colour; closed nose with hints of wild berry/cassis; intense palate, packed with red-/blackcurrants and mulberries. Excellent tannin structure and an enduring aftertaste. Tank sample of **98** reveals the difference between an 'SA' vintage (13,3% alc.) and a 'European' one (12,4% alc). Very similar to late-developing **95**, only now starting to open up. Matured in mix new/old oak up to 2 yrs. No **96**.

★☆ Merlot Overgaauw a local pioneer of this grape. Latest **98** a classic: bigger (at 13,6% alc.) than pvs, more tannin, darker colour, bigger extract, more spice in aftertaste. Needs another yr to show its potential followed by 2 more yrs in bottle. Mint/eucalyptus plus strawberry/raspberry/cherry in nose, all reverberating warm, full and deliciously long palate. 18 mths 2nd fill barrels. Bigger structure than **97** soft, rich, warm on release, with emphasis on choc-cherry fruit. Gently oaked 2 yrs, mostly 2nd fill Fr. 13% alc.

✿ Shiraz Quintessential spicy, smoky bacon aromas with rich, ripe pepper and plum pudding in **98** (for 1999 CWG Auction). Very youthful, needs 6—8 yrs to mature. Fermented/matured yr 50/50 new Fr/Am oak, followed by 6 mths 2nd fill barrels. From youngish (6 yr old) vines. 13,7% alc.

★☆ Tria Corda Outstanding dry red blend, featuring only the finest grapes in the finest years. **98** sees formula change, malbec replacing cab f for a 60:25:15 cab s, merlot, malbec blend. 12,8% alc. "It was such a great year for malbec, so we used it," Chris Joubert explains. The result is a spicier nose/taste and darker colour. Less of a food wine than pvs, though its big mouthfeel makes it very approachable. Commercial considerations aside, Chris Joubert would sell these in reverse chronological order — **99**, **98**, **97** — latter a long haul wine. No **96** "the quality just wasn't there." Joubert's favourite? "**97** has more mystique and mystery. This is a philosophising wine." **98** creamy, spicy nose, oak (18 mths small Fr) well integrated. Luscious mouthfeel, restrained, tight, huge tannin structure. More approachable than **97** which an 'umbrella' wine: gales of fruit under an umbrella of oak. 15 mths 100% Fr 1st fill. Big, tight, classic, gravelly Bdx style. Layers of peppery, earthy, cherry fruit with mint/bluegum hints. 60%

cab s, 25% merlot, 15% cab f. 12,8% alc. Promise of 8–10 yrs maturation. **95** a stunner (slightly less cab s, more cab f), longer (2 yrs) in small Fr oak.

- ✿ **Pinotage-Cabernet Franc 98** 55/45 blend. Best drinking 4/5 years, keep up to 8. 3rd fill Fr oak. Spicy nose, plum jam palate. More in your face than complex, intense **97**, with plum-packed nose, sweet-ripe cherry flavours, peppery finish. 60/40 blend. Pinotage from 30 yr old vines. Yr 3rd fill barrels.

- ✿ **Touriga Naçional-Cabernet Sauvignon** New And now for something completely different…highly unusual (in Cape) varietal combo featuring touriga's ethereal perfumes and cab's organising tannins — this **97** a 65/35 blend; intensely deep, almost black; dazzling bouquet of violets echoing in palate with aniseed and cinnamon; firm but ready tannins for now and up to 3 yrs. No **98**. Special bottling of upcoming **99** to be released for Makro.

- ✿ **Chardonnay 99** a nostalgic backwards glance at the older buttery Cape styles, emphasizing viscosity and weight. This partly achieved by natural yeast ferment (4 wks as opposed to 2 — not to be repeated as "too risky"), and partly by 7 mths Fr oaking, which well woven into the remarkably dense texture. Peaches/lemons/limes waft above and through the richness, to much-needed leavening effect. **98** SA's champion wood-matured white on SAYWS 1998.

- ✿ **Sauvignon Blanc** ▼ Chris Joubert moving away from reductive winemaking, allowing more lees contact than pvsly. This and more mature vyds impart greater intensity to **00**, filled with fresh green fruit, firm acids carry through to very dry finish and long aftertaste.

- ✿ **Sylvaner** The one and only Cape example, first bottled here in 1971. **98** maturing gracefully, kerosene notes becoming more evident along with initial spicy/peach aromas and good, full body. Touch of sugar, 5 g/ℓ, for smoothness. Good match for Cape Malay cuisine. No **99**.

- ✿ **Cape Vintage** Latest **98** ✿✿ breathtaking intensity, mouthfeel; luscious 'cakemix' fruit-and-nuts layered with minerally tannins and aromatic spirit. Top Cape 'port' and ✿✿ rating in SA *Wine*'s July 2000 blind tasting. Labelled 2000 Cape Vintage Reserve 1998 and sold in handsome 500 ml bottle with special wooden presentation case. Modern drier, higher-alc style (80,8 g/ℓ sugar, 20,3% alc); from six Douro varieties: touriga, tintas b/f/r, souzão, cornifesto, 20 mths oak, barrel selection, no filtration. Bigger, better than pvs perfumed **90** from tintas b/f, souzão, cornifesto, malvasia rey.

· ·

Overhex

Worcester (see Worcester map) • Tasting & sales Mon–Fri 8.30–4.30 • Cellar tours for groups by appointment • Small conference centre • Views • Wheelchair-friendly • Owners 17 shareholders • Manager Hennie Verster • Winemaker AB Krige (since 1996) Consulting winemaker Rod Easthope • Consulting viticulturists VinPro, Rod Easthope • Production 6 200 tons 95% white 5% red • PO Box 139 Worcester 6849 • Tel (023) 347-5012 • Fax (023) 347-1057 • E-mail overhex@intekom.co.za

REVOLUTIONARY FORCES have taken over this cellar. Formerly just another co-op, perhaps best-known for its battle to get the Wine & Spirits Board to recognise a curiosity 'ice wine', it blazes into the new millennium radically transformed, a cellar with the world in its sights. In just one year, everything — from vineyard to bottle to market targets — has changed for the better. How did they do it? Not with loads of fancy new equipment — the only new purchase was a mash cooler — but with attitude. This started with the growers — a conveniently small group representing 8 family farms. "We took them through a mind-shift session," explains winemaker AB Krige, "starting back at the basics." Cape-based Kiwi Rod Easthope (sweeping away viti-vini-cobwebs all over the country) and VinPro viticultural consultants motivated new approaches from ground to cellar. Marketing strategist Lucy Warner added fresh focus. Three close-targeted "New Era" ranges are the result. Rod Easthope says: "Rarely have I worked with such a motivated team." Lucy Warner enthuses about the Overhexers' "determination and enthusiasm". And AB Krige is simply over the moon: "I used to dream of making wines this good … it has been a momentous transformation!" Note: the wines below, all 00, were tasted very young and could not be rated realistically. However, the overall impression is of great improvement across the board; all should rate ✻ to ✻✻ on current form.

The Hex range

Premium collection, after the Hex River "which brings life and fulfilment to the inhabitants of the region".

Shiraz Probably the pick of this crop, exceptionally promising with supercharged fruit stretching the palate with sap until checked by ripe tannins and a fine, fragrant framework of oak from new Fr/Am barriques. Strapping 13,8% alc. 1 000 cases. **Pinotage** Not available for tasting. **Chardonnay** Barrel fermented, sur lie, malo — all stops pulled for super-smoothness and flavour extraction. Ripe peach and mango are the fruit anchors, woodsmoke/butterscotch add fullness and complexity, lees contributes some creaminess to properly dry, long finish. High 13,8% alc lends its own smoothing effect. 1 000 cases. **Chenin Blanc** Another swashbuckler with kick-boxing flavour and alc (13,8%). Lemonade in the nose, splashing into background smoky/toasty/vanilla from stave fermentation; mouthfilling lemon and, especially, lees with oak. Mid-palate, sweetish impression from ripe fruit/alc, though finish is distinctly dry. 1 000 cases. **Noble X** Fully fledged botrytised dessert from colombard, a mystery mid-2000, only some subdued dried apricot/botrytis whiffs giving clues about the future of 'X'. 13,6% alc, 6 g/ℓ acid, 66 g/ℓ sugar. 500 ml. 1 000 cases.

Silumku range

Recognises the 'father figure' of the cellar hands at Overhex; "the most gentle of gentlemen you could hope to meet". **Cabernet Sauvignon** Fascinating explosion of ripe, precisely defined fruit (blackberry/cherry) with amazingly soft tannins. **Pinotage** Very youthful, unformed but showing fine structure, deep flavours of ripe banana and more aromatic fynbos/scrub. Big, full (13,5% alc), dry finish. Oak-staved. 1 000 cases. **Chardonnay** Broad spread of tastes as result of oaking/sur lie vinification: lemon/lime and creamy lees, plus richer butterscotch and barley sugar layered in vigorous, fresh, full palate (13,6% alc) with fine thread of acidity. Finish is dry, lingering. 14 000 cases. **Chenin Blanc** Lots of fresh guava/passionfruit and tropical flavours crammed into big punchy palate (13,6% alc) with rounded mouthfeel. Dry zest in finish. Well made. 1 000 cases. **Sauvignon Blanc** Assertive acids dominate here mid-2000, subdued sweet-hay tones.

Hexagon range

Dry Red Relaxed quaffing style with generous cherry/plum fruit in lightly smoky background. Accommodating tannins and soupçon of invisible sugar for smoothness. Cinsaut, shiraz, ruby cab. 13% alc. 12 000 cases. **Dry White** Informal easy drinker from chenin/chardonnay; full (13% alc), flavoursome with honeysuckle fragrance and lemony dry finish. 15 000 cases.

Overmeer Cellars

No-frills quaffing range launched by Stellenbosch Farmers' Winery in 1996 to challenge the co-op and other boxed wines on price. Lately with portion non-SA grapes. Only the Late Harvest is available in glass. All NV.

Selected Red ✻ Snappy choc-cherry, plum tones; quite a long finish. Med-bodied. Grapes ex-SA, Spain, Argentina. **Premier Grand Cru** ✻ Fairly neutral nose, some subdued guava; clean, crisp finish. High turnover helps ensure freshness. **Stein** ✻ Technically semi-sweet, but smooth rather than syrupy; some grapey/tropical fragrances. **Late Harvest** ✻ Fractionally sweeter, fuller version of Stein; uncloying.

Paddagang Wines

Tulbagh (see Tulbagh map) • Tasting & sales 7 days a week 10—4 Tasting fee R5 p/p • Paddagang Restaurant • Owner Paddagang Wines • Winemaker Michael Krone • PO Box 303 Tulbagh 6820 • Tel (023) 230-0394 • Fax (023) 230-0433

THE wittily labelled 'Frog Alley' range takes its name from the characterful old-Cape restaurant on the frog route from riverside into Tulbagh town. The eatery and adjoining wine sales/tasting locale are run, and the wines selected, by a group of friends (and made by Michael Krone, winemaker at Tulbagh Co-op). The labels — a play on the amphibian theme — are among the most charming and original in the Cape.

✿ **Brulpadda** Individual port-style sweet fortified dessert with creamy choc depths, toffee richness. Good winter warmer. **NV** (as are all below) from ruby cab/pinotage.

Paddajolyt ✫ 😊 Light, sappy mouthful of cherries, best lightly chilled in summer. Unwooded cinsaut. Moderate 11,8% alc.

Paddarotti ✿ Unambiguously merlot; raspberry/strawberry tones, juicy palate with just a soupçon of tannin. **Paddamanel** ✿ Unoaked cab/merlot blend; bright berry fruit, light, undemanding. **Paddadundee** Unwooded chardonnay. Untasted. **Paddasang** ✫ Light-bodied sauvignon. **Paddaspring** Current bottling well past its best. From colombard. **Platanna** ✫ Semi-sweet chenin, floral easy drinker. **Paddapoot** ✿ Hanepoot fortified dessert; sweet, honeysuckle scented, citrusy finish. 16,4% alc.

Panarotti's

FOOD FRIENDLY NV house wines for SA pizza/pasta chain, Panarotti's, by Simonsig. Well chosen for moderate alcohol, well balanced styles.

Red ✫ Juicy, fruit-laden blend including ruby cab, pinotage, pinot; takes well to chilling when enjoyed with hearty Italian fare. **Dry White** ✫ Varietal cocktail including mostly clairette blanche, colombard, bukettraube; sweet talcum whiffs and bone dry, simple limey flavours. **Stein** ✫ In popular semi-sweet mode, lowish 11,5% alc. Aromatic notes from bukettraube, gewürz. **Vin Doux Sparkling** ✫ A 'sweetie' with pin point bubble and luscious grapey whiffs in lively party style.

Papillon see Van Loveren
Papkuilsfontein see Tukulu
Paradyskloof see Vriesenhof
Paul Bonnay see Pick 'n Pay

Paul Cluver Estate

Elgin (see Walker Bay map) • Tasting & sales Mon—Fri 9—5 Sat 9—1 No charge for individual tasting R10 p/p for groups of 8 or more • Picnic baskets in summer • Viewing deck • Art gallery • Summer sunset concerts in forest amphitheatre end Oct—March • Owner Paul Cluver • Winemaker Andries Burger (since 1997), with Patrick Kraukamp (since 1997) • Vineyard manager Wayne Voigt • Marketing manager Andries Burger • Production 8 000 cases 120 tons 60% white 40% red • PO Box 48 Grabouw 7160 • Tel (021) 859-0605 • Fax (021) 859-0150 • E-mail pcwine@cluver.co.za or andries@cluver.co.za • Website www.cluver.co.za

THE CLUVERS' De Rust farm (dating back to 1795) glides into the new millennium having introduced a new dimension to the Cape flavour spectrum. Generally considered the closest, climatically, to Burgundy (pinot noir very much at home here), this area is all about restraint, fruity delicacy, elegance. And the new-generation Paul Cluver team — including winemaker son-in-law Andries Burger — are determined to keep it that way. They've initiated a local guild of growers, and are encouraging their neighbours to start boutique cellars instead of selling off all their sought-after fruit. Because property prices in Elgin are relatively low compared to those in Stellenbosch, for example, a land-grab by big, bulk producers is a distinct possibility, and Burger and friends are anxious that the unique personality of this appellation's wines is not drowned or homogenised — and that the Paul Cluver motto of "handcrafted fine wines" remains true. So an Elgin wine route could be just up the road.

✿ **Cabernet Sauvignon** Individual offering from cool climes; classy, restrained yet characterful in market crowded with sameness. These attributes arrayed in **98** ✿✿, probably finest to date and improving in bottle. Serious looking deep, almost black colour; fine minerally/pebbly texture with aromatic tobacco whiffs. Reserved but not ephemeral (13% alc). 15 mths Fr oak, 60% new. 7 yr old vines. For now and over next 5 yrs. Richer than pvs **97** ✿, slightly vegetal nose, signature pebbly, tobacco/cedar tones plus pencil shavings. Barrel sample of **99** somewhat lean, reflecting difficult cab season here. **00** more fruit, higher extraction.

✿ **Pinot Noir 98** top pinot in 1999 SA Wine tasting, has become even more complex in bottle (though optimal drinking still several yrs out). Brilliant ruby colour; redcurrants, cherries, some violets, coffee and lanolin in sleek, velvety glove. Dijon clone, 11 mths Fr oak, 40% new. **00**, sampled from cask, hints at similar form to excellent **98**. No **99**.

✿ **Chardonnay** Latest **99** upscale from pvs, richer colour (lovely orangey tones) and palate, greater elegance, balance. Lemon/lime integrated with fine-grained oak. 13,5% alc. 100% new Fr casks, 6 mths then 3 mths 2nd fill. Promising **00** barrel sample, possible 'single vyd' release; Burgundian overtones, honeyed flavours. **98** ✿, with less new oak (80%, 9 mths), developing ripe, creamy complexity.

✿ **Gewürztraminer** Delicate, almost fragile **00** appears lighter and touch sweeter than pvs (though at 13% alc not evanescent) some litchi, hints of rose petals. On sweetish side of off-dry (10 g/ℓ sugar). Continues more refined style set by **99** which strikingly perfumed, petally. No **98**.

✿ **Weisser Riesling Special Late Harvest** Viscosity now more apparent in palate of **99**, growing in bottle with fragrant marmalade/pineapple tones. Liberal spoon sugar (27 g/ℓ sugar) cut by tangy acidity. 14% alc.

✿ **Weisser Riesling Noble Late Harvest 99**, first release, overlooked by SA consumers but snapped up at Nederburg Auction by Dutch chain Great Grapes. Cream of ripe crop, honey-gold richness mirrored in botrytis intensity, generous mouthfeel (14,2% alc.); reined in by high natural acids (11,5 g/ℓ). *Wine* ✿. 600 ℓ production, not oaked. **00** even higher alcohol (15%) though flavours initially not as intense.

✿ **Weisser Riesling** Still seeking a consistent style (but meanwhile reflecting vintage variations in intriguing, always interesting ways). Taut, Mosel-like austerity in off-dry **97**, now with evolved 'paraffin' tones. Extraordinary richness, verging on unctuousness in **98** ✿, acidic backbone straining under combined weight of 30% botrytis, 17 g/ℓ sugar, 14% alc. Latest **00** returns to Germany and taut, apricot/grapefruit nervousness; varietal meat/spiciness in nose. Dryness, penetrating acidity need (and will aid) some bottle maturation. No **99** — all went into NLH/SLH.

Sauvignon Blanc ✿ **00** youthful pale straw, lemony aromas and fresh acidity, well fleshed (13,5% alc.) **Sauvignon Blanc Barrel Fermented** ✿ Popular in small restaurant trade. **00** sparingly oaked, giving run to good fruit, acids; better varietal character than **99** which richer, aromatic.

Perdeberg Co-op

Paarl (see Paarl map) • Tasting & sales Mon—Fri 8—12.30, 2—5 • Cellar tours by appointment during harvest • Wheelchair-friendly • Owners 46 members • Winemaker Kobus de Kock (since 1989) • Vineyards 2 500 ha • Production 18 000 tons (6 000 cases own label) 60% white 40% red • PO Box 214 Paarl 7620 • Tel (021) 863-8244/8112 • Fax (021) 863-8245 • E-mail pwynk@iafrica.com

LONGTIME winemaker Kobus de Kock may be famously reticent but his wines speak volumes. A new red wine cellar will virtually triple the red wine production capabilities by 2007 to satisfy the demands of wholesalers. A newcomer to the small, inexpensive range is shiraz. "I think it's going to be excellent," says the winemaker, indulging in a totally out of character bit of trumpeting. "Because such a minute percentage of our production goes into our own-label wines, we bottle only the good stuff." And judging by demand, more of the good stuff would be in order.

Pinotage Reserve 99, with firm oak-spicy grip, a new high for this pvsly demure label. Next-up 00 tasted in awkward youth, so rating's provisional. Ripe, sturdy (13,8% alc), plummy mouthful still lashed by oak/tannin. Standard (unoaked) **Pinotage** 00 bigger than above (14,5% alc), positively packed with ripe plummy tannin with banana hints. 578 cases each. 98 ABSA Top Ten finalist.

Hanepoot NV (98) tasted last yr earns extra (✶) for good bottle development. Honeysuckle fragrance carries charmingly through to finish, which delicately spirity, non-cloying. 17,5% alc. 578 cases.

> **Cinsaut** At over 14,5% alc, value priced 00 not one to quaff standing up. Pleasing cinsaut strawberries in broad, fresh non-jammy palate. 13,5% alc. 578 cases. **Chenin Blanc Dry** Always quaffably fresh, inviting. 00 offers Perdeberg's trademark guava plus exotic jasmine perfume. Still amazing value at under R10 ex-cellar. 13,1% alc. 578 cases.

Shiraz 00 barrel sample savoury/earthy; with potential for higher rating on release. ±14% alc. 578 cases. **Semillon Reserve** 99 less striking yr down the line. Some delicate citrus tones. 13% alc. 578 cases. **Cinsaut Liqueur Wine** Most unusual/characterful NV fortified dessert with curious sweet sugarcane/savoury effect with tobacco (!) whiffs. Somehow works. 18% alc. **Cabernet Sauvignon-Merlot** Unremarkable 99 quaffer succeeded by riveting, attention-seeking 00, brandishing violets/lead pencils/mint — the whole modern Cape claret number. Distinct but soft tannin, charry oak in unfinished sample all point to starry (?) future. 13,5% alc.

Perdeberg Wines see Vinfruco
Petit Rochelle see Mont Rochelle

Philip Jordaan Wines

Worcester • Not open to the public • Owner/winemaker Philip Jordaan • Viticultural consultant Schalk du Toit • Vineyard 1 ha • Production 100% red • PO Box 55 Rawsonville 6845 • Tel (023) 349-1601 • Fax (023) 349-1581 • E-mail dutoitcellar@intekom.co.za

"SINGLE-VINEYARD": big names are falling over themselves to identify, within their multiple hectares, neat little parcels of vines — these to be individually giftwrapped and presented to those they'd most like to impress. Du Toitskloof Winery cellarmaster Philip Jordaan doesn't have to choose between this hill, that ridge, the other dale. His vineyard is a single vineyard, no more than 1 ha of 10 year old cabernet franc. It all goes into the one wine below, which kicked off in style with the 98 vintage winning the Wine of the Month Club's "best unusual red" category. Jordaan calls it an any-occasion red, but does suggest one specific food-mate:

springbok fillet with his own "kamikaze marinade". (Recipe enquiries directly to him, not us, please.)

⚛ **Cabernet Franc** Individual dry red, probing style, improving by the vintage. Variety's spicy/high toned aromatics immediately strike in **99**, with green pepper piquancy to palate's contrasting ripe plum, minerally oak. Similar structure and feel to first release **98**, with some emphatic tannins and dry, elegant finish. Good now, but should improve over 2–3 yrs (though Philip Jordaan suggests you drink within 5 yrs of harvest). 8 mths oaked. ±13% alc.

. . . .

Pick 'n Pay

Enquiries Elsa Gray • Tel (021) 934-5018 • Fax (021) 934-8975 • E-mail egray@pnp.co.za

THIS nationwide chain of SA supermarkets and hyperstores covers all the bases, from starched tablecloth showpieces to summer party sloshers. And, for bubbly fans, some affordable sparkling perk-me-ups.

'Corporate' range

> **Dry Red** ⚛ 🙂 Exuberant, well-priced quaffer; bright juicy red fruit; **99** soft, pleasantly balanced. Ruby cab/merlot/pinotage blend; unwooded, full-bodied (13,5 alc). From Van Loveren. Drink young.

Cabernet Sauvignon ⚛ Very fresh, mouthcoating though not heavy **99**, with refined blackberry/sweet mulberry/cassis fragrance. Lightly oaked. From Helderberg. **Pinotage** Untasted. From Darling Cellars. **Ruby Cabernet-Cabernet Sauvignon 99** made by Bergsig. Untasted. **Chardonnay** ⚛ Reliable oak-matured version; gentle, good on its own or with food. **99** with ripe lemon-lime, some dusty oak, touches of butterscotch. From Backsberg. **Chenin Blanc 99** Unwooded, ex-Darling Cellars. Untasted. **Sauvignon Blanc** ⚛ **00** lightish, brisk, youthful, for well-chilled drinking this summer. From Savanha. **Special Late Harvest** ⚛ Lightish and easy, versatile: lightly chilled as aperitif, dessert partner or solo. **99** with soft litchi fruit, not too sweet. 100% gewürz. By Robertson Winery. **Shiraz 00** from Van Loveren. Untasted. **Rosé** ⚛ **99** luminous brick red; sweet cherry flavours; lightish undemanding summertime drink. Ex-Savanha. **Chardonnay** Unwooded, ex-Goudini Winery, not ready for tasting. **Blanc Fumé** ⚛ Lightish bodied/toned **99** very quaffable, pleasant gooseberry/tropical tones, grain of sugar enhances smoothness. 100% unwooded sauvignon blanc ex-Robertson Winery. **Blanc de Blanc** ⚛⚛ Among fastest movers in this range. Guavas, fresh-cut grass and sunshine in **00**, just dry blend colombard/sauvignon from Van Loveren. **Johannisberger** ⚛ Good standalone quaffer, or partner for spicy food. Lightish, flowery unwooded blend white muscadel/colombard/gewürz from Robertson Winery. **99** with grapey hints, smooth, lightly spicy. Not too sweet.

Fab With Food range

Shrewdly packaged, consumer friendly wines offering one-chop solution to perennial culinary conundrum: what wine with what food? Range (untasted) includes:

Fantastic with Fish Unwooded sauvignon. **Chic with Chicken** Lightly wooded chardonnay. **Cool with Curry** Off-dry, light/med-bodied colombard/gewürz. **Divine with Dessert** SLH from colombard/gewürz. Also **Marvellous with Meat**, Perfect with Pasta, both imports.

'No Name' range

5 ℓ bag in boxes sold under P 'n P's in-house 'No Name' brand. Untasted. **Dry Red**, Rosé, **Dry White**, **Dry White Light**, **Stein**, **Late Harvest**.

'Vinipak' range
500 ml budget packs by Robertson Winery. Untasted. **Dry Red**, **Dry White**, **Stein**, **Late Harvest**.

Ravenswood range
Budget bag in box range by Robertson Winery. Untasted. 5 ℓ vats: **Dry Red**, **Rosé**, **Premier Grand Cru**, **Light**, **Stein**, **Late Harvest**, **Johannisberger**. 2 ℓ packs: **Grand Cru**, **Stein**, **Late Harvest**.

Paul Bonnay range
Budget-priced NV sparklers by Robertson Winery. Untasted. **Rouge**, **Brut**, **Vin Sec**, **Vin Doux**.

. . . .

Pierre Jourdan see Cabrière
Pierre Simond see Winecorp
Pinehurst see Môreson
Pinotage Company see Claridge

. . . .

Plaisir De Merle

Simondium (see Franschhoek map) • Tasting & sales Mon—Fri 9—5. Sat 10—1 Open public holidays except religious days) • Self-guided cellar tours as above Guided tours by appointment • Bring your own picnic by arrangement • Conference facilities for max 30 people with meals • Tourgroups • Gifts • Walks by arrangement • Views • Proclaimed conservation area • Owner Stellenbosch Farmers' Winery • General manager Hannes van Rensburg (since 1990) • Winemaker Niel Bester (since 1993) • Farm manager Freddie le Roux (since 1982) • Vineyards 400 ha • Production 700 tons 35 000—40 000 cases own label 75% red, 25% white • PO Box 121 Simondium 7670 • Tel (021) 874-1071/2 (wine sales) • Fax (021) 874-1689 Cellar tel/fax (021) 874-1488 • E-mail nbester@sfw.co.za • Website www.plaisirdemerle.co.za

THIS IS Stellenbosch Farmers' Winery's show-piece, show-off, show-the-way property: its imaginative winery architecture broke the traditional gabled and Cape-Georgian mould; it's hosted every VIP visitor to the winelands on its 1 000 ha and in private guesthouse; and from the first 93 vintage it reached out for a modern, gentler, earlier drinking wine style, a departure from tough-tannin, leave-it-to-the-grandchildren sorts of reds. Winemaker Niel Bester acknowledges SFW's Duimpie Bayly and Ch Margaux *regisseur* Paul Pontallier (the first of today's stream of French consultants to the Cape) as the biggest influences on his approach to the fruit grown specifically for Merle in 80 ha of the 400 ha vineyards (the rest goes to Nederburg/SFW). New plantings here include more shiraz; cabernet franc and additional petit verdot are in the pipeline. And the experimental wines Bester has made from young nebbiolo and sangiovese vines look "very promising". More than 'promising' — in fact excellent — is this range's presentation, lauded in SA's first packaging awards initiated by Grape.

⚜ **Cabernet Sauvignon** This opened a new, gentler, low-acid, soft-tannin chapter for Cape cabs when launched; was an SAA/Veritas selection for first 3 consecutive years. Fans will welcome return to form in **98**'s ⚜ unexpected dip. Generous vintage, **98** almost opulently fruity with well defined plum/raspberry jam (though not jammy) flavour, woodsmoke (both from 12—14 mths in casks, some new, and dollop shiraz — smidgeon merlot also contributor). 'Sweet', gently gripping tannins rounded by 14,3% alc. 17 000 cases.

⚜ **Merlot** Regaining some of the lustre of first release **95** VG, SAA trophy runner-up, which helped establish property's red wine credentials. Thumbprint meaty/minty/sweet violet array in latest **98** ⚜, supple with dry tannins yet sweetish viscosity from mouth expanding 14,4% alc. Yr 3rd fill casks. 3 300 cases. **97**, **96** both ⚜, less striking.

⚜ **Shiraz** Am oak's initially prominent vanilla/spice now absorbed, allowing extra-ripe choc-berries to gain ascendancy in **98** *Wine* ⚜. 50/50 Am/Fr oak. 14,3% alc. 1 000 cases. **99** ⚜ sample steps up into higher dimension: aromatic black berry succulence with truffles/pepper/liquorice. Fine, polished example with potential to improve.

🔥 **Cape Red Blend** Niel Bester's contribution to the Cape red debate (prompted by controversial 1999 Diners Club Competition). **97** full-bodied Bdx-style mix (50% cab, 20% merlot, 10% petit verdot) with aromatic shiraz overlay. Deep flavoured, good ripe blackberry/cherry, shiraz pepperines which contrasts well with sweet violet scent. 13,7% alc leaves sweetish parting impression.

🔥 **Chardonnay** Characterful, elegant and improving by the vintage, though **98** already quite honeyed, ready for drinking over next yr./2. **99** 🔥 ▼ in different league ("Best chardonnay I've made"); 100% barrel fermented, like pvs, but better quality cask imparts understated smoky-oak/vanilla sophistication to rich lees/lime/barley sugar. 90% new oak, partial malo. 13,3% alc. 3 800 cases.

🔥 **Sauvignon Blanc** ▼ Aromatic, individual style (much prized in Europe) with spice/wild herb/'buchu' aromatic constant amid vintage driven fruit variation. Promising when tasted for pvs ed, **99** has developed splendid creamy concentration (partly from 4 mths on lees), tropical/gooseberry richness matched by racy acid; some citrus zest in finish.13,3% alc. Released after yr. 2 000 cases. This and future unwooded. **98** 10% barrel fermented. **96**, **95**, **94** VG (100% oaked), all SAA.

Petit Verdot New **99** barrel sample (unrated) makes dramatic, front-of-stage entrance with great inky depths, cracked pepper/cinnamon excitement and layered choc/summer flower/cherry hedonism. Showstopper, originally planned for a blend (subsequently abandoned), small portion destined for blending with cab; future of remainder undecided. **Sangiovese** New **99** sample reveals fragrant, floral side of this classic Italian variety, plus more familiar spicy cherries; fairly prominent tannins enhance already weighty impression, though the whole retains some elegance. Potential 🔥.

. . . .

Plantation see International Wine Services
Pongrácz see JC le Roux
Porcupine Ridge see Boekenhoutskloof

. . . .

Porterville Co-op ▼ ℣

Swartland (see Swartland map) • Tasting & sales Mon—Fri 8—1; 2—5 Sat 8—11 • Cellar tours by appointment • Conference centre • Shady picnic spot (bring your own basket) • Owners 115 members • Winemaker André Oberholzer (since 1996) • Viticulturist André Oberholzer & Bennie Liebenberg • Production 15 000 tons 25 000 cases • PO Box 52 Porterville 6810 • Tel (022) 931-2170 • Fax (022) 931-2171

"I wish people would talk less nonsense about wine. Wine is made with passion. It should be drunk with passion and respect," is a cry from the heart of winemaker André Oberholzer who plies his craft in paragliders' paradise, Porterville, with its off-road trails and magnificent mountaintop Groot Winterhoek wilderness area. This scenic stretch of the Swartland was subjected to some pretty extreme weather last year: first exceptionally wet then exceptionally dry; exceptionally cool then exceptionally hot. But this man for all seasons expects some rather "exceptional" wines from the 2000 harvest to match.

🔥 **Pinotage Reserve** ▼ Breathes more rarefied air, quality wise, in **99**. Swashbuckling new-Cape style with deep wells of flavour matched by high vaulting alc (± 14%). Yr small oak adds spicy overtone to long, enveloping plum/pepper flavour. 1 200 cases.

Enigma 🔥 Keep-em-guessing blend offers the following clues: cherry, plum, toast, woodsmoke plus 'sweet' chewy tannins and med/full body. If your answer's shiraz, cab, merlot you're probably cribbing from pvs ed. Add splodge pinotage and you'd be right. Yr small oak. 640 cases. **Vin Rouge** 🔥 Those old BBQ companions, pinotage and cinsaut, ready to light your fire with this plummy/smoky **NV**; lightish toned with refreshingly moderate 12% alc. 500 cases. **Rosé** ✿✿ Pretty light rose colour introduces sweet tropical aromas of mainly guava, plus some strawberry. Drier than pvs for a more cuisine-friendly feel. **NV** (00) 90% colombard, rouged with pinotage. 300 cases. **Sauvignon Blanc** ✿✿ Clean cut-grass, some gooseberry, good tangy finish. **00** well made med-bodied quick quaff. 300 cases. **Emerald Riesling** ⚑ Pleasant, swiggable **00**, more vinous than fruity with bright finish. Med-bodied. Best in yr of harvest. 200 cases. **Late Vintage** ⚑ Quietish nose but better tropical flavour, sweet and simple. **NV** from chenin. 400 cases. **Red Jerepiko** ✿✿ Silky textured **NV** fortified dessert with gentle strawberry wafts and pleasing tingle of alc. Cinsaut/cab/pinotage blend. 17% alc. 1 000 cases. **Golden Jerepiko** ✿✿ Rich old-gold hue sets the tone for expansive muscat aromas/flavours in this **NV** fortified dessert, from low-cropped hanepoot. Dried herb/minty scents in orange zesty, spirity palate. 17% alc. 1 000 cases.

Pinotage ✿✿ 😊 Value quaffing hardly gets fresher or more flavourful than this. Fair amount of gentle tannin keeps the lid on springy cherry/raspberry fruit, some oaky hints from wood-chipping add extra interest. High alc (13,4%) needs watching. 550 cases. **Chenin Blanc** ✿✿ 😊 Soft papaya fruit beckons in **00**, smoothed by few grams sugar for crisp, lightish summer refreshment. 530 cases. **Chardonnay** ✿✿ 😊 Ripe peach, touches of lees and lime, sweet vanilla and pear make charming, flavoursome quaffing. Drink-young **00** with fairly moderate 12,7% alc. 500 cases. **Premier Grand Cru** ✿✿ 😊 All too often PGCs are bland; here's one with pizzazz: billowing sweet-pea fragrance, fresh tropical taste. **NV** (00) from colombard, not too alcoholic at 12,7% alc, not raspingly dry. 500 cases. **Blanc de Blanc** ⚑ 😊 Latest **NV** bottling revisits pvs lightish no-worries tippling formula: tropical fruit salad lightly sweetened and lifted by acid. Chenin/colombard (50/50). 800 cases.

....

Post House Cellar ♟ ♟ ♟

Stellenbosch (see Helderberg map) • Tasting by appointment • Owner/winemaker/viticulturist Nicholas Gebers • Vineyards 35 ha • Production 12 tons (900 cases own label) 70% red 30% white • PO Box 5635 Helderberg 7135 • Tel/fax (021) 842-2409 • E-mail ngebers@iafrica.com

A JAUNTY red post box beside the cellar is all that remains of rural Raithby's postal hub, destroyed by fire in the early 1900s. But the nostalgia continues in Nick Gebers' wines, featuring 'postage stamp' front labels with captivating cherub motifs. Today the old post house is home to the Gebers family and Nick Gebers' tiny low-ceilinged cellar. Inside is a neat wall of barrels, outside a little warehouse ('air conditioning' courtesy of hay-bales on the roof). All rustic and artesian and fun. "I don't believe in fiddling around with wines," is Gebers' philosophy, "wine has to make itself."

* **Merlot** Chunky style with abundant fruit and youthful tannins needing to smooth in bottle. Latest **99** improves on pvs; shows black cherries, herbs and eucalyptus. **98** more individual, earthy; with savoury nuances and irascible tannins demanding min 4 yrs. Naturally fermented in open tanks, 35% new oak; unfiltered. Power alcs at ± 14%. ± 110 cases.

* **Cabernet Sauvignon 99** a far cry from pvsly reviewed **97** ⚑, **98** ✿✿, both more rustic and sinewy. Latest shows complexity, structure, balance, with black cherry/tobacco/cedar whiffs from 35% new oak; tannins noticeable but suave. Barrel sample tasted, could rate higher on release. Vinification/alcs as above. ± 170 aces.

Chenin Blanc ⚑ **00** idiosyncratic, almondy, oaky from fermentation in 20% new Am casks. Punchy 13,8% alc. 180 cases.

....

Quantum see Lost Horizons

Radford Dale

Stellenbosch • Not open to the public (wines made at Onderkloof winery, Sir Lowry's Pass) • Owners Alex Dale & Ben Radford • Winemaker Ben Radford, with Gill Radford & Gus Dale • Viticulturist Lorna Roos • Vineyards 7 ha • Production ± 45 tons 3 000 cases 65% red 35% white • 67 Hillcrest Road Somerset West 7130 • Tel/fax (021) 852-3380 • E-mail vinum@netactive.co.za

BEN RADFORD and Alex Dale remind you of what wine's all about. Or should be. Of course they can talk the talk, walk the walk. They come to the Cape from the Barossa Valley and Burgundy (where they first met), with detours wherever vines grow and wines flow. Low key Radford, winemaking chief of the new Winecorp operation, has made some of the Cape's most gorgeous modern wines during his six years here; high voltage export specialist Dale, over the same period, has shown an uncommon grasp of Cape wine's problems and potential. But these qualifications are by the way in this joint venture of like minds. In a field where many take themselves and their 'art' very seriously, and in a region where wine, if not quite a religion is certainly politics, it's almost shocking to see the simplicity of the Radford Dale raison d'être. Fun. Enjoyment. Unpretentiousness. "There is too much smoke-and-mirrors in this industry," says Dale. "Too much snobbery, mediocrity and confusion. Radford Dale will always be uncomplicated, reliable, and — we hope — eminently gratifying. Enjoyment is the key, locked into quality. The overriding merit is the notion of sheer fun."

✿ **Merlot** As convincing, delicious a merlot as one could wish to find in Cape. Class (and temptation) shimmer through intense **99** spicy, meaty fragrances, silky, sweet-fruited flavour, compact minerally core. Plenty of staying power for another 4–6 yrs. New/used oak, mainly Fr, some Am, 1 yr; periodic micro-oxygenation (controlled injection of oxygen) for finer tannins, overall polish. Through malo. 525 cases. Sinewy, long **98** will benefit from yr/two before opening, age further 4–6. Helderberg fruit. Oak-matured, mainly Fr casks, 70% new. 13% alc.

✿ **Chardonnay** "A bunch of my sceptical Burgundian mates" are the people with whom Alex Dale would most like to share this splendid, elegant **99**, with more than hint of harmonious Old World flowers, oatmeal, roasted hazelnuts. Plus New World tropical limes, creamy palate weight, lovely focused length. Enjoyable now, with promise of future pleasure over 2 yrs at least. All barrel fermented, yr Fr/Am oak (80/20). Regular lees stirring; fined/filtered but not cold stabilised. 550 cases. Fine follow-up to rich, savoury **98**.

✿ **Shiraz** Barossa boy Ben Radford may be at the controls, but this **99** dial veers towards France: elegant (though no shortage of savoury intensity), Rhône-like flavour array (black pepper, chocolate, whiff wild herb). But there's some Aussie smoked bacon, too, and sweet cinnamon spice. Bit lean when tasted mid-2000, just after bottling, but R/D wager the pleasure index will climb, so give yr or more before pulling cork. Oak matured, 75% Fr barriques, balance Am, 75% new. Malo in cask. Unfiltered. 97 cases.

Rainbow Nation see Natural Corporation
Ravenswood see Pick 'n Pay

Remhoogte 🍷 🍷 🍷 🍷

Stellenbosch (see Stellenbosch map) • Tasting, sales, cellar tours by appointment • Bring your own picnic • Tourgroups up to 20 people • Walks • Views • Exhibition of hunting trophies (southern African antelope) • Owner Murray Boustred Trust • Winemaker Murray Boustred, with Jean Daneel • Consulting viticulturist Johan Pienaar • Farm manager Nickie Hannekom • Vineyards 35 ha • Production ± 250 tons (± 40 tons ± 3 000 cases own label) 100% red • PO Box 2032 Dennesig 7601 • Tel (021) 889-5005 • Fax (021) 889-6907 • E-mail remhoogte@adept.co.za

THERE ARE HORSE paddocks and lovely walks up to the Simonsberg on this rustic property (in a good neighbourhood, with L'Avenir and Morgenhof nearby), which recently applied for estate status. The cabernet and merlot from the 2000 harvest are "fantastic", enthuses owner Murray Boustred, who has evolved from construction/property development tycoon to hands-on maker of complex wines (the Merlot 98 made the Top 10 chart in *Wine*). The cellar has been enlarged to handle 150 tons and they're concentrating on quality red wines only, growing production each year. "My therapy is the bush," says Boustred, who takes to the saddle when he cannot escape to the wilds. The wines were not available for tasting for this ed. Pvs included (pvs rating in brackets)" **Merlot 98** (✿✿), **Pinotage 97** (✿✿), **Cabernet Sauvignon 95** (✿✿).

. . . .

R & de R-Fredericksburg see R&R

. . . .

R&R

Simondium (see Paarl map) • Tasting & cellar tours by appointment • Owners Anthonij Rupert & Baron Benjamin de Rothschild • Winemakers Schalk-Willem Joubert (since 1997), Clive Radloff (since 1997), Yann Buchwalter (1999) 90% red 10% white • PO Box 55 Simondium 7670 • Tel (021) 874-1648 • Fax (021) 874-1802 • E-mail info@fredericks‌burg.co.za • Website www.fredericksburg.co.za

JUST THE INITIALS OF, arguably, the leading wine wine familes of France and South Africa, the Ruperts and Rothschilds, now headline the wines from this joint production venture. It's a new-generation partnership, between Benjamin, son of the late Baron Edmond de Rothschild, and Anthonij, son of Dr Anton Rupert, and while its home-base in the Cape, the ambience is decidedly French. A tricouleur draped the cellar door when we visited, signifying France's Euro 2000 football victory. Bordeaux winemaker Yann Buchwalter (there's to be French assistance for Schalk-Willem Joubert and Clive Radloff in the cellar every vintage) is probably still celebrating. Pomerol guru Michel Rolland visits four times a year to consult and keep R&R on track, pursuing "greatness without bigness" and "the subtlety of the French classics", that sort of elusive, inspirational thing. Pick ripe, focus on elegance: those were the two basics Joubert first picked up from Rolland and they remain central, but he's recently added a new motivational chant: "Under-promise, over-deliver." The goal of world class wines is easier said than done, but drawing nearer by the vintage.

✿✿ **Baron Edmond** Further wood maturation (for total 24 mths in 100% new Fr oak) and softening in bottle have added extra nuances — and star wattage — to this long-nurtured, prestige claret. Maiden **98** — eventually available to an expectant market from Oct 2000 — announces itself with dramatic inky colour, waves of blackcurrant/forest fruit aromas woven with aromatic cedarwood, Bdx-like hint of tar. Restrained ripe fruit flavours with tobacco leaf complexity, fine merlot mineral thread. Firm dry tannins, persistent finish hint at long-term ageing potential (2008 at least). Merlot/cab (60/40), grapes selected in prime vyds, blended during vinification. 13,5% alc.

✿ **Classique** New 'Left Bank' version of blend above (merlot the junior partner here — 40%), with aspirations to same A-league quality. Maiden **98** "elegant rather than bold" says Schalk-Willem Joubert, echoing the cellar's motto. Vibrant ruby; nutty, earthy aromas, asphalt whiffs precede ripe raspberry/bramble array, mineral earthiness, hints of mushrooms. Firm but non-combative tannins allow access to refined berry fruit, unimpeded flavour flow into finish. Fr oak aged, all new barrels. 13,2% alc.

✿✿ **Baroness Nadine Chardonnay** Compelling, convincing Cape chardonnay, neither New nor Old World — best of both. First release **98** gaining refined opulence: shimmering golden colour with suggestion of green; subtle bouquet of ripe quince, hazelnut; tangy lime fruit embroidered with restrained oak spice, palate-lifting alc. Components seamlessly gathered into delicious chalky mouth-ful with penetrating finish. Mainly w-facing Pine Ridge, Bleskop vyds. Mix nat-ural/inoculated yeast, fermented/aged 14 mths new oak, 100% malo. Superlative now and through 2002.

....

Reserve Centenaire see Morgenhof

....

Reyneke Wines

Stellenbosch (see Stellenbosch map) • Tasting & sales weekday mornings or by appointment • Cellar tours by appoint-ment • Walks • Views • Uitzicht B&B cottages • Owner Reyneke Family Trust • Winemaker James Farquharson (since 1998) • Viticulturist James Farquharson "with some helps/tips from Rob Easthope" • Vineyards 20 ha • Production 160 tons (±35 tons ±2 000 cases own label) 70% red 30% white • PO Box 61 Vlottenburg 7604 • Tel/fax (021) 881-3517 • E-mail reyneke@netactive.com • Website www.reynekewines.co.za

"BASICALLY, we're making wine in a garage. And oh yes, a converted milking shed!" smiles James Farquharson, one half of this Polkadraai Hills partnership with Johan Reyneke (artist wife Mila Reyneke also keenly involved when not sketching en plein air or practising karate kicks). They met while Farquharson was looking at ways to control vineyard snails in an environmentally friendly way, and landed up on the Reyneke aerie, Uitzicht. "We're two guys of 28 and we are committed to make it work, so we have to do everything on the cheap," he explains modestly, but the wines certainly don't convey this impression. Reyneke looked at his partner one day and said: "I know you can make good wine, but the trouble is — you have to learn to SURF!" Thus began another apprenticeship for the winemaker who admits ruefully that he ended up unplaced in the first Vintners Classic — but his surf buddy came in a very unshabby overall third. Yet this is no endless beach party: eco-friendliness is taken very seriously (Johan Reyneke an Environmental Philosophy postgrad). And the farmhands here are among a handful in Cape with shares in the business.

✿ **Cabernet Sauvignon** ▼ Handsome new packaging, good whiffs tobacco pouch/pencil shavings hint at serious **98** intent. This confirmed in juicy, mouth-watering flavour of crushed blackberries, fine structure with glossy tannins and well toned body. Approachable, but better in 1–2 yrs. Oak aged, mixed cooper-age. 13,5% alc.

✿ **Cabernet Sauvignon-Merlot** New ▼ **99** shows the increasingly rare, more delicate side of Cape reds. Pretty damson/prune scented fruit, soft easy mouth-ful, juicy, lightish, but has all the right flavours, not overripe. Refined, with good oaking. 80/20 blend. Yr Nevers/Vosges casks, 40% new. 13% alc. 575 cases.

Sauvignon Blanc ⚹ New Delicate grass/veld flowers, still touch of guava fermen-tation character; fresh, very lively with piercing acidity which needs bit of time to settle. "No frills dry white," summarises winemaker. 250 cases.

....

Rhebokskloof Estate

Paarl (see Paarl map) • Tasting & sales daily 9—5 including all public holidays • Formal tasting/cellar tour by arrange-ment, R7 p/p • Cellar tours by arrangement during tasting hours • Restaurant (see Eat-out section) • Estate grown extra virgin olive oil • Conferences • Play area for children • Tourgroups • Views • Conservation area • Wheelchair-friendly • Owner Rhebokskloof Farming & Trading (Pty) Ltd • Winemaker/viticulturist Daniël Langenhoven (since 1998) • Viticulturist Werner de Villiers (since 1999) • Vineyards ± 100 ha • Production 500 tons 60% white 40% red • PO Box 7141 Noorder-Paarl 7623 • Tel (021) 863-8386 • Fax (021) 863-8504/393 • E-mail rhebok@iafrica.com • Website www.rhebokskloof.co.za

COMPLETE WITH LAKE and stately swans, the environment is an integral part of this gorgeous Cape property — it straddles two valleys and borders Paarl Nature Re-serve (a portion of the mountain is leased from the Reserve) — where shy rhebok can still be spotted in the vineyards. All very nice for winemaker and keen cyclist

Daniël Langenhoven, who keeps the wheels turning in the cellar. Last year saw the release of Rhebokskloof's first shiraz and there's an ongoing and extensive planting programme with a shift of focus to reds.

🍀 **Chardonnay Sur Lie** Big, open, oaky chardonnay, breakfast-special-style (marmalade on buttered toast), highly concentrated yet balanced with integrated wood in **99**. 13% alc. 500 cases. These can age a few yrs, developing creamy butterscotch/caramel richness, as 98 is starting to do.

🍀 Requiem 98 back-tasted mid-2000, still headed for future opulence: tropical fruit salad, soft honeyed tones and quite developed riesling (100%) minerally kerosene edge now apparent, all brushed with variety's signature spice. Continued patience will be rewarded. 14,61% alc.

Cabernet Sauvignon 🍀 Still on the up, **97** has lost its initial youthful tannic friskiness, allowing ripe berry fruit with tobacco/cedar fragrance to bloom. Oaked, 20% new casks. 13,3% alc. 1 500 cases. **Gamay Noir** 🍀 Some Burgundian 'damp cellar' sniffs in **98**, which unexpectedly developing into something special. Sophisticated smoky cherry notes, still fresh fruit and downy tannins. Should go very well coq au vin/venison. Not oaked. 13% alc. 500 cases. **97** VG. **Merlot** 🍀 Difficult-to-read 98 tightly shut mid-2000. Some dusty oak, light fruit, tight tannin the main features. 33% yr Fr oak, some new. 13% alc. **Pinotage** ☆ New Not an easy drink: raspy tannin, pinotagey bitterness partially leavened by only **98** modest fruit. Portion oak aged. 12,8% alc. 800 cases. **Dry Red** 🍀 **99** lightly oaked quaffer features the now customary juicy/creamy cherries, plums, spicy green pepper, light tannins for summer sloshing. Gamay/merlot/cab/pinotage. Could be lightly chilled. 13% alc. 3 500 cases. **Chardonnay Grande Reserve** 🍀 More restrained, Old World version of Sur Lie above, drier, less oaky: Fresh, lively citrus flavours and dry finish in **99**. Barrel fermented. 13,5% alc. 400 cases. **Grand Vin Blanc** 🍀 Peach melba richness in fat, viscous **00**, with strapping 13,8% alc which needs equally broad palated food or a comfortable couch. Chardonnay/sauvignon (75/25). Partly barrel matured. 1 000 cases. **Rhebok Dry White** ☆ **NV** more texture than fruit; honeyed/floral and some muted tropical tones in **99**. Bouquet Blanc 🍀 **00** summer sipper fragrant with narcissus, muscat and tropical fruit. Chardonnay/chenin/hanepoot mix. 14% alc. **Weisser Riesling Special Late Harvest** 🍀 New Out of the blue pops this instantly aged, heavily honeyed **97**. Past its best; some stalky, bitter end notes. 13,3% alc. 500 cases. **Tamay Brut Sparkling** 🍀 Attractive dryish sparkler; gently fizzy, whiffs of riesling in unexpectedly developed bouquet. Chardonnay/riesling, splash hanepoot. **NV** (99). Big 13,5% alc. 400 cases.

Rickety Bridge 🍷 🍷 🍷

Franschhoek (see Franschhoek map) • Tasting & sales daily 10—5 Tasting fee R5/tasting refundable on purchase • Cellar tours by arrangement • Gifts • Views ("This is Franschhoek, after all") • Wheelchair-friendly • Owner Duncan Spence • Winemaker Boela Gerber (since 1998), with Dawid Gqirana (since 1998) • Viticulturist Boela Gerber • Vineyards 16 ha • Production 120 tons 65% red 35% white • PO Box 455 Franschhoek 7690 • Tel (021) 876-2129 • Fax (021) 876-3486 •

"I'M VERY HAPPY with the semillon here," reports Boela Gerber, young winemaking whiz who, as then-deputy to André van Rensburg was poised to take up residency in the Stellenzicht cellar before being lured away with the prospect of whipping the Rickety Bridge vineyards and cellar into shape. "Actually, I'd plant the whole farm with semillon and shiraz, they're so good. Being so small, we'll stick to varieties which have proven themselves," continues Gerber, a confirmed francophile whose crushes in Bordeaux have left him disdainful of local wineries turning out showpieces lashed with American oak. "I want to make food wines with structure and elegance. The French are best at this." Rickety Bridge's new owner, UK entrepreneur Duncan Spence, is content to let the maverick do his thing. Which includes after-hours mountain biking and fly-fishing with his wine-mate Adi Badenhorst of Rustenberg.

✿ **Shiraz** This cellar's signature, heaped with awards: debut **96** gold on Veritas; **97** *Wine* ✿✿ current **98** ✿✿ Michelangelo gold, *Wine* ✿✿. **98** light coloured but not lacking intensity: cracked pepper/woodsmoke/green pepper/spice and toasty oak all resonate in big, extra-long palate with mulberries at the core. 13,6% alc. Unblended preview of **99** for Mar 2001 release, rated ✿ mid-2000. Deeper hued, more minerally than pvs, but not quite as concentrated. On form of pvs, however, wattage could rise with time. 13,2% alc. These from single vyd on own farm, "fruit always excellent — no need for fancy techniques". Mix Fr/Am casks. 140 cases.

✿ **Merlot** Fragrant style with clean, well judged oak backing; usually some floral/earthy hints with oak-spicy vanilla perfume. **98** features scents of red roses (of which Claudia Schiffer, with whom winemaker would like to share this wine, might approve), some choc-nut richness and the house's signature firmness in palate. Upcoming **99** (sample, pre-blending) richer, more mouthcoatingly tannic. 13,2% alc.

✿ **Paulinas Reserve 96** VVG, SAA has acquired mellow tones of woodsmoke/ripe berries, and though softly abundant tannins could carry the wine through winemakers' projected 7–8 yrs, we suggest you enjoy it now and over next 1–2 yrs while at its best. 18 mths Fr oak, new/used. After farm's founder, Paulina de Villiers. Special label, bottle, individual box. 400 cases.

✿ **Chardonnay** ▼ Expansive barrel fermented/aged style, deeply flavoured, excellent with food. Complex, inviting **99** bouquet of pineapple/marmalade/toasted almonds, some peach/vanilla echoes in smooth, soft centered palate with 'sweet'/dry finish. Yr in casks, mainly new, partial malo. 13,9% alc. 400 cases.

✿ **Semillon** ▼ "Best 10 casks (out of ±72), made for food — smoked trout, spicy chicken, pork …" Winemaker's culinary inspirations come alive when tasting **99**, with intricate spicy/toasty lime, peach pip, vanilla nuances, fragrant hints of lemon grass. Full-bodied (13,5% alc). Yr new Fr/Am oak. 230 cases.

✿ **Sauvignon Blanc** ▼ **00** headlong downhill racer, holding nothing back in the flavour stakes: tropical guava/pineapple/mango; almost sweet fruit impression which satisfyingly cut with fine-tuned acid. Pvs **99** cloaked in similar Caribbean togs of sweet melon and mango. 13,2% alc. 280 cases.

Cabernet Sauvignon ✿ **99**, for Mar 2001 release, firm but nicely fleshed with comfortable fruit. Good maturation potential. 15 mths new Fr barriques. 500/450 cases.

Duncan's Creek range

New:

Dry Red ✿ "Eating, laughing, sharing style," Boela Gerber borrows a famous Cape white-wine slogan to describe **99**, 100% cab with cassis, strawberry and some tobacco whiffs; easy drinking for now and for 2–3 yrs. 18 mths oaked. 13,6% alc.
Dry White Bright fruit from initial peach/guava waft to crisp herbs/cut-grass finish. **00** (sample — unrated) positively gulpable, so watch that 13,7% alc. Chenin/sauvignon. These 200 cases each.

Rider's Drift Wines

New ▼

Stellenbosch (see Stellenbosch map) • Tasting by appointment • Owner Bolognesi Marketing & Distribution (Pty) Ltd • Production 2 450 cases 50% red 40% white • PO Box 919 Stellenbosch 7599 • Tel (021) 886-5080 • Fax (021) 886-5081 • E-mail info@ridersdrift.co.za • Website www.ridersdrift.co.za

A PRIVATE, international marketing/distribution operation specialising in customers' own-labels and house brands is behind this range of consumer friendly quaffers. Wines below all 99.

Western Cape Pinotage ✿ 😊 Soft, satisfying, plummy quaff with some smoky-oak notes for added interest. 13% alc. **Cinsaut-Cabernet Sauvignon** ✿ 😊 So barbeque-cordial, should be draped with a string of sausage. Built-in woodsmoke, raspberry softness to glide smoothly from fireside to table.

✿ **Paarl Pinotage** ◥ Marginally more concentrated, serious, than counterpart above; good soft black cherry fruit, some plummy depths with enough supple tannin to uncork now or keep yr/2. 13% alc.

Chenin Blanc-Chardonnay ‡ Honeyed bottle age imparts some gentle charm, but probably better in flush of youth. Lightly oaked. 13% alc.

. . . .

Riebeek Cellars

Riebeek Kasteel (see Swartland map) • Tasting & sales Mon—Fri 8—5 Sat 8.30—12 (closed public holidays) • Cellar tours by appointment • Bring your own picnic • Wheelchair-friendly • Owners 63 shareholders • Cellarmaster Zakkie Bester (since 1999) • Winemaker Eric Saayman • Consulting viticulturist Paul Wallace (VineWise) • PO Box 13 Riebeek Kasteel 7307 • Tel (022) 448-1213 • Fax (022) 448-1281 • E-mail riebeek@mweb.co.za

THESE DAYS it would appear that you have to drive all the way to this Swartland cellar to pick up A Few Good Men. Three-quarters of the limited-quantity wines in this range are allocated for export, the remainder kept for sale from the cellar itself, where you may find more good men than you bargained for. High-energy new cellarmaster Zakkie Bester (who was winemaker at De Wet in Worcester for over a decade), has joined innovative winemaker Eric Saayman. Another facet here is sports development (soccer, rugby and cricket) for the local community, a promise of even more good men to come from this cutting-edge cellar in the quaint village of Riebeek Kasteel. The range, not tasted for this edition, includes (pvs ratings in brackets): Riebeek range: **Pinotage 98** (✿✿), **Pinotage-Tinta Barocca 98** (✿✿), **Chardonnay 00, Chenin Blanc 00, Chenin Blanc Bush Vine 00, Anaïs 99** (‡), **Brut NV** (99) (‡), **Hanepoot NV** New; A Few Good Men range: **Cabernet Sauvignon 98** (✿✿), **Shiraz 98** (✿✿); Cape Table range (1 ℓ value packs): **Cellar Red, Cellar Rosé, Chardonnay, Cellar White, Cellar Gold**.

. . . .

Rietrivier Co-op

Montagu (see Klein Karoo map) • Tasting & sales Mon—Thu 8—5 Fri 8—3 • Cellar tours by arrangement • Play area for children • Tourgroups • Views • Owners 45 members • Manager/winemaker Chris-Willem de Bod (since 1999) with Petrus Bothma (since 1994) • Vineyards 300 ha • Production 6 000 tons (2 500 cases own label) 95% white 5% red • PO Box 144 Montagu 6720 • Tel/fax (023) 614-1705 • E-mail pingeye@lando.co.za

THIS CO-OP has kept its wines to itself and its 45 members for the past few years. Now, good news for curious consumers in general — and travellers through the beautiful Montagu valley in particular — is that new manager-winemaker Chris-Willem de Bod's doors are open for tasting and buying. Classic red and white varieties are being planted here; colombard and chenin blanc are not destined to remain the majority grapes for much longer. Wines below all New to this ed.

✿ **Montagu Muscadel** In an area recognised for this sweet fortified dessert style, here's a standout. **00** winks at you through luminous coral-pink gauze, billows muscat/honeysuckle/spicy cinnamon which echo in spirity palate. 300 cases.

Chardonnay ‡ Fermentation with oak chips creates super-charry effect in hot, alcoholic (14%) dry palate. 300 cases. **Colombard** Off-dry **00** untasted. 300 cases. **Late Vintage** ✿ Pleasing tropical tones in gentle **NV** sweet dessert, lightish effortless quaffing. 300 cases. **Hanepoot ✿ 00** intensely spirity fortified dessert, some low key muscat flavour. 300 cases.

> **Petite Rouge** ✿✿ 😊 Light coloured/toned **NV** which glides effortlessly across the palate, ends softly in wafts of sweet strawberries. **Petite Blanc** ✿✿ 😊 No-frills lightish semi-dry **NV** quaffer with peach/dried apricot charms. Super-fresh cut of acidity finishes cleanly. This and Rouge above 500 ml screw-tops. 36 000 bottles. **Sparkling Vin Doux** ✿✿ 😊 Fans of sweet bubbly styles need look no further than this lightish, fresh, well made **NV** for bargain tippling. Muscatty, creamy texture. 300 cases.

Rietvallei Estate

Robertson (see Robertson map) • Not open to the public Tasting & sales at Bergkelder (see that entry) • Cellar tours by appointment • Owner/winemaker/viticulturist Johnny Burger • Vineyards 142 ha • Production 2 000 tons 95% white 5% red • PO Box 386 Robertson 6705 • Tel (023) 626-4147 • Fax (023) 626-4514

IT'S quite a leap from the rustic Klaas Voogds riverside to the sophisticated hotspots of Stockholm, but Johnny Burger's warming Red Muscadel dessert, still based on his grandfather's hand-written recipe tacked up behind the cellar door, seems to be a tipple *sans frontiers*. Having conquered Sweden, hunter/winemaker Burger's closing in on his next quarry: a red wine cellar which he hopes to build to make a long hankered-after Cabernet Sauvignon.

✿✿**Red Muscadel** 🏆 Among the gems of this fortified dessert style in Cape; deep flavoured, intensely sweet but seldom cloying. Current **98** with uncharacteristic (but good) dried-fruit-nuts character, some cherry/quince tones in palate (in contrast to more standard floral/muscat perfume). But same broad viscous palate, tangy spirit which leaves palate refreshed. Bushvines, some 91 yrs old. Bargain priced. 17,4% alc.

Chardonnay ✿✿ Partially barrel fermented **98** holding in there, though honeyed bottle age now beginning to sideline the fruit. Suggest drink up. 13,5% alc.

Rijk's Private Cellar   New 🍷 🍷 🍷

Tulbagh (see Tulbagh map) • Tasting & sales daily 9.30—4.30 • Cellar tours for large groups by appointment • Restaurant and luxury guest house (see Stay-over section) • Conference facilities • Play area for children • Tourgroups • Gifts • Walks • Views • Wheelchair-friendly • Owner Neville Dorrington • Winemaker Charl du Plessis (since 1999) • Consultant viticulturist Johan Wiese (since 1996) • Farm manager Boet Eddy (since 1996) • Vineyards 31 ha • Production ± 15 000 cases 80% red 20% white • PO Box 400 Tulbagh 6820 • Tel (021) 230-1622 • Fax (021) 230-1650 • E-mail wine@rijks.co.za • Website www.rijks.co.za

IF ANYONE succeeds in putting traditionally white-wine Tulbagh on the New World red-wine map, on present form it will be Charl du Plessis. This was made clear when the young ex-Boland winemaker clanked offstage with a slew of 2000 Young Wine Show gold medals for first-crop wines which had been entered "just to see whether we're going the right way". The sparkly infants had been born in the modern cellar on Neville Dorrington's Rijk's farm, which stretches scenically below Tulbagh's mountain fringe and features a gourmet eat-out, luxury sleep-over, herb garden and conference centre. "Things at Rijk's have been approached professionally from the very beginning," du Plessis states. "We do everything on a small scale. There are 31 ha under vines, with no single block larger than one hectare." The plan, he reveals, is to groom the oak-fermented Chardonnay for the cellar's starring role. We predict, however, the promising reds below won't remain in supporting roles for very long. Wines below all **00**, most were sampled too young for realistic assessment.

Pinotage Sniff, taste and feel your excitement grow. This massive (14,5%) but balanced, ripe and wonderfully silky customer, though far too young for a conclusive assessment, seems headed for the Cape big league. One to watch. To go through 18 mths Am (mainly), Fr oak schooling (as are reds below). 400 cases. **Shiraz** (unrated). Young Wine Show gold plaudits here (and for Merlot, Chardonnay below) mark this as a serious Cape shiraz contender. (Winemaker remarks, on less weighty note, "the only wine which can handle rich barbecued galjoen".) Strapping 14% alc. 500 cases. **Merlot** Four ✶s winking? Densely woven cloak of black fruits, embroidered with choc. 13,9% alc. 500 cases. **Cabernet Sauvignon** More refined than blockbusters above, but plenty of charm, balance (even at weighty 14% alc). Too young to rate. 430 cases. **Chardonnay** Mid-2000 showing juicily ripe tropical vanilla. New Fr oak fermented/aged. 13,4% alc. 260 cases. **Chenin Blanc** "I'm still learning," winemaker allows, but unrated preview shows he has the knack. Ripe pears and tingly acidity. Partly barrel fermented 13,5% alc. 550 cases. **Sauvignon Blanc** ✶✶ Green apple/gooseberry tang in this early drinker, plenty of ripe sauvignon fruit. 13,5% alc. 270 cases. **Semillon** Two single blocks, night harvested, yielded 260 cases, showing smoky vanilla oak, passionfruit and kiwi. Big wine at nearly 14% alc. Unrated.

. . . .

Rite Wines see Shoprite Checkers
River see International Wine Services
River's Edge see Weltevrede

. . . .

Robertson Winery

Robertson (see Robertson map) • Tasting & sales Mon—Thu 8—5 Fri 8—4.30 Sat 9—1 • Cellar tours by appointment • Conference/function hall • Miniature wine museum • Owners 42 members • General manager Bowen Botha • Production manager Lolly Louwrens • Winemaker Francois Weich, with Eduard Malherbe • Consulting viticulturist Briaan Stipp (VinPro) • Production 24 600 tons 87% white 10% red 3% rosé • PO Box 37 Robertson 6705 • Tel (023) 626-3059 • Fax (023) 626-2926 • E-mail info@robertsonwine.co.za or sales@robertsonwine.co.za

BACK TO THE future at this modern, industrious Robertson-town winery, with its resonant address at No 1 Constitution Street. Originally an offshoot of the Castle Wine & Brandy Company, one of the major producers of 'Cape Smoke', Robertson has once again turned its hand to brandy production and hopes to release the contents of the first few barrels, which "maturing quietly in oak and looking extremely promising" according to production manager Lolly Louwrens, in about 3—4 years. Though these nostalgic drops may briefly steal the limelight, it's the enormous wine production lines which continue to form the guts of this operation, handling 25 000 tons of grapes from 43 member farms and producing over 18-million litres of wine a year. Beyond its own ranges, the winery runs a booming bottling/filling business — Pernod-Ricard's complete Long Mountain, Gecko Ridge and La Fontaine ranges, for example, are filled on the premises. On the eve of its 60th anniversary (founded 1941), the winery unveiled a R10-million red-wine production facility to accommodate an envisaged 2005 crush of 8 000 tons of black grapes — a fourfold increase. "We're a busy winery," says Louwrens laconically.

Wide River range

Cellar's flagship 'Reserves'

✶ **Cabernet Sauvignon** ▼ Modern, well made cab, **98** carefully oaked to show off ripe berry/plummy fruit. Good minerally texture with long approachable tannins for now or for 3—4 yrs. 13% alc. **99** preview up a level: juicier, better structure.

✶ **Retreat Sauvignon Blanc** ▼ New World mouthfilling style, high kicking alc (14%) and most attractive. Pure sauvignon 'green' aromatics ('khaki' bush, nettle, cat's pee) plus riper passionfruit nuances. Clean, zesty, balanced. Vyd selection.

✿ **Special Late Harvest** Limpid buttercup yellow colour introduces delicate **99** botrytis dessert. Rose petal, freesia bouquet; extra-smooth, almost viscous texture that carries to gently sweet finish with hints of botrytis. A good partner for fresh, sappy fruit salad.

✿ **Almond Grove Weisser Riesling Noble Late Harvest** Standout wine of range and contender for A-league status in Cape. First release **99** *Wine* ✿✿ botrytised riesling in full, elegant flight. Lime/apricot fragrances with ripe peaches and bits of marmalade/caramel in palate. All taper gently to bright, crisp, clean finish. **00**, untasted, flew out of cellar. 9,5% alc. 375 ml.

✿ **Red Muscadel** New Classic example of this signature regional fortified dessert style. Luscious, spirity **NV** with billowing muscat/honeysuckle perfume, intensely sweet, silky yet lively.

Chardonnay ✿ Seriously oaked in **99**, barrel fermented/aged 10 mths — which too obvious when tasted mid-2000. May come together, so perhaps give time. 13,5% alc. **Late Vintage** ✿ **99** lightish 'banana boy' flavours, overwhelming sweetness.

Robertson range

✿ **Cabernet Sauvignon** Sampled young, **00** showed more promise than pvs. Vanilla savouriness framed by good long tannins. Lightly oaked. 13% alc.

✿ **Special Late Harvest 99** particularly good yr for this consistent botrytised sweet dessert, from gewürz. **00**, sampled young, promising. Zippier, with all pvs lemon-lime/honey/botrytis woven with tingly acidity. Med-bodied.

Merlot 00 too young to rate conclusively, but showing ✿ potential. Concentrated plums, some violet wafts, fragrant toasty oak. 13% alc. **Pinotage** New Too early to pin stars on unwooded **00** tank sample. Some acetone/ester top notes, earthy undertones. 13% alc. **Shiraz** New **00** still in formative stages (so unrated). Bouquet tightly closed, some smoky plum, black pepper, vanilla notes. Potential ✿ (?). **Chardonnay** ✿ Tropical-toned **00** with buttery vanilla palate, clean dry citrus finish. Lightly wooded. 13,3% alc. **Chenin Blanc** ✿ Lightish **00**, gentle, no-ceremonies just-dry swigging; some lemonade tones. **Colombard** ✿ Made off-dry in drink-young **00**, lightish tropical/pineapple tang, tastes smooth rather than sweet. **Beaukett** ✿ Semi-sweet white dessert from gewürz/colombard/muscadel. Petally, smooth **00**, lightly spicy. **Late Vintage** ✿ Lightish, well made **99** white; sweet, clean, effortless. Chenin/muscadel. **Red Muscadel 99**, tasted as sample, in present form rates ✿. More toffee-choc character than muscat. **Port** ✿ Promising **99** infant of pvs ed has grown into handsome adult, with swirling shiraz-like woodsmoke (though that grape not in blend of ruby cab, merlot, cab); tastes dryish and more spirity than 16% alc would suggest.

Ruby Cabernet ✿ 😊 Seldom fails to please. Brightly coloured, med-bodied **99** offers sappy blackberries/plums, supple drinkability. **00** (sample) more of the same. **Dry Red** ✿ 😊 Charming anytime fun wine with bright raspberry taste. Lightish ruby cab/merlot/cinsaut blend. **NV**. **Sauvignon Blanc** ✿ 😊 **00** rung above pvs; reductive treatment from vyd to cellar delivers vibrant palate tension, good minerally threads.13,2% alc.

Silversands range

Chardonnay ✿ Good vinous qualities in **00**, full bodied (± 13% alc) unpretentious dry quaffer. Lightly wooded. 13,5% alc.

'Varietal' 2 ℓ box range

On release, SA's first certified bag-in-box wines with varietal labels/vintage dates.

Sauvignon Blanc ✿✿ ☺ **00** pick of these bag-in-boxes. Bright nettle/ripe gooseberry freshness, herby touches, mouthfilling dry flavour. 13% alc.

Chardonnay ✿✿ Lightly oaked, lively peach/pear flavours shine through; soft, gentle dry finish. 13,6% alc.

Vinipak range

Good-value, hike/picnic/beach party 'combiblocs' in 500/1 000 ml. All NV.
Dry Red ✿✿ See under Robertson range above. **Dry White** ✿ Lightish varietal allsort, smooth, surprisingly elegant. **Late Harvest** ✿ Light (10% alc), sweet, pleasant quaffer.

. . . .

Robert's Rock

LIFESTYLE RANGE by KWV aimed at foreign 'wendis' (wine enthusiasts, no disposable income) in 25–35 year age group. Robert Gordon a military man and colourful figure of the early Cape who gave his name to one of the pearl-like rocks on Paarl Mountain. Labels below WO Western Cape. See also KWV International, Cathedral Cellar. KWV's ranges generally not for sale in SA, though regularly selected to fly with SAA.

✿ Cabernet Sauvignon-Merlot Half a degree up the pleasure scale in lightly oaked **98** ✿✿, fairly firmly structured yet strong fruity presence, choc-cherry tastes in good long dry finish. 65/35 ratio. **97** juicy, full but not quite as much oomph.

✿ Shiraz-Malbec Shiraz's gutsy spice, malbec's broadening tang add up to quite a serious Rhône-style red in **99**. Vibrant fruit kept under control by 6 mths barrelling in seasoned casks. 58/42 blend. 12,9% alc.

✿ Chardonnay-Semillon Winning recipe here: 55/45 ratio in **00**, chardonnay briefly dipped in oak (2 mths) for creamy finish; semillon gives savoury lime/mineral character. Can safely keep couple of yrs, **99** ✿✿ fresh, very drinkable though not as characterful.

Pinotage-Pinot Noir ✿✿ **98** not as successful as pvs. Latest 70/30 blend quite tannic; lacks plummy flavours to fill the mid palate (and consumers' trolleys?). Yr 2nd fill oak. **Chenin Blanc-Chardonnay** ✿✿ Drink-soon **00** charming medley of biscuity chardonnay, sappy tropical fruits with guava predominant. Lightly oaked. Good value 60/40 blend.

. . . .

Rob Roy

POPULAR 5 ℓ range from Robertson Winery. Untasted for this ed, the range includes: **Dry Red**, **Dry White**, **Late Harvest**.

. . . .

Robusto Wines   New ▼

Not open to the public • Owner/winemaker/viticulturist Teddy Hall • Vineyards 3 ha • Production 6,5 tons 60% white 40% red • PO Box 2868 Somerset West 7129 • Tel 083-461-8111 • Fax (021) 881-3514 • E-mail winemaker@kanu.co.za

IT'S THE DREAM of most winemakers to own their own label and Kanu/Goedgeloof cellarmaster Teddy Hall, having given up his day job in the business world (and transplanted his young family from Pretoria) to study viticulture & oenology at Stellenbosch, has now taken the plunge. In 2000 he made the Chenin below from Hall-managed vines on a breezy Koelenhof hill, where the view is enough to make any grapes dance and sing. Probe this fungi-truffling gourmet (with a weakness for splashy cigars, which he can't — yet — afford) for a table partner for the Chenin and you get a mouthful: pan fried Cape salmon, butternut gnocchi with sage butter, aubergine and mozzarella bake and whew! freshly picked strawberries.

✿ **Chenin Blanc** Chenin evangelist Teddy Hall believes this formerly ubiquitous, now increasingly endangered variety is the "Cape cult grape of the future". This **00**, a 'robusto' in its own way, might just help prove him right: intense, plump, luscious fruit; fresh-sliced apple, mint and honey with sweet oak spice from new oak; sweetness again in palate balanced by tangy fruit acid. Low-cropped (5 t/ha), fermented/aged 8 mths Fr barriques. 300 cases.

. . . .

Rocheburg see Arlington
Rock Ridge see Vinfruco
Roland's Reserve see Seidelberg

. . . .

Romansrivier Winery

Wolseley (see Worcester map) • Tasting & sales Mon—Fri 8—5 Sat 8.30—11.30 • Cellar tours by appointment • Bring your own picnic • Conference/reception facilities for up to 200 guests • Views • Wheelchair-friendly • Owners 43 members • Winemaker Albie Treurnicht (since 1998) • Viticulturist Hanno van Schalkwyk (VinPro) • Production 7 200 tons (6 000 cases own label) 95% white 5% red • PO Box 108 Wolseley 6830 • Tel (023) 231-1070/80 • Fax (023) 231-1102 • E-mail romans@cybertrade.co.za

A PREMIUM wood-matured Cabernet-Ruby Cabernet blend has joined the league at this mountain-ringed winery (with its breathtaking price range — all wines under R20!). Winemaker Albie Treurnicht leads the entrepreneurial approach — recently extended to include an experimental block with six "alternative" cultivars. "We have planted petit verdot, barbera and sangiovese, among others, to determine their suitability to our specific conditions" (Romansrivier is about 40 km from Worcester in the direction of Wolseley). Experimentation, innovation and entertainment at this cellar have three sources — a Swiss export market (the Ceres Merlot and Cabernet Sauvignon), Inus Muller (currently production manager at Stellenbosch Vineyards and the one who set Albie Treurnicht firmly on the wine path) and Treurnicht's hobbies (cooking, fishing and mountain biking).

✿ **Koelfontein Merlot** ⟍⟋ Cellar can't meet demand for this flagship red, vyd selection from cool-climate Koelfontein farm. Good varietal expression (aromatic plums, violets, some green pepper hints plus blackberry/raspberry); juicy tannins tapering to long fresh finish. Yr barrelled, none new. 13,4% alc. 300 cases. **97** SAYWS gold.

Vino Rood ✿✿ ☺ "Sales double annually," reports Albie Treurnicht. Strawberries, twist of pepper, supple tannins for instant, succulent quaffability. Medbodied blend cinsaut/ruby cab, lightly Am oak-aged. 600 cases.

Cabernet Sauvignon-Ruby Cabernet ✿✿ 𝐍𝐞𝐰 **98** potentially very good wine, though needs time, careful monitoring to catch at peak. Terrific bouquet of berries/green pepper/eucalyptus leaf, some fragrant medicinal whiffs; dusty oak and sweetish fruit presently lashed by tannins. Give min 2 yrs to settle. 51/49 blend, new-barrel fermented, aged 12 mths ("My pet project of that yr," says winemaker). 280 cases. **Ceres Chardonnay** ✿✿ Partly oaked **99** has lost its chirpy vibe since last tasted. Better young. 12,6% alc. 300 cases. **Mosterthoek Sauvignon Blanc** ✿✿ **00** nettly/cut-grass tastes, perky dry finish. Med-bodied sauvignon for early drinking, from single vyd block. 300 cases. **Grand Cru** ⚱ Unpretentious drink-soon quaffer, lightly honeyed, not too dry. **NV** (00) chenin/chardonnay. 1 500 cases. **Colombard** ✿✿ Off-dry **NV** (00) offers usual bouncy guava mouthful, mouthwatering acid which needs food. Drink soon to catch at best. 600 cases. **Ceres Vin Blanc** ⚱ Latest med-bodied **NV** (00) from colombard, unusually low-keyed; tech-

. . . .

nically semi-sweet yet briskly acidic. 900 cases. **Jerepico** ✿ Good everyday/night fortified sweet dessert from hanepoot, full, clean-spirited. Regional show class winner. 17% alc. **NV** (98). 260 cases. **Ruby Port** ⚡ **NV** (98) Earthy prunes, glow-producing whack of spirit (19% alc), ideal for winter warming. Tinta b/ruby cab, yr seasoned barrels. 200 cases. Also available: **Mosterthoek Cabernet Sauvignon 98** not ready for tasting.

. . . .

Roodendal

LIMITED VOLUME cabernet sauvignon, generally made every second year, usually in odd years. 1979, maiden vintage, styled to precise specs: grapes ex-Coastal region, young vineyards in light soils on higher slopes. Never advertised, and so sought after, it quickly sells out. By Stellenbosch Farmers' Winery.

Cabernet Sauvignon ✿ Current **97** good and ready: some secondary whiffs creeping in — tobacco, cigarbox, cedar; velvet cassis juiciness in light frame of tannin. Small portion oaked. Med-bodied; aged 2 yrs in bottle before release.

. . . .

Roodezandt Co-op

Robertson (see Robertson map) • Tasting & sales Mon—Fri 8—5.30 Sat 9—12.30 • Cellar tours by arrangement • Wheelchair-friendly • Owners 53 members • General manager Abé Rossouw • Winemakers Christie Steytler (since 1980), with Elmo du Plessis (since 1999) • Consulting viticulturist Briaan Stipp (VinPro) • Vineyards ±1 500 ha • Production ±24 000-27 000 tons (7 000 cases own label) 93% white 7% red • PO Box 164 Robertson 6705 • Tel (023) 626-1160 • Fax (023) 626-5074 • E-mail roodez@intekom.co.za

BALTUS Kloppers, recently retired stalwart (nearly 40 years on the Board), gives his resounding name to the new flagship, Balthazar Classic. Made from cabernet sauvignon, it's a statement of this energetic Robertson co-op's quality intentions and barometer of the move from overwhelmingly white to an ever larger proportion of red wine. Adding momentum to the swing is fresh face Elmo du Plessis, who reports that the 53 growers work hand in glove with him, winemaking chief Christie Steytler (another seasoned hand: 2000 marked his twentieth year here) and vineyard guru Briaan Stipp. "With reds especially, we pick for ripeness," du Plessis says, "we don't only go on sugar levels." They award members with certificates for quality grapes, so it's hardly surprising that they have a loyal local clientele and a healthy European export market.

✿ **Balthazar Classic 98** VG a worthy tribute to this industrious cellar's chairman of the past 25 yrs. Warm stewed mulberries/strawberries with hints of choc, sown together by dense but supple tannin with a keen vanilla edge. Yr Fr oak. 12,4% alc. **99** barrel sample reveals striking deep colour/flavour, aromatic sweet redcurrants and oak spice, well (but not over-) extracted fruit. Promising.

✿ **White Muscadel** This traditional Cape dessert a regular show winner. **00** ✿, sampled young, already very drinkable; bright yellow-gold, 'oily' whiffs of marmalade/coconut, super-silky unctuous muscat flavour with seamlessly absorbed spirit. 17,5% alc. ±450 cases. **98** absolutely gorgeous now; complex, smooth, intense, beautiful bottle age richness emerging. Clearly a slow starter, now beginning to fly. Unbelievable bargain at R13 from cellar door.

> **Cabernet Sauvignon** ✿ ☺ **98**'s ready and a pleasure to drink: plump cassis, nice toasty oak and soft, creamy finish. Yr small Fr casks. 12,5% alc. ±1 400 cases. **99** not available for tasting. **Sparkling Demi Sec** ⚡ ☺ Party animal, this frisky, light (10% alc) bubble with balanced sweetness and delicate apple/marzipan aromas. Unpretentious and fun. Carbonated. 500 cases.

Keizer's Creek ✿ Latest **NV** (00) bottling unusually assertive, earthy/smoky/stewed fruit tones best with rustic fare. Standard ruby cab/cab/merlot mix, unwooded. 13% alc. 2 000 cases. **Colombard 00** (sample, unrated) fragrant with jasmine/melon touches and dry kiwifruit tang. Good summer quaffer. 13% alc. ±600 cases. **Sauvignon Blanc** ✿ Assertively fresh **00** lightish in all departments; some muted pear/green pea tones. Dry. ±600 cases. **Colombar-Chardonnay** ✿ **00** crisp, full-bodied dry white with fruit salady tastes and hints of sherbet. ±600 cases. **Late Harvest** ✿ **NV** Supple, slip-down semi-sweet with light peachy finish, some marmalade tones from bottle age. Med-bodied. ±300 cases. **Special Late Harvest** ⚘ Richer version of above (also muscadel/chenin); perfumed jasmine/talcum/candy floss; sweet, soft lingering fruit salad tastes. Med-bodied. ±1 500 cases. **Red Muscadel** ⚘ Ethereal topaz/ruby colour sets the tone for **98** fortified dessert's delicate rose petal/strawberry sweetness, which carries softly into lightly spirity finish. 17,1% alc. ±250 cases. **Port 00** tank sample very promising: ripe smoky fruit, sweet vanilla wafts swirling in luscious choc palate. 10% alc. ±450 cases. Good 'SA style' — no Portuguese varieties — from ruby cab, as was still-available **98** ✿, now showing soft, smoky tones. Not unsatisfying. Oak aged.

Rooiberg Winery

Robertson (see Robertson map) • Tasting & sales Mon—Fri 8-5.30 Sat 9—3 • Cellar tours by appointment • Light lunches/refreshments in tea garden during tasting hours. Or bring your own picnic • Wheelchair-friendly • Owners 35 members • CEO/exports Johan du Preez (since 1996) • Winemakers Tommy Loftus (since 1989), Eben Rademeyer (since 1996), Pieter van Aarde (since 1998) • Viticulturist Stefan Joubert (since1998) • Vineyards 720 ha • Production 150 000 cases 85% white 15% red • PO Box 358 Robertson 6705 • Tel (023) 626-1663 • Fax (023) 626-3295 • E-mail rooiberg@wine.co.za • Website www.rooiberg.co.za

RUSSIANS and Japanese are this bustling co-op cellar's most far-flung fans; locals know why. We've long rated it one of the goodies (good value, good taste) and the glamorous self-service buying and tasting area sets new standards for cellar-door shopping. (Whatever you bear away, or mail-order, don't miss the absolutely cracking Red Jerepiko.) Four different meso-climates influence the 720 ha of lime-rich vineyards which belong to Rooiberg's 35 member-farmers, giving winemaker Tommy Loftus and his team the scope to turn out a wide array of wine styles, for any and every palate or occasion, invariably winning a swathe of awards. Newcomers to the range are a Semillon and a Merlot — as always, from this cellar, ungreedily priced.

⚘**Roodewyn** ▼ At ±R13 98 this **98**'s a steal. A 'Cape blend', as was pvs, cab/merlot/pinotage, jam-packed with ripe cherry fruit. Thumping 14% alc.

⚘**Red Muscadel** Stunning **98** just gets better, though its tone is changing from full blown muscat to dusty sweet stewed fruit; in palate you'll now find perfumed roses and spun silk. Initial spirity tang starting to slide into unctuousness, suggest think about drinking up — a not unpleasant prospect. 17,6% alc.

⚘**Red Jerepiko** ▼ This cellar's calling card and one of SA's perennial top unwooded fortified desserts. **96**, from pinotage, growing ever richer, more velvety in bottle. Now with smoked meat, some prune/plum whiffs and wonderfully sweet pinotagey flavours which, at table, would be outstanding with blue cheese. Three VVG since **91**. 18% alc.

⚘**Cape Ruby Port** ▼ Still-impressive **95** VVG with fine, super-intense smoky prune carrying through very well into soft, med-sweet palate with hints of raisins. Exceptionally well priced at ±R20 from the new, luxe tasting room. Yr Fr oak. Tinta b/souzão/cab f. 18,6% alc. **97** SAYWS class winner, **96** VG.

Cabernet Sauvignon ⚘ High toned, full-bodied **98** showcases ripe picked creamy cassis, spicy vanilla and mulberry/redcurrant compote. Attractive wine.

Merlot ✿ New Arresting mix of contrasting tastes/textures — green olives/menthol/tar — living happily in surprisingly soft, very full, chocolatey **98** palate. 14% alc. **Pinotage** ⚘ Invariably attractive example. **98** silkier than many pinotages, with fine-grained tannins and really vibrant plum/mulberry fruit. Bountiful 14% alc adds to 'sweet', fat profile. **Shiraz** ⚘ Cherries/mulberries and fragrant pepper in dry, light-toned (though full bodied — 13,8% alc) **98** easy drinker. **Selected Red** ✿ **New** **00** cocktail of 5 varieties serves up smoky/savoury aromas and full, dry, almond tastes. 13% alc. **Rosé** ✿ **New** Vibrant ruby/pink **00**, lightish, with spicy organic cherries; pronounced sweetness cut by tart acid for sweet-sour effect. Ruby cab/sauvignon. **Sauvignon Blanc** ✿ Not a stunning yr for this grape, but **00** shows deft handling in delicate cut-grass/pear array with flinty-dry seafood-friendly finish. Enjoy young. **Semillon** ✿ **New** Fine first release **99** packs plenty of varietal character into med/full, dry frame: aromatic beeswax/honey and, to finish, creamy lanolin plus fleeting impression of sweetness. **Premier Grand Cru** ✿ NV (99) Lightish bodied, properly bone-dry, as always, yet easy, non-aggressive. Supple herbal/grassy tastes. **Bukettraube** ✿ Sweet but balanced juiciness in **99**, light-bodied and stacked with unusual (for this variety) baked apple tones. **Late Vintage** ★ NV (99) Equal partnership colombard/chardonnay, semi-sweet with dusty/herbal whiffs. Light 10% alc. **Special Late Vintage** ✿ Soft, lightish semi-sweet **99** with attention seeking pineapple bouquet, fruit salad flavours. From chenin. **Brut Sparkling** ✿ Busily-bubbly dry **99** showcases sauvignon's dusty lemon grass tones; dollop smoothing (not sweetening) sugar ensures soft exit. Carbonated. **Vin Doux Sparkling** ★ 99 real 'wedding bubble' — reassuringly sweet, pretty and lightly floral from soupçon gewürz, here partnering chenin. Carbonated, light (7,5% alc).

Cape Riesling ✿ 🍷 Variety's thumbprint fresh-cut hay mingles with citrus in **00**, made fresh, crisp and bone dry for instant summer rejuvenation. **Chardonnay** ✿ 🍷 Here's an **00** charmer for fans of the unwooded, wraparound-fruity style: lime/marzipan in zippy dry palate with grapefruit twist. ASAP quaffing. **Chenin Blanc** ✿ 🍷 Crowd pleasing sweetish version, **00** with 'dusty' guavas from nose to tail. Really attractive juicy mouthful at negligible R10/bottle. **Colombard** ✿ 🍷 Sweetish version of this Robertson speciality; **00** shyly peachy/apricotty in nose, juicier/livelier in palate with tapering sherbety tang. **Rhine Riesling** ✿ 🍷 This winemaking team knows a thing or two about fruit/acid balance. Try **00** and see: fragile floral fruit, brush of sugar wrapped in zesty acid. Summer refreshment deluxe. Moderate 12% alc. **Flamingo Vin Doux Sparkling** ✿ 🍷 Wonderfully frivolous fizz with billowing rose petal bouquet and sweet strawberry taste. Low 8,5% alc won't dampen the party spirit. Yes, it's flamingo pink.

Rosenburg see Uiterwyk

Rozendal Farm   🍷 🍷 🍷 🏚

Stellenbosch (see Stellenbosch map) • Sales by appointment • Luxury auberge with restaurant and many amenities • Owners Kurt & Lyne Ammann • Winemaker Kurt Ammann • Production 2 000–3 000 cases 100% red • PO Box 160 Stellenbosch 7599 • Tel (021) 883-8737 • Fax (021) 883-8738 • E-mail rozendal@mweb.co.za

WE first alerted wine drinkers to restaurateur Kurt Ammann's red in this guide's 1984 edition. An 83 blend was his debut vintage. "Excellent flavour, body and balance," we said. By the 1986 edition this description had blossomed, like the wine, into "lovely, complex and full-flavoured but not heavy... showing off a mellow richness from small oak maturation which has imparted a cedary aspect to the beguiling bouquet". In the 1990 guide we urged: "If you can lay your hands on an 83 Rozendal, do not pass up the opportunity. Even better, drink it." . We asked how he'd made this gem. "I don't know," he said. "I'm still trying to find out. Perhaps I knew too little." In the case of his wine then and since — the awards and acclaim have continued to roll — perhaps Rozendal is better experienced than dissected. Try to squeeze it into a tobacco pouch or spice rack and you reduce its individuality, render the mysterious banal. The current release, 98, not available for tasting. But

... in the spirit of our recommendation a decade ago: find it, sample it (at the Ammanns' auberge with their immaculate food, maybe), judge its star quality personally. In our book, its singularity, and subtle and supple pleasures, have always rated ✿ or more. Nothing has changed, and we're hoarding our own last bottle of fine 95.

. . . .

Ruitersberg see Ruitersvlei

. . . .

Ruitersvlei Estate

Paarl (see Paarl map) • Tasting & sales Mon—Fri 8.30—5.30 Sat 9—2 • Belgian/French restaurant/bistro open daily for lunch & dinner (closed Sun evening/Mon; closed Tue during winter) Tel/Fax (021) 863-3959 • Guesthouse/B&B Tel (021) 863-1517 • Gifts • Views • Wheelchair-friendly • Owner Faure Holdings (John Faure) • Marketing manager Belinda Faure-Griessel • Bottling manager Riaan Richter (since 1999) • Winemaker Dominique Waso (since 1999) • Vineyard manager Sheryl Butler • Vineyards 300 ha • Production 1 500 tons 60 000 cases 50% red 50% white • PO Box 532 Suider-Paarl 7624 • Tel (021) 863-1517 • Fax (021) 863-1443 • E-mail ruitersv@iafrica.co.za

HAVE YOU TRAVELLED overseas recently? Internationally seasoned winemaker Dominique Waso's reply to our question — "No, too much work to do" — shows how wise John Faure was to listen to his four daughters and take this family property public in 1996. Lift-off was instant, with all the siblings involved from the ground up (sister Sheryl the OC vineyards). Ruitersvlei, previously an anonymous supplier to merchants (port varieties a speciality), has become a booming example of a revitalised, new-age Cape estate; buyers pant specially hard after its high-performance Cabernet (local show champion in 99, against very stiff competition). Dominique Waso reports "huge demand for red wine, more than double the previous year". New plantings are streaming in — the vineyards have been expanded to 300 ha with the emphasis on reds, and cabernet franc the latest recruit to the ranks. Two new ranges, the export-only Ruitersberg, and the John Faure, have been launched. The special Destiny wines have been made — available only at an annual charity function on the farm or the tasting room, part of their proceeds ploughed into Ruitersvlei's social development programme.

✿✿ **Cabernet Sauvignon Reserve** Massive, concentrated Paarl cab, classically Fr barrique aged, from low crop vyds yielding around 4 t/ha. 98 almost decadently ripe, but buttressed by tannin and fresh of acidity. Upcoming 99 not yet bottled and already couple of victory laps (class winner at Paarl, national young wine shows). Succulent cassis/cherry, fragrant mint, minerals, spicy oak, polished tannins — all in balance; interminable finish. These ± 14% alc.

✿ **Merlot Reserve** Something of a paradox: often quite pale but behind delicate exterior uncommon intensity, plum, cherry, vanilla oak plushness. As in **98**, with yielding tannins, 'sweet' palate impression from strapping 14,5% alc. Latest **99** (from barrel) potentially best to date; fragrant oak and lively tannin backdrop.

✿ **Cabernet Sauvignon-Merlot** New ▼ 60/40 blend, components assembled from lots destined for Reserves. So not a bantam in this heavyweight range though lightly priced at around R25 ex-farm. Refined tannins, expensive cigarbox whiffs, fragrant spicy oak mingle with sweetly ripe fruit in fine first-release **99**. 13,4% alc.

✿ **Shiraz-Merlot** New ▼ Fresh face in this guide, but well known and much loved by customers; so much so limited supplies of shiraz from new vyds, destined for standalone bachelorhood, hastily married off for this 50/50 blend. "Damn!" laments winemaker. **99** ripe plums, smoky/spicy tones, savoury tastes with bits of fruitcake. Long dry tannins. Enough substance for now or for 3–5 yrs. 13,3% alc.

✿ **Paarl Riesling** ▼ Pvs labelled simply 'Riesling', so no hint this is in fact SA riesling (crouchen blanc). Unusual, striking **99** of last ed developing delightful mellow tones, signature straw whiffs joined by honey/beeswax in fairly rich palate. Latest **00** almost clone of pvs, only more youthfully flushed.

✿**Sauvignon Blanc** Winemaker suggests you try **00** with freshly landed galjoen or abalone. Though med-bodied, has more than enough guts, bright acidity to take on linefish/shellfish richness. Limited release. Pvs **99** ✿✿ lightweight in all respects.

✿**Four Sisters** New Classically styled MCC brut sparkle, pinot noir from next-door Landskroon,14 mths on lees; small quantity released Sep 2000, remainder will be on lees ± 36 months. Boiled sweets/toast/butterscotch in crisp, clean, harmonious **NV**. 12% alc.

Chardonnay Reserve ✿✿ Early-peaking **99** not living up to promise. Drink up. **00** (cask sample) cut above; minerally, vanilla/toasted nuts and lively, unusual nectarine whiffs in complex array. Partly barrel fermented/aged. **Chenin Blanc-Chardonnay** Untasted. **Pinotage** Not tasted for this ed. **Shiraz** ✿✿ 36 yr old single vyd is origin of this lightly oaked **99** with smoky shiraz savouriness, herbaceous nuances in tannic finish. **Mountainside White** ✿✿ **99** Undemanding, fresh summer splash; some tropical tones, zesty finish. Off-dry, med-bodied. Colombard/Cape riesling/muscat d'alexandrie (50/40/10 formula "an accident", acknowledges winemaker: "Had to fill the tank!".

Cinsaut-Cabernet Sauvignon ✿✿ ☺ Cut above ordinary quaffer, yet extra-drinkable. Juicy raspberry/blackberry, peppermill grind, appetising savoury hint in **00**, lightly glossed with invisible sugar. 13% alc. **Mountainside Red** ✿✿ ☺ Chunky, lightly savoury **99**, early/easy campfire quaff (14% needs watching), mainly cinsaut, ruby cab, tinta b, carignan, with touch smoothing (rather than sweetening) sugar. Lightly chill in summer. **Chenin Blanc** ✿✿ ☺ This **00** bit more serious than pvs, but no less gulpable. Med/light-bodied, twist of lemon enervates clean, tropical palate.

John Faure range

✿**Port** New 🏆 Renewed interest in this category ahead of 2000 Diners Club competition. This **NV**, low cropped tinta b from 96/97 vintages "and dash very old port", 'old Cape' style: gentle nutty, wild berry tastes, good spirity touch. Puckering dry finish (66 g/ℓ sugar). **Cabernet Sauvignon-Shiraz** ✿✿ **97** has become more interesting in bottle, some good savoury, tobacco tastes now, with blackberry/strawberry. Tannins drying, so best drunk soon.

. . . .

Rupert & Rothschild Vignerons see R&R

. . . .

Rustenberg Wines ♟ ♟ ♟

Stellenbosch (see Stellenbosch map) • Tasting Mon–Fri 9–4.30 Sat 9–12.30 • Sales Mon–Fri 8–5 Sat 9–12.30 Closed Sun, Good Friday/Easter, Christmas • Cellar tours by appointment • Tourgroups • Walks/hikes by arrangement • Views • Wheelchair-friendly • Owner Simon Barlow • Winemaker Adi Badenhorst (since 1999) • Viticulturist Kevin Watt • Vineyard manager Nico Walters • Vineyards 100 ha • Production 600 tons, 46 000 cases 75% red, 25% white • PO Box 33 Stellenbosch 7599 • Tel (021) 809-1200 • Fax (021) 809-1219 • E-mail wine@rustenberg.co.za • Website www.rustenberg.co.za

RUSTENBERG PETER BARLOW, this distinguished 318-year-old property's loftiest line-out jumper (recently rave-rated by the world's most influential wine critic, Robert Parker) was on the bench in millennium year, injured. The fires that incinerated various Stellenbosch mountainsides scorched through the prime cabernet block of the single vineyard dedicated to give homage to owner Simon Barlow's late father. There'll be no PB 2000. Parker's 92 out of 100 score for the 96 ("may be the finest red wine I have ever tasted from South Africa"), made by then-winemaker Kiwi Rod Easthope, throws down the gauntlet to new *chef de cave* Adi Badenhorst, but

here's a youngster with a notable Cape pedigree to background his working experience locally, in California, and at Ch Angelus in Bordeaux. His grandfather was
farm manager of Groot Constantia for 45 years; his father presides at Constantia
Uitsig, was formerly at Buitenverwachting. Rustenberg's recent turn-around, from
old Cape landmark (with gracious matching architecture) to new era standard set-
ter, is, of course, not based on a single high flying label, nor on winery pyrotechnics
alone. There is a new cellar, linked by winding (to avoid the roots of centuries-old
oaks) underground tunnel to the old; there is a new bottling line, and lifts to ease
workers' loads; there is a chic new tasting room. But even more crucially, viticulturist Kevin Watt, vineyard manager Nico Walters, and a motivated, empowered
staff contingent are delivering the goods from the ground up — these 100 ha of
vines on the southern slopes of Simonsberg.

✿✿Peter Barlow Standard-bearing red in classic style, quintessential stamp of
Stellenbosch, Rustenberg and class. Lays stake in reclaiming the property's
former brilliance, based on unstinting standards set by present day owner Simon
Barlow's late father, Peter. 100% cab from single site, healthy virus cleaned 12
yr old vines. Cropping cut to 6 t/ha — the single bunch per shoot limit makes a
"profound difference," says Barlow. Next **98** dense inky black, perfumed pencil
lead, cedar/cigar box aromatics interleaved with floral violets, all understated.
Ripe fruit foil for expertly managed tannins; never blowsy; oozes elegance.
Measured oak belies generous 20 mths maturation. 13,9% alc. **97** *Wine* ✿✿, 90
rating in *Wine Spectator*, also a rare red with true fragrance, concentration;
beguilingly soft tannins. Splendid **96** ✿✿, 92 rating in *Wine Spectator*. Sample
99 has opulent ripe fruit 'devouring' the oak, 75% new. Releases to date all
Seguin Moreau cooperage.

✿Rustenberg Second in listing, not in quality. Latest **98** strong colour (Barlow
believes the cool summer nights in the vineyards are the secret to their colours),
leaf tobacco scents; ripe, near chunky red berry fruits — all reined in by chiding
tannic structure. 100% cask aged 20 mths. 13,8% alc. 3 000 cases. Fascinating
vertical tasting in mid-2000 showed sample **99** ripe, brimming with red berries/
black cherry/cassis; **97** ✿✿ refined, still fresh, forthcoming crushed forest floor
fruits, oak spice and violet scent. Definite notch up on maiden **96** SAA, International Wine Challenge gold (1999), 91 rating in *Wine Spectator*, leafy, moist
tobacco, lanolin softness and firm acidity; ready. All share sumptuous deep-pile
red velvet texture. Blend settling at 85% cab s, 10% merlot, 5% cab f.

✿✿Five Soldiers Statement white lavished with attention. Only 500 cases. Single
virus cleaned vyd guarded by five tall stone pines, 'Chardonnay' does not appear
on label — 100% natural yeast fermentation (which can take months), Yr 100%
new wood, 100% malo. All to garner more complexity, more fatness/viscosity.
All this and more in next **99**: tropical melons give way to toasty, buttery richness, endless length elevated by tart crispness. 14,3% alc. Extrovert **98** ✿✿ bold
and broad, lashings of lime marmalade on hot toast as the butter melts in. Like
99, muscular (alc 14,5%), both different to initial understated **97** which has
developed quicker than hoped for.

✿✿Stellenbosch Chardonnay ▼ Firmly ripe, assertive, confident style reflecting cool Helderberg terroir of sibling farm, Nooitgedacht. **99** "on target at where
we are aiming" — and that's high. Fresh lemon/lime zippy fruit supports main
act of rich, creamy palate, at once minerally and fleshy. Excellent fruit concentration and confident oaking. 13,8% alc. 1 800 cases. **98** boldly scented, flavoured to match; ripe lemons, piles of fresh toast. Best grapes (1–2 bunches
per shoot) picked only when seeds are ripe (as for reds), fermented in 50% new
wood, all Fr, natural/inoculated yeasts;100% malo, 10 mths sur lie in wood
without sulphur, 'natural fining' by oak.

❀ **Stellenbosch Sauvignon Blanc** Ripe tropical fruit in **99**; passionfruit/melon/bell-pepper back-ground. Fat, ripe palate balanced by juicy acidity. Full-bodied, fleshy.

❀ **Q.F.2** Worthy successor to cellar's 1st NLH-style dessert, the fully botrytised **97 Q.F.1**, from chardonnay. **00**, from sauvignon, sparkles with green tinge, super 'berry' richness, crisp twist stops cloying in its tracks. Twinges of Tokay in winemaking — 40% botrytis enriched grapes soaked on skins, barrel fermented (30% new oak), long lees contact. **Q.F.1 97** *Wine* ❀ Rich, weighty, redolent with botrytis, sweet citrus flavours, waxiness well balanced by tight acidity. Named because of the Friday afternoon dash into the cellar for a "quick fix" after the week's work.

❀ **Stellenbosch Brut** Cap classique released for the millennium; followed previous bubbly made for Rustenberg centenary. Set to become regular feature with 2 future tranches in the wings. Growing straw-yellow; biscuity/bready/lees and yeast, hazelnuts/lime freshness in palate. Crisp, refreshing, albeit somewhat austere. Made by the book (Rod Easthope even claims to have dusted off his oenology texts for this one) from 70% Nooitgedacht chardonnay, 30% pinot noir, whole-bunch-pressed, 18 mths on lees. 11% alc. **NV** (97).

Brampton range

Good value label; flamboyant fruit driven market led whites, fleshy reds; focus firmly on varietal fruit.

❀ **Old Vines Red** Everyday red with style, substance, without a second bond. Blend depends on what's available: mainly cab s, merlot, cab f and some pinot noir, mostly old vines. **99**'s ✔ lightish ruby colour belies intense flavour to come: chewy raspberry/cherry fruit, tobacco leaf spice, firm tannic tail. 18 mths seasoned oak ("Royal treatment for the bottom end"). 13,3% alc. 3 800 cases. **98** less fleshy; dried herbs/dusty tobacco/tea leaf aromas, will evoke nostalgia in lovers of the old style Cape reds.

❀ **Cabernet Sauvignon-Merlot** Here you get "sweetness for your money" — juicy, jammy mouthfilling red blend with in-your-face-fruit — to ape Rosemount 'diamond label' range. **99** jam-packed with red cherry fruit, all dominated by 40% new oak, all Am. Oxidative pumping over, malo in wood. 13,5% alc. 3 500 cases. Gulp-down style, as seductive as **97** *Wine* ❀. **98** more challenging, more structure, formality.

❀ **Chardonnay** ✔ Unequivocal chardonnay in showy, extroverted fruity style (although ⅓ barrel fermented). Lastest **99** emits spumes of ripe tropical melons, orchards of citrus from nose to mouth, tightly bound (though 4 mths on lees adds breadth). 13% alc. 3 000 cases. **98** also ripe peachy fruit, melon/butterscotch nuances, muscat notes of old clones. Palate still firm.

Sauvignon Blanc ❀ Well defined style maintained by Badenhorst in his first **00** foray here, but crisper/grassier than previous. Protection of primary fruit character shows in piles of tropical tones in nose, plus more conventional gooseberries/nettles in full palate. **99** full and ripe, fresh acidity sustains life. **Port** ❀ **94** Attractive SA-style port, sweet and welcoming, with some refinement. Fruitcake flavours offset by freshness of 20% cab s. Brilliantly ruby-hued, based on 80% souzão.

. . . .

Rust en Vrede Wine Estate ∇ ∇

Stellenbosch (see Stellenbosch map) • Tasting & sales Mon—Fri 9—5 Sat Oct—Apr 9—4 May—Sep 9—3 • Owner Jannie Engelbrecht • Winemaker Louis Strydom (since 1998) • Production 280 tons 20 000 cases 100% red • PO Box 473 Stellenbosch 7599 Annandale Road Stellenbosch 7600 • Tel (021) 881-3881 • Fax (021) 881-3000 • E-mail info@rustenvrede.com • Website www.rustenvrede.com

HERE's a strong contender for an estate which represents the spirit and dynamism of new-generation Cape wine. Owner Jannie Engelbrecht, whose sinuous swerves at full throttle made him a star Springbok rugby wing, executed his last, clever sidestep a couple of years ago, and left the field open for son Jean, a former airline pilot. And is he flying! With winemaker Louis Strydom (ex-Saxenburg), and marketing manager Neil Buchner, this young, hungry and driven trio has notched up a hectic number of air miles raising foreign consciousness about this specialist red-wine estate. Jean Engelbrecht says: "You have to shake the hand, kiss the baby, rather like being a politician. Our wine is sold into many restaurants and we want to meet all our customers." Back on the farm, the winds of change blow pretty briskly too. Of the 30 ha under vines, 25 ha have been replanted, and for a relatively small estate like this to employ a fulltime viticulturist (since November 1999) is both unusual and significant. Drip irrigation, to de-stress young vines, is the next big project. In time, the range will probably be pared down to just the one, flagship R&V blend. The Tinta Barocca is to be the first casualty — 2000 its last vintage. A second label, Guardian Peak (after the mountain overshadowing the estate), will main-feature an export blend of cabernet and shiraz, with a dash of upcoming mourvèdre (a souvenir of Louis Strydom's season in southern France).

✿ **Rust en Vrede Estate Wine** All R&V team's energies now directed towards ultimate goal of single *grand vin*, à la the top Bdx châteaux. To be expressed through this cab-dominated Cape blend, always featuring shiraz, merlot; annual production driven solely by quality. Arresting **96** ✾ among top reds of (challenging) yr, 92 rating in *Wine Spectator*, *Wine* ✾. Rich cherry/blackberry array, exotically spiced, mouth filling. Good ageing potential to ±2007. Slighter **97** ✿ reflects cool, old-clone disfavouring vintage; will need more careful monitoring to catch at best, probably before 7th birthday. Present cab astringency cushioned somewhat by plush shiraz/merlot component, sensitive oaking which plumps out fruit. But would benefit from couple of yrs' rounding in cellar. 13% alc (Strydom's ideal between 13,5%–13,8%) **93** VVG, **94** VG, SAA.

✿ **Shiraz** Consistently top-rated example, from **98** with added oomph from some young virus-free clone. Outburst of hedonistic smoky, spicy fragrance, with cedar/toast to deepen. Delicious savoury-rich mouthful, contrasted by surprisingly delicate texture (and palish ruby hue). Will have become more pliable by June 2001 release, and thereafter will gain lushness over 5–7 yrs. 16 mths, 50/50 new Fr/Am barrels (no Am oak vulgar sweetness, despite high proportion). Pvs **97** ✾ one of the best made at R&V, shows power of excellent shiraz vintage. Packed with mulberries, estate's trademark shiraz aromatics. 15 mths Am barriques.

✿ **Cabernet Sauvignon** Even with new virus-free vines coming on-stream, elegance remains hallmark of this cellar's cab. Such easier-ripening material not available in cool **97** ✿, mirrored in lighter than usual texture (though fullish 13% alc), firm acid core, relatively developed herby, sweet mint tones. Finely calibrated oak binds into pleasant-drinking whole; but this shorter term than pvs (possibly now–2003). 18 mths new Radoux barriques; 6,3 g/ℓ acid. **96** sold out.

✿ **Merlot** The red chosen for 1993 Mandela/De Klerk Nobel Peace Prize Dinner in Oslo. **89** featured on that occasion; **99**, separated by exactly 10 vintages, still a special-occasion wine: silky, succulent, enhanced by ripe, wrap-around tannins; poised acidity provides welcome length, elegance. Fr oak matured, all used barrels. Delicious follow-up to **98** ✾, probably best ever from this cellar. Mouth-coating ripe plums framed by supple tannin and quite a fresh lift of acidity. Allier barriques, 6 mths; 13,4% alc.

✿ **Tinta Barocca** Traditional Port variety, but no longer a hint of portiness in this completely restyled, vibrant (but not unserious) number. **99**, like pvs **98**, brims with welcoming spicy cherry warmth; mouth-filling freshness. Easy fruit neatly contrasted by solid, ripe tannins (includes 10% cab stiffening). Drink now with flavoursome pasta or hold for 2 yrs. Edges rounded by 11 mths older Fr barrels. 13,8% alc.

Rusthof see Mooiuitsig

Rylands Grove see International Wine Services

Sable View

EXPORT RANGE launched 1990; marked Stellenbosch Farmers' Winery's re-entry into the international market, post apartheid.

❀ **Cabernet Sauvignon** Latest **98** departs from customary compact, understated mode: forward charry black berries/cherries in well balanced palate. Satisfying. For now or over next few yrs. 13% alc.

❀ **Chardonnay** Bigger, better defined flavours in this much improved wine, oaked **99** with butterscotch, vanilla creaminess, freshened with marmalade tang.

❀ **Muscat d'Alexandrie** Specially for Asian market. Super-smooth **99** glides across palate trailing garlands of exotic flowers and fruits. Though sweetish, ends crisply clean. Lowish 10,5% alc.

Sauvignon Blanc ❀ Latest keeps the breathless pace set by **99**. Bursts of gooseberry, guava, cut grass in med-bodied **00**, racy lemon conclusion.

Sandown Bay

CAPE Wine Master, seafood forager and accomplished cook Dave Johnson styles this small negociant range to sit comfortably with tastebuds and pockets. See also Newton Johnson and Cape Bay. Wines below all **00**, all **New**.

Cabernet Sauvignon ❀ 😊 Outfitted with herbs, mint, sweet plums and dab of tannin for relaxed outdoor supping. Chez Johnson, there'd be beef & abalone casserole on the table. 12,5% alc, unoaked. 1 100 cases. **Pinotage** ❀ 😊 Sweet ripe plums, bit of charry oak, tweak of tannin; young and quaffable. 13,5% alc. 2 200 cases.

Chardonnay Exotic smelling (of jasmine, passionfruit) unoaked number with lots of soft, citrus flavour. Sample, unrated. 1 050 cases.

Savanha   🍷

Stellenbosch (see Stellenbosch map) • Tasting & sales daily 9—5 at Spier Wine Shop (see Spier Cellars), or by appointment Tasting fee R12 p/p • Cellar tours by appointment • Owner Winecorp • Winemakers Stéphane de Saint Salvy (reds) Christo Versveld (whites) • Consultant (Naledi, Sejana) Alain Mouiex • Viticulturists Gerrie Wagener (Afrika Vineyards), Johan Smit • Production 2 000 tons 35% red 65% white • PO Box 99 Lynedoch 7603 • Tel (021) 881-3690 • Fax (021) 881-3699 • E-mail winecorp@iafrica.com

THIS is part of Winecorp, the newest big player in the Cape winelands, and the wines are designed to occupy a very specific slot in the group's portfolio. The name of the red-winemaker perhaps gives the strongest clue: Stéphane de St Salvy is obviously French (as is super-consultant Alain Moueix), and a refined, more Old World style is the mission here, both in the Savanha range and the two top-of-the-tree labels, Naledi Cabernet and Sejana Merlot. (All distributed in Europe and the USA by the same company that handles Romanée-Conti.) New white winemaker Christo Versfeld, fresh from travels in Burgundy, has his sights set on the classics, too. His background includes a stint at that most excellent of co-op wineries, Nuy. 2000 was the last harvest handled at the old Berg & Brook cellars at Simondium. Activity centre in future is a newly-built cellar at Spier; grape-supplies come from prime areas where contract-growers work under the critical eye of seasoned Gerrie Wagener (ex-Boschendal and Vergelegen), who now heads Winecorp's viticultural operations. *Note:* Berg & Brook no longer exists as a label. The streamlining here also sees the following ranges/labels culled: Benguela Current, Agulhas Bank, Cheetah Valley, Pierre Simond and Guess.

⚜ **Sejana Merlot** Lofty aim here — hinted at in seSotho name, meaning 'trophy' (or 'drinking cup') — to produce attention/accolade grabbing yet accessible Cape merlot. World-class intentions underscored by inclusion of the first release in a Bdx-marketed 'best of both hemispheres' six-pack (rubbing shoulders with Pétrus). **99** very fresh smelling, blackcurrant juice with incipient violets, meaty warmth. Palate shows greater sophistication, potential complexity than pvs, needs further yr/2 to develop. Yr Fr barriques, 30–40% new. 1 400 cases. Back-taste of **98** mid-2000 prematurely tired (✦), with unheralded porty tones.

⚜ **Naledi Cabernet Sauvignon** The name means 'star' in seSotho — sparkly quality recognised by judges of inaugural 2000 Grape Packaging Awards who accorded this and stablemate above 'Best in SA' status. **99** with mint/cassis familiarity, minerally freshness give way to broader flavour richness; well-judged oak and polished dry tannins. Overall compact feel despite 14,2% alc. Dbnville/Paarl grapes, vinified separately; malo, yr in barrel, 30–40% new. 1 700 cases. **98**, back-tasted mid-2000, has come off the boil (⚜); not as striking as pvsly.

Savanha range

⚜ **Merlot** Latest **99** ⚜ not a typical SA style (imprint of blue-blooded Frenchman Stéphane de St. Salvy evident here); quite likely an acquired taste, but one worth acquiring. Ripe meaty/smoky plum aromatic exuberance tracked by sleek yet bustling feel. Under this trim, fruity veneer lies promise of richer things to come, though with right dishes — nothing too strongly flavoured — could be opened now. 10 mths Fr oak, 25% new, rest 2nd fill; malo in barrel. 13,8% alc. 4 900 cases. Opulent, finely structured **98** more recognisably South African.

Cabernet Sauvignon ⚜ Distinct family resemblance between this **99** and Merlot above, though more youthful profile here thanks to green walnut/blackberry/minerally grip. Drink now (as Stéphane de St. Salvy agrees many of his countrymen would do) or cellar 4–5 yrs. 3 000 cases. **Shiraz** ⚜ Dominated by 'sweet' spicy notes of Am oak, challenging freshness in **99**. 1 800 cases. **Chardonnay** ⚜ Marked change of style with **00**: accent now on freshness, tropical/limey fruit; oak's buttered-toast tones only lightly spread. Uncomplicated, tasty though pre-bottling sample leaves overplayed residual sweetness. 2 000 cases. **Semillon** ⚜ Latest **00** aimed at restaurant trade, styled to accompany many dishes. Unfinished sample reveals pleasant winey aromas, some lemon whiffs; fuller, weightier feel in mouth balanced by clean, citrus flavours, unobtrusive oak. Teaspoon sugar will encourage accessibility. 13,8% alc. 1 000 cases. **Sauvignon Blanc** ⚜ For youthful, well-chilled drinking. **00** lightish style, revealing cooler Dbnville flinty/chalky tones. Brisker edges of acid smoothed by soupçon sugar. Lowish 11,5% alc. 2 000 cases.

Savisa see Sonop

SA Wine Cellars

Stellenbosch • Marketing director Nico van der Merwe • PO Box 184 Stellenbosch 7599 • Tel (021) 888-3200 • Fax (021) 887-0728 • Toll-free tel 0800-225-400 • Website www.sawinecellars.co.za

SALES, marketing and distribution company within Distillers Corporation handling the wines of the following estates: Alto, Allesverloren, Fort Simon, Jacobsdal, Le Bonheur, Meerlust, Neethlingshof, Rietvallei, Theuniskraal and Uitkyk, as well as Bergkelder, Drostdy Cellar, Durbanville Hills, JC le Roux and Stellenzicht (all individually listed in this guide).

Saxenburg ♟ ♟ ♟ ♟

Stellenbosch (see Stellenbosch map) • Tasting & sales Mon—Fri 9—5 Sat 9—4 Sun 10—4 (Oct-May) Tasting fee R1,50 per wine • Cellar tours by appointment • Guinea Fowl Restaurant • Gifts • Conferences • Views • Lunchtime pony rides for children Sun & public holidays • Variety of small game permanently on view • Owners Adrian & Birgitte Bührer • Winemaker/viticulturist Nico van der Merwe (since 1991) with Koos Thiart (since 2000) • Vineyards 70 ha • Production 350 tons, 50 000 cases (300 tons, 25 000 cases under own label) 80% red 20% white • PO Box 171 Kuils River 7580 • Tel (021) 903-6113/6313 • Fax (021) 903-3129 • E-mail saxfarm@iafrica.com • Website www.saxenburg.co.za

'CONSISTENTLY EXCEPTIONAL' might well serve as a summary of Saxenburg in general, but to be precise, it was how we described the Private Collection (PC) Sauvignon Blanc last edition, and there's no reason to revise that opinion — in fact, no 2000 version to review. The super-warm harvest season was stressful for some whites (though watch out for dazzling reds), and winemaker Nico van der Merwe simply didn't think the Sauvignon exceptional enough to qualify for the elite PC club. It's such unswerving commitment to maintaining standards across the board (not only for the property's super-wines, the Cabernet, Shiraz and Merlot) that has made Saxenburg a new(-ish, over the past decade) Cape star and a hot favourite in 18 export countries. Including picky France, where Van der Merwe also makes the wine at Adrian and Birgit Bührer's 16th century Ch Capion, near Montpellier, shipping some of it back to create the unusual bi-national Grands Vins below (and see in cyber-detail on Saxenburg's own website). He's certainly flown a long way beyond his childhood dreams. Growing up in dusty, dry Hopefield, his greatest ambition was "to work in an area where there was more water!"

❀ **Private Collection Cabernet Sauvignon** "Nice vintage cab for better occasions," says Nico vd Merwe self-deprecatingly, neglecting to mention this is one of the Cape's grandest, single vyd selection from the own farm, expensively oaked. Elegance, linearity, liveliness of current **97** reflects the cooler vintage. Swathes of ripe fruit, traditional Cape green-walnuts, dark berry tones in keeping with overall classic bearing; reverberating length. Oak sensitively used. Yr Fr barriques, 90% new. 550 cases. **96** ❀, earlier ready vintage, with suggestion herbaceousness, forward cassis charm. *Wine* ❀. **95** SAA, *Wine* ❀. **94** VG, *Wine* ❀. Standard **Cabernet Sauvignon** ❀ Shade less serious, described by vdM as "poolside wine". **98** possibly most accessible of regular range reds, bit more developed. Open, almost meaty nose (winemaker suggests partnering with "a lot of nice kudu biltong" — air-dried meat!). Good weight. Yr Fr barrels, 20% new. 13% alc. 3 000 cases. Tuck into **96**, **98** while waiting for **97**, and deliciously long, elegant **95**.

❀ **Private Collection Merlot 97** ❀ might have wowed local palates, but latest **98**, single vyd selection with serious demeanour, restraint, is the Europeans' choice, winemaker reveals. Like other **98** PC reds, this currently a brooder, for contemplation not instant gratification ("and substantial, complex dishes," adds burly vdM). But many further intricacies will come with time. New oak (90%, all Fr) adds fresh spice, cedar to underlying richness. Impressively long, polished finish. 5—10% cab blended for structure. 13,5% alc. 1 000 cases. **97** big, long, refined, with dark-fruit opulence. **96** ❀ lighter-textured, charming silky feel, sweet red-plum flavours, well oaked. From **95**, 100% S'burg grapes, cooler slopes. **95**, **94** opulent, dense but never brash. Probable best drinking order: **96**, **94**, **95**, **97**, **98**. Regular **Merlot** ❀ Fully ripe, plummy tones in **98**; big, juicy mouthful, slightly more tannin grip than usual for standard range, which identified by accessible fruity charm; yr or 2 will bring pleasing harmony. Includes 15% cab. 13,5% alc. Yr Fr oak, 10% new. 3 000 cases.

❀ **Private Collection Pinotage** Single vyd selection from own farm, evincing Burgundy-Rhône overtones in rich, concentrated **98** ❀ ripeness. More traditional pinotage 'sweetness', rusticity well contained; no finishing pinotage bitterness either. Yr Am oak, 20% new. 13,5% alc. 1 000 cases. **96** *Wine* ❀; **95**

SAA, Wine ✿ . Standard **Pinotage** ✿✿, like other 'regulars' in range, requires bit more time to reach comfortable drinkability. **98** appealing smoky, dried-fig fruits, wrapped in vibrant juicy structure. Am oak matured, 10% new, 1 yr. 13% alc. 2 000 cases.

✿✿**Private Collection Shiraz** Vd Merwe's annual bi-hemispheric experience with this variety (at Ch Capion, S'burg) evident in this riveting Cape shiraz. Brilliant tightrope-walk between potency, restraint again in **98**, which gives impression of coming-of-age for farm's flagship. Like other PC reds of vintage, currently more introspective; undeveloped fruit hints at macerated raspberries/violets, dusted with minerally spice. But flavours are already rich, concentrated (as is 14% alc), the finish deliciously spicy and dry. Oaking similar to pvs: mix Burgundian, American casks, 20% new, but more 2nd fill than usual. 30% Stbosch grapes. 3 000 cases. All releases to date, exclusively under PC label, burly, warm individuals. **97** seductive, Rhône-like. **96** SAA (runner-up red wine trophy) chewy-rich but, like **92**, peaking earlier. **95** rich, spicy, very fine.

✿✿**Saxenburg Shiraz Select** (SSS in pvs ed) Much along lines of PC above though — incredibly — bigger, richer, gorgeously savoury (a meal in itself!). Cask fermentation a key here, giving more fruit concentration. **97** locally styled young Hermitage, about as massive, demanding. Infanticide to open before 2002/3, too early to predict peak age. Through malo in Burgundy barrels, yr Fr, 2nd fill Am oak (50/50). 13,5% alc. 200 cases. Latest **98** a worthy follow-up. Again Stbosch grapes, vyds "a little closer to Stbsch town than pvs", gravel soils vs pvs decomposed granite. Used Am oak-fermented, then just under yr Fr ±40% new, 14+% alc. 180 cases. Sold by similar methods as pvs: portion on 2000 CWG Auction, remainder released later only from farm. ±R500/bottle.

✿✿**Gwendolyn** First and arguably most successful in blended range named after Bührers' children; Gwendolyn younger daughter. Inaugurated **96**. Current **98** reflects all warmth, generosity of vintage; inviting savoury/herby attractions, concentrated flavour, fine partnership of cab/shiraz (60/40). Yr Fr/Am oak, 20% new. Own grapes. 13,5% alc. 1 500 cases. **97** dry, tangy spice, dark fruits.

✿✿**Manuel** Well-modulated cab/merlot blend (70/30), named after Bührers' eldest son. **98** ✿✿ compact but not lean; plummy merlot in driving seat, strapped in by fine, dry tannins. Give 12–18 mths in bottle, then, on vdM's advice, enjoy with maritime cuisine. Stbosch/Dbnville grapes, Yr Fr oak, 20% new. 13% alc. 1 500 cases. **97** fine-boned with minerally, blackcurrant freshness, softening merlot. 3–4 yr maturation potential.

✿✿**Private Collection Chardonnay** Pvsly part of regular range, now labelled 'PC', better reflecting v high standard. **99**, like pvs, striking and refined (seemingly exclusive attributes when alcs tip 13,5%). Latest bit more obviously tropical in youth, usual hazelnut-clove played down but should grow with time; full, supple mouthfeel; spirited backbone for longer development (this also to round off few noticeable oaky edges). "Try with lots of Norwegian salmon," vdM ventures. 100% barrel-fermented/matured 10 mths, 50/50 new/used Fr oak, through malo. 13,5% alc. 1 200 cases.

✿✿**Private Collection Sauvignon Blanc** Consistently exceptional yet easy-to-enjoy but **00** not considered special enough for PC label, so none released. **99** with trademark tropical elegance; balance, fruit/acid integration, good for further 2 yrs. 13,4% alc.

Grand Vin Rouge ✿✿ ☺ Easy, satisfying, med-bodied quaffer. Happy **NV** French/SA marriage (70% Capion grapes, 30% S'burg). Latest (98/99) usual all-sorts mix: cabs s/f, merlot, syrah, grenache, cinsaut, but less carignan than pvs. Lightly oaked. 2 500 cases.

Grand Vin Blanc ⚘ Softly fleshed, flavoursome, well-priced **NV** dry white with sufficient presence for most fish, light meat dishes, interest for solo satisfaction. Cross-hemisphere blend: equal parts **00** S'burg chenin, **99** Capion chardonnay. Local's more flaunting tropical ripeness cut by French pebbly, citrusy tang. 5 000 cases. **Private Collection Natural Sweet Le Rêve de Saxenbourg** ⚘ Lightish **NV** (98) non-botrytised dessert, 50% chenin, equal parts gewürz, riesling. Spicy citrus scents; sweetish-clean finish. 375 ml. 3 000 cases. **Private Collection Le Phantom Brut Cap Classique** ⚘ Lightish, gentle **NV** (**94**) sparkler "for the young and energetic". Pinot/chardonnay, min 48 mths on lees; good biscuit flavours, dryish finish. 300 cases.

Scali

Paarl • Not open to public • Owners/winemakers Willie & Tania de Waal • Viticulturist Willie de Waal • Vineyards 3 ha • Production 10 tons 485 cases 100% red • PO Box 7143 Noorder-Paarl 7623 • Tel (021) 863-8349 • Fax (021) 863-8383 • E-mail schooneoord@kingsley.co.za

WILLIE AND TANIA de Waal don't just admire the world's great wines from afar, they camp right up close and personal to the objects of their passion. The fifth-generation De Waals to farm these 340 ha on the slopes of the Perdeberg, they delivered grapes from its 90 ha vineyards to Boland Cellars (for prize-winning chenin and other labels). And so they might have gone on, in the obscurity of what Tania de Waal fondly calls "the outback", had their working relationship with the grapes not intensified into a full-blown affair. They took their toothbrushes and tents and camped out in Europe, specially smitten by the vineyards of the Rhône; Australia followed; France seduced again (highlight a Burgundy harvest — "fantastic!"). Eventually they could no longer resist. They got permission from Boland to keep back 10 tons of their best grapes, renovated the old stone cellar on the farm (Willie de Waal's grandfather used to make port for KWV), and produced their own first wine, just 485 cases of 99 Pinotage due for 2001 release. It is "the beginning of our pursuit of, and passion for the ultimate wine".

⚘ **Pinotage** Individual style, loads of personality, more shiraz character than pinotage (de Waals pushing envelopes here?), but fine intensity. Deep-layered **99** with black choc, woodsmoke, minerals and some green stalks/minty wafts; viscous plums lead good initial attack though mid-palate tapers quickly to dry, puckering finish. Deserves time to develop. Yr Fr/Am oaked, 50% new. ±13% alc.

Scarborough see Cape Point Vineyards
Scholtzenhof see Ken Forrester

Sedgwick's

VENERABLE OLD CAPE BRAND, now owned by Stellenbosch Farmers' Winery.

Old Brown Sherry ⚘ **NV** The original SA old brown (originally produced 1886), and still the fisherman's favourite warming drop. Actually a jerepigo/sherry blend; deep mahogany colour, rich, sweet, pronounced raisiny character. **Government House Port** ⚘ **NV** Ruby style dessert, launched 1911 and despite relative lightness, IWSC gold medal holder. Forward prune-like aromas/flavours, some clean earthiness and lick choc for extra smoothness. Large oak cask aged min 18 mths.

Seidelberg Estate

Paarl (see Paarl map) • Tasting & sales Mon—Fri 9—5 Sat/Sun/public holidays 10—4 Tasting fee R6 for 5 wines • Cellar tours by appointment • Olive & Vine Restaurant (see Eat-out section) • Conference/function centre • Tourgroups • Gifts • Walks • Views • Wheelchair-friendly • Owner Roland Seidel • Winemaker Nicolaas Rust (since 1999) •

Viticulturist Conré Groenewald (since 1999) • Vineyards 85 ha • Production 20 000 cases 80% red 15% white 5% muscadel • PO Box 505 Suider-Paarl 7624 • Tel (021) 863-3495/6 • Fax (021) 863-3797 • E-mail ebr@new.co.za • Website www.seidelberg.co.za

WINEMAKER-MANAGER Nicolaas Rust's wish list includes "building this farm into one of the best in the Cape winelands" and, off-duty, "relaxing with a glass of good wine somewhere cellphones don't ring". Given that the latter device is the new — and all-invasive — coloniser of South Africa, his first wish looks much likelier to be granted. Hamburg-born Roland Seidel (re-establishing his native-country's links with this historic property between Fairview and Landskroon; it was German-owned in 1691) is pouring resources into vineyards and cellar expansion. There are now 85 ha of mostly red-wine varieties on this 420 ha spread backed by Paarl mountain, and old vineyards are being grafted over to newly fashionable (in the Cape) viognier and mourvèdre. Consumer-friendliness extends to the Olive & Vine cellar-restaurant, and picnic lunches outside, with full-frontal Table Mountain view. The increasingly impressive wines are listed by Louis Latour on the export market.

Roland's Reserve range

✿ **Merlot** Sets a _big_ cat among the Paarl pidgeons with massively ripe, explosively fruity **99**; minerally oak and whack of tannin hardly able to contain the mulberry/blackberry/sweet violet flavours, which reverberate for ages. Would be a pity to open all this untamed power too early; give 4 yrs min, then try again. 14% alc. 400 cases.

✿ **Pinotage** Estate's "first ever pinotage" — and **99** seems to be making up for lost time: powerful, mouth expanding with variety's 'sweet' juicy presence (here as mulberry/ripe banana), concentrated yet firmly constrained by sweet tannins which need 2–4 yrs to relax. Oak aged, 14,5% alc. 800 cases.

✿ **Cabernet Sauvignon** This in different mode to above swashbucklers; **99** compact, almost demure in cassis/ripe black cherry garb and firm tannic girdle with fragrant oak. Gives impression of a much better wine waiting to be freed, so don't hurry; give few yrs and see how it develops. 14% alc. 600 cases.

Seidelberg range

✿ **Cabernet Sauvignon-Merlot** Step up for this 50/50 blend in unoaked, full-bodied **99**, starring a fine cherry/raspberry bouquet which permeates the balanced sappy palate. 1 200 cases. **97** VG

✿ **Chardonnay** ⬇ Now luxuriously settled into fat, toasty/butterscotchy style cleverly tweaked with plenty of crisp citrus. **99** full-bodied (13,5% alc), enduring; should age interestingly. **98** entirely fermented in new Fr oak. **00** not tasted.

Chenin Blanc ✿ Wearing its age gracefully, **98** with intricate citrus/herb and sweet honey interplay. Rich and full, long tapering finish. Super food wine, well priced. **Sauvignon Blanc** ✿ 98 in flinty-dry unwooded style, quite plump palate (nettles, figs), frisk of sweetness in finish. 12,5% alc. **Sauvignon Blanc-Riesling** ✿ Rarely seen as a combo on labels in Cape, but nothing unfamiliar about the sweet-hay/figgy whiffs in **99**, which appears bigger than its 11,5% alc would suggest.

De Leuwen Jagt range

✿ **Red Muscadel** ⬇ Sophisticated fortified dessert with honeysuckle/herb tones to ripe cherry/sweet plum, some pepper and warming spirit on the tongue. For solo sipping on a furious winter's night. 18,5% alc. **NV**. 1 000 cases.

> **Chenin Blanc** ✿ 😊 Here's a companionable quaffer to buy now and drink tonight while all the wonderfully fresh sherbety tang's still popping out of the bottle.

Merlot �★ Lots of texture (mainly dry tannin), but only shy hints of sweet strawberry/plum fruit in **00**. Perhaps needs time to relax/develop. 13,2% alc. 1 200 cases.

Cabernet Franc-Merlot ✿ **99** equal blend makes for interesting flavour combination of green pepper/raspberry/coffee/choc plus some cherry on the top. Unwooded. Tight tannins need time or saucy rump steak. 13% alc. 1 200 cases. **Chardonnay** ✦ Unwooded, undemanding **98** more alive than expected; full-bodied tropical/melon tones still reasonably quaffable. 13,5% alc. 1 000 cases. Preview of **00** cause for some excitement ... **Sauvignon Blanc** ✿ New Green apple crispness in **00**; mixes with tropical fruit salad in brisk dry palate. **Nuance** ✦ New Delicate hay whiffs hint at Cape riesling provenance of this lightish **99** blend with white muscadel, showing bit of honeyed age. 1 000 cases.

. . . .

Sentinel see Coppoolse Finlayson

. . . .

Ship Sherry

NOT 'SHERRY', but jeripigo-style fortified which has achieved the status of trusted companion, especially among bluecollar workers in the Eastern Cape. By Stellenbosch Farmers' Winery.

NV ✿ Somewhat neutral but clean, well made, not oversweet.

. . . .

Shoprite Checkers

National wine buyer Stephan Eksteen • PO Box 215 Brackenfell 7561 • Tel (021) 980-4000 • Fax (021) 980-4075

"TO BUY DIRECT from the farm or producer, locally and internationally, to ensure the lowest possible price" is the consumer focused mission of Stephan Eksteen, wine buyer for this national supermarket chain which sources and sells the in-house OddBins and Rite ranges below, as well as a wide selection of wines from many of the leading Cape wineries.

OddBins range

Cabernet Sauvignon Bin 85 ✿ New Here's the bargain of this range: partially oaked **99**, offering super full-bodied cab flavours, sleek tannins, smoothly dry oak. Satisfying. 13,6% alc. 1 000. **Ruby Cabernet-Cabernet Sauvignon Bin 142** ✿ ☺ Warm spicy-plummy **00**, lightly oaked, offers ripe 'sweet' fruit, though finishes firmly dry. Good table partner for Karoo lamb, observes Stephan Eksteen. 1 500 cases. 13,% alc.

Cabernet Sauvignon-Merlot Bin 34 ✿ New **99** features just the right dollops tannin, sweet berry fruit, and body to cut the fat of a succulent BBQed sausage. Cask aged 12 mths. 13,8% alc. 1 000 cases. **Cabernet Sauvignon-Merlot Bin 86** ✿ Here's an instantly aged **95** still with good sweet-tasting, oak-fragrant berry fruit. Fresh acidity suggests drink soon. 600 cases. **Ruby Cabernet-Merlot Bin 146** ✦ New Stephan Eksteen suggests you try full-bodied, unoaked **00** with equally robust ostrich stroganoff with mashed potato. 13% alc. 1 200 cases. **Chardonnay Bin 129** ✦ New Individual style med-bodied **99**; pungent, lemony. 600 cases. **Chenin Blanc Bin 137** ✦ New Granny Smith apple in fresh, easy **00**. Lightish, softly dry. 1 000 cases. **Sauvignon Blanc Bin 49** ✦ Some lightish passionfruit flavour, strong 'grainy' acidity which really needs food. 1 500 cases. **Colombard-Chardonnay Bin 87** ✿ From the 'home' of colombard, Rbtson, and it shows: fresh guavas, herbs, earth and citrus — all jostling in lightish, not-too-dry palate. 1 500 cases. **Sauvignon Blanc-Chardonnay Bin 139** ✦ New No-formalities quaffing **00**, simple, lightish grass/guava tones, citrus finish. 1 000 cases. **Stein Bin 39** ✦ New Pleasantly contrasting green apple flavour and honeyed sweetness in **00**. 2 000 cases.

. . . .

Rite range

House-brand 5 ℓ boxes from Robertson Winery. Untasted for this ed, but track record suggests ✿-✿✿ quality. **Dry Red**, **Grand Cru**, **Rosé**, **Stein**, **Late Harvest**.

. . . .

Signal Hill ▼

Franschhoek (but see Stellenbosch map) • Tasting & sales by appointment • Owners Ridon Family Vineyards (Pty) Ltd and The Wine Factory cc • Winemaker Jean-Vincent Ridon (since 1997), Lawrence Buthelezi (since 1999) • Viticulturist Marietjie Marais • Vineyards 4,5 ha • Production 1 200 cases 50% red 45% dessert 5% white • PO Box 1050 Stellenbosch 7599 • Tel (021) 880-0908 or + 33 15 301 3167 • Fax (021) 880-0508 • E-mail ridon@iafrica.com • Website www.signalhillwines.co.za

JEAN-VINCENT RIDON'S stormy affair with the Cape continues. After a nerve-racking 99 crush ("hope not to have too many like it in my life"), the flamboyant descendant of 14th century Loire vignerons, pvsly winemaker at Ashanti (where he made this small range for his own account), in the 2000 vintage found himself "seeking asylum in the middle of fermentation". Hastily transferring to the Agusta cellar in Franschhoek, he found time to make an experimental icewine (which, he's certain, the Wine & Spirit Broad "will kill me for"), as well as a Chardonnay and a Pinotage featuring "French and African wood". Though the young Frenchman has embraced SA with energy and passion (he's the driving force behind the increasingly influential Air France–Preteux Bourgeois winemaking competition), he remains attuned to the Old World: "Even when the finances are low, I force myself to go back to France as soon as I can to regenerate my classic spirit, and to avoid falling on the easy side of winemaking."

✿ **Cabernet Sauvignon** ▼ In pvs ed we asked of **98**, can Jean-Vincent Ridon make a dull wine? Conclusion: impossible. With follow-up **99** (featuring splash shiraz), he proves the point: whiffs Bourneville cocoa/bitter coffee/creosote (!) — all washing with warm summer fruits over weighty (13,9% alc), tarry palate to persistent, dry, still tannic finish. It all works rather well, though too early to anticipate development. 25% old clones ex-Klapmuts, balance new Simonsberg bushvines, very low-yielding. Yr Fr oak (25% new). Not filtered/stabilised, so expect a sediment. **98** with dash ripe banana (!). **97** *Wine* ✿✿.

✿ **Pinot Noir Barrel Fermented** Experimental cask fermentation in **98** turned out so well, it's repeated in latest **99** with perhaps even more Burgundian result: waves of woodsmoke/ripe strawberries/fungi spilling into really mouthcoatingly — but ripe — tannic palate, which should settle with time. Grapes ex-F'hoek; unusually 100% fermented in open new small Fr barrels; cask-aged on lees. 13% alc. No **00**.

✿ **Vin de L'Empereur** Deliciously different golden dessert from muscat d'alexandrie (hanepoot). Natural table partner for foie gras or, J-V R suggests, postdinner finale of tangy apricot tart. Unusual riesling tones with minty/eucalyptus/honeysuckle scents in **98** *Wine* ✿✿, sweet-sour flavours, initial background oak now fully absorbed. Clean citrus finish. Grapes (no botrytis) from Simonsberg (Paarl side).13% alc. **99** not ready for tasting. This and below 375 ml.

✿ **Vin de L'Empereur Crème de Tête** Luscious **98** botrytis dessert with golden syrup/marmalade and lightly caramelised tones, all reverberating in penetratingly sweet palate. Back-tasted mid-2000 lacks initial cleansing acidity (may be in awkward phase); suggest careful monitoring. *Wine* ✿✿, Michelangelo gold, wine mail order club selection. "Hand-selected", 40 yr old bushvine muscat d'alexandrie ex-Simonsberg farm. Barrel-fermented in all-new oak. 12% alc, 6,5 g/ℓ acid, 221 g/ℓ sugar.

. . . .

Silversands see Robertson Winery
Silumku see Overhex

Simonsig Estate

Stellenbosch (see Stellenbosch map) • Tasting & sales Mon—Fri 8.30—5 Sat 8.30—4 Tasting fee R5 p/p • Cellar tours Mon—Fri 10, 3 Sat 10 (max 8 unless by arrangement) • Owners Malan family (Simonsig Estate Partnership) • Winemaker Johan Malan (since 1981), with Van Zyl du Toit & Debbie Burden • Viticulturist Francois Malan (since 1980) • Marketing Pieter Malan • Vineyards 286 ha • Production 2 100 tons 150 000 cases 50/50 red/white • PO Box 6 Koelenhof 7605 • Tel (021) 888-4900 • Fax (021) 888-4909 • E-mail wine@simonsig.co.za • Website www.simonsig.co.za

WINE INDUSTRY DOYEN Frans Malan may be officially retired, but he still worries about the customers. And though occasionally patrons with overdue accounts may be a particular focus, the booming family business, radiating from Stellenbosch into nearly two dozen wine markets, is ample evidence that Malan and sons Pieter, Francois and Johan know how to keep consumers happy. Among the first to grasp the value of personal contact, they put up welcome signs and spread the red carpet for visitors. Egging colleagues to follow suit, they helped put the Stellenbosch Wine Route on the map. "South Africans can't afford to spend as much on a bottle of wine as they used to, so we have to have other labels to keep this market," says Pieter Malan. So while Simonsig remains the core brand, the Malans have created a Family Vintners range — non-estate wines from own/purchased fruit — and launched these into 22 export markets with great success. Consistency, a wide range of premium and well priced products, and a sound business ethos drive this operation, visited by 70 000 people annually. And if recent ratings by the US *Wine Spectator* are a guide, the price-quality ratio here is among the best.

✿ **Shiraz** Higher star rating indicative of improving shiraz quality in Cape — Johan Malan not lagging here or in 'show reserve' arena (see below). Striking inky/plum hues open **98**, cracked peppercorn, redcurrant whiffs, earthy farmyard undertones rebound in full yet well mannered palate. Understated vanilla from ±33% Am oak; rest Fr, 25% new, 19 mths.

✿ **Merindol Syrah** (Shiraz Reserve in pvs ed) Scrutinise family crest on any Simonsig bottle and see the words 'Sigil Malan de Merindol', reference to Huguenot origins in Europe. This excellent **97** reserve, from oldest vyds, combines Australian ripe fruit, Rhône hillside scrub tonality; dense plum hue, ripe cassis and smoky whiffs; persistent finish with subtly supportive oak (18 mths mainly new Fr, some Am). *Wine* ✿.

✿ **Pinotage Red Hill** Old bush vines, yielding 8 t/ha, expansively oaked (unlike standard bottling — see below). Second release **98**, just bottled when tasted, closed but showing huge potential: elegant tannin structure framing full red berry flavours. Full-throated oaking (20 mths mostly Am, one third new), hardly noticeable, through for style reasons Johan Malan's inclination to favour Fr cooperage in future. **97** SAA.

✿ **Pinotage** "Doesn't need wood," declares Johan Malan, referring to pinotage in general (though expensively oaked Red Hill above makes its own case). **99** certainly none the worse for lack of oak adornment: full frontal blast of stewed plums, tar, forest floor; concentrated curranty mulberry packing fruity punch in juicy palate.13,6% alc. **98** awarded 89 rating by US *Wine Spectator*; mail order club best value selection. **97** ✿, SAA. **89** tasted at the cellar Jul 2000 showed glimpses of Burgundian greatness, though pure pinotage.

✿ **Tiara** Unflashy but excellent Bdx blend, with statuesque Cape/Old World presence in **98** despite youth (unrated in deference to request, but easily matches pvs). Blend 60% cab, 40% petit verdot, 34% merlot, 2 % cab f — real Bdx cépagement. Smoky, earthy notes, elegant sweetly tuned fruit. 17 mths Fr oak, 63% new, few Am casks as condiment. Muscular 14% alc. For the long haul. **97** Best New World Red in UK *Decanter* monthly roundup, "one of the greatest vintages ever" states Malan. Much less (4%) petit verdot (though he feels latter holds more promise than merlot in Cape). These have been shown to age rewardingly — **94** still lively. **95** SAA, VVG.

☘**Frans Malan Reserve** Cape blend honouring Frans Malan, Cape wine pioneer, entrepreneur, free thinker and still vigorous eminence here. Features pinotage — somewhat controversially, though jury's still deliberating 'proper' Cape red makeup. In **98** the home boy grape is 50% of blend, with 20% merlot, 30% cab. Complex smoky, plum pud aromas, finely judged oak (Fr/Am new/2nd fill); fine-grained berry flavours. Rung above **97** ☘ (though SAA, VVG), touch more cab (33%).

☘**Chardonnay** ▼ Long regarded as Cape benchmark (with bonus of accommodating price). **99** powerful citrus/butterscotch and dense, juicy lime. Some toasty overtones. Barrel fermented/aged 10 mths Fr oak. 13,2% alc. Taut acidity points to another vintage worth cellaring. These can develop well, acquiring complex hazelnut/marzipan flavours with age. **98** VVG, **97** IWSC gold, **96** VG.

☘**Gewürztraminer** ▼ Special Late Harvest style, brilliant yellow-gold, trademark rose garden/litchi aromas, ripe melon/kiwi flavours. **99** ☘ with elegantly poised sweetness (31 g/ℓ), most attractive. **98** greater length, even some cellaring potential.

☘**Cuvée Royale** Distinctive, powerfully flavoured cap classique, very dry, good acidity gives length, maturation potential. Current **92** led by chardonnay (though blended with 16% pinot); 7 yrs on lees/in bottle make for exceptionally complex apple/sourdough bread aromas. Pvs **91** marked 30 yrs of Simonsig wines.

☘**Kaapse Vonkel** Ground-breaker approaching 30 yrs as first commercial cap classique. **96** a 'sparkling Cape blend' — 15% homespun pinotage adding local colour to 50% chardonnay, 35% pinot. Red grape body/fruit to the fore; 4 yrs on lees, plus some bottle maturation give more weight, complexity than when reviewed last yr. Honeyed croissant nose, firm, quite weighty palate, all combine to satisfy. 8 g/ℓ sugar.

☘**Vin de Liza** Peach/apricot toned NLH from bukettraube, named after revered Malan matriarch. Elegant in standout slim 375 ml bottle. **99** ☘ delicate potpourri of dried fruits, whiff honeyed botrytis; not too sweet (96 g/ℓ sugar). Departs from old Cape style 'sticky nobles'. **98** even drier (85 g/ℓ), more substance.

Chenin Blanc ☘ 🙂 **00** More than 25 000 cases of this firm, peach/melon flavoured dry white produced — many for the US. 15% colombard adds freshness; firm structure ensures interesting cellaring possibilities for yr or three.

Cabernet Sauvignon ☘ Poised, urbane red, more Old World than New, reflecting vintner's classical, thoughtful approach. **98** as polished as pvs, well fleshed with plummy fruit (dash merlot peeping through), some background smoky, earthy aromas. 18 mths Fr oak. **Sauvignon Blanc** ☘ Seldom a blockbuster, but **00** good varietal identity for this hot vintage. Lemon, nettle whiffs, firm dry, creamy flavours. Nearly 14% alc adds balanced texture, presence. **Vin Fumé** ☘ One of the first Cape wooded sauvignons; still very popular in restaurants (not just because of non-greedy price). **99** bone dry, generous creamy fruit salad nose; firm, food-friendly zesty finish. **Weisser Riesling** ☘ One of the Cape's few standouts (though always low keyed), with good ageing potential — an **87** delighted recently. Just-dry **99**, with dash morio muscat, starts quietly, gentle floral, herbal notes; orange rind, grapefruit, sour cream flavours lead to juicy farewell. **Mustique** ☘ Exotic, aromatic trio bukettraube, riesling, morio muscat (just some of the 20 varieties on Malan's palette). **99** surprisingly dry for 12,5 g/ℓ sugar, creamy, honeyed aromas. **Franciskaner** ‡ **00** Floral whiffs and gulpable semi-sweet fruit from well blended bukettraube, chenin and gewürz.

Simonsvlei International

Paarl (see Paarl map) Tasting & sales Mon—Fri 8—5 Sat 8.30—4.30 (also Sun during Dec/Jan) Fee R5 for 6 tastings • Cellar tours by appointment • Luncheons Mon—Sat 12—3 Tel (021) 863-2486 (children's menu available) • Tourgroups (guided tours including meals available) • Function/conference facilities • Views • Wheelchair-friendly • Owners 73 shareholders • Consulting viticulturist Kobus van Graan (VinPro) • Vineyards 1 400 ha • Production 220 000 cases 80% white 20% red • PO Box 584 Suider-Paarl 7624 • Tel (021) 863-3040 • Fax (021) 863-1240 • E-mail info@simons-vlei.co.za • Website www.simonsvlei.co.za

EVERYTHING'S happening on the double here. In fact, people thought they were seeing double when they spotted MD Kobus Louw perched on the roof. He was left high and dry after he'd remarked that he'd "sit on the roof" if the cellar achieved a double gold at Veritas, which it did, for its Hercules Paragon Shiraz 97. The liquid assets at this modern Paarl co-op turned company are certainly on an upwardly mobile swing. And not just the wines: the website is being redesigned and will soon boast the latest Internet technology; the vat cellar has just been upgraded; there's a new grape classifying system in place; and the operation in its entirety is being ISO 9000 quality assurance accredited. All very exciting and challenging for incoming winemaker Francois van Zyl (ex Groote Post), who was set to start here just as the guide went to press. But this industry leader was not without its setbacks: the death of chairman Phillip Louw in a car accident was a sad moment in the history of Simonsvlei.

Hercules Paragon range

❀ **Cabernet Sauvignon** Developing profitably in bottle, **98** now offers some secondary tobacco whiffs over minerally strawberry fruit. Some ripe but firm tannins suggest this has legs for another 3—5 yrs min. Med-bodied. Yr 2nd fill Fr oak, malo in barrel. 2 000 cases.

❀ **Merlot** Paragon of these flagships, med/light-bodied **98** gaining polished complexity in bottle. Initial tightness giving way to fragrant juiciness (wafts of violet, raspberry, cherry), supple tannins ripe with promise. 1 000 cases.

❀ **Shiraz** Opulence glimpsed in pvs ed starting to emerge from pvsly austere **98**. Some richer plummy tones, plus signature varietal aromas of woodsmoke/clove/cinnamon peeping through. But needs more time. 1 000 cases. 13% alc. **97** VVG, SAA, wine mail order club selection.

❀ **Sauvignon Blanc** New Nod to the Old World in austere, bone-dry **00** with spread of 'green' flavours: grass/herbs/nettles plus riper gooseberry. Food wine, med/full-bodied. 700 cases.

❀ **Semillon** Notch up scale from pvs, **99**'s burnished yellow-gold reflects wide-angle lime/lees/bush tea/honey flavour spectrum. Med-bodied. 1 000 cases. This, like **98** ❀❀, wine mail order club selection, needs another yr to gain flesh, shed initial acidic tartness.

Simonsvlei range

❀ **Shiraz** Attractive lightly oaked style. Herby/savoury **99**, med-bodied; some mulberry/plum and supple tannins. 2 000 cases.

❀ **Cabernet Sauvignon-Merlot** ✔ Signature mulberry tones in easy **99**, sweetly ripe palate and soft dry finish. Slightly better than a quaffer, but without pretensions. Value at R20 ex-cellar. 13% alc. 2 000 cases.

❀ **Humbro Red Jerepico** ✔ Recent bottlings have bumped this popular **NV** sweet fortified dessert into a higher star bracket. Coppery colour, muscat/plum fragrance and fleshy non-cloying palate. Red muscadel. Wine mail order club selection. 2 000 cases.

❀ **Humbro Hanepoot** ✔ Latest **NV** bottling raises the quality stakes (and value — this R13 ex-winery). Perfumed honeysuckle/freesia bouquet; sweet, spirity yet light and refreshing. Lightly chill or pour over ice for a fragrant summer cooler. 2 000 cases.

✿ **Premier White Muscadel** ▼ Invariably excellent unctuous fortified dessert; limited quantities, premium priced. More luscious than jerepigos above, more glow inducing. **96** with supercharged muscat fragrance, intriguing white pepper sprinkles; viscous palate which ends with a honeyed flourish. 500 cases. **95** *Wine* ✿.

✿ **Port** More traditional style fortified dessert. Latest release sees home boy pinotage dropped from team — shiraz/tinta b scrum together in **97**, with smoky choc-raisin tastes, savoury tang, nice lifting spirit in finish. **96** ✿ similar smoky/savoury prune aromas.

✿ **White Port** Individual example, one of tiny handful of this style in Cape. Curious spread of **98** sensations: tropical fruit to hazelnuts to peppery vanilla. But all mingle quite elegantly in spirity palate with (curious, not unpleasant) green banana finish. Chenin, developing well in bottle. Fine looking packaging. 500 cases.

Cabernet Sauvignon ✿ Undemanding med/full-bodied **99** with rhubarb/strawberry/light vanilla charms, well toned tannins which glide to easy dry finish. 2 000 cases. **Pinotage** ✿ Ripe plums and chunky tannins in 98, some understated dustiness in bone-dry finish. 2 000 cases. **Chardonnay** Tank sample of **00** too young to rate. Pvs **97** ✿. 2 000 cases. **Premier Chenin Blanc** ✿ Bracingly dry, almost austere **00** needs food (winemaker's suggestion of Mediterranean vegetables not a bad call). 5 000 cases. **Sauvignon Blanc** ✿ Light/med-bodied **00** very fresh, zippy, dry. Light gooseberry, cut grass tastes. 5 000 cases. **Premier Bukettraube** ✿ Uncomplicated, easy semi-sweet; **00** with delicate muscat scent, mellow fruity tones and zesty acidic finish. Lightish 11% alc.

Mount Marble range

Simonsrood ✿ 🙂 NV Popular everyday red with easy charm. Blend cinsaut/cab/tinta b. Med-bodied. 3 000 cases. **Vin Doux** ✿ 🙂 Sherbety sweet carbonated sparkler with bright, mouthfilling foam; straightforward yet satisfying.

Blanc de Blanc ‡ NV Bone dry and quite austere; clean lemon-guava fragrance. Wine mail order club selection. 2 000 cases. **Riesling** ‡ Well made, if not wildly exciting Cape riesling; tangy dried apricot/peach, fresh straw in dry finishing **00**. Suggest drink early. 5 000 cases. **Bouquet Blanc** ★ New Rather ordinary **NV** with some flowery, honeyed tones. 5 000 cases. **Stein** ✿ NV Nicely balanced light bodied off-dry finishing with a citrus twist. 3 000 cases. **Late Vintage** ✿ NV Supple, sappy flavours, honeyed/floral sniffs. No-frills quaffing. 3 000 cases. **Special Late Harvest** ‡ Some tropical, honeyed sweetness in **99**, with enough acidity for now — but not for keeping. 3 000 cases.

. . . .

Slaley Cellars ♈ ℞

Stellenbosch (see Stellenbosch map) • Tasting by appointment • Sales Mon—Fri 9—4 Sat & public holidays by appointment • Owners Hunting family • Winemaker Christopher van Dieren (since 1998) • Vineyard manager Jaco Mouton (since 1999) • Vineyards 80 ha • Production 450 tons (150 tons/12 000 cases own label) 90% red 10% white • PO Box 119 Koelenhof 7605 • Tel (021) 882-2123 • Fax (021) 882-2798 • E-mail chris@slaley.co.za • Website www.slaley.co.za

BELGIAN-BORN, Bordeaux-trained Christopher van Dieren's first work-berth was at Ch Giscours. Coming to the Cape 10 years ago, he crewed in the Nederburg, SFW and Simonsig cellars before becoming winemaking captain of this ship; vineyard manager Jaco Mouton is also ex-Simonsig. Commodore of the fleet is Lindsay Hunting, from a British ship-building dynasty, hence Slaley's maritime labels and the tendency to lapse into watery allusions. Not that earth and sky aren't part of the chart: Broken Stone (referring to ancient beacons found on the farm) is the second-label range; the Huntings' aeronautical manufacturing history will feature on a third, probably Reserve range. It was the 98 Shiraz which shot this newcomer to the very upmarket Simonsberg block (in own-winemaking terms, after supplying Nederburg for 40 years) into the South African stratosphere. Shiraz again featured in a blend with cabernet which also won Veritas double-gold. But don't expect carbon copies in future. Van Dieren's French-dressing inclines him towards a Rhône style Syrah, not a New World Shiraz; and his heart really belongs to the classic Bordeaux blend. Land ahoy? Keep your eyes peeled.

✿ **Hunting Family Shiraz** Maiden **97** *Wine* ✿ product of an ill-fated joint venture, as was show-stopping **98 Reserve** ✿, which was finished during dissolution of the partnership. Latter took honours at every level (*Wine* ✿, VVG, Michelangelo gold), for good reason. But this was a stylistic one-off. New winemaker van Dieren has sights firmly set on Côtes du Rhône rather than Barossa; shows in follow-up **99** (under Hunting Family label — Reserve to be used again for two-barrel submission to Nederburg Auction in time): good spicy pepper nose with cinnamon hints, but lacks fruit intensity in palate. Sample **00** shows tremendous promise, elegant grip and flavour intensity to come. The violent tides of style need to settle before consistent quality flows.

✿ **Hunting Family Merlot** New "With this one will we redeem ourselves," says van Dieren of the upcoming **99**, 1 000 cases sold-out prior to release. (60% exported to Germany, USA; find it locally at Makro.) Heady perfume of scented violets, full of sumptuous dark choc/red berry flesh. Soft tannins provide backbone to ripe fruit, fragrant oak (50/50 Am/Fr) and stalwart alc (14%). Next **00** bigger, better from restricted yields (7 t/ha).

✿ **Hunting Family Chardonnay** Sea-change of shiraz style above mirrored here: **98** emphatically New World, stone fruit flavours densely layered with coating ripe butterscotch, leesy vanilla in expansive palate (100% barrel fermented, 20% new Am, 50% through malo; 13,2% alc.). Now ends trifle bitter. Next **99** deliberately more 'Continental' — lemon/lime fruit centre-stage with viscous melting-butter off left. Tangy, more elegant. All Fr oak. Hint botrytis adds pineapples, not sugar.

Broken Stone range

✿ **Cabernet Sauvignon-Merlot** New **99**, for release 2001, eventually destined for Slaley range and flagship status. Vibrant, precocious colour; nose packed with brambles, blueberry, oak dominates in youth. Beautifully refined palate, ripe tannins firm up the ensemble. Most promising, as is sample **00** to follow: perfumed all-Fr oak (80% new) more serious fruit/structure (Van Dieren's Bdx experience coming to fore). 77% cab s, rest merlot. Cab f/petit verdot set to join the fray in future.

✿ **Cabernet Sauvignon-Shiraz** Wild peppery spice of **98** VVG, SAA, *Wine* ✿ resonates in palate with soft red berries, pimento, touch anise. Firm texture of cab promises good development. 17 mths 20% Fr, 80% Am oak (half new). 13,5% alc. Next **99** ✿ more shiraz (35%), but higher yields (12 t/ha) dilute flavour. Still, most agreeable spiced raspberry, soft tannins. Easy ending, easy drinking.

Cabernet Sauvignon ✿ New **99** tobacco interleaved with juicy blackcurrant/cherry, soft and fresh. German oak, rest 2nd fill Am, Fr. Will be popular. **Pinotage** ✿ Currants/strawberries join ripe plums in sappy drink now **97**. Next **98** *Wine* ✿ more wild, gamey, fully ripe with jammy banana, herbal-remedy edge. Unequivocal pinotage held back by bitter finish. **Sauvignon Blanc** ✿ Fresh tropical fruit, succulent green melon, touch gooseberry in **00**. As far from asparagus as van Dieren can get: easy fresh flavour is his aim. Forward **99** developing cat's pee/bottle age cardboard nose.

Simunye see Backsberg

Sinnya

UK BORN Master of Wine (and accomplished cook) Richard Kelley is behind this Afro-accented brand ('Sinnya' the San equivalent of 'Breede River'), grown by various Robertson wine farmers and owned/marketed by Vinimark.

Pinotage New Preview of infant **00** (too unformed to rate realistically, but with ⚜ potential) reveals 'sweet' banana/mulberry tones, exuberant tannins. 13% alc. **Merlot-Cabernet Sauvignon** ⚜ Lightly oaked **99**, with splash ruby cab, in unusually gruff mood when tasted mid-2000. Subdued, astringent (but should work well with gastronome Richard Kelley's foodie pairing: traditional BBQed 'skilpad' (minced game liver in fatty caul). ±13% alc. 7 000 cases. **Chardonnay** ⚜ Chicken Kiev's on Kelly's menu here, prompted by **00**'s plumpness, broad vanilla tones. 13% alc. 5 000 cases. **Colombard-Chardonnay** ☆ Clean, fresh, though unexpectedly not very characterful **00** (pvs much zingier). Med/full-bodied, partially oaked. 2 000 cases.

Siyabonga

Wellington • Not open to the public • Owners Graham Knox & Alain Moueix • Winemaker Etienne Charrier (since 2000) • Viticulturist Francois Baard (since 1999) • Vineyards 12 ha • Production 5 000 cases (1 350 own label) 60% white 40% red • PO Box 1209 Wellington 7654 • Tel (021) 864-3155 • Fax (021) 864-1744 • E-mail doolhof@mweb.co.za

A CAPE WINE FARM as an agent of revolution? This is exactly what you'll find on this 80 ha Wellington property owned by writer-entrepreneur Graham Knox, scene of a remarkable literacy, life-skills and economic empowerment programme designed to change the lives of workers and employers alike, ripple out to the neighbours, and serve as a pilot-project throughout the winelands. Pre-schoolers, scholars and adults are all learning, Knox and his wife Diane included (they're being taught Afrikaans). A multi-disciplinary team from the University of the Western Cape is in charge, funded by the SA Wine Industry Trust. Infused with a new sense of purpose, workers are redeveloping the vineyards, planting cabernet and merlot, building roads. These first wines from Siyabonga ("we give thanks") aren't politically correct sops to social conscience. They're quite good enough to stand on their own.

⚜ **Pinotage** Statement pinotage with flesh and muscles for the long haul. **99** grabs your attention with swirling bouquet of woodsmoke and plum; rich mulberry in big, firm palate with generous layerings of red berries. Not a facile wine: current astringent tannins need couple of yrs — should be well worth the wait. Low yielding (4 t/ha) vyd on own farm. Partly barrel fermented, aged 12 mths new/2nd fill Fr oak. 250 cases.

⚜ **Severney** First in envisaged range of small volume, premium blended whites. Complex collage of floral, tropical, citrus flavours and tastes in quietly delicious **00**, mainly barrel fermented semillon, chenin, chardonnay with splash unoaked sauvignon. Sampled immediately post-bottling (July 2000) still somewhat unsettled, but should develop harmony by early 2001. Some grapes from neighbour. 13% alc. 1 200 cases.

Slanghoek Winery

Worcester (see Worcester map) • Tasting & sales Mon—Fri 8—12.30, 1.30—5.30 Sat 10—1 • Cellar tours by appointment • Grietjiesdrift Guesthouse & Restaurant 100 m from cellar, open daily tel (023) 349-3161 (023) 349-3121 • Tourgroups • Walks • Views • Owners 25 members • Winemakers Kobus Rossouw (since 1993), Henri Swiegers (since 1996), Christo Pienaar (since 1998) • Viticulturists As above, with VinPro consultants • Vineyards 1 600 ha • Production 23 000 tons (12 000 cases own label) 86% white 14% red • PO Box 75 Rawsonville 6845 • Tel (023) 349-3026 Fax (023) 349-3157 • E-mail slanghoek@lando.co.za • Website www.slanghoek.co.za

THE QUALITY—PRICE RATIO at this cellar is already amazing enough; heaven knows how much better it could get now that its 25 members' vineyards have been fitted with neutron water-sensors, and 5 weather stations are monitoring the various meso-climates in this beautiful valley. Vines which clearly have been living in style — you do not win the national young wine championships year after year, as Slanghoek does, with abused grapes from low-class neighbourhoods — will now have the equivalent of 5-star room-service. Slanghoek's values remain irreproachable. Kobus Rossouw and his crew — Christo Pienaar and Henri Swiegers (son of Giel of Vredendal and KWV repute) — have introduced varietal Sauvignon, Chenin and Chardonnay to the line-up, and are launching the "informal" Vinay range, but it's desserts which are the specialities of the menu here.

❀ **Noble Late Harvest** ⑦ Handsomely packaged, carefully made botrytised dessert; at its best one of SA's finest, as evidenced by **99** ❀, SA champion NLH. All the more remarkable for non-greedy price. This and first release **98** ❀ from riesling. Formula changes to 50/50 chenin/hanepoot in latest **00** ❀, showing usual potent fruit intensity, with sweet-sour pineapple/quince piquancy and good shake of 'dusty' botrytis. Sweetest of these, in analysis and taste, despite bracing 9 g/ℓ acidity, in flush of youth seems a shade ponderous, almost unctuous where **99**, with gorgeous kumquat/dried fruits ensemble remains wonderfully tingly, uncloying. **98** fuller, richly sweet, improving in bottle. 250 cases.

❀ **Port** ⑦ Since **97** in more modern style, less sweet than pvs. Stewed prunes, spice and pepper in latest **98**, slice of fruitcake in palate, good spirity finish. 500 cases.

Cabernet Sauvignon ❀ Charming earlier maturing style (within 2–4 yrs). Brilliant youthful purple glow in **99**, cassis, cherries and just a hint of green olive. Some nice dry, ripe tannins. Customary sensitive oaking. 800 cases. **Pinotage** ❀ 𝐍𝐞𝐰 Unwooded **00** looks bright and young; tastes it too. Good minerals and red fruit stuffing, very dry finish. "Barbeque wine," say winemakers, unpretentiously. 13,5% alc. **Shiraz** ❀ Bold purple colour matched by striking Karoo scrub aromatic flourish; **99** quieter than pvs, so give bit of time to fill out. Lightly oaked. **Chardonnay** 𝐍𝐞𝐰 Barrel-fermented **00**, sampled from cask mid-2000, too embryonic to rate realistically, but solid platform of fruit should carry the finished wine to ❀ maturity. **Chenin Blanc** ❀ 𝐍𝐞𝐰 **00** infant still swaddled in fermentation character when tasted, already offering mouthfilling tutti-frutti flavours, refreshing cut of acid. Just off-dry. 1 000 cases. **Sauvignon Blanc** ❀ 𝐍𝐞𝐰 Appealingly fresh **00** New World style, invisible grain sugar plumps palate, smoothes brisk acidity. Lowish 11% alc. **Chardonnay-Sauvignon Blanc** ❀ Though formula changes to off-dry in latest **00** 50/50 blend (**99** dry), honest, good value swiggability remains. Lower altitude 11,4% alc. 1 600 cases. **Vinay** ❀ 𝐍𝐞𝐰 Refreshing, carefree off-dry quaffing the goal, which **00** attains with zingy, papaya-scented sauvignon, chenin, colombard blend. 500 and 1 000 ml. 1 600 cases. **Riesling-Sémillon** ❀ Hugely popular, inexpensive 50/50 blend; off-dry in analysis but certainly not sweet tasting. SA riesling's seabreeze/ozone aroma to the fore in **00**, semillon's broadening texture needs few mths to kick in. Lowish 11,6% alc. 1 500 cases. **Special Late Harvest** ❀ Barely off the vine when sampled, **00** delicate hanepoot dessert needed only time to get up to speed of **99** ❀. Latest offers sherbety litchi/lime bouquet, good sugar-acid tension. **97**, **96** VG. 800 cases. **Rooi Jerepiko** ⚝ Penetratingly sweet fortified dessert, from pinotage; showcases the local variety's aromatic red fruits, plus deeper molasses/caramel and raisin tones. Usual acid uplift missing in both current **99** and incoming **00**. 500 cases. **98**, **97** VG. **Soet Hanepoot** ❀ This cellar known for the delicacy, elegance of its sweet muscat d'alexandrie fortified desserts. Current **97** all honey and raisins; initial freshness starting to fade, so best drunk up. 500 cases. **95** VVG, **94** SA Champion. **Vonkelwyn NV** Sweet sparkling charmer not available for tasting. Pvs rated ❀.

Snake River see Linton Park

Somerbosch Wines

Stellenbosch (see Helderberg map) • Tasting & sales Mon—Fri 9—5 Sat 9—1 • Cellar tour by arrangement • Views • Wheelchair-friendly • Owner Roux family • Winemakers Marius & Japie Roux • Viticulturist Marius Roux • Vineyards 80 ha • Production ± 700 tons (250 tons 15 000 cases own label) 60% red, 40% white • PO Box 12181 Die Boord 7613 • Tel (021) 855-3615 • Fax (021) 855-4457 • E-mail enquiries@somerbosch.co.za • Website www.somerbosch.co.za

WHEN off-road enthusiast and winemaker Marius Roux isn't in the vineyards or cellar with brother Japie, he hangs up his 'gone fishing' sign, loads the family into the Landrover and hits the backroads to the bush or coast. The Rouxs (pharmacist wife Yolande, toddling James and, soon, a sibling) like to live and work in harmony with nature. Not that time stands still on their property in the foothills of the Helderberg. They've just moved into a new wine pressing cellar, expanding the facilities by 50%. They've had to. The 2000 merlot is already flexing its muscles and "looks like becoming a big one. We're really excited," say Marius and Japie Roux. They'll also be making the first shiraz from young vines this year — another eagerly awaited addition to the family.

✿ **Cabernet Sauvignon** Winery's top seller, developing fruitfully in **98**. Ripeness the key here, imparting succulence which follow-up **99** ✿ lacked when tasted mid-2000. Strict tannin, herbal/eucalyptus tones all need time to relax and grow. 13,6% alc. 2 200 cases. Yr 1st–3rd fill oak.

✿ **Merlot** This variety's undoubtedly found a niche here, showing quite distinctively with exotic scrubby/herbal perfumes and wafts of sweet violet. **99** also features youthfully exuberant tannins needing time, but the sturdy mulberry fruit-centre should stay the distance. ± 14% alc. 1 300 cases. Yr in casks, none new. **98**, markedly softer in youth, drinks well now.

✿ **Pinotage** Settling into its own style, which is full, almost brash and (perhaps something in these soils exactly midway between SOMERset West and StellenBOSCH), uncommonly aromatic. Tomato jam's the quirky scent in **99**, with more conventional banana/plum/spicy oak; plenty of fruity tannin to go 3–5 yrs. Sample tasted, potentially ✿ on release. 50% new Am oak, also new/used Fr. 450 tons.

✿ **Fine Ruby Port** New The Roux brothers in quieter mood with this attractive **NV** fortified dessert from cab. Spicy flavours of prunes, cinnamon and cloves, good spirity aromas. ± 18% alc. 350 cases.

Chardonnay New Sample of partially oaked **00** too unformed to rate but brimming with potential. 14% alc. 1 000 cases. **Chenin Blanc** ✿ Oak and acidity on verge of gaining upper hand in **99**; suggest drink soon. 14,3% alc. 450 cases.

Cabernet Sauvignon-Merlot Reserve ✿✿ 😊 Deftly oaked **97** has evolved into a smooth, satisfying drink. Fascinating crimson/blue colour, tobacco-fragrant strawberries, soft but dry tannins. Good unpretentious food wine. 12,9% alc. 800 cases.

Seugnet Rouge ✿✿ New 😊 (Say: soo-*nay*) **99** summertime special starring super-ripe cinsaut strawberries, cab raspberries and a long, soft lazy finish. Alc nudging 14% could prove very relaxing. Not oaked. **Sauvignon Blanc** ✿✿ 😊 Laid-back quaffing in gooseberry/grassy **00**, pleasant crisp dry finish. 13% alc. 800 cases. **Seugnet Blanc** ✿ New 😊 Lovely outdoorsy tippler with prepacked picnic of tropical fruit/tinned asparagus. Bright, bouncy med-bodied flavours, dry finish. This **99** and Rouge above 1 000 cases each.

Sommelier's Choice

PO Box 1 Cape Town 8000 • Tel (021) 465-8707 • Fax (021) 465-8709 E-mail sales@wineconcepts.co.za • Website www.wineconcepts.co.za

VALUE FOR MONEY in-house range of Wine Concepts, Cape Town based wine consulting/broking business run by Mike Bampfield-Duggan (of Upper Crust Restaurant fame), Murray Giggins and architect Derrick Henstra.

First is a lightly oaked **Chardonnay 98** (not available for tasting), to be followed by a **Shiraz 99**.

Sonnigdal see Goue Vallei

Sonop Wine Farm

Paarl/Stellenbosch (see Paarl map) • Tasting, sales, cellar/vineyard tours by appointment • Bed & breakfast at Sonop Farm • Owner Jacques Germanier Group/SAVISA (Pty) Ltd • Managing director Bernard Fontannaz • Winemaker Alain Cajeux • Vineyards 74 ha (own) Production 120 000 cases 60% red 40% white • PO Box 1142 Stellenbosch 7599 • Tel (021) 887-2409 • Fax (021) 886-4838 • E-mail office@sonop.co.za

"WE STARTED in 1991 with one farm," says Bernard Fontannaz, explaining just how far this path-breaking, export-achievement-award winning operation has grown (it's part of Jacques Germanier's Swiss-based multinational negociant businesss). "Now there are several farms, wineries as well as long term partnerships with growers across the winelands." And, on the drawing board, a new high-tech cellar. Keeping pace with expansion is the rate of transformation into ecologically sound organic production. A fresh note of enthusiasm creeps into Fontanaz's voice when he recalls that when Sonop farm at Paarl was bought "the soil was like concrete. Now the top 20–40 cm are soft and alive and full of earthworms. Everything goes back into the soil — stalks, pomace, even kieselguhr from the filtration line (which helps keep the soil alkaline). It's not the prettiest vineyard, but it's full of life!" A slow, steady process, the conversion is being done a block at a time and will be complete by 2002. Meanwhile the Winds of Change project, channelling funds to the Sonop farm staff, is flying. From every case of Winds of Change wine sold in the UK, a donation of £1 is made, funded equally by SAVISA, wholesalers and retailers.

African Legend range

Cabernet Sauvignon ✷ Early drinking **00**, interesting blend warmer/cooler climate fruit Stbosch/Paarl/Worcester. Reasonable concentration, some berries/plums, tannins still gangly. **Merlot** ✷ Light bodied **99** with some wine-gum flavours, dry finish. No oak. **Pinot Noir** ✷ Light, easy drinking **00**; honest wine, smells and tastes like pinot. No oak. **Pinotage** ✷ Mouthwatering glassful. **00** whiffs of high-toned sweet cherries followed by soft, easy fruit, interesting dry finish. Not oaked. **Shiraz** ✷ Old-boy-club leather and smoke introduction to med-bodied **00**, then sweet redcurrants; some richness and dry tannins. 30% small oaked. **Chardonnay** ✷ **00** pleasing peachy fruit, subtle oak overlay; fullish with creamy palate and dryness from oak returning in finish. Well priced. **Chenin Blanc** ✷ Gentle almond blossom aroma with hints of pear; **00** more flavour/weight than many at this price. **Colombard** ✷ Ripe peachy fruit climbs out of the **00** glass; light and lean, crisp acidity. **Sauvignon Blanc** ✷ **00** Good dry white will appeal to many for summer, but lacks varietal character.

Bredasdorp range

Ruby Cabernet ✷ **00** lesser wine than pvs, very soft with sweetish fruit and earthy, tannic finish; bit clumsy. **Rosé** ✷ One of few dry rosés, and very welcome for warm climate quaffing. **00** lovely raspberry aroma with hints of chocolate box.

Fullish, dry. **Sauvignon Blanc** ✷ Good varietal character with charm and fresh appeal. **00** youthful, cut-grass with hints of tropical and passion fruits.

Cape Levant range

Cabernet Sauvignon ✺ **97** Tired aromas, stalky; sweetish fruit and dry dusty tannins. **Merlot** ✺ Some dusty berry flavours in savoury-dry **99**, very dry finish. **Pinotage** ✷ Unusual concentration at this price level, with good **99** varietal character. Sweetish red cherry fruit gives way to dry finish, something of a signature for this cellar. Some 20% barrel aged. **98** SAA.

Sonop range

Cabernet Sauvignon ✷ Individual **00** aromas of roasted/toasted nuts, which some will love, others may hate. Lovely ripe fruit spreads across palate, with ripe tannins to match, long dry finish. 40% aged in new Am oak. **Merlot** ✷ Very easy to drink, better than average commercial versions. **99** stars blackcurrant, supported by wood. Nicely rounded fruit, some flesh, soft tannins 10% oaked. **Pinotage** ✷ **00** embryonic when tasted, shy sweetish raspberry fruit, some stalkiness. Ripe, quite dense plummy fruit, still awkward but not overpowering tannins. Should be approachable mid-2001. Not wooded. **Chardonnay** ✷ **99** Pretty spring flowers fragrances with hint old clone muscat. Despite 13% alc, tastes light, fresh. Balanced with long finish. No oak. **Chenin Blanc** ✷ Waves of fresh ripe yellow peach/spiced apples. **00** a plump version, well stuffed and fleshy, acid comfortable. **Sauvignon Blanc** ✷ Very lean, dry in **00** with aggressive acidity, not much varietal character.

Morgan (Cilmor) range

✦ **Cabernet Sauvignon** Charming, subtle style, not bombastic or self important. **00** wafts dark berries, cinnamon, eucalyptus and cedar. Med-bodied; some savoury tones plus fresher leafy notes. All new clone, 10% barrel aged.

✦ **Cabernet Franc** Gorgeous fragrance of hawthorn with delicate leafiness in this lighter **99** version of cab f. Svelte fruit, poised and elegant, offers redcurrants, good dry tannins and quite dry finish.

Merlot ✷ Still scratchy **99** tannins need another yr/2 or rustic food (spicy BBQ ribs?). Fresh leafy notes, some dark berries nicely concentrated, promising. **Pinotage** not tasted. **Shiraz** ✷ Sniff those **99** smoky/leathery scents and you know they are shiraz. Med/full bodied; sweet ripe fruit, large dollop alc (13,5%), fine-grained dry tannins, vanilla from Am oak all add interest. **Chardonnay** ✷ Waft of oak/caramel in **00**, bigger, fatter than pvs with ripe peaches and cream. 20% oaked, combination staves and barrel. **Chenin Blanc** ✷ Fresh lemon zest, hint of pears in **00**, light/easy with fine tangy acid. **Sauvignon Blanc** ✷ Youthful spring flowers, fresh guava aromas in **00**, fresh crispy fruit, though lacks true sauvignon punch.

Cape Soleil range

Organic line-up certified each year by Dutch organisation Skal, following full on-site inspection of farm/cellar and all records. Range trimmed to following wines:

Merlot ✷ Delicately fruity, lighter style **00**, restrained dark-berried fruit, still emerging. Supple feel, firmed by 10% Fr oak, none new. **Pinotage** ✷ Latest **00** already well settled down in mid-2000. Sweet red cherry aromas which translate easily into palate, ripe fleshy fruit with soft acidity making an already accessible glassful. **Shiraz** ✷ Newest **00** (barrel sample), in contrast to pinotage, still unsettled, stalky; full-bodied, some richness/earthiness, but needs to settle. 15–20% Am oak. Young vyds (1993). **Chardonnay** ✷ Med-bodied rather than rich **00**, pleasing creaminess backed by wood spice. Fresh floral aromas, some sweet-oak vanilla. 40% barrel fermented, new Seguin Moreau casks. **Sauvignon Blanc** ✷ Pretty, blossomy fruit with good touches sauvignon grass/green peppers in **00**. Fresh, lightish, good fruity mouthful features tropical melange and gentle acidity.

Kersfontein range

Exclusive to Direct Wine UK.

✿**Pinotage** Immediate impression of immense ripeness — signature of many wines from **00**. Bold sweet red cherries, wood well tucked away; chewy texture with big structure which should develop with interest. 30+ yr old low-cropping bushvines, 20% oaked, all Fr.

✿**Cabernet Sauvignon** New 'Hot', stalky fruit strangely combined with cool eucalyptus in **00**, very individual. Broad-shouldered, ripe, with ripe tannins to match; light sweetness.

Cabernet Franc New ✿ **00** initially flourishes cool leafy notes, then concentrated warm redcurrants/raspberries; carefully crafted tannins for earlier drinking.

Winds of Change range

Sales from this line provide assistance to Sonop farm employees. Except for Pinotage-Cabernet Sauvignon, all New.

✿**Semillon-Chardonnay 99** a banger: high-toned semillon citrus peel/smoke, then chardonnay sweet peach scent. Super ripe, rounded palate. Expands and grows in the mouth.

Merlot-Pinotage ✿ New Perfumed black cherry fruit beckons in **99** 60/40 blend; pretty, soft, no tannin to speak of. **Pinotage-Cabernet Sauvignon** ✿ Good dark-berried fruit concentration, attractive ripeness in **99** 60/40 blend; tannins still unyielding, so give another 1–2 yrs. Lightly oaked. **Pinotage-Shiraz** ✿ From **00**, styled for "off-the-shelf drinking," says Fontannaz. Plump, sweet berry fruit, puffs of smoke/vanilla; soft tannins. **Chardonnay** ✿ **98** big, bold statement of fat peachy ripeness, sweet caramel and lees. Somewhat quick finishing.

Out of Africa range
New

Notch higher up the price scale; 25 000 cases each.

✿**Pinotage** Fragrant version, a **99**, with raspberry fruit and chocolate, and no pinotage sweetness. Excellent fruit concentration, seductive black velvet texture but tannins come back on finish, should soften soon as they are ripe, not harsh. From 25 yr old vines in Dbnville. Used Fr casks.

Cabernet Sauvignon ✿ Welcoming friendly style. Dusty/smoky **99** attractive mix of older-clone dryness, newer-vine sweet plummy structure. **Chardonnay** ✿ Early preview shows mid-weight, lively **00** with some fatness and length. Toasted nuts/sweet vanilla of oak, plus citrus which spreads easily across the palate. **Sauvignon Blanc** ✿ Pleasant grassiness, good whiff tropical passionfruit, zesty green apples in **00**; fullish, rounded, finishes bit quick. Grapes from Dbnville.

Sparkling range
New

NV carbonated bubbles, strikingly packaged in embossed, frosted bottles, aimed to appeal to 18–25 year olds.

Tribal Sparkling Wine, ✿ Will Europe believe this is what local tribesmen and women are drinking? Bright, energetic bubble, charmingly off dry with fresh zesty flavours. All chenin. **Elixir** ✿ Bouncy fruit, easy charm. Prettily padded by soupçon sugar. Trendy label will appeal to young consumers.

Diemersdal range

✿**Cabernet Sauvignon** Sophisticated wine with beautiful balance. Full blast of roast/toasty fruit in **99**, loads of ripe plums, touches wild herbs/ground coffee in background of good oak. Generous, fleshy, ripe dark mulberry fruit balanced by good acid, fine-grained tannins showing signs of softening. 20% new Am oak, 20% used Fr.

✿**Chardonnay** Butterscotch and luscious peachy fruit in current **99**. Fat juicy mouthful, well rounded and fleshy but disciplined by good whack of oak.

Shiraz ✿ Greets you with loads of dark berried fruit, nice smoke/leather touches, concentrated fruit. **99** tannins held in check to classically dry finish. Still in formative stage, may rate further star with time. **Pinotage** ✿ **99** unusually rustic version, shows meaty/dusty wood tones with none of variety's distinctive sweet notes. Forbidding tannins. **Merlot** ✿ Sweet cassis cordial and eucalyptus wafts contrast with dry finish with touch of bitterness. Some fleshy fruit in fairly demure **99**. **Sauvignon Blanc** ✿ Assertive grassy attack in **00**, followed by green pepper/fig. Tangy, zesty, with good sauvignon capsicum/herbs to please aficionados. Despite generous alc (13,2%) has Loire like style and feel.

. . . .

Southern Right Cellars   ▽

Walker Bay • Tasting & sales at Wine Village (see Hermanus Heritage Collection) • Owners Anthony Hamilton Russell & Kevin Grant • Winemaker Kevin Grant (since 1994) • Viticulturist Stephen Roche (since 1998) • Vineyards 23 ha • Production 105 tons 9 300 cases 60% white 40% red • PO Box 158 Hermanus 7200 Tel (028) 312-3595 • Fax (028) 312-1797 • E-mail hrv@hermanus.co.za

WHALES in nearby Walker Bay enjoy it — every bottle contains a donation to conserving the Southern Right species which calves here. Oenophiles in the far-off USA love it — "Wow! Is this good wine!" enthuses a Boston newsletter. But while partners Anthony Hamilton Russell and Kevin Grant credit all the intrinsics like soil and slope and microclimate and stringent grape selection, perhaps what shines through most clearly is that both are having huge fun with this growing sideline to their respective owner and winemaker day-jobs at nearby Hamilton Russell Vineyards. Southern Right began as a gleam in their eyes — the challenge "to make something great" from local grape pinotage, and a recognisably South African version of sauvignon blanc — "somewhere between the overt fruit of New Zealand and the tight, restrained Loire styles". And while grapes will still be bought in, from joint-venture vineyards with private growers in the area, they now have their own 113 ha property in the Hemel-en-Aarde valley, with Walker Bay sea views, "a perfect place for a cellar" (love at first site?) and stony, clay-rich soil they believe to be ideal for pinotage."

✿ **Pinotage** "Vinosity rather than rusticity" is the aim, which realised more completely in **99** ✿ than pvs. Fruit more expressive, mouthfeel broader; greater complexity, roundness. Mid-palate better fleshed with fruit, with no pinotage acetone or bitterness. Own, Walker Bay, Western Cape fruit. 10 mths small Fr oak, 50% new. 13,7% alc. 1 700 cases. **98** as big (14% alc), but tighter; initial tannic rush needed longer to settle; good dry finish. Peek at **00** reveals ample berry fruit, huge tannins, incipient savoury notes dominated by varietal's banana fragrance. **97** ABSA Top 10, *Wine* ✿.

Sauvignon Blanc ✿ Complex cool-climate sauvignon; New Zealand perhaps uppermost in **00** — better flesh, less demanding freshness than pvs– though Sancerre never out of sight. Recapitulates pvs reductive style (which 'freezes' aromas/flavours, necessitating yr or so to 'thaw'). Floral notes with minerals/pebbles, fragrant gardenia in palate. Single vyd. 8 700 cases. 13,2% alc. Better vintage than **99**, initially piercingly fresh, grassy (though Air France–Preteux Bourgeois laureate).

. . . .

Spar

PO Box 1589 Pinetown 3600 • Tel (031) 701-8401 or (012) 998-4737 • Fax (031) 701-2030 or (012) 998-4738 • E-mail richard.alessandri@spar.co.za or saexvino@mweb.co.za

"THERE'S a friendly Spar wherever you are", reads the marketing slogan of this supermarket group, which means you don't have to travel any distance for a well priced drop. Beyond a wide selection from some leading wineries, Spar offers its own Country Cellars and Carnival ranges (100 000 cases sold annually — see separate entries). These are selected and managed by an independent wine committee according to very specific styles. In a further demonstration of wine dedication,

Spar was the biggest of the supermarket buyers at the 2000 Nederburg Auction — snapping up more than 700 cases at a value of over R670 000.

. . . .

Spice Route Wine Company

Swartland (see Swartland map) • Tasting & sales at Fairview (see that entry) • Cellar tours by appointment • Owner Charles Back • Winemaker Eben Sadie (since 1998) • PO Box 645 Malmesbury 7300 • Tel (022) 487-7139 • Fax (022) 487-7169

WHEN Eben Sadie speaks of "liquid passion" he's not referring to wine alone, though he pours so much intensity into the dramatic numbers below it's a wonder they don't turn to solids. Sadie is a surfer; when he can (all too rarely) tear himself away from this West Coast winery, his escape route heads straight to the nearest big breaks; in June 2000 he organised the first Vintners Surf Classic for equally stoked 'brothers' who wave-ride all over the wine world. When he talks barrels, they might easily be of the tubular sort, not those ruled by the men he describes as "the kings" of Spice Route's two maturation cellars (one French-perfumed, the other a New World blast): Jackson Kriel, Martin Welkom and Paul Khunyuza, tutored by visiting French winemakers, have fine art degrees in topping and racking. Sadie himself exemplifies the fervent, near-fanatical young blood transfusing the Cape wine scene, and is building a strong case for admission to its master-class. In just 3 vintages Spice Route has become a cult label, its wines as radical and explosive as any wave, winning umpteen awards and roaring off export shelves. He keeps constantly in mind, and ranged (emptily) on his kitchen shelves, the wines he most admires — mainly Côte Rôtie, it appears. The route to making great wine, he believes, is drinking great wine. And, when necessary perhaps, blowing your mind open in the perfect barrel?

'Flagship' range

✿✿ Merlot 99 ✿✿ striking, assured follow up to impressive **98**, Air France–Preteux Bourgeois finalist. Later vintage resonatingly rich; area's red earth nuances underpinning macerated red plums/dark bitter choc. Soft yet concentrated/structured; firm, dry tannins only enhance echoing, spicy intensity. Sympathetically oaked, as are all Eben Sadie's wines: 18 mths, all Fr, 50% new. Cooperage also important in forging structure: Vicard reining in variety's natural voluptuousness. 14,3% alc. As with pvs, destined for grand maturity.

✿✿ Pinotage 99 ✿✿ same genre as massive, inky **98** *Wine* **✿✿**, more readily recognisable varietal stamp than 'standard' range, but with thoroughly modern class. Intricate array dried bananas/figs/summer fruit corseted, augmented by whiffs toasty Fr oak. Oak also delicious savoury influence in finish, contrasts overall viscosity, creaminess. Despite size, concentration (yield minuscule 2,5 t/ha) and assertive (though glossy) tannins, nothing vulgar, out of place with this individual. (One can quite see why a visiting Brazilian sommelier has mooted variety as suitable for Amarone style.) 13,5% alc. 18 mths Fr barriques, 40% new.

✿✿ Syrah Standout, in many ways, in this trio of superb **99** Flagships, one of thrilling new-genre SA shirazes. Encapsulates both power/grace of variety; concentrated opulence, overall 'darkness' of character — black spice/roasted meat/savouriness — only adding to richness, veiled complexity. "Was slowest developer in oak. Will take years to mature — 15?" speculates Eben Sadie. Classically barrelled; 18 mths Fr oak, 30% new; malo in oak after 6 weeks on skins. Perfectly balanced 14,5% alc/6,1 g/ℓ acid. For all sophistication, has warm, 'big bear' personality of **98** *Wine* **✿✿**, rounded, but vibrantly dry.

'Standard' range

✿ Shiraz With Flagship Merlot and Syrah above, dominates this cellar's **99** reds; chalk and cheese compared with **98** **✿✿**, which trifle too oaky, short. Though

99 matured 85% Am oak, one-third new, impression is brooding Fr style: deep, dark, quite minerally, savoury roasted meat/red earth concentration, all bolstered by 14,5% alc; absolute delicacy of fruit makes for amazing contrast; finest, driest tannins. Rousing white-spice finish epitomises wine's liveliness, individuality. Among SA shiraz elite. **98** spiced with 7% each grenache/carignan.

🌺 **Pinotage 99** well differentiated from Flagship and, like its Shiraz stablemate, better than **98** 🌺. Differs from traditional style in silky texture (made possible by sheer dry tannins); smoky/spicy dark flavours reflect European sophistication; total absence of bitterness. Like partners in Standard range, already approachable but plenty still to give. Subtle two-thirds Am oak, balance seasoned Fr 13,6% alc.

🌺 **Cabernet Sauvignon-Merlot** If maiden **98** *Wine* 🌺 was a voluptuous charmer, **99** evinces as many delights with more subtlety, restraint. Ripples rather than waves of meaty/black truffle/cassis elegance; purity highlighted by fine texture, oak halo. All carried out pianissimo; so let *it* do the talking, which it can already, though has build for min 8 yrs. Am/Fr oak, 30% new Am barrels. 13,8% alc.

🌺 **Chenin Blanc** Dazzling **98** some act to follow, and if **99** 🌺 is less extrovert, it lacks nothing in style, personality; could well out-live its predecessor. Ripe canned mango/passionfruit/pineapple intensity, overlaid with some oxidative decadence; palate similarly linear, tight (lees stirring kept to minimum, to avoid flabbiness), emphasises purity of chenin fruit, also sturdy 14% alc. Dash sugar (4,5 g/ℓ) helps pull whole together. **98** similar treatment, analysis; more lush. Both barrel-fermented, older Fr oak, 8 mths sur lie. From 36 yr old bushvines. Unfined/filtered.

🌺 **Viognier** New Boring is a word unknown in this cellar; witness this electrifying maiden **00**, subtly scented with dried apricot/wild flowers/herbs; richly textured, graceful yet packed with spicy vibrancy, power. "Zero human intervention" vinification (basket pressing, natural ferment, no fining/filtration — last unusual in Cape whites) delivers amazing purity, sophistication. Concentration from minuscule yield — 1 bunch per vine — from less than 1 ha. Barrel-fermented, all 3rd fill Fr oak.

Andrew's Hope range

🌺 **Sauvignon Blanc** ▼ (Pvsly Long Walk) **00** best to date, something of a shining light in generally dim sauvignon vintage. Tangy gooseberries/rhubarb/figs/passionfruit (all scintillatingly pure — result of night harvesting?) cartwheel athletically across palate. Yet sufficient weight, ripe flinty acids for intensity, length. Enjoy while youthfully charming, before end 2001.

Cabernet Sauvignon-Merlot 🌺 Fit-all style for those who want nothing more than good fruit, quality winemaking with accessibility and right price. **00** exceptionally fruity without being brashly up-front, chewily supple with firm yet non-aggressive tannin kick. 50/50 blend, Fr oak staves. 13,4% alc.

. . . .

Spier

THE BATTLE over who owns the Spier Wine Estate name at press time had not been resolved. And if the lawyers still haven't been able to sort out the differences between 'Spier Wine Estate' on the Polkadraai road (home of Kanu wines — see Goedgeloof), the throbbing 'Spier' tourist complex on the Lynedoch road with its 'Spier Home Farms' on the Annandale road (see Spier Cellars), well, what chance do we have? We can only direct you to our winelands map of the disputed territories, and move on …

Spier Cellars

Stellenbosch (see Stellenbosch map) • Tasting & sales daily 9—5 Tasting fee R6 p/p (informal tasting, R12 p/p for conducted tasting) • Cellar tours by appointment • Jonkershuis & Taphuis restaurants, also Farmstall & Café Spier • Luxury hotel • Tourgroups • Conferences/banqueting • Gift shop • Conservation area • Facilities for children • Vintage train • Walks • Views • Wheelchair-friendly • Owner Winecorp • Winemaker Frans Smit (since 1995) • Viticulturists Gerrie Wagener (Afrika Vineyards) since 2000, Simon Springthorpe (since 1996) • Vineyards 75 ha • Production 1 200 tons 60% white 40% red • PO Box 1078 Stellenbosch 7660 • Tel (021) 809-1143 • Fax (021) 809-1144 • E-mail francoisvdw@spier.co.za • Website www.spier.co.za

THESE CELLARS have now become an epicentre for various Winecorp ranges (see entry), and HQ for Afrika Vineyards, its viticultural operation. This is headed by one of South Africa's brightest stars in the field, former Vergelegen and Boschendal GM Gerrie Wagener, who keeps a close eye on the existing 75 ha of vineyards — another 90 ha due for development. Frans Smit continues to turn out award-winning wines and has been inspired by a recent visit to the south of France and the Rhône. Meantime, two hotels are going up (the second a R300-million Ritz-Carlton), plus golf courses. The performing arts programme has been twinned with London's Broomhill Opera, under artistic director Mark Dornford-May, offering anything from King Kong to Carmen in the open-air amphitheatre. The multiple restaurants flourish, the tourist trains run on time, Springbok rugby players get married and US First Ladies attend conferences here.

Private Collection

✿ Cabernet Sauvignon (Reserve in last year's ed.) Attention grabber in classic Cape style — walnuts, roasted coffee/chocolate warmth, expensive cigar box whiffs among the usual headline features. All delivered in **98** with restrained power, harmony, 100% cab needing no other mid-palate filler. Low 4 t/ha yield provides concentration necessary for freshening 6,6 g/ℓ acid. Excellent potential over next 6—8 yrs. Alc just under 13%. 14 mths 70/30 new/used Fr oak, malo in barrel. *Wine* ✿, VVG.

✿ Merlot (Reserve in pvs ed) Our first look at post-assemblage **98** (final blend not available in time for pvs guide) shows strong but not overdone new oak influence, which adds dimension, richness to savoury, meaty character. Healthy deep ruby colour, full body and compact, yet pliable tannins all suggest proper ripeness until acid harshness kicks in on tail; will need careful monitoring to catch at best. *Wine* ✿, VVG. 13,4% alc, 6,5 g/ℓ acid. 14 mths 100% new Fr oak.

✿ Chardonnay Reserve in last year's ed. **98** only vintage to date, sold out. Next **01** under Private Collection label.

Sauvignon Blanc ✿ New **00**, tasted young, set to be one of yr's success stories. Inviting smoky, gooseberry intensity, promising more with time. Big, grippy mouthful, packed with ripe fruit. Technically off-dry, 8 g/ℓ natural residual sugar harmonises steely acid, creates accessibility. Purists will sniff, but watch this fly out of the cellar. 13,9% alc.

'Regular' range

✿ Cabernet Sauvignon ▼ Frans Smit hits all right notes in this mid-price range. Here, as with Chardonnay below, achieves more than just simple satisfaction, accessibility. Well-proportioned **99** modern version of traditional Cape style, endowed with bright blackberry/roasted nut, cedary oak. Plus juicy bounce that will accommodate those who prefer their reds young, vibrant. 13% alc. 5 000 cases.

✿ Sauvignon Blanc ▼ Usually some pyrotechnics here, but **00** ✿ degree less showy, intense than pvs. Comfortable spring flower bouquet, sprightly medium body and clean, grassy bite. Fashioned into balanced, pleasurable — and early drinking by invisible 3,8 g/ℓ sugar. **99**, **96** SAA.

❀ **Chenin Blanc Barrel-Fermented** (Chenin Blanc in pvs ed) Frans Smit's first attempt at wholly cask-fermented chenin looks most promising. Fr oak beautifully integrated in **00**, allowing grape's pure honeysuckle/floral notes to blossom. Delicate yet flavoursome, leesy, roundly dry. Should fill out with time, reveal further complexity (and gain probable higher rating). 50/50 new/used Fr oak, 7 mths on lees, frequent lees-stirring. 13% alc.

❀ **Noble Late Harvest** Consistently gorgeous dessert, to be discontinued — much to disappointment of enthusiasts. Swansong **98** features expensive 24-ct gold brilliance, youthful spicy, dried-apricot nose enriched (but not overpowered) by botrytis; zippy feel, underlying richness hinting at greater opulence with time. 13,5% alc, 138 g/ℓ sugar, all-important 8 g/ℓ de-cloying acid. **97** slightly fuller, drier (105 g/ℓ sugar), super follow-up to bemedalled **96** VVG, *Wine* ❀, Michelangelo double-gold. 375 ml. These old-vine bukettraube, oak fermented/aged 18 mths, 60% new.

Pinotage ❀ New Ben Radford, group chief winemaker, suggests present consumer preference is for "anything that doesn't smell like (old-style) pinotage!" This sparky-fruity, quaffable **99** should please modernists without alienating traditionalists, who will find nostalgic redcurrants/tart plums/aromatic spice and sweet-fruit finish. Lightly oaked. **Chardonnay** ❀ Easy but not simple **99**, generously layered with juicy peaches, melons. Pineappley zest provides moreish freshness. Subtly Fr oak enriched. Best over next 12–18 mths. 60/40 cask/tank-fermented. 13% alc. **Symphony** Everyday blended dry white. **Bouquet Blanc** Pvs mainly semi-sweet bukettraube/riesling.

. . . .

Springfield Estate

Robertson (see Robertson map) • Tasting & sales Mon—Fri 8—5 Sat 9—4 • Cellar tours by appointment • Bring your own picnic • Play area for children • Walks • Views • Wheelchair-friendly • Owners Abrie & Jeanette Bruwer • Winemaker/viticulturist Abrie Bruwer • Vineyards 150 ha • PO Box 770 Robertson 6705 • Tel (023) 626-3661 • Fax (023) 626-3664 • E-mail springfield@minds.co.za

IT'S DE RIGUEUR to serve "nice ripe runny cheese" (the natural, unpasteurised sort, of course) and fresh, just-baked bread with Abrie Bruwer's Cabernet Sauvignon 98 — don't even think of salted crackers: "Only when shipwrecked!" proffers this adamant and decidedly off-beat Robertson estate winemaker. If it's Springfield you're drinking, and you're not marooned, it simply must be accompanied by the right stuff (which this fourth-generation wine farmer is in the habit of producing). Bruwer describes the 2000 harvest as "hot and difficult". His philosophy of minimal intervention meant that he had to make peace with the estate's very rocky soil (the farm was previously called Klipdrift, Afrikaans for stone drift) on the banks of the Breede River. With a minimalist make-do set-up par excellence, Bruwer jokes that he does not have figures on the total tonnes produced by Springfield: "We don't possess luxuries such as scales". Although if they did, they'd surely be tipped in his favour.

❀ **Cabernet Sauvignon** ▼ **98** reprises francophile Abrie Bruwer's more refined style. Supple, fragrant dry tannins enclose abundant mulberry/blackberry and sweet ripe cherry, which jostle in palate with minty tones and savoury green pepper, charry oak furnishing an extra dimension. Natural yeast ferment on whole berries, resolutely minimal handling; yr Fr oak, 50% new. 13% alc. This a mix of all farm's cab vyds; single vyd 97 version due in 2004.

❀ **Méthode Ancienne Chardonnay** "Made in the ancient style of Burgundy" (barrel fermented with natural yeasts), only released when Abrie Bruwer satisfied with quality — which, he wryly notes, has been only twice in 5 attempts — **97** SAA and this current remarkable **99**, creamily complex and deliciously serious. Sweet toned white peach/honeysuckle fragrances in vanilla backdrop; limey lees further extend the mouthfilling richness, which brilliantly balanced by vibrant dry acidity. Terrific now, with potential for even greater intricacy over time. 14 mths Vosges casks, 70% new; 3–4 mths on fermentation lees, no stirring; no fining/filtration. 13,5% alc.

✿ **Wild Yeast Chardonnay** ✔ Mostly unwooded version of above, natural yeast fermentation imparts extra floral dimension to beautiful ripe peach/lees/citrus complexity in **98**. Same lip-smacking creaminess, tingly acidity as above. Single vyd, tank fermented (3 mths), yr on fermentation lees without addition of sulphur. 13,5% alc. 2 000 cases. **99** not available for tasting.

✿ **Special Cuvée Sauvignon Blanc** Muscular, uncompromising, unwooded style, individual and very good. **00**, from coolest vyd on estate, not quite as 'sauvage' as pvs: herbaceous/nettly attack cushioned by more 'popular' gooseberry/ripe peach tastes (but still with excellent varietal expression). Racy dry finish. 12,5% alc.

✿ **Life from Stone Sauvignon Blanc** Further refinement of Springfield approach to this grape: vyd composed 70% of rock fragments. **00** worthy follow-up to well travelled maiden **99** (SAA, Air Namibia, BA, Blue Train). Immediately strikes as closer to Loire styles: flinty, steely, very fresh and mouthfilling. Ripe fruit flavours of the warm **00** vintage (gooseberry/melon/fig) contrast with mouth-wateringly crisp, cool acid.

> **Colombard-Chardonnay** ✿ 😊 Good gulpable everyday drops with some style. **00** begins and ends with chardonnay citrus/pear; middle's nicely filled with colombard tropical fruit and bright acid.

- -

Spruitdrift Winery

Olifants River (see Olifants River map) • Tasting Mon—Fri 8.30—5 Sat 8.30—12 • Sales 8—5.30 Sat 8—12 • Cellar tours on request Mon—Fri 8.30—5 Sat 8.30—11.30 • Traditional barbeque (snoek/meat) for 15—60 people by arrangement • Conference centre for up to 40 delegates. Book ahead • Owners 85 members • Winemaker Erik Schlünz (since 1996) • Consulting viticulturist Jeff Joubert (since 1996) • Production ± 30 000 tons • PO Box 129 Vredendal 8160 • Tel (027) 213-3086 • Fax (027) 213-2937

CAPE LOBSTERS (on the front labels) and splashy fields of wildflowers are some of the non-wine assets of this West Coast co-op, established in 1968. Members' vineyards stretch along the Olifants River and its irrigation arteries, covering a vast area from Koekenaap and Trawal to Vredendal. Some of the top-performing parcels are a cool breeze from the Atlantic. A close-knit community, all take pride in wine maker Erik Schlünz's achievements and efforts — latterly including a lift in red-wine quality and varietal character.

✿ **Merlot** Standout **99** reflects general improvement in this cellar's reds, which continues in latest **00**. Serious mulberry depths, layers of ripe plum, sweet violets, soft choc; some quite harsh tannins still. Sampled very young, so unrated, but most promising. High kicking 14,9% alc. 98 VG.

✿ **Hanepoot Jerepiko** A warming fortified drop for misty days. **NV** splendidly scented with muscat, honey, freesia and honeysuckle. Soft and unctuous yet finishes with bright spirity tang. Also good alfresco sipper over ice. Screwtop.

Cabernet Sauvignon Too unformed to rate, but potentially ✿, **00** offers good solid quaffing with extra pizzazz from deep fruit flavour, good oak/vanilla backing and long supple tannins. Satisfying, though high 13,9% alc needs watching. **98** VG inaugurated this label's improved form. **Pinotage** ⚥ Perhaps most challenging of these reds, **99** somewhat subdued yet recognisably pinotage; some unripe banana and tough tannin in palate. Needs (and would be good with) robust casseroles, venison and similar dishes. 14,4% alc. **Ruby Cabernet** Preview of **00** suggests this will earn the same rating as lightly oaked **98** ✿, with deep-piled, almost 'sweet' mid-palate and generous plummy, smoky tones. Soft dry finish. 13,4% alc.

Shiraz New Plucked from barrel (so unrated), and still massively tannic, **00** revealed dark minerally/earthy tones, long twirls of smoke. **Rosé** ✻ **NV** Features spruced livery with cellar's 'Cape lobster' logo. Spruced taste, too: fragrant tropical fruit salad and good sugar/acid balance. Delicate coral colour for summer/pool prettification. Lowish 11,8% alc. **Chardonnay** Latest **00** tasted pre-bottling (not rated) showed better than pvs. 'Sweet' pears, bits of peach in smooth palate with unexpected warming alcoholic glow (13% alc not particularly high). Potential ✻. **Chenin Blanc** Pre-bottling taste of **00** substantially zingier than pvs: fresh tropical breezes, cocktail of guava/pineapple, which finishes bone dry. ± 13% alc. **Sauvignon Blanc** Too young to rate, med-bodied **00** should settle into pvs ✻ easy quaffing mode with fresh, fruity cut grass/bell pepper tones, brisk, refreshing acidity. **Premier Grand Cru** (★) Very ordinary **NV**, well past its best. Also in 1 ℓ box. **Rapsodie** ✿ Light/med-bodied semi-sweet **NV** with delicate guava, muscat aromas. Clean, fresh smooth and quite sugary. **Stein NV** Untasted. **Late Harvest** ✿ Simple, easy, honeyed; sweet yet lightish 11% alc. **NV**. Also in 1 ℓ box. **Special Late Harvest** ✻ Jasmine scented **99**, gentle, sweet fruit salad tones tweaked with drop of acid. 100% chenin. Light/med-bodied. **Doux** ✻ New Frisky carbonated bubbles with some fresh-fruit tastes; clean and creamily sweet. **NV**. **White Muscadel Jerepigo** ✻ **97** fortified dessert gaining some complexity, richness in bottle, fragrant rose petals/litchi/spice; tropical fruit salad flavours taper languidly to spirity, and unexpectedly dry finish. Chill lightly for aperitif. Screwtop.

Spur

THIS POPULAR SA family steak restaurant chain links its house wines to its cow punching Western theme. Food friendly NVs with lowish alcohols. By Simonsig.

Buffalo Red ✿ Supple, quaffable blend of ruby cab, pinotage, pinot — super with steak. **Desert Moon** ✿ Delicate floral whiffs and dry, crisp lemony flavours. Mostly clairette blanche, colombard, riesling. **Autumn Rain** ✿ Juicy, aromatic blend of bukettraube, gewürz, chenin in popular semi-sweet mode. **Sparkling Rain** ✿ Hits the spot with rich, sweet grapiness. Carbonated blend of aromatic varieties; lively pin-point bubbles.

S/SW New

SOUTH/SOUTH WEST — "easy drinking, sociable" wines from African Wines & Spirits in fashionable 1 000 ml bottles. S/SW geographical reference to Cape wine country.

Ruby Cabernet-Merlot ✻ Smooth, lightish cherry flavours in honest, outdoorsy **99**, uncomplicated and nice. **Chardonnay-Chenin Blanc** ✻ Refreshing pear-toned **99**, with some bright chardonnay citrus for flavoursome, undemanding sipping.

St Elmo's

PIZZA AND PASTA demand food friendly, uncomplex wines, and the successful St Elmo's chain offers family diners value for money with this NV range by Simonsig.

Dry White ✿ Crisp, lemony blend of (mostly) clairette blanche, colombard, bukettraube. Simple floral aromas and bracing finish, which good with seafood. **Red** ✿ Ruby cab, pinotage and some pinot blended into supple, juicy pasta tipple — even better when lightly chilled. **Stein** ✿ From aromatic varieties including bukettraube, gewürz; in popular semi-sweet style with uncomplicated appeal. Undemanding 11,5% alc.

Steenberg Vineyards

Constantia (see Constantia map) • Tasting & sales Mon—Fri 8.30—4.30 Sep—Feb also Sat 9—1 Tasting fee R5 p/p for tour groups • Cellar tours by appointment • Cape-Continental restaurant • Five-star Steenberg Country Hotel • Championship golf course • Owner Johnnies Industrial Corporation (Johnnic) • Winemaker Nicky Versfeld (since 1996), Christa von la Chevallerie (since 2000) • Viticulturist Herman Hanekom (since 1990) • Production 500 tons 38 800 cases 60% white 40% red • PO Box 10801 Steenberg Estate 7945 • Tel (021) 713-2211 • Fax (021) 713-2201 • E-mail info@steenbrg.co.za or sales@steenbrg.co.za • Website http://users.iafrica.com/s/st/stf-wine/

THE BUZZ about this historic farm, latterly transformed into upper-crust golfing and residential estate, started with the first vintage in 93. Production from vineyards established by the man who grew Boschendal, Herman Hanekom, was so tiny that it only just quenched the thirst of the directors of Johnnic, the industrial giant which owns this property. Ordinary mortals were kept waiting for their share — and nothing sharpens the appetite more. There was a stampede for the first public release. The 94 Sauvignon Blanc, made by Nicky Versfeld — then at Welmoed — was instantly greeted with a flurry of excited p-words — potential, promising, pretty amazing for young vines, and wine made in a borrowed cellar. By 96 the new kid on this very exclusive, mountain- and maritime-influenced Constantia block had proved more than precocious. A star Merlot established its red street cred, with the accomplished Versfeld now in command of Steenberg's completed own-cellar. At the new sensation of the international art world, the Tate Modern in London, there are only 19 wines on the restaurant list — 4 come from Steenberg, including its first vintage of Nebbiolo. What? Why are they introducing new players instead of playing to their known strengths? Hanekom says the vineyards are young, and they're still experimenting, "still finding our way". They don't look the least bit lost to supporters here and abroad — even the French clamour for their Shiraz and Merlot.

Steenberg range

Merlot Queen-pin of range, though Catharina below an alter ego. **98** Best Merlot Worldwide on 2000 IWSC; dense, vibrant yet soft with minerally/choc/peppermint-cream restraint. Its nature, as is typical of whole farm style, demands contemplation (over several bottles?), never is all immediately apparent. Combination New World flair/Old World solid structure, modulation; latter attributes will ensure successful development over next 6–8 yrs. 14% alc. Yr new Fr barriques. Barrel sample **99** equally tantalising; bit more forthcoming — vintage characteristic — though greater complexity; mellifluous, fine tannins with all-important dryness counteracting 14% alc.

Catharina Constantia ladies have style and class, showing the gentlemen the way. Catharina (after Catharina 'Tryn' Ras, feisty four-times-widowed first owner of this historic (1682) farm, originally known, rather exhaustingly, as Zwaanswyk aan de Steenbergen) is emulating Christine, her much-admired counterpart at Buitenverwachting; both are blends. **98**, second release, bears distinguishing stamp of farm's merlot — with cab s, shiraz, cab f (42/40/15/3) — but has own strong personality. Ripples with mineral spice, bitter choc elegance. Down-duvet soft, initially emphasises youthful fruity sweetness, but structure kicks in, giving rounded dry length. Promises more savouriness with age, which this absolutely deserves/needs. Barrel-matured both as separate varieties (yr new Fr oak), and as blend (6 mths 2nd fill). 13,4% alc. **97** cab/merlot (70/30) merges strength with elegance. Polished prior to blending, 17 mths new Fr oak.

Cabernet Sauvignon Styled to please classicists/traditionalists. Quietly sophisticated **98** mixes cassis/cigar box subtlety with suggestion of ripe plums; very sleek, mouthfilling; initial light-textured does not hint at richer, more expansive yet still dry finish. Satisfying now; should grow over next 4–5 yrs. 12,7%

alc.**97** ✿ more imposing, complex than pvs. Fr oak maturation set at ± yr, 50% new. Also available in magnums.

✿**Pinot Noir** "Future of this table wine style depends on where we go with the bubbly," says Nicky Versfeld. On current showing of fine **99** we'd suggest it would be a pity to discontinue something so promising. More demonstrative, characterful than ready-to-drink **98**; **99** delivers fanfare of scintillatingly pure fragrance: cherries/raspberries/fresh truffles/autumn leaves. Fruit delicacy echoed in palate with good concentration, generous weight, but will require 2–3 yrs, maybe more, to break through persistent, though fine, tannin barrier to reach peak. 13,3% alc. Oak important but not dominant roleplayer: 9 mths 225 ℓ Fr oak, 50% new. Malo in barrel. Burgundian clone, 113.

✿**Chardonnay** (Wooded) Barrel fermented version growing as vines mature. **99** confidently structured with good aging potential. Some quite Burgundian tones, roasted hazelnuts/oatmeal/citrus zest expanded by creamy mouthfeel. Perfect New/Old World mix-'n-match of great finesse. Yr Fr oak, 30% new; only 70% 2nd fill portion through malo. Low 4,5 t/ha yield. 13,5% alc. Barrel sample **00** shows same family stamp and promise.

✿✿**Sauvignon Blanc Reserve** ▼ This thoroughbred and Merlot most sought-after wines in all countries where farm's wines are sold. **00** ✿, like all since **94**, should not disappoint though reflects richness of vintage; trifle more forward than usual, tropical/figgy depths sustained by chewy lees richness, invisible 6,3 g/ℓ acid accelerator. Hugely concentrated, this is not a wine for faint-hearted; will require bouillabaisse, paella, creamy seafood or chicken pasta — and several hours' digestion. 13,2% alc. **99** fulfilled our expectations ("will outshine even medalled **98**, **97** both *Wine* ✿" we suggested last ed) by taking SAA white wine trophy; thrilling combination of power and grace with pervasive cool, minerally ripeness. Regular **Sauvignon Blanc** ▼ In-house referred to as 'Loire' style, usually distinctly different from Reserve, via earlier accessibility, 'sweet' nettly juiciness. But **00** ✿ bears closer resemblance to Reserve; quite tropical, fat, tad 'lazy' — loper rather than sprinter; but may still get into its stride. 13,2% alc, 6,3 g/ℓ acid.

✿**Semillon** (Wooded) ▼ Lavish ripeness of **00** favours this 100% oak-fermented version, judging from mid-2000 barrel sample. Oak (including judiciously applied 30% new) reins in, adds structure, simultaneously expands pickled lemons/fresh honeycomb character, rich texture. Emphatically bold, statement wine but well-balanced, with good aging potential. 14% alc, 6,1 g/ℓ acid. **99**, also with grassy tang of unwooded vintage-mate. Fine future anticipated.

✿**Semillon** (Unwooded) Same source as version above, which takes **00** ✿ towards ripest end of scale; retiring lemony/honeycomb flavours, more blustery 14% alc. Will probably perform best with food. **99** altogether more individual, tighter fruit feel, similar to sauvignon's dried green-grass perkiness; filling out with age.

✿**Steenberg 1682 Brut** This property's first MCC, sold out in pre-millennium rush. Impressive debut: lots of Champagne-like rich, toasty lees, creamy persistence, vibrant fine bubble, dry. Chardonnay/pinot noir (93/7) blend from 97 vintage (though **NV**). Next is equal mix 99/98, ratio 70/30 chardonnay/pinot noir. Tasted prior to dosage 'sweetening', showed fine toasty lees array, pinprick bubble, good freshness. Should rate at least ✿. Also in magnums.

Shiraz ✿ Heads for Fr elegance rather than Aussie grunt, though both maiden **98**, **99** include soupçon Am oak "as bit of lift for fruit". Barrel sample **99** promises sleekness, refinement; tasteful spice, violets, texture as tender as well-hung fillet, some meaty savouriness too. Oak matured mainly second fill Fr, 10% Am tiny portion new. 13,4% alc. **Nebbiolo** ✿✿ **99**, improvement on maiden **98**, starts with strong ruby hue. Built in similar robust, astringent style but fruit weighs in with greater concentration, achieves better balance; though violets/minerals/cherry pip combination essentially delicate, uncomplicated. Vibrant, clean, dry feel makes this a natural with richer though not too-strongly flavoured dishes. Yr Fr oak, 10% new; malo in barrel. 12,6% alc. **Chardonnay** (Unwooded) ✿✿ **00** more varietal oomph than maiden **99**; quite forceful citrus/oatmeal/smoky aromatics; richly mouthfilling, well-rounded persistence. 13,7% alc. **Catharina** New Goal is flagship white blend partner to red above. Unfinished sample **00** too young to assess. Composed of 52% Reserve sauvignon/38% unwooded semillon/10% barrel-fermented semillon; components as under individual labels. Good structure, interesting rich/fresh fruit contrast; should develop well with age, rate minimum ✿.

Motif range

Rouge Sec ✿✿ ▼ Consistently hits all right quality/value/ready-to-go buttons. **99** matches soft berry charm with form, rounded dryness and length. 70/30 cab/merlot blend; 12 mths in barrel, none new. **97** VG. **Rosé Sec** ✿✿ Dryness, food-friendliness only constants in this glimmering ruby pink **00** unwooded cab/shiraz blend — **99** multi-mix of virtually every variety on farm. Fresh, vigorous cassis, red berry aromas; full-bodied, sufficient personality/concentration to team up with duck, rare rack of lamb. 13,4% alc. **Rosé Semi-Sweet** ⚥ New **00** same wine as above, sweetened to 18 g/ℓ sugar; diminishes individuality though still balanced, pleasant summer sipping. **Blanc Sec** ⚥ Ripe but not overly dramatic unwooded sauvignon/semillon blend; spruced up with drop muscat de frontignan in **00**. Balanced, anytime quaffer. **98** VG.

Sauvignon Blanc-Muscat (Jasmine in pvs) ✿✿ ☺ **00** refined fruity 55/45 blend; polished muscat de frontignan scents add daintiness/length to fuller sauvignon. 6 g/ℓ sugar balanced to please both dry and sweeter palates. **99** hanepoot/sauvignon blend.

Stellenbosch Farmers' Winery   ♟ ♟ ♟ ♟

See Stellenbosch map • Tasting & sales Mon—Fri 8.30—5 Sat 10—1 • Cellar tours Mon—Thu 10 & 2.30 Fri 10 only Booking essential Tel (021) 808-7569 • Oude Libertas Restaurant (see Eat-out section) • Oude Libertas Amphitheatre for summer twilight concerts • Cellarmaster Razvan Macici • Winery manager Jan le Roux • PO Box 46 Stellenbosch 7599 • Tel (021) 808-7911 • Fax (021) 887-1355/886-5414

THIS VENERABLE COMPANY, 75 years old in 2000, has not merely reflected the South African wine industry's history, it's created, revolutionised and driven it. SFW's Chateau Libertas and La Gratitude were launched in 1932 and 1936 respectively, offering the first light (and dry) alternatives to the heavies and fortifieds available to local consumers ("elephant blood" wines, a later MD of the company, Ronnie Melck, called them). Lieberstein, launched in 1959, then reeled in the huge shoals of those who still wanted their wines sugar-coated. In just 5 years it became the biggest selling bottled wine in the world; South Africa's wine-producing direction had changed, irrevocably. Tassenberg on the everyday red drinking front, Zonne-bloem at the dinner table, and Grand Mousseux, sparkling at a million weddings, made indelible impressions: big-branding, in the Cape, was an SFW invention. Innovation continues today at a furious pace under hot new cellarmaster Razvan Macici (Masters degrees from the Universities of Bucharest and Stellenbosch), with previous cellar chief Wouter Pienaar working with viticulturists to boost the quality of the grapes and wine SFW buys in. The giant is about to begin roaring again with the significant improvements across the board, particularly in the lower-priced ranges. And as this guide went to press, the potential merger between SFW and Distillers Corporation was delayed due to evaluations of both companies by independent merchant banks. The proposed name for the new liquor giant is South

African Distilleries & Wines. More history in the making? . See separate entries for SFW brands.

. . . .

Stellenbosch Vineyards

Stellenbosch (see Stellenbosch map) • Tasting/sales/meals/refreshments at Welmoed, Helderberg, Eersterivier (see individual entries for details). Sales also at Twin Oaks, Main Road, Somerset West Tel (021) 852-7307 • Managing director Hermann Böhmer • Group head winemaker Chris Kelly (since 1998) • Viticulturist Francois de Villiers (since 1998) • Vineyards ±2 500 (growing to 3 000 by 2005) • Production 14 000 tons (rising to 19 000 by 2005) 700 000 cases 63% white 36% red 1% rosé • PO Box 465 Stellenbosch 7599 • Tel (021) 881-3870 • Fax (021) 881-3102 • E-mail info@stellvine.co.za

"WE'VE proved you don't need to be small to produce top quality wines," says Hermann Böhmer, MD of this potent transformation of a handful of co-op cellars into one modern dynamo, and, most crucially, their 150 farmer-members into "contract growers" with a new take on their contribution to the wine process. The company sends them to pick up tips from some of the best coaches in the world, with a core group of growers 'training' in Australia most recently; Di Davidson, a leading Aussie viticultural consultant, will be a vital force in Operation Red Alert, a drive to expand red-wine plantings. The raw material at SV's disposal has always been good — much of the cream of the Stellenbosch crop comes from these farmers' vineyards — and is slated to grow even better. The winemakers who take over the baton are well travelled too. 'International' is the key word here, and while "we are not trying to make Australian wines, just learning from a country with a climate and conditions similar to ours", Kiwi Chris Kelly, group winemaking chief, has just brushed up on advances Down Under, and taken (and passed) a show-judging course there. Mike Graham, the French-speaking winemaker based at Welmoed, worked the 99 vintage in the Ardèche; Elizabeth Augustyn headed from the Helderberg satellite cellar to Villa Maria in New Zealand for her latest harvest experience. Böhmer's vision of SV as "one of South Africa's premium wine companies" is coming into focus.

Genesis range

- ✿ **Cabernet Sauvignon** Those who enjoyed maiden 97 (almost exclusively SAA First Class passengers) will immediately recognise family likeness in **98**. Refined spread of roasted nuts, warm hay woven with subtle cassis; robustness of vintage evident only in greater concentration — overall profile one of sophisticated restraint, polish. Single vyd fruit perfectly complemented by 13 mths 80/20 Fr/Am oak, some new. ±13% alc. 1 000 cases.

- ✿ **Shiraz 98** like team-mate above, fast out of the starting blocks: more concentrated, richer than maiden **97**, otherwise carries over all that yr's warm choc/pepper features, spicy vibrancy, resonating finish. Somehow achieves this power-packed action with polish, finesse. Kelly & Co seem to be specialising in fanfare wines; this'll be another. 13,3% alc. Yr new/used Fr/Am oak. 1 000 cases. Limited quantity magnums available; these extra 3 mths barrelled; slighter greater viscosity (also presently more oak-spicy, with bottle size, potential for good ageing). **97** outspoken but not vulgar. Diners Club Award finalist.

- ✿ **Chardonnay** New White counterpart to above flagships; **99** patently in same league; beams personality. Received full, new barrel treatment, which presently still riding fruit, should not be of concern as built to mature; tight, fine-boned structure, packed with intricate flavours (none stands out), dense creamy texture expanded by blossoming citrus lift in tail. Successfully walks the tightrope of generosity, elegance. Single vyd; low-cropped (3 t/ha); 40% spontaneous ferment; 100% through malo. Yr oaked. 550 cases.

. . . .

Kumkani premium range

⚜ Sauvignon Blanc Our enthusiasm for **99** *Wine* ⚜, tasted in unfinished form for pvs guide, if anything has increased. Brims with southern hemisphere confident intensity: ripe tropical tones revved up with cool climate green peas/rhubarb — delicious combo of full fruity succulence, accelerated/lengthened by fresh integrated acid. Cool, clean feel, balanced with plenty flavour; New Zealander Chris Kelly's touch evident here. 2 000 cases.

⚜ Shiraz-Cabernet Sauvignon New Can SA be as successful with this partnership as Australia? **98**'s further evidence that it can. Shiraz leads with inviting meaty/spicy tones, cab powers engine-room with structure/ageability, also some roasted coffee bean richness; whole achieves something greater than 60/40 parts. Possibility of improvement over next 5–8 yrs, though balanced, sufficiently rounded for present enjoyment. Yr mainly Fr oak, some new. Finalist 1999 Diner's Club Award. 1 000 cases.

Versus ⚜ This 1 000 ml innovation continues on its starry path. Latest accolades, apart from scores of happy fans, SA Institute of Packaging's Gold Pack Award ('Oscar' of glass packaging of any sort), Grape inaugural Packaging Award Top Ten. **00** (switching for a moment to applauded package's *contents*) probably best to date. More fruity substance, though not overwhelmingly alcoholic; chenin's tropical/honeysuckle fragrance dusted with enlivening dollop of sauvignon; friendly soupçon sugar provides unfussy drinkability with interest. Kelly's good news is "there's plenty of this quality". **Infiniti** ⚜ "Going to be a noisy wine, like Versus," predicts marketing manager Geoff Harvey. Apart from the popping of the cork, he means it's going to be backed by a lot of PR fuss. As sparkling shiraz, first commercially available red of its kind for SA, should generate it's own brouhaha. Has grown over past year; retains lots of ripe blackberry fruit backed by flattering yeasty complexity; fuller palate too, adopting more shiraz choc savouriness, complemented by soft texture, surging, creamy mousse. Non-imposing 20 g/ℓ sugar, so will partner all meat/poultry dishes featuring rich sauces. "Also very popular ice-cold as an aperitif in Australia," confirms Kelly. Base-wine fermented on skins, oak aged before 2nd fermentation. **NV. Infiniti Vintage Brut** ⚜ New Bubbly fundi Mike Graham's experience/sure hand evident in **99** chardonnay/pinot noir blend (95/5). Tasted prior to 'sweetening' (in this case more 'rounding') dosage addition ($\pm$3–4 g/ℓ) already shows characterful toasty lees, creamy texture/mousse yet gives overall impression of lightness. Pre-finish rating; may well go up with little more time to integrate, settle down.

Stellenbosch range

Only bottled when sufficient volume remains after SV's other brands completed.

Jerepigo ⚡ 😊 Light-textured white fortified dessert, fresh minty/grapey tones; clean, not oversweet finish; ideal poolside sipper chilled/over crushed ice. From hanepoot. **NV (99)**.

Radiant Red ⚡ Cab/merlot/cinsaut from **97**. None since. **Blanc de Noir** ⚡ Last was **99**; no **00**. **Dry Steen** ⚡ **00** full-bodied, straightforward ripe melon tones cut by steely but balanced acid. **Weisser Riesling** ⚡ Lightish off-dry **99**. No **00**. **Special Late Harvest** ⚡ **00** unambiguous ripe grapey aromas, sweetness controlled by balanced freshness. **Ruby Port** ⚡ **NV** Dark ruby, generous earthy currant wafts; fruitily sweet.

Stellendrif   New

Stellenbosch • Tasting & sales at Louiesenhof (see that entry) • Owner/winemaker/viticulturist Fanie Cilliers (SHZ/Kuün Wines) • Vineyards ± 20 ha • Production 1 200—1 500 tons • 70% red 30% white • PO Box 6340 Uniedal 7612 • Tel/fax (021) 887-6561

ONE-MAN BAND Fanie Cilliers finds time to hit the ground running (half-marathons), then catches his breath long enough to simply enjoy his own Stellenbosch vineyards. The current yield, untasted for this edition, includes Cabernet Sauvignon 98, with merlot still in the barrel at time of going to press and a pinotage planned for 2001. These wines may be tasted at Louiesenhof.

. . . .

Stellenryck

WELL-ESTABLISHED small premium range from the Bergkelder, reserved for classic varieties and better vintages, and now moving to a vineyard based focus. Preview peek at two from 2000 vintage — Chardonnay and a new Semillon — reveals plenty to look forward to here, with a focus on good fruit selection. Tasting & sales at the Bergkelder (see that entry).

⚜ **Cabernet Sauvignon** Released when more mature than most locals — a big bonus added to reliability. Current **95** with attractive notes of cassis and green pepper on cedary background. Some elegance in palate, and plenty of sweet berry fruit leading to tight but lengthy finish. 13% alc. Fr oak, 70% new. Serious, multi-layered **94** ⚜ showed as one of top cabs of vintage. **93** VG, *Wine* ⚜; **92** VVG; **91** VVG, *Wine* ⚜. **93** first in more modern, approachable idiom.

⚜ **Chardonnay** Soft sheeny gold of **99** delivers notes of buttered toast and marmalade (but at 13% alc not recommended for breakfast). Rich lime/toast/butterscotch palate, with good acidity and lingering finish. Barrel fermented. Will develop a few years, like delicious and elegant **98** ⚜.

⚜ **Sauvignon Blanc** With some grassiness, lots of guava, passionfruit and mango to smell and taste on **00**. Big supportive acidity ushers in good, crisp finish. Pvs: **97** ⚜; **95** VVG, trophy at IWSC 1996, *Wine* ⚜. Before **96** wooded, labelled Blanc Fumé.

Stellenzicht Vineyards

Stellenbosch (see Stellenbosch map) • Not open to the public, except by prior arrangement Tasting & sales at Neethlingshof Estate (see that entry) • Owner Lusan Holdings • Winemaker Guy Webber (since 1998) • Vineyards Jaco van den Berg (since 1998) • Production 626 tons 50 000 cases 70% red 30% white • PO Box 104 Stellenbosch 7599 • Tel (021) 880-1103 • Fax (021) 880-1107 • E-mail nee@mweb.co.za • Website www.neethlingshof.co.za

THIS IS A DAUNTINGLY SERIOUS — and expanding — operation but after only two vintages the (quintessentially?) relaxed Guy Webber seems even less stressed now than at his previous, much smaller cellar posts in Stellenbosch. Hands in pockets, rocking back and forward, he chuckles loudly at every opportunity, parrying remarks about the turnover of winemakers here and at sister estate Neethlingshof (about 10 in as many years) with: "I'm a lover not a fighter, ha, ha." Besides, he says, "I don't see these as anyone's personal or ego wines, Guy Webber's wines. They're Stellenzicht Vineyards wines. And there's such a thing as a vintage." He's also a team man. "When it gets really hectic during the harvest, we install the braai at the back and keep the coals and spirits going through the night with a bit of a party." The reds coming out of Stellenzicht may have been harvested by his predecessors, André van Rensburg, now at Vergelegen, Boela Gerber at Rickety Bridge, but they've been managed — 'elevated' the French say — by Webber; and they include a number of wonderful ones. The latest vintages haven't been easy for whites — in the extreme heat and drought of 2000 it was something of a miracle they rescued anything much at all. "It was the dew in January that saved us," he says. "Also, Van Rensburg is a bit of a genius with sauvignon, you have to give him that, even if genius is a big word." The real inference is that Webber accepts the challenge — but, too perhaps, that he believes he knows a thing or two about reds, which he does. Some streamlining here — generated by Webber and the

. . . .

new management — plus the introduction of a potentially exceptionally interesting and good value range — Stellenzicht Stellenbosch.

❀ Founder's Private Release Minute quantities of 100% cab **97**, given very respectful, forelock-tugging treatment in cellar — 90% new oak 26 mths! Specially selected fruit. Presently barely approachable, mouth-tingling, grippy, minerally, even slightly metallic. Probably needs 3–4 yrs to reveal potential more obviously, when, seems likely, will begin to turn into one of those wines that are both brittle and feline ("elegant?"); then should stand well apart from current vogueish fruity, soft hug-em-and-forget-em reds. A 10-yr projection guess? It could become a still lean but complex, toasty claret, retaining quite lively fruit with supple texture: chic, even graceful, with vestiges of astringency faded. But quite hard to see that now. 420 cases.

❀ Cabernet Sauvignon Serious, unflamboyant, with growing record of consistency; VVGs for both **95**, **94** former with blackcurrants, mulberries, lick of oak, ripe cassis flavours in palate; some leafiness. Latest **96** ❀ from less rich yr offers hay-like nose, med-bodied palate of pleasant berry fruits. 8 600 cases.

❀ Merlot Easy, clean-fruited succulence a hallmark of this label; latest **97** ❀ provides more of same; relatively simple, juicy effort, with quite dryish finish. (Long time in used oak — ❀ for 30 mths, 13,4% alc.) 3 700 cases. **95** VVG, SAA continues to bloom. Perfumed with violets, ripe plums; richly flavoured with more plums, hints tobacco, coffee. ±6 mths Fr oak.

❀ Pinotage 99 terrific — and remarkably soft, uncharacteristically fine balance on palate for such young pinotage. Boiled sweets, varietal flavours leavened by mix of spices and succulent plumminess. Seriously bold — 14,5% alc, yr in oak (about 25% new) 1 800 cases. Follows first **98** *Wine* ❀, also flourishes ripe plums, redcurrants spiked with cloves, toasty vanilla (small Fr oak). Both with ageing potential, at least 4–6 yrs.

❀❀ Syrah A Cape icon since **94** VG introduction and probably first (non-auction) Cape red to break the R100 barrier — back in 1995/96. Catapulted to fame after an upset win over Australia's fabled Grange (91) — judged by an international panel at Oz-SA Wine Test in 1995. Now rationed to 3 bottles per person — and NO tasting sample to decide whether you like it or not! Outstanding **95** (no **96** — considered a lesser Stbosch vintage, when it was relegated to Shiraz below VVG!) **97** *Wine* ❀ great, **98** ❀❀ a stunner; dramatic wafts of dark cherries, ripe plums and — part of all great syrahs' inimitable add-ons — twists of the pepper grinder. Fills the mouth with dry herbs, some Karoo bush, smoky oak, dark chocolate. Nudging a whopping 15% alc, but excusable in such beautifully weighted showcase. Lavishly decorated (at Sélections Mondiales, Michelangelo etc). **98** *Wine* ❀ should grow into a **94**. Next up **99** different, reflects less fruit-laden harvest for perhaps a more approachable — less emphatic result. (14 mths in oak, 87% new, mostly Fr) Intense, deep, almost opaque colours accompany rich mocha/dark chocolate aromas; fine pedigreed, balanced persistence; should reach drinkability yr or 2 ahead of broader shouldered, more peppery **98**. 1 500 cases. Key contributor is the terroir — single vyd, 11 yrs old, called Plum Pudding Hill. Low yield (2,25 t/ha). Malo in small oak, all new; Fr and 12% Am barrels, about yr, depending on vintage.

❀ Shiraz Second-ranking label for this variety but very impressive too; excellent show record. **98** ripe, rich chocolatey — supple, despite its big, wide mouthfeel. Some Rhône pepperiness, liquorice as well. A rounded, complete wine, bereft of coarse tannin. Oaked ±yr, ❀ new, 14,3% alc. 1 800 cases. **97** ❀ features ripe plum, same liquorice, just hint of vanilla (small Fr oak). Deep rich palate; spicy aftertaste, long and clean. Good for current drinking, but will go 4–6 yrs. 13,45% alc. Pvs. **89** VVG, **90** VG, **93** SAA, **96** VVG.

❀ Stellenzicht Billed as property's second red flagship — after Syrah above; blend cab s/f, merlot; only prime fruit, fermented separately. Barrel aged, 30%

new. No need for second fiddle billing in **97** ✿✿ with malbec for first time: smashing vintage has hauled in a super red. Nose should be accompanied by roll of drums. Deserves another deep breath or two. Purple-black hues. Hugely rich, silky textured with broad array of ripe berry, spicy scents. Some liquorice, violets too. Cab 60%, merlot 25%, cab f 10%, malbec 10%; 100% new Fr oak 2 yrs. 900 cases. Skipped **96**. **95** VG fine follow-up to **94** *Wine* ✿.

✿ **Merlot-Cabernet Franc** To be discontinued after latest release **97** ✿✿, which, if not as complex as some of its stablemates above, characterised by pleasant cinnamon, sweet cloves whiffs, friendly supple texture (13,5% alc, 56% merlot, 44% cab f; 2nd fill casks 14–24 mths.) Good price-quality match (about R24 bottle ex-source). 5 000 cases. **96** bold impression in palate, choc-fruitcake, mulberry flavours. Pliable tannins. Grape varieties fermented separately, aged small Fr oak before blending. 13+% alc. **94** VG. **95** VVG.

✿✿ **Cuvée Hans Schreiber** (Last of these labels, since S'zicht came under Lusan corporate umbrella.) **98** Chardonnay (follows massive 97 Sauvignon). Power, complexity here; big-boom nose delivers ripe white peaches, melon flavours. Creamy-textured palate; almost sweetish notes countered by spicy oak. Barrel-fermented/matured 8 mths 86% Am oak, balance Fr. 14,12% alc.

✿ **Chardonnay 98** ✿ best to date. Complex nose: ripe yellow peaches, some tropical fruits, oaky spice. **99** lime-rich colour backdrop to buttery/lime/floral aromas and full, spicy, big rounded palate; some twist in finish but overall, ample charm rather than crisp bite. Barrel-fermented/aged ±9 mths, 80% new oak. 13% alc. 4 800 cases. Pvs several gold medallists at Sélections Mondiales, *Decanter* Top 100 in **95**, **96** VVG, SAA. **97** *Wine* ✿, Air France–Preteux Bourgeois trophy.

✿ **Sauvignon Blanc** Difficult, hot, fruit-sapping vintage especially for sauvignon **00** ✿. Result was more plain flint/grass character than customary tropical fruitiness. Solid rather than showy fresh star it usually is. (13,6% alc.) 2 700 cases. **99** also considered so-so sauvignon vintage, but this label seemed to defy the trend with a corker, rich but racy. VVGs, *Wine* ✿ regular occurrences since **95** SA champ.

✿ **Semillon Reserve** Highly, widely acclaimed. Cape Wine Academy trophy for best SA white at IWSC 3 yrs running until current release **99**, whose lime-rich finish and uncompromisingly dry palate confirm its niche — a singular food wine (specially for frontal-fruit-averse drinkers). Rather, there's some dry herb character, weighty palate feel (14,2% alc, only new barrels, 3 mnths). 750 cases. **98** ✿✿ a beauty, its more than 15% alc clearly a plus for international judges. Powerful lemon, herb, vanilla-oaky scents. *Wine* ✿. These have potential to grow, given 5–6 yrs. Barrel-fermented/aged Fr barriques. **97** *Wine* ✿, Air France–Preteux Bourgeois trophy; **96**, **95** VG.

✿ **Sauvignon Blanc-Chenin Blanc** Untasted **00**. Pvs **99** unoaked; highly aromatic, floral. Just-dry answer to everyday drinking with some style. **95** SAA, VG.

✿ **Sauvignon Blanc-Semillon** Alternative for chardonnay/chenin-weary drinkers, good at table. Partly oak-fermented **99** (with 30% semillon; 13,3% alc) offers quiet aromas — in late 2000, wisp of smoke. Rich palate with some citrus fruit, but signature flavours are nuts, even hint tobacco. Long finish. 3 300 cases. Regular VG, VVG, SAA.

✿ **Fragrance** To be discontinued after **99** ("A pity" says winemaker Webber, "it's always a draw at shows and events, people come back again and again to the counter and ask for more. I've had to tell some thirsty old ladies it's run out." Muscats morio/alexandrie, white muscadel combination. Whoppingly-scented **99** ✿ with tropical-fruit and the spices of the bazaar, plus accents of passion-fruit/gooseberry. Off-dry balance (9,5 g/ℓ sugar, 12,6% alc. 2 300 cases. **96** VVG.

✿**Weisser Riesling Noble Late Harvest** To be discontinued — leaving this specialist niche to sister estate Neethlingshof. **98** *Wine* ✿ good 6–10 yrs to go to allow elegant intensity of bouquet to evolve, full complexity to develop. Beautiful already, though: pronounced lime-fruity scents, aromatic herby hints, no botrytis excess. Rich, full, finely-balanced palate. Almost searingly fresh (8,3 g/ℓ acid). Unwooded 12,9% alc, 133 g/ℓ sugar. 1 000 cases. **96** *Wine* ✿, VGG.

Stellenzicht Stellenbosch Series

Inexpensive range, blends of grapes/wines from Lusan's Stellenbosch vineyards, Stellenzicht, Le Bonheur, Uitkyk, Neethlingshof, Alto.

✿**Sauvignon Blanc 00** composite of 4 Stbosch vyds (of Lusan's five, only red-wine Alto missing) — and some might even say improvement on most SBs from the estates! Interesting exercise to compare them blind. This a fair, weighty example, some attractive tropical gooseberry fruit, clean quite crisp balanced palate. 13% alc. 9 300 cases.

Triplet ✿ **98** blend, cab s/f (70/22) with merlot; easy, no frills — no awkward edges either — dry red, partly oaked; good dark plum hues, some fruity prune flavours; dusty-dry nose; quite supple, simple finish. 12,9% alc. 13 000 cases.

Chardonnay ✿ **00** eminently drinkable. Lime colours, lime-marmalade tastes, delicious, uncomplicated but some oak backing. Purists might quibble about quite prompt fall-off — but not at cool (±R12/bottle) price! 8 600 cases.

. . . .

Steytler see Kaapzicht
Stonecross see Deetlefs

. . . .

Stonewall Wines

Stellenbosch (see Helderberg map) • Tasting & sales Mon—Fri 9—5 Sat 9—1 • Cellar tours by appointment • Guest-house (meals by arrangement) • Owner De Waal Koch • Consultant winemaker Ronell Wiid (since 2000) • Viticulturist De Waal Koch • Vineyards 80 ha • Production 400 tons (2 500 cases own label) 70% red 30% • PO Box 5145 Helderberg 7135 • Tel (021) 855-3675/083-310-2407 • Fax: (021) 855-2206

DE WAAL KOCH is keeping busy with his small Stonewall range, made in the refurbished cellar (ca 1828) on his Happy Vale farm below the Helderberg. Exports are booming (90% goes to the UK and Denmark), and there's a keen focus on reds: by the end of 2001, the plan is to have an 80/20 red/white ratio in the vineyard. Exiting stage left is chenin, and striding into the limelight are shiraz, cab, merlot and pinotage. Which should please the new consultant winemaker, Ronell Wiid, Diners Club laureate and something of a red wine specialist.

✿**Cabernet Sauvignon** New The house style emphases power, concentration, though here not without some refinement, assisted by delicate floral, sweet-oaky scents. **98** still quite grippy, so no need to rush; try in 2–3 yrs, by which time tannins should have begun to relax. 13,4% alc.

✿**Ruber** (pvsly Cabernet Sauvignon-Merlot) Forceful claret style, more power than finesse but plenty of charm, flavour, intensity; ripe tannins for 5+ yrs keeping. Newest **98** perceptibly oaky still, though not dominating 'sweet' wild berry, mocha, cherry tones. Give couple of yrs to settle. 14% alc. **97** VG.

✿**Chardonnay** ▼ Rung up ladder in **98**, whose smoky, toasted nutty charms contrast attractively with 'sweet' melon flavour. Given abundance of primary fruit, seems no rush to drink — should happily go couple of yrs. 13,2% alc.

Sauvignon Blanc ✿ Lightly oaked **99** has lost its initial aromatic attack, gained light, mellowing lick of bottle age. Still good fruit, freshness; nettle, cut grass, green pepper in bright tapering finish. Lightish 11,5% alc.

Stony Brook

Franschhoek (see Franschhoek map) • Tasting & sales Mon—Sat 9—1 Tasting fee R5 p/p refundable with purchase • Facilities for children • Views • Owners Nigel & Joy McNaught • Winemaker Nigel McNaught • Consulting viticulturist Paul Wallace (VineWise) • Vineyards ±14 ha • Production 50 tons, 3 000—4 000 cases 70% red 30% white • PO Box 22 Franschhoek 7690 • Tel/fax (021) 876-2182 • E-mail mcnaught@iafrica.com

"HANDS-ON" doesn't completely convey Nigel McNaught's engagement level at this 22,5 ha property, the second he and wife Joy have successfully transformed from ordinary farm into singular vineyard (Rickety Bridge the first spot they re-colonised in Franschhoek). You'd have to add "feet-first" and "head-on" and "heart-and-soul in". A medical doctor in his previous life (and still helping out at the local clinic), McNaught's passion for wine was stoked by a post-matric stint as a cellar-rat under Günter Brözel at Nederburg. He and wife Joy became "absolutely dedicated consumers" — surely the best sort of education for any winemaker — but polishing off the end-product wasn't enough; they wanted to get stuck in from the start — and did. Still do. From ground level to the bottle, from deliveries to writing the least clichaic press releases in the winelands, the McNaughts do the lot. From these 14 ha of vineyards and converted fruit-packshed winery, and these untrained *émigrés,* comes a series of personality-plus extroverts (no frail, pale patients in this ward).

✿ **Cabernet Sauvignon Reserve** Mexican waves of applause for first-cap **98** VVG, *Wine* ✿, wine mail order club selection; powerful, densely extracted Franschhoek cab, admirably complex: mint/eucalyptus, choc and black cherries, spicy oak peeping from velvety curtain of fruit. Some long, ripe tannins in satisfying conclusion. ± Yr oak, 50% new. 14% alc. 380 cases. Regular **Cabernet Sauvignon** ✿ Blend of own/Agter Paarl fruit in **99**, commendable follow-up to maiden **98**. Latest offers classic blackcurrant fruit, well rounded, highish 13,5% alc absorbed into firm, cedar-fragrant structure. ±Yr Fr oak, some new.

✿ **Pinotage** Springbok with red wine jus is the McNaughts' all-SA food recommendation for **99** ✿, the all-SA grape being trucked in from Malmesbury/Darling for this second release. Some chewy tannins certainly can do with such sturdy fare, or 2–3 yrs in bottle to meld with sappy red berry centre. 320 cases. Maiden **98** *Wine* ✿. These 10 mths Fr/Am oak (50/50). ±13,5% alc.

✿ **Reserve** NEW Promising debut in **99**, classically styled Bdx blend of mainly cab, merlot, with dashes petit verdot, malbec. Very good savoury backdrop, forward but soft berry fruit, easy tannins. Potential to develop splendidly (and gain further half-star at least). 11 mths Fr barriques, mainly new. 13,3% alc. 440 cases.

✿ **Annie's Wine** Highly individual first attempt at Sauternes-style NLH ("heaps of botrytis in 1997"), will appeal to adventurous palates: booming botrytis presence with unusual smoky lime/lees and sprigs herbs, chardonnay-like citrus (though from sauvignon) in finely textured palate. Barrel fermented/aged 15 mths, new Fr/Am oak. Honours artist friend Anne Marais. Uncertified.

Shiraz ✿ Currently available **98, 99** feature some aggressively wild, animal smells yet attractive, well defined varietal fruit, soft tannins and juicy finish. **99** ±yr barrelled 50/50 Fr/Am oak. 14% alc. 520 cases. **Chardonnay** ✿✿ **99** slenderer feel than pvs (though 13% alc not insubstantial); 100% fermentation/ageing in Allier casks adds length though not much breadth. Might gain some flesh in bottle. **97** *Wine* ✿. **Semillon** ✿ Some initially rough **98** edges have yielded to lanolin smoothness; honeyed bottle age in flavoursome dry palate broadened by 14% alc. Try with blackened fish or crayfish curry. 8 mths Fr casks, some new. **Sophie's Choice** ✦ NEW Sauvignon/semillon, pleasant off-dry quaff. 300 cases. **Vert** ★ NEW Stop/start vinification in this off-dry **99** semillon, with fermentation eventually fizzling out with residual sugar of 12,6 g/ℓ. Oxidative, sherry-like, highly individual. 200 cases. **Rose de Vert** NEW ✿ handsomely packaged sweet dessert from mutated, now red-grape-bearing semillon vyd. Goes well with ripe camembert and other soft French-style cheeses, report the McNaughts. Full, mouthfilling (15% alc, 35 g/ℓ sugar) yet dainty, almost ethereal **98**. 500 ml. 1 200 bottles.

. . . .

Stormberg

Wellington • Not open to the public • Owner/winemaker Koos Jordaan • Consulting viticulturist Andrew Teubes (VinPro) • Vineyards 32 ha • Production 2 500 cases 100% red • 20 Aurora Street Paarl 7646 • Tel 082-776-3540 • Fax (021) 872-4912 • E-mail kooskit@mweb.co.za

"DAUNTING" is Koos Jordaan's impression of the competition for shelf space in the UK, where he fact-found in 2000 wearing a notepad and two hats: Stormberg, his own small boutique venture, buying in grapes while 32 young hectares mature, and Historic Wines of the Cape, an even fresher presence which markets the wines of a select group of wineries including Hanneli Rupert-Koegelenberg's La Motte (Jordaan's a director of Historic, with ex-SFW colleague Duimpie Bayly and associates). But Jordaan, who was "born under a vine", is undaunted by the market rough and tumble. He learned, on a trip Down Under in 1995, that "small can be good". So, armed — "at last" — with proper packaging he's ready to "improve and make Stormberg a success".

Cabernet Sauvignon-Shiraz ⚘ New Australian-style fruit amplitude in **98**, bright strawberries and other red fruits in lighter-bodied, gentle tannin frame. Blend includes "my very precious Durbanville shiraz, which was originally planned as a single wine," reveals Koos Jordaan.

. . . .

Sumaridge

Walker Bay • Tasting & sales possibly from Apr/May 2001 — phone for details • Owner Lorraine Cellars (Pty) Ltd • Winemakers Mike Dobrovic (consultant, 2000 vintage); Greg de Bruyn with Bartho Eksteen (from 2001) • Viticulturist Greg de Bruyn, advised by Eben Archer • Vineyards 28 ha • 45 tons (rising to 450) 2 500 cases (rising to 40 000) 55% white 45% red • PO Box 1413 Hermanus 7200 • Tel (028) 312-2824 • Fax (028) 312-1097 • E-mail gregdb@icon.co.za

THINGS are — quite literally — all over the show at this brand-new establishment in the Hemel-en-Aarde valley. At press time the Sauvignon was at Goedgeloof waiting for labels, the Chardonnay at Mulderbosch ready for bottling, the Merlot in barrels at neighbouring Newton Johnson. Sitting in the hot seat, hoping not to drop any catches, is new Cape Wine Master, trained architect and, from 2001, resident winemaker Greg de Bruyn. Between remote controlling his workload in a flourishing Gauteng partnership, he's overseeing the building of the winery (designed by you-know-who), planning the vineyards, managing the farm, branding the products and handling distribution. There's also an eatery to be designed and built. But de Bruyn and wife Les are unfazed by all these pressing deadlines, and the plan remains to be open to the public in time to greet the arrival of the first whales of the 2001 season.

⚘ **Sauvignon Blanc** Bracing freshness the signature here, maiden **00** still needs to gather its ripe gooseberry, fragrant pear, cool citric elements into harmonious unit. So give bit of time, perhaps even 12 mths from harvest, and drink solo or with butter-basted grilled linefish. 13,2% alc. 1 180 cases.

. . . .

Swartland Wine Cellar

Swartland (see Swartland map) Tasting & sales Mon—Fri 8—5 Sat 9—12 • Owners 102 members • Production head Olla Olivier (since Jun 1996) • Winemakers Andries Blake red wines (since 1996), Abrie Beeslaar white wines (since 1999) • Marketing manager Marius Kotzé • Quality control Marius Prinsloo • Production 1,2 million cases 76% white 20% red 4% rosé • PO Box 95 Malmesbury 7300 • Tel (022) 482-1134/5/6 • Fax (022) 482-1750 • E-mail swynkelder@mbury.new.co.za

NOT ONLY among the very best value locally, this friendly, affordable range now charms and cheers consumers in more than two dozen countries including Britain and the United States. Exports are roaring (in the Netherlands, Swartland is the largest wine supplier world-wide to the Albert Hein retail chain), and offshore sales now represent half of the total. And where easy-swigging bag-in-box wines represented 50% of production just a few years ago, they're down to just 10%. By contrast, wines sold in glass have soared to 60% (the remaining — very good — fraction appears on shelves in SA and around the world in other people's bottles including, locally, Woolworths'). And, with global demand swinging ever further towards red, Swartland is ready with a present-day vineyard mix of 40% red and 60% white, rising to 50/50 by 2004. One of the first co-ops to go down the good-wine trail, Swartland is now positively leaping towards its quality goal. Which is one good reason to swing into the airy visitor centre on the fringe of Malmesbury.

Reserve range

Only made in exceptional years.

✿ Cabernet Sauvignon-Merlot ▼ A serious red in any company. **99** intense and full-flavoured. Blackberries/red cherries densely packed, fragrant with sweet violets, coffee and choc. Ripe tannins give just the right firming grip to juicy/spicy fruit. Last was **97**, harmonious, balanced and, like **99**, ready to drink, and probably not for long ageing. 70/30 blend, 6 mths small oak. 13% alc.

Pinotage ✿ Lightish **00** throws together ripe plums/bananas and youthfully puckering tannins. Suggest give bit of time to relax/develop. Some pvs have been excellent — **96** ABSA Top Ten.

'Standard' range

✿ Cabernet Sauvignon Improves with each vintage. **00** ✿ features sappy mulberries, sweet vanilla from 3–6 mths in small Fr oak; sweet ripe tannins and a really long finish. Like pvs **98**, harmonious, balanced, and a great bargain at R20 ex-cellar.

✿ Shiraz ▼ Pvs vibey **98**, with toasty/savoury fruit, gets topped by strapping **99** ✿, decidedly warming from 15% alc but balanced, not unmanageable. Flavour packed black/red fruits, whiffs woodsmoke/new leather; lazy viscous texture which goes exceptionally well with food. **97/99** *Wine* ✿.

✿ Colombard ▼ Exceptionally expressive fruit in **00**; stacked with guava and honeysuckle; rich, sweet tasting yet with lingering, very smooth, bone-dry finish. 12,5% alc.

✿ Vintage Port 97's initial oak/tannin attack has softened considerably; now tastes smooth, supple and rich with roasted almond/prune/fruitcake all dusted with spice. Dry in the modern style (90 g/ℓ sugar). Plenty of room still for development. Tinta b/cab/shiraz. 17% alc. Small oak 13 mths. *Wine* ✿.

Pinotage ✿ Velvety **00** spotlights the sweet-fruity persona of this grape; deep plummy flavours, banana/cinnamon whiffs come together in round, generous palate which ends crisply dry. **Merlot** ✿ Small Fr oak aged **99** shows good bottle development; ripe, sweet mulberry dominates, some plummy/savoury snatches. Fuller than pvs at 13,5% alc. **Tinta Barocca** ✿ Not many varietal bottlings in Cape; this is a good one. **00** soft, earthy without porty overtones; lightly charry fruitcake tones supported by ripe mulberry. Bushvines; unoaked. 13,5% alc. **Rosé** ✿ Good red wine aromas/flavours; lively; 13,5% alc lends substance in palate. At dryish end of semi-sweet. **NV. Blanc de Noir** ✿ Semi-sweet blush, always with dryish finish for quaffing solo or at table. Perfumed, med-bodied **00** with pear/quince and some spun sugar aromas. From pinotage. **Chardonnay** ✿ Rounded, mouthfilling **00** with citrus/tropical tones and light brush of oak. Long zesty finish. 13% alc. **Fernão Pires Light** ✿ Ideal lunchtime tipple with low alc of 9%. Delicate limey **00**, off-dry and lively. **Riesling** ✿ Cape riesling's signature sweet-hay aroma mingles with citrus/dried apricot in fresh, full-flavoured **00**. Gentle dry finish. **Bouquet Blanc** ★ **NV** Won't ruffle any feathers. Gentle, light semi-sweet. Touch of muscat grapiness. **Bukettraube** ‡ Smooth, soft semi-sweet **00** with confectionery shop perfumes of honeysuckle, jasmine, malva. Light 10,5% alc. **Stein** ⚶ Lightish semi-sweet chenin with firm acidity which ensures ripe tropical tastes refresh, don't cloy. **NV**. **Late Vintage** ‡ Richer, full-bodied version of Stein above with bit of age and some honeyed tones. **NV** from chenin. 13% alc. **Natural Sweet** ⚶ Sweet, lightish charmer; soft honeyed feel, pretty rather than serious. **NV**. **Hanepoot** ⚶ **New** Attractive lemony fortified dessert; **99** very smooth marmalade/muscat through to tingly finish. 16,5% alc. **Hanepoot** ★ **New** Powerfully sweet, raisiny, coarse. **NV**. 19% alc. **White Jerepico** ‡ **New** Tropical melons from start to finish of this **NV** fortified dessert from chenin; full, sweet; tangy 19,5% alc. **Red Jerepico** ⚶ **New** Pinotage infuses this fortified dessert with plummy/earthy tastes and bits of fruit cake; full, smooth and warming. 18,5% alc. **NV**. **Port** ⚶ Modern, bright, pleasing ruby style fortified dessert with plum/raisin tones and little scoops of earth hinting at tinta b provenance. Good dry spirity finish. Very well priced at under R15 ex-cellar.

Dry Red ⚶ 😊 Super everyday red; good chewy style with loads of plummy fruit, sweet/savoury twist to tail. Unoaked blend pinotage, cab, tinta b. **NV**. **Steen** ⚶ 😊 Delightful **00** early drinker with exuberant tropical fruit flavours of guava/passionfruit/papaya; ripeness creates sweet impression on tongue but finishes dry, lemon zesty. **Sauvignon Blanc** ⚶ 😊 **00** fresh cut-grass/sweet gooseberry romp in ultra-fresh palate with smooth acidity, long finish. Amazing value. **Premier Grand Cru** ⚶ 😊 Crisp and bone-dry, ideal foil for seafood and fish. Latest **NV** (00) with supercharged guava/passionfruit; frisky, fresh with whiff of orange peel in tail. Lightish bodied chenin/colombard/clairette blanche mix. **Blanc de Blanc** ⚶ 😊 Pretty floral fragrances, hints of jasmine; juicy fruit. Charming lightish dry **NV** from colombard/chenin. **Cinsaut** ⚶ 😊 Quaffer with a lot to offer (including 14% alc, which hardly noticeable). Savoury/toasted hazelnuts/fragrant scrub all mingle with ripe strawberry in unwooded **00**. Hardly a tannin in sight.

Sparkling range

All carbonated, NV, budget priced.

Cuvée Brut ⚶ **New** Crisp, refreshing dry bubbles from sauvignon; fills the mouth with fruity froth, finishes tangy-clean. **Demi Sec** ⚶ **NV** Crowd-pleasing sweetish bubbles; sauvignon perfumed with bit of hanepoot; festively fizzy. Lowish 11,7% alc. **Vin Doux** ⚶ Sweeter version of Demi-sec above, slightly more honeyed; will please many. **Rosette** ⚶ Low alc semi-sweet sparkler with active, creamy mousse. Pinotage, here with mainly chenin, hanepoot, imparts the deepish blush. 8,5% alc.

Boxed range

Untasted for this ed, but on track record, solid ‡/⚶ quality. 5 ℓ casks: **Grand Cru**, **Blanc de Blanc**, **Stein**, **Late Harvest**; 2 ℓ casks: **Grand Cru**, **Stein**, **Late Harvest**.

Sylvanvale Vineyards

Stellenbosch (see Stellenbosch map) • Tasting & sales daily 9—6 Fee R5 p/p refundable on any purchase • Cellar tours by arrangement • Vineleaf Restaurant with children's menu (see Eat-out section) • Picnics by arrangement • Luxury 40 room hotel • Conferences • Tourgroups • Play area for children • Gifts • Walks • Views • Wheelchair-friendly • Owner David Nathan-Maister • Consultant winemaker Martin Meinert (since 1999) • Consulting viticulturist Lorna Roos (since 1998) • Vineyards 6 ha • Production 2 500 cases 50% red 30% white 20% rosé • PO Box 68 Stellenbosch 7599 • Tel (021) 882-2012 • fax (021) 882-2610 • E-mail devon @ iafrica.com • Website www.sylvanvale.co.za

"TO REFLECT our tiny patch of this beautiful valley in hand-made wines of character and intensity," is *bon-vivant* hotelier David Nathan-Maister's aim, and 2000 was a bull's-eye vintage for the 6 ha of vines surrounding his Devon Valley Hotel. This rural inn could walk straight into the international *Guides de Charme* series, with its serene setting, classy country cuisine, award-winning wine (and malt whisky) list, and enough character(s) to stage a small opera. (David N-M lists wine — "make it, drink it, love it" — women, his wife and 2 daughters — and song as his hobbies — he presents a Sunday afternoon opera radio programme.) His own wine, fashioned by Martin Meinert, grown by Lorna Roos, went beyond hand-made to hand-snapped, beyond intensity to almost solid flavour, in the case of the Vine Dried Chenin in 2000. "We made numerous passes through the vineyards, snapping the bunches on the stems, thus allowing the grapes to dry out on the vine while preserving acidity. The aim was a blockbuster!" Some pinotage was steered along the same route, and has emerged rather like a dry port.

⚜️**Pinotage Reserve** Highly individual statement-making style showing richness, weight (14% alc), swirling perfumes of plum/mulberry/spice and just a suggestion of eucalyptus in latest **99**. More obviously oaked than pvs, giving extra spicy/vanilla lift to the super-dense fruit. Single vyd ±30 yrs old. Yr Fr oak, none new. First release **98** also very fine; similar intensity/weight, mouthcoating but supple tannin. Still on the up. Small quantities — ±800 cases.

⚜️**Dry Pinotage Rosé** Properly dry and flavour packed, good on its own and versatile with food. **99** holding well, savoury/spicy raspberry/plum still enticing, as is the vibrant ruby-pink hue. No **00**.

⚜️**Laurie's Vineyard Chenin Blanc 98** sole release to date ageing gracefully. Bright buttercup yellow; full (alc nearly 14%), some honeyed richness further fleshing the broad passionfruit tones; dried peach nuances in the bouquet. Good bone-dry finish excellent with food. ±20 yr old vines. Unwooded.

Vine Dried Pinotage Wildly individual Late Harvest style, informally subtitled 'Recioto di Pinotage', picked at 38–40 °B and casked 12 mths. 16% alc, 4 g/ℓ sugar. Untasted. **Vine Dried Chenin Blanc** Here's another of those quirky, windmill-tilting numbers Sylvanvale specialises in: super-concentrated chenin (for 'recipe', see intro above), new-barrel fermented in Fr oak (very unusual in Cape) for an individual, full-throated style probably with enough guts and structure to go the intended 10 yrs. **00** (sample) highly intense dried apricot/pineapple/Cape gooseberry perfumes and leesy hints melding with quince and exotic peach pip/nutmeg in viscous, sweet-sour palate. Should rate min ⚜️ on release. 210 g/ℓ sugar ±30 yr old vines. 200 cases.

. . . .

Table Mountain

THIS RANGE by Stellenbosch Farmers' Winery was first released into the Japanese market in 1997 and fast became a top seller.

⚜️**Cabernet Sauvignon** Good contrasting savoury/fruitcake tones in **98**, full bodied/flavoured with touch of peppery spice. Versatile table accompaniment. 13% alc.

Chardonnay ⚜️ Zesty, med/full-bodied **99** with fragrant citrus/tropical attractions and good dry finish.

. . . .

Table Peak

EXPORT range for Matthew Clark, UK, by Vinimark.

Ruby Cabernet ⚜️ 🍷 Vivid ruby-hued, med-bodied **00** offers sappy blackberries/plums, supple drinkability.

Colombard ✿✿ Lightish off-dry **00** with tropical pineapple tang, tastes smooth rather than sweet. For carefree early drinking.

Talana Hill see Vriesenhof

Tasheimer Goldtröpfchen

THESE RHINE-STYLE 'droplets of gold' which started the semi-sweet white wine revolution in SA in the 1950s being phased out by owners Stellenbosch Farmers' Winery.

Tassenberg

BIGGEST SELLING RED in SA, launched 1936; associated with good times by generations of South Africans. The red wine shortage in Cape led to an addition to the label in 1997: "Produced in SA and Argentina, filled in the RSA". Current blend includes Spanish, Chilean, Argentinean fruit, carefully chosen to resemble the SA cinsaut used. By Stellenbosch Farmers' Winery.

> **NV** ✿✿ ☺ Warmly satisfying, cherry/plum profile with winegum sappiness; touch of spice and smooth palatability. Med-bodied.

Taverna Rouge

LIGHTLY sweet (unusually for red), budget priced NV blend from SA Wine Cellars. Now a blend of oak matured wines from Spain/SA. Not tasted for this ed (pvs rating ✿✿).

Tesco see Vinfruco

TenFiftySix Winery

Franschhoek (see Franschhoek map) • Tasting by appointment • Owner Michael Falkson • Winemaker Gerda Willers (since 1999) • Viticulturist Toll Malherbe • Vineyards ± 3 ha • Production ± 3 500 cases 50/50 red/white • PO Box 244 Milnerton 7435 • Tel (021) 551-2284 • Fax (021) 551-2487 • E-mail charbrey@new.co.za

"AT FIRST I made wine by the seat of my pants," recalls Michael Falkson, property developer, self-taught winemaker and owner of this small Franschhoek farm, quirkily named after the number of its title deed. "I actually thought it all quite easy. Then a local magazine referred to my Veritas gold winning sauvignon as 'cat's pee'. I freaked. I didn't know it was a positive!" Since those early days Falkson's perfectionism, boosted with lots of outside advice, has won loyal fans at home and in the UK and Germany. He's now ceded the main winemaking responsibility to consultant Gerda Willers, who will keep a practised eye on the established rows of cabernet and the younger semillon vines, soon to be followed by merlot.

Cabernet Sauvignon ✿✿ Latest is **99** (though **98**, **97** still available from farm); undemanding savoury aromas of green pepper, mulberry, joined by spice and fragrant herbs in full (13,2% alc) but gentle palate. **Sauvignon Blanc** ✿✿ **00** extrafresh lemon-zippy tones prefaced by pears, and some gooseberries in bouquet. Try with popcorn and peanuts, says Michael Falkson, quirkily. ± 13% alc. Also-available **99** quieter, softer. **Blanc Fumé** ✿✿ Lightly oaked sauvignon; aromas/flavours more muted than above, lowish 11,9% alc, yet **99** has enough substance to go well with richer foods like traditional spicy braised smoorvis. Also available (not tasted): **Chardonnay 99**, **Chenin Blanc 97**, **MCC 98**.

Thandi Wines

Elgin (see Elgin/Walker Bay map) • Tasting & sales at Paul Cluver (see that entry) • Winemaker Patrick Kraukamp (since 1996) with Andries Burger • Farm manager Christo Nel • Consulting viticulturist Eben Archer • Vineyards 26 ha • Production 6 800 cases 54% red 46 • white • PO Box 48 Grabouw 7160 • Tel (021) 859-0605 • Fax (021) 859-0150 • E-mail pcwine@cluver.co.za • Website www.cluver.co.za

WITH FRUIT FARMING currently in something of a slump — particularly apples, the major crop in this cool Elgin area — the wine-growing segment of this forestry, fruit and vine empowerment project must do more than come to the party. It's got to get up on the table and dance. And so it has, with Thandi's debut wines immediately rocking off the shelves of UK supermarket chain Tesco in 1999, and the new-millennium crop — up more than 25% to 100 000 litres — increasing the momentum. You could, if you liked, buy this label simply on its New South Africa credentials — it was the lifeboat launched to save the forestry workers' village of Lebanon, threatened by privatisation, and represents a joint venture between the workers' community trust and Paul Cluver wines. But that wouldn't satisfy winemaker Patrick Kraukamp — presently working out of the Cluver cellar — nor the original motivator of this project, Paul Cluver, who says: "We have a very good story here, and the legitimacy of that story is important. But we have to be able to show the goods in terms of actual empowerment of workers *and* the quality of the wine." The intentions are admirably serious — and so far so good …

✿ **Chardonnay** Two versions. For Benelux/German markets: **Cape of Good Hope** ✿✿ **99** golden yellow; rich, creamy, pineapple/grapefruit-pith concentrated in full but fresh palate; grapefruit tang enhances broad mouthfeel; balanced finish. Fr oak, 30% new, rest 2nd fill, 6–8 mths. No malo. 13,5% alc. For UK market, the better of the pair: **Elgin 99** more elegance, crisp finish, fresh acidity, no malo for fresh flavours.

Pinot Noir ⚡ **99** has colour/flavour many red wines would die for: striking deep shades; very ripe, almost fruit-cordial intensity; serious oaking (3rd/4th fill barrels, 11 mths). But here, it's possibly de trop: there's not enough structure, balance or elegance to round it all up and package it convincingly. Taste from **00** barrels much more striking (thanks to improved techniques including cold maceration, pumping over with aeration, punching down of cap etc etc). Far superior to **98**, singled out by British wine writer Richard Neill in his pick of New Word wines; attractive, clean fruit, accessible and easy drinking. **Cabernet Sauvignon** ⚡ **97** first release; fruit from Overgaauw/Koopmanskloof. Deep red; herbaceous nose, 'buchu' vegetal flavour spectrum plus fruit and mint. 12,5% alc.

Thelema Mountain Vineyards

Stellenbosch (see Stellenbosch map) • Tasting & sales Mon–Fri 9–5 Sat 9–1 • Tourgroups by arrangement • Views • Wheelchair-friendly • Owner McLean Family Trust & G H Webb • Winemaker Gyles Webb • Viticulturist Aidan Morton • Viticultural consultant Phil Freese • Vineyards 50 ha • Production 350 tons 25 000 cases 60% white 40% red • PO Box 2234 Stellenbosch 7601 • Tel (021) 885-1924 • Fax (021) 885-1800 • E-mail thelema@adept.co.za

EVERYTHING has a price, they say. But it would have to be pretty serious to tempt winemaker Gyles and marketing director Barbara Webb and family off this lovely farm, with 50 ha of vineyards precision-marching up the slopes of Simonsberg. Perhaps it's the excellence of these vineyards, given extra oomph with the latest trellising and pruning systems via Californian consultant Phil Freese; perhaps the promise of new plantings — shiraz and cabernet franc; perhaps the spanking new extensions to the cellar with its staggering mountain view; perhaps the internationally acclaimed wines, considered models of modern Cape excellence. Whatever, though the farm is not on the market, Webb is constantly fending off fishing expeditions. Which of course — Thelema fans may rest easy — he had no intention of accepting. (In any case, who could afford to buy the human, hardworking family element that has been so integral to Thelema's transformation from obscure fruit farm to Cape eminence?) More serious than such incidents were the raging scenes from Apocalypse Now early in 2000 as runaway fires swept over the Western Cape mountains. Thelema's new dam supplied blaze-fighting helicopters, and Webb lost 1 000 young vines. Even worse was the fume factor, about which Webb is characteristically honest: a lot of wine emerged smelling (and tasting) of smoke. Your Thelema wines will be in even shorter, more select supply than usual. Though boosted this year by a quirky one-off Pinotage (grapes from Stellenbosch University's experimental vineyards), Webb's dictum remains "make less, but better".

✿✿**Cabernet Sauvignon** Sumptuously delicious modern Cape cabernet, with international cult following to match. Squid-inky colour, intense perfumed bramble nose, rich deep-roasted coffee announce — with full flourish — return of the inimitable Thelema 'phoenix' heraldry in latest **97** ✿✿: classic blackberry/mulberry fruit, velvety mouthfeel offset by diamond-edge of relative youth. Ripe minty imprint less aggressive than pvs, elegance from long, cool growing season. 20 mths serious ("and expensive," laments Webb) Fr oak, 40% new. 10 % merlot adds mid-palate flesh. *Wine* ✿✿. Preview of full-ripe **98**: closed mid-2000, may be released end 2000 (depending on readiness and marketing policy review). These upscale from **96** ✿, brilliant winemaking in challenging vintage, though probably earlier drinking. *Wine* ✿. Fabulous 95 ✿✿, *Wine* ✿ maturing elegantly. Cedar, cassis piled over choc-mint; berry fruit opening; lengthy departure. **94** Diners Club winner. Around 13,5% alc; cab grapes from clones 163 and 46. Also **CWG Auction Reserve** ✿✿, firmest, finest, densest cab — magnified by spicy all-new oak maturation — selected for this prestige label. Last was **95** voluptuous, sensationally rich.

✿**Merlot** Gyles Webb's 'other red' — yin to the above cab's yang: gutsy, firm, needing ±5 yrs from harvest, yet even in youth ripe with the property's watermark plush berry bouquet; fleshy warm palate, balanced finish. **98** pre-bottling sample holds savoury secrets, which thrusting tannins will yield with time. **97** gaining Italian style muscularity, gamey decadence leavened by grassy, red/blueberry freshness. **96** more herbaceous, less meaty, for early drinking, as is **95** with smoked meat aroma lightened by minerals, herbs. Limited new oak (10%) in 20 mths small barrel maturation. 13,5% alc. **CWG Merlot** Departure from Webb's propensity to offer cab at auction. **98** a distillate of all above attributes — and more: immense fruit intensity, savoury black olive, pimento succulence shrouded in huge ripe tannin; American oak's perfumed vanilla completes the cornucopia.

✿**Pinotage** New "First," says Gyles Webb, "and last!" Cape's indigenous grape given the Webb-o-matic treatment in **98** — and the result is positively puissant. Unambiguous wild, gamey flavours, ripe banana, coffee, spice. Generous dollop Fr/Am oak (18 mths), plus far-from-demure 14,8% alc sure to be instant hit. Bought-in grapes.

Shiraz Gyles Webb quietly chuffed with **00**, 1st crop from leased vineyards, adding fresh colour to palette. Hermitage-like richness, concentration, with associated pepper/spice aromatic density. Unrated.

✿**Chardonnay** Swords may be crossed in rarefied circles about the 'classicism' of this wine, but the paying public probably couldn't care less. **99**, sampled in infancy for pvs ed, has developed into emphatic, rich, buttery mouthful with trademark ripe lime marmalade/pineapple flavours, creamy texture. Crop down 40%, new Fr oak component up to 50% (11 mths). Just-dry 4 g/ℓ residual sugar and 14,4% alc fill any spaces left in palate. Will be hugely popular. Painstaking vyd preparation, separate block vinification, yeast diversity and meticulous logging of cellar performance part of Webb's strategy to ensure best barrel selections. Yet vintage always a factor: **98**, something of a deviation in Thelema's style, explodes in late 15% alc rush; but beams with character of its own (prized by *Wine Spectator*, which bestowed lofty 91 rating). Super **97** *Wine* ✿, though no pushover at 14% alc, more congruent with Thelema style: zesty, grapefruit punch of long ripened fruit, rich finish. **95** SAA. **94** WINE ✿, top of SAA chard selections **Reserve Chardonnay 97** ✿ wowed the crowds at 2000 Nederburg Auction with stratospheric white wine price of R250/bottle (original plan to avoid rationing by "drinking it all ourselves" overcome by market demand and good business sense). Showcase choice for New York Wine Experience.

✿ **Ed's Reserve** Singularly unusual chardonnay from clone 166, with super-potent grapey muscat features which not even "severe wooding" can diminish (fans wouldn't dream of it anyway). Named after "famous mother-in-law" and chef-de-tasting-room Edna McLean. Even bigger (is it possible?) in this latest (3rd) **98** release: 15,6% alc, prompting Webb, asked when he would drink, to reply: "When I'm not too thirsty!" Pungently petally, delicately spicy (akin to sweet-scented viognier) **97** survives substantial 14% alc. Webb, "conceding defeat in attempting to craft it into a conventional chardonnay", suggests: "Enjoy it for it's natural exuberant self". No shortage of same, in bottle or the tasting room. First **96** labelled "A Dry White" — back label owned up to its chardonnay provenance.

✿ **Sauvignon Blanc 00** sees return to form and style — in spite of drought, heat and fires — after two out-of-character vintages (though fans of pvs nervy, knife-edged style — **97** the benchmark — will have to hope for a cooler 01 vintage). Fresh floral nose, ripe tropical melon and guava, fleshy gooseberry. 13,7% alc. Racier, flintier and better balanced than **99**, which had the stuffing knocked out of it by harvest heat; and imposing **98**, jam-packed gooseberry fruit, formidable 14,2 % alc and touch of sugar.

✿ **Muscadel** New to this ed. Fortified **NV** dessert with golden amber, nutty rather than raisiny tastes. Density, flavour surpasses pvs (and other more frivolous offerings). Rich, not too sweet (194 g/ℓ sugar), not too weak (18% alc). Blend 93, 96 vintages. Next (98, 00 blend) created in sherry-like solera barrel system of maturation — shows in rich 'oloroso' style. Arresting very cold.

Rhine Riesling ✿ Returned to range in **99** after over-ripe **98** not released. Latest **00** perfumed, delicate in Germanic just off-dry style (4,7 g/ℓ sugar). Deliciously undemanding, but kaleidoscopic at table. Webb treats himself to mature **93** when in need of reward (these cellar well without overt terpenes). **Muscat de Frontignan** ✿ **00** true to variety with grapey, rose bud nose; but palate has substantially more grip than most. Refreshing chilled. Lighter (13% alc.), drier (9 g/ℓ) than nearly semi-sweet **99**. Super-ripe **98** not released.

· ·

Theuniskraal Estate ♀

Tulbagh (see Tulbagh map) • Tasting & sales by appointment Mon—Fri 9—12, 1—5 • Cellar tours by appointment • Winemakers Kobus & Andries Jordaan • Viticulturists Rennie, Kobus, Andries & Wagner Jordaan • Vineyards 130 ha • Production ± 1 500 tons ± 20 000 cases 87% white 13% red • PO Box 34 Tulbagh 6820 • Tel (023) 230-00687/88/89 • Fax (023) 230-0690 • E-mail info@theuniskraal.co.za • Website www.theuniskraal.co.za

THINK THEUNISKRAAL and a crisp Riesling springs to mind as fast as a mirage in the desert. But right now this 18th century family estate at the north-west end of the Tulbagh valley is seeing red, with more red varieties being planted, red wine facilities being added to the pressing cellar and a new red wine label. They've also learnt a thing or two about marketing from the Aussies. Quite a substantial spread for the youngest Jordaan — the fourth generation since oupa Andries Jordaan began the proud family tradition of winemaking — to cut his toddler teeth on.

✿ **Semillon-Chardonnay** Rises above its iconic stablemate in **00**, even showing potential for development. Some complexity from light barrelling — nutty tones

over butterscotch/vanilla — expansive mouthfeel with creamy fruit salad flavours and supple dry finish. 56/44 blend, 13,7% alc. ± 3 800 cases

Riesling ✿✿ First 'estate' white wine in SA — 53 yrs on market and still a crowd
pleaser: 16 000 cases/yr. Though winemakers recommend "drink as soon as you
can", **99** demonstrates these don't keel over immediately. Cape riesling's dry
thatch nicely layered with honey, bone-dry finish with pleasing crunch. Med-bodied. **00** not available for tasting.

. . . .

Three Rivers see Bon Courage

. . . .

Tokara

Stellenbosch (see Stellenbosch map) • Tasting, sales, cellar tour hours to be announced • Restaurant (please call —
details not available at press time) • Views • Wheelchair-friendly • Owner GT Ferreira • Cellarmaster Gyles Webb •
Winemaker Miles Mossop (since 2000) • Vineyard manager Eddie Smit (since 1997) • Vineyards 43 ha • Production
700 tons max 60% red 40% white • PO Box 662 Stellenbosch 7599 • Tel (021) 887-8561 • Fax (021) 887-8556

THE LONGER THE ANTICIPATION, the greater the expectations, the more intense the
pressure: can South African financial wizard GT Ferreira (of the FirstRand banking
group) extend his golden touch to wine? Is cabernet sauvignon red? The vineyards
of this sensationally sited property in the prime Banhoek area of Stellenbosch
(views from its slopes to Table Mountain and across False Bay) have been developed by Thelema's Gyles Webb, regarded by many as the Cape's most accomplished winemaker, and a complete fanatic about growing vines properly. Webb
only has to slip over the fence to get to his consulting cellarmaster's office in a
designer winery which makes everyone else's no-expense-spared edifices seem,
well, rather parsimonious. Ferreira chooses his next door neighbours well. Other
good choices here: young Miles Mossop (son of Cape Winemaster and port producer Tony) moves confidently into his first plum winemaking job after Stellenbosch
University studies and a year in California and Australia. And Etienne Bonthuys, the
most dramatic of chefs, does his thing here in an equally dramatic restaurant. So
far, so good. But what about the wines? Patience. It's taken a year or three to find
a suitable name — Tokara it now is, after Ferreira's two teenagers, Thomas and
Kara. It probably won't be until mid-2001 that the first fruits from these vineyards
are released. The suspense continues …

. . . .

Towerkop see Ladismith
Tradouw see Barrydale

. . . .

Travino Wines

Olifants River (see Olifants River map) • Tasting & sales Mon—Fri 8—1; 2—5 • Phone ahead for cellar tours • Owners
47 members • Winemaker/manager Alkie van der Merwe (since 1995) with JC Coetzee (since 1995) • Consulting
viticulturist Jeff Joubert (VinPro) • Vineyards ± 600 ha • Production 9 075 tons 90% white 10% red • PO Box 2 Klawer
8145 • Tel (027) 216-1616 • Fax (027) 216-1425 • E-mail travino@kingsley.co.za

"No charge!" insists eternally upbeat Alkie van der Merwe, who speaks in excla-
mation marks, of tasting fees at this co-op winery. "A satisfied wine buyer is
enough payment!" And if you visit during the spring wild-flower season, you'll have
the combined "splendour" of what's in your glass and what's blooming outside.
While passionate about the West Coast, van der Merwe is also a keen traveller. He
recently visited China ("to see where our exports have been going"), and France, to
pick up tips for the upcoming red wine cellar. On which subject he might also
consult older brother Nico, of Saxenburg red-wine fame — sibling rivalry, he jokes,
spurred him into winemaking, which (another joke) he describes as an ideal training
ground "for a career in politics!!"

Merlot 00 (sample, not rated) potentially better than pvs; strict tannin balanced by full fruit. **99** ☆☆ juicy berries in savoury background. Lightish 11,7 alc. 500 cases. **98** VG. **Pinotage** ☆☆ Smoky/savoury **99**, initially softly plummy, turns firmly tannic in finish. Lightly wooded. Lightish 11,6% alc. 500 cases. **98** SAYWS gold. **00** (sample) promising. **Shiraz 00** tasted pre-final make-up, unrated. Remaining (oaked) portion sold to AvdM's brother Nico for his Wilhelmshof label. 12,4% alc. 400 cases. **99** ☆ smoky/tarry character. **Classic Dry** ★ New Subdued nose and earthy tones. Definitely dry. **NV**. **Grand Rouge** New ☆☆ With light lick of sweetness, AvdM says, to smooth the way for novice red wine drinkers. Ripe plums, some savoury/herby notes, smooth. Med-bodied. **NV**. 500 cases. **Chardonnay** ☆ Soft barley sugar/honey tones in **00**. 13,4% alc. 250 cases. **Sauvignon Blanc** ☆ Undemanding **00**, very fresh, short finishing. 500 cases. **Blanc de Blanc** New ★ Chardonnay/chenin made semi-sweet "for sundown sipping". **NV**. 400 cases. **Special Late Harvest** New ☆ Pineapple/banana tastes, ample sweetness in **00**. 13% alc. 400 cases. **Muskateer** New ☆☆ Experimental **98** fortified dessert from red muscadel, 50% oaked 1 yr. Arresting bright brick red, almost fluorescent; marmalade/marzipan and, in sweet-spirity palate, dabs of choc. Sweet toothed will love this. 16,1% alc. 250 cases.

Trawal see Travino

Twin Oaks see Du Preez Wine

Tukulu

Darling • Tasting & sales at Oude Libertas, Stellenbosch • See Stellenbosch Farmers' Winery • Owners SFW, Leopont 98 Properties, Maluti Groenekloof Community Trust • Winemaker Carmen Stevens • Vineyards To be expanded to 330 ha • Enquiries Carina Gous tel (021) 808-7911

THIS VAST, R32-million West Coast property (so far 180 ha under vines and growing) is at the leading edge of 'development projects' (or if you prefer, 'empowerment ventures') in the Cape. Kick-started by SFW, with the local community and a group of black liquor retailers the majority shareholders, Papkuilsfontein's winemaking operation is headed by accomplished Carmen Stevens — the first 'woman of colour' to hold such a position in South Africa. All very fine, but does the 'development' tag signify — as it can do — that these wines may not yet be quite up to speed? That they're more feel-good than taste-good? The answer here is an emphatic NO! The infant Pinotage we previewed last year has grown into a stunner. (There's development for you.) The 2000 Chenin is a wow. So if Tukulu's admirable background lends extra nuances to every sip, well and good. But absolutely no slack needs to be cut here …

☆☆**Pinotage** New ✓ In pvs ed we peeped at this **99** sleeping (in oak) infant and predicted: "Should pack a hefty punch". That it certainly does: massively concentrated, almost cordial-like berry fruit folded into charry vanilla, long, spicy tannins. The arrangement initially strikes as sweet, yet tapers to lipsmacking dry conclusion. Exceptional. Yr small oak, 25% Am. Burly 14% alc.

☆☆Chenin Blanc Something about these red Tukulu soils — type first identified on a KwaZulu-Natal farm of same name — coaxes best qualities from these ancient, low cropping vyds (miniscule 3–4 bunches/vine): good concentration, fresh lemony acidity in 99 and now, in arresting 00 ☆☆, more richness, intensity yet admirable restraint. Unlike pvs, these forthright gooseberry/guava/milled pepper tones need no oak embroidery; they stand alone mouthfillingly, despite the relatively slender body (12% alc). Very different chenin.

Tulbagh Co-op

Tulbagh (see Tulbagh map) • Tasting & sales Mon—Fri 8.30—5 Sat 9—1 Closed religious public holidays • Views • Wheelchair-friendly • Owners 70 members • General manager Neil Watson • Public relations Madeleine du Toit • Winemaker Michael Krone (since 1997) with Stefan Smit • Vineyards 1 000 ha • Production 10 000 tons • PO Box 85 Tulbagh 6820 • Tel (023) 230-1001 • Fax (023) 230-1358 • E-mail tkw@tulbaghwine.co.za • Website www.tulbaghwine.co.za

MICHAEL KRONE, of wine's First Family in Tulbagh (the TJ and NC Krones), would like to "create an estate mentality" among this co-op's 70 members, whose vineyards stretch over 1 000 ha. Recent visits to Germany, Holland and London's International Wine Trade Fair have reinforced his quest for quality. "We will have to be careful that we aren't upstaged by the newer kids on the block, Chile and Argentina," he says. We'd say that for friendly, well-priced quaffability, this ever-improving range fits the consumer bill anywhere.

> **Cabernet Sauvignon** ✿ NEW ☺ Unpretentious everyday stuff; supple tannins make the strawberries/blackcurrants very easy to swallow. Med-bodied. 2 500 cases. **Merlot** ✿ ☺ Honest, undemanding pasta-style quaffer. Full-bodied **99** with ripe, rounded plums/violets/coffee. Unwooded. 13,3% alc. **Brut** Energetic fruity dry bubbles to share, so winemaker says, with SA aquastar Penny Heyns at the poolside. Lightish, refreshing. NV. 3 000 cases.

Camelot ✿ Super-soft, almost tannin-free **99** cab/merlot mix; pungent plums/peppers and good savoury-dry aftertaste. Med-bodied. 1 500 cases. **Chardonnay** ✿ NEW Wood-fermented **00** tastes lightly of oak, but more of ripe peaches and tropical fruit. Finishes fresh, clean. 13,6% alc. 1 000 cases. **Seminay Blanc** ✭ "Beach BBQ wine". **00**, like pvs, tropically attired, whiffs of lime in soft, sweetish, med-bodied palate. Chardonnay/sauvignon/semillon. 2 000 cases. **Vin Doux** Carbonated sweet fizz from colombard/pinotage with charming candy floss/tropical tastes. Lowish alc (10,6%).

Drink Eezi range

2/5 ℓ 'barrel bags'.

Claret ✭ Simple, earthy, dry. **Blanc de Blanc** ★ Lightish, ordinary, very dry, some cinnamon spice. **Stein** ✭ Vaguest tropical hints, surprisingly dry. **Late Harvest** ✭ Sweet, lightish fruity tastes.

Also available (not tasted): **Late Harvest NV**. 2/5 ℓ bag in boxes: **Dry Red**, **Grand Cru**, **Extra Light**, **Stein**, **Late Harvest**.

Twee Jonge Gezellen Estate

Tulbagh (see Tulbagh map) • Tasting & sales Mon—Fri 9—4 Sat 10—2 Closed Sun, Christmas, New Year's Day, Good Friday Tasting fee quoted on request for large groups • Cellar tours Mon—Fri 11, 3; Sat 11 • Tourgroups by appointment • Views • Wheelchair-friendly • Owner/winemaker Nicky Krone ("since ± the year dot") • Vineyard 120 ha • Production 1 500 tons • PO Box 16 Tulbagh 6820 • Tel (023) 230-0680 • Fax (023) 230-0686 • E-mail tjg@mweb.co.za

"APOLOGIES for being so late — you ask so many questions!" Nicky Krone's referring to the forms we send every year to all participants in this guide asking (among others), what's new in your winery? The response from this warm family farm is always worth waiting for, not just for the invariably entertaining snippets (winemaker Leon Mostert bid farewell in 2000 to realise his dream of running a fast food outlet), but also for Nicky Krone's reflective, often witty, elegantly penned replies. "We're re-establishing red varieties as well as viognier, and starting a new range of varietal wines under the 'Krone' banner, to be released towards the middle of 2001". And? "Our eldest son NC jnr is back after further studies and recently married to another wine fanatic who also just happens to be a chartered accountant. When he and Kathleen started going out together, we could see that young NC's days were 'numbered' …".

✤ **Krone Borealis Brut** A bottle-fermented sparkling blend of 50–50 chardonnay/ pinot; finer, riper, more subtle than most cap classiques, consistently shines in competition: pvs **94** _Wine_ ✤, **93** won Nicky Krone 1995 Diners Club Winemaker of Year award. Named after the constellation of stars, the Corona Borealis (Krone, crown, corona, all synonyms) created by god of wine Bacchus, who flung his gem-studded crown into the heavens to impress one of the ladies in his life. The romance continues, albeit at a slightly less breathless pace, in **97** ✤. Starts, as always, with classic biscuit aromas, then lovely, lees creaminess on a good toasty base and, despite a whisper of sweetness mid-palate, finishes with cleansing, almost austere dryness. The bubbles, energetic and persistent, not as extraordinarily fine as pvs. "NB", (Mary Krone underlines the capital letters), "no added preservatives", which may be what makes this the best-selling bubbly of choice for health devotees.

TJ 39 ✢ Blend riesling (39 is the clone number), sauvignon, chardonnay, chenin retains long track record of dependability with vitality, good dry white table companion. Lunchtime-lightish alc at ± 12%. **00** (tank sample, as are all still-wines below, so may rate marginally higher on release) delicate lemony nose, perky-fresh palate. 6 000 cases. **TJ Schanderl** ✤ A dainty bouquet in **00**, but tantalisingly perfumed with sweet pineapple; crisp, fresh muscat (de frontignan) flavours; rivetingly dry finish (though technically contains few grains of sugar). Lightish 12% alc. **TJ Light** ✤ Not only for the diet-conscious, though endorsed by the Heart Foundation. **00** "blend of early ripening, fruity varieties", daintily perfumed (hints of honeysuckle/muscat), soft, gentle, off-dry taste, with clean finish. Low-low 8,5% alc, but more charisma than many "lights". **TJ Night Nectar** ✤ Becomes a Natural Sweet from **00** (pvs officially Semi-Sweet), but still mainly chenin with spattering gewürz. Rose and honeysuckle fragrances, whisper of botrytis, clean, fresh and much lighter than pvs at 7,5% alc. 6 000 cases. **TJ Rose Brut** ✤ Snazzy salmon pink colour tells you which section of the deli counter to visit when foodmatching this "designer sparkling wine" (mainly pinot, chardonnay, unwooded, with extended lie-in on lees for authentic yeasty effect). Tastes lightly of candied/ baked apple, perked up with explosive, mouthfilling bubbles to dry, almost savoury finish. Feathery texture enhanced by lowish 11,7% alc. **NV**. 5 000 cases.

Two Oceans

EVEN if the eye-catching labels wrongly claim that the Atlantic and Indian oceans meet at Cape Point, this is a good value range. Made at the Drostdy cellar.

Cabernet-Merlot ✤ Unwooded and friendly **00**, ripe baked aromas, soft tannins and plum pudding flavours, with acid kicking in to give a savoury finish. High 13,5% alc. **Rosé** ✢ New Pale coppery-pink, scent of pale pink roses, pale flavours. Just off-dry; for export only. **NV**. **Sauvignon Blanc** ✤ Ripe gooseberries much in evidence in **00**, leading to a savoury lip-smacking finish. **Semillon-Chardonnay** ✤ New Good varietal nose with lemon/lanolin notes in **00**. Firm, crisp balance leads to citrus adieu.

Uiterwyk Estate   ♈ ♈

Stellenbosch (see Stellenbosch map) • Tasting & sales Mon—Fri 10—4.30 (Oct-Apr) Mon—Fri 10—12.30; 2—4.30 (May-Sep) Sat 10—4.30 year round • Tasting fee R5 p/p for groups 10 + • Cellar tours during harvest by appointment • Owners Danie & sons • Winemakers Chris de Waal (white wines (since 1978), Daniël de Waal (red wines, since 1990) • Marketing Pieter de Waal • Production 1 000 tons ± 22 000 cases 50/50 red/white • PO Box 15 Vlottenburg 7604 • Tel (021) 881-3711 • Fax (021) 881-3776 • E-mail info@uiterwyk.co.za • Website www.uiterwyk.co.za

GIVEN one word to encapsulate the style of this historic estate and the three brothers who run it, you might choose 'understatement'. There's no flash here. But — you'd have to insist on rather a strong 'but'. Because their wines are definitely attention-grabbers, even if, in a typically De Waalian way, they don't present themselves brashly. Daniel de Waal (reds) and Chris de Waal (whites) would far rather express themselves in suave French than strident 'Strine in their wines — though when upcoming shiraz joins the range ("we've got the right soils here — poor, gravelly") it's likely to sound bilingual. "I like Rhône shiraz, it's elegant. But sometimes it's thin. I like the spice in Aussie shiraz. But not the sweetness. Falling between the two — that would be lovely," Daniel de Waal says. "Elegance" is his non-negotiable, however extrovert a wine. He carefully chooses the pinotage to go into his Estate Cape Blend from older vineyards — "it must be big and bring fruit and creaminess, but it must also bring elegance". And he admires cabernet franc (and will bottle it solo in 2001) "because of its elegance". Chris de Waal's Sauvignon Blanc and Viognier are also made with the power-cum-finesse combination in mind.

✿✿Pinotage 'Top of the Hill' World-class red, regardless of variety. Since first release **96** ✿✿ single vyd selection, ± 45 yr old vines, new Nevers oak barrelled ±22 mths, racked half-yearly. Showered with awards: **96** *Wine* champion pinotage of 1998; **97** ABSA Top Ten, *Wine* ✿✿. Follow-up **98** 'declassified', blended with Estate assemblage and standard Pinotage below: leaf-roll virus prevented grapes from attaining physiological ripeness, explains Daniël de Waal, so result not up to usual standard. But regular **Pinotage** ✿✿ pumped up with splash 'Top of the Hill' continues to fly. **98** extra-concentrated (and more densely tannic), though plush fruit delivers less obvious spicy banana/ripe fig/ summer fruit than pvs. Even in this robust yr avoids sometime pinotage coarseness, though there's a hint– not unpleasant — of bitterness. 13,2% alc. 18 mths small Fr oak, 40% new. Gentle-tannined fruit from younger vyds, dash merlot usually included for extra softness. Yields kept to 5 t/ha. **96** VVG, ABSA Top Ten; **95** VVG. Regular Nederburg auction selection. Most need 4/5 yrs minimum.

✿✿Estate Cape Blend Outstanding cab-based blend, proudly waving the SA flag with routine infusion of pinotage (not more than 35–40%, however, owing to the local grape's feistiness). **98** ✿ (for release April 2001) acquires ageability from power of vintage. Big, robust, as other **98**s in range, with extra dimension only blending can achieve. Led upfront by elegant cab f (45%, largest percentage to date), whose leafy, spicy fragrance lifts overall fruit profile; 30% merlot injects stronger Bdx character. Fully absorbed oak adds complementary richness. Usual velvety sophistication presently restrained by dry, taut tannins; should gain opulence with time. 22 mths Fr oak, 60% new, rest 2nd fill. 13,5% alc. Smaller portion pinotage (from Top of the Hill vyd) due to vintage difficulties (see above). Since **94** has featured cab f (**97** 40%, 30% each pinotage/merlot, **96** *Wine* ✿ 40% with equal part pinotage, 20% merlot) — cab s rejected as clashing with merlot/pinotage components. Will change from **00**: "We can now see from earlier wines, in longer term cab s will provide better aging potential."

✿Merlot Serious dry red since **96**, *Wine* ✿ benefiting from increasing variety of vyd aspects — from north to south — and soils — from gravelly loam to clay. This first reflected in **97**; latest **98** sees north/south vyds equally represented. Result is deep lustrous ruby, intense plummy, minerally ripeness; creamy texture, very fresh, long flavours. Build and tannins demand good 3–4 yrs. 18 mths small Fr oak, 30% new. 13% alc. Before **96** these rated mainly ✿.

✿Shiraz NEW Here lies (pinotage) maestro Daniël de Waal's next challenge. Maiden **99** an impressive start, boosted by instantly 'mature' vyds (20 yr old vines, with grafted-on buds from neighbour, Overgaauw — so this, interestingly, step-sibling to Chris Joubert's Gilga and Kevin Arnold's Shiraz). As with other Uiterwyk reds, France an influence here: on advice from friends in Rhône, portion spent 3 mths on viognier lees in new oak ("for elegance", though winemaker concedes efficacy of method hard to judge). Less doubtful is northern Rhône elegance, fruit delicacy; chocolate, roasted spice suavely bound into mouthfilling velvety texture. Nothing too forceful, outspoken, yet no shortage of presence. 15 mths Fr oak, 30% new.

Cabernet Sauvignon ✿ Two vintages to be offered during currency of this guide: **97** ✿ charming, refined, showing house's European restraint, dryness. Already drinking well, so enjoy over next 2–3 yrs while waiting for **98**, more robust, also quite closed and probably longer lived, judging from youthfully recalcitrant tannins. 13% alc. Both Schleip clone, 18 mths Fr oak, 30% new. **Sauvignon Blanc** ✿ **00**, from same single vyd as super **99** ✿, opens with pure gooseberry, grassy promise; turns somewhat leaner in palate with quite prominent acid in infancy. Will probably settle after few mths but not achieve same weight, richness as pvs. 13,3% alc, 7,2 g/ℓ acid. **Viognier** ✿ One of handful in Cape of this trendy white variety. Small portion of first **99**, matured in new Fr oak, reappears in follow-up **00**. Adds breadth, weight (rich taffeta rather than **99**'s satiny swish), structure and, probably, ageing potential (**99** already showing bottle age). Peach pip, apricot less extrovert than pvs, but more concentrated, longer, better food style (Malaysian cuisine, per the de Waals). 13,5% alc. **Chardonnay** ✿ **98** filled out with 15% oaked portion from pvs vintage. No **99**. **Chardonnay Reserve** ✿ **98** serves up good breakfast of toast, gently pickled lime confiture and suggestion of roast hazelnut on the side. Supple, fruity feel, despite generosity of 80% new oak; smoothly dry finish. Also freshness to benefit from further yr/18 mths maturation. Barrel-fermented, all Fr oak, on lees extended 15 mths.

Rosenburg range

For UK restaurants; also sold locally. **Cabernet Franc-Pinotage** ✿ Plummy pinotage to fore in **97**; smooth, friendly dry finish. Yr rounding in older oak barrels.

··

Uitkyk Estate ▼

Stellenbosch (see Stellenbosch map) • Tasting & sales Mon—Fri9—5 Sat 9—12.30 Closed Sun • Owner Lusan Holdings • Manager/winemaker Theo Brink (since 1994) • Production 869 tons 62 796 cases • PO Box 3 Elsenburg 7607 • Tel (021) 884 4416 • Fax (021) 884 4717

PRE-2000 HARVEST fires delayed Theo Brink's experiments with this elegant Simonsberg farm's more exotic grapes — mourvèdre and nebbiolo among the recent transplants. Which will ensure that, for the present, all eyes (and palates) will remain focused on the stalwarts, which include the very distinguished Cabernet whose name echoes that of the flamboyant former owner, Baron von Carlowitz. Within these refined viticultural ranks, one vineyard occupies a special station. "It's a six year old plot — the best one on the property", explains affable Brink (talented son Theo jnr plies the family trade in the Kanu/Goedgeloof cellar). Whereas most Uitkyk vineyards are planted with 3 300 *stokkies* per hectare, this one's a claustrophobic 8 300. Which seems to faze neither the vines nor Brink, who continues to garner plaudits for his super-concentrated, sumptuous wine.

✿ **Carlonet** Venerable Cape institution, increasingly lustrous since standout **93**. Mulberries, cassis and plums with dusting of cedar in **97** version, powerful, solid and savoury, with firm tannic structure. Lurking fruit should leap with few yrs' development. 100% cab; 13,5% alc; Fr oak, 50% new. **96** ✿ VG, *Wine* ✿, difficult Cape vintage, with vegetal twist; well balanced with pleasant savoury dry finish. **95** ✿ with stunning 'sweet' profile, super-supple.

✿ **Chardonnay Reserve 99** Bursting with toast aromas, and citrus hints. Creamy rich palate, spiced with cloves but dominated by oak (11 mths new Fr), finishing on citrus note. Same emphatic oakiness still showing on **97** VG.

··

✿ Sauvignon Blanc Melon and unusual pumpkin aromas in **99** ✿; well balanced and rich, with crisp pineapple/green apple finish. 13% alc. **98** almost baroque richness, power. Effusive gooseberry, figs, grass in **97**.

Cabernet-Shiraz ✿ Cherry, cedar and medicinal notes on still youthful but approachable **97**, with big, dry tannins. 13,3% alc; mix new/ 2nd fill Fr oak. **96**, rated ✿ in previous ed, awkward (✱) when retasted mid-2000.

Uitvlucht Winery

Montagu (see Klein Karoo map) • Tasting & sales Mon—Fri 8.30—5.30 Sat 8—12 • Cellar tours by appointment • Owners 45 members • Winemaker Kootjie Laubscher (since 1993) • Production 7 000 tons 15 000 cases 95% white 5% red/dessert • PO Box 332 Montagu 6720 • Tel (023) 614-1340 • Fax (023) 614-2113

"EVERYTHING'S the same as last year," says Kootjie Laubscher, "except we have a Cabernet and a Merlot." Which might not seem like front page news, but when you consider the overwhelming proportion of white wine vines in these scenic vineyards, the arrival of this particular twin is a reason to break out the (local, of course) bubbly and raise glass to a bright red future. The following wines, untasted, are on the current list: red: **Cabernet Sauvignon** New, **Merlot** New; **Ruby Cabernet**; dry white: **Sauvignon Blanc**; **Blanc de Blanc**; off-dry: **Colombar**; semisweet: **Chenin Blanc**; **Late Harvest**; sparkling white: **Vin Doux**, **Vin Sec**; fortified desserts: **Red Muscadel**; **White Muscadel** (these also in 250 ml); **Muscat de Frontignan**; **Port**.

Upington see Oranjerivier Wynkelders

Upland Estate New 🍷 🍷 🍺 🍷

Wellington (see Wellington map) • Tasting, sales, cellar tours by appointment • Self catering cottages Tel (021) 864-1184 • Walks • Views • Owners Edmund & Elsie Oettlé • Winemaker/viticulturist Edmund Oettlé • Vineyards 13 ha • Production ±700 cases 100% red • PO Box 152 Wellington 7654 • Tel (021) 082-731-4774 • Fax (021) • E-mail oettle@intekom.co.za

DR EDMUND OETTLÉ and his electrical engineer wife Elsie seem to plan their lives by the decade. He spent 10 years as a fulltime vet before they both opted for life on this 46 ha property perched above the Wellington valley. It was a change, if not a holiday, as they quickly had to develop new skills, starting with the age-old agricultural activity of keeping the bank manager at bay. They began to make their own wine (foot-pressed in old concrete baths); and laboriously built up a hand-made cellar. Later, egged on by neighbour Roger Jorgensen, he concocted his own brandy kettle and distillery (frugally taking care of 10 ha of chenin and SA riesling). Come the dawn of another decade, another millennium, and the Oettlés make another swerve: changing lanes from Fisantekuil Farm to Upland Estate; going public with their first wine and first 'grappa' (the brandy's due in 2001); doing it all organically. Hand-grown, hand-made. Meantime, while managing all the above, they also bred peregrine and other resident falcons and the indefatigable Doc picked up a PhD in electron microscopy.

✿ Cabernet Sauvignon Wellington-size (±14% alc) cab with character and charm to match. First release **98** better than follow-up **99** (sample), tannins better managed though both generous, fleshy, almost fruit-cordial blackcurrant intensity. At table, the Oettlés like to pour this with venison or game birds, or full flavoured cheese. Own vyds. Yr 300 ℓ 2nd fill Fr/Am oak. 250 cases.

Merlot ✿ New oak vanilla, generous ladle alc (14%) give this maiden **98** an immediately warm, friendly air, enhanced by cherry liqueur/choc box tones and sweetly ripe fruit/tannins. Enjoy now while soft and comfortable. Grapes from Upland marketing manager Erich Maske's Klein Waterval farm next door. Yr Fr barriques. 100 cases.

Uva Mira Vineyards

Stellenbosch (see Helderberg map) • Tasting by appointment • Sales Mon—Fri 9—4 • 3 self catering, fully serviced guest cottages • Views • Owners Weedon family • Consulting winemaker Jan 'Boland' Coetzee (since 1996) • Consulting viticulturist Eben Archer • Vineyards 18 ha • Production 5 000 cases 80% white 20% red • PO Box 1511 Stellenbosch 7599 • Tel/fax (021) 880-1682 • E-mail uva.mira@softswitch.co.za

DES WEEDON, the driving force behind this farm, with a lofty position on the Helderberg and wraparound views, died in 2000 after battling a long illness. A lot of what has been achieved here can be put down to sheer hard work. But there's also been an element of luck involved: last year saw another exceptional harvest with the good deep mountain soils providing excellent buffering against drier conditions. The very first crop of home grown roobernet is being blended with merlot to produce "an authentic Cape-style red blend". Also indigenous are the proteas, pincushions and leucondendrons that they grow and export. They've been concentrating on the vineyards and when plantings are finished, there'll be a 70% red to 30% white mix. The three-level manor house has just been completed, then there's a cellar to be built, seven trout-stocked dams to maintain and 850 olive trees to tend to on this busy farm, which borders right on the Helderberg Nature Reserve. With Denise Weedon at the helm, these 'Special Grapes' will continue to flourish.

✿ **Chardonnay 00**, sampled in youth, most promising: full, weighty mid-palate with clean, intense soft fruit auguring well for development. Light citrus/tropical bouquet with mango perfume not overpowered by maturation in 2nd fill Fr oak. **99** ripe, soft and very long. **98** ✿ intense, polished, with all-round balance.

Sauvignon Blanc 00 not ready for tasting. Pvs **99** (✿) partly barrel fermented.

Van Loveren

Robertson (see Robertson map) • Tasting & sales Mon—Fri 8.30—5 Sat 9.30—1 No tasting fee • Owners Nico & Wynand Retief • Winemakers Bussell Retief (since 1993) & Phillip Retief (since Dec 98) • Viticulturists Hennie Retief (since 1991) & Neil Retief (since 1998) • Production 3 000 tons 150 000 cases • PO Box 19 Klaasvoogds 6707 • Tel (023) 615 1505 • Fax (023) 615 1336 • Email vanloveren@lando.co.za

"IT'S A BIG world out there," says Bussell Retief, reflecting on recent marketing trips to Singapore and London. "There's a lot of potential, but lots of competition. The market mostly wants red wine and good service." Always alert to meeting needs, Van Loveren is rapidly approaching its goal of upping its red wine to 50% of total production (previously 70% was white). Not that white wine is being forgotten — witness the new Four Cousins 1 000 ml bottle, stylishly packaged and bearing the pictures (in a characteristically modest way) of the four Retief men involved in the farm. So the range remains wide, the prices keen, the welcome warm, and the tasting-venue garden as lush as ever.

✿ **Cabernet Sauvignon-Shiraz 99** has ripe plummy fruit, with overtones of capsicum and chocolate. Firm, smooth and nicely balanced, with well-integrated oak influences.

Shiraz New **99** Gold on the Young Wine Show, but untasted by us. **Blanc de Noir Shiraz** ✿ Dry, salmon coloured **00**, would look good and taste well on the lunch table, wafting smoky red berries about. **Blanc de Noir Red Muscadel** ⚥ The sweet version, with grapey, camphor-cream aromas; wears its 15 g/ℓ of sugar lightly. **Reserve Chardonnay** ✿ After yr in bottle, **99** woody/citrussy to sniff at, simple lime-cordial to taste; nice and fat, but sourish finish. **Spes Bona Chardonnay** ✿ **00** untasted. Unwooded, undemanding lemony quaffer in **99**. **Cape Riesling** ⚥ **00** untasted. Whiffs of hazelnuts and honeysuckle in just-dry **99**. **Pinot Gris** ⚥ Honey, bubblegum aromas in **00**, weighty (13,5% alc) and dryish. **Sauvignon Blanc** ✿ Attractive, full-frontally flavoured and just-dry **00**, nicely balanced, and gliding silkily and crisply down the throat. **Blanc de Blanc** ✿ **00** 60/40 blend of colombard and sauvignon, redolent of guavas, grass and sunshine. Just dry. **Vino Blanc** ✸✸ Very good value quaffer, light and easy, dry. 500 ml screwtop. **Colombar-Chardonnay** ✸✸ Fruitily and florally aromatic 70/30 blend in **99**; soft, with crisp pear-drop endnotes. **Colombar** ✸✸ **00** unsampled; normally a good tropically-fruited and sweetish example of this Robertson speciality. For early drinking — **99** tiring mid-2000. **Fernão Pires** ✸ Herby flavours in **99** and richly soft texture; 7,8 g/ℓ sugar. **Rhine Riesling** ✸ **00** untasted. **99** showing some pleasing petrolly development, with honeysuckle and pineapple; just off-dry (7 g/ℓ sugar). **Special Late Harvest Gewürztraminer** ✸✸ A golden bowl of rose petals in developed **99**. Light and not too sweet (38 g/ℓ sugar well balanced by acid), with satisfyingly tangy marmalade twist. **Red Muscadel** ✸✸ Rosy-amber **99**, geraniums and raisins to sniff and an opulently sweet, rather spiritous palate. 200 g/ℓ sugar; lowish 16,5% alc.

River Red ✸✸ ☺ Ripe, plummy red fruit aromas in **99**; soft and pleasantly balanced, with baked, 'sweet' flavours; from 50/25/25 ruby cab, merlot, pinotage. Unwooded, 13,5 alc. The Retiefs enjoy it somewhat chilled in summer. Also in **NV** 500 ml screwtop. **Semillon** ✸✸ ☺ Very pale **00**, with notes of bubblegum and lanolin; dry and intense, crisply satisfying stewed apple and rhubarb finish. **Four Cousins River White** ✸✸ New ☺ Touch of muscadel adds intrigue to colombard (65%), sauvignon (30%) **00**, softened by unobtrusive touch of sugar. Sure to be a winner in its handsome high-shouldered 1 000 ml bottle.

Papillon range

Colour-coded butterflies feature on these budget priced **NV** carbonated bubblies. **Brut** ✸ Light, dry and cleanly crisp, with masses of bubbles vigorously pushing out grassy-straw notes. 60/40 colombar/sauvignon. **Demi-sec** ✸ Candy-floss aromas from this riesling/white muscadel blend, and a quite crisp uncloying finish; 36 g/ℓ sugar. **Vin Doux** ✸ Amber-pink beneath the fragrant froth. Simply sweet (80 g/ℓ sugar). Red muscadel.

Vaughan Johnson's Wine & Cigar Shop

Cape Town • Sales Mon—Fri 9—6 Sat 9—5 Sun 10—5 • Wheelchair-friendly • Owner Vaughan Johnson • Victoria & Alfred Waterfront Pierhead Cape Town 8001 • PO Box 50012 Waterfront 8002 • Tel (021) 419-2121 • Fax (021) 419-0040 • E-mail vjohnson@mweb.co.za

IS IT THE WINE, is it the cigars, is it the regular stimulation of world travel and travellers (for some, his Waterfront shop is a bigger attraction than the cable-car)? Is it the new adrenalin of a branch in super-cool Dublin? Whatever, though Vaughan Johnson's recently made his (elegant) way to a half-century, Cape Town's sleekest purveyor of taste-sensations hasn't lost the 20-something energy which switched him off his first career in accountancy and plugged him into the wine business. Not that he's ever loosened his grasp of bottom lines and cost discrepancies; it's just that the VJ wine balance sheet is all about reconciling price with quality. The numbers must add up to good value. This is the continuing theme of his own ranges — the cheeky names and unpretentious packaging sing along too — and why they're so popular. So how does this constant taker of the consumer pulse, here and abroad, diagnose the future for South African wine? As outspokenly as ever: "Robust, earthy, enveloping, deeply satisfying — Shiraz — is our greatest hope for growth and recognition." We trust he's taken suitable cover from the pinotage artillery …

These all **NV**. **Sunday Best** ✸✸ Tailor-made red companion to a Sunday roast. Ripe raspberries and strawberries invite you to sit, whisps of smoke swirl about your nose and full, generous flavours fill your palate to a long, firm conclusion. Bright ruby colour looks good at table, too. 13% alc. **Captain's Claret** ✸✸ New Light fruity red with sweet jammy flavours and a brilliant ruby colour. Honest everyday fare, very reasonably priced. **Good Everyday Red** ✳️ Succulent cherries are everywhere in this super little sipper: in the cherry-red colour; in palate, with food-cordial savoury/minerally twist, and in finish, which lingers pleasingly. **Sunday Best** ✳️ This is the white version of above, similarly built for comfortable and versatile food matching. Easy, dry; some tingly lemon fruit and a long firmish finish. 12,5% alc. **Really Good White** ✳️ Latest zippier than pvs, with good herby/dusty aromas, mouthfilling taste and crisp but not sharp finish. Good on its own or with seafood. 12,5% alc. **Great Waterfront White** Not tasted. **Good Everyday White** ✳️ No-frills quaffing style underlined by plain brown paper label (reappears on red version above). Nothing cut-price about the flavour though: plenty of tropical guava and a light pleasing dustiness; quite brisk acid keeps the tone light, refreshing. 12,5% alc.

> **Really Good Red** ✳️ 😊 Here's a chic red number to sip sedately or pour with your meal. Bright red fruit nicely touched up with expensive-smelling cedar wood and spice, firmish tannins and long, lip-smacking finish which will continue satisfying for yr/2. 12,5% alc. **Seriously Good Plonk** ✳️ 😊 Cheerful, perky white offering succulent fresh-fruit flavours — guavas, green apples — and brisk dry finish. Unpretentious screwtop. 12,5% alc. Red version not ready for tasting.

Van Zylshof Estate

Robertson (see Robertson map) • Tasting & sales by appointment • Owners Chris & Andri van Zyl • Winemaker/viticulturist Andri van Zyl (since 1983) • Vineyards 30 ha • Production 450 tons 99% white 1% red • PO Box 64 Bonnievale 6730 • Tel (023) 616-2940 • Fax (023) 616-3503 • E-mail vanzylshof@lando.co.za

THE Asparagus Association of Limburg in the Netherlands took such a liking to Andri van Zyl's Chenin, they appointed it official Asparagus Wine of 2000 — giving up an ancient tradition of French Pinot Blanc! Who knows what honour they might have bestowed had they tasted van Zyl's sometimes asparagusy Sauvignon. But KLM pipped them to the post and nabbed it for their international flights. And, for the first time in two years, the airline found themselves out of stock in less than three months. One of Robertson's smallest estates, Van Zylshof crushed the first cabernet in 2000 and hope to ultimately raise their red wines to the same high altitude as their whites.

🌸**Chardonnnay** 🏆 Friendly, approachable style with bit of complexity from partial ageing in Fr oak. **00** toasted hazelnuts over ripe pear, some extra richness from lees, concluding lime/lemon tang. 13,5% alc. 1 600 cases.

🌸**Riverain Chardonnay** 🏆 Unwooded version. **00** showcases estate's fragile peach/pear flavours, with fresh lemons/limes in briskly dry conclusion. 13% alc. 1 000 cases.

🌸**Chenin Blanc** Crowd pleaser since debut **97**. Latest med/full-bodied **00** features fresh tropical fruit, lemonade zest, briskly dry finish. Broadening rather than sweetening 4 g/ℓ sugar. 5 000 cases.

Sauvignon Blanc ✳️ Clean, dry grass/pineapple flavours in unwooded **00**; zippy acid makes this a natural seafood partner. 12,5% alc. 3 000 cases.

Veenwouden 🍷 🍷

Paarl (see Paarl map) • Tasting, sales, cellar tours by appointment • Tasting fee R100 p/bottle if no purchase made • Max 6 people per tasting — "we are a small cellar" • Owner Deon van der Walt • Winemaker Marcel van der Walt (since 1995) • Viticulturist Charles van der Walt (since 1990), with Marcel van der Walt (since 1993) • Production 80 tons 5 500 cases 100% red • PO Box 7086 Noorder-Paarl 7623 • Tel (021) 872-6806 • Fax (021) 872-1384 • E-mail veenwouden@intekom.co.za

ABSENTEE-OWNERSHIP, especially of a property as small and specialised as this, can often be a disaster. Switzerland-based South African tenor Deon van der Walt is a frequent flyer-in, but his singing engagements take him all over the world, and while Paarl has its cultural monuments, an opera house is not among them. A remarkably strong, symbiotic family support system — brother and ex-golf pro Marcel the winemaker, father Charles the vineyardist — is the anchor here. But, inspirationally speaking, Deon van der Walt is never far away. In fact, he's as close as the bottles lining his brother's office — there's a Ducru-Beaucaillou, there's a Margaux; here's an Opus One, and a Pingus (the new Spanish cult wine at a R1 000 a throw). They're the sort of aspirational wines Deon van der Walt picks up on his travels, and brings home to taste blind against Veenwouden. "Only the best" is their yardstick, and Marcel vdW ventures "we're getting there". The vineyards are still relative babies — average age 7 years in the next-up 98 — and he believes more maturity will raise quality. Those who have marvelled at Veenwouden's outstanding consistency since the first 93 — it's emerged from nowhere to capture international attention vintage after vintage — clearly should book for forthcoming attractions right now. (Including a Shiraz from the small vineyard near Wellington which they've recently acquired.) And be prepared to pay front row prices. Already the cost of the Classic has rocketed from around R60 to R100 a bottle. But the hike is symptomatic of huge demand, short supply, and the rising costs of maintaining a savage crop curtailment system. In the Veenwouden vineyards during the 'green pruning' period, you're ankle deep in sacrificial bunches of grapes. Quantity will never lead to quality in the Van der Walts' book — this co-written with old friend Michel Rolland, the Pomerol guru, who has given long distance and on the spot advice. Marcel van der Walt's experience in Rolland cellars, including Le Bon Pasteur, provides yet another reason for reviewing this family production as one of the classiest acts in town.

⚝⚝ **Merlot** Since stunning **93** debut, one of Cape's finest, most consistent merlots, garlanded with local and international awards. Latest **98**, probably best to date, again mirrors this winery's obsession with fruit quality (international consultant Michel Rolland doctrine — "only the finest, cleanest, ripe fruit" — fully absorbed here), ruthless selection the norm (4-5 t/ha yield). Thereby is coaxed precocious complexity, sophistication from vines barely 7 yrs old (younger than permitted for the Grand Vin in Bdx). Notable too in **98** is greater individual personality, broader sweep of resonating aromas, more echoing concentration (usual sturdy alc, regular dash cab important contributors). Yet nothing obtrusive or overdone: profile remains sophisticated, classic (Marcel vd Walt's oenological compass set to the Right Bank in Bdx, where he worked in Rolland's Bon Pasteur cellar). Oaking regime set at 2 yrs 80% new Fr barriques. 14% alc. 2 500 cases. **97** armfuls of accolades including *Wine* ⚝, gold 2000 IWSC, silver Concours Mondial de Bruxelles.

⚝⚝ **Veenwouden Classic** Golf pro turned winemaker Marcel vd Walt cards a hole-in-one with this dramatic, dark-hued **98** ⚝⚝, like its team mate above, championship winning material — powerful, more muscular than the Merlot (thanks to strength of cab, 50% of blend with 36% merlot, 12% cab f, 2% malbec). So more patience required here (though no lesser reward): 9-12 yrs probably, 3-4 recommended for present authoritative tannins to unleash sumptuous underlying fruit. Current linear theme continued with taut lead pencils, cassis and dusty spice. Expensive new Nevers cooperage, also part of regime, adds final polish to Bdx-like aura. 2 300 cases. 14% alc. **97** showed earlier tender sweet ripeness, backed up by usual dryish finish. Similar impressive award haul as above wine including Urkunde Grand Prix Dégustation in Hamburg, gold Bdx International Challenge du Vin. **96** oozes confident, expensive cedar/lead pencil, minerally spice. Air France–Preteux Bourgeois trophy. **95** ⚝⚝ fine black fruits, cedary fragrance, though less overtly sumptuous.

✿✿ **Vivat Bacchus** This range's 'easy drinker' ("full of music and fun", say the vd Walts, hence reference to tippling song from Mozart's *Abduction from the Serail*), but not frivolous. **98** (and future) styled similarly to above wines: firmer, fuller, longer in oak (14 mths, half new), though retains malbec's distinctive high-toned, minerally quality. Fresh, deep, supple flavours within fine frame of tannin. Mainly merlot, malbec, plus 20% mix cabs f/s. 13,5% alc. 700 cases.

✿✿ **Chardonnay 98** released, reluctantly, with supposed rush-reducing R150/btl price tag ("Actually we'd like to keep it for our own parties, so if people really want a bottle, I'm afraid they'll have to pay") — yet flew out of the cellar. Follow-up **99** ✿✿ promises equally brisk sales. Uncommon breadth and structure, properly sufficient alcohol (touching 13%) and incipient Burgundian ripe, dry quality of roasted hazelnuts (empty bottle of Olivier Leflaive Puligny-Montrachet in vd Walt's office a clue to the general stylistic direction). Classically barrel-fermented/aged, all new Fr oak, 14 mths, through malo. 130 cases.

Vendôme Wines

Paarl (see Paarl map) • Tasting & sales Mon—Fri 9.30—4.30 Sat 9.30—12.30 • Cellar tours by appointment • Cheese platters by arrangement • Views • Wheelchair-friendly • Owner Jannie le Roux • Winemaker Jannie le Roux jnr • Vineyards 40 ha • Production 1 000 cases own label 60% red 40% white • PO Box 36 Huguenot 7646 • Tel (021) 863-3905 • Fax (021) 863-0094 • E-mail lerouxjg@icon.co.za • Website www.wine.co.za/vendome

THIS is the small private venture of Boland Cellars chairman (and deputy chair of the KWV group) Jannie le Roux, with his son Jannie jnr, the 10th generation to farm here on a tributary of the Berg River, just outside Paarl. The French name is no marketing gimmick; this family's Huguenot connections stretch back to the arrival of 17-year-old Jean le Roux in the Cape in 1687; the farm's original name was Klein Parys (Little Paris). Jannie jnr has been fired up by recent travels through Bordeaux, California and Australia, and while he may not — yet — be an established member of the group of "young, new-generation, innovative winemakers" he most admires, watch this place. Better still, pop into its very atmospheric tasting room. Father's experience and son's fresh approach (which includes using natural yeasts in the red winemaking) make a good-looking combination. And we cheer the Xhosa on the trilingual label. Laduma!

Chardonnay-Chenin Blanc ✿✿ Melon-toned **99** quaffably dry, floral/talcum powder sniffs in soft, juicy palate. 100 cases.

Cabernet Sauvignon ✿✿ Earthy, gamey undercurrents and whiff of eucalyptus in med-bodied, small oak aged **99**; cassis through to easy dry finish. 100 cases. Also available, but not ready for tasting: **Merlot-Cabernet Sauvignon** Unwooded; **Cabernet Sauvignon-Cabernet Franc-Merlot** Small oak aged. **Red Blend** Merlot/cab, unwooded, **Chardonnay** Barrel fermented.

- -

Venus see Vinfruco

- -

Vera Cruz Estate

Stellenbosch • Tasting & sales at Delheim • Owners Hans Hoheisen & MH 'Spatz' Sperling • Winemaker Conrad Vlok (since 2000) • Viticulturist Victor Sperling • Production 2 000 cases • PO Box 10 Koelenhof 7605 • Tel (021) 882-2033 • Fax (021) 882-2036 • E-mail veracruz@delheim.com

REGISTRATION as an estate allows these warmer-climate vineyards nearer Klapmuts, long the source of some of Delheim's top wines, to show their class less anonymously. The range, always a 'cellarmaster's barrel selection', may vary from vintage to vintage.

✿ **Shiraz 99** in elegant, restrained style. Yr Fr oak (60% new) show in both nose/palate mid-2000, but with time, spicy vanilla notes will meld with lurking plum/raspberry fruit and seasoning of cracked peppercorns. Very good acid/tannin balance; lengthy dry finish. 13,9% alc. Maiden **98** IWSC 2000 gold.

✿ **Pinotage** NEW Gamey/smoked meat/wild berry aromas in **98**, vanilla whiffs from Am oak. Typical sweetish pinotage entry, hallmark mulberry/sweet estery notes of carefully selected sappy fruit. Soft, supple impression aided by combo sturdy alc, lowish acid, apparent sweetness in finish (13,7% alc, 5,4 g/ℓ acid, 3,2 g/ℓ sugar).

✿ **Sauvignon Blanc** NEW Full-bodied **99**; subtle nettle/grapefruit/capsicum whiffs; broad entry, supple citrus flavours and crisp acidity. Generous still-fresh mouthful maturing gracefully, due to careful reductive winemaking.

✿ **Chardonnay** NEW **99** brilliant lemon-straw; elegant pear/peach and lemon-grass whiffs with just a hint of sweet, toasty oak (despite 9 mths new barrels, lees stirred fortnightly). Supple, sweet entry leads to crème brulée finish, with ripe peaches-and-cream farewell.

- -

Verdun Estate

Stellenbosch (see Stellenbosch map) • Tasting & sales Mon—Fri 9—5 Sat 9—1 Tasting fee R10 p/p (includes tasting glass) • Cellar tours by appointment • Bring your own picnic by arrangement • Play area for children • Walks/mountain biking by arrangement • Views • Wheelchair-friendly • Owners Tolken family • Winemaker Jan van Rooyen (since 1999) • Viticulturist Pieter Rossouw (since 1997) • Vineyards 81 ha • Production ±450 tons 65% red 35% white • PO Box 79 Vlottenburg 7604 • Tel (021) 886-5884 • Fax (021) 887-7392 • E-mail verdunestate@verdun.co.za

"FULFILLING and demanding" is how Jan van Rooyen, ex-Klein Simonsvlei/Niel Joubert, describes his wine career. With interests spanning ancient history, philosophy and the latest technology, he's found a match in this historic Stellenbosch estate, named after the WW1 battleground. The 81 ha marching up the Bottelary Hills have been seen extensively replanted with, among others, cabernet franc, petit verdot, malbec and semillon, destined chiefly for future blends. "We want to produce a full Bordeaux red as well as a Cape blend," explains owner Francois Tolken, who bought the property in 1995 and restarted the winemaking operation. Other firsts (in the new era) include the bottling of a Pinotage and harvesting of the first shiraz.

✿ **Theresa** Flagship claret of this revitalised estate; named after a Tolken daughter (aka Twiggy). Splendid debut **97** VG maturing beautifully. Concentrated cassis strikes as sweet initially, then turns fragrant with light balsam/tobacco/cedar perfumes; long tannins wrap up an elegant package. Cab/merlot (80/20), aged 18 mths new Fr oak. 13% alc. 970 cases.

✿ **Cabernet Sauvignon** Debut **97** still hiding some of its considerable allures. Initial oakiness has stepped aside, giving centre stage to ripe mulberry fruit, tobacco whiffs. Ample fine-grained tannins suggest there's no rush to uncork; try again in ±2 yrs. 15 mths 100% new Fr barriques. 12,7% alc. 770 cases.

✿ **Merlot** First **99** delivering on early promise with dark choc/berry aromas of remarkable intensity given cooler yr. Overall effect is vinous rather than varietally typical. 12—15 mths 100% new Fr oak. 13% alc. 1 350 cases.

✿ **Chardonnay Reserve** Serious chardonnay, cask fermented/aged, attractively peachy and ripe with broad, weighty flavours which linger well. Sur lie 11 mths. 13,5% alc. 320 cases.

✿ **Chenin Blanc** Delightful **98** set the pace for this partly barrel fermented, just-not-dry style. **99** ✿ not quite par, though offers some broad, assertive oak-spicy/leesy flavours. 13,5% alc. 1 600 cases.

Pinotage ✿ NEW Off to good start with cinnamon scented **99**, all sweet cherries and vanilla from 13 mths new Fr oak. Despite sturdy 13,7% alc, tastes pleasingly light, though some brash young tannins need bit of time to settle. 1 250 cases.

Sauvignon Blanc ✿ 99 starts slowly with muted bouquet but soon perks up with lively, fleshy palate with passionfruit/melon (soupçon barrel matured). Tapers to demure dry finish. 13,5% alc 1 040 cases.

Interlude range

Gamay Noir ✥ This grape was the 'old' Verdun's speciality, made in **97** for first time since 1983. Latest **99** features cherries; lively even slightly tart tones. Not oaked. 12,4% alc. 1 080 cases. **Blanc** ✥ Yet another formula change in **99** (to chardonnay/gewürz/chenin); this version's relaxed, undemanding, vinous rather than fruity. Dry, unoaked. 13,5% alc. 2 700 cases.

. . . .

Vignerons du Monde

Franschhoek • Tasting & sales at Mont Rochelle • Owners Graham de Villiers & Achim von Arnim • Production 2 000 cases PO Box 334 Franschhoek 7690 • Tel (021) 876-3000 • Fax (021) 876-2367 • E-mail petitrochelle@wine.co.za

> **Sauvignon Rouge** ✥ 😊 "New wine for the new millennium from a new partnership," say Franschhoek wine partners Graham de Villiers (Mont Rochelle) and Achim von Arnim (Cabrière) of their delightful dry rosé, blend sauvignon blanc/cab sauvignon, made in the Mont-R cellar. **99** lovely luminous pale ruby colour; gentle, perfumed raspberry/cherry tastes which linger for ages, smooth almost viscous texture through to the gently dry end. "Must be chilled," insists Mont-R winemaker Justin Hoy, correctly. ±2 000 cases.

. . . .

Vergelegen

Stellenbosch (see Helderberg map) • Tasting & sales daily 9.30—4.30 (including Sun during season), except Christmas, Workers' Day (May 1st), Good Friday. Tasting fee R5 p/p • Guided winery tours daily 10.30; 11.30; 15.00 (no tours in winter) • Lady Phillips Restaurant, Rose Terrace (see Eat-out section) • 'Interpretive Centre' depicting farm's history • Gifts • Tourgroups • Walks • Wheelchair-friendly • Owner Anglo American Farms • Winemaker André van Rensburg (since 1998) • Viticulturist Niel Roussouw (since 1995) • Vineyards 105 ha • Production 43 000 cases 58% red 41% white 1% NLH • PO Box 17 Somerset West 7129 • Tel (021) 847-1334 • Fax (021) 847-1608 • E-mail jdawson@vergelegen.co.za • Website www.vergelegen.co.za

FEW OF THEM can say it, but most of them know it. Vergelegen is a mouthful but no serious international wine writer would dream of leaving this historic property — vines first planted in 1700 — off the Cape A-list. But what's its global rating? That's the question corporate owners AmFarms and winemaker André van Rensburg want to answer quickly and conclusively. International icon-status is their mission. "I have only one goal: to position Vergelegen as one of the top 100 wine names in the world," says van Rensburg. Single vineyard wines (like the dramatic Schaapenberg Sauvignon) will drive the process; more vineyards are being planted, to bump up the current 105 ha (plenty of space on these 3 000 ha mountainsides and sea-facing slopes, where scientific irrigation is the latest priority). All Vergelegen wines will reflect this particular sense of place; buying-in grapes will become a thing of the past. Shiraz, the variety that made van Rensburg famous at Stellenzicht, is among the new plantings. The one-off below comes from a vineyard near his previous stamping ground that's now been uprooted; there was understandably no reply to Van Rensburg's cheeky fax offering to buy Hans Schreiber's Stellenzicht crop to provide 'continuity' … So the fans will just have to wait for the first authentically Vergelegen-rooted shiraz: it's due in about 8 years.

✥ **Show Reserve** Complex, daring cab franc-led blend, calculated, unabashedly, to heap maximum cachet on Vergelegen marque. Cheval Blanc *president* Pierre Lurton, with whom AvR would most like to share this wine, one of very few likely to taste super-scarce **98**, just 250 cases and developing into something exceptional. Dashes merlot, cab s (23%/14%), 17 mths 100% new Fr oak which already absorbed in massive, super-ripe palate, braced with mouthcoating ripe tannins. Long life ahead: 10–15 yrs.

✿✿**Cabernet Sauvignon** Beautiful, classically styled cab (if not varietally pure: dashes merlot, cab f (7%/6%) for extra complexity (and quantity — this latest **98** relatively munificent 5 000 cases compared to paltry 500 in **97**). **98** textbook cassis, blackcurrants. Oak, dominant when tasted for pvs ed, starting to integrate; but deserves more time: 10–15 yr lifespan. 21 mths 100% first fill Fr casks. 13,8% alc.

✿✿**Vergelegen** This property's flagship, currently classic Bdx blend (next decade could be 100% shiraz (?), from warmer, northerly Rondekop vyds. Still only one **98** release — and what a release: arresting 'cold stones' mineral quality in palate, dark cherry fruit, thrilling acidity. Exceptional complexity, balance, intensity. We and winemaker agree: this for deepest corner of cellar. Will give enormous pleasure 15–20 yrs from now. 75% cab, 20% merlot, 5% cab f, tiny 4,5 t/ha yield. 22 mths 100% new Fr oak. 13,8% alc. 2 000 cases.

✿✿**Syrah** New A bold statement (AvR not inclined to anything less); nods towards crackerjack Australian style but with its own identity (not a Stellenzicht clone) **99** grapes picked extra ripe (13,6% alc); intense, rich colour; spicy, peppery seasoning with black cherries, plums in palate; long ripe tannins for the long haul (10 yrs). Keep 3 yrs before evaluating progress. 15 000 bottles, 11 000 for CWG auction. 13 mths small oak, 30% Am, rest Fr), 50% first fill.

✿**Merlot 98**, first release since **95**, needs couple more yrs in bottle. With dash invisible cab; rich plummy red colour, mocha in nose, ripe berry flavours; good fruit intensity from maturing 8 yr old Vergelegen vines. 17 mths Fr oak, 50% new. 13,8% alc. 3 000 cases.

✿**Mill Race Red** ▼ Top value Bdx blend, since **98** with more of everything. **99** ✿ crosses threshold into the big leagues (still with minor price tag). Sleek black berries, some aromatic wild scrub; better balance, intensity than pvs. Blend cab, merlot, cab f (48/44/8), 16 mths Fr oak, 30% first fill. 10 000 cases. **98**, plush **97** (with 40% merlot) SAA. "Can/will handle any occasion," states winemaker.

✿✿**Show Reserve White** New Semillon devotee AvR passionately convinced these marine-facing Schaapenberg hills among Cape's finest semillon terroirs. Here's proof: **99** intensely honeyed, layered with marmalade, citrus plus spicy oak. Variety's 'oiliness' showing in luscious dry palate. 100% semillon, 9 mths all new oak (50/50 Fr/Am). Keep 3–4 yrs to give honey character time to develop, then enjoy over next 10 yrs.

✿✿**Chardonnay Reserve** Serious, meticulously made chardonnay; miniscule 700 cases from single vyd on lower Schaapenberg hill, miserly 5,5 t/ha yield, 3½ month natural ferment ("seriously nerve-wracking"), yr 100% new oak. Style set by Anglo executives, who insist on continuation of New World course charted by predecessor. 13,7% alc. **99** butter biscuits in nose, good citrus flavours. Initially more oaky than **98**, with broad, powerful flavours which not overstated. Oak and lime integrated in 'oily lemon peel' mode unveiled in **96** VG, SAA White Wine of 1998. **97** SAA, *Wine* ✿. Standard **Chardonnay** ✿ Urbane, fragrant, vinified to accentuate fresh citrus fruit — though **99** still dominated by oak mid-2000. Big (13,5% alc.), broad-toned with complex layers of butter, oakspice, lime. 100% Vergelegen grapes for first time; all barrel fermented/aged 9 mths Fr oak, 60% first fill. Only partial malolactic ("in a warm climate, malo destroys flavour"). Optimal drinking in 2 yrs.

✿✿**Schaapenberg Sauvignon Blanc** (Reserve in pvs ed) Dramatic, powerful sauvignon, among the best in Cape, characterised by flinty-fruity raciness, varietal purity enhanced by minimalist winemaking; no oak. Tightly coiled and brooding at first, needs time to show its best. Schaapenberg "our definitive single vyd", on high windy ridge looking out over Gordon's Bay, where elements perform their own crop thinning (to meagre 4,5 t/ha); so miniscule production (500 cases) which instantly snapped up. **00**, characteristically closed mid-2000, needs yr at least (and will continue to improve over next half-dozen vintages). Big, gusty (14%), stylistically closer to steely **98** ✿ SAA, *Wine* ✿, Michelangelo double-gold. These tighter than **99** SAYWS grand champ, which more profusely flavoured, riper. Standard **Sauvignon Blanc** ✿ Consistently excellent, sophisticated sauvignon combining variety's bracing freshness and sleek, almost viscous mouthfeel (partly from dash semillon, now a standard fixture à la Australia). Mainly own grapes in **00**, which nods to the Loire in shy green-fruit nose, soft, not too aggressive. More expressive/varied palate, covering grass to asparagus to tropical fruit. 13,5% alc. 9 300 cases. Softer than deliciously racy, assertive **99** with surprisingly polished mouthfeel for so 'loud', aromatic a wine. **96–98** SAA (latter runner-up White Wine trophy, best SA dry white IWSC, *Wine* ✿).

✿ **Vin de Florence** Versatile, well priced off-dry white; fragrant, zingy, enormously quaffable. Now also with extra staying power (pvs tended to become flabby after yr). **00** touch sweeter than pvs (8,6 g/ℓ sugar); muscat, ginger in nose, fresh green Granny Smith apples. Good aperitif; also match for spicy Thai cuisine/curries. Chenin, sauvignon, hanepoot, semillon blend. Vintaged from **99**; pvs NV (**97, 98**) bottlings SAA.

✿ **Noble Late Harvest Semillon** Since first **98** a standout sweet botrytised dessert, deeply flavoured, invigoratingly fresh. **00** new recipe: unwooded, sweeter at 120 g/ℓ sugar, botrytis character initially muted. Very delicate, almost frail despite high alc (14,5%); usual rapier acidity (8 g/ℓ). In present slimline form a (delicious) aperitif; but will gather intense honeyed lusciousness with time. Very different to instantly sumptuous **99**, oak fermented/finished, big, relatively dry (14,5% alc, 100 g/ℓ sugar). **98** rich, complex, drinking very well now; will go another 5 yrs min.

Pinot Noir ✿ First labelled pinot from this area in ages; first from this farm. **98** just a small foretaste: 250 cases. Rich colour though fairly light, reflecting youngish vines struggling on wind-battered slopes. Not overly complex but elegant, for earlier drinking — now-2004. 14 mths Fr oak, 10% first fill

....

Vergenoegd Estate   � ⱱ ⱱ

Stellenbosch (see Stellenbosch map) • Tasting & sales Wed 2–5. Sat 9.30–12.30 • Views • Wheelchair-friendly • Owners Haydn Wright & John Faure • Winemaker John Faure • Viticulturist Haydn Wright • Vineyards 100 ha • Production 600 tons (5 100 cases own label) 100% red • PO Box 1 Faure 7131 • Tel (021) 843-3248 • Fax (021) 843-3118 • E-mail enquiries@vergenoegd.co.za

HIGH ALTITUDE VINEYARDS on this historic family estate mean 13 m above sea level! It may be on the Helderberg Wine Route but it's really an appellation all of its own, so close to False Bay — and the salty underground lair that lies beneath this portion of the 'Cape Flats' — that viticulturist Haydn Wright surely had to teach his new cabernet, merlot and shiraz vines to swim before embarking on the 10-year replanting programme that is transforming the vineyards. (Particularly the merlot, which prefers the farm's low-altitude, riverside ground — all of 10 m above sea level.) It's more than the power of suggestion which leads the cognoscenti to detect a unique Atlantic Ocean tang in the wines from these 100 ha. John Faure, the 6th generation of his family to do his thing here in the cellar (now increasingly filled with new French barrels) has raised its modern reputation to new heights.

✿ **Reserve** ▼ Flagship Médoc-style blend, understated (and so perhaps underrated by market currently more attuned to big, showy styles); initially tight but develops very well with time, which latest **98** will do; so suggest buy, lay down and watch it command high Nederburg Auction prices by the end of the decade. Very French, powerful yet restrained. Dramatic inky appearance, presently quite austere, firmly structured, but balanced. 61/21/18 cab, cab f, merlot. **97** ✿

softer initially, reflecting higher proportion merlot (32%, with cab 50%, cab f 18%). **96**, from lighter yr, not as rich as standout **95** ✿ VG, *Wine* ✿.

✿ **Cabernet Sauvignon** Latest **98** ✿ back on par with acclaimed **95** VG, *Wine* ✿ (still showing spicy mineral fragrances). **98** most attractive cassis nose, good wild berry fruit, firm tannins, dry finish. Yr first fill Fr oak. Prospect of good ageing. 1 440 cases. **96** ✿✿ starting to show its age; lightweight **97** ✿✿.

✿ **Merlot** Quite tight, restrained style; fragrant, always with hint of mint. Needs 3–5 yrs to develop. Latest **98** reined-in, almost austere black plum flavours, ripe tannins; mocha and again plums in bouquet. Yr Fr/Hungarian oak, none new. Improvement on **97**, which initially more succulent, softer, persistent. Mouth-filling though not big. Plums layered with mint and cinnamon. This richer than more eucalyptus-like **96** VG. **95** subtle, aromatic, minty.

✿ **Shiraz** Latest **98** inky black old Cape style blockbuster, lashings of oak from yr in first fill Fr casks. Still closed, decade away from optimal drinking. White pepper and nuts in palate. Single-vyd version being considered (go for it! we say). **97** ✿✿ more approachable, peppery nose, fruit gums in palate, long aftertaste. *Wine* ✿. **96** ✿✿ gamey, elegant rather than opulent; fine tannins.

✿ **Port** Crossover Cape/Portuguese style, nodding to the Douro in relatively dry profile (88,5 g/ℓ sugar), good flavour intensity. 100% tinta b, in alluvial soils, destined to be grubbed-up (woodsman, spare that tree!). **96** rich, complex fruit-cake tones of raisins, dried fruit, marzipan, bits of orange peel, 'sweet' cloves and almonds; all echoing in chocolatey finish. 2 yrs used barriques. 18,9% alc. 400 cases. This drier; more persistent than pvs **95** VG, *Wine* ✿, offering cranberry, dried currant aromas. **74** ✿✿ in *Wine*'s 'Golden Oldies' tasting, so potential here for long, fruitful maturation.

Versus see Stellenbosch Vineyards

Viljoensdrift Wines & Cruises

Robertson (see Robertson map) • Tasting & sales Sat 10—2 at tasting venue or by appointment • From Jan 2001, sales also daily at new cellar Mon—Fri 9—2 or by arrangement • Picnic baskets by arrangement • River raft/tasting area for groups of 15 or more by arrangement • Small conferences • Breede River cruises Sat 12 (weather permitting) or by appointment Adults R20, children under12 R10 • Owners Viljoen family • Winemaker Fred Viljoen • Viticulturist Manie Viljoen • Farm manager Jaco Kotze (since 2000) • Vineyards 60 ha • Production 1 000 tons • PO Box 653 Robertson 6705 • Tel (023) 615-1901 • Fax (023) 615-3417 • E-mail viljoensdrift@lando.co.za • Website www.wine.co.za

THIS must be one of the most atmospheric wine 'experiences' in the country: where else can you sample either on terra firma, in a Breede riverside tasting room, or on a double-decker raft (floating past indigenous flora and fauna, doing a spot of bass-fishing); picnic baskets an optional extra? Fred and Manie Viljoen restored the old cellar on this 300 ha fruit and wine farm in 1998, reactivating a family tradition begun 180 years before, when the first generation of Viljoens made dessert wines here, and 'Cape Smoke' brandy. The brothers were "enraptured by the result". As were visiting Dutch buyers: the Netherlands remain Viljoensdrift's sole export market. All this rustic informality is deceptive: there's a lot of thoroughly modern activity going on here. They're following the Integrated Production of Wine (IPW) system, which sets stringent scientific standards for environmentally friendly wines.

Cabernet Sauvignon ✿✿ 🍷 Supercharged cassis/mulberry breakdance/hip-hop/can-can across the palate, pausing only to note some grippy tannins in unwooded dry **00** finish. 13% alc. 2 000 cases.

Pinotage ✿✿ Minerally, plummy **00** bit more guts than pvs; quite strident tannin/dry finish call for hot coals and some well-hung meat. Not oaked. 13,5% alc. 3 000 cases. **Shiraz** New **00** untasted. 14,8% alc. 1 000 cases. **Chardonnay** ✿✿ **00**

improves on pvs with generous citrus/tropical tastes; some smoky/marmalade whiffs, clean lemon-fresh finish. **Semillon** ✦✦ "Enormous effort" went into tweaking these vyds, resulting in pleasing med/full **00** with bright, fresh lime/leesy tastes and now standard sprinkle of spice. 1 000 cases. **Colombar-Chenin Blanc** ✦✦ Jasmine/peach/citrus fragrances in gently dry, drink now **00**, with delightful juicy finish. "Best to date," say the Viljoens. 12,5% alc. 2 000 cases.

Villiera Wines
✦ ✦ ✦

Paarl map • Tasting & sales Mon—Fri 8.30—5 Sat 8.30—1 • Self-guided cellar tours during tasting hours • Guided tours by appointment • Winter art events last Sat of July, 1st Sat of Aug • Owners' Annual St Vincent's Day dinner closest to 22nd Jan • Owners Grier family • Winemakers Jeff Grier (since 1984) with Anton Smal (since 1991) • Viticulturists Simon Grier (since 1983) & Christie Franse (since 1990) • Vineyards 300 ha • Production 1 800—2 500 tons 160 000 cases 40% white 33% red 6% rosé 21% sparkling • PO Box 66 Koelenhof 7605 • Tel (021) 882-2002/3 • Fax (021) 882-2314 • E-mail villiera@mweb.co.za

WHILE MANY of his SA colleagues are having a love affair with shiraz, eloquent and infinitely likeable winemaker Jeff Grier (serious stature and recognition in the industry notwithstanding, he remains firmly earthed in his family values — the extended Grier clan runs the star-studded Villiera show) finds variety the spice. According to him, merlot is currently the most planted international varietal from Bordeaux to Chile but "SA needs a consumer-friendly style" (which Villiera consistently provides). Pinotage is "versatile but will always be a bit gimmicky — it's what zin(fandel) is to the Californians". Hence Villiera uses pinotage in bubbly and mixed reds as "a Cape blend should include pinotage from a marketing point of view". They're not giving up on their sell-out Bush Vine Sauvignon either. Hence vineyard expansion, masterminded by Jeff Grier's cousin Simon, brilliant viticulturist and perfectionist, focuses on both sauvignon blanc and merlot. For the rest, Villiera is consolidating what's there rather than starting new ventures, yet always keeping the price exceptionally affordable. Co-winemaker Anton Smal is more hands-on in the cellar these days. Prize money from the winning Merlot-Pinotage 98 in the Paarl Vintners Red Blend Challenge, funded this surfer's trip to test the wines and waters at Margaret River recently.

✦ **Merlot Reserve** ✔ Villiera's assured, comfortable style rises to 'statement' level here (though, characteristically, no over-statement). **98** first to be released (**97** reviewed last ed held back for further maturation). Ripe, creamy fruit, dense but not roughly over-extracted. Minty tones initially suggest cab until voluptuous, springy tannins sweep across palate; some incipient meatiness in concentrated, complex flavour array. Careful oaking (yr Fr. casks, 80% new) adds to sophisticated, sleek profile. Delicious now, but all in place for beneficial 5—7 yrs' ageing. 14,5% alc. Single vyd, 6 yrs. Occasional bottling. 500 cases. Regular **Merlot** ✦ Reliable, versatile red "for dinner parties or civilised barbeques" (or airborne meals: frequently flies with SAA). **98** forward ripe plum-jam succulence, lightish texture (though at 14+% alc no shortage of body), fine tannins. Not so much development potential as some pvs but tasty, easy to enjoy over next 2—3 yrs. 6 500 cases.

✦ **Shiraz** ✔ Melt-in-the-mouth **99** plumbs great depths of flavour, partially new oak adds fragrant spice to already savoury/wild boletus mushroom decadence. Sturdily built (10% cab stiffening) yet great fruit delicacy, abetted by yielding tannins. Malo complete. 8 mths Am casks. 13,3% alc. 500 cases. No **98**. **97** also delicious; smoky, raspberry/black cherry garb, accessorised with leather and spice. 16 mths oak, 50% new. Single bushvine vyd.

✦ **Merlot-Pinotage** ✔ (Auction Reserve, for CWG, in pvs ed) Convincing candidate for ultimate Cape Blend (already winner of 1999 Paarl Vintners' Challenge for best Wineland Red Blend). Local hero pinotage, often unruly marriage partner, seamlessly incorporated in this 73/27 blend. Merlot treated as in Reserve above; much same results; pinotage yr Am oak — brings extra fresh tobacco leaf, spicy nuances, more juicy succulence without shouting its presence. Thoroughly modern (Cape?) feel but not lacking old-fashioned backbone. 14,8% alc, 3.6 g/ℓ sugar. Seriously parsimonious R38.50 ex-farm price. 500 cases. **97** ✪✪ dense raspberry fruit; soft, spicy, lingering. 70/30 mix. Pinotage from 20-yr-old dryland bush vines, low yielding. 18 mths new Fr oak. Unfiltered.

✤**Cru Monro** ▼✔ Consistency, quality trademarks of farm's flagship red, a cab-merlot fusion which frequently out-matures (easily spans 10 yrs) others with more lofty ambitions. Greater cab presence (though typical 55/45 ratio) in **98** imparts tighter, more compact, savoury-dry tannin structure. No shortage of rich, dark-berried fruit waiting in wings — time alone required to harmonise. Echoes of both traditional Médoc elegance and modern ripeness; whole an SA statement. 13,5% alc. 3 800 cases. **97** fine minerally texture, dense but non-aggressive tannin. Similar to **96** VVG, also with Villiera's signature merlot. **95** succulent. **94 SAA**. All Fr. Oak matured, +- 12 mnths, 45% new in **98**.

✤**Chenin Blanc** ▼✔ The peoples' chenin? Astonishing price/quality ratio (±R16 ex-farm) makes this a worthy candidate. Judges' chenin too: never out of the top 5 in *Wine*'s Chenin Challenge (**98** overall winner), **99** SAA. Also admired, covertly, by cutting-edge chenin producers from the Loire: "I always enjoy watching their faces when they're impressed but pretend to dislike the style," Grier grins. Which deliberately at riper end of scale, rich, weighty (from 40% barrel-fermented portion), spiced with tropical/pineapple fragrance. All nicely balanced, just dry (4 g/ℓ sugar). **00** follows fullness, intensity of pvs, consistency of all vintages. 14% alc. 10 000 cases.

✪✪**Bush Vine Sauvignon Blanc** ▼✔ Combined consistency/quality, with a little help from scarcity value, makes this — deservedly — one of SA's few cult sauvignons. "Flavour window was matter of hours rather than days," Jeff Grier explains importance of well-timed harvesting in fiery **00** which, even tasted in infancy, clearly shows class, concentration. Deep fumé, flinty nose; weighty, luscious palate with slow-motion explosion of passion fruit/gooseberry, echoing finish; all achieved without over-strident alcohol. Hugely rewarding mouthful in youth, room for growth over 2–3 yrs. Will doubtless reap similar rewards (local and international) to pvs. 1 500 cases. **99** SAA, sumptuous, long with pineapple/herbaceous complexities. **98** ✤ recalls the Loire (though perhaps leaner than the French model); **97** ✤ Diners Club winner, *Wine* ✤ richer, more generous apricot tones. Single vyd, 25 yrs old.

✤**Sauvignon Blanc** ▼✔ Front-row Cape sauvignon, in lively, earlier-drinking style. Quantities limited only by grape supply (not by demand). **00** "not an easy year", but both this and bush vine version reach usual impressive standard with apparent ease. Touch lighter, more zesty but no less intense than pvs, picked earlier "because the flavours were there". Grassy, passion fruit character, decisively clean, fresh. Deserves to be enjoyed over 12–18 mths (with seafood pasta, per Jeff Grier). From trellised vyds. 9 000 cases. **99** SAA, full of herbaceous fragrance, gooseberry/tropical touches. **97** *Wine* ✤.

✤**Blanc Fumé** ▼✔ Ultra ripe tropical, gooseberry scented sauvignon, 70% barrel-fermented for extra spicy, marzipan oomph and richness. **00** generous, succulent, but also firmly built, allowing for development over 3–5 yrs. Try with smoked salmon, BBQ chicken. Old, low-yielding vines. 13,5% alc. 2 000 cases. **99** ripe, concentrated. **98** less herbal, fresher than quite flinty **97**.

✤**Rhine Riesling** ▼✔ One of the Cape's most characterful rieslings. **00** not one to drink in a hurry (if you can resist its youthful charms): with bit of age — Grier reckons it can benefit from 3–8 yrs — should pick up on intensity, develop drier feel. Gentle pickled lime, peppery ripeness; spicy, semi-dry palate, with keen, clean acid tail. Winemaker obviously has tender spot for this variety; he'd like to share it with Thai salad, coronation chicken and Lynne, his wife. 7 g/ℓ sugar. 1 500 cases.

✿ Tradition Rosé Brut ✅ Everything about this MCC bubbly conjures up fun-filled summer days. On release, whispering delicate red fruit notes, palest blush hue; with age, more bready, ginger-biscuit richness. Deliciously light, creamy feel; the most demanding thing about this wine would be reaching out for another bottle. Mainly pinot, chardonnay with 10% pinotage vinified as light red. Invisible 8 g/ℓ sugar. 2 500 cases.

✿ Monro Brut Première Cuvée ✅ (Named **Millennium Cuvée** for run-up to 2000) Villiera's top-of-the-range (yet unpretentiously-priced) bubbly, combination of pvs Carte d'Or (three SAA MCC trophies) and Vintage Tradition. Latest **95**, rich bready, biscuity bouquet; contrasting creamy fresh flavours emphasised by fine, soft bubble. Luscious now, yet structure to benefit from further ageing. Classically brut at 7 g/ℓ sugar. Five-star packaging. An individual, according to Grier, able to span moods from parties to philosophy. Equal partnership pinot with barrel-fermented/matured chardonnay, min 4 yrs on lees. 1 500 cases. **Brut 2000** Stylishly packaged MCC to celebrate the millennium and 15 yrs of Cap Classique on this farm. A one-off; sold out.

✿ Tradition Brut ✅ Consistent, hugely popular **NV** sparkle, affordable and, thanks to local-yokel pinotage in varietal mix (with 45% pinot, 20% each chardonnay, chenin), truly a 'Cap' Classique. Latest bottling (**98**) features trademark elegance, sea-fresh scent, gentle leesy/biscuity character. Medium body, zippy pin-prick bubble, hint of citrus and non-sweetening dash sugar add to overall perk-me-up/aperitif style. With yr or 2 can fill out with benefit. Also available in 1,5 ℓ and 375 ml. 15 000 cases.

✿ Chenin Blanc Noble Late Harvest ✅ New A dessert inspiration from Jeff Grier's trip to the Loire, courtesy of winning SA *Wine*'s Chenin Challenge, and another example of this winemaker's enormous versatility. Preview of **00** reveals extraordinary contrast of unctuous fruit, riveting acidity; rich botrytis tones freshened by variety's bright honeysuckle perfume. When to enjoy? "When my (just-about teenage) kids are in their 20s," ventures Grier. Hand-selected berries, harvested at 40 °B. Aged in mix new 225 ℓ, older 300 ℓ Fr barrels. 13% alc, 180 g/ℓ sugar, 12 g/ℓ acid. 375 ml. Release date end 2000. 500 cases.

✿ Port ✅ Jeff Grier in bi-hemispheric mode with this tasty, accessible LBV dessert: Portuguese styling (higher alc at around 20%, lower sugar at ±90 g/ℓ) yet SA-orientated varietal mix of mainly pinotage, plus shiraz, gamay. Result is individual, 'authentic' example with properly dry finish for long ageing. Latest **97** ✿ features creamy choc-berry aromas/flavours; pleasant grip, 2½ yrs in barrel. Pvs: **96** austere but not lean; **95** ✿ VVG, *Wine* Top Ten, richer, both same varietal mix with pinotage playing lesser role.

Cabernet Sauvignon ✿ Laid-back, polite sort of cab, well-behaved at table. Ripe plum jam aromas in latest **98**, nicely-judged tannins offset jammier notes in palate. Trimmer profile than pvs (yet not lean), for earlier drinking. **Pinotage** ✿ Since maiden **97** VVG, *Wine* ✿, showcases the appealing characteristics of this home-grown grape. Fruity-succulent **99** features smoky/spicy aromatics and red-berry, dried-fig richness. Sturdy 14% alc seamlessly absorbed in beautifully polished finish. **Chardonnay** ✿ Epitomises house style of satisfaction without excess. **00** fruity but not simple aromas; toasty/yeasty, some banana scents with lively citrus-zest core. Ready-to-drink creamy roundness. Good with pigeon or duck, opines winemaker. 13,3% alc. 1 800 cases. **Gewürztraminer** ✿ Shows how charming this rare-in-Cape variety can be. Packed with fragrant litchis and spice; but never exhaustingly exotic. **00**'s richness (partly from 14% alc) freshened by clean, minerally tones. Try with lamb curry, spicy Thai chicken. Best over next year. 1 900 cases. **Sonnet** ✿ Invariably captivating off-dry quaffer, smoothing grain sugar calculated to satisfy both sweet and dry-toothed. **00** lightish, succulent, alive with floral/spice freshness. Muscat ottonel laced with chenin, splash gewürz. 4 000 cases.

Blue Ridge range

Mainly for export, but available in some stores and from farm. Good value.

> **Rouge** ✦✦ 😊 Drink-me-now **99** delivers plenty of soft, savoury aromas/flavours. Rhônish mix mainly shiraz with carignan, gamay. 8 000 cases. **Blanc** ✦✦ 😊 Not-so-ordinary everyday white. **00** polished, dry and deliciously long. Very ripe chenin freshened with equal portion sauvignon. 13% alc. 16 000 cases.

Villiersdorp Co-op

Worcester (see Worcester Map) • Tasting & sales in season Mon—Fri 8—6 Sat 9—5 otherwise Mon—Sat 9—2 • Cellar tours by appointment • Breakfasts, light meals, coffees/teas Mon—Fri 9—5.30 Sat 8—4.30 in season, otherwise Mon—Sat 9—1.30 • Conferences for ± 30 delegates • Farmstall • Gifts • Wheelchair-friendly • Owners 70 members • Winemaker/manager to be appointed • Viticulturist Danie Conradie • Production 7 000 tons 97% white 3% red • PO Box 14 Villiersdorp 6848 • Tel (028) 840-1120/51 • Fax (028) 840-1833

SEASONED JP Steenekamp — 20 years at this cellar with its far-flung vineyard plots — left in 2000 to concentrate on his Swellendam farm, where cattle and milk are the focus. (No replacement had been named at time of going to press.) Meanwhile the 70 growers have been encouraged to plant more red varieties, which currently account for only 3% of the total. Merlot, cab and shiraz are going into the ground near Villiersdorp in 2001, and the plan is to keep planting until the ratio swells to 30%.

✿ **Hanepoot Jerepiko** ✔ With antique steam engine on front label, keeps improving. Orange zest gives latest (**NV**) bottling its distinctive tang; orange again in palate with hanepoot's signature honeysuckle. Fresh, vigorous and rather nice. 18% alc. 200 cases.

Cabernet Sauvignon New **99** sample leads with minerally dark berries, some richness and youthfully angular tannins which will need a short while to relax. Potential ✦✦. **Cabernet Sauvignon-Merlot 98** ✦✦ was the champ red wine on Worcester show, so follow up **99**, tasted from tank, should be at least as good. Ripe plummy fruit, nice chalky undertone and lively tannins, which should soon settle. **Ruby Cabernet** ✦✦ **99**'s 'green' tones, exuberant freshness need time (winemaker says 5 yrs) or rich cuisine. 13,3% alc. 250 cases. **Rosé** ✦✦ Super alfresco wine, tweaked with a bit of sweetness, lowish alc (11,5%), to ensure swiggability. Delicate light coral colour, bright rose/fresh apple tones, joined by tropical fruit in fresh, smooth palate. Crisp, non-aggressive finish. 245 cases. **Chenin Blanc** Offdry **00** wafts variety's guava aromas; quiet nose but friskier palate. Enjoy in bloom of youth. Med-bodied. 270 cases. **Colombard** ✦✦ Drink soon **00** with fresh guava, spoon sugar raises swiggability. 12% alc. 560 cases. **Sauvignon Blanc** ⚡ **00**'s fragile apple/cut-grass freshness must be appreciated soon to catch at best. 13% alc. 250 cases. **Colombard-Chardonnay** ⚡ Med-bodied **00**, with this wine's signature contrast between 'sweet' tropical fruit and arrestingly dry palate, really needs rich food (grilled yellowtail?). 270 cases. **Late Vintage 00** (sample) clean apple/pineapple crunch, fairly dry and refreshing. Possible ✦✦. **Demi-sec Sparkling** ✦✦ Bright, fruity carbonated **NV** with uninhibited bubbles, honey/muscat tastes. Colombard/hanepoot. 240 cases.

Vinfruco

Stellenbosch/London • Vinfruco (UK) Farnham House Farnham Royal Buckinghamshire SL2 3RQ England • Tel +44 (1753) 64-7093 • Fax +44 (1753) 81-8821 • Vinfruco (SA) Pinotage House Brandwacht Office Park Stellenbosch 7600 • Tel (021) 886-6458 • Fax (021)886-6589 • E-mail dalena_koen@capespan.co.za • Website www.arniston-bay.co.za

MORE than a million cases of wine are shipped from the Cape annually by this export-only operation. Its mainstream varieties are the fashionable reds, shiraz and merlot, and local hero pinotage, and its headline brand (with own website and posters in the London Underground) Arniston Bay, which with the debut of a Rosé now covers the colour spectrum. Initially a buyer of finished wine, in 1999 Vinfruco began to short circuit the production chain, and now directly buys 2 500 tons of grapes; it has its own blending and 'final processing' quarters at Perdeberg winery, and a 3 000 barrels facility at Koopmanskloof, all overseen by production director Anton du Toit. Three groups of wines are marketed: Vinfruco's own brands; estate and other partner-producer labels, including the Thandi 'empowerment' range (see separate entry); and buyers' own brands, tailored to international retailers' specs. Europe remains the primary focus; but now also targeting Japan.

Arniston Bay range

Slickly packaged brand with wide appeal.

Ruby Cabernet-Merlot ✤✤ Gulpable juicy style, plenty of smoky mulberry fruit, mouthfilling (13,5% alc), vibrant plummy colour in **99**, gently dry finish. Not oaked. **Rosé** ✤✤ New Charming, quaffable newcomer to this growing (in Cape) category. Fresh, pretty from nose to gently dry tail: vivid fuchsia pink; rich stewed fruit nose with hints of raspberries, succulent cherry taste. Low-level alc for no-worries lunch-time sipping. **Chenin Blanc-Chardonnay** ✤✤ Flies off UK high street shelves thanks to good price:quality ratio. Blend Paarl/Rbtson fruit in crisp, tangy **99**, clean floral fragrance with honeysuckle whiffs. Feathery texture from non-sweetening grain sugar. 13% alc.

Oak Village range

Pinotage ✤✤ Current unwooded **98** starts out warmly with smoky red berries, suggestions prunes/eucalyptus, yet finish is sinewy, dry, needing richer cuisines such as casseroles, venison. Med-bodied. **Vintage Reserve** ✤✤ Despite resounding name, **99** an approachable, unpretentious unwooded cork to pop now. Sappy cherries, light tannins, fine dry finish. Med body. Very drinkable. Cab/merlot, splashes cinsaut, shiraz. **Chardonnay** (unoaked) ✤✤ Floral, fruit salad headlines in creamy peach/apricot palate in 99. At peak, so go ahead and enjoy. 13,4% alc. Chenin Blanc ✱ Lightly floral 99 doesn't need a crutch of oak to achieve desired swiggability.

Following available but untasted for this ed: **Pinotage-Merlot 99** New, **Sauvignon Blanc 99**.

Oak Village Barrel Selection New

Specially chosen casks from catchall Coastal appellation.

✤ **Cabernet Sauvignon** Textbook cassis/vanilla bouquet, expansive mulberry fruit/liquorice whiffs in **97**, supple sweet-oaky finish. Med-bodied. Yr casks, mainly Fr. 2 000 cases.

Shiraz ✤✤ **98** will appeal to Rhône fans: dense choc/redcurrants, peppermill complexity, fine tannins. Finish, by contrast, quite uncomplicated (so just missed ✤ rating). Yr Fr/Am casks. 2 000 cases.

Groot Geluk range

Exclusively for Netherlands market.

Cinsaut-Shiraz 99 60/40 blend, 13% alc. Untasted. Pvs rating (✱). 2 940 cases. **Chardonnay Reserve 99** 6 mths oaked. 12,7% alc. Untasted. Pvs rating (✤✤). 1 320 cases. **Chenin Blanc** New Unwooded, dry. 12,7% alc. 3 237 cases.

Kaapse Hoop range

For Dutch market. **Rosé 00** dry, from pinotage. 13,1% alc. Untasted. Pvs rating (✿✿). 2 130 cases. **Chenin Blanc Eerste Pluk** (Early Release) **00** unwooded, dry. 12,5% alc. Untasted. Pvs rating (✿✿). 6 292 cases.

Rock Ridge range

Cabernet Sauvignon ✿✿ **98** Comfortable plummy mouthful, some cassis/green olives in fairly taut, minerally finish. 100% barrelled 1 yr. 13% alc. 10 000 cases. **Pinotage** ✿✿ New Some good pinotage character in Am barrelled (8 mths) **99**. Mulberries/violets/light eucalyptus reappear in fleshy, full-bodied palate. 13,5% alc. **Chardonnay** ✿✿ Modern, partially cask fermented **99** VVG, quite punchy with bright green-asparagus/passionfruit and toasty hints. 13,5% alc.

Cape Reflections range

✿ **Chardonnay** Latest **99** gear up on first release **98**. Later vintage fuller, richer, creamy butterscotch texture in harmony with spicy fruit salad aromatics. Well judged acidity. 13,6% alc. 1 000 cases.

Venus range

Venus ✿✿ Crisp, characterful méthode champenoise sparkler from chardonnay/pinot noir, min 2 yrs on lees, brut-style but not aggressively dry. Festive mousse, good apple/lemon bouquet and some yeasty/honeyed flavours. Undaunting 11% alc.

Koopmanskloof range

Cabernet Sauvignon ✿✿ More traditional Cape style, but not lacking character or flavour. Fr cask aged **97** offers smoky red berry whiffs, savoury tastes, slightly dusty oak aromas in good dry finish. 3 770 cases. **Pinotage** New **99** Fr/Am cask aged. Not available for tasting.

Other ranges/labels available (not ready for tasting): **Bin 121 Merlot-Ruby Cabernet, Eikestad Cinsaut-Shiraz, Eikestad Chenin Blanc, Klein Begin Cabernet Sauvignon, Klein Begin Sauvignon Blanc-Chardonnay, Klein Begin Pinotage, Perdeberg Sauvignon Blanc, Tesco Cabernet Sauvignon, Tesco Merlot-Cinsaut.**

. . . .

Vinum   New

Stellenbosch • Not open to the public (wines made at Onderkloof winery, Sir Lowry's Pass) • Owners Martin Gebers, Edouard Labeye, Christophe Durand, Alex Dale • Winemaker Edouard Labeye (since 1999) with Gill Radford • Viticulturist Lorna Roos • Vineyards 8 ha • Production 17 tons 1 200 cases 100% red • 67 Hillcrest Road 7130 Somerset West • Tel/fax (021) 852-3380 • E-mail vinum@netactive.co.za

ALEX DALE, who seems to have sprouted new turbocharged wings since leaving Longridge (see another flight of his fancy under Radford Dale) should hate Vinum to be judged on its looks. That sort — any sort — of discrimination has to be anathema to someone who writes (on each neck-tag) of new-frontier South Africa rising like a phoenix "from the furnace of past evils". But then the man must change this wine's packaging. Sexy as it stands, if you lie it down — well, try it and see if you can escape the seductive eye-contact of its extraordinary label. No wonder it transfixed the crowds at OddBins' London trade fair. Fortunately there's substance to all this style. Here's a unique collaboration of "four passionate wine minds" — Stellenbosch vineyard-owner Martin Gebers, winemaker Edouard Labeye and cooper Christophe Durand (both French), and marketing man-of-the-world Dale (officially a Brit). Let alone stealing a march on New World competitors, Dale and partners are giving some satellite Bordeaux producers something to chew on …

✿ **Cabernet Sauvignon** Bright, focused, sassy **99** cab, not too tiringly new-fangled (all familiar smells and tastes are here: walnuts, olives, tobacco pouch, cassis and lick of new oak) but thoroughly modern, including high-tech vinification (Labeye-advocated micro-oxygenation — injection of controlled amounts of oxygen into the must/wine) plus upmarket, innovative packaging. ±Yr casked, Fr/Am oak (75/25). 1 200 cases.

. . . .

Vinimark

Directors Tim Rands, Cindy Jordaan, Guys Naudé • PO Box 441 Stellenbosch 7599 • Tel (021) 883-8043/4 • Fax (021) 886-4708 • E-mail info@vinimark.co.za • Website www.vinimark.co.za

INDEPENDENT Stellenbosch wine merchants styling various ranges, including Kleindal, Cullinan View and Table Peak (see those entries) in conjunction with local partners for export.

. . . .

Virginia

THE "WINE FOR MEN who enjoy being men" seems to have gathered quite a female following too, with the actual male to female consumption ratio about 3:2. One of SA's largest selling whites for many years, it's sold in glass; the old gallon jar now metricated to 4,5 ℓ. By Stellenbosch Farmers' Winery.

Semi-dry **NV** ✿, surprisingly fresh ripe-guava aroma; soft, smooth, swiggable.

. . . .

Vlottenburg Winery

Stellenbosch (see Stellenbosch map) • Tasting & sales Mon—Fri 8.30–5 Sat 9—12.30 • Tasting fee R10/ R6 (includes international taster/tumbler glass) • Owners 22 members • Winemaker Kowie du Toit (since 1973) with P G Slabbert (since 1997) • Viticulturist P G Slabbert (since 1997) • Vineyards ± 1 000 ha • Production 8 000 tons 65% white 35% red • PO Box 40 Vlottenburg 7604 • Tel (021) 881-3828/9 • Fax (021) 881-3357 • E-mail vlottenb@netactive.co.za

AFTER returning from a study trip to Australia, the 22 Vlottenburg growers confidently pronounced their reds much better than the Aussie versions. Not only that, the locals believe they outperform any farmer Down Under when it comes to canopy management. Fans of this model Stellenbosch co-op know and lament that only a small fraction (5%) of these canopy-managed vines get to strut their stuff under the Vlottenburg label — the remainder of the 6,7-million litres trundle down the road to SFW for their various ranges. Happily there are plans to extend the Vlottenburg Limited Release range, and improvements to the red wine making facilities might just see some extra cases up for grabs.

✿ **Merlot 98** finest merlot yet from this cellar. Sweet violets greet you, ripe plums/blackberries/choc lead you into soft, rich toasty/oaky/woodsmoke palate with whiffs of freshly made espresso. **97** ✿ fat, juicy, toasty.

✿ **Shiraz** After promising debut in **98**, follow-up **99** keeps the aromatic fireworks going with heathery spice/smoky oak and savoury touches. Sturdy tannins need matching with cuisine if you plan to open now, but probably better to wait yr/2.

✿ **Reserve** Mix shiraz/cab (60/40) with minty touches to blackberry/dark cherry. Some high-toned smokiness and big but ripe tannins which need a bit of time to relax. **96** VG.

✿ **Cabernet Sauvignon** Fresh, generous **99** mouthful of mulberries/green pepper tapers to quite a puckering finish, which begs a bit of time. Intensity, balance suggest this will be a satisfying drink in, say 2–3 yrs. **Cabernet Sauvignon Limited Release** Special **97** bottling back-tasted mid-2000 appears to have peaked prematurely. Now offering some baked/savoury tones, dry tannins.

✿ **Chardonnay** For those who prefer a richer style, **99** and follow-up **00** ✿ offer buttery toast/vanilla plus some leesy tones to the variety's citrus crispness. Well made and satisfying. 4 mths Fr oak. 13% alc.

✿ **Muscat de Hambourg** Sunset-pink **99** fortified dessert developing with distinction in bottle. Intensely fragrant with complex candy floss/jasmine/freesia/

honeysuckle bouquet. Very sweet but non-cloying. 16,5% alc balanced, pleasingly tingly. Unusual variety in Cape.

Rouge ⚘ So quaffable, it all but pours itself. Strawberries/ripe banana in latest **NV** bottling, sappy fruit and silky tannin. Uncomplicated but satisfying cinsaut/pinotage. 1 ℓ screwcap. **Blanc de Blanc** ⚘ Guava/passionfruit lead the way to instant, unpretentious quaffing in this **NV** 1 ℓ screwcap. Inside are off-dry sauvignon/chenin, made fresh and bouncy "to share with your neighbour", per Kowie du Toit.

....

Pinotage ⚘ **99** (sample) angular when tasted mid-2000, needs time to shed more rustic overtones. Yr Fr oak. **Chenin Blanc** ✿ Back in the line-up with **00** sociable sipper; tropical tones and brisk finish despite generous dollop sugar. **Sauvignon Blanc** Gooseberry/nettle/cut-grass ripeness, relaxed acidity in full-bodied, dry **00** sample, with ⚘ potential. 13% alc. **Gewürztraminer** ⚘ Honeysuckle/rose petal perfumes in **00**, sweet yet refreshing, doesn't cloy. Good aperitif and food partner. **Late Harvest** ⚘ 🆕 Relaxed, undemanding semi-sweet with low (10% alc) and plenty of tropical flavour for sipping outdoors in summer. Chenin/riesling/bukettraube mix. **Hanepoot NV** Not ready to taste for the ed. Pvs rating ⚘.

....

Von Ortloff 𝖸 𝖸

Franschhoek (see Franschhoek map) • Tasting, sales, cellar tours by appointment • Owners/winemakers/viticulturists Georg & Evi Schlichtmann • Vineyards 15 ha • Production 75 tons (50 tons 2 940 cases own label) 55% white 45% red • PO Box 341 Franschhoek 7690 • Tel (021) 876-3432 • Fax (021) 876-4313 • E-mail vortloff@mweb.co.za

"HAVING MANAGED quite a lot of planned/unplanned circumstances since we started our vine/wine life," say Georg and Evi Schlichtmann, "we sometimes wonder what's still in the pipeline." During a 2000 night out — he, retired BMW executive, in Cape Town; she, celebrated international architect, further flung on business in Germany, got their answer: a terrifying bushfire which "perversely" flared and sputtered for two weeks, miraculously without causing significant damage. Undeterred, the irrepressible couple are pressing ahead with their plan to extend the current 15 ha on the Franschhoek river, mainly sauvignon, chardonnay, merlot and cabernet, up the Dassenberg mountain (securing a bigger overdraft for this and other projects was "one of the highlights" of the year). It seems nothing can dampen the spirits of this energetic and stylish couple, whose Merlot scooped an inaugural Grape Packaging Award in 2000. But even Georg Schlichtmann ("MD, delivery boy, accountant… you name it") can't help sighing: "There's no such a thing as relaxing away from the winery/vineyards."

⚘ **No 7 Merlot** 🏆 Steps up into ⚘ league with exceptionally smooth, harmonious **99**, seductive cherry/plum bouquet, excellent length, brilliantly accessible with promise of good ageing up to 5 yrs. 9 mths small oak, 15% new. 14% alc well integrated. 970 cases. Pvs **98** cherry/plum tastes, delicate violet fragrance. Preview of 'special reserve' — 20% portion of **99** earmarked for extended barrelling (release in 2001): extra concentration/complexity with house's signature smoothness. Good ageing potential.

⚘ **Cabernet Sauvignon-Merlot** Steady line of improvement since tightly wound **96**. Follow-up **97**, with higher proportion merlot, friendlier, more approachable. **98** ⚘ encompasses both of these styles: generous fruit (cassis/plums) and choc, plus quite strong charry oak and tannins, which will need time to meld. 14–16 mths small oak, some new. 13% alc.

⚘ **Chardonnay** Elegant barrel fermented **99** with tropical/toast/vanilla, somewhat lighter/fruitier tone than pvs **98** with 'dark' butterscotch/fudge/pear spectrum. Thumbnail refined drinkability remains, however; long dry finish with now standard 9 mths ageing in med/heavy toast barriques well absorbed. 13% alc. 620 cases.

Sauvignon Blanc ✿ Ripe picked **00** offers more gooseberry than grass; body to match the rich flavour, all balanced by bright acidity. Hand labelled bottle makes chic alfresco luncheon partner. 14% alc. 660 cases.

- -

Vredendal Winery •

Olifants River (see Olifants River map) • Tasting & sales Mon—Fri 8—5.30 Sat 8.30—12.30 (tasting venue closes half-hour earlier) • Cellar tours 10, 5 during harvest • Bring your own picnic • Fully-equipped conference centre for ±45 delegates • Audio-visual presentation • Gifts • Owners 160 members • Winemakers Alwyn Maass (since 1997), Len Knoetze (since 1999), Pieter Verwey (since 1999) • Viticultural consultant Jeff Joubert • Vineyards 3 300 ha • Production 70 000 tons • PO Box 75 Vredendal 8160 • Tel (027) 213-1080 • Fax (027) 213-3476 • E-mail vredwine@kingsley.co.za

"CORRECT grape-farming and top winemaking" is this huge winery's motto, and in the super-hot vintage of 2000 it was put to the test. The nearby Atlantic Ocean, and the Olifants River always deliver their quota of cool-down breezes and liquid refreshment to this semi-desert Namaqualand area; canopy management — offering individual bunches the optimum ratio of sunshine to shade — is practised on a vast scale. (This co-operative has 3 300 ha of vineyards to draw on, grown by 160 farmers.) With ripeness and intensity the buzzwords in modern Cape winemaking, and full-bodied, higher-alcohol reds in demand in the marketplace, heat piled on warmth can be a plus-factor. But just to be on the safe side farmers were also paid incentives to dawn-harvest the more sun-susceptible customers like sauvignon blanc. And quality control was so rigorous (you cannot pass off a burnt raisin to cellarmaster Pieter Verwey as a ripe grape) that though vineyard sources had expanded by 300 ha since the previous vintage, the total 2000 yield was down by 7 000 tons — to a mere 70 000! It's this sort of intensive-care ("both in bulk and boutique wines, separately and delicately handled," they point out) which gives Vredendal its good name, and its record as one of South Africa's biggest exporters.

✿ **Maskam Cabaret** ▼ Friendly, well made drink now red blend of cab/ruby cab with warming cherry/blackberry flavours, touches of sweet oak and clean finish. 13,5% alc. 1 500 cases. **96** VG. **94** Jan Smuts Trophy for best SA wine of year, Top 5 of *Wine* 'co-op selection' tasting.

✿ **Maskam Hanepoot Jerepiko** ▼ Sweet fortified dessert starring muscat d'alexandrie in full fragrant flight. First release **98** from block selected by ace viticulturist Andrew Teubes. Next **99** ✿, SAYWS champion, steps up the pace with complex interplay among muscat, honeysuckle, ripe peach and mango. Richness checked by well judged alc (17%). Amazing value at R11/bottle ex-winery. 1 500 cases.

Namaqua Selected Red ✿ New ☺ Soft, easy style with savoury green pepper, strawberry and pleasing hints of char. **99** "blend of noble varieties" designed for washing down pizza, pasta (with tomato) or casseroles, say winemakers. 13% alc. 1 000 cases. **Chardonnay-Colombard** ✿ ☺ Med-bodied **00** with clean guava/papaya fruits; fresh and well made. Nice dry finish. From chenin. 13% alc. 1 000 cases. **Goiya Kgeisje** ✿ ☺ Pronounced Hoya-heyshe, joined by firm click; meaning 'first wine' in the Kung language. Winery's top seller (500 000 cases annually). Recipient of inaugural 2000 Grape Packaging Award. Effortlessly quaffable **00**, as always, meant to be uncorked as fresh as possible to catch the delicate tropical tones. Chardonnay/sauvignon blend, unwooded, off-dry (7 g/ℓ sugar).

Gôiya G!aan ✿ String together three aromatic red grapes — shiraz/ruby cab/pinotage — and you get a vibrant mouthful with plenty of good scents to sustain

PARADYSKLOOF

CABERNET SAUVIGNON/MERLOT

1996

12.0% BY VOL

J H H COETZEE
VRIESENHOF
PARADYSKLOOF
STELLENBOSCH

750 ML

STELLENBOSCH WYN VAN OORSPRONG

interest (herbs, wild scrub, bit of char). Current **99**'s sweet tannins, balanced acidity complete an attractive, immediately drinkable package. Name directly translated from Kung — the San language □ means 'wine red'. Not oaked. 13% alc. **Namaqua Dry Red** ☼ Pleasantly contrasting fruit cake/savoury tastes, shortish finish. All-sort blend, **NV**. 13% alc. **Namaqua Grand Cru** ☼ Muted tropical tones, honeyed dry white. **NV**. 12,5% alc. 1 000 cases. **Namaqua Dry White** ☼ Plain, no-faults grapey dry sipper from chenin/colombard. **NV**, med-bodied. **Namaqua Selected Stein** ★ **00** semi-sweet chenin shows some tropical/honeyed tones. 12,5% alc. 1 000 cases. **Namaqua Late Harvest** ☼ **New** **NV** (00) chenin brushed with fresh honey, slathered with sweetness. No-complications tipple. 12% alc. 1 000 cases. **Maskam Port** ☼ Deep ruby **97** unexpectedly tired mid-2000. Meaty/earthy tones and some tough tannins. Ruby cab. 18,6% alc. 500 cases. **Maskam Red Muscadel** ★ Deep coppery **98**, gentle muscat character, very sweet. 17,5% alc. 1 500 cases.

Also available in 3/5 ℓ casks (Namaqua label, untasted): **Grand Cru**, **Stein**, **Late Harvest**. This cellar also produces a range of witblits and brandy.

Vredenheim Estate

Stellenbosch (see Stellenbosch map) • Tasting & sales Mon—Fri 9—5 Sat 9—2 Fee R1/wine • Cellar tours by appointment • Barrique Restaurant for lunch/dinner Tue—Sun • Reception/conference hall (catering included) • Play area for children • Tourgroups • Gifts • Views • Walks • Mountain biking • Wheelchair-friendly • Owner/viticulturist C Bezuidenhout • Winemaker Elzabé Bezuidenhout (since 1987) • Vineyards 80 ha • Production 1000 cases 60% red 40% white • PO Box 369 Stellenbosch 7599 • Tel (021) 881-3878 • Fax (021) 881-3296 • E-mail vredenheim@global.co.za

THIS 300 YEAR OLD Vlottenburg cellar — frequently hired out for weddings, birthdays and other celebrations — is an engaging family venue, with Angus cattle, horses, sheep, antelope and the odd ostrich to greet you. You can eat outdoors in summer (the Barrique Restaurant offers picnic lunches in season by arrangement). The annual harvest festival takes place on the last Saturday in January, a chance to release your inner winemaker and foot-stomp your very own wine. Stellenbosch artist Piet Grobler designed the quirky and colourful labels on Vredenheim's wines.

Vredenheim 208 ❀ Flagship blend cab/shiraz/tinta b with super-intense pepper tone, some savoury tastes in **97**. At table, Elzabé Bezuidenhout pours this with oxtail, traditional potjiekos casseroles or venison. Yr oaked. 473 cases. **Cabernet Sauvignon** ☼ **New** Blackberries, some jammy/porty tastes, dry tannins in **97**, yr oaked. 13% alc. 370 cases. **Merlot** ❀ Coffee/choc mainly, some plums and wraparound tannins in **98**. **Dry Red** ★ **96** oaked cab/merlot blend with coffee/choc tastes, robust tannins.

Vriesenhof–Talana Hill–Paradyskloof

Stellenbosch (see Stellenbosch map) Tasting & tours by appointment • Sales Mon—Thu 8.30—1; 2—5 Fri 8.30—1; 2—4 Closed on weekends and public holidays • Lunch/dinner by Annette Coetzee by arrangement • Owner/winemaker Jan 'Boland' Coetzee • Production 21 000 cases 80% red 20% white • PO Box 155 Stellenbosch 7599 • Tel (021) 880-0284 • Fax (021) 880-1503 • E-mail vriesen@iafrica.com • Website www.vriesenhof.co.za

BOLAND Coetzee's feminine side is on the lees, in 2 French oak barrels (different coopers) just inside the doorway of his maturation cellar. "After 21 years, we need a surprise," he says, and the upcoming revelation is a 2000 Pinot Noir — first fruits from young vines just outside the tasting room. This former Springbok rugby flank, who originally put Kanonkop Pinotage on its road to fame, has been wanting to add to his stable of reds for some time. The 2000 is an interesting wine, from Dijon clones, firm in the palate with amazing fruit; the potential is there. It's 2 decades since he and his family took a sabbatical in Burgundy — but the memories of his season in the Drouhin cellars there are clearly still vivid. As is his recollection of slinking past the SA plant quarantine authorities with another Burgundian souvenir

— cuttings of chardonnay, smuggled into this country in his infant son's nappy. This, of course, has nothing to do with the fact that his version of this classic French white is one of the most fragrant around.

✿✿ **Vriesenhof Kallista** Flagship Bdx blend; classically, firmly structured for long term pleasure rather than instant gratification ... But hang on, does a softer side of Boland Coetzee wink in **98**? Merlot's an equal partner here (50% of blend), with cabs s/f (35/15); result is greater than usual approachability, riper tannin structure than, say, **97**, with 50% cab. Terrific wine: inky black, cab f's swirling perfume; rounded and long. Probably earlier maturing than **97**, refined, gravelly, elegant, needing 5 yrs from vintage for fruit to come to the fore. Barrel tasting of **00** components promise abundant fruit with signature firmness, glossy tannins and vegetative cab whiffs from JBC's favourite clone 46 ("the old veldskoen clone"). **96** leaner, more vegetal. Older vintages show herbaceous austerity — prized by traditionalists.

✿✿ **Vriesenhof Cabernet Sauvignon** Latest **98** typical Helderberg vegetal tones plus tobacco, sensitively oaked (20% new Fr, balance second fill). Deeply coloured; blackcurrant/earth tones and firm tannins. And no mint — "that's for cowboys". Longer-lasting probably than **98** Kallista, but shorter legs than **97** ✿✿, with dense cassis in firm palate. **99** barrel sample offers strong nutty flavours.

✿✿ **Vriesenhof Pinotage 98** for those who hanker after the more traditional style: huge tannins without bitterness, broad mouthfeel; plums/spice/bananas with medicinal sniffs, impression of sweetness in finish. 13 mths new oak. Tame in comparison to **97**, something of a sleeping giant, fashioned (partly by 20 mths new oak) for the long haul; less obvious than **98**, more fragrantly spicy, still-muted fruit and tannic grip which need yrs to develop and relax. **00** hailed by JBC as "a pinotage year." Barrel samples intensely coloured, firm tannins and no hint of greenness.

✿✿ **Talana Hill Chardonnay** Fr style **99**, nervous, taut, good minerally quality. 'Oily' palate with lemon zesty, fairly austere finish. Less perfumed than **98** with peach/apple pie flavours and dry chalky/lemony tang.

Talana Hill Royale ✿✿ **98** somehow lacks the generosity of vintage; perfumed but lean, hardish tannins (though JBC "fairly happy"). Merlot/cab f (75/25) blend. **Paradyskloof Pinotage** Untasted. **Vriesenhof Chardonnay** ✿✿ **99** forward vanilla and honey echo in palate with soft buttery tones. 35% new wood, 8 months. This, like pvs, longer term wine which needs time to reveal its generous charms. **Paradyskloof Sauvignon Blanc-Chardonnay** ✿✿ Good value **99** simple, easy and fruity, good dry finish.

. . . .

Waboomsrivier Co-op   ⚑ ⚑

Worcester (see Worcester map) • Tasting, sales & cellar tours Mon—Fri 8–5 Sat 8-10 • Views • Wheelchair-friendly • Owners 50 members • Winemakers Chris van der Merwe (since 1987) & Wim Viljoen (since 1991) • Consulting viticulturist Pierre Snyman (VinPro) • Vineyards 883 ha • Production 11 360 tons (60 tons, 4 000 cases own label) 62% white 38% red • PO Box 24 Breede River 6858 • Tel (023) 355-1734 • Fax (023) 355-1731

THEY may be in rural Worcester, but the Waboomers are thinking international trends and sexy varieties, and planning accordingly. The first crop of sangiovese is already in tank; petit verdot and malbec went into the ground in 2000, and cab franc will be the new kid in the block in 2001. "You've got to be market driven and offer greater variety to the customer," explains Chris van der Merwe. They sell just 2% of production in bottle under the in-house Wagenboom label; rest goes to merchants in bulk. New French cellar technology is proving to be "quite transforming", vdM reports, particularly for cab and shiraz. Which means local fans as well as palates in Canada, Holland and Switzerland will find even more to rave about in the future.

Ruby Cabernet Young, cheeky 99 never saw a barrel, so no oaky encumbrance to exuberant fruit pastille flavour. Lightly chilled, a versatile summer playmate. 13,7% alc. Screwtop. 276 cases.

Cabernet Sauvignon ✸ **99** flagship easy, accessible; supple palate gently firmed by tannin. 13% alc. 389 cases. **Pinotage ★** Oak-chipped **99** no longer the sprite we tasted for pvs ed. Better in flush of youth. 14% alc. 279 cases. **Blanc de Blanc** ☼ Gently dry, med-bodied chenin/semillon for right-now quaffing. Fresh guava, meadow flowers in **00**. 280 cases. **Perlé** ☼ Late harvested semi-sweet chenin, lightly spritzed. 280 cases. **Chenin Blanc Late Harvest** ☼ Delicate semi-sweet **99**, some whispered fruit salad tones. 288 cases. **Rubellite Sparkling ★** Vividly coloured, volcanically fizzy semi-sweet **NV** (99), chenin/pinotage. 277 cases. **Port** ✸ More jerepigo than authentic port, but pleasant, not unctuous; some Christmas cake, dusty oak highlights. **NV** (95). Ruby cab. 397 cases.

Wagenboom see Waboomsrivier

Wamakersvallei Winery ♆ ♆ ♆

Wellington (see Wellington map) • Tasting & sales Mon—Fri 8—5 Sat 8.30—12.30 • Cellar tours by appointment • Picnics by arrangement • Gifts • Owners 45 members • Winemakers Chris Roux (since 1970), Pieter Rossow (since 1975) • Consultant viticulturists VinPro • Vineyards 1 600 ha • Production 11 500 tons (10 000 cases own label) 65% white 35% red • PO Box 509 Wellington 7654 • Tel (021) 873-1582 • Fax (021) 873-3194 • E-mail wamakers@mweb.co.za • Website www.wamakersvallei.co.za

WHEELS are turning at this anything but staid old co-op in the 'Valley of the Wagon Makers'. Wamakersvallei's approach is fresh, forward thinking, and its funky new logo depicting a swinging hammer hits the spot. They've got their act together, keeping up with marketing and production developments, and making wines honed to market specs for Ashwood and Cape Wine Cellars, among others. They intend to focus on their own range, to which end they've appointed a viticulturist to work in conjunction with an additional winemaker (not chosen at time of going to press). Chris Roux, winemaker here for three decades, does however allow himself one distraction: frequent trips to Newlands — his son Chean played for the Stormers and captained the WP team in the last Currie Cup.

✸**Merlot 99** Something of a find at R15 ex-cellar, **99**'s full of merlot coffee grounds, extra-sappy full-bodied fruit, good dry finish (a signature of this winery). 1 950 cases.

Cinsaut ✸ **98** light, succulent choc/savoury dry red to try, so winemakers recommend, with traditional waterblommetjie bredie. 2 500 cases. **Celebration 2000** ✸ Striking packaging, equally attention-getting perfumed tropical fruit are stars of this lightish-bodied sparkling, made semi-dry for smoother sipping. Super wine, and a snip at R12 ex-cellar. From sauvignon. ±900 cases.

Cabernet Sauvignon ✸ Tasty, very savoury light-bodied red with herby aromas translating easily into palate, still with brush of tannin. 3 000 cases. **Pinotage** ✸ "Share it with your sweetheart," suggest Chris Roux/Pieter Rossow, who made this red-cherry-toned **99** in an usually restrained, almost demure style (so we suggest you wait yr to let it grow, then share). 13,5% alc. 3 000 cases. **Chenin Blanc** ☼ **00** pleasant everyday drink, modestly fruity, non-aggressively dry. Lightish 11,5% alc. 1 000 cases. **Sauvignon Blanc ★** Unusual muscat scents in **00** bouquet;

lightish with soft (5 g/ℓ) acidity. 1 500 cases. **Stein** ✵ Ripe summer fruit and hint of hay in just off-dry **NV**. **Late Harvest** ✵ Soft, shy but not unpleasant semi-sweet **NV**. **Fishermans Jerepigo** ✵ Designed to thaw a frosty sea dog's soul. Very sweet yet delicate, bright hanepoot florals. 17,5% alc. 1 200 cases. **Jagters Port** ✵ **NV** 'Hunter's Port' just right for campsite quaffing: suitably 'wild' herbs/peppers, really warming alcoholic finish. 19% alc. 1 100 cases. Also available but not tasted: **Duke of Wellington Victory Red 97** pinotage/ruby cab. **Chardonnay 99** unwooded. **Riesling 99**.

. . . .

Wandsbeck see Agterkliphoogte

. . . .

Warwick Estate

Stellenbosch (see Stellenbosch map) • Tasting & sales Mon—Fri 10—4 Sat 9—1 Nov—Apr or by appointment Closed Christmas, Family Day, New Year's Day, Easter Tasting fee R5 p/p refundable with purchase • Wheelchair-friendly • Owners Stan & Norma Ratcliffe • Winemaker Anna-Mareè Mostert (since 1999) • Winegrower/viticulturist Nicholas Dowling (since 1998) • Vineyards 75 ha • Production 350 tons, 20 000 cases 89% red 10% white 1% rosé • PO Box 2 Muldersvlei 7607 • Tel (021) 884-4410 • Fax (021) 884-4025 • E-mail cellarinfo@warwickwine.co.za • Website www.warwickwine.co.za

IN A YEAR which saw South Africa thumped by Australia in every sporting field, Bravo Warwick! And Viva chardonnay! on this once red-only property in the prime Muldersvlei bowl of Stellenbosch. Sparky co-owner (with husband Stan) Norma Ratcliffe, now free-ranging outside her former domain of the cellar ("style guidance counsellor" she labels herself) was finally convinced that her dabbles with white wine were more than an indulgence when her 99 Warwick trounced all Oz and Kiwi opposition in the Cowra Tri-Nations Chardonnay Challenge. So prematurely triumphal had the Aussies been that the prize — a ticket to Burgundy for the winning winemaker — had been booked ex-Sydney ... Though the Ratcliffes' son Michael, studying in Adelaide prior to taking over general farm management duties at the end of 2000, could conceivably have made that flight, sheepish organisers speedily (sheepishly?) did some re-routing to and from Cape Town. Anna- Mareè Mostert, ex-Mont Rochelle cellar in Franschhoek, has a dynamic act to follow here. In our questionnaire to winemakers for this edition we asked them to name a first XV of their peers; where Norma Ratcliffe's name did not appear we can only cry Sexism! Few competitors of any gender on the Cape's still non-level playing field have contributed with such distinction to South Africa's image than this intuitive, self-taught winemaker. She remains the local maestrina of cabernet franc; her latest statement-wine, the Three Cape Ladies blend, features some of the bush-vine pinotage with which she's also challenged old stereotypes (this vineyard was hardest-hit by the runaway fires during the harvest of 2000; 3–4 ha. were lost). Nursing this back to health is viticulturist Nick Dowling, with Californian input from consultant Phil Freese.

✤ **Trilogy** ⚐ Marked by triple antique marriage cup motif and fine, understated claret style reflecting Ratcliffe's Bdx experience in the 1980s. Latest **98** too young to measure at tasting mid-2000 but in same style, albeit a touch less generous. 13% alc. 3 000 cases. A little harder than seminal **97**, Michelangelo gold, concentrated garnet colour; individual, fragrant nose of violets/tobacco leaf with tarry tones. Ripe but restrained blackcurrant fruit eased by meaty merlot (39%) contribution, sappy 7% cab f tying up any loose ends. Mineral, stony backbone for acid, tannin; fine, measured finish. 12,5% alc. **96** variant of generally lighter vintage, full of well-fleshed fruit emerging from behind tannin veil. **95** ripe, deep fruit concentration, malleable finish. Previously about 60/30/10 cab s/merlot/cab f. 18 mths 225 ℓ Nevers/Allier/Vosges oak, 30% new.

✤ **CWG Auction Reserve** To date best selection of Trilogy barrels have been offered at auction under Femme Bleue label. Future likely to see move away from both this label and Bdx-style blend. **99** from pinotage (to emulate **96**, **95** auction bottlings of that grape): big, broad-framed, billowing scents of cherries/spice; minimal sweet banana/cloves pulp, excellent perfumed fruit in densely meshed tannins.

⚜Three Cape Ladies 97 Cape-style blend cab/merlot/pinotage (40/40/20) didn't win 1999 Diners Club competition but will turn heads with striking packaging — and no less remarkable wine. Shimmering ruby, fleshy choc/roasted chestnuts/plum fruit in packed palate, riper than usual but still with trademark Warwick mineral ring. 13% alc. 2 yrs Fr oak. 400 cases.

✹Cabernet Franc For a variety that can be austere/anorexic alone, along comes full, fleshy **98** ⚜ with ripe berry fruit to offer the counterpoint. Currently fortified by huge (but ripe) tannins, this should open into generous savoury (green olive/pimento) mouthful over 5 yrs. Now more beneficent than **97**, latter result of cool, extended ripening season, strenuous cropping. Closed but will be a stunner. Fine Fr oak keeps grassy/sappy fruit in purdah. Brambly nose sweetened by pepper; classic cab refinement with cherry/mocha. Ripe tannic structure, 13% alc, for lasting finish; needs time to show its true excellence. **96** earthy, more rustic, quiet. **95** SAA, *Wine* ⚜ carried off 1997 IWSC Dave Hughes Trophy. Run of quality started with **94** *Wine* ✹.100% varietal (except for **93**), moderate alcs., easy acids. Oak regime now 20 mths Fr oak, 30% new.

⚜Old Bush Vine Pinotage ✅ 00 may be at some risk due to devastating fires, but tank sample **99** delicious in full but not flippant fruit style. Nose scattered with heady fynbos/heather/violets. Palate sturdy, well framed and bolstered by 13,5% alc. Purple-hued **98**, with dash merlot, more obvious boiled sweets/banana/liquorice. Pulpy ripe palate pops with soft, sweet fruit. Welcome dark choc finish. 13,5% alc. More retiring **97** developing tawny tints, stewed fruit/ripe plums flow on fleshy palate. **96** *Wine* ⚜ new-wave style. **95** VVG sweeter, juicier. Yr small, med-toast Fr oak reins in pinotage's wilder flashes, provides classy, firm finish. From old bushvines, 8 t/ha yields.

⚜Merlot ✅ New **98** continues run of super **97** but altogether bigger, fuller, more earthy/robust. Fleshy bitter choc, chunkier tannin and chewy, lipsmacking richness, 13% alc in support. Glance at dense St Emilion examples. 13,8% alc. 1 080 cases. Delicate **97** still purple, fragrant whiffs meat/milk choc/soil/wood. Fine tannins softening but will last. Both step up from **96** ⚜, mint/violets/mulberry fruit with elegance of pvs. With touch cab. **95** SAA, **94** SAA, VG.

⚜Cabernet Sauvignon 98 "yummy" summer berry compote; black cherries vie with cassis/mulberry in juicy mouthful. 13,5% alc. 1 200 cases. Easier, more relaxed than taut **97** ✹, redolent of cigar box, tense acid/tannin structure leavened by choc-caramel breadth. Rich palate. Average 5 t/ha, 14 mths new/2nd fill med toast Nevers/Allier oak.

⚜Chardonnay ✅ "Having lost the cricket, rugby, hockey and netball, at least we came back with some dignity with the Chardonnay prize," says Ratcliffe of the Tri-Nations triumph secured by **99** to add to SAA First Class listing, Michelangelo gold. Barrel sample **00** confirms no flash in the pan: peachy fruit nestled in rich creamy wood, already deliciously melded into full palate. Will be as excellent as winning **99**. Hazelnut complexity to creamy mouthful cut by limey tang. Has developed superbly — "pity it's mostly drunk" laments Anna-Mareè Mostert. Potent ripe tropical **98** *Wine* ⚜ swaggering 14% alc. ready. **97** initiated new style, more modern and drinkable than maiden **96**.

Waterford ❡ ❡

Stellenbosch (see Stellenbosch map) • Tasting & sales Mon—Fri 9—4 No fee • Landowners Jeremy & Leigh Ord • Company owners Jeremy & Leigh Ord, Kevin Arnold • Winemaker Kevin Arnold (since Nov 1997) • Viticulturist Bob

Hobson (since 1999) • Production 20 000 cases 70% red 30% white • PO Box 635 Stellenbosch 7599 • Tel (021) 880-0496 • Fax (021) 880-1007 • E-mail waterfordhil@icon.co.za

IF "FAMILY FARM" conjures up for you a picture of rural simplicity, of country folk quietly rusticating away, we urge you to get connected. Sepia tints are out, digital images are in, and nowhere is this more evident than at the very sophisticated, definitively new-millennium property on the slopes of the Helderberg. Yes, it's a family venture — the hands on deck belong to Jeremy and Leigh Ord, Kevin and Heather Arnold, and their assorted children. But, as befits a partnership between an IT magnate (Ord's Didata group went public on the London Stock Exchange mid-2000) and a cutting-edge winemaker (Arnold reborn, in his own creative space at last), here thoroughly modern forces are at work. In every way, Waterford is a new-era showpiece. The Cape-Mediterranean winery is a triumphant blend of style and efficiency. The tasting room, conceptualised by Heather Arnold (a winelands style-icon herself), has already featured in South Africa's top décor magazine. The actual winery, built round a courtyard featuring the Waterford hallmark — a double-decker fountain — draws on Kevin Arnold's investigations round the wine-world: dressed in stone and wood from the farm, it's a model of practicality, with just about everything except the winemaker on labour-saving wheels. The packaging, by local guru Anthony Lane, is super-chic, with the fountain embossed on the Waterford bottles.

✿**Kevin Arnold Shiraz** Carries name/stamp of illustrious winemaker, but firmly part of Waterford range. Subtitled, after owners' children, to emphasise family focus here. First **98** 'Robert Charles', the eldest A. *Wine* ✿, Grape inaugural excellence in packing award. Piercing pan-roast spices, deep roast coffee, fantastic savoury intensity in firm, full but not overbearing palate. Soft, ripe tannins offset dark fruit. Easy to drink but utterly serious. Next **99** 'Lloyd Francis', another A (the O children to feature later), even better; tingling spice threaded with rich plum, delicious balanced mouthful flecked with liquorice/pepper, prospects good for long term growth. "Gives me goosebumps," says Arnold. We agree. Grapes from Overgaauw. 13,5% alc. Small Fr oak.

✿**Cabernet Sauvignon** 'Cosmopolitan' provenance while Waterford winery was being built and until vineyards up to speed: first release **98** made at Spier, aged at Neil Ellis, blended and bottled at Waterford! Cherry/blackberry bouquet, spicy oak around palate with clean fruit, ripe tannins, lingering elegance. Ripe, juicy and tasty; already better than when tasted for pvs ed; balanced, supple tannin should reward further 4–6 yrs in bottle. 11 mths new oak, 35% Am, 13,5% alc. *Wine* ✿.

✿**Chardonnay** Barrel sample **00** entrenches "in-between" style Arnold seeks: in-between fruit and oak — with elegance per house philosophy. Striking limey character dominates wood at present, latter showing in balanced **99** with melon, faint cashew aromas. Smooth, clean palate features duet buttery vanilla/measured citrus fruit.

✿**Sauvignon Blanc 00** mid-2000 too recently bottled for fair assessment, but signs of gentler, more grassy, better balance than pvs. **99** packed with gooseberry/sweetcorn/herbs. Crisp acid, grapefruit lighten load of powerful palate. Selected for FinAir — "perhaps the 14% alc. attracted them," jokes Kevin Arnold. Own farm grapes, 9 yr old vines, 50–50 bush/trellis). First **98** on small scale.

Pecan Stream ✿ **New** Sassy new second label, more frivolous but clearly branded 'Waterford'. 90/10 chenin/chardonnay blend deliberately less obviously fruity, more gravity, aimed at table. **00** has gentler oak (all chardonnay barrelled), fresher fruit than **99** which retains tropical fruit but honeyed. Full, round and ripe palate handles 14% alc.

Webersburg

Stellenbosch • Not open to the public • Owner Fred Weber • Viticulturist Braam Steyn (since 1996) • Vineyards 40 ha • Production 60-80 tons 3 500 cases 100% red • PO Box 3428 Somerset West 7129 • Tel (021) 851-7417 • Fax (021) 852-5280 • E-mail weber@iafrica.com

THIS PROMISING BOUTIQUE WINERY produces only cabernet sauvignon at present, but their merlot comes into production this year and by 2002 should be going into bottle (a very handsome bottle, if the current packaging standard is maintained) both varietally and in a blend. The maiden 96 was quickly bought up at the London Wine Trade Fair; and Fred Weber showed the 97 at his British importer's stand there in 2000. He learned at the Fair, he says, that high quality is the most important thing for export success. And, not surprisingly, he doesn't seem unduly worried.

Cabernet Sauvignon Cassis emerges from subtle framing of rather dusty cedar and herbs in **97**. Full-flavoured, silky palate, with savoury acidity lifting the plentiful fruit, firm but gentle tannins, and a satisfyingly lingering dry finish. Restrained, classic styled wine, wearing its 18 mths of new Nevers oak well. 12,9% alc. Showing signs of maturing well, though with plenty of beneficent time to go.

Welgegund Wines

Wellington • Not open for tasting/sales • Guest-house/B&B Tel Ron Spies 082-453-4787 • Owners Alex & Sheila Camerer • Winemaker Marthinus Broodryk (Bovlei Winery) • Viticulturist Ron Spies (since 1995) • Vineyards 28 ha 63% red 37% white • Production 122 tons • PO Box 683 Wellington 7655 • Tel (021) 864-1185 • Fax (021) 873-2683 • E-mail rac@icon.co.za

WELLINGTON — "a good, warm Mediterranean climate" — is the ideal spot to grow carignan in SA. So say Alex & Sheila Camerer, Gauteng business/political movers/shakers who've owned this pretty Wellington farm since the mid 1908s. Here they grow some of the less than 80 ha of carignan in the Cape, and though "the history of this grape in SA is a collection of old records, reminiscences and rural legend," the Camerers hope to raise the status of the variety through low cropping and ripe picking. The wine below is made by Marthinus Broodryk at Bovlei co-op, which eagerly buys the rest of the Welgegund's produce — the farm is recognised as the cellar's best source of cinsaut.

Carignan Perky, attention-grabbing red berry/baked plum in **00** dry red. Zippy flavours, soft tannin add to all-round tippleability. Good picnic wine, say Alex & Sheila Camerer. Lightly oaked. ±500 cases.

Welgemeend Estate

Paarl (see Paarl map) • Tasting & sales Wed 2—4 Sat 9—12.30 or by appointment • Owner Hofmeyr family • Winemaker Louise Hofmeyr (since 1991) • Manager/viticulturist Ursula Hofmeyr • Vineyards 12,6 ha • Production 3 500 cases • PO Box 1408 Suider-Paarl 7624 • Tel (021) 875 5210 • Fax (021) 875 5239 • E-mail welgemeend@worldonline.co.za

THERE COULD BE no better tribute to the memory of Billy Hofmeyr, who died in mid 2000, than the progress evidenced in recent years at one of the Cape's first boutique wineries. Pioneer of local Bordeaux blends, Billy left behind a feisty partnership of always vital wife Ursula and daughter Louise who took over all aspects of the farm after his incapacitation from Alzheimer's some 10 years ago. Winemaker Louise is firmly committed to a classic approach (in the tasting room, long shelves of empty bottles of Europe's finest reveal her continuing vinous education and pleasure in wine). So no oaky, alcoholic blockbusters here: Welgemeend never enters competitions and the wines are not designed to overwhelm immediately and easily. Hofmeyr has made numerous improvements during her reign in the cellar, including introducing a second label wine in the early 1990s to allow for rigorous selection for the flagship labels. With an achieved confidence based on an understanding of what her vineyards offer in the varying seasons, vinification tweakings have been consolidated more recently with reduced level of fining (only egg-white) and filtering, and since 1998 the total abandonment of acidification and innoculated yeasts.

✿✿ Estate Reserve ✅ Current **98** and **97** a year on, reveal new high for this, the first Cape Bdx blend and one of the few with established track record of consistently expressing its terroir origins. **98** still youthful deep ruby; concentrated, rich but elegant, complex flavours too seamlessly integrated for facile comparisons (though hallmark mineral, red fruit, mocha, black olives, cigar box all present). Triumphant supple balance: big, fine tannins, savoury natural acidity, unobtrusive contribution of oak (30% new, 18 mths). 36% cab, 40% merlot, 24% cab f. Alc unusually bold at nearly 13%, reflecting hot vintage. **97** more restrained but very fine. Recommendation: tuck away both vintages at least 5 yrs and enjoy early matured **96** simpler, lighter (but not lightweight), thoroughly pleasant and most claret-like of all. **95**, **94** showing characteristic elegance and balance, **95** readier to drink now, but both deserve few more yrs (this label noted for ability to age).

✿ Amadé ✅ Remarkably successful, uncopied Cape interpretation of Rhône blend: approx third each shiraz, grenache, (now mostly non-estate) pinotage. Extraordinary value for serious (though not grand) wine, with ability to age interestingly. Spicy, strawberry, mineral aromas/flavours, extra ripeness of grenache in current **98** ✿ adding herby richness to fine tannin structure. Mostly older oak maturation, 12 mths.

✿ Douelle A different nod to Bdx, 38% malbec dominating (with 28% cab, 22% merlot, 12% cab f). **98** youthful crimson; hints of mulberry, caramel/toffee; beguiling wildness — particularly appreciated by foreigners, here and abroad. Fresh, elegant, firm but non-aggressive tannins, subtle oak, crisp, slightly medicinal finish. **97** ✿ with juicy mulberry, cinnamon aromas, sweet woodsmoke whiff.

✿ Soopjeshoogte 98 ✅ shows that barrels not quite good enough for the top wines still offer very satisfying, excellent value drinking. Estate Reserve's virtues here in slightly reduced form Minerally red-fruit aromas, touch of green pepper. Firm, well-balanced structure. 50% cab, with merlot, cab f. Fleshier than **97** ✿, with dried fruit, fennel, nutty qualities.

- -

Wellington Co-op　　　　　　　　　　　　　　　　🍷

Wellington (see Wellington map) • Tasting & sales Mon—Fri 8—5 • Owners 50 members • Winemaker Gert Boerssen (since 1980) & Koos Carstens (since 1991) • Vineyards 1 530 ha Production 10 500 tons 20 000 cases 65% white 35% red • PO Box 520 Wellington 7654 • Tel (021) 873-1163/1257 • Fax (021)873-2423 • E-mail wellwyn@iafrica.com

THIS Wellington co-op is an old fiddle (1906) playing a brand new tune under the baton of seasoned cellar-orchestrators Gert Boerssen and Koos Carstens. The contemporary rhythm is red — nearly two-thirds of the crush is now made up of black-skinned grapes, and though most of the finished product still finds its way into bottle anonymously under third-party labels, a portion is bottled for the in-house brand and exported to five countries in Europe. Locally, these characterful Wellington reds and whites have earned a reputation for good value and drinkability.

Cinsaut-Ruby Cabernet ✿ 😊 Round, soft, succulent **99**, quaffs easily thanks to cinsaut's comfortable strawberry/raspberry tones. Team with pasta/pizza, and note a possible comeback from flamboyant 15% alc. **Chenin Blanc** ✿ 😊 Happily unscathed by warm **00** harvest; fresh, zippy green-apple acidity and riper guava flesh in dry palate. Drink tonight if not sooner. 13% alc.

Cabernet Sauvignon ✿ Usually swiggable cab has an unexpected edge of dry tannin in **98**, which needs something BBQed, say, or rustic casserole for smoothing. Yr Fr oak. **Merlot** ✿ **97** is gliding into mellow maturity; soft pulpy red berries/plums throughout, with just a gentle squeeze of tannin at the end. After dinner, try with choc mousse, winemakers advise. 13% alc. **Pinotage** ★ Oak-aged **98** showing very mature character. Better young and fresh. **Shiraz** ✿ **97** acquiring not unpleasant 'baked' tone as it ages, some good shiraz woodsmoke and pepper wafts. Lightish feel despite 13,5% alc. **Chardonnay** ⚲ Clearly took a knock in extra-warm **00**. Muted aromas, short on flavour. **Sauvignon Blanc** variety's usual bite more like a pleasing nibble in **00**, tropical-toned with fragrant mango, low 5 g/ℓ acidity. Pulls up quite short.

Welmoed Wines

Stellenbosch (see Stellenbosch map) • Tasting Mon—Fri 9—5 Sat 9—4.30 Sun 10—3.30 Sales Mon—Fri 9—5.30 Sat 9—3 Sun 10—4 • Cellar tours by appointment • Duck Pond Restaurant for lunch daily Tel (021) 881-3310 Also private functions • Head winemaker Chris Kelly • Winemaker Mike Graham (since 1999) • PO Box 456 Stellenbosch 7599 • Tel (021) 881-3800 or 881-3870 • Fax (021) 881-3434 or 881-3102

SUPPLIED by well-situated vineyards, many brushed by Atlantic Ocean-breezes, this winery is now part of the Stellenbosch Vineyards group (see that entry).

Reserve range

✿ **Cabernet Sauvignon** Serious yet unintimidating, and hugely enjoyable company (pretty well sums up both this wine and the Chris Kelly/Mike Graham winemaking duo). They nominate "lucky girls" as preferred partners when drinking this wine. Elegance, fruity charm in **99** ✿. Cassis, softening mint, linked by hint dusty oak. Rounded, firm finish. 9 mths 300 ℓ Fr oak. Pvs **97** elegant cassis/coffee, ripe tannin frame.

✿ **Shiraz** 🄽🄴🅆 Baby brother to Genesis (Stbosch Vyds' flagship range), from different, single vyd (27 yr old bushvines). Everything on gentler scale, though **99** captures variety's essential vibrancy. Plenty of grape to chew on, nose/tail peppered with white spice; rolls over tongue in long chocolatey waves. Perfect partner to Cape Malay dishes.

✿ **Merlot** At the ripest end of ripe, **99** ✿ held together/saved from over-ripeness by solid frame, subtle oaking. Voluptuous plummy mouthful, unintimidating tannin for current drinking. Best over next yr/two. 14,3% alc. Fr/Am oak aged. **98** luscious, with sweet minerally plums.

✿ **Sauvignon Blanc** ▽ "Precision harvesting" key to **00**'s success in difficult vintage. Brims with ripe figs, melons, even suggestion of rhubarb, guava; the whole luscious fruit salad repeated in palate. Weight/concentration contrast with vivid acid spine, which should be going strong until at least mid-2001. But why bother: there are 11 000 cases to tide over until then! 12,8% alc. **98** *Wine* ✿.

Pinotage ✿ 🄽🄴🅆 Chris Kelly not particularly fond of traditional pinotage, so this **00** styled for like-minded consumers. Big, soft, juicy; quiet red berry fruits touched up with sweet-oak vanilla; absolutely no astringency/bitterness. 30% Fr oaked, 9 mths. 13% alc. **Chardonnay** ✿ For those who hanker after a fuller, more oak-enriched, but not oaky, chardonnay. Partly barrel-fermented **00** broad, tropical, soft vanilla tone; supple if short on complexity. **Chenin Blanc** ✿ Barrel-fermented portion enriches **99** without swamping smooth honeysuckle/lime marmalade. Full bodied, balanced; good fruity persistence. 13,9% alc.

Selection range

Pinotage ⚲ Foursquare **99**; straightforward redcurrants, touch of burnt rubber; robust, some varietal astringency. Lightly oaked. **Chenin Blanc** ✿ Unashamedly fruity, juicy **00**; very ripe melon/honey character reflected in sturdy alc (13,7%), though soupçon sugar brings it all together.

> **Sauvignon Blanc** ✿✿  Quiet yet satisfying gooseberry **00**; ripe, lively acidity, good fruity persistence all styled to ensure second bottle is opened immediately. **Blanc de Blanc** ✿✿ Ripe papaya/melon-toned chenin with crisp, freshening sauvignon. **00** full flavoured, long, dry.

Weltevrede Estate

Robertson (see Robertson map) • Tasting & sales Mon—Fri 8—5 Sat 9—3.30 • Cellar tours by appointment • Traditional lunches Mon—Sat 12—2.30 Or bring your own picnic • Self-catering cottage • Play area for children • Tourgroups • Gifts • Walks • Conservation area • Mountain biking • Views • Wheelchair-friendly • Owner Lourens Jonker • Winemaker Philip Jonker with Riaan Liebenberg (since 1999), Sam Davids (since 1972) Viticulturist Philip Jonker with Herman Kitshoff (since 1995) • Vineyards 100 ha • Production 1 400 tons • PO Box 6 Bonnievale 6730 • Tel (023) 616-2141 • Fax (023) 616-2460 • E-mail weltevrede@intekom.co.za • Website www.weltevrede.com

PHILIP JONKER, fourth generation grower on this friendly Bonnievale estate, is on a mission to transform his heritage into wine. "I was born here. It's my calling," he states. Not that this youngster's tradition-bound. International exposure — a swing through Europe, with pit-stop at the London Wine Trade Fair among his recent walkabouts — are helping to fine tune his winemaking game which, he professes, is "still at Craven Week level". A record small harvest, with "very good quality due to compact berry size and concentration of flavour" got the millennium off to a cracking start for this keen water sports enthusiast, who regards his wife, Lindelize, and father Lourens (stalwart of KWV) his main winemaking inspirations. The range has been restructured into a flagship, Oude Weltevreden, a "single-variety, terroir-specific" range, Weltevrede, and fruit-driven early-drinking collection, River's Edge. Quality and value are the goals throughout: "Even if someday a bottle of Weltevrede costs more than R1000, it will be money well spent," assures Philip Jonker.

Oude Weltevreden range

✿✿ **Chardonnay** Selected vats from top vyd, limited quantities, barrel fermented. "Looking for a Burgundian character," says Philip Jonker, who believes this first **98** VG, *Wine* ✿✿ will age "at least 5—10 yrs". Yet back-tasted mid-2000, already showed less acid uplift than pvsly, heralding onset of flabbiness. Still very attractive, however, is the butterscotch richness checked by citrus piquancy. Suggest monitor carefully. 13,5% alc. 350 cases.

Merlot-Cabernet Sauvignon ✿✿ First dry red from this estate, traditionally made. **98** fairly elegant cassis/lead pencils bouquet; ripe fruit and firm dry finish. SAYWS gold. Fr oaked, malo in barrel. 12,5% alc. 210 cases.

Weltevrede range

✿✿ **Chardonnay** Altogether convincing in **98**, fine balance of citrus/tropical fruit and vanilla oak. **00** sample in similar mould: very nice buttery mid-palate refreshed with delicate lime/orange-zest, crisp citrus finish. Barrel fermented/aged 3 mths Fr oak. 1 500 cases.

✿✿ **Ovation Rhine Riesling** Natural Sweet Botrytised dessert back-tasted mid-2000 showed some advancing terpene characters in **99** bouquet; appeared clumsy, acid/sugar balance out of kilter. ✿✿ on present form. Needs watching. 12,5% alc. 750 cases.

✿✿ **Philip Jonker Brut** Improving Blanc de blancs MCC from 100% chardonnay. **95** sold out; no **96**, **97**. **98**, released in time for "real millennium" previewed in last ed offered satisfying honey/butterscotch flavours, highly energetic bubble.

✿✿ **Cape Muscat** Benchmark Cape fortified muscat dessert, opulent and concentrated but not overpowering. Handsome appearance applauded by judges of Grape's inaugural excellence in packaging awards. **98**, from muscat de hambourg, distinguished by silky milk chocolate, rich caramel and toffee/malt layers, with fragrant 'sweet' tea-leaves and lightly spirity finish. Mouthfilling and very long. Stunning with choc mousse. Will be interesting to follow development. 17% alc. 375 ml. 380 cases.

Rhine Riesling ⚘ Fast-track development of riesling in Cape highlighted in off-dry, med-bodied **98** SAA. Huge terpene bouquet with waxy nuances. 1 500 cases.
Gewürztraminer Fragile rose petals plus this wine's trademark, fresh honey, in off-dry med-bodied **00** (sample). Delightful solo or with aromatic cuisine, soft cheese. Should rate ⚘ on release. 1 600 cases. **Oupa Se Wyn** ⚘ Flavourful fortified dessert from red muscadel, portion ex-vyd planted 1926, now national monument. **99** balanced, not too sweet, flavours per **98** but fresher: spice and raisins layered with tar/malt/toffee. Low (for this style) 15,5% alc. 1 500 cases.
Ouma se Wyn ⚘ (Honours grandma Lisbeth Jonker.) Consistently delicious fortified dessert from single vyd white muscadel. Usual complex white flower bouquet replaced with rose petal perfume in latest **99**; clean, well defined flavours. Lightish 15,5% alc. **97** VVG. 800 cases. Also available (untasted): **Sauvignon Blanc**.

River's Edge range   New

> **Colombard** ⚘ ☺ The whole Robertson guava orchard ("our limestone rich terroir," explains winemaker), with melon/citrus backing in super-fruity, fresh, lightish **00**. 2 500 cases.

Blanc de Noir ‡ Pack this semi-sweet blush and punnet ripe strawberries for an instant picnic treat, say Lindelize and Philip Jonker. Boiled sweets in **99**, to be enjoyed soonest. Red muscadel. 1 500 cases. **00** not tasted. **Cape Riesling** ‡ Plump, muscat-scented **99** beginning to loose its zing. Drink up. 1 400 cases. **Chardonnay** ⚘ Sparky lemons/limes from nose to dry palate, satisfying **00** summer standalone or casual lunch partner. Unwooded (estate's first). 13,5% alc. 1 500 cases. **Sauvignon Blanc** ⚘ Grass in nose, mango in palate make a compatible pair in gentle, well made, drink-soon dry **00**. Med-bodied. 4 000 cases. **Muscat-Colombard** ⚘ Fragrant combo of muscat/tropical tones in lightish **00**, gently dry for easy satisfying quaffing. 800 cases. Also available (untasted): **Blanc de Blanc**.

....

Weskus see Winkelshoek

....

Western Wines

Not open to the public • Winemaker Rhyan Wardman • Production 400 000–500 000 cases • Western Wines Ltd, Glazeley, Bridgnorth, Shropshire WV16 6AB United Kingdom • Tel +44 174 678-9411 Fax +44 174 678-9501 • E-mail manager@western-wines.com • Website www.western-wines.com

"A TOUCH of vanilla, a sprinkling of pepper, and job well done," reads a red wine review in UK journal *Red & White*, "bottle it and ship it to Britain where they just can't get enough of this kind of thing." The subject happens to be the Kumala Merlot-Ruby Cabernet 99, but it might be any one of this explosively successful range owned by Western Wines of the UK and made locally under the internationally seasoned eye of Kiwi Rhyan Wardman. The newly appointed winemaker consults to the various Boland, Breede and Olifants river partner cellars, and oversees production and blending of the wines which now tumble into mainly the UK (but also Europe, Far East and US markets) at the astonishing rate of half a million cases a year. James Reid, Scots-born anchor for Western Wines in SA, says: "We're now selling the brand into virtually all the major supermarket and high street retailers in the UK. We've increased our spending and broadened our advertising campaign to include the general UK press and sports fixtures." Winner of a local Grape excellence in packaging award, the 'regular' Kumala range will soon include some single varieties such as Chardonnay and Pinotage. And this is just the beginning: "Our plan," reveals Reid, "is to develop Kumala from UK-SA brand into a global one."

Kumala range

✿ **Cabernet Sauvignon** Reserve Multi-layered **99** dense with red and black berry fruits (extra complexity from splash merlot), plus signature chewy tannin which could partner rustic food or be left to soften for yr/2. Spicily smooth texture, long finish. Oak well integrated. Stbosch fruit. 60% in new/2nd fill Radoux barriques, 14 mths; malo in barrel. 13,4% alc. 8 000 cases.

✿ **Merlot Reserve 99**, with dab cab, floral/violet scents over ripe plummy fruit, rich smoky oak background. Softish tannins for now or for keeping 2–4 yrs or with full flavoured cuisine. Stbosch fruit. New/2nd fill Radoux barriques, malo in barrel. 13,3% alc. 1 000 cases.

✿ **Cabernet-Shiraz** Roundness, balance are standout features of **00**, partly wooded 60/40 cuvée. Full, ripe mulberry/strawberry gliding to smooth long finish in very light smoky background. Super wine. 13% alc.

✿ **Colombard-Chardonnay** Spring-fresh **00** showcases pear/guava and fragrant honeysuckle with suggestion of vanilla oak. Immensely pleasing drink-young style, plumped by invisible sugar and broadened by partial malo. 70/30 blend, portion oak-staved. 12,8% alc. Worcester provenance.

Ruby Cabernet-Merlot ✿ 😊 They should patent the formula for this stylish everyday drink, succulently soft and quite warming (though alc not particularly high at 12,8% alc). 60/40 blend in **00**, partially oaked.

Merlot-Ruby Cabernet ✿ Ripe and plummy, some violets and green pepper savouriness adding frisson of complexity to **00** satisfying sipper. 60/40 blend, portion oak-staved. **Cinsault-Pinotage** ✿ Undemanding but most agreeable, well-crafted, touches of mulberry/strawberry and eucalyptus. Almost sweet farewell, clipped by good dry tannin. Lightly wooded 50/50 mix in **00**. **Semillon-Chardonnay** ✿ Well-made, crisp, nicely defined herby/hay-like flavours in **00**, some lemon/lime, clean dry finish. 60/40 mix, portion of semillon oak-staved, lees stirred for extra creaminess. 12,7% alc. From Worcester. **Chenin Blanc-Chardonnay** ✿ Fresh lemonade served here, plus white-peach and citrus with slick of oak on the side. Bright, med-bodied **00** summer-picnic wine or partner for lighter curries. 65/35 blend, 40% oak-staved. McGregor origin. **Sauvignon Blanc-Colombard** Med-bodied **00** sample shows ✿ promise in basket of crisp lemon/pear/tropical fruits and fragrant cut grass. Finish is brisk and dry. 50/50 blend ex-Worcester.

WhaleHaven Wines ⚑ ⚑ ⚑

Walker Bay (see Walker Bay map) • Tasting & sales Mon—Fri 9.30—5 Sat 10.30—1 Closed Sun & religious holidays • Tourgroups by appointment Fee R8 p/p • Animal farm for children • Owners Storm Kreusch, Robert & Maryke Middlemann, Dr & Mrs Alberto Bottega • Winemaker Storm Kreusch (since 1995), Anton de Vries (since 1997) • Production 6 000 cases • Private Bag X10 Hermanus 7200 • Tel (028) 316-1633 • Fax (028) 316-1640 • E-mail whwines@itec.co.za
EXPANSION AND SUCCESS are in the fragrant air of this small winery, founded in 1995. Winemaker Storm Kreusch, after having two daughters, now has a new crusher/destalker called Spitnick and a forklift named Moby Dick, as well as an extended cellar to cope with a 30% increase in production. Which is just as well for admirers, as WhaleHaven has now started exporting to countries as far apart as Canada and Malaysia and getting promises from the English press of being 'catapulted into international pinot stardom'. This, added to a second top-of-the-class rating for Pinot Noir in local *Wine* magazine taste-off. All the red grapes come from Oak Valley farm in Elgin, where this Stellenbosch University-trained and locally and internationally experienced winemaker works closely with the resident viticulturist. And

her name? Apparently it's an abbreviation of 'stormwind' a happy translation of 'Gail' by an Afrikaans schoolteacher, which has stuck, however inappropriately, to this firmly serene woman.

🐾 **Oak Valley Pinot Noir** Tasting together all four vintages thus far, and being struck by the development of **97** and **98**, suggests the extra half-star for these, entirely from new-clone grapes. **98** with raspberry aromas, gamey hints, voluptuous palate of velvet. Elegant, restrained, in more classic than New World manner, but also succulent and marvellously undisguised by excessive wood (mix of new/older Fr oak). 13% alc. **97** topped local pinot tastings for *Wine* 🐾 (as did **96**), travelled with the Blue Train; touch less powerfully structured, but possibly even finer, longer lasting. Both will amply reward few years' patience. Unfiltered. Maiden **95** 🐾 (pure BK5 clone) and more complex **96** 🐾 (14% BK5), both drinking well; earthy, farmyardy sweetness.

🐾 **Cabernet Franc Chélene** New After Kreusch's daughter, who pressingly announced her imminent arrival while Storm was racking this wine. **97** a once-off unfortunately, as it is a deliciously successful experiment. Fragrant with mineral, violet tones, silky elegant palate; good balance, touches of spice and herbs, long finish. Unfined, unfiltered (and just a bit cloudy), bottled by hand.

🐾 **Oak Valley Merlot** Minty chocolate and fruit-cake, as well as medicinal quality in **98** lead to fleshy, slightly baked, soft-tannin palate. 8 mths Fr oak. **97** 🐾 shade less rich and structured.

🐾 **Oak Matured Chardonnay** Intelligent, restrained wooding in **98** allows panoply of lovely, almost perfumed, aromas to emerge. Hints of nuts, butter, citrus lead to well-integrated silky palate, lingering crisp finish. Genuinely dry, and not too powerful at 13,2% alc. Grapes from Kaaimansgat near Villiersdorp; fermentation/maturation mix new/older Fr oak, 9 mths on lees. **97** from Elgin/Walker Bay grapes: nuts and apricot aromas, creamy/citrus flavours and refreshing acidity.

🐾 **Sauvignon Blanc Millenium** [sic] Twist of herbiness adds interest to usual melons, guavas, passionfruit in non-reductive **00** from Walker Bay grapes; broad flavours with good integrated acidity. Should be even better with 6–12 mths in the bottle. 13% alc.

Cabernet Sauvignon Oak Valley 🐾 Fragrant brambleberry and cassis, with hint of coffee in **97**, plenty of fruit and good grip of tannin, 'savoury' acidity. 13% alc.

Baleine Noir 🐾 Fun wine with a touch of the serious (or vice-versa?). Whiffs of stalky mintiness, cherry in **98**, soft fruit-laden tannins and slight natural petillance from semi-carbonic maceration of mostly merlot (15% cab f). A food wine, suggests Storm, and best lightly chilled.

Wide River see Robertson Winery

Wildekrans Estate　　　　　🍷 🍷 🍷 🍷

Walker Bay (see Walker Bay map) • Tasting & sales daily 8—5.30 at Orchard Farm Stall on N2 near Grabouw (closed Christmas Day) Tasting for tourgroups by appointment • Cellar tours by appointment • Breakfast, lunch, snacks, farm produce available at Orchard Farm Stall, or bring your own picnic • Play area for children • Proclaimed conservation area • Wheelchair-friendly • Owner Bruce Elkin, EK Green • Winemaker Jacques Fourie (since 1997) • Viticulturist Barry Anderson (since 1990) • Vineyards 50 ha • Production 400 — 500 tons, 10 000 cases (150 tons, 8 000 cases own label) 60% red 40% white • PO Box 200 Elgin 7180 • Tel (021) 859-5587 • Fax (028) 284-9872/ (028) 284-9902 • E-mail houw@mweb.co.za

THE FORCES of nature have been slipped a copy of this estate's strategy documents it seems: the focus is on intensifying fruit flavours from the 50 ha vineyards — and that's exactly what a pre-Christmas hailstorm achieved. The crop was halved; concentration was naturally boosted: the vintage of 2000 is good, powerful news. Perhaps even better than 98 — which produced a Pinotage rated best of all tasted by the UK's *Wine* magazine, and a Chardonnay selected for the Nederburg Auction. Owner Dr Bruce Elkin and winemaker Jacques Fourie have a double vision here: building the Wildekrans reputation for a "serious" range (like the Barrel Selection Pinotage, all new French oak and bush vines) and single vineyard wines — as well as offering easy, everyday-drinkers. Made across the board "as naturally as possible" with what Fourie believes are essentials for winemakers — "romance and daring".

✿✿ Pinotage Barrel Selection First release **98** introduced a new benchmark for pinotage in this cool Walker Bay area. **99** ✿ restates the case in this powerfully concentrated, earthy/tarry follow-up. Deepest purple/plum colour mirrors mulberry/choc/blackberry intensity, which spills into palate to taut, vibrant mocha finish. Like pvs, delicious in infancy, but deserves time to reach maturity. Only 408 cases. Low-cropping bushvines. Yr new Fr oak. 14% alc. Also in 1,5 ℓ magnums. Standard **Pinotage** ✿ **99** repeats vibrancy of pvs, red/wild berry whiffs reverberate in juicy palate with fennel and understated oak spice from yr in 2nd/3rd fill Fr casks. Strapping 14% alc doesn't intrude. 825 cases.

✿ Cabernet Sauvignon Standout **98** VG, with splash pinotage, best since **96** proudly clanked off with Jan Smuts trophy as SA national grand champ. Warm blackcurrant/eucalyptus, firm minerally texture and bone-dry finish, in classic claret style. Yr Fr oak, some new. 14% alc. 1 422 cases.

✿ Merlot Given the choice, Jacques Fourie wouldn't share **98** with anyone: "I'm crazy about merlot and want this one all to myself." Plush, enveloping style (14% alc) strawberry/cassis and hints plum in ripe, sweet tasting palate, which silkily glides to clean dry finish. Good food wine. 422 cases. **97** accessible on release, elegant.

✿ Osiris Flagship Bdx blend in elegant, creamy style, with vanilla/mocha richness nicely contrasted with ripe tannins and dusty, dry finish. Ample plum (almost plum-*pudding*)/cherry flavours, plus smoky/spicy aromas in **98**, sole release to date. Half cab and equal merlot, cab f. Yr Fr oak. 14% alc. After Egyptian god of agriculture.

✿ Sauvignon Blanc ▼ Attractive **00** with ripe melon/fig and, more pungently, capsicum aromas, turning to brightly illuminated lemony tastes and tart, attention grabbing finish. 12% alc. 500 cases. Credible follow-up to Loire-like **99** ✿, with flinty/racy palate, fine steely finish. Good maturation potential.

✿ Semillon ▼ Yr down the road, full-bodied **99** seriously delicious. Figgy whiffs a la Australia's Margaret River; fat, sleek yet structured (partly by 14% alc) with almost edible toast-and-marmalade finish. 3–4 mths Fr oak, none new. 365 cases.

Chenin Blanc ✿ 🍷 Tasty example of more serious, oaked Cape chenin: toasted nuts over fruit salad and cream. 3 mths in wood plus low (5 g/ℓ) acidity smooth **00**'s edges. 13,5% alc. 976 cases.

Cabernet Franc-Merlot ✿ Bruce Elkin a big fan of this blend — 90/10 ratio in **99** (cab f slightly higher proportion than first **98**). Smoky 'green olive' aromas with wild berries; some resonant earth/leather, which contrast pleasingly with ripe cassis. Good youthful quaffing with some maturation potential. ±Yr oaked. 13,5% alc. 583 cases. **Chardonnay** ✿ **00** barrel sample oak-driven mid-2000, but plenty tropical fruit waiting in wings to restore the balance. 6 mths, new/2nd fill Fr oak. 334 cases. **Caresse Marine** ✣ Attractive (both taste and looks — winner of Grape inaugural excellence in packaging award) **00** returns to this guide as dry chenin/semillon blend with tangy kiwifruit and extra-dry, seafood-friendly finish. 13,5% alc. 605 cases.

Wilhelmshof

Stellenbosch • Not open to the public • Owners Nico & Petra van der Merwe • Winemaker Nico van der Merwe • Production 25 tons 2 000 cases 100% red • PO Box 12200 Stellenbosch 7613 • Tel/fax (021) 903-9507

THESE FIRST OWN-LABEL WINES are bringing immense pleasure to Nico van der Merwe who, as incumbent winemaker at Saxenburg, has built a following that stretches around the world. It's not just that the self-admitted maverick gets free reign here. Much of the fun comes from working with his signature grape, syrah, of which it seems he can't get enough (he's been working back-to-back crushes annually at Saxenburg and its twin, Ch Capion in the south of France, for several years). For his solo act, van der Merwe's aiming for "Rhône-style mature red wines for medium prices". Future plans are to build up a market for his label, and move production of the grapes (and in the long run vinification) to quiet Bot River, where he and super keen, highly informed wife Petra, a partner in the adventure, have some land they are champing to develop.

✿Robert Alexander Shiraz Draws gasps of astonishment, disbelief at blind tastings: can these really be extra toasty Olifants River vyds? Answer is yes: 95% from (here's the secret) *cooler* Vredendal slopes (remainder ex-Stbosch), made to vdM's specs by his brother, Robert Alexander van der Merwe (aka Alkie), cellarmaster at Travino. Blueprint is stylish, drinkable Côtes du Rhône, which **99** evokes: generous spice and chocolate; warm, savoury tastes; dense, supple texture, rounded dryness. Good now, can mature few yrs. 7–8 yr old vines, 10 t/ha yield; 10 mths used casks; bottled at S'burg. 13% alc. 1 500 cases.

Mas Nicolas Too young to rate, this first release **99** shiraz/cab shows all vd Merwe's thumbprint richness, polish, balance. Minerally spice, wild scrub tones of shiraz clearly defined, as is cab's cassis freshness, yet both harmonious. Statement wine, world apart from Gwendolyn cab-shiraz made by vdM at Saxenburg. 60/40 Kuils River/Stbosch fruit. Yr Fr oak, 60% new. To be released only after 2½ yrs, when should rate min ✿. 13,5% alc. Price around R120/bottle. 500 cases.

Windfall

Robertson • PO Box 802 Robertson 6705 • Tel/fax (023) 626-4498

IRREPRESSIBLE EDDIE BARLOW had barely touched down on his new farm in the Agterkliphoogte Valley when the former SA all-rounder was tapped by the Bangladeshi cricket authorities to coach first the development team, and latterly the national side. So off he took, leaving a live-in manager and flying viticulturist Eugene van Zyl to tend the replantings of pinotage, merlot, ruby cab and viognier. His and wife Cally's fine-wine making aspirations were further stumped when 'Bunter' collapsed at his Dhaka home after suffering a stoke in early 2000. Bouncing back, the formidably determined Barlow hopes to bottle something this year, "so we may get one of our mates to do it". Meanwhile the 2000 crop was sold off in bulk.

Windmeul Co-op

Paarl (see Paarl map) • Tasting & sales Mon—Fri 8—12.30; 13.30—5 • Cellar tours by appointment • Owners 54 members • Manager/winemaker Danie Marais (since 1999) • Winemaker Hugo Lambrechts (since 1999) • Viticulturist Paul Wallace (VineWise) • Production 9 200 tons (1 500 cases own label) 70% white 30% red • PO Box 2013Windmeul 7630 • Tel (021) 863-8043/8100 • Fax (021) 863-8614 • E-mail windmeul@iafrica.com

HERE'S LIQUID frustration for you. Such very nice wine in such short supply. Only a relative trickle of the crop handled by this cellar — making 1 500 cases — appears under its own label, available directly to the public. The rest disappears anonymously into other people's bottles. So it's advisable to be very quick off the mark to sample the latest attractions here, which feature more reds by the vintage from the 54 member-growers of the co-op — and updated cellar technology to match. Winemaker Hugo Lambrechts, fired up by a recent visit to California, and equally new manager Danie Marais are enthusiasm personified.

✿ **Cabernet Sauvignon-Merlot** 🏆 String of VGs for this well made, unpretentious New World style red, all the more attractive for its amazingly low price. **98** heralded fresh level of excitement with excellent tannin structure, well-defined succulent fruit. Follow-up **99** (sample) same quality/character but less immediately accessible, plum-pud and coffee/choc opulence bound by tight tannins which need probably 2–3 yrs to relax. Yr 225 ℓ Fr casks. ± 13% alc. ± 250 cases.

✿ **Cabernet Sauvignon** 🏆 Latest **99** (barrel sample) potentially better than **98**, which set New World forward-fruity tone combined with sappy, ready tannin. **00**'s mulberry/cassis joined by sweet choc and cinnamon in deep-flavoured palate. Yr Fr oak. 13,5% alc. 350 cases.

✿ **Merlot** 🏆 Tangy acidity and supple tannin set the stage for **00** sweet-violet/ripe plum/roast coffee performance, with extra cinnamon spice for interest; very long fruitily-sweet finish. 375 cases. Sample tasted; promises improvement on **98**, with fine mineral texture. Yr Fr oak. 13,5% alc

Chenin Blanc ✿✿ 😊 Vibrant, tropically outfitted **00** tastes charmingly fresh, ends zippily dry. Unwooded. 500 cases.

Pinotage NEW Extra-ripe picked (26 °B), oak-matured **00** (barrel sample) shows great promise: lashings of sweet plums/cherries in a chalky basket, wrapped with succulent tannins which coat the palate and trail to crisp dry finish. 270 cases. **Chardonnay 00** (sample) satisfying mouthful of lime and lees, some toasty/smoky oak and sweetish ripe-fruit impression; touch of butterscotch and citrus in bright, fresh finish. Fr oak fermented/matured. Potential ✿. 270 cases. **Merry Mill Red** Let's-party **NV** quaffer features fresh summer-berry aromas and lip-smacking tastes. In friendly 500 ml 'dumpy'. Unrated.

. . . .

Winds of Change see Sonop
Wine Concepts see Sommelier's Choice

. . . .

Winecorp

Chairman Faisal Rahmatallah • CEO Johann Laubser • Group winemaker Ben Radford • Vineyards & viticulture Gerrie Wagener • Brand executive Renske Minnaar • National sales manager Bryan Culhane • PO Box 99 Lynedoch 7603 • Tel (021) 881-3690 • Fax (021) 881-3699 • E-mail winecorp@iafrica.com

EPITOMISING THE NEW-MILLENNIUM shake-up in the South African wine industry, this group represents a basket of brands for which Winecorp provides an umbrella service. The corporate mission, says chairman Faisal Rahmatallah, goes beyond claiming local pole position; Winecorp's engines are being tuned to take on the world. While centralisation anchors the operation, with shared bottling, shipment, marketing and exports (British MW Adrian Garforth heads Winecorp Europe), admin/finance and viticulture services (through Afrika Vineyards, overseen by ex-Anglo Gerrie Wagener), diversity is the core production principle. Australian Ben Radford, the winemaking chief, is not overseeing a giant fruit salad here. Each winery is specifically dedicated to a style, or a region or even a price tier. For details of Winecorp's stable of ranges, refer to separate entries under Spier, Longridge, Savanha and Capelands.

. . . .

Winelands see International Wine Services
Wine Village see Hermanus Heritage Collection

. . . .

Wine Warehouse

Tasting & sales at Enoteca outlets (Cape Peninsula) Newlands: Mon—Fri 10—9 Sat 9—7 City (Buitengracht Street): Mon—Fri 9—8 Sat 9—5 • Tourgroups • Gifts • Conferencing • "Definitely no mountain biking!" • Monthly Wine Fair • Regular tutored tastings • Wheelchair-friendly • Owners Oscar & Andrea Foulkes • Production 80 000 cases • PO Box 16571 Vlaeberg 8018 • Tel (021) 424-4060 • Fax (021) 424-9196 • E-mail oscar@wine-warehouse.co.za

IN CALIFORNIA, 'garage' wines are all the rage — they're the micro scale, hand sculpted, after hours creations of, say, plastic surgeons or commodity brokers — anybody but fulltime winemakers — emanating from anything but conventional wineries. Difficult to find, impossibly priced, but for the raves in the sniffazines, you might suspect they were more urban legend than reality. Oscar Foulkes' wine business did begin in a garage; he isn't a winemaker (commentating on races of the horsey sort was more his nosebag); wines like his Mystery range have been a runaway success. But happily for everyday consumers, he's not the Cape cousin of the US *garagiste*. Quite the opposite. Good old-fashioned value and friendly, non-snooty wines in respectable quantities (80 000 cases), cost-savingly packaged, are what he ferrets for in winelands here and abroad, and what he, with wife Andrea, purveys — plus many other goodies — in the couple's chic Enotecas in Cape Town.

Oscar's Easy Red ✿ ☺ Easy's the word — on eye (Grape Packaging Award winner), palate, pocket — but not insipid: good earthy strawberry tang; quite European feel. For drinking young, lightly chilled, "with sushi, spicy curries, classic European — whatever". SAA selection, Wine of the Month Club best value red blend. Ruby cab, cinsaut, pinot noir. 500 ml screwtop. 36 000 cases. **Mystery Dry Red** ✿ ☺ Quality/value reprised in latest (**NV**), lurid purple/plum colour, succulent plum, berry, fruitcake tastes, usual broad easy palate. Chill lightly for carefree summer splashing. Unoaked ruby cab/cinsaut. 13,5% alc needs watching here and in white below. 8 800 cases. **Mystery Dry White** ✿ ☺ Bit of a formula switch (from straight chenin to chenin/chardonnay), but who's noticing? Slaphappy gulpability's unchanged: lemon/dried apricot tang in **00**, dollop sugar for extra-smooth mouthfeel. Monster bargain at ±R9. 13,5% alc. 8 800 cases.

Mystery Reserve Sauvignon Blanc Latest 00 not ready for tasting, but on track record should rate at least ✿. Best-seller in range. 8 000 cases. **Mystery Melon** ✿ Bags of ripe pineapple (from Ferdinand de Lesseps grapes?) in latest version of this light, carefree, sweetish **NV**, with delicate nip of acidity for freshness. Earns extra marks for originality, non-grabby pricing. 2 000 cases. **Mystery Reserve Brut Cava** Bottle fermented sparkle from Spain, so unrated. 1 000 cases.

Winkelshoek Wine Cellar

Piketberg (see Swartland map) • Tasting & sales Mon—Fri 8-5 Sat 8—1 Tasting fee R1 p/p • Restaurant daily 8 am—9 pm • Gifts • Owners Hennie Hanekom & Jurgens Brand • Winemaker Hennie Hanekom (since 1984) • PO Box 395 Piketberg 7320 • Tel (022) 913-1092 • Fax (022) 913-1095 E-mail winhoek@intekom.co.za

HENNIE HANEKOM's jauntily labelled Weskus quaffing range is available for tasting and sale from the restaurant/visitor centre at the N7/R44 intersection near Piketberg. Also available are sherries and a variety of spirits. The range, untasted for this ed, includes **Vin Rouge**, **Grand Cru**, **Blanc de Blanc**, **Late Harvest**, **White/Red Muscadel/Jerepiko**, **Hanepoot**, **Ruby Port**.

Woolworths

Category manager (wine/beverages) Howard Kotze tel (021) 407-2530 • Selection manager (wine/beer) Allan Mullins tel (021) 407-2777 wwamu@woolworths.co.za • Assistant selector (wine/fresh juices/beer) Jenny Ratcliffe tel (021)

407-2956 wwjrat@woolworths.co.za • Senior Buyer (wine/beverages/beer) Ivan Oertle tel (021) 407-2762 wwioe@woolworths.co.za • Selector's assistant John Leukes (021) 407-2853 wwjle@woolworths.co.za

WHY DOES this nationwide chain give its wine team such dreary designations? Cape Wine Master Allan Mullins is 'selection manager'; colleague Ivan Oertle is 'senior buyer'; new recruit Jenny Ratcliffe is 'assistant selector'. They sound like a bunch of bureaucrats, providing just another stock item on the Woolies shelves. Nothing could be more misleading. Mullins whirls about the winelands in a fever of enthusiasm so infectious that he's got many of the best winemakers in the Cape giving these wines their very personal touch, and others panting to join the band. Keeping him (more or less) on the straight and narrow for 10 years (with never the slightest disagreement) has been Ivan Oertle, exactly the sort of calm and collected maestro of minutiae necessary to turn wild schemes into practical realities, keep tabs on the 250 000 cases Woolies now sells per year. Naturally, Oertle is an acute taster and trend-spotter himself. Jenny Ratcliffe, sparkling daughter of Norma and Stan of Warwick Estate, was into wine practically from the moment she was born. These people aren't just sourcing and purveying a product, they're finding and delivering excitement and romance. And, of course, outstanding value. The pity, in the past, has been that not every Woolies features wine, but that's about to change: there'll be specialist wine stores in every branch by 2002, all fitted out with wooden wine boxes — not a sterile shelf in sight.

Reserve range

Exclusive to Woolworths; all in suitably smart livery featuring imported bottles.

- **Cabernet Sauvignon** ✔ Villiera's Jeff Grier's are the hands which created pvs **97** *Wine* ✿ and current **98** ✿✿ for this flagship range. Latter from exceptional red wine yr, so marginally fuller, richer, though resolutely classic, restrained (where Signature cab below is in-your-face), harmonious enough for drinking but with enough creamy fruit concentration for development over 5-7 yrs. 13% alc.

- **Pinotage** Powerhouse **98** showcases pinotage at its ripest. Inky purple glow, fruity richness dressed in smart new oak; blockbuster flavours, some raspberry high notes, texture of tender steak (good accompaniment too). Yr Fr oak, all new. In distinctive long-necked brown bottle. From Kaapzicht.

- **Cabernet-Shiraz** This probably 'readiest' of the Reserves, though **97** could go few more yrs. Plum pudding, some cigarbox (from Fr oaking), hint stewed fruit. Classic rather than trumpeting style (so won't interrupt dinner conversation unnecessarily). From La Motte.

- **Grenache-Syrah** The now customary off-beat, individual tastes here in sappy profusion: peppery spice, wild herbs, gamey excitement. **99** also features soft tannins for interesting solo sipping or at table with venison, casseroles and other dense-textured dishes. From Ken Forrester. ±13% alc.

- **Chardonnay Reserve** ✔ Even chardonnay-averse consumers should find something pleasurable to sniff/taste in gracefully complex **99**; with oak perfectly balanced to set off soft, creamy chardonnay fruit, create harmony, agreeable dryness. Full-bodied but not heavy. Satisfying. Barrel selection from Neil Ellis's Stbosch chardonnays. 13,5% alc.

- **Wild Yeast Chardonnay** New ✔ Creamy, mouthfilling lees, lemons and limes star in this **98** chardonnay, fermentation with natural yeasts adds complexity (some tangy nettle, herby extras). Full-bodied (13,5% alc), rich and delicious. From Springfield.

- **Barrel Reserve Chenin Blanc** ✔ Rich honey, almond tastes in **99**, darkly smoky/toasty undertones and hint of botrytis. Supple, juicy texture. Passionate chenin image-booster (and restaurateur/vintner) Ken Forrester's an influence here, though this version is less lavishly oaked than his own bottling. Outstanding value at ±R24 ("R50's more like it!", boggles Forrester). 13% alc.

✿ **Constantia Reserve Sauvignon Blanc** No **99**, so **00** "rushed in" — Buiten-verwachting, source of the wine, known for late-blooming sauvignons, so no mad rush to uncork; give bit of time for powerful, almost massive gooseberry/capsicum flavours to develop. On other hand, tastes rather good now ...

Noble Late Harvest Chenin Blanc Barrel Reserve ✿ Immediate impression of mellow ripeness carries through into **99** palate where an arrangement of fruits (peach/apricot/melon) brushes with botrytis. As with pvs **98**, lively finish, lowish 76 g/ℓ sugar ensure compatibility at either end of a meal (though generous 13,8% alc needs watching if you plan to start, rather than end, here!). Delicious now, should mature interestingly. Partially barrel-matured. 375 ml. From Ken Forrester. **Fields of Gold** ✿ New Evocatively named **NV** dessert reveals itself in silky waves of penetrating sweetness. More texture/honey than fruit, but attractive, if somewhat offbeat, flavours. From Ashanti. 500 ml.

Signature series

New

Incidental range, only in exceptional vintages.

✿ **Cabernet Sauvignon** Bushy tailed Bruce Jack of Flagstone (cellar at the V&A Waterfront in Cape Town) kicks off this prestige range with **99** cracker from selected Helderberg fruit. Defiantly New World, it bowls you over with whacks of dense flavour (berries, cherries, tobacco — the whole cab number, including melt-in-mouth choc). Massive, almost bulky, it deserves time to mellow and grow.

Millennium Collection

Features the following wines: Celebration (in frosted bottles) and Collection (in bottles imported from France).

✿ **Celebration Cabernet Sauvignon-Merlot** Rich savoury **98** tones contrast pleasingly with ripe red cherries and plums; soft dry tannins. From Swartland Winery.

✿ **Millennium Collection Shiraz-Cabernet Sauvignon Reserve 98** developing seductive Rhônish touches of silky choc, aromatic spice and savoury plums (Fr clone features here). Brush of Am oak adds more spice, vanilla roundness to cab's firm structure. From La Motte.

✿ **Millennium Collection Chardonnay Reserve** Stylish, sensuous wine which packs its almost opulent riches into a sleek, firmly dry frame. **98** firm toasty, limey bouquet; creamy, leesy-rich palate which tapers to fine citrus finish. Barrel fermented. From Neil Ellis (Stbosch origin).

✿ **Millennium Collection Brut Reserve NV** Soft, creamy feel, enhanced by streams of finest effervescence, very pure, refined, fresh dough/baked bread tones. High pinot content (60%, remainder chardonnay) lends satisfying mouth-filling quality. 3 yrs ageing on lees. From Villiera.

Celebration Sauvignon Blanc ✿ See under Vins de Cuvée above. **Celebration Cuvée Brut** ✿ Lightish carbonated sparkler with some richness, creaminess, from high proportion chardonnay. Though labelled extra-dry, this **NV** not aggressive.

Terroir range

These reflect specific regional character, winemaking culture. Limited availability, no more than 500 cases of one-off wines; labels change regularly.

✿ **Cabernet Sauvignon** Cab in slim, tailored mode, not exhaustingly alcoholic (12,5%). **97**, like Merlot below, which from same farm/vintage, growing mintier, more herbaceous with time (reflection of cooler clime?). 'Sweet' ripe fruit still more than match for prominent but supple tannins. Origin Wildekrans.

✿ **Cabernet Sauvignon-Merlot** Rich, muscular red, improving in bottle. **97** reflects warmth of Bottelary area's west-facing vineyards; intensely fruity (but not fruit driven), balanced by dense, lush tannins. One for winter, game dishes. Ex-Kaapzicht.

✿ **Semillon** Released with yrs' bottle age, **99** offers fine complexity, plenty of character. Old World aura, almost 'wild' (some pleasing cheesy smells, green olive tastes); very dry, so versatile at table. From Wildekrans.

Merlot ✿ **97** acquiring eucalyptus/choc flavour spectrum, some woody elements to go with the stewed fruit. Tough tannins suggest this for further keeping (short term only) or now the more rustic portion of your culinary repertoire. *Wine* ✿. From Wildekrans.

Premium range

✿✿ **Cabernet Sauvignon-Merlot** ✅ Suggest buy now before they change their minds! Bargain priced at R40, deserves to be elevated into the Reserve collection. **98** (excellent vintage) open, generous, wonderfully ripe, mouthfilling berries with swirling violets, tobacco, mocha. With classic Neil Ellis firmness, restraint. 13,0% alc.

✿ **Rhine Riesling** ✅ Now offered young (prior to **99** aged a bit before release). Latest **00** off-dry with perky floral, peppery aromas; equally racy palate. Charming in youth, but track record suggests will mature well. From Villiera.

> **Grand Rouge** ✿ **99** arguably best value in entire range. It's tasty (plenty of concentrated, sweet-ripe blackberry fruit with oaky hints) and though not designed as stayer, could age few yrs if needed. But somehow that's unlikely. From La Motte.

Merlot ✿ Smart packaging (evoking refined opulence of Rupert-Koegelenberg owned La Motte, where this **99** was made), smart tastes ("juicy and sexy", per Allan Mullins): ripe merlot plums fragranced with violet, soft tannins and breezy acidity. 13% alc. **Shiraz** ✿ **98**, with smoky/toasty tones and savoury zing, something to pour before, during and after Sunday BBQ. Perhaps even lightly chilled. Big 13,5% alc. From Rooiberg. **Bush Vine Shiraz** ✿ Different source to above, so different taste but same soft, smooth drinkability. **98** husky, full-bodied almost rustic; heather, wild scrub scents. Oak matured. 13% alc. From Swartland. **Cabernet Franc-Merlot** ✿ 'French' character about **99** bouquet, though palate touch jammy, dense, with spicy depths. Good long finish. Oak matured 50/50 blend from Seidelberg. **Sauvignon Blanc** ✿ Bot River's cooler climate reflected in **00**'s pure gooseberry, chalky sleekness complemented by moderate 12,5% alc. Very fresh finishing. From Wildekrans. **Chardonnay-Pinot Noir** ✿ Versatile white table companion (from Cabrière, with its own upper crust restaurant attached), delicate orangey tones in lightish **00**. Extra-ripe raspberry/strawberry fruit tastes almost sweet yet finishes crisply dry.

Vins de Cuvée

Mid priced ("under-priced, actually, because we're just nice people") cork-closed range — whites under R20, reds under R30). 750 ml bottles. Some of these also in new Flexibles range — see below.

Pinotage ✿ Big, robust, 'sweet', juicy **98**. Warm climate pinotage with banana touch, tangy dry finish. Customer favourite from Rooiberg. **Maison Rouge** ✦ Friendly everyday **NV** red. Quietly fruity, soft, unassertive tannins. Ruby cab, cinsaut, cab, merlot blend ex Ashwood. **Rosé** ✿ Shimmering pink off-dry **00** showcases bright, smooth tropical fruit and brisk acidity for refreshing summer quaffing. Chenin, muscat, pinot blend from Villiera. **Blanc de Noir** ✿ Versatile off-dry sundowner or partner to Provençal-type dishes. **99** now showing some honeyed bottle development to original redcurrant/wild strawberry tang. From Swartland. **Chardonnay** ✦ Limes, buttered toast in **00**, med-bodied and most agreeable. Portion oaked for smooth spicy interest. From Robertson Winery. **Chenin Blanc** ✦ Off-dry

00 for enjoying in youthful prime, when dainty tropical tones still fresh, lively. From Rooiberg. **Sauvignon Blanc** ✷ Ultra-zesty **00** drinks easily, gratifies; green pepper, nettle tones which should still be fresh and breezy ±yr from now. From Robertson Winery. **Chenin Blanc-Chardonnay** ✷ Smooth, tropical with light oaky spice and some ginger tang. Firm, good body/balance, sound dry finish. Chenin portion barrel fermented, matured 4 mths. From Seidelberg.

Cabernet Sauvignon ✷ 😊 Invariably good early quaffing, **99** with uninhibited black/red berry fruit; juiciness emphasised by near-invisible tannins. Lightly oaked. From Bergsig. **Cape Riesling** ✷ 😊 Generous splash Rhine riesling raises the quaffing quotient in latest **00**. Fresh, spritely hay/honey flavours mill in good dry palate. Can age a bit. From Weltevrede. **Blanc de Blanc** ✷ 😊 Compatible, quaffable chenin/sauvignon equal partnership in latest (**NV**) bottling; cut grass/guava ripeness, easy dry finish. From Villiera. **Muscat-Colombard** ✷ 😊 Good curry wine, says Ivan Oertle; appetising apéritif too, especially in drink-young **00** with reduced sugar level for more sophisticated feel. Some exotic papaya scents. From Weltevrede.

'Selected' range

Dry Red ✷ Soft, juicy, uncluttered mulberry, spice flavours. More likely to be found in shoppers' trolleys than any of the bottled reds. NV 'All-SA' blend cinsaut, ruby cab. From Simonsvlei. **Cape White** ✷ 12 000 cases of this low priced NV crowd pleaser purchased annually. Lightish bodied, zippy tropical whiffs; bit of sweetness for extra charm, drinkability. Colombard from Rooiberg. **Late Harvest** ✱ 'People's wine' with near-universal appeal. Ripe, slightly raisiny, clean; lowish sugar for smoothness rather than sweetness. From Simonsvlei.

Three Springs range

In distinctive blue bottles (from Uruguay, nogal). White available at special promotional price of ±R15 until mid-2001.

Red ✷ Lots of varieties and even two different countries (SA, France) go into this **NV** blend. But no need to piece them all together: just open and enjoy the light, fruity, peppery/savoury flavours. From Saxenburg. **White** ✷ **00** gem of a dry white: soft, butterscotchy, smoky, with super-drinkable lime zestiness throughout. Lightly oaked semillon/chardonnay. From Delheim.

'Lite' range

Bianca Light ✱ Note the dieter-friendly low alc (9,5%). Which sometimes equates to insipid, but not here: plenty of aromatic flavour (fresh grapes/muscat/peaches) and even bit of body. Deservedly popular off-dry. From Delheim.

Nouveau range

Gamay Noir ✷ 😊 Juicy and packed with bright, fragrant fruit for buying/drinking today (don't keep this or Blanc below hanging about — not made to age). Good on its own or with picnics, leisurely patio meals.

Blanc ✷ Irresistible quaffing style: fruity, juicy, satisfying. Party waiting to happen. Above **00**s from Villiera.

'Zesties'

New

Friendly, affordable range for wine-newcomers. From Ashwood.

Juicy Red ✷ 😊 Glides smoothly across the palate; plenty of (juicy, yes) cherry flavour, grind of pepper, too, for partnering with food. **Zesty White** ✷ 😊 Sappy, gulpable style: tropical fruit salad flavours, smooth and mouthfilling. Ex Ashwood/Bergsig/Wamakersvallei.

Méthode cap classiques

✵**Vintage Reserve Brut** (blue label) Terrifically rich, sensuous and just a bit decadent. **93** with delicious biscuity, new-baked-bread flavours extended by slow, fine bubble. Brisk dry finish. Sophisticated table partner (oysters, caviar, crayfish etc) but also solo sipper, anytime morale booster. Pinot/chardonnay (60/40), 5 yrs on lees, 18 mths on cork. From Villiera.

✵**Brut** (Red label) Dew-fresh pinpoint bubble with hints of toasty biscuits and yeast. Friendly, affordable and fun. Versatile, too: breakfast kick-starter, patio pick-me-up, sundown sipper. Super example of this unintimidating style, from Villiera's Jeff Grier; who practically invented it. Pinot noir, chardonnay, pinotage, chenin. Moderate 12,5% alc. Flies off the shelves. **NV**.

✵**Brut Rosé** See-through lacy lingerie-pink sparkler, easily appreciated through transparent bottle. Easygoing strawberry/raspberry flavour with just a touch of yeast to remind this is a 'proper' MCC. Pop today and pour with anything from carpaccio to strawberries and cream. Traditional pinot noir/chardonnay with colour input from pinotage. From Villiera.

Basic sparklers

Spumanté Rosé ⁂ Romantic sunset-pink semi-sweet fizz sends out quaff-me-quick invitation with chewing gum, wild strawberry flavours and cinnamon tang. Low 9,5% alc. **NV** from red muscadel. Ex-Rooiberg, **Brut** ⁂ Perky **NV** bubbly with liveliness enhanced by grassy hints from 70% sauvignon blanc (balance chardonnay). Dry but soft feel, effected by grain sugar, ensures ongoing popularity. From Rooiberg. **Spumanté** ⁂ Hugely popular honeysuckle-scented light fizz, fresh, smooth but not oversweet. **NV** gewürz/chenin mix.

'Flexibles' **New**

500 ml, 1 ℓ, 2 ℓ vintage-dated varietal wines in flexible packs. From Robertson Winery. **Dry Red** ⁂ Same as Selected Cape Red. **Merlot** ⁂ Sniff here and be reminded of baked cherry pudding, which might be a good, if unusual, after-dinner accompaniment, though **00** versatile enough to partner savoury dishes too. **Chardonnay** ⁑ See under Vins de Cuvée above. **Sauvignon Blanc** ⁂ See under Vins de Cuvée above. **Blanc de Blanc** ⁑ Bright, tropical, refreshing. Chenin with splash colombard. Softly dry. **Late Harvest** ⁑ Same as Selected Late Harvest above.

Bag in boxes

Following in 500 ml, 1 ℓ 'combiblocs', 5 ℓ boxes. Filled 'on demand' for freshness; all NV, medium-bodied, 11-11,5% alc. from Simonsvlei. **Dry Red** ⁂ Same as Selected Cape Red. **Premier Grand Cru** ⁑ Flies off shelves faster than any other in the range. Same as Blanc de Blanc above. **Stein** ⁑ Chenin in very laid-back mood. Shyly sweet. **Bouquet Blanc** ⁑ Fragrant grapey flavours, (from dash aromatic hanepoot), smooth rather than sweet. Also: popular **Glühwein**, **Sangria** and various wine 'coolers'.

Yellow Cellar see Helderkruin

Yonder Hill

Stellenbosch (see Helderberg map) • Tasting, sales, cellar tours by appointment • Views • Wheelchair-friendly • Owners Naudeé Family • Winemaker/viticulturist David Lockley (since 1998) • Vineyards 10 ha • Production 100 tons 8 000 cases 90% red 10% white • PO Box 914 Stellenbosch 7599 • Tel (021) 855-1008 • Fax (021) 855-1006

DAVID LOCKLEY once said of Yonder Hill's cellar: "I call it a peep show. You can see all of it no matter where you stand." Fortunately the cellar was enlarged in time for the 2000 harvest: "Space at last! The underground cellar works well, the new cooling plant is a dream," continues this quirky mechanic turned winemaker, whose wines are "destalked, crushed, fermented and matured to the sounds of classical music". "Wine was always my hobby, now it's my job," he remarks with immense satisfaction. (And cars would now seem to be his hobby: he's restoring a Karmann Ghia at the moment.) During the recent building, some bottles of iNanda were encased in the fireplace in the tasting centre — "the boss doesn't know I used the good stuff" he quips — for future archeologists to discover. Lucky them — it was one of the great years for this red blend. This busy winemaker (he's always tinkering, weighing, measuring bunches, experimenting with oak, or leaf cover) operates on an instinctive level: "I wait until I dream about harvesting, then I bring in the grapes," he says, but always harvesting too late rather than too early. "You can't ever get rid of those green flavours once they're there." Now he's on a personal quest to produce "the best merlot in the world".

✿ **Cabernet Sauvignon** New Elegance, restraint hallmarks of maiden **98**, from cleaned-up old clones emitting familiar green pepper/plum/mulberry tones, folded with subtle fragrant cedary oak. Ample youthful tannins deserve time to soften. 18 mths Fr oak. 13,5% alc.

✿ **Merlot** ✔ Signature rich, mocha/savoury notes joined by violets/plums/black choc in complex **99**, with thimble cab. Mouthfilling flavours enriched by vanilla from 2 yrs new Fr oak; enveloping 'sweet' tannins, which augur well for development over 5–6 yrs. 13% alc. Pvs **98** big but balanced. **97** minerally, chocolate mousse character.

✿ **iNanda** Meaning 'beautiful place', Old-world-style blend of cab/merlot/cab f, proportions depending on vintage — 80/13/7 in latest **98**. Cracked/green pepper, ripe berries in concentrated form with long, ripe, charry tannins. Balanced; structure to improve 6–8 yrs. 13,5% alc. **97** restrained, sappy elegance, **96** concentrated, fleshy.

Chardonnay ✿ Fruit-led (as opposed to -driven), racier style. Gentler oaking (no malo) lets bright citrus shine through. **00** starts with lemon/lime, light leesy tones, then some toasty oak carrying into crisp finish. Very drinkable ("beside the pool," winemaker suggests), with some elegance. 12,5% alc. 4 mths Fr casks, none new. Also available (not tasted for this ed): **Deux Cabernets 96** cabernet duo: sauvignon/franc (70/30).

Zanddrift Vineyards   ▼ ▼ ▼ 🏠

Paarl (see Paarl map) • Tasting & sales Mon—Fri 10—5 • Cellar tours by appointment • Guest house • Functions/function facilities by arrangement • Tourgroups • Views • Owner Zanddrift Vineyards (Pty) Ltd • Winemaker Yvonne le Roux • Consultant winemaker Mark-Carmichael-Green • Consultant viticulturist Paul Wallace • Vineyards 29 ha • Production ± 8 000 cases 90% white 10% red • PO Box 541 Suider-Paarl 7624 • Tel (021) 863-2076 • Fax (021) 863-2081 • E-mail zanddrift@yahoo.com • Website www.zanddrift.co.za

THE BELL TOWER of an old stone chapel built by Italian prisoners of war in the early 1940s marks the entrance to this compact and modern wine cellar (and sometimes concert venue — the Western Cape Music Education Project recently performed a classical music programme here). Since the departure of Riaan Marais, Yvonne le Roux has taken over the management of the winery, assisted by seasoned consultant Mark Carmichael-Green. "We work extremely well together," she comments. The farm's 29 ha are planted mainly with white varieties — with small pockets of pinotage.

✿ **Semillon Reserve** Individual, attractive **00** starts with familiar lemon/lime scents and some smoky vanilla, then turns aromatic in palate with mixed savoury herbs before morphing again into a fruity finishing flourish. All works quite delightfully. 12,5% alc. 300 cases.

❀ **Chapel d'Or** Striking **98** botrytis dessert from chenin with high-toned tropical nose, hints of ripe mango; viscous but light (11,8% alc) texture which gains citrus/quince overtones mid-palate and in finish. 350 cases.

Capella Reserve ❀ 😊 Quaffable **00** features a smooth, dry salad of kiwifruit, lime and guava, infused with broadening 13% alc. Chenin blanc. ±800 cases.

Cabernet Sauvignon ★ **98** dry red with some cooked/almondy tones. 13% alc. 1 650 cases. **Pinotage** ❀ No put-down intended when we say med-bodied **98** is made for BBQ sloshing; pre-smoked (charry ripe plums), rustic (some stalkiness), robust (plenty of active tannin to slice through fatty boerewors). 2 000 cases. **Chapel Cellar Route 303** ❀ Aperitif-style blend Cape riesling/colombard, **00** offering attention-grabbing contrast between delicate, almost sweet honeysuckle/litchi bouquet and ultra-crisp dry palate. Lightish 11,5% alc. 4 500 cases. **Tuscany Spring** ❀ Zingy lemon/lime character immediately conjures up visions of freshly landed seafood. Full-bodied **00** quite weighty (13% alc), with broad leesy tastes and zesty lemonade finish. 1 800 cases.

. . . .

Zandvliet Estate

Robertson (see Robertson map) • Tasting & sales Mon—Fri 9—5 Sat 9—1 • "Lots of friendly dogs for friendly children" • Tourgroups • Gifts • Bring your own picnic • Views • Wheelchair-friendly • Owners Paul & Dan de Wet • Winemaker Johan van Wyk (since 2000) • Viticulturists Dan de Wet & Wouter Theron • Vineyards 176 ha • Production 1 500 tons 50 000 cases 50% red 45% white 5% rosé • PO Box 36 Ashton 6715 • Tel (023) 615-1146 • Fax (023) 615-1327 • E-mail shiraz@lando.co.za • Website www.zandvliet.co.za

THE E-MAIL ADDRESS of this lovely old farm sums up its new-millennium focus: Shiraz. 'Zandvliet is Shiraz, and Shiraz is Zandvliet', goes their slogan, and to further underscore the point, Zandvliet is to become a shiraz-only label. It's been a natural progression: long before this variety became fashionable in the Cape, it was Zandvliet's strongest suit, winning every sort of award from the first 76 vintage. Affable Paul de Wet knew in his bones he'd picked the right horse. And yet. Frustratingly, while consumers became Bordeaux blend-besotted and chardonnay-crazed, shiraz simply seemed to plod along. No longer. And nowhere are they readier for the modern thirst for this variety than here in these chalky hills (Kalkveld). With Californian viticultural magician Phil Freese and brother Dan de Wet in the saddle, new high-land vineyards have been established and older ones fine-tuned. New styles have been exhaustively probed — Paul de Wet and Johan van Wyk, who has taken over the fulltime winemaking portfolio, have been juggling French, American, even Russian oak; filtering minimally or not at all; testing various fermentation techniques in a drastically modernised cellar. And they've introduced a new range, Equus. This alludes to the estate's history as a leading race horse stud; now wine's the main feature of the race card here. The new-generation Zandvliet is streaking down the home straight.

Zandvliet range

❀ **Kalkveld Shiraz French Oak Matured** Marked style change since **96** 're-launch' of this oldest, best-known Robertson shiraz producer. This (and Am casked version below) from youthful plots on chalky hills (kalkveld in Afrikaans), prepared in conjunction with international vineyard guru Phil Freeze. Unfiltered, "grown, made and *bottled*" on estate; handsomely packaged. Latest **98** all-new Fr oaked, 13 mths; deeper tinted, tighter, more focused than pvs **96** (no **97**). The **98** persistent, choc-berry flavours, super whiffs cassis, fennel, sweet spicy oak. These for those who prefer more classical, less obvious vanilla-oaky topping. Unfiltered. **99**, all-new oak, should be best yet. 13,3% alc. 2 600 cases. no **97**.

❀ **Kalkveld Shiraz American Oak Matured** Demonstrative, more extrovertly 'sweet' than above. More New World style, scented vanilla notes persist in palate; but dry elegant finish in current **98**. Serious dark plummy colours, bold cassis aromas, lacks above's swirling complexity but finishes with pleasant, ripe tannin softness. From very hot, dry year. All new casks (pvs **96** included some used oak), also unfiltered. 13,4% alc. 1 500 cases. Next **99** more concentrated (5 t/ha yield),more fruit stuffing, more grip.

❀ **Chardonnay** **99** first under new Zandvliet label: bold, clean-flavoured with some firm pineapple/lemon fruitiness alongside understated oaky-yeasty elements. Barrel-fermented, 4 mths aged, Fr/Am/Russian oak (75/20/5), all new. 1 300 cases. **98** ❀ full, dry, with fresh citrus bite. Impact-alcs at 13,5%–14%.

Shiraz ❀ Traditional Zandvliet label. No new oak. Much liked by traditional, new oak-shunning Cape-shiraz fanciers since first **75** vintage. Current **97** follows long established, leanish, unflashy style. 13,5% alc. 7 000 cases.

Equus range   New

❀ **Cabernet Sauvignon-Merlot-Shiraz** Complexity from 23 different single vyd parcels, individually oaked, portion new casks, remainder used; assembled for 60/40/20 final ratio. And what a ratio! **99** deepest plum centre, crimson edge; fragrant leaves, wild berries, puffs of woodsmoke; savoury tannins tasting distinctly Old Worldish in their elegant ripe intensity. Non-intrusive New World expansiveness: 14% alc. This a mere foal: give at least 5 yrs for max pleasure. 2 600 cases.

❀ **Equus Chardonnay** "Accessible quaffing" the aim here, but this emphatically not a jolly swigger. Plump (13,8% alc), unabashedly fruity (though 50% barrel fermented), but crisp acidity keeps a bridle on latent excess. 1 400 cases.

Astonvale range

Marketed by Bar Valley Wines, PO Box 55, Ashton 6715. Tel/fax as for Zandvliet. All wines Robertson origin, very reasonably priced at well under R20 ex-farm.

Colombard New 😊 Bright pear/guava attractions in medium-weight **00**. Really fresh, clean. Paul de Wet cuts to the chase when suggesting an occasion to suit this wine: "Quaffing." Chill well. 4 000 cases.

Shiraz ❀ Fast-forward to **99** for smoky, green olive tones; strawberries-and-cream texture, brush of oak. Lightly chill in summer. 13,5% alc. 4 300 cases. **Chardonnay** ❀ Spicy unwooded **00**, good grip; lime fruit makes impact on palate, tangy fruit salad in finish. 13,7% alc. 5 000 cases. **Sauvignon Blanc** ❀❀ **99** shy aromas, flinty gooseberry tastes, easy dry drinking. 13% alc. 4 000 cases. **Colombard-Sauvignon Blanc Créme** ❀❀ **00** again 80/20 blend, dryish, some candy floss, talcum flavours, quite broad, but not as hefty as pvs (12,4% alc.). 4 000 cases.

- -

Zandwijk see Kleine Draken
Zevenrivieren see Zevenwacht

- -

Zevenwacht Estate

Stellenbosch (see Stellenbosch map) • Tasting & sales Mon—Fri 8—5 Sat & Sun 9.30—5 R12.50 (includes international tasting glass) R6 if own glass is used Tumbler & tasting R9 • Cellar/vineyard tours by appointment • Restaurants, picnic basket/barbeque baskets etc • Cheese tasting on request • Guest cottages • Conference centre • Banqueting facilities • Traditional 'lapa' for outdoor functions • Helicopter pad • Children's play park • Cheese factory • Professional Chef's School • 4x4 trail • Views • Owners Harold & Denise Johnson • Winemaker Hilko Hegewisch (since 1995) • Viticulturist Francois Baard (since 1997) • Production 1 100 tons 75 000 cases 55% white 45% red • PO Box 387 Kuils River

7580 • Tel (021) 903-5123 • Fax (021) 903-3373 • E-mail sales@zevenwacht.co.za • Website www.zevenwacht.co.za

PEOPLE-FRIENDLY Zevenwacht really has it all, with a heli pad, 4x4 trail, children's play park and top-notch SA cuisine (there's a professional chef's school too). They've just installed an ultra-modern R2-million bottling, labelling and de-palletising line. Soft-spoken winemaker Hilko Hegewisch declares it "very flexible," which it no doubt has to be in order to accommodate the disparities in bottle sizes: from 375 ml to a walloping 27 ℓ, with 1 ℓ bottles (for duty-free at Johannesburg International), magnums and 3 ℓ in between. They've also upgraded equipment with brand new tractors and bulldozers. Awards have been thick on the ground with Veritas golds, silvers and bronzes. Say cheese and you'll see many smiles around here, too — the all-natural Farmhouse Cheddar (uncoloured, preservative and flavourant free) has been declared a champion. Visitors can view the traditional English farmhouse method at the modern cheese factory.

Zevenwacht range

✿Shiraz On form of pvs the celebrity here since dramatic **97** *Wine* ✿ performance (though other reds below nipping at these heels). Concentration, fragrant warm spices the keynotes, promise of fine development. **98** elaborated on these qualities with alluring peppery warmth, ripe fruit and some chewy tannins that needed 2–3 yrs. Current **99** ✿✿ more sinewy style, elegant with generous if not showy fruit. 100% oaked, 13 mths. Preview of **00** absolute cracker: densest berry fruit packed into powerful (14,5% alc) spicy/peppery frame.

✿Pinotage Juicier **00** style dictated by export market (Hegewisch would prefer more 'classic' approach); mulberries/blackcurrants, some ripe banana, subtle oak presence (only 25% barrelled); late picking shows in sturdy 13,5% alc. **98** ✿✿ with Ribena-like fruit, soft tannins. **97** *Wine* ✿.

✿Chevalier ▼ Satisfying Bdx-style blend, undramatic but flavourful and ungreedily priced. **98** SAA; current **99** 55/45 cab/merlot blend, 100% oaked ± 13 mths. Good minerally threads to well padded berry/cherry ensemble. 3 000 cases. 13,1% alc. **96** SAA, *Wine* ✿.

✿Zevenrood ▼ Unvarying quality/value dry red, with the latest 00 bottling (**NV** on label) showing benefits of redoubled efforts in vyds (including new irrigation network); mainly cab with merlot, splash shiraz; pops with flavour, ripe berries, bits of green pepper; juiciness in mouth with just the right amount of tannin. Briefly oaked. 20 000 cases.

✿Chenin Blanc ▼ Fuller vintage mirrored in **00**, mouthfilling, boldly flavoured with this farm's signature citrus/apple in palate; good contrast between ripeness and fresh acidity. 5 g/ℓ sugar smoothes without sweetening. 13% alc. Big seller: 86 000 cases.

Bouquet Blanc ✿✿ 🍷 Delightful, scented, smoothly sweet aperitif from gewürz, dashes hanepoot, riesling, chenin. Real feel-good wine — pleases crowds *and* show judges with honeysuckle/jasmine/rose petal perfume, freshened by bright acidity. "Can't make enough," reports Hilko Hegewisch.

Cabernet Sauvignon 98 tasted for pvs ed rated ✿, dry tannins needing plenty of time to meld with fruit/oak. **99** not tasted. **00** sampled from barrel different league to pvs, result of concerted vyd management, stringent selection, warm vintage picked ripe (shows in punchy 13,5% alc). Great intensity, richness, 'sweet' chocolatey berries/cherries and coffee spiced with cinnamon/vanilla; long firm tannins all point to future ✿ potential. **Merlot** New ▼ Variety pvsly all went into Zevenrood blend; from **99** (not available for tasting) fruit considered good enough for solo performance. **00**, from barrel, exceptionally rich, promising. Velvety berry fruit with choc/smoke/cigar box/tobacco complexity, sweet tannins and great persistence. Could rate ✿✿ on release. **Blanc de Noir** ✿ Increasingly popular, 'correctly' made blush (only black grapes, fermented as red wine), properly dry and full flavoured. **00** with strawberries, plums and violet perfume, satisfying on its own or with food. **Chardonnay** ✿ By popular demand, fruitier style since **96**; latest **00** only 10% oaked to show off ripe peach/melon; firmish mouthfeel takes well to food. **Sauvignon Blanc** ✿ Reductive vinification means these start slowly, reach best 2–3 yrs from harvest. Full-bodied/flavoured **00** should age better than most pvs; 'sweet' impression from ripe fruit and assertive 13,5% alc. Some muscatty/green pepper tones; crisp finish. 5 000 cases. **Blanc de Blanc** ✿ Refreshing, well priced easy-drinker with more character/interest than most of this style; **00** intense flavours of fruit salad and sherbety lemonade, lip-smackingly dry finish; crisp acid makes you want another sip. Mainly chenin with dabs chardonnay, riesling. 13% alc. 25 000 cases. Also available, not tasted: **Gewürztraminer 99**, Pinot **Noir-Chardonnay 99**.

Zevenrivieren range

These from Harold Johnson's Banhoek vyds, made at Zevenwacht.

- ✿ **Cabernet Sauvignon** ▼ **99** difficult, warm yr, ably handled, only fraction (20%) oaked to preserve softer fruit flavours from young vines. Mulberry, touch of cigarbox/tobacco; firm tannins for good keeping.
- ✿ **Chardonnay** ▼ Hot **00** vintage brings this label to life with beautiful ripe, soft mouthful, lighter-toned than Zevenwacht version above but full-bodied (13,5% alc), deep-flavoured. Ripe peach and all the good things from oak: vanilla, toast and butterscotch. Big improvement on pvs. Partially barrel-fermented, 100% new casks, 10 mths.

Sauvignon Blanc ✿ **00** quiet when tasted mid-2000 (reductively made, so should perk up with bit of time). Chalky sleekness in mouth with cut-grass/green pepper/gooseberry; bracing finish. Unwooded, 13,1% alc.

· ·

Zomerlust

BUDGET range in 2/5 ℓ casks by Robertson Winery for Vinimark. Range, untasted for this ed, includes: **Dry Red**, **Blanc de Blanc**, **Stein**, **Late Harvest**.

· ·

Zonnebloem

Stellenbosch • Tasting & sales at Oude Libertas See Stellenbosch Farmers' Winery • Owner Stellenbosch Farmers' Winery • Cellarmaster Razvan Macici • Winemakers Jan de Waal (reds) • Razvan Macici (whites) • Assistant winemaker Carmen Stevens • Winery manager Jan le Roux • Production 212 000 cases 65% red 35% white • PO Box 46 Stellenbosch 7599 • Tel (021) 808-7911 • Fax (021) 883-2603 • E-mail cedge@sfw.co.za • Website www.zonnebloem.co.za

WHEN you're this well established — roots stretching back a couple of centuries — when you're really, truly ubiquitous — your produce proudly arrayed on winelists and wine store shelves from Bredasdorp to Bryanston — what do you do to stay on top? You get a blood transfusion — beginning with a new talented young cellarmaster (articulate Razvan Macici, Romanian-born football fanatic and authentic cool dude); a bright, passionate young team (Carmen Stevens, deputy winemaker, who also looks after the rising-star Tukulu range; brand manager Chris Edge, hotelier in a former life, surfer and partner — by marriage — of one of the hottest gourmet caterers around). Season this fresh-faced youth with super-experienced, salt-of-the-earth Jan de Waal, eminence here since 1969. Splurge on a brand new, deluxe cellar (price tag: R38-million), handling both warehouse-size batches and thimbleful 'show reserves'. Kick-start it all — red wine facilities go on-stream this year, remainder in 2002 — and voila! "Zonnebloem has a long tradition," reflects Razvan Macici. "My responsibility is to be the keeper of the good quality of the wines. This means preserving flavours from the vineyard into the bottle, to give wines with intense fruit, good drinkability."

Fine Art label

Ch Mouton Rothschild-inspired range launched 1996, featuring unique front-label paintings by local artists. Limited edition — only 5 000 ℓ of each — from single vyd sources. Reds all matured in 100% new oak.

✿ **Cabernet Sauvignon** New Currently reigned-in, but should grow more expansive over 4-8 yrs. Components, certainly, all in position: some deep-piled berry fruit, warm smoky/toasty aromas and good dollop of tannin.

✿ **Merlot** New Very ripe, almost succulent tannins are key to **99**, bestowing a gliding smoothness to rich, full (13,6% alc), balanced, sweet-oaky palate. Choc and perfumed violets add opulent touches.

✿ **Shiraz** Exceptional fruit concentration in **99** ✿, recalling both the Rhône and Australia in densely extracted, aromatically intense character. Lasting impression, however, is sinew rather than muscle (despite rippling 14% alc.). Pvs **97** good dollop vanilla-oak, whiff of roast/toast, some medicinal character.

✿ **Sauvignon Blanc** Razvan Macici ecstatic about the latest release, from selected cool climate lots, low cropped (4 t/ha), reductively handled for max freshness, vitality. **00** ✿ positively brims with exotic passion fruit, pineapple, nettle aromas; palate dominated by 'sweet' fruit which tapers to bracing yet balanced flinty-dry finish. Last was **98**, which deserved its 'reserve' status in tricky sauvignon yr.

Standard range

✿ **Cabernet Sauvignon** Unflashy, food-friendly style, remarkably good considering the large quantities. **98** — warmer, more generous vintage — reflected in light (attractive) tarry touch, sweet-tasting (though analytically dry) ripe fruit. **97** ✿ shade less intense, some initially austere tannins.

✿ **Merlot** "*The* vintage!" beams Razvan Macici, referring to **98**. We agree: quite possibly finest to date under this label. Enormously mouthfilling (13,5%) yet not overdone; the full merlot house in bouquet/palate: sweet violets, green pepper, blackberry, dark choc. **97** ✿ undomineering, so good at table.

✿ **Pinot Noir** New Not the thrusting long-haul Millennium pinot of pvs ed (though portion of those grapes diverted into this **97**). Well fruited but currently lacking bit of flesh, so give time for strawberry, cherry amplitude to increase.

✿ **Pinotage** ▼ One of the Cape's more reliable, flavoursome pinotages. Latest **98** ✿ (clearly an exceptional red vintage for this cellar) something of a standout. Fullness, ripeness are keywords, with plum/morello cherry freshness and brush of oak for instant roundness, longer-term keepability. 13,5% alc. **96** tangy, seamlessly oaked.

✿ **Shiraz** Romania, Rhône and the Cape meet in **98** ✿, and the result is electrifying — and distinctly Old World. Generous but refined layers of fruit, tangy-spicy, scented with violets and heather. Sturdy 14% alc fully integrated. Accessible, with fine structure for keeping. **97** suave, understated; **96** intense, sensuous.

✿ **Lauréat** Stylish Bdx blend, cabs s/f with merlot (62/13/25) in latest **98**. Understated, as usual, nothing booming but nothing missing either; toasty oak, merlot's coffee aroma and new clone minty sprigs all present and accounted for. 13,5% alc. **97** similar, perhaps bit lighter, more immediately approachable, earlier maturing.

✿ **Chardonnay** Steady improvement over past few vintages sees this support player grow into headline act in **99** ✿. Partial barrel fermentation/ageing imparts rich butterscotch, lees, toast to offset bone-dry lime piquancy. Best out of 60 entrants in wine mail order club taste-off. **98** rounded, generous, balanced.

✿ **Sauvignon Blanc** 120 000 litres of supercharged fruit in **00**, stringent vyd selection providing the extra octane. Good spectrum of flavours, from green pepper/grass to gooseberry/guava, giving broad, gusty satisfaction.

✿ **Blanc de Blanc** ❱ Usual med/full-bodied 85/15 chenin/sauvignon mix, but uncommon concentration, spunk in **00**: bolt of chenin guava touched off by flinty/grassy sauvignon spark. Super-fresh (partly from careful reductive handling), balanced.

✿ **Rhine Riesling** Fast-forwarding once more after back-pedalling in **98** ✿✿. **00** generously proportioned (13% alc — feature of vintage), some lemon/floral tones and good palate tension (partly achieved by dropping residual sugar to near-dry 5 g/ℓ). No **99**.

✿ **Special Late Harvest** ❱ **98**, tasted for 2 pvs eds, has become seriously gorgeous. Wafts of pineapple, honey joined by whiffs botrytis/beeswax. Good tug of acidity keeps the whole arrangement in balance.

✿ **Noble Late Harvest 96**, first in 7 yrs, seems happy to continue indefinitely (or until next version arrives). Some unusual ripe banana scents emerging, though overall well-acidified freshness remains. Mainly chenin, dash riesling. Low range 11,5% alc.

Premier Grand Cru ✿ Colombard/chenin (50/50) in foodie mode, good with many cuisines including seafood. **00** fuller than pvs, ripe, good lemony tang in bone-dry but not austere palate. Certainly not an afterthought in this range.

Complete general index

This is a summary of wines featured in the A–Z section. New labels in **bold** type.

STILL WINES

White wines

Single varieties

Bukettraube Boland, Bovlei, Cederberg, Du Toitskloof, Goue Vallei, Koelenhof, Lutzville, Rooiberg, Simonsvlei, Swartland

Chardonnay (unwooded) Agterkliphoogte, Ashwood, Bloemendal, Bloupunt, Bon Courage, Botha, Bouchard Finlayson, Bovlei, **Brandvlei**, Constantia Uitsig, Coppoolse Finlayson, Cordoba, Darling Cellars, De Wetshof, De Zoete Inval, Die Krans, Dieu Donné, Drostdy, Excelsior, Franschhoek Vineyards, Goedverwacht, Goue Vallei, **Groote Post**, **Hildenbrand**, Hilltop, Hinterland (Hartswater), Jonkheer, **Joostenberg**, Kleine Zalze, **Kloovenburg**, Langverwacht, **La Petite Ferme**, Linton Park, Louisvale, McGregor, Mont Rochelle, Montagu, Mooiuitsig, Mulderbosch, Natural Corporation, **Nietvoorbij**, Nuy, Opstal, Overhex, Pick 'n Pay, Riebeek, **Sandown Bay**, Seidelberg, Spar, Steenberg, Table Mountain, TenFiftySix, Trawal, Van Loveren, Van Zylshof, Vinfruco, Vlottenburg

Chardonnay (wooded) **Agterkliphoogte**, Altydgedacht, Amani, Ashanti, Ashton, Ashwood, Astonvale, **Audacia**, Avontuur, Backsberg, Badsberg, Beaumont, Bellingham, Bergsig, Blaauwklippen, Bloupunt, Boland, Bon Courage, Bonnievale, Boplaas, Boschendal, Boschkloof, Bouchard Finlayson, Brampton, Buitenverwachting, Calitzdorp, Cape Wine Cellars, Cape Wine Exports, Cederberg, Chamonix, Claridge, Constantia Uitsig, Coppoolse Finlayson, Cordoba, Darling Cellars, De Wet, De Wetshof, Deetlefs, Delheim, Dellrust, Die Krans, Dieu Donné, Douglas Green, Du Toitskloof, Durbanville Hills, Eikehof, Eikendal, **Fairview**, Fat Bastard, **Flagstone**, Fleur du Cap, Fort Simon, Glen Carlou, Goede Hoop, Goedvertouw, Goedverwacht, Goudini, Graham Beck, Groot Constantia, Groot Eiland, Hamilton Russell Vineyards, Hartenberg, Hazendal, Helderkruin, **High Constantia**, Hoopenburg, **Ingwe**, IWS/Pacific Wines, **Joostenberg**, JP Bredell, Jordan, Kanu, Klawer, Klein Constantia, Kleindal (Vinimark), Kleine Zalze, KWV/Cathedral Cellar, L'Avenir, **La Couronne**, La Motte, Laborie, Laibach, **Lanzerac**, Le Bonheur, Leidersburg, Libertas, Lievland, Linton Park, Long Mountain, Longridge, Lost Horizons, Louiesenhof, Louisvale, Louwshoek, Lutzville, Malan Family Vintners, Meerendal, Meerlust, Merwespont, Middelvlei, Middlepost, Alphen Mondial, Mont Rochelle, M'reson, Morgenhof, Mount Rozier, Mouton-Excelsior, Mulderbosch, Napier, Nederburg, Neethlingshof, Neil Ellis, Nelson's Creek, Jonkheer, Nordale, Onderkloof, Overgaauw, Pick 'n Pay, Plaisir de Merle, Porterville, R&R, Radford Dale, Rhebokskloof, Rickety Bridge, **Rietrivier**, Rietvallei, **Rijk's**, Robertson, Romansrivier, Rooiberg, Ruitersvlei, Rustenberg, Sable View, Savanha, Saxenburg, Seidelberg, Shoprite Checkers, Simonsig, Simonsvlei, Sinnya, Slaley, **Somerbosch**, **Sommelier's Choice**, Sonop, Spar, Spier, Spier Estate, Springfield, Spruitdrift, Steenberg, **Stellenbosch Vineyards**, Stellenzicht, Stony Brook, Swartland, Talana Hill, Thandi, Thelema, Tradouw (Barrydale), Tulbagh, Uiterwyk, Uitkyk, Uva Mira, Van Loveren, Van Zylshof, Veenwouden, **Vendôme**, **Vera Cruz**, Verdun, Vergelegen, Viljoensdrift, Villiera, Vinfruco, Vriesenhof, Warwick, Wellington, Welmoed, Weltevrede, Whalehaven, Wildekrans, Windmeul, **Woolworths**, Yonder Hill, Zandvliet, Zevenrivieren, Zevenwacht, Zonnebloem

Chenin blanc (unwooded, dry, sometimes called steen) Arlington, Ashwood, Avondale, Bergsig, Bernheim, Boland, **Brandvlei**, Cape Wine Cellars, Cape Wine Exports, Coppoolse Finlayson, Darling Cellars, Deetlefs, Drostdy, Du Preez, Du Toitskloof, Fair Valley, Goue Vallei, Groene Cloof, **Hildenbrand**, IWS/Pacific Wines, Jacaranda, Kaapzicht, **Kanu**, Kleine Zalze, KWV, Laibach, Landskroon, Leidersburg,

Libertas, Long Mountain, Lost Horizons, McGregor, Mellasat, Mont Destin, Montagu, Mouton-Excelsior, Napier, Old Vines, Onderkloof, Opstal, Perdeberg, Pick 'n Pay, Porterville, Rickety Bridge, Riebeek, Seidelberg, **Shoprite**, Simonsig, Simonsvlei, Spar, Spruitdrift, Stellenbosch Vineyards, Swartland, Sylvanvale, Van Zylshof, Villiersdorp, Vinfruco, Wellington, Windmeul, Zevenwacht

Chenin blanc (unwooded off-dry/semi-sweet, sometimes called stein) Autumn Harvest, Backsberg, Bernheim, Boschendal, Bovlei, Cederberg, Delheim, Dellrust, Douglas, Du Preez, Eersterivier, Franschhoek Vineyards, Goudini, Hazendal, Helderberg, Huguenot, Kellerprinz, Klawer, Kleindal (Vinimark), Landskroon, Lieberstein, Lutzville, McGregor, Montagu, Natural Corporation, Overmeer, Perdeberg, **Robusto**, Romansrivier, Rooiberg, Rosenburg, **Shoprite**, **Slanghoek**, Somersbosch, Spar, Swartland, Vaughan Johnson, Virginia, Waboomsrivier, Welmoed, Woolworths

Chenin blanc (wooded) Amani, Ashanti, Beaumont, Cederberg, Chamonix, De Trafford, Die Krans, Dieu Donné, Eikendal, Fairview, Fort Simon, Franschhoek Vineyards, Glen Carlou, Helderberg Reserve, IWS/Pacific Wines, Jordan, Kaapzicht, Ken Forrester, Kleine Zalze, L'Avenir, Laibach, Landskroon, Long Mountain, Longridge, M'reson, Morgenhof, Mulderbosch, **Muldersvlei**, Nederburg, **Old Vines**, Oude Wellington, Post House, **Rijk's**, Reyneke, Rickety Bridge, Ruitersvlei, Savanha, Sonop, Spice Route, Spier, Swartland, Tukulu, Verdun, Villiera, Welmoed, Wildekrans, Woolworths Reserve

Clairette blanche De Wet, Goudini

Colombard (dry) Agterkliphoogte, Ashton, Bernheim, Bon Courage, Douglas, **Du Toitskloof**, Goedverwacht, IWS/Pacific Wines, Klawer, Langverwacht, Nuy, Robertson, Roodezandt, Sonop, Swartland, Zandvliet

Colombard (off-dry/semi-sweet) Bonnievale, Botha, McGregor, Montagu, Nuy, Overhex, **Rietrivier**, Romansrivier, Rooiberg, Uitvlucht, Van Loveren, Villiersdorp, Weltevrede, Woolworths

Fernão Pires Nuy, Swartland, Van Loveren

Gewürztraminer Altydgedacht, Ashton, Bergsig, Bon Courage, Bovlei, Delheim, Douglas, Groot Constantia, Koelenhof, Landzicht, **Meerendal**, Neethlingshof, Paul Cluver, Villiera, Vlottenburg, Weltevrede, Zevenwacht

Hárslevelü Lemberg

Muscat d'Alexandrie (unfortified) Eersterivier, L'Émigré, Libertas, Sable View, Swartland

Muscat de Frontignan (unfortified) De Wet, Montagu, Thelema, Twee Jonge Gezellen

Pinot blanc Cordoba, **Lanzerac**, Nederburg

Pinot Gris L'Ormarins, Van Loveren

Riesling (Cape or SA) Boland, Bon Courage, Boschendal, Bovlei, De Wet, Du Toitskloof, Fleur du Cap, Goudini, KWV, Mooiuitsig, Nederburg, Nuy, Rooiberg, Ruitersvlei, Simonsvlei, Swartland, Theuniskraal, Uitkyk, Van Loveren, Woolworths

Riesling (emerald) Porterville

Riesling (Rhine or weisser) Backsberg, Buitenverwachting, Clairvaux, De Wetshof, Delheim, Groot Constantia, Hartenberg, Jordan, Kaapzicht, Klein Constantia, KWV, La Bri, Lievland, Long Mountain, **Merwida**, Nederburg, Paul Cluver, Rhebokskloof, Rooiberg, Simonsig, Slanghoek, Stellenbosch Vineyards, Thelema, Van Loveren, Villiera, Weltevrede, Woolworths, Zonnebloem

Sauvignon blanc (unwooded) Altydgedacht, Ashton, Ashwood, Astonvale, Avondale, Avontuur, Backsberg, Beaumont, Bellingham, Blaauwklippen, Bloemendal, Boland, Bon Courage, Boplaas, Boschendal, Bouchard Finlayson, Bovlei, Brampton, **Brandvlei**, Buitenverwachting, Cape Point Vineyards, Cape Wine Cellars, Cape Wine Exports, Cederberg, Clos Malverne, Constantia Uitsig, Coppoolse Finlayson, Cordoba, Darling Cellars, De Meye, De Wet, De Wetshof, De Zoete Inval, Delheim, Dellrust, Die Krans, Drostdy, Du Preez, Du Toitskloof, Durbanville Hills, Eersterivier, Eikendal, Excelsior, Fairview, Fleur du Cap, Fort Simon, Franschhoek Vineyards, Freedom Road, Goede Hoop, Goedvertrouw, Goedverwacht, **Goudini**, Goue Vallei, Graham Beck, Groot Constantia, **Groot Eiland**, **Groote Post**, Hartenberg, **Havana Hills**, Hazendal, Helderberg, Helderkruin, Hoopenburg, **Ingwe**, **Joostenberg**, Jordan, Kaapzicht, Ken Forrester, Khanya, Klawer, Klein Constantia, Kleindal (Vinimark), Kleine Zalze, Knorhoek, Koelenhof, KWV/Cathedral Cellar, **Land's End**, L'Avenir, La Bri, **La Couronne**, La Motte, Laborie, Laibach, Landau du Val, Landskroon, Lemberg, L'Émigré, Lievland, Linton Park, Long Mountain, Longridge, Lost Horizons, Louwshoek-Voorsorg, **Lushof**, Lutzville, Malan Family Vintners, McGregor, Meerendal, Mont Rochelle, Mooiplaas, Mooiuitsig, M'reson, Morgenhof, Mount Rozier, Mouton-Excelsior, Mulderbosch, Natural Corporation, Nederburg, Neethlingshof, Neil Ellis, Nelson's Creek, Jonkheer, Nuy, Onderkloof, Overgaauw, Paul Cluver, Pick 'n Pay, Porcupine Ridge, Porterville, Rickety Bridge, Robertson, Romansrivier, Roodezandt, Rooiberg, Rosenburg, Rustenberg, Sable View, Savanha, Saxenburg, **Seidelberg**, Simonsig, **Simonsvlei**, Simunye, Slaley, **Slanghoek**, Somerbosch, Sonop, Southern Right, Spar, Spice Route, **Spier**, Springfield, Spruitdrift, Steenberg, Stellenbosch Vineyards, Stellenzicht, Stony Brook, Swartland, TenFiftySix, Tradouw (Barrydale), Trawal, Uiterwyk, Uitkyk, Uitvlucht, Van Loveren, Van Zylshof, Verdun, Vergelegen, Villiera, Villiersdorp, Vinfruco, Vlottenburg, Wellington, Welmoed, WhaleHaven, Wildekrans, **Woolworths**, Zevenrivieren, Zevenwacht, Zonnebloem

Sauvignon blanc (wooded, sometimes called Blanc Fumé) Amani,　Ashanti, Backsberg, Bartho Eksteen, Bon Courage, Boschendal, Chamonix, De Wetshof, Eikendal, Elephant Pass, Jordan, Kanu, Ken Forrester, La Motte, Makro, Mulderbosch, Nederburg, Paul Cluver, Pick 'n Pay, Plaisir de Merle, Ruitersvlei, Simonsig Fumé, TenFiftySix, Uva Mira

Semillon (unwooded) Bloemendal, Bon Courage, Cape Point Vineyards, Franschhoek Vineyards, Helderkruin, IWS/Pacific Wines, Klein Constantia, **La Petite Ferme**, Lutzville, Steenberg, **Stony Brook**, Viljoensdrift, Villiersdorp

Semillon (wooded) Backsberg, Boekenhoutskloof, **Boschendal**, Constantia Uitsig, Deetlefs, Delheim, Doornkraal, Eikehof, **Fairview**, Franschhoek Vineyards, Landau du Val, Nederburg, Neethlingshof, Perdeberg, Rickety Bridge, **Rijk's**, Savanha, Simonsvlei, Steenberg, Stellenzicht, Stony Brook, **Vergelegen**, Wildekrans, Woolworths

Schönberger Hartenberg

Sylvaner Overgaauw

Therona Oranjerivier

Viognier Fairview, **Spice Route**, Uiterwyk

Blends

Chardonnay-sauvignon blanc (unwooded) Ashwood, Bellingham, Botha, Chamonix, Craighall, Douglas Green, Fort Simon, Jordan, **La Couronne**, Laibach, **Linton Park**, Lost Horizons, McGregor, Meerendal, Shoprite Checkers, Simonsvlei, Slanghoek

Chardonnay-sauvignon blanc (wooded) Craighall, Nederburg, Paradyskloof, Pick 'n Pay, Rhebokskloof, Weltevrede

Other chardonnay blends (unwooded) Agulhas, Arlington, Ashwood, Blaauwklippen, Bon Courage, Bonnievale, Boschendal, Bouchard Finlayson, Clairvaux, Constantia Uitsig, Coppoolse Finlayson, Goudini, Graham Beck, Haute Cabrière, Kleine Zalze, Long Mountain, **Meerendal**, Natural Corporation, Nederburg, Nelson's Creek, Opstal, Overhex, Rhebokskloof, **Rider's Drift**, Robertson, Romansrivier, Roodezandt, Rooiberg, Saxenburg, Shoprite Checkers, Simonsig, Sinnya (Robertson Valley Wines), Springfield, Theuniskraal, Tradouw (Barrydale), Tulbagh, Van Loveren, Verdun, Vendôme, Villiersdorp, Vinfruco, **Waterford**, Woolworths, Zevenwacht

Other chardonnay blends (wooded) Arlington, Ashanti, Ashton, Boschendal, Douglas, **Fort Simon**, Franschhoek Vineyards, La Bri, Langverwacht, Longridge, McGregor, Nordale, Riebeek, Ruitersvlei, Simonsvlei, Woolworths, Zevenwacht

Other white blends (unwooded, usually labelled blanc de blanc) Amani, Ashwood, Astonvale, Autumn Harvest, Avondale, Avontuur, Bellingham, Blue Ridge (Villiera), Bradgate, Buitenverwachting, **Darling Cellars**, De Wetshof, Delheim, Doornkraal, Douglas, Drostdy, Eikendal, Franschhoek Vineyards, Groot Constantia, Hartenberg, Jacques Pinard, Jean Daneel Wines, Kellerprinz, Klawer, L'Avenir, La Bri, Landzicht Grand Cru, L'Émigré, Longridge Bay View, Lutzville, Malan Family Vintners, Mont Rochelle, Mooiuitsig, Motif (Steenberg), Nederburg, Neil Ellis, Nuy, Onderkloof, Overmeer, Panarotti's, Pick 'n Pay, Rickety Bridge, Slanghoek, Spier, Spruitdrift, Spur, St. Elmo's, Stellenbosch Vineyards, Stellenzicht, **Stony Brook**, Swartland, Tulbagh Co-op, Twee Jonge Gezellen, Van Loveren, Vaughan Johnson, Viljoensdrift, Vinfruco, Waboomsrivier, Welmoed, Weltevrede, **Woolworths**, Yellow Cellar (Helderkruin), Zellerhof (Huguenot), Zonnebloem

Other white blends (unwooded, off-dry/semi-sweet) Altydgedacht, Ashwood, Avontuur, Bellingham, Boplaas, Boschendal, Botha, **Brandvlei**,Calitzdorp, Cape Wine Cellars, Clairvaux, Darling Cellars, De Wet, Delheim Goldspatz, Die Krans, Doornkraal, Douglas Green, Douglas, Du Toitskloof, Eikendal, Franschhoek Vineyards, Goue Vallei, Groot Constantia, Groot Eiland, Groot Eiland, Hanseret (Eersterivier), Koelenhof, Landskroon, Landzicht, Longridge Bay View, Lost Horizons, Malan Family Vintners, Motif (Steenberg), Nederburg, Nelson's Creek, Panarotti's, Pick 'n Pay, Porterville, Riebeek, **Rietrivier**, Robertson, Roodezandt, Ruitersvlei, **Simonsvlei**, Simonsig, Spar, Spier, Spruitdrift, Spur, St. Elmo's, Stellenzicht, Swartland, Tasheimer Goldtröpchen, **Trawal**, Twee Jonge Gezellen, Van Loveren, Vergelegen, Villiera, Vlottenburg, Wellington, Woolworths, Zevenwacht

Other white blends (wooded) Hartenberg, Morgenhof, Stellenzicht, **Siyabonga**

Pink wines

Blanc de noir Avontuur, Barrydale, Bergsig, Bon Courage, Boplaas, Boschendal, Clairvaux, Culemborg (Douglas Green), Darling Cellars, De Wet, De Zoete Inval, Douglas, Du Toitskloof, Goue Vallei, Klawer, Laborie, Lutzville, Mooiuitsig, Neethlingshof, Swartland, Van Loveren, Weltevrede, Woolworths, Zevenwacht

Rosé (dry) Ashanti, Bellingham, De Zoete Inval, **Franschhoek**, Hartenberg, Libertas, Motif (Steenberg), Nederburg, **New Beginnings**, Newton Johnson, Savanha, Sonop, Sylvanvale, Villiersdorp, **Vinfruco**, Warwick

Rosé (off-dry/semi-sweet) Agulhas (Merwespont), Backsberg, Bernheim, **Cape Gables**, Cape Wine Cellars, **Clairvaux**, **Darling Cellars**, Delheim, Dieu Donné, Douglas Green, Fairview, **Franschhoek Vineyards**, Goudveld, **Groot Eiland**, **Hartswater**, Koelenhof, Kellerprinz, L'Avenir, **Lanzerac**, **Long Mountain**, **Lost Horizons**, **Louwshoek**, Makro, **McGregor**, Nederburg, **Oranjerivier**, Pick 'n Pay, Porterville, **Rooiberg**, Shoprite, Spar, Spruitdrift, Swartland, **Two Oceans**, Woolworths

Red wines

Single varieties

Barbera Altydgedacht

Cabernet franc Avontuur, Bellingham, Blaauwklippen, Fairview, **High Constantia**, KWV/Cathedral Cellar, Landskroon, Sonop, Warwick

Cabernet sauvignon Allesverloren, Alto, Altydgedacht, **Annandale**, Arlington, Ashanti, Ashton, Ashwood, Audacia, Avondale, Avontuur, Backsberg, Bellingham, Bergsig, Bernheim, Bertrams, Beyerskloof, Bianco (De Heuvel), **Bilton**, Blaauwklippen, Bloemendal, Boekenhoutskloof, Boland, **Bonfoi**, Boplaas, Boschkloof, Botha, Bovlei, Brenthurst, Buitenverwachting, Calitzdorp, Cape Wine Cellars, Cape Wine Exports, Carisbrooke, Cederberg, Chamonix, Clos Malverne, Coleraine, Constantia Uitsig, Coppoolse Finlayson, Cordoba, Culemborg (Douglas Green), Darling Cellars, De Meye, De Trafford, De Wet, De Zoete Inval, Delheim, Die Krans, Diemersdal, Dieu Donné, Doornkraal, Douglas Green, Drostdy, **Du Plessis,** Du Preez, Du Toitskloof, Eaglevlei, Eersterivier, Eikehof, Eikendal, Excelsior, Fairview, Fleur du Cap, Franschhoek Vineyards, Genesis, Goede Hoop, Goedvertouw, Goudveld, Goue Vallei, Graceland, Graham Beck, Grangehurst, Groene Cloof, Groot Constantia, Groot Eiland, Hartenberg, Helderberg, Helderkruin, **High Constantia**, **Hildenbrand**, Hoopenburg, Huguenot, IWS/Pacific Wines, **Joostenberg**, Jordan, Kaapzicht, Kanonkop, **Kanu**, Khanya, Klein Constantia, Kleindal (Vinimark), Kleine Zalze, Knorhoek, KWV/Cathedral Cellar, L'Avenir, **La Couronne**, La Motte, Laborie, Laibach, Landskroon, Landzicht, Le Bonheur, Le Riche, Leidersburg, Libertas, Lievland, Linton Park, Long Mountain, Longridge/Bay View, Lost Horizons, Louisvale, Louwshoek-Voorsorg, Lutzville, Makro, Malan Family Vintners, Meerendal, Meerlust, Mellasat, **Merwida**, Merwespont, Middelvlei, Middlepost, **Mischa**, Mons Ruber, **Mont Rochelle**, Mooiplaas, Mooiuitsig, M'reson, Mount Rozier, Mouton-Excelsior, Napier, Natural Corporation, Nederburg, Neethlingshof, Neil Ellis, Nelson's Creek, **Nietvoorbij**, Jonkheer, Nuy, **Onderkloof**, Opstal, Oude Wellington, Overgaauw, Paul Cluver, Pick 'n Pay, Plaisir de Merle, Porcupine Ridge, Post House, R&R, Remhoogte, Reyneke, Rhebokskloof, Rickety Bridge, Riebeek, **Rijk's**, Robertson, Romansrivier, Roodendal, Roodezandt, Rooiberg, Ruitersvlei, Rust en Vrede, Rustenberg, Sable View, **Sandown Bay**, Savanha, Saxenburg, Seidelberg, **Shoprite** Checkers, Signal Hill, Simonsig, Simonsvlei, **Slaley**, Slanghoek, Somersbosch, **Sonop**, Spar, Spier, Springfield, Spruitdrift, Steenberg, Stellenzicht, Stony Brook, Swartland, Table Mountain, TenFiftySix, Thandi, **The Cabernet Company**, Company Thelema, Uiterwyk, Uitkyk, **Upland**, **Vendôme**, Verdun, Vergelegen, Vergenoegd, Viljoensdrift, Villiera, **Villiersdorp**, **Vinfruco**, **Vinum**, Vlottenburg, Vriesenhof, Waboomsrivier, Warwick, Webersburg, Wellington, Welmoed, Whalehaven, Wildekrans, Windmeul, Woolworths, **Yonder Hill**, Zevenrivieren, Zevenwacht, Zonnebloem

Carignan Fairview, Welgegund

Cinsaut Arlington, Clairvaux, Darling Cellars, Franschhoek Vineyards, IWS/Pacific Wines, Landskroon, Perdeberg, Mont Rochelle, Swartland, Vinfruco, Waboomsrivier, Yellow Cellar (Helderkruin)

Gamay Noir (see also under Nouveau) Fairview, Kleine Zalze, Rhebokskloof, Verdun, Woolworths

Malbec Ashanti, Backsberg, **Bellevue**, Fairview

Merlot **Altydgedacht**, Arlington, Astonvale, Audacia, Avontuur, Backsberg, Badsberg, Bellingham, Bernheim, **Bilton**, laauwklippen, Bloemendal, **Bloupunt**, Boland, Boplaas, Boschendal, Boschkloof, Botha, Bovlei, Calitzdorp, **Camberley**, Cape Wine Cellars, Cape Wine Exports, Coleraine, Constantia Uitsig, Coppoolse Finlayson, Cordoba, Culemborg (Douglas Green), Darling Cellars, De Trafford, Delheim, Dellrust, Dieu Donné, Douglas Green, Drostdy, **Du Plessis**, Du Toitskloof, Durbanville Hills, Eikehof, Eikendal, Fairview, Fleur du Cap, Fort Simon, **Fraai Uitzicht**, Franschhoek Vineyards, Goue Vallei, Graceland, **Graham Beck**, **Groote Post**, Hartenberg, Helderkruin, Hoopenburg, IWS/Pacific Wines, JP Bredell, Jacaranda, Jacques Pinard, Jonkheer, Jordan, Kaapzicht, Kanu, Klawer, Kleine Zalze, Koelenhof, KWV/Cathedral Cellar, Laborie, **La Couronne**, Laibach, Landskroon, Libertas, **Linton Park**, Longridge, Longridge Bay View/Capelands, Lost Horizons, Louiesenhof, Louisvale, Louwshoek-Voorsorg, Meerendal, Meerlust, Meinert, Mont Rochelle, M'reson, Morgenhof, Mount Rozier, Mouton-Excelsior, Natural Corporation, Nederburg, Neethlingshof, Nelson's Creek, **Nietvoorbij**, Overgaauw, Overhex, Plaisir de Merle, Porcupine Ridge, Post House, Radford Dale, Remhoogte, Rhebokskloof, Rickety Bridge, Riebeek, **Rijk's**, Robertson, Romansrivier, **Rooiberg**, Ruitersvlei, Rust en Vrede, Savanha, Saxenburg, Saxenburg, Seidelberg, Shoprite Checkers, Simonsvlei, Somerbosch, Sonop, Spar, Spice Route, Spier, Spruitdrift, Steenberg, Stellenzicht, Swartland, Thelema, Tradouw (Barrydale), Trawal, Tulbagh Co-op, Uiterwyk, **Upland**, Veenwouden, Vera Cruz, Verdun, Vergelegen, Vergenoegd, Villiera, Vinfruco, Vlottenburg, Warwick, Wellington, Welmoed Reserve, Whalehaven, Wildekrans, Windmeul, **Woolworths**, Yonder Hill, Zandvliet, Zonnebloem

Mourvèdre **Beaumont**

Nebbiolo Steenberg

Petit verdot **Plaisir de Merle**

Pinot Noir Avontuur, Backsberg, Barefoot, **Bon Courage**, **Boschendal**, Bouchard Finlayson, Claridge, Eikendal, Glen Carlou, Goedvertrouw, Goudveld, **Groote Post**, Hamilton Russell Vineyards/Ashbourne, Haute Cabrière, Hoopenburg, Klein Constantia, Meerlust, Muratie, Neil Ellis, Paul Cluver, Signal Hill, Sonop, Steenberg, Thandi, Vergelegen, Whalehaven, Zonnebloem

Pinotage Altydgedacht, Ashanti, Ashwood, Avontuur, Backsberg, Badsberg, Beaumont, **Bellevue**, Bellingham, Bergsig, Bernheim, Beyerskloof, Blaauwklippen, Boland, **Bonnievale**, Boplaas, Botha, Bouwland, Bovlei, Cape Wine Cellars, Cape Wine Exports, Cederberg, Claridge, Clos Malverne, Coppoolse Finlayson, Culemborg (Douglas Green), Darling Cellars, De Wet, Deetlefs, Delheim, Dellrust, Diamant Rouge, Die Krans, Diemersdal, Douglas, Drostdy, Du Toitskloof, Durbanville Hills, Eaglevlei, Eersterivier, Fairview, Fleur du Cap, Franschhoek Vineyards, Goede Hoop, Goedvertrouw, Goudini, Goudveld, Goue Vallei, Graham Beck, Grangehurst, Hidden Valley, Groene Cloof, Groot Constantia, Groot Eiland, Helderberg, Helderkruin, Hidden Valley, Huguenot, IWS/Pacific Wines, JP Bredell, Jacobsdal, Kaapzicht, Kanonkop, **Klawer**, Kleindal (Vinimark), Kleine Zalze, **Kloovenburg**, Knorhoek, Koelenhof, KWV/Cathedral Cellar, L'Avenir, Laborie, Laibach, Landskroon, Landzicht, Lanzerac, L'Émigré, Longridge/Bay View, Louwshoek-Voorsorg, Makro, Malan Family Vintners, Mellasat, Middelvlei, Mooiplaas, Mooiuitsig, M'reson, Morgenhof, Mount Rozier, **Mouton-Excelsior**, **Muldersvlei**, **Natural Corporation**, Nederburg, Neethlingshof, **Neil Ellis**, **Nietvoorbij**, Nelson's Creek, New Beginnings, **Newton Johnson**, Jonkheer, Onderkloof, Overhex, Paradyskloof, Perdeberg, Pick 'n Pay, Porterville, Remhoogte, Rickety Bridge, **Rider's Drift**, Riebeek, **Rijk's**, **Robertson**, Romansrivier, Rooiberg, Ruitersvlei, Sable View, **Sandown Bay**, Savanha, Saxenburg, **Scali**, Simonsig, Simonsvlei, **Siyabonga**, Slaley, Somerbosch, Sonop, Southern Right, Spar, Spice Route, **Spier**, Spruitdrift, Stellenzicht, Stony Brook, Swartland, Sylvanvale, **Thelema**, The Pinotage Company, Trawal, Uiterwyk, **Vera Cruz**, Viljoensdrift, Villiera, Villiersdorp, **Vinfruco**, Vlottenburg, Vriesenhof, Waboomsrivier, Warwick, Wellington, **Welmoed**, Wildekrans, **Windmeul**, Woolworths, Zevenwacht, Zonnebloem

Pontac Hartenberg

Ruby Cabernet **Agterkliphoogte**, Coleraine, Douglas, Drostdy, Du Preez, Goudini, Goudveld, Hilltop, Hinterland (Hartswater), Langverwacht, Long Mountain, Longridge Capelands, Lutzville, McGregor, **Merwida**, Oude Wellington, Robertson, Sonop, Spruitdrift, Uitvlucht, Villiersdorp, Vinfruco, Waboomsrivier

Sangiovese **Boplaas**, **Plaisir de Merle**

Shiraz **Ashanti**, Allesverloren, Altydgedacht, Arlington, Ashton, Avondale, Backsberg, Barefoot, Beaumont, Bellingham, Bertrams, Blaauwklippen, **Boekenhoutskloof**, Boland, Bon Courage, **Bonnievale**, Boplaas, Boschendal, Bovlei, Cape Wine Cellars, Coleraine, Coppoolse Finlayson, Darling Cellars, De Meye, De Trafford, Delheim, Dellrust, Diemersdal, Douglas Green, **Du Plessis, Du Preez**, Du Toitskloof, **Eikehof**, Fairview, Fort Simon, Genesis, Gilga, Goede Hoop, Graham Beck, Groot Constantia, **Groot Eiland**, Hartenberg, **Havana Hills**, Helderberg, Helderkruin, Hoopenburg, JP Bredell, Kaapzicht, Kanu, Khanya, Klein Constantia, Kleine Zalze, **Kloovenburg**, KWV/Cathedral Cellar, La Motte, Landskroon, L'Émigré, Lievland, Linton Park, Longridge, **Louwshoek**, **Luddite**, Middelvlei, **Mischa**, M'reson, Mouton-Excelsior, **Natural Corporation**, Nederburg, Neethlingshof, **Neil Ellis**, Nelson's Creek, Overgaauw, Pick 'n Pay, Plaisir de Merle, Rickety Bridge, Riebeek, **Rijk's**, **Robertson**, Rooiberg, Ruitersvlei, Rust en Vrede, Savanha, Saxenburg, Simonsig, Simonsvlei, Slaley, Slanghoek, Sonop, Spice Route, Steenberg, Stellenzicht, Stony Brook, Swartland, Trawal, **Uiterwyk**, **Van Loveren**, Vera Cruz, **Vergelegen**, Vergenoegd, Villiera, Vlottenburg, Wellington, **Welmoed**, Woolworths, Zandvliet/Astonvale, Zevenwacht, Zonnebloem

Tinta Barocca Allesverloren, Beaumont, Darling Cellars, Die Krans, Rust en Vrede, Swartland

Zinfandel **Ashanti**, Blaauwklippen, Fairview, Hartenberg

Blends

Cape 'Bordeaux' (blend of cab and/or merlot with any/all of the following cabernet franc, malbec, petit verdot) Avontuur, **Avondvrede**, Backsberg, **Bellevue**, Bertrams, Beyerskloof, Blaauwklippen, **Boschendal**, Boschkloof, Bouwland, Bovlei, Bradgate, Brenthurst, Buitenverwachting Buiten Keur, **Camberley**, Claridge, Clos Malverne, Constantia Uitsig, Cordoba, Craighall, **De Toren**, De Trafford, De Wet, Diemersdal, Dieu Donné, Durbanville Hills, Eersterivier, **Eikendal**, Fairview, Glen Carlou, Goede Hoop, Graham Beck, Grangehurst, Groot Constantia, Gouverneurs Reserve, Hartenberg, **Havana Hills**, Helderberg, Jacaranda, Jean Daneel Wines, Jonkheer, Jordan, Kaapzicht, Kanonkop, **Kanu**, Klein Constantia, Klein Gustrouw, Kloofzicht, Koelenhof, KWV/Cathedral Cellar, L'Avenir, La Bri, **La Couronne**, La Motte, Laborie, Laibach, Le Bonheur, Le Riche, Lemberg, L'Émigré, Lievland, Louiesenhof, Louisvale, Makro, Malan Family Vintners, Meerendal, Meerlust, Meinert, Mont Destin, **Morgenhof**, Motif (Steenberg), Mouton-Excelsior, Mulderbosch, Muratie, Napier, Nederburg, Neethlingshof, Neil Ellis, **Nietvoorbij**, Nuy, Overgaauw, Paradyskloof, Perdeberg, **Reyneke**, **R&R**, Rickety Bridge, Rozendal, Rustenberg, Saxenburg, Seidelberg, **Shoprite**, Simonsig, Simonsvlei, Sinnya (Robertson Valley Wines), **Slaley**, Somerbosch, Spar, Spice Route, Steenberg, Stellenzicht, **Stony Brook**, **Stormberg**, Swartland, Talana Hill, Tradouw, Tulbagh Co-op, Uitvlucht, Veenwouden, **Vendôme**, Verdun, Vergelegen, Vergenoegd, Villiera, Villiersdorp, **Vinfruco**, Vredenheim, Vriesenhof, Warwick, Welgemeend, Weltevrede, WhaleHaven, Wildekrans, Windmeul, Woolworths, Yonder Hill, Zevenwacht, Zonnebloem

Other dry red blends with cabernet Alto Rouge, Ashwood, Avondale, Beaumont, Bellingham, Bonnievale, Boplaas, Boschendal, Botha, Brampton, Calitzdorp, Cederberg, **Clos Malverne**, Coppoolse Finlayson, Cordoba/ Mount Claire, **Darling Cellars**, De Zoete Inval, Delheim, Douglas Green, Drostdy, Eikendal, Glen Carlou, Goedverwacht, Graham Beck, **Grangehurst**, Hartenberg, Hazendal, Huguenot, IWS/Pacific, Kaapzicht, Kanonkop, Ken Forrester, **Khanya**, Kleine Zalze, Koelenhof, KWV, Laibach, Lievland, Longridge Bay View, Lost Horizons, Lutzville, Makro, Malan Family Vintners, Mont du Toit, Morgenhof, Nederburg, Opstal, Oude Wellington, Panarotti's, Pick 'n Pay, Plaisir de Merle, Porterville, Rhebokskloof, **Rider's Drift**, Roodezandt, Rooiberg, Ruitersvlei, Rust en Vrede, Saxenburg, Shoprite Checkers,

Simonsig, Slaley, Somersbosch, Sonop, Spar, Spur, St. Elmo's, **Stellenbosch Vineyards**, Swartland, Uitkyk, Van Loveren, Vaughan Johnson, Vinfruco, Vlottenburg, Vredenheim, Warwick, Woolworths, **Zandvliet**, Zevenwacht

Other dry red blends Arlington, Ashton, Ashwood, Avontuur, Backsberg, Barrydale, **Bergsig**, Bonnievale, **Brandvlei**, Cape Wine Cellars, **Carneby Liggle**, Coppoolse Finlayson, Dellrust, Doornkraal, Douglas, Drostdy, Du Toitskloof, Fairview, Fort Simon, Goudini, Groot Constantia, Hanseret, Helderberg, Huguenot, IWS/Pacific Wines, **Joubert-Tradauw**, Kanu, Klawer, **Laibach**, Landskroon, Long Mountain, Longridge Bay View, Lost Horizons, Merwespont, Middelvlei, Montagu, **Muldersvlei**, Naked Truth, Nelson's Creek, Overgaauw, Overmeer, Pick 'n Pay, Riebeek, **Rietrivier**, Romansrivier, **Rooiberg**, Rosenburg, Ruitersvlei, Simonsvlei, Spar, Tassenberg, **Trawal**, Tulbagh Co-op, Uiterwyk, Van Loveren, Vaughan Johnson, Villiera, Vinfruco, Vlottenburg, Welgemeend, Wellington, **Woolworths**

Dessert wines

Unfortified

Late Harvest Ashton, Autumn Harvest, Bonnievale, Boplaas, Calitzdorp, Cape Wine Cellars, Culemborg, De Zoete Inval, Delheim Spatzendreck, Die Krans, Drostdy, Goudini, Goudveld, Heerenhof, Kellerprinz, Klawer, Lutzville, McGregor, Mooiuitsig, Overmeer, Riebeek, Roodezandt, Spar, Spruitdrift, Swartland, Tulbagh, Uitvlucht, **Vredendal**, Waboomsrivier, **Woolworths**, Zellerhof (Huguenot)

Special Late Harvest Ashton, Backsberg, Bergsig, Blaauwklippen, Bon Courage, **Bonnievale**, Botha, Bovlei, Cape Wine Cellars, Darling Cellars, Delheim, Dieu Donné, Drostdy, Du Toitskloof, Eikendal, Fairview, Goudini, Hanseret, Hartenberg, Huguenot, Kaapzicht, Klawer, L'Émigré, Lutzville, Nederburg, , Paul Cluver, Pick 'n Pay, Roodezandt, Rooiberg, Ruitersvlei, Shoprite Checkers, Simonsig, Simonsvlei, Slanghoek, Spar, Spruitdrift, Stellenbosch Vineyards, Swartland, Van Loveren, Vlottenburg, Weltevrede, Zonnebloem

Natural Sweet Ashanti, Avontuur, Beaumont, Boschendal, De Wetshof, Delheim, Doornkraal, **Grünberger**, Klein Constantia, Laibach, Meerendal, Nederburg, Saxenburg, Signal Hill, Simonsig, Swartland, **Sylvanvale**, Vredenheim, Zonnebloem

'Straw' Wine De Trafford, **Fairview**

Noble Late Harvest (From botrytis-affected grapes) **Amani**, Ashanti, Avontuur, Boland, Bon Courage, Cederberg, De Wet, De Wetshof, Delheim, Dieu Donné, Groot Constantia, **Joostenberg**, Ken Forrester, **Kanu**, Klein Constantia, Lievland, Morgenhof, Nederburg, Neethlingshof, **Overhex**, Robertson, Romansrivier, Rustenberg, Signal Hill, Simonsig, Simonsvlei, Slanghoek, Spier, Stellenzicht, Stony Brook, Vera Cruz, Vergelegen Sémillon, Woolworths, Zonnebloem

Fortified

Non-Muscat White Die Krans, KWV, Pierre Jourdan

Non-Muscat Red **Barefoot**, Boplaas, Botha, Doornkraal, Douglas, Fairview, Jacaranda, Laborie, Landzicht, Louwshoek-Voorsorg, Mons Ruber, Perdeberg, Porterville, Rooiberg, Slanghoek, **Swartland**

Muscat Hanepoot
Bergsig, Bonnievale, Boplaas, Bovlei, **Brandvlei**, Calitzdorp, De Wet, Doornkraal, Douglas, Du Toitskloof, Fairview, Goudini, Goue Vallei, Groot Eiland, Huguenot, Kaapzicht, Klawer, Koelenhof, Landzicht, Louwshoek-Voorsorg, Mons Ruber, Mooiuitsig, Muratie Amber, Opstal, Overhex, Perdeberg, Porterville, **Rietrivier**, Romansrivier, Simonsvlei, Simonsvlei, Slanghoek, Spruitdrift, Stellenbosch Vineyards, **Swartland**, Villiersdorp, Vlottenburg, Waboomsrivier, Wellington

Morio Muscat Landskroon

Muscat de Hambourg Vlottenburg

White Muscadel **Avondale**, Ashton, Boland, Bon Courage, Boplaas, Calitzdorp, Clairvaux, Die Krans, Goue Vallei, Graham Beck, Grundheim, Huguenot, Klawer, Landzicht, McGregor, Mons Ruber, Mooiuitsig, Nuy, Roodezandt, Simonsvlei, Spruitdrift, Uitvlucht, Weltevrede

Red Muscadel **Agterkliphoogte**, Ashton, Boland, Bon Courage, Boplaas Red Dessert, Clairvaux, De Wet, Doornkraal, Douglas, Du Toitskloof, Grundheim, Huguenot, Klawer, KWV, Landzicht, Louiesenhof, McGregor, Montagu, Mooiuitsig, Jonkheer, Nordale, Nuy, Overhex, Riebeek, **Rietrivier**, Rietvallei, Robertson, Roodezandt, Rooiberg, Seidelberg, Simonsvlei, Spruitdrift, **Trawal**, Uitvlucht, Van Loveren, Weltevrede

Cape 'port', white Boplaas, Doornkraal, KWV, Simonsvlei

Cape 'port', red Allesverloren, Alto, Ashton, Axe Hill, Beaumont, **Bergsig**, Bertrams, Blaauwklippen, Boplaas, Botha, Bovlei, Brampton, **Calitzdorp**, De Wet, De Zoete Inval, Dellrust, Die Krans, Doornkraal, Douglas, Douglas Green, Du Toitskloof, Franschhoek Vineyards, Glen Carlou, Goue Vallei, **Goudini**, Groot Constantia, Grundheim, Helderberg, Helderkruin, Huguenot, JP Bredell, **KWV**/Cathedral Cellar, Landskroon, L'Émigré, Louiesenhof, **Louwshoek**, Makro, McGregor, Mons Ruber, Mooiuitsig, **Morgenhof**, Muratie, **Nietvoorbij**, Overgaauw, Riebeek, Robertson, Romansrivier, Roodezandt, Rooiberg, **Ruitersvlei**, Simonsig, Simonsvlei, **Somerbosch**, Slanghoek, Stellenbosch Vineyards, Swartland, Vergenoegd, Villiera, Villiersdorp, Waboomsrivier, Wellington

SPARKLING WINES

Méthode Cap Classique (champenoise)

White Ambeloui, Ashanti Pearls, Avontuur, Backsberg, **Barrydale**, Bloemendal, Bon Courage, Boschendal, Buitenverwachting, Cabrière, **Chamonix**, Dieu Donné, Douglas Green, Graham Beck, Helderkruin, JC le Roux, Klein Constantia, Longridge, Môreson, Morgenhof, Nederburg, **Ruitersvlei**, Rustenberg, Saxenburg, Simonsig, Steenberg, TenFiftySix, Twee Jonge Gezellen, Villiera, Vinfruco, Woolworths

Rosé Avontuur, Cabrière, Villieram Woolworths

Red Graham Beck, Stellenbosch Vineyards

Non-MCC Sparkling

White (dry, often carbonated) Agusta, Bellingham, Boland, Boplaas, Botha, Bovlei, Country Cellars, Delaire, Du Toitskloof, Eikendal, Here XVII Souverein, JC le Roux, Kaapzicht, Klawer, La Cotte (Franschhoek Vineyards), McGregor, **Merwida**, Naked Truth, Nederburg, Papillon Brut (Van Loveren), Paul Bonnay, Riebeek, Rooiberg, **Sonop**, **Stellenbosch Vineyards**, **Swartland**, Tulbagh, Wine Warehouse, Woolworths

White (off-dry/semi-sweet) Cinzano, Grand Mousseux, JC le Roux, Nuy, Boplaas, Bovlei, Calitzdorp, Cape Chamonix, Die Krans, Doornkraal, Eikendal, Grand Mousseux, Jean le Riche, Koelenhof, La Cotte (Franschhoek Vineyards), McGregor, Mont d'Or Naked Truth, Nederburg, Panarotti's, Papillon (Van Loveren), Paul Bonnay, Rhebokskloof, Riebeek, **Rietrivier**, Roodezandt, Rooiberg, Simonsvlei, Slanghoek, Spur, Swartland, Trawal, Villiersdorp , Woolworths, Boland, Country Cellars, Die Poort, Huguenot, Jac Canard, Kaapzicht, Lutzville, Montagu, **Sonop**, Tulbagh, Uitvlucht

Pink (dry) Twee Jonge Gezellen

Pink (off-dry/semi-sweet) 5th Ave Cold Duck, Bergsig, Huguenot, Rooiberg, Swartland, Waboomsrivier, Woolworths

Red (off-dry/semi-sweet) Cinzano, Grand Mousseux, JC le Roux, Paul Bonnay Rouge

Perlé Wines
Ashton, Autumn Harvest, Bergsig, Capenheimer (Monis), Culemborg (Douglas Green), Die Poort, Grünberger (Bergkelder), Waboomsrivier

SPECIALISED STYLES

Kosher Wines
Kleine Draken

'Light' & Low-Alcohol Wines
(Note: Some labels duplicated elsewhere.) 5th Avenue Cold Duck (SFW), Bergsig, Boplaas, Calitzdorp, Cinzano, Country Cellars (Spar), De Wet, De Wetshof, Drostdy, Fleur du Cap, Grand Mousseux (SFW), Grünberger (Bergkelder), Hartswater, JC le Roux, Landzicht, Rooiberg, Swartland, Trawal, Twee Jonge Gezellen, Woolworths

Nouveau
Woolworths

Sweet Red (unfortified)
Avontuur Dolcetto, **Sylvanvale**

Winegrowing areas

FROM A 17TH-CENTURY experimental vineyard in the Dutch East India Company gardens below Table Mountain, South Africa's vignoble over more than 340 vintages has spread over a large area. Grapes are now grown in close to 60 officially declared appellations covering in excess of 100 000 hectares. Since the introduction of the Wine of Origin scheme in 1972/3, production zones have been designated 'regions', 'districts' and 'wards' — the latter being smaller geographical units whose soil, climate and ecological factors are officially, though not universally, considered distinctive. 'Estates', the smallest category of the WO system, consist of single farms or multiple properties run as a unit. In this guide, only officially registered estates — at press time there were close to 100, though some do not produce under their own label and some do not make wine at all — are referred to as 'estates'. This distinguishes them from what in officialese are 'private wine cellars', 'co-operatives' and 'producing wholesalers'. The following are some of the more important cultivation zones:

Constantia Sometimes referred to as the cradle of wine making in the Cape, Constantia is a standalone ward within the umbrella Coastal Region. A leafy zone on the south-east of the Cape Peninsula facing into the Atlantic ocean, Constantia is cooled by sea breezes from two sides: south-easters across False bay and northerly gusts over Constantiaberg, the scenic mountain spine. A first-division viticultural area focused since the earliest days on fine wine production. Recognised for whites generally, sauvignon blanc in particular.

Durbanville A Coastal ward in transition, poised between rustic tradition and headlong development. Among the original farmland planted to vines (the Starke family property, Meerendal, boasted 60 000 vines as early as 1716), these rolling hills are starting to move out of the anonymous shadow of bulk wine production into the glare of solo stardom. Important quality factors include deep, water retentive soils, cooling summer nighttime mists and climatic influences from both Table and, more marginally, False bays. Recognised for sauvignon blanc, merlot.

Klein Karoo Known locally as Kannaland, after the otherwise nondescript family of succulent plants whose dream inducing properties are legendary, this harsh yet striking inland region once was washed by a prehistoric ocean. Now it is semi-arid scrubland — perfect for ostrich farming but something of a challenge for wine growers who rely on irrigation for their vineyards. Similarities (in climate, if not soil) with the Douro Valley of Portugal have inspired some local vintners, principally around the quaint village of Calitzdorp, to apply their talents to 'port' increasingly with results that impress even the Portuguese. Recognised for 'port' styles, other fortifieds.

Olifants River In these most northerly Cape grape growing areas, you will find more than just sun baked sleepy wineries producing no-frills *vin ordinaire*. Quality moves are afoot here epitomised by the Vredendal Co-operative (single largest winery in South Africa, handling a mega-harvest of 70 000 tons annually), where a programme is underway to pinpoint and separately bottle the most promising fruit from top-performing individual farms and vineyards. Cooler upland zones such as Piekenierskloof, an Olifants River ward proclaimed in 1999, are promising developments. Recognised for everyday reds, fortifieds.

Orange River This is the hottest, most northerly Cape growing area, and the 4th largest, with more than 15 000 ha (close to 15% of the national vineyard) in river beds along the sprawling Orange. Overwhelmingly a white grape area: the three main varieties are sultana (10 500 ha, mainly for drying), colombard and chenin. But plantings of reds, especially merlot, shiraz and pinotage, are spreading five times faster than white.

Paarl Paarl appellation has many different mesoclimates, soils and aspects and thus succeeds with a wide range of styles/varieties. The ward of Wellington, originally known as Limietvallei (Frontier Valley), is shedding its Sleepy Hollow image with some promising wines, especially reds, from properties mainly on higher ground. Franschhoek, founded by 17th-century Huguenots and now a millionaire's playground, falls within this viticultural district. Paarl is recognised for shiraz and, more recently, viognier/mourvèdre grown on warmer slopes; Franschhoek recognised for chenin, semillon.

Robertson 'Valley of vines and roses' is Robertson's tourism slogan — and it's appropriate. Since the turn of the previous century upstream Brandvlei Dam has regulated the flow of the Breede River. A dependable supply of water has seen the flowering of over 40-million vines and innumerable blooms of all sorts, including splendid splashes of roses. Though a warmer area, Robertson traditionally has been white wine country. However, recently there have been hints of red-wine promise, especially shiraz. Significant features include cooling late afternoon south-easters during summer, and limestone soils. Recognised for chardonnay, colombard for brandy, everyday whites, sparkling.

Stellenbosch To many, this intensively farmed district around the town of Stellenbosch is *the* red-wine producing area in South Africa. Yet many of its whites (and bubblies and fortifieds) also feature in the SA premier league. Key contributors to quality are the cooler mountain slopes, variegated soil types and breezes off False Bay which help moderate summer temperatures. Officially designated wards within the district are Jonkershoek Valley east of Stellenbosch town; Simonsberg, encompassing the south-western foothills of Simonsberg mountain; and the appellations of Bottelary, Devon Valley and Papegaaiberg north-west of the town. Further subdivisions are likely in the future. Recognised for cabernet, pinotage, shiraz, sparkling.

Swartland Traditionally associated with big, booming reds, this sunny, previously neglected wheat and tobacco area north of Cape Town since the early 1990s has shown it can yield top-table white wines too. Now the district is on a new roll, especially the Groenekloof vineyards nearer the cooling Atlantic, and the more established precinct of Malmesbury. Inland, scenic Tulbagh with its mountain skirted vineyards, in the past has concentrated on white varieties. But there is now a small movement towards planting reds. Recognised for pinotage, shiraz, sauvignon blanc.

Walker Bay To the adage that the best wine is made within sight of the ocean, the wine-growing fraternity of Walker Bay might add: "And within sight of a whale's flipper". They would be referring to the Southern Rights which return every year to calve in the waters off Hermanus, the ward's main town. Since the 1980s some of the Cape's splashiest wines have come from this maritime area south-east of Cape Town which, with the cool climate Elgin vineyards, resorts under the official Overberg District appellation. Recognised for pinot noir, chardonnay and aromatic pinotage.

Worcester This is the big daddy of SA winedom, measured by the number of vines planted — close to 60-million, or nearly 20% of the national vineyard. Bulk of production is distilled into brandy — the world's biggest array of potstills is a much ogled feature of the district capital of Worcester — and most of the remainder goes directly to wholesaling producers. But small quantities are bottled under own labels, and these often represent good value for money. Traditionally vineyards were sited in fertile alluvial soils; now they are starting to move up into the hills. Recognised for fortified muscadel, hanepoot.

Wine of Origin-defined Western Cape Production Areas

Region	District	Wards
Breede River Valley	Robertson	Agterkliphoogte
		Bonnievale
		Boesmansrivier
		Eilandia
		Hoopsrivier
		Klaasvoogds
		Le Chasseur
		McGregor
		Vinkrivier
	Worcester	Aan-de-Doorns
		Goudini
		Nuy
		Scherpenheuvel
		Slanghoek
	Swellendam	Buffeljags
		Stormsvlei
Klein Karoo		Montagu
		Tradouw
	Calitzdorp	
Coastal	Cape Point	
		Constantia
	Tygerberg	Durbanville
	Paarl	Franschhoek Valley
		Wellington
	Stellenbosch	Jonkershoek Valley
		Papegaaiberg
		Simonsberg-Stellenbosch
		Bottelary
		Devon Valley
	Swartland	Groenekloof
		Riebeekberg
	Tulbagh	
Olifants River	Lutzville Valley	Koekenaap
		Spruitdrift
		Vredendal
		Piekenierskloof
	Overberg	Walker Bay
		Elgin
	Douglas*	
	Piquetberg	
		Hartswater*
		Lower Orange*
		Cederberg
		Ceres
		Herbertsdale
		Rietrivier (Free State)*
		Ruiterbosch
		Swartberg

Boberg (fortified wines from Paarl & Tulbagh)

*Officially designated Northern Cape geographical unit
Source: SAWIS

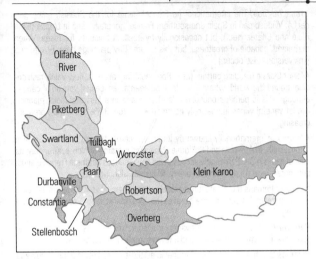

- Olifants River
- Piketberg
- Swartland
- Tulbagh
- Worcester
- Paarl
- Klein Karoo
- Durbanville
- Robertson
- Constantia
- Stellenbosch
- Overberg

. . . .

Grape varieties mentioned in the guide

LEGISLATION requires the presence in the wine of only 75% of the stated variety (85% for exports). Blends may only name component parts if those components were vinified separately, prior to blending; then they are listed with the larger contributor(s) named first. Figures given for proportion of national vineyard are for 1999 (latest available).

Red-wine varieties

Cabernet sauvignon Adaptable and internationally planted black grape making some of the world's finest and longest lasting wines. And retaining some of its inherent qualities even when overcropped in poorer soils and climates. Can stand alone triumphantly, but frequently blended with a wide range of other varieties: traditionally, as in Bordeaux, with cab franc, merlot and a few minor others, but also in South Africa, for example, sometimes partnering varieties such as shiraz and pinotage. Number of different clones, with differing characteristics. 6,7% of vineyard area, and steadily increasing (2,5% in 1987).

Cabernet franc Like its close relative cabernet sauvignon, with which it is often partnered, a classic part of the 'Bordeaux' blend, but in SA and elsewhere also used for varietal wines – particularly on the Loire. Insignificant vineyard area.

Carignan Hugely planted in the south of France, where it is not much respected. But there, as in SA, older, low-yielding vines can produce pleasant surprises. Insignificant vineyard area.

Cinsaut Cinsault in France. Another of the mass, undistinguished plantings of southern France, which only occasionally comes up trumps. Used to be known locally as hermitage, the name reflected in its offspring (with pinot noir), pinotage. 3,6% of vineyard area, and decreasing.

Gamay noir Although produces some serious long lived wines in Beaujolais, its use for (mainly) early and easy drinking in Beaujolais, often using carbonic maceration, is the model mostly copied in SA. Insignificant vineyard area.

. . . .

Grenache (noir) The international (ie French) name for the Spanish grape garnacha. Widespread in Spain and southern France, generally used in blends (as in Rioja and Chateauneuf), but occasionally by itself. A favourite for rosés. When restrained, capable of greatness, but this is rare. Tiny plantings here. (White and pink versions also occur.)

Merlot Classic blending partner (as in Bordeaux) for cabernet, now wildly fashionable around the world, where it tends to be seen as an 'easier' version of cab — although this is perhaps because it is often made in a less ambitious manner. Merlot varietal wines increasingly common in SA too. 3,6% of vineyard area, increasing.

Mourvèdre Internationally known by its French name, though originally Spanish (monastrell). In Australia and California also called mataro – which is, strangely, its official name in SA. Particularly successful in some serious southern French blends, and increasingly modish internationally. Miniscule plantings here.

Nebbiolo Perhaps the greatest red grape to have scarcely ventured from its home — Piedmont in this case, where it makes massive, tannic, long lived wines. Minute plantings here.

Petit verdot Use of this excellent variety in Médoc limited by its late ripening. Now appearing in some local blends, and a few varietals. Tiny quantities.

Pinotage South Africa's 'national grape' is a 1920s cross between pinot noir and cinsaut ('hermitage'). Became unfashionable in the 80s, with only a few champions, but now has cachet and some international success. Made in a range of styles, from simply fruity to ambitious, well-oaked examples. 5,5% of vineyard area, increasing.

Pinot noir Notoriously difficult grape to succeed with outside its native Burgundy, but SA, along with the rest of the New World, now producing excellent examples, especially as use of BK5 clone wanes. Usually matured in wood; seldom at bargain price. Very small proportion of the vineyard.

Ruby cabernet US cross between cabernet sauvignon and carignan, designed for heat tolerance. Rather rustic, used mostly in cheaper blends. 1,5% of vineyard area.

Shiraz Better known as syrah outside SA and Australia (and on some local labels too). Internationally increasing in popularity, with northern Rhône and now also Australia as its major domiciles. Clearly happy in warmer climates, shiraz is seen by many as the great hope for SA wine. Made here in a variety of styles — generally wooded, often with American oak. 3,3% of vineyard area, increasing (0,7% in 1987).

Tinta barocca Elsewhere spelt 'barroca'. One of the important Portuguese portmaking grapes, which is now its primary role in SA, usually blended. Also used for some varietal unfortified wines, and namelessly in some 'dry reds'. Insignificant vineyard area.

Touriga naçional Important Portuguese port-making grape, now usefully grown here for similar ends, along with tinta francisca, tinta roriz and souzão. Tiny plantings.

Zinfandel The quintessential Californian grape (of European origin, and the same as Italy's primitivo), used here in a small way for big wines. Tiny plantings.

White Wine Varieties

Chardonnay In the Cape, as elsewhere, many new vineyards of this grape have come onstream in recent years, with wines showing a wide range of styles, quality and price. Generally used varietally, but also in blends. Often heavily wooded in more ambitious wines. 5,7% of vineyard area, has increased greatly (0,7% in 1987), now stabilising.

Chenin blanc South Africa has more chenin (locally also called steen) vineyards than even France's Loire Valley, the variety's home. Used here for everything from generic 'dry whites', though to ambitious sweet wines, to brandy. Some notable table-wine successes in recent years, in a sea of overcropped mediocrity. 23,8% of vineyard area, declining fast (33% in 1987).

Colombar(d) One of the mainstays of brandy production in the Cape, colombard (usually without the 'd' in SA) also used for numerous varietal and blended wines, ranging from dry to sweet — seldom wooded. 11,2% of vineyard area, increasing.

Gewürztraminer Readily identifiable from its rose petal fragrance, best known in its Alsatian guise. In the Cape usually made in sweeter styles. Insignificant vineyard area.

Hanepoot Traditional Afrikaans name for muscat d'alexandrie, the Cape's most planted muscat variety (see also muscadel below). 4,3% of vineyard area (some for raisins and table grapes)

Muscadel Name used here for both muscat de frontignan and muscat blanc à petits grains (both red and white versions). The grape associated with the famous Constantia dessert wines of the 18th century today is used chiefly for dessert and fortified wines and for touching up blends. Red and white versions together 1,2% of vineyard area.

Muscat See Hanepoort and Muscadel.

Riesling The name a source of confusion to consumers, and of distress to the producers of what is known in its great homeland, Germany, simply as riesling and here officially as Rhine or weisser riesling. In SA, standing alone, 'riesling' usually, and officially, refers to Cape riesling (sometimes called Paarl or SA riesling), a much inferior grape properly known as crouchen blanc, mostly used here anonymously in blends, and sometimes varietally. Rhine/weisser riesling frequently in off-dry style here, in blends or varietally, some botrytised dessert examples — and developing terpene character much earlier in SA than in cooler climates. Cape riesling 2,7% of vineyard area, decreasing; Rhine/weisser 0,6%. Note: in this guide 'riesling' with qualification refers to the latter.

Sauvignon blanc Prestigious vine most associated with eastern Loire regions, Bordeaux and, increasingly, New Zealand — whose wines have helped restore fashionability to the grape. The Cape version no longer a poor relation of these. Usually dry, but some sweet wines; sometimes wooded, more often not (former sometimes called fumé blanc). 5% of vineyard area, increasing.

Semillon The present small hectarage devoted to semillon is a far cry from the early 19th century, when the grape, also known as 'groen' (green) grape, a reference to its bright foliage) represented 93% of all Cape vines. Sometimes heavily wooded. Now 1% of vineyard area.

Viognier Increasingly fashionable noble variety internationally, spreading out from its home in the northern Rhône, now showing promise here. Usually only lightly wooded, if at all. Insignificant vineyard area.

The major SA wine styles

Blanc de blancs White wine made only from white grapes; also a term for champagne (and **méthode cap classique**) made only from white grapes/chardonnay.

Blanc fumé or **fumé blanc** Dry white made from sauvignon blanc, not necessarily finished in wood (nor smoked, smoky).

Blanc de noir A pink wine (shades range from off-white through peach to pink) made from red grapes.

Brut See sugar or sweetness, sparkling wine.

Cap classique See méthode cap classique.

Carbonated See sparkling wine.

Cru Meaning 'growth' in French, or the vineyard responsible for the provenance of a wine, as in Grand Cru, denoting a great vineyard, or Cru Bourgeois, of lesser quality. See premier grand cru.

Cultivar Grape variety (a contraction of 'cultivated variety').

Cuvée French term for the blend of a wine.

Demi-sec See sugar or sweetness.

Dessert wine A sweet wine, to accompany the dessert, but not necessarily only so; the French deploy their usual insouciance famously in drinking sweet Sauternes and Barsac at the start of a meal with pâté de foie gras.

Dry to sweet See sugar or sweetness.

Fortified wines Increased in alcoholic strength by the addition of spirits, to 16% or more alcohol by volume.

Grand cru Literally 'great growth' but in SA denoting the producer's own subjective, unofficial rating of a wine.

Jerepiko or **jeripigo** A red or white wine, fortified with grape spirit prior to fermentation starting; very sweet, with considerable unfermented grape flavours.

Late Harvest Sweet wine made from late harvested and therefore sweeter grapes. See **sugar or sweetness**.

Méthode cap classique (MCC) See sparkling wine.

Noble Late Harvest Sweet dessert wine exhibiting a noble rot (botrytis) character, from grapes infected by the botrytis cinerea fungus. This mould, in warm, misty autumn weather, attacks the skins of ripe grapes, causing much of the juice to evaporate. As the berries wither, their sweetness and flavour become powerfully concentrated. These nobly-rotten grapes yield some stunning dessert wines. By law, grapes for NLH must be harvested at a minimum of 28° Balling and residual sugar must exceed 50 g/ℓ.

Nouveau Term originated in Beaujolais for fruity young and light red, usually from gamay and made by the carbonic maceration method. Bottled a few weeks after vintage to capture youthful, fresh flavour of fruit and yeasty fermentation.

Premier grand cru Unlike in France, not an officially recognised rating in SA, simply a dry white.

Perlant, perlé, pétillant Lightly sparkling, carbonated wine.

Port Fortified dessert with improving quality record in Cape since late 1980s, partly through efforts of SA Port Producers' Association which recommends use of word 'Cape' to identify the local product. Following are SAPPA-defined styles: **Cape White**: non-muscat grapes, wood aged min 6 mths, any size vessel; **Cape Ruby**: blended, fruity, components aged min 6 mths, up to 3 years depending on size of vessel. Average age min 1 yr. **Cape Vintage**: fruit of one harvest; dark, full-bodied, vat-aged (any size); **Cape Vintage Reserve**: fruit of one harvest in yr of "recognised quality". Preferably aged min 1 yr, vats of any size, sold only in glass; **Cape Late Bottled Vintage (LBV)**: fruit of single "yr of quality", dark, full-bodied, slightly tawny colour, aged 3–6 years (of which min 2 years in oak); **Cape Tawny**: wood matured, amber-orange (tawny) colour, smooth, slightly nutty taste (white grapes not permitted); **Cape Dated Tawny**: single-vintage tawny.

Residual sugar See sugar or sweetness.

Rosé Pink wine, made from red or a blend of red and white grapes. The red grape skins are removed before the wine takes up too much colouring.

Sparkling wine Bubbly, or 'champagne', usually white but sometimes rosé and even red, given its effervescence by carbon dioxide — allowed to escape in the normal winemaking process. **Champagne** is sparkling wine that undergoes its second fermentation in the bottle. Under an agreement with France, SA does not use the term 'champagne', which properly is a geographic appellation describing the sparkling wines from the Champagne area. Instead, **méthode cap classique** (MCC) is the SA term to describe sparkling wines made by the classic méthode champenoise. **Charmat** undergoes its second, bubble-forming fermentation in a tank and is bottled under pressure. **Carbonated** sparklers are made by the injection of carbon dioxide bubbles (as in fizzy soft drinks). See also **sugar or sweetness**.

Special Late Harvest SA designation for a dessert style. Grapes must be harvested at a minimum of 22° Balling sugar (quite normal for even dry wines) and have a maximum of 50 g/ℓ of residual sugar.

Stein Semi-sweet white wine, usually a blend and often confused with steen, a grape variety (chenin blanc), though most steins are made partly from steen grapes.

Sugar or sweetness In still wines: extra-dry or bone-dry are wines below 2,5 g/ℓ in residual sugar content, undetectable to the taster. A wine legally is dry up to 4 g/ℓ. Taste buds will begin picking up a slight sweetness, or softness, in a wine — provided its acidity is not excessive — at about 5–6 g/ℓ, when it is still off-dry. But by about 8–9 g/ℓ a definite sweetness can be noticed. However, an acidity of 8–9 g/ℓ can render a sweet wine fairly crisp even with a sugar content of 20 g/ℓ plus. Official sweetness levels in SA wine are:

Still wines	Sugar (g/ℓ)	Sparkling wines	Sugar (g/ℓ)
Extra dry	≤ 2,5	Extra dry/brut	≤ 15
Dry	≤ 4	Dry/sec	15–35
Semi-dry	4–12	Semi-sweet/demi-sec	35–50
Semi-sweet	4–30	Sweet/doux	> 50
Late Harvest	20–30		
Special Late Harvest (SLH)[1]	≤ 50		
Natural Sweet (or Sweet Natural)	> 30		
Noble Late Harvest (NLH)[2]	> 50		
Naturally dried grape wine (straw wine)[3]	> 30		

[1] Grapes must be harvested at 22° Balling or more, i.e. ripe.
[2] Must have at least 30 g/ℓ sugar-free extract, grapes harvested at 28° Balling or more.
[3] Potential alcohol must be at least 16% by volume.

Varietal wine From single variety of grape. In SA must consist of 75% or more of the stated grape — BUT 85% or more if exported.

Vintage In SA primarily used to denote year of harvest. Not a substantive quality classification (a 'vintage' port in Europe means one from an officially declared great port grape year.)

· ·

Some recent Cape vintages

South African vintage variations are relatively insignificant. Dry hot summers are the norm. Even when they aren't, as in 1996, the vastly different conditions in widely scattered growing areas — 350 km north and east — make any comments generalisations at best. Also, many areas and producers plant a formidable mix of grapes ripening across the picking season to stagger the harvest. The lack of uniformity extends to soil types, clones and climates within the same regions. Vineyard practices themselves and wine-making techniques are changing so fundamentally and extensively that they are the important determinants of individual vintage quality variations. The comments below are therefore very general. With some exceptions, Cape dry whites should probably be consumed within a year.

2000 Something of a viticultural *annus horribilis*: soaring harvest temperatures for the third season running; generally parched conditions with costly fire damage in some zones; freak hailstorms which destroyed entire crops in parts. These adversities restricted total output to about 900-million litres, below 1999's 914-million. But improved vineyard management contributed to healthy, intensely-flavoured fruit and the prospect of some very exciting, fleshy, long-lived reds. By and large the wow-factor is lower among the whites, though as in 1999 there are fine chardonnays, semillons, chenins and even sauvignon blancs.

1999 Some excellent chardonnays, a few sauvignon blancs and semillons, but on the whole whites lack concentration and flavour. The reds, like 1998, are fat and alcoholic but show less fruity opulence.

1998 Fat, alcoholic wines generally: whites tend to lack flavour intensity; reds big, booming but flavoursome, excellent maturation potential. Undoubtedly a red-wine year.

1997 Mixed year: a number of both reds and whites outclass previous vintages, but some producers who lacked the courage to wait for their vineyards to ripen make green and thin wines.

1996 Cool season marked by several sets of late showers in many areas; but a record yield overall. Very average quality reds, mainly for early drinking. Patchy whites; some good chenins and sémillons. Not a great year.

1995 Very dry and hot vintage — and even lower yields in many varieties than in 1994. A ripe year, for big but concentrated reds with good maturation potential.

Recent above-average red wine years: 1991, 1992, 1994, 1995, 1997, 1998, 1999. The 1970s: a rough rule of thumb, the even years were usually more favourable for reds (of only academic interest now, the uneven years, marginally cooler, favoured whites.) The best of the 1970s was undoubtedly 74; but it is rare to find any that have hung in. A few 78s are passable. Very little excitement elsewhere. The 1980s: again, even years generally favoured reds (82, 84, 86), but uneven 'white' years 87 and especially 89 produced some remarkable reds.

. . . .

Some winetasting terms used in this guide

Short of a ready description? Here are a few frequently used words, phrases and explanations that may be helpful.

Accessible, approachable Flavours and feel of the wine are harmonious, easily recognised; it is ready to drink.

Aftertaste The lingering flavours and impressions of a wine; its persistence — the longer, the better.

Alcohol Produced by yeasts fermenting the sugars in the grape. An essential component of wine, providing fullness, richness and, at higher levels, sometimes an impression of sweetness. Also a preservative, helping keep wines in good condition. Measured by volume of the total liquid. Most unfortified table wines in SA vary between 11% and 14% by vol; fortifieds range from about 16% to 21%.

Astringent Mouth-puckering sensation in the mouth, associated with high tannin (and sometimes acid).

Aroma Smells in the bouquet, or nose.

Attack First sensations on palate/nose — pungent, aggressive, quiet, etc.

Attractive Having some (modest) positive attributes; pleasant.

Austere Usually meaning unyielding, sometimes harsh.

Backbone The wine's well formed, firm, not flabby or insipid.

Baked 'Hot', earthy quality. Usually from scorched/shrivelled grapes which have been exposed too long to the sun, or from too warm a barrel fermentation, especially in some whites.

Balance Desirable attribute. The wine's chief constituents — alcohol, acid, tannin, fruit and wood (where used) — are in harmony.

Bead Bubbles in sparkling wine; a fine, long-lasting bead is the most desirable. See also mousse.

Big Expansive in the mouth, weighty, full-bodied, as a result of high alc or fruit concentration.

Bite or grip Imparted by tannins and acids (and alcohol in fortified wines); important in young wines designed for ageing. If overdone can impart undesirable bitterness, harshness or spirity 'glow'.

Bitter Sensation perceived mainly on the back of the tongue, and in the finish of th e wine. Usually unpleasant though an accepted, if not immediately admired character of certain Italians wines. Sometimes more positively associated with the taste of a specific fruit or nut, such as cherry-pip or almond.

Body Fullness on the palate.

Botrytised Exhibits a noble rot/botrytis character, from grapes infected by the botrytis cinerea fungus (see 'Noble Late Harvest', page 418).

Bottle age Negative or positive, depending on context. Positively describes development of aromas/flavours (i.e. complexity) as wine moves from youth to maturity. Much prized attribute in fine whites and reds. Negatively, bottle-age results in a wine with stale, empty, or even off odours.

Buttery Flavour and texture associated with barrel-fermented white wines, especially chardonnays; rich, creamy smoothness.

Charming Usually used in the context of lighter, simpler wines. Sometimes synonymous with 'sweet' (both as in 'sugary' and 'dear').

Classic Showing similar characteristics of the finest examples of European classics of claret, burgundy etc; usually associated with balance, elegance, subtlety.

Coarse Rough, unbalanced tannins, acid, alcohol or oak.

Complexity Strong recommendation. A complex wine has several layers of flavour, usually developing with age/maturation. See bottle-age.

Corked Wine is faulty; its flavours have been tainted by yeast, fungal or bacterial infections from the cork. It smells of damp, mouldy bark in its worst stages — but sometimes it's barely detectable. In a restaurant, a corked wine should be rejected and returned immediately; producers are honour-bound to replace corked wine.

Creamy Not literally creamy, of course; more a silky, buttery feel and texture.

Crisp Refers to acidity. Positively, means fresh, clean; negatively, too tart, sharp.

Deep and depth Having many layers; intense; also descriptive of a serious wine.

Dense Well-padded texture, flavour-packed.

Deposits (also sediment or crust) Tasteless and harmless tartrates, acid crystals or tannin in older red wines. Evidence that wine has not been harshly fined, filtered or cold-stabilised.

Dried out Bereft of fruit, harder constituents remaining, tired.

Earthy Usually positive, wine showing its origins from soil, minerally, damp leaves, mushrooms etc.

Easy Undemanding (and hopefully inexpensive).

Elegant Stylish, refined, 'classic'.

Esters Scents and smells, usually generated by alcohols and acids in wine. A wine can be described as 'estery' when these characteristics are prominent.

Extract An indication of the 'substance' of a wine, expressed as sugar free or total extract (which would include some sugars). 18 g/ℓ would be low, light; anything much above 23 g/ℓ in whites is significant; the corresponding threshold for reds is around 30 g/ℓ.

Fat Big, full, ample in the mouth.

Finesse Graceful, polished. Nothing excessive.

Finish The residual sensations — tastes and textures — after swallowing. Should be pleasant (crisp, lively) and enduring, not short, dull or flat. See also **length**.

Firm Compact, has good **backbone**.

Flabby Usually, lacking **backbone**, esp. acid.

Flat Characterless, unexciting, lacking acid. Or bubbly which has lost its fizz.

Fleshy Very positive, meaning a wine is well fleshed out with warm texture and grape flavours.

Flowery Floral, flower-like (i.e. the smell of rose, honeysuckle, jasmine etc). Distinct from **fruity** (i.e. smell/taste of papaya, cantaloupe, grape! etc)

Forward rather than shy; advancing in age too; mature.

Fresh Lively, youthful, invigorating. Closely related to the amount of acid in the wine and absence of oxidative character: a big, intensely sweet dessert without a backbone of acidity will taste flat and sickly; enough acid and the taste is fresh and uncloying.

Fruity See floral.

Full High in alcohol and extract.

Gravelly With suggestions of minerally, earthy quality; also firm texture.

Green Usually unripe, sour; sometimes simply youthful.

Grip Often almost literally, gripping, firm on palate, in finish. Acid, tannin, alcohol are contributors.

Heady Usually refers to the smell of a wine. High in alcohol; intense, high toned.

Herbaceous Grassy, hay-like, heathery, can also indicate under-ripeness.

Hollow Lacking substance, flavours.

Honey or **honeyed** Sometimes literally a honey/beeswax taste or flavour; a sign of developing maturity in some varieties or more generally a sign of bottle age.

Hot Burning sensation of alcohol in finish.

Intensity, also **concentration** No flab, plenty of driving flavour.

Lean Thin, mean, lacking charm of ample fruit.

Lees/leesy Taste-imparting dead yeast cells (with skins and other solid matter) remaining with wine in tank/barrel (or bottle in the case of méthode champenoise sparkling wines) after fermentation. The longer the wine is 'on its lees' (sur lie) the more richness and flavour it should absorb.

Light Officially wines under 10% alcohol, also light in body (and usually short on taste); a health-conscious trend in both reds and whites.

Lively Bouncy, fresh flavours.

Long or **length** Enduring; wine's flavours reverberate in the palate long after swallowing.

Maderised Wine smells/tastes oxidised and flat; colour is often brownish. Overmature.

Meaty Sometimes suggesting a general savouriness; but also literally the aroma of meat — raw, smoked etc. Often applied to merlot, shiraz, sometimes cabernet.

Mousse Fizz in sparkling wines; usually refers also to quality, size and effervescence of the bubbles. See also **bead**.

Mouthfeel, **mouthfilling** Texture; feel; racy, crispness (fine with appropriate dishes) or generous, supple, smooth.

Neutral What it says, neither here nor there.

New World Generally implies accessible, bold, often extrovert (in terms of fruit and use of oak). **Old World** embraces terms like subtle, complex, less oaky, more varied and generally more vinous (than fruity). See also **classic**.

Oaky Having exaggerated oak aromas/flavours (vanilla, spice, char, woodsmoke etc). Young wines can outgrow oakiness, older ones less readily. Oak balanced by fruit in young wines may lessen with age, but over-oaked young wines (where fruit is not in balance) will become over-oaked old wines.

Palate Combination of flavour, taste and texture of a wine.

Perfumed or **scented** Strong fragrances, fruity, flowery, animal etc.

Plump Well fleshed in a charming, cherubic way.

Porty Heavy, over-ripe, stewed; a negative in unfortified wine.

Rich Flavourful, intense, generous. Not necessarily sweet.

Robust Strapping, full bodied (but not aggressive).

Rough Bull-in-a-china-shop wine, or throat sand-papering quality.

Round Well balanced, without gawkiness or jagged edges.

Sharp or **tart** All about acid, usually unbalanced. But occasionally sharpish, fresh wine is right for the occasion.

Short or **quick** Insubstantial wine, leaving little impression.

Simple One-dimensional or no flavour excitement.

Stalky Unripe, bitter, stemmy.

Stewed Over-ripe, cooked, soft, soggy fruit.

Structure Vague word, usually refers to the wine's make up (acid, tannin, alcohol) in relation to its ageing ability; if a wine is deemed to have "the structure to age" it suggests these principal preservatives are in place.

Stylish Classy, distinguished; also voguish.

Supple Very desirable (not necessarily subtle), yielding, refined texture and flavours. See also **mouthfeel**.

Tannic Tannins are prominent in the wine, imparting, positively, a mouth-puckering, grippy, tangy quality; negatively, a harsh, unyielding character.

Tension Racy, nervous fruity-acid play on the palate. Often associated with German riesling.

Terpenes Strong, floral compounds influencing the aromas of especially riesling, gewürz and the muscats; with bottle-age, terpenes often develop a pungent resinous oiliness.

Texture Tactile "feel" in the mouth: hard, acidic, coarse and alcoholic; or, smooth, velvety, warm.

Toasty Often used for barrel-fermented and aged wines showing a pleasant biscuity, charry character.

Vegetal Grassy, leafy, herby—in contrast to fruity, flowery, oaky. Overdone, a no-no.

Yeasty Warm bread or bakery smells, often evident in barrel-fermented whites and méthode champenoise sparkling wines, where yeasts stay in contact with the wine after fermentation.

....

Some winemaking terms used in this guide

A few brief reference explanations. See also Winetasting terms.

Acid and **acidity** The fresh — or, in excess, sharp or tart — taste of wine. Too little acid and the wine tastes dull and flat. In South Africa, winemakers are permitted to adjust acidity, either by adding acid — at any stage before bottling — or by lowering the acid level with the use of calcium carbonate. See also **volatile acid** and **malolactic**.

Barrels (barrel-aged; barrel-fermented) Barrique is a French word for ±225l barrel. Vat is a term generally used for larger (2 000–5 000 ℓ) wooden vessels. Barrels are generally 225–500 ℓ oak casks. Wines are pumped into barrels to age, pick up oaky flavours, etc. When must or fermenting must is put into barrels, the resulting wine is called barrel-fermented.

Volatile acid (VA) That part of the **acidity** which can become volatile. A high reading indicates a wine is prone to spoilage. Recognised at high levels by a sharp, 'hot', vinegary smell. In South Africa, most wines must by law be below 1,2 g/ℓ of VA; in practice, the majority are well below 1 g/ℓ.

Whole bunch pressing or **cluster pressing** Some Cape cellars use this age-old process of placing whole bunches directly in the press and gently squeezing. The more usual method is to de-stem and crush the grapes before pressing. Whole bunch pressing is said to yield fresher, cleaner must, and wine lower in polyphenols, which, in excess, tend to age wines faster and render them coarser.

Wood-fermented/matured See barrels.

Yeasts Micro-organisms that secrete enzymes which convert or ferment sugar into alcohol. Naturally present in vineyards and on grapes but locally, wild yeasts are usually still killed by addition of sulphur, and cultured yeasts are used. The wild yeasts in the Cape were generally thought unsuitable in the past, especially for white musts. Lately, a few growers have begun to experiment with "wild ferments", i.e. using natural vineyard yeasts, for both red and white wines. There have been some excellent results.

The main SA wine competitions & awards

South African wine-growers are encouraged to push the quality-envelope by a number of annual awards bestowed by liquor-industry bodies and independent companies with ties to the wine-trade. Here are some of the main wine-accolades conferred each year.

Diners Club Winemaker of the Year Probably the single most coveted SA wine prize, inaugurated in 1981. An international wine luminary presides over the judging panel; a different category is chosen each year and announced far in advance, giving local producers enough time to experiment, fine-tune and even plant new vineyards. Categories from 2000-2005, in order: 'Port', Chenin Blanc, Pinotage, Brandy, Innovative Red Blends, Sémillon Blends.

Michelangelo International Inaugurated in 1997, this contest is run under the rules of the Office Internationale de la Vigne et du Vin (OIV) and judged by a combined international/local panel. Highest accolade is the Grand Medaille d'Or:

ABSA Bank/PPA Top Ten Competition run by the local Pinotage Producers' Association with a major local financial institution. Aim is to set international quality targets for vintners of South Africa's home-grown variety, pinotage.

SAA Selections Not a competition, but an annual singling-out of wines to fly with the national airline, South African Airways, on domestic and international routes. To stock the carrier's airborne-cellar, a panel of local and overseas judges evaluates entries from across the winelands (there no longer are constraints on submissions). The top-scoring red, white, bubbly and "port" receive the SAA Trophy.

South African Young Wine Show This major event, covering five broad categories and 70 "classes", was inaugurated in 1975 to gauge the quality of 'infant' wines prior to finishing and bottling, thereby recognising wineries who sell in bulk to producing-wholesalers and thus otherwise would remain anonymous. Grand champion receives the General Smuts Trophy.

Veritas Hosted by the South African National Wine Show Association, this major competition recognises top market-ready wines across a wide range of categories. Gold, double-gold, silver and bronze medals are awarded. Star-performers may affix the Veritas logo to their winning wines.

Air France–Preteux Bourgeois Classic Staged with leading French cork importer, Preteux Bourgeois, and Air France under the rules of the OIV. Rewards SA wines with the best ageing potential. Recognition is given in five categories, and judges also select an overall winning wine.

Wine routes, trusts & associations

FOR localised information about regional official wine routes and wineries, contact these organisations:

Calitzdorp Wine Route Tel (044) 213-3312 (ask for Tourism Information) Fax (044) 213-3302.

Constantia Wine Route Tel (021) 794-1810 (ask for André Badenhorst) Fax (021) 794-1812.

Durbanville Wine Route Tel 083-310-1228 (cellular) Fax 96-5631 E-mail nitida@ct.lia.net.

Helderberg Wine Route Tel (021) 852-6166 Fax (021) 851-1497 E-mail hwr@mweb.co.za Website www.helderbergwineroute.co.za.

Klein Karoo Wine Trust Tel/fax (028) 572-1284 (Riaan Marais).

Olifants River Wine Trust Tel/fax (027) 213-3126 Cell 083-701-9146 (Sanmari van der Westhuizen).

Orange River Wine Trust Tel (054) 332-4651 Fax (054) 332-4408 E-mail marketing@owk.co.za.

Paarl Wine Route Paarl Vintners Tel (021) 872-3605 Fax (021) 872-3841 E-mail paarl@wine.co.za Website www.paarlwine.co.za.

Robertson Valley Wine Route Tel (023) 626-3167 Fax (023) 626-1054 E-mail info@robertsonwinevalley.co.za

Stellenbosch Wine Route Tel (021) 886-4310, Fax (021) 886-4330, E-mail info@wineroute.co.za Website www.wineroute.co.za.

Swartland Wine Route Tel (022) 487-1133 Fax (022) 487-2063 E-mail swartlandinfo@wcaccess.co.za.

Tulbagh Wine Trust Tourism Office Tel/fax (023) 230-1348 Website www.tulbagh.com.

Vignerons de Franschhoek Tel (021) 876-3062 Fax (021) 876-2964/2768 E-mail franschhoek@wine.co.za Website www.franschhoekwines.co.za.

Wellington Wine Route Tel (021) 873-4604 Fax (021) 873-4607 E-mail welltour@cis.co.za Website www.visitwellington.com.

Worcester Winelands Association Tel (023) 342-8710 or (023) 342-8720 Fax (023) 342-2294 E-mail manager@worcesterwinelands.co.za Website www.worcesterwinelands.co.za.

Some specialist tour operators

Adamastor & Bacchus John Ford conducts tailor-made tours for small groups to wine farms not usually accessible to the public. Photography an additional speciality. Tours can be conducted in German and Norwegian. Tel/fax (021) 439-3169 • Cell 083-229-1172 • E-mail johnford@iafrica.com.

André Morgenthal Offers specialist wine tours to off-the-beaten-track cellars, and conducts innovative 'out-tastings' in your home or venue of choice. Carefully chosen wines and food create a synergistic experience, complete with cigars and all the trimmings. Tel (021) 887-6583/082-658-3883 • E-mail wynsacci@hotmail.com.

The Capevine Special interest tour operator Annette Stals will organise the consummate Cape winelands experience to facilitate your enjoyment of wine, architecture, history, gardens, regional cuisine and beautiful scenery. Tel (021) 913-6611 • Tel/fax (021) 913-4580 • E-mail capevine@iafrica.com.

Vineyard Ventures Super-experienced guides Gillian Stoltzman (082-893-5387) and Glen Christie (082-920-2825) specialise in small groups, tailor-making each sipping-safari to visitors' tastes — off the tourist beat. Tel (021) 434-8888 • Fax (021) 434-9999 • E-mail vinven@iafrica.com.

Vintage Cape Tours Private and tailor-made tours for the discerning food and wine lover   specialist wine guides in English, German, French and Afrikaans. Tel (021) 872-9252 • Tel/fax (021) 862-1484 • Cell 082-553-8928 or 082-656-3994 • E-mail vctours@adept.co.za • Website www.vintage-cape.co.za.

Window On Cape Wine This quality, visual winelands presentation is portable, personalised and includes a tasting. Ideal for conference entertainment or tour groups. Meryl Weaver also does specialised full or half day winelands excursions — Satour registered guide. Tel/fax (021) 889-1002 • E-mail mvweaver@iafrica.com.

. . . .

Armchair tours of the winelands

E-scapes *Cape Town, The Fairest Cape of all* (German: Kapstadt), *Images of Cape Town and the Winelands* (German: *Eindrucke von Kapstadt und den Weinbaugebieten*) and other titles. Contact Tania Tel (021) 852-9390 • E-mail e-club@kingsley.co.za.

Sovereign Videos *Winelands of the Cape* Includes 28 top estates. Tel (021) 423-3043 • Fax (021) 423-3056.

. . . .

Wine education

Accolade Wine Appreciation Experienced Cape Town-based wine taster/educator Claude Felbert offers his introductory wine appreciation course, which includes $\pm$ 11 hours of tuition and an exam for those who wish to write it, at least 8 times a year. Higher-level individual 'varietal courses' are also offered, along with twice-yearly detailed tasting programmes with sections on common wine faults. Courses for 10 or more people are held in other centres by arrangement. Tel (021) 712-4245 or 083-261-8863; E-mail accolade@worldonline.co.za.

Cape Wine Academy Official education body for the SA wine industry, headquartered in Stellenbosch and with a branch in Johannesburg and centres in Durban, Pretoria, Bloemfontein, Port Elizabeth, Knysna, Windhoek and Harare. Runs theory and tasting courses at several levels, also examinations. New courses include wine service, an Introduction to Wines of the World and skills workshops for cellar workers. The Principal is Christine Rudman.

Stellenbosch: Tel (021) 808-7597/7547 Fax (021) 883-9179; Johannesburg: Tel (011) 783-4585/6 Fax (011) 883-2356; Durban: Tel/fax (031) 564-5067; Pretoria Tel/fax (012) 333-1978; Bloemfontein: Tel (051) 430-3174 Fax (051) 448-6076; Port Elizabeth (Jaco Schoeman): Tel (041) 504-3872 Fax (041) 504 3744; Harare (Bunny Landon): Tel 09263 913 538 40.

Cape Wine Master The successful completion of tasting/theory examinations set since 1983 by the Cape Wine and Spirit Education Trust have qualified 43 wine aficionados for the CWM title. Their institute of Cape Wine Masters holds seminars, runs tasting workshops, charts trends, names a Wine Personality of the Year, etc. Chair Christine Rudman is also Principal of the Cape Wine Academy (above). There are three Honorary Members: Phyllis Hands, Dave Hughes and Colin Frith. Contact: Stellenbosch Tel (021) 808-7591 Fax (021) 886-4568

· ·

Stay-over in the winelands

FEATURED below are guest lodges, hotels, country inns, B&Bs and self-catering cottages in the winelands, many of them on wine farms: look for the 🍷 symbol below the individual entries in this guide. All these establishments have restaurants, swimming pools, gardens/terraces, parking and televisions et al (unless stated to the contrary). All rates are for standard double rooms unless otherwise specified, for example per person (pp), breakfast included (B&B) or on a dinner, bed and breakfast basis (DB&B). The stay-overs featured below describe their own attractions.

Breede River Valley

Fraai Uitzicht 1798 Klaas Voogds East (R60), between Robertson & Ashton • R430 B&B, R370 self-catering • Major credit cards accepted (excl AmEx) • Owners Axel Spanholtz & Mario Motti • Tel/fax (023) 626-6156 • E-mail fraai.uitzicht@lando.co.za • Website www.lando.co.za/fraaiuitzicht

Fraai Uitzicht 1798, the historic wine and guest farm at the foothills of the Langeberg mountains in the Klaas Voogds Valley, is a delightful place. With long farm walks, a wealth of bird life and spectacular views across the Robertson 'Valley of Wine and Roses', it is the perfect place to relax and experience the beauty and tranquillity of nature. Attentive hosts and luxury guest cottages, each with open fireplace, braai facilities and a big private veranda, await you. There's a fresh mountain water pool, a bamboo forest, and beautiful herb, flower and rose gardens surrounded by vineyards and fruit orchards. The restaurant serves generous country fare (see separate Eat-out entry). Fraai Uitzicht 1798 is central to many attractions, including the Robertson Valley Wine Route.

Merwenstein Guest Farm Swellendam Road, 6 km from Bonnievale • R350 B&B • Major credit cards accepted • Owners Hugo & Heidi van der Merwe • Tel/fax (023) 616-2806 • E-mail merwenstein@lando.co.za • Website www.merwenstein.co.za

In the magnificent Breede River Valley, 40 km from Swellendam and Montagu, you will find this wine and fruit farm. Take an informative walk with the owner and glean first-hand information on cultivating grapes. Dinners combining African flavours and Merwespont wines are shared with your host and make for evenings worth remembering. The en suite rooms have private entrances and patios. It is within easy walking distance of Merwespont Winery, Lys se Kombuis and the Tokkelossie Museum. Outdoor options include a river cruiser and a golf course nearby.

Mimosa Lodge Church Street, Montagu • R375 pp DB&B • Green Season from R185 pp B&B • Breakfast R40, dinner R95 for non-residents • Owners Yvette & Andreas Küng • Tel (023) 614-2351 • Fax (023) 614-2418 • E-mail mimosa@lando.co.za • Website www.mimosa.co.za

Firmly established in Montagu, this carefully restored historic building exudes charm, warmth and friendliness. The decor is vibrant and colourful. The 9 comfortable en suite bedrooms have modern facilities, while the 3 suites offer luxury and tranquillity. The garden with its black-marbled pool is surrounded by the Lodge's own apricot orchards. Mimosa Lodge is renowned for its creative cuisine by owner Andreas Küng. The highly acclaimed table d'hôte changes daily, and special dietary requirements are gladly catered for. The Lodge's own wine cellar provides the perfect match for an excellent dinner.

Constantia

Hampshire House 10 Willow Road • R390–420 B&B • No restaurant • Major credit cards accepted • Owners Ricky & Carole Chapman • Tel (021) 794-6288 • Fax (021) 794-2934 • E-mail stay@hampshirehouse.co.za • Website www.hampshirehouse.co.za

Set in the idyllic Constantia wine valley, Hampshire House was a 99/00 finalist in the AA/SAA Accommodation Awards. It provides the perfect base from which to explore the picturesque Cape Peninsula, with easy motorway access to Table Mountain, the V&A Waterfront, the winelands and beaches, as well as excellent local restaurants. Five individually decorated en suite bedrooms have king-sized or twin beds, satellite television, CD player, radio alarm, bar fridge, overhead fan and cosy underfloor heating in winter. There's a pool and secure off-street parking. English and continental buffet breakfasts are available. You can enjoy a drink in the Hampshire Arms, a cosy pub with a comprehensive winelist.

Mount Heron Swaanswyk Road, Tokai • Rate R600 B&B • No restaurant • Major credit cards accepted (excl Diners) • Tel (021) 712-5983 • Fax (021) 715-7460 • E-mail mtheron@iafrica.com

Mount Heron is a handsome country house set in 2½ acres of secluded gardens, between Steenberg Golf Course and Tokai Forest. Stylishly decorated bedrooms are en suite and have pure cotton linen and luxurious bathrobes, TV with M-Net, radio alarms and hairdryers. The Constantia Wine Route (with five of the Cape's leading cellars) and excellent restaurants are five minutes' drive away. There's a large swimming pool, secure off-street parking. It's a non-smoking establishment, no children allowed.

Franschhoek

Auberge Clermont Robertsvlei Road • Tel (021) 876-3700 • Fax (021) 876-3701 • E-mail clermont@mweb.co.za • Website www.clermont.co.za

This magnificent auberge has been created in a historic wine cellar surrounded by chardonnay vineyards. The scent of roses, lavender and rosemary is everywhere. The 6 luxe en suite rooms have been individually decorated in Provençal style with great attention to detail. Underfloor heating and ceiling fans ensure year-round comfort. The generous bathrooms have double basins, heated towel rails and separate showers. There is a pool and tennis court on the premises, and a three-bedroomed self-catering villa alongside a formal French garden. Clermont is 1 km from the village centre and close to its associate restaurant, Haute Cabrière (see separate Eat-out entry).

Auberge du Quartier Français Cnr Berg & Wilhelmina Streets • R1 210 room only, R1 800 DB&B • Major credit cards accepted • Tel (021) 876-2151 • Fax (021) 876-3105 • E-mail res@lqf.co.za • Website www.lqf.co.za

Le Quartier Français is a sanctuary of intimacy and comfort. Set behind a bright Provençal façade with white-washed stone walls, the 15 suites are decorated in modern Cape Provençal style, individually furnished with brightly coloured fabrics, deep down duvets and king-sized beds wrapped in Egyptian linen, with log fireplaces for winter. The two suites have separate living rooms, air conditioning and private swimming pools set in secluded gardens. Le Quartier Francais also features a trendy cigar bar, a lounge, a patio restaurant, the main restaurant (see separate Eat-out entry for Le Quartier Français), an intimate courtyard and a well-stocked library.

Cathbert Country Inn Franschhoek Road, Simondium • R350 pp sharing • Major credit cards accepted • Owners Roger & Ann Morley • Tel/fax (021) 874-1366 • E-mail info@cathbert.co.za • Website www.cathbert.co.za

Wake up to country quiet, clean air and glorious views, just 40 minutes from Cape Town. Cathbert Country Inn — a 99/00 AA/SAA Accommodation Awards finalist — is in the heart of the winelands at the foot of the majestic Simonsberg mountains, perfectly placed for touring Paarl, Stellenbosch and Franschhoek. Individually appointed suites, all with private verandas, opening onto dam, vineyard and mountain views, have all the trimmings: a comfortable sitting area, TV, minibar, underfloor heating, fireplace and ceiling fans. Breakfast at leisure on a sunny garden deck or in the restaurant overlooking the pool; gourmet dinners are also served. Mountain walks, bird watching and many fine golf courses nearby take care of the great outdoors. Airport transfers can be arranged.

Franschhoek Country House Main Road • From R275 pp B&B (R550 per room) • Major credit cards accepted • Tel (021) 876-3386 • Fax (021) 876-2744 • E-mail fch@mweb.co.za • Website www.ecl.co.za

Wallow in luxury and some serious indulgence at this upmarket country house in the fetching Franschhoek Valley. The restored manor house and former perfumery, which dates back to 1890, has 14 rooms and suites, most with fireplaces and balconies, with all the expected comforts and amenities, including satellite television. A swimming pool is set in tranquil gardens with mountain vistas. Guests can enjoy lunch or dinner at the famous in-house Monneaux restaurant (see separate Eat-out entry), which is known for its exquisite menu and wine selection.

La Couronne Hotel Robertsvlei Road • R1 560 B&B • Major credit cards accepted • Tel (021) 876-2770 • Fax (021) 876-3788 • E-mail reservations@lacouronne-hotel.co.za • Website www.lacouronnehotel.co.za

La Couronne, 'the crown' of Franschhoek, is positioned in what is undoubtedly one of the most beautiful settings in the world. The small luxury hotel, set among the vines of the La Couronne wine estate, offers a complete winelands experience, with fine dining and a vast selection of South African and international wines (see separate Eat-out entry). Guests are invited to a private tasting in the estate cellar, and can enjoy a horse ride, a walk through the vineyards, or trout fishing in one of their mountain ponds. During the harvest season guests are encouraged to become involved in the winemaking process.

La Petite Ferme Pass Road • R375 pp sharing B&B • Owners Dendy Young family • Tel (021) 876-3016/8 • Fax (021) 876-3624 • E-mail lapetite@iafrica.com

La Petite Ferme is set high above Franschhoek (a vantage point from which it catches the last rays of the afternoon sun) with breathtaking views of orchards, vineyards and the lush valley below. Luxury, elegance and comfort are amount, with 3 delightful private cottages set among the vineyards, each with private patio and plunge pool; the spacious bedrooms have fireplaces, TV, bar fridges, heaters and ceiling fans, and bathrooms with roomy oval tubs and showers. Country-style breakfasts are served in the cottage, cooked farm breakfasts in the restaurant (see separate Eat-out entry).

Résidence Klein Oliphants Hoek 14 Akademie Street • R250 pp B&B • Major credit cards accepted • Owners Ingrid & Camil Haas • Tel/fax (021) 876-2566 • E-mail info@kleinoliphantshoek.com • Website www.kleinoliphantshoek.com

The Résidence Klein Oliphants Hoek is named after the original name for Franschhoek, once the foraging place of roaming elephants. The guesthouse is a beautifully renovated 1888 English missionary station, with 6 spacious en suite rooms and splendid views of the surrounding mountains. The original small school under the shade of the large oak has been converted into an elegant 7th suite with a private entrance and garden. There are fireplaces in both the lounge and restaurant. Your multilingual hosts Camil and Ingrid, who have international catering experience, will host private dinners on request. Cooking classes in the open kitchen at the old wood stove will inspire you to explore European-African cuisine.

The Dartrey Lodge Guest House 5 Dirkie Uys Street • From R145 pp sharing, B&B • Tel/fax (021) 876-3530

Historic homesteads, mountain panoramas and vineyards are all part of the scenic Four Passes Route, and The Dartrey Lodge is a perfect base from which to absorb this wonderful Cape region. May and Les Wright welcome guests to their 1898 Victorian home, which offers spacious and comfortable en suite bedrooms with separate entrances set in a lovely garden with mountain views. Each has a ceiling fan, oil heater, clock radio and tea tray. Enjoy the television, library, cosy lounge and log fire in the main house on those chilly days. A full English breakfast is served at leisure in the charming dining room. The Dartrey Lodge Portfolio Collection and Satour accredited. Excellent restaurants are within easy walking distance.

Houw Hoek

Wildekrans Country House opposite Houw Hoek Farm Stall on the N2 • R350 B&B • Meals available on request • Major credit cards accepted • Owners Barry Gould & Alison Green • Tel (028) 284-9827 • Fax (028) 284-9624 • E-mail wildekrans@kingsley.co.za

Wildekrans is on a fruit farm in the peaceful and scenic Houw Hoek Valley, surrounded by mountains, just an hour's drive from Cape Town. Three en suite bedrooms in the old homestead (1811) are furnished with four-poster beds. Two cottages are set in the tranquil garden and pear orchard. All are also available for self-catering holidays. Relax in the large English country garden or at the pool. Leisurely walks, hikes and mountain bike trails begin at the foot of the garden. Appreciate the Wildekrans collection of contemporary South African art. Visit the Walker Bay wine route and beaches.

Paarl

Grande Roche Hotel Plantasie Street • R1 750 B&B • Major credit cards accepted • Tel (021) 863-2727 • Fax (021) 863-2220 • E-mail reserve@granderoche.co.za • Website www.granderoche.co.za

Grande Roche has become a legend in South Africa with an array of awards including the 1995 'Tourism Hotel of the Year Award' for "incredible attention to detail, impeccable grounds, excellent food and superb levels of luxury" and the American-based international Andrew Harper Award given to outstanding country estates exuding warmth, charm and excellence. This South African gem overlooks vineyards and rugged mountains and its sprawl of individually decorated suites are a gentle alternative to the hurly-burly of big city life. You can relax in the pools, go biking or play tennis on site, enjoy excellent golf nearby, go to the gym or indulge in a massage given by the hotel's private masseur. It's the ideal base from which to explore the entire Cape region. (See separate Eat-out entry for Bosman's.)

Kleinplaas Country House 39 Upper Bosman Street • R380 B&B • Major credit cards accepted (excl AmEx) • Owner Narine Troost • Tel (021) 863-1441 • Cell (082) 458-8284 • Fax (021) 863-1441 • E-mail troost@iafrica.com

You'll find Kleinplaas high up on the slopes of Paarl Mountain, in the shadow of Paarl Rock. Stylish en suite double bedrooms with fireplaces open onto a terrace with views over the garden, Berg River Valley and towering Drakenstein mountains in the distance. A private self-catering cottage with fireplace, surrounded by vineyards and forests, is also available. Kleinplaas is close to historic sites, wine routes and highly acclaimed restaurants. There's hiking and mountain biking on the farm. It's wheelchair-friendly, has secure parking and children are welcome.

Laborie Guest House Taillefert Street • R255 pp B&B • Major credit cards accepted • Owners KWV International (Pty) Ltd • Tel (021) 807-3271 (For reservations, contact Elma Brand) • Fax (021) 863-2221 • Website www.kwv-international.com

Laborie Guest House is situated on the historic Laborie Estate in Paarl and is set amid beautifully landscaped gardens, with gorgeous views of Paarl Mountain and the Paarl Valley. It comprises six tastefully decorated double bedrooms, each with its own bathroom. A full English breakfast is served in the magnificent Manor

House. Facilities include an elegant sitting room for visitors' use, safe parking and an eco-friendly wine hiking trail on the estate. The well-known Laborie Restaurant offers luncheons and dinners (see separate Eat-out entry).

Lanquedoc Guest Cottages Klein Drakenstein • Self-catering cottages: 2 en suite bedrooms R825 per night in season, R600 per night out of season; 1 en suite bedroom R495 per night in season, R360 per night out of season • Continental breakfast on request, R25 pp • Major credit cards accepted • Tel (021) 862-3368/3190 • Fax (021) 862-3258/6300 • E-mail lanque@iafrica.com

The historic Lanquedoc Farm invites you to experience a working olive farm in the heart of the Cape winelands. Set at the foothills of the Klein Drakenstein mountains in the fertile Paarl Valley, luxurious self-catering cottages provide accommodation of the highest standard for the discerning traveller. There's a magnificent pool with covered pavilion, braai facilities in the garden, spectacular mountain bike and hiking trails through olive groves, vineyards and buchu plantations, as well as easy country walks, crackling log fires and unforgettable scenery. Lanquedoc's superior extra virgin olive oil and black mission olives — processed on the farm — are available for purchase by guests.

Pontac Manor Hotel & Restaurant 16 Zion Street • R790 B&B • Major credit cards accepted • Owners Desire & Tim Orill-Legg; Stanley Carpenter • Tel (021) 872-0445 • Fax (021) 872-0460 • E-mail pontac@iafrica.com Website www.pontac.com

Tucked beneath Paarl Rock, Pontac Manor, dating back to 1723, has been beautifully restored to its original Victorian splendour. The hotel, with its warm, old-world atmosphere and air of timeless sophistication, offers 16 tastefully decorated and spacious bedrooms with en suite bathrooms, set in a large, sculpted garden with pool. From the broad terrace, guests can enjoy a magnificent view over the valley to the mountains beyond. The newly opened 'Restaurant at Pontac' offers fine dining with an African flair. Interesting dishes with delicate sauces please every palate. Light meals and refreshments are served throughout the premises. Well-equipped meeting facilities for up to 22 people are offered in the new Conference Suite, while the Board Room accommodates up to 12 delegates.

Somerset West

Die Ou Pastorie Country House & Restaurant 41 Lourens Street • R650 B&B • Major credit cards accepted • Owner Garry Roberts Tel (021) 852-2120 • Fax (021) 851-3710 • E-mail info@dieoupastorie.co.za • Website www.dieoupastorie.co.za

This historical monument with its gracious period antiques dates back to 1819, yet offers every modern convenience for the discerning traveller of today. Situated in the Helderberg basin, which is central to all the major tourist attractions in and around the Cape Town area, Die Ou Pastorie lies close to the winelands routes of Stellenbosch, Franschhoek, Paarl and Helderberg. The 16 en suite bedrooms are located in the well-manicured gardens in two 'pavilions' separated by the extensive herb garden. The rooms are classically decorated in Victorian style, capturing the spirit of luxury. The restaurant with its elegant dining rooms, situated in the original parsonage, has a warm and intimate atmosphere where continental cuisine and an award-winning winelist provide a memorable dining experience (see separate Eat-out entry).

Willowbrook Lodge 1 Morgenster Avenue, off Lourensford Road • R1 210 B&B • Major credit cards accepted • Owners Janik and Serge Olchanetzky • Tel (021) 851-3759, Fax (021) 851-4152 • E-mail willowb@iafrica.com • Website www.willowbrook.co.za

Willowbrook Lodge is situated on the banks of the tranquil Lourens River on the outskirts of Somerset West, a stone's throw from the 300-year-old historic Vergelegen wine estate and two minutes' drive from Erinvale Golf Estate. French owners Janik and Serge Olchanetzky preside over a haven of tranquillity and informal elegance. This is an atmosphere in which you immediately feel welcome. Each of the 11 rooms have en suite bathrooms, underfloor heating and are carefully sited in an enchanting Cape 'discovery' garden. The renowned French-style gastronomic restaurant, which has been consistently rated as one of the 10 best in the country, offers à la carte menus (see separate Eat-out entry). It is a place where fresh flowers, antiques, works of art and paintings create a very special backdrop to memorable cuisine. Excellent award-winning short winelist. Willowbrook Lodge is a member of the prestigious Relais & Chateaux group.

Stellenbosch

Aan die Oewer Guesthouse Jonkershoek Valley • R550 B&B • Major credit cards accepted • No restaurant • Tel (021) 887-9385, Fax (021) 887-2418 • E-mail aandieoewer@iafrica.com • Website www.aandeoever.co.za

This riverside guesthouse is situated just outside historic Stellenbosch in the lush Jonkershoek valley. Special care is taken to cater for those in need of silence, tranquillity and a relaxed atmosphere — in fact, they'll find themselves cushioned in comfort. This area is perfect for hiking and cycling. Aan die Oewer is only 3,5km from the buzzy town of Stellenbosch with its excellent restaurants and surrounding wine estates.

Devon Valley Hotel Devon Valley Road • R650, including full farmhouse breakfast • Major credit cards accepted • Owners David & Lee Ann Nathan-Moister • Tel (021) 882-2012 • Fax (021) 882-2610 • E-mail devon@iafrica.com

A Stellenbosch landmark for over 50 years, the Devon Valley Hotel offers stunning views, cosy rooms, innovative Cape country cuisine and the finest winelist in the winelands (see separate Eat-Out entry for The Vineleaf). Walk through the beautiful gardens, gaze over their own vineyards or just sit on the patio, admire the view and sip a glass of their award-winning Sylvanvale wine. At night, sit in front of the log fire at the Cat & Moose bar, and savour one of their 120 single malt whiskies — the largest selection in Africa!

Graceland Vineyards Stellenrust Road • R150–225 B&B • Tel (021) 881-3121 • Fax (021) 881-3341 • E-mail pmcn@iafrica.com • Website www.gracelandvineyards.com

Graceland Vineyards is well situated between Stellenbosch and Somerset West, surrounded by the award-winning wineries on the Helderberg Wine Route. This peaceful estate offers traditional South African hospitality with two spacious, uniquely decorated guestrooms offering every comfort. For the energetic there is a large swimming pool, a tennis court as well as bicycles and several golf courses nearby. Sample the latest cabernet sauvignon or merlot vintage and enjoy a tour of the barrel cellar. Full breakfasts are served overlooking the tranquil garden and vineyards. There are many excellent restaurants nearby.

L'Avenir Wine Estate Guest House Klapmuts Road (R44), north of Stellenbosch towards Paarl • R330 B&B • Major credit cards accepted • Meals on request • Owners L'Avenir Wine Estate Pty Ltd • Tel (021) 889-5001 • Fax (021) 889-5258 • E-mail lavenir@adept.co.za • Website adept.co.za/lavenir/

This is a wine lover's heaven: 9 en suite bedrooms set around a large pool on a wine estate with 70 hectares of prime vineyards to wander in, cellar tours and award-winning wines at cellar prices. Relaxed and unhurried luxury, only five minutes from Stellenbosch, 20 minutes from the airport and the beaches of the Strand, 50 minutes from Cape Town. Conference facilities are available.

Natte Valleij Farm Klapmuts Road (44), 12 km north of Stellenbosch towards Paarl • R160 pp, including full breakfast • Self-catering cottages: Vineyard Cottage from

R375 per day; Cellar Cottage R250 per day • Owners Charles & Charlene Milner • Tel (021) 875-5171 • Fax (021) 875-5475 • E-mail milner@intekom.co.za

The historic Natte Valleij farm is situated in the prime winegrowing Muldersvlei bowl, renowned for its award-winning reds. The farm nestles under the Simonsberg mountains and is surrounded by many well-known estates. There's a B&B option as well as two self-catering cottages: Vineyard Cottage (circa 1714) can sleep 6 in 3 double bedrooms, with 2 bathrooms, sitting room and dining room; Cellar Cottage sleeps 2 to 4. Both cottages have their own stoep and braai facilities. The secluded swimming pool is set in a large garden. You can fish for bass in the farm dam or go for long walks through forests or up the mountain. Charles and Charlene Milner offer friendly hospitality and welcome the opportunity to share with you the ambience of a bygone era.

The Village at Spier Lynedoch Road (R310) • R950 • Major credit cards accepted • Owners Spier Management Pty Ltd • Tel (021) 809-1100 • Fax (021) 881-3141 • E-mail info@spier.co.za • Website www.spier.co.za

Magnificent natural surroundings, graceful architecture and the inherent elegance of Spier make The Village a perfect place for conferences or holidays. Situated 10 minutes from Stellenbosch, 15 minutes from Cape Town International and 25 minutes from Cape Town CBD, The Village is within strolling distance of a diverse range of facilities. These include no less than 7 swimming pools, 4 restaurants, 2 pubs, a wine centre, an 18-hole golf course, an equestrian centre, the cheetah park, a vintage steam train, an art collection, as well as the conference centre. Spier is also well known for it music festivals and other performances in the open-air auditorium.

Stellenbosch/Kuils River

Zevenwacht Wine Estate, Country Inn & Vineyard Cottages Zevenwacht Estate, Langverwacht Road, Kuils River • From R350 B&B • Major credit cards accepted • Owner Harold Johnson • Tel (021) 903-5123 • Fax (021) 903-3373 • E-mail reservations@zevenwacht.co.za • Website www.zevenwacht.co.za

Set in the winelands, the inn is part of the wine estate with its magnificent historic Cape Dutch manor house which houses the restaurant. A working wine farm, Zevenwacht has a range of quality wines grown and produced on the estate. A traditional farmhouse cheddar is also produced on the estate. Luxuriously appointed en suite rooms command sweeping views of the winelands and the vineyard cottages each have 3 en suite bedrooms sharing a private sitting room. A self-catering chalet with 4 en suite rooms, also with magnificent views of Table Mountain and Table Bay, is another option.

Wine and cheese tastings, a swimming pool, tennis courts and a sauna enhance the experience.

•Swartland

Samoa Hotel Central Street, Moorreesburg • R190 pp • Major credit cards accepted • Tel (022) 433-1201 • Fax (022) 433-2031

Visitors to the Swartland and its wine route will find the Samoa Hotel in Moorreesburg a veritable oasis. The ambience is warm and luxurious, complete with a 19th-century open wood fireplace to welcome winter visitors and an inviting patio and pool for summertime relaxation. The rooms are beautifully designed and decorated. The De Kraal Restaurant, with its legendary steaks, also offers ever-changing menus to suit every palate. A conference room and full-sized snooker table complete the picture.

Tulbagh

Hunters Retreat Guest Farm Ruimte Farm • R300–R390 B&B • Major credit cards accepted • Tel (023) 230-0582 • Fax (023) 230-0057 • E-mail esther@lando.co.za • Website www.lando.co.za/huntersretreat

Hunters Retreat Guest Farm is an accredited B&B, located 1,4km from the town of Tulbagh, with 7 spacious en suite rooms — some with fireplaces — in a lovely country setting with beautiful mountain views. Take time out, with wine estates, hiking trails and historical Church Street to explore, horse riding for the adventurous, or less strenuous activities like lounging around the pool or having a braai under the lapa. The charming chapel on the farm is perfect for country weddings and there's a venue for small receptions. You'll find good restaurants in the nearby village.

Lemberg Wine Estate and Guest House Off the R46 • R350 per couple per night, excl food (R125 discount for South Africans) • Owners Uschi and Klaus Schindler • Tel (023) 230-0659 • Fax (023) 230-0661 • E-mail schindler@lando.co.za • Website www.kapstadt.de/lemberg

The guesthouse is a magnificent rondavel, set on 21 ha next to a lake, perfectly appointed for privacy. This is an exclusive suite, tastefully decorated, with a fully equipped kitchen, bedroom with king-sized bed, en suite bathroom with shower, cosy lounge, fresh flowers and fruits, veranda and garden leading to the lake. Breakfasts, gourmet lunches or evening dinners are served in the guesthouse or at the lake's edge. The ideal place from which to explore the beautiful Cape in all directions and good advice is offered on enjoyable half-day or day trips to the many places of interest around the estate. Visitors will enjoy a personal wine tasting and informative cellar tour — they produce 3 distinctive and carefully crafted wines. Let the hedonist in you enjoy being pampered with personal, attentive service.

Rijk's Private Cellar & Country Estate Main Road • Double R656 B&B; Twin R556 B&B • Major credit cards accepted • Tel (023) 230-1006 • Fax (023) 230-1125

Rijk's is a wineland getaway of immense charm and tranquillity. Set on the outskirts of the historic and picturesque Tulbagh Village is the gracious country house, overlooking a lake from its vantage point among the vineyards. Rijk's offers friendly country hospitality in a relaxed farm atmosphere, with luxurious en suite bedrooms, each room opening onto a private patio, and all with majestic mountain views. Visit Rijk's own private cellar and winery with its range of superior wines, cellar tours and tastings. Enjoy classic cuisine in Rijk's Restaurant or on the sunny patio. Explore the surrounding wine farms, historical village with 32 national museums, and scenic mountain passes, or simply relax next to the pool and observe the bird life.

. . . .

Plan your stay

FOR additional accommodation options, brochures and local advice, contact the information offices and/or publicity associations of the wine areas you plan to visit.

Franschhoek Publicity Association Tel (021) 876-3603 Fax (021) 876-2768 E-mail info@franschhoek.org.za.

Helderberg Tourism Bureau Tel (021) 851-4022 Fax (021) 851-1497 E-mail info@helderbergtourism.co.za

Hermanus Tourism Bureau Tel (028) 312-2629, Fax (028) 313-0305 E-mail infoburo@itec.co.za

McGregor Publicity Association Tel (023) 625-1954 Fax (023) 625-1630

Paarl Publicity Association Tel (021) 872-4842, Fax (021) 872-9376 E-mail paarl@cis.co.za

Robertson Tourism Bureau Tel (023) 626-4437 Fax (023) 626-4290 E-mail info@robertson.org.za

bosch Publicity Association Tel (021) 883-3584 Fax (021) 883-8017 E-mail
kestad@iafrica.com

Wellington Tourism Bureau Tel (021) 873-4604 Fax (021) 873-4607 E-mail well-tour@cis.co.za

West Coast Tourism Bureau Tel (022) 714-2088 Fax (022) 714-4240 E-mail bureau@kingsley.co.za

Worcester Tourism Bureau Tel (023) 348-2795 Fax (023) 347-4678 E-mail records@worcmun.org.za

Some wine & food partners

Here are some recommendations on matching cuisine and wine:

Artichokes Make most wines taste like heavy metal. Drink water, or squeeze lemon onto the chokes, which somehow seems to tone down the tinny edges, and team with a high-acid, fresh dry white.

Asparagus A difficult customer. A dry white with lots of flavour, like fresh sauvignon.

Avocado Riesling, white port.

Barbecue See Braai below.

Beef Roast: Cape Bdx blend, cabernet, cabernet franc, merlot, pinot, just about any serious red. Cold roast beef: room for a bit of light here, reds that can take a spot of chilling, pinot, also rosé, blanc de noir, sparkling dry rosé. See also Stews below.

Biltong (savoury air-dried meat snack, usually sliced) Not usually partnered with wine, but try robust shiraz (or beer).

Bobotie (spicy ground-meat, usually lamb) Many possible wine-partners: try dry sparkling, fresh young chenin, riesling, pinotage or other reds made in fruity, easy-drinking styles.

Bouillabaisse Fresh young white, sauvignon, dry rosé.

Braai (the traditional barbecue, a national institution) The wine partner would depend on what's being braaied, but whether meat, fish or fowl, choose a wine with character and muscle, not a fragile little thing that would be overwhelmed by the smoke for a start.

Carpaccio Meat: Just about any red. *Fish:* chardonnay, MCC.

Charcuterie Simple fresh reds.

Cheese A good cheddar can be very good with an elegant red or ruby port. Cream cheese is better with full-bodied whites — try sémillon or chardonnay. Goat's cheese: full-bodied white or dry red. Blue cheese: as long as it's not too powerful, good with rich dessert whites such as NLH and port.

Chicken Roast: best red or white. Chicken pie: try light to medium shiraz or young pinotage.

Chinese MCC, dry (or dryish) white with flavour; riesling.

Chocolate Difficult. Demi-sec bubbly, red muscadel, Cape Pineau des Charentes (see Laborie, Louwshoek-Voorsorg). Or wait and have a glass of dry champagne after the choc mousse.

Crudités Simple dry white.

Curry Pinotage-punting Beyers Truter of Kanonkop recommends (what else?) pinotage; Giorgio Dalla Cia of Meerlust suggests cabernet or a Cape Bdx blend. Fish curry: chardonnay is good, especially when coconut milk is an ingredient. A cheerful, very slightly off-dry (and slightly pétillant) chenin blend is fine too. Also blanc de noir. Sweetish Cape-Malay curries: try matching the spice with gewürz or young riesling or contrasting with sauvignon.

Desserts See Chocolate above.

Duck Fruity young red, champagne, shiraz, off-dry riesling, pinot.

Eggs Not great for or with any wine, but a simple omelette calls for a simple glass of red.

Foie gras Sweet white, NLH/SLH, MCC, merlot.

Fruit MCC, sweet sparkling wine, Late or Special Late Harvest, hanepoot jerepiko or rosé. Strawberries: with cream: NLH; without cream: Uiterwyk's Pieter de Waal recommends a light red. Beware of citrus fruits as they can overpower/ sour a wine.

Game birds Rosé, pinot or Cape Bdx blend. Remember, the darker the meat, the darker/stronger the wine. Guinea fowl: Pinot or merlot.

Ham Young pinot; fresh, juicy red.

Hamburgers Dry, simple red.

Ice-cream (If not too sweet): good bubbly.

Karoo lamb and mutton Roast: best red (cabernet, merlot etc.). Chops: shiraz or young cabernet. Try to avoid mint sauce — it distorts the taste of even minty, new-clone cabs. Stews: light red.

Kidneys Full red, riesling, chardonnay.

Liver Fruity, forceful young red, maybe pinotage.

Mushrooms Pinot.

Mustard sauce Light red, pinotage.

Nuts Port after a meal; sherry before; nutty desserts: MCC.

Oxtail Shiraz.

Pasta Seafood: sauvignon, down-table chardonnay; cream, cheese, egg, meat, tomato sauces: sturdy red.

Pastries and cakes SLH.

Pâté Champagne, gewürz, riesling, pinot.

Phutu or Mealie Meal (SA equivalent of polenta) Sturdy red.

Pizza Depends on ingredients, but also see pasta above.

Pork Off-dry white, fruity red, rosé, zinfandel. Pinotage with spare ribs. In Portugal, roast suckling pig is often teamed with bubbly.

Quiche Full fruity white, riesling, gewürz, sylvaner.

Rabbit Depends on how it's cooked, and the ingredients. Anything from great to simple, red or white.

Ratatouille Light, fruity red, rosé, blanc de noir.

Risotto Fish: medium-bodied dry white; mushrooms: pinot.

Salads Go easy on the vinaigrette — vinegar (or even too much lemon juice) affects wine. A prickly fresh white or rosé with a Salade Niçoise. Chardonnay with a grand shellfish salad. Or something non-serious like a blanc de noir. Or top up one's water table.

Seafood Caviare MCC.

Fish Kurt and Lyn Ammann of Rozendal recommend dry red. If that doesn't appeal, dry sparkling, MCC or dry white (sauvignon or chardonnay/chardonnay blend) are safe choices for saltwater; more delicate white or MCC for freshwater. Grilled: sauvignon; cream sauce: chardonnay, chardonnay blend. With red-wine sauce: red used in recipe or pinot. Smoked: crisp aromatic white, sauvignon, full-bodied (wooded) chardonnay, gewürz or riesling, dry or with a touch of sugar. Sushi: a not-too-grand (nor too rich) chardonnay.

Salmon Chardonnay or fruity non-tannic young red.

Sardines (grilled) Crisp pétillant white, young red.

Smoorvis (braised fish, usually lightly spicy) Frisky (off-dry) chenin, chardonnay or young pinotage.

Snoek Assertive dry white, young red or pinotage.

Sole Grilled: sauvignon or Cape riesling. Sauced: chardonnay.

Trout Young riesling

Shellfish Grilled, boiled, steamed or cold (with mayonnaise): sauvignon, crisp young chenin or off-dry riesling. Rich sauce: MCC or chardonnay-sémillon blend. Piri-piri: this spicy/hot sauce calls for a light pétillant white.

Calamari (squid) Sauvignon, dry white blend or light red.

Cape salmon (geelbek) Racy sauvignon.

Crab Riesling or off-dry chenin.

Crayfish (Cape rock lobster or kreef) Sauvignon or chardonnay.

Elf (shad) Chardonnay, dry chenin or Cape riesling.

Galjoen Sauvignon, chardonnay or cabernet blanc de noir.

Kingklip Chardonnay or wood-matured white.

Langoustine (deep-sea, from SA's East Coast) MCC, chardonnay.

Mussels Sauvignon or chenin. Smoked: wooded chardonnay.

Oysters MCC, sauvignon, lightly wooded or unwooded chardonnay.

Perlemoen (abalone) Chardonnay or sauvignon.

Prawns Chardonnay or sauvignon.

Snacks Of the canapé sort: aperitif white, fruity, dry to off-dry, kir, sparkling white/rosé, blanc de noir, dry sherry.

Snails Chardonnay, pinot, dry riesling.

Sosaties As for curry.

Soufflés Cheese: red; fish: white; dessert: dessert white.

Steak Red wine: cabernet, merlot, shiraz — take your pick. Robert and Gabi Christianus of Wagon Wheels & Gabi's recommend vintage champagne. Pepper steak: somehow smoothes tannins, so doesn't need a mellow old bottle.

Stews and bredies Hearty red. Fish casserole: fresh young white, sauvignon or dry rosé. Waterblommetjie bredie: sauvignon, chardonnay, young pinotage or merlot.

Sweetbreads Chardonnay, or fine claret, pinot.

Thai Draughts of cool fresh dry white for the chilli-hot dishes. Lemon grass, coconut milk and good chardonnay go surprisingly well together. A chilled nouveau style could hold its own.

Tongue Gently dry white, fruity red.

Tripe Hearty red, simple dry white or dry rosé. With tomato: dry red. With onions or white sauce: off-dry chenin or chenin-blend.

Turkey Zinfandel, dry rosé, pinot.

Veal Take your pick, depending on preparation. With vitello tonnato try a chilled, light red.

Vegetables Sauvignon.

Venison Powerful pinot, pinotage, shiraz or mature Cape Bdx blend.

For more about the wine styles mentioned here, see page 417.

. . . .

Eat-out in the winelands

MANY WINERIES offer light lunches or picnics: look for the 🍷 symbol above the individual entries in this guide. The restaurants featured below describe their own culinary styles, menus and attractions.

Constantia

Cloete's at Alphen Alphen Drive • Classic cuisine • Lunch/dinner daily • Major credit cards accepted • Convenient parking • Tel (021) 794-5011 • Fax (021) 794-5710 • E-mail reservations@alphen.co.za • Website www.alphen.co.za

Cloete's at Alphen is in the elegant 18th-century manor house, a national monument, on the historic Alphen Estate at the gateway to the Constantia Valley. Enjoy classic à la carte meals in an atmosphere of past intrigue, surrounded by antiques and paintings from the Cloete family collection. The restaurant specialises in small private functions. If you are looking for something more casual, try the memorabilia-filled Boer 'n Brit in the Jonkershuis or the terrace in the dappled shade of ancient oaks.

Constantia Uitsig Spaanschemat River Road • Mediterranean influences • Lunch 12:00–14.30, dinner 19:30–21:00 (every day in season) • Booking advised • Fully licensed • Corkage R18 • Children welcome • Wheelchair-friendly • Major credit cards accepted • Non-smoking in dining rooms • Tel (021) 794-4480 • Fax (021) 794-310 5 • E-mail cuisine@iafrica.com • Website www.uitsig.co.za

Housed in the original manor house under the shade of 100-year-old oaks and with sweeping views of the Constantia Valley the restaurant, awarded Top 10 status in SA, offers widely varied Mediterranean cuisine and, to complement your meal, the winelist offers the best of the Cape. Constantia Uitsig also offers accommodation in 16 luxurious garden suites with private patios, 2 swimming pools, guest lounge, cricket oval, wine tastings, helicopter flips and their second restaurant, **La Colombe**, tel (021) 794-2390, fax (021) 794-7065. Situated on the historic wine farm La Colombe, with direct frontage onto the pristine blue swimming pool and manicured gardens, offers fine Provençal cuisine. Rated as one of the Top 5 restaurants in SA. Dashing French-born chef Franck Dangereux changes the menu daily according to the season and what's available.

Parks 114 Constantia Main Road • Global cuisine • Dinner Mon-Sat • Booking advised • Corkage R25 • Children welcome • Wheelchair-friendly • Major credit cards accepted • Non-smoking • Tel (021) 797-8202 • Fax (021) 797-8233 • E-mail bibendum@iafrica.com • Website www.parksgroup.com

New visitors and ever-growing numbers of regulars are assured of a warm welcome and professional service at Michael and Madeleine Olivier's popular Constantia restaurant. Guests dine in the rooms of the beautifully restored house, set in a pretty garden. The atmosphere is elegant but relaxed. Parks' signature dishes — blackened fish and duck confit — are retained by popular demand. The daily chef's selection menu offers interesting and unusual dishes using fresh, seasonal ingredients. Desserts are scrumptious and, while fresh fruits and sorbets always feature, the main emphasis here is, quite frankly, sinful. Both the food and the extensive winelist offer flair and quality at a fair price.

Peddlars-on-the-Bend Spaanschemat Road • Country fare • Open daily 11:00–23:00 (pub), 12:00–23:00 (restaurant) • Closed Christmas Day • Booking advised • Corkage R10 • Children welcome • Wheelchair-friendly • Major credit cards accepted • Non-smoking 80% • Tel (021) 794-7747/50 • Fax (021) 794-2730.

Peddlars-on-the-Bend has become one of Cape Town's most popular destinations for locals and visitors alike. Warm country charm, a lovely garden setting under a huge oak tree and a reputation for quality service make this an irresistible venue. The menu offers generous (but reasonably priced) portions of wholesome country food: hearty casseroles in winter, good steaks, fresh linefish and tasty pasta. Award-winning winelist (Diners Club) showcases the area but ventures further afield too; includes some special buys from private cellars and auctions. Good selection of local brandy; Cognac and cigars.

Franschhoek

Ballon Rouge 7 Reservoir Street • Modern European cuisine • Open 7 days a week, 7:00–23:00 • Booking advised • Corkage R10 • Children welcome • Major credit cards accepted • Non-smoking section • Tel (021) 876-2651 • Fax (021) 876-3743 • E-mail info@ballon-rouge.co.za • Website www.ballon-rouge.co.za

Ballon Rouge is comfortably niched as a modern-style brasserie, with a wide-ranging menu. It is owned and run by the Morgan family, who have had considerable experience in the catering field in London. Chef David Hoffman was trained by Rory Morgan, whose experience in European restaurants is apparent in the country-fresh fare offered on the à la carte menu, supplemented by exotic dishes and daily specials, all served in a warm and friendly atmosphere. The winelist has won a Diners Club award each year since 94 and continues to be a winning feature of the restaurant.

Bread & Wine Happy Valley Road, La Motte • Modern country fare • Open Wed-Sun, except during season • Booking advised • Children welcome • Wheelchair-friendly • Major credit cards accepted • Tel (021) 876-3692 • Fax (021) 876-3105 • E-mail linda@lqf.co.za • Website www.moreson.co.za

Surrounded by vineyards and lemon orchards, the newly spruced up Bread & Wine restaurant on the Môreson Martin Soleil wine farm is a place to indulge the senses. Modern country fare tempts the palate with flirtatious combinations of food and award-winning wines. Feast on delicious local produce, home-made breads, sausages, cured meats and pickles. Bread & Wine is a relaxed and rustic setting for informal family lunches, business lunches and dinners, weddings and larger functions.

Haute Cabrière Cellar Restaurant Pass Road • International cuisine • Closed for 2 weeks annually, usually in July • Booking advised • Children welcome • Wheelchair-friendly • Major credit cards accepted • Non-smoking section • Tel (021) 876-3688 • Fax (021) 876-3691 • E-mail hautecab@iafrica.com

High up on the Franschhoek Pass and overlooking the beautiful valley you'll find the award-winning Haute Cabrière Restaurant in a magnificent mountain cellar. Here two prodigious winelands talents, chef-patron Matthew Gordon and wine-grower Achim von Arnim, present a true marriage of food and wine. The cuisine is international, the standard world class. All dishes are available in full- and half-portions — try several to mix and match with the wines, which are all available by the glass or bottle. Wonderful fresh fish, succulent lamb, fresh home-made pasta, salads from the farm and a great selection of delicious modern cuisine will take you into a new dimension in eating out. (See separate Stay-over entry for Auberge Clermont).

La Couronne Robertsvlei Road • New World cuisine • Open daily • Booking advised • Corkage R25 • Children welcome • Major credit cards accepted • Non-smoking • Tel (021) 876-2770 • Fax (021) 876-3788 • E-mail reservations@la-couronnehotel.co.za • Website www.lacouronnehotel.co.za

Situated on the slopes of the Franschhoek foothills and blessed with spectacular views of the valley, this small luxury hotel's restaurant conveys true elegance, and has already been voted one of the the top 50 most exciting restaurants in the world by Condé Nast Traveler. Patrons can relish modern international cuisine and an intelligently structured winelist. Alfresco dining on the terrace completes the romantic setting that is the hallmark of the La Couronne experience. As chef Peter Goffe-Wood puts it: "Our challenge is to do the breathtaking location justice." (See separate Stay-over entry.)

La Petite Ferme Pass Road • French country cuisine • Open Mon-Sun • Booking advised • Corkage R8 • Children welcome • Major credit cards accepted • Non-smoking • Tel (021) 876-3016/8 • Fax (021) 876-3624 • E-mail lapetite@iafrica.com

Three generations of the Dendy Young family have been involved in the restaurant, with the help of manageress Natalie, winemaker Mark's cousin — this enables him to concentrate on the farm's increased vintage. The wines made here are exclusively available on the winelist or in limited quantities to patrons of the restaurant. Rainbow trout is deboned and smoked on the farm, a house speciality continued along with a summertime favourite, Plum Crazy, made from home-grown Santa Rosa plums. The Malay-influenced menu features tried and tested recipes with an innovative twist, changed with the seasons. Three luxury guest suites, overlooking the beautiful valley, feature private patios with plunge-pools and are stylishly decorated for the ultimate experience in tranquillity, privacy and warm hospitality.

Le Provençal Restaurant Main Road • Franco-Japanese • Open for lunch every day, dinner Tues-Sat • Booking advised • Tel (021) 876-2065 • Fax (021) 876-2066 • E-mail restaurant@agustawines.co.za

Experience chef Richard Carstens' Franco-Japanese cuisine at this frequently awarded restaurant. Accolades scooped in the last two years include: Top 6 in Cape Review; top 100 in Wine magazine; top 10 in Tony Jackman's Cape on a Plate, voted one of the top 50 most exciting new restaurants in the world in Condé Nast Traveler. Enjoy the superb selection of Franschhoek wines on the terrace in the vineyard.

Le Quartier Français 16 Huguenot Street • Cape-Provençal cuisine • Open 7 days a week, breakfast, lunch & dinner • Booking advised • Corkage R15 • Children welcome • Wheelchair-friendly • Major credit cards accepted • Non-smoking • Tel (021) 876-2151 • Fax (021) 876-3105 • E-mail linda@lqf.co.za • Website www.lqf.co.za

Le Quartier Français, with its vibrant and colourful cigar bar, spacious, airy restaurant, panoramic view of the mountains and lavender-filled gardens, lends itself to chef Margot Janse and her team tickling your tastebuds. Innovative dishes such as olive oil poached salmon trout with a smoked salmon fritter, cucumber and seaweed, or grilled springbok loin in a balsamic broth with Brussels sprouts, roast onion, mushrooms and curried gnocchi, are served in the restaurant. In the bar or on the terrace, try the lamb burger with creamed avocado, marinated tomatoes and pickled cucumber on a toasted foccacia. Meals are complemented by an award-winning winelist (Diners Club Winelist awards since 94) featuring local wines. (See separate Stay-over entry.)

Monneaux Franschhoek Country House, Main Road • Fusion with Eastern influences • Open 7 days a week, breakfast, lunch & dinner • Booking advised • Corkage R20 • Wheelchair-friendly • Children welcome • Major credit cards accepted • Non-smoking section • (021) 876-3386 • (021) 876-2744 • fch@mweb.co.za • Website www.ecl.co.za

Situated at the Franschhoek Country House (see separate Stay-over entry), the Monneaux Restaurant is named after the building, which was once a perfume-producing factory. Voted one of the top restaurants in SA, the modern French fusion cuisine is innovative, prepared with fresh well-sourced ingredients and exquisitely presented. Lunches are served under a spreading pepper tree in the gardens while dinner is served in the understated yet elegant dining room or enclosed verandah. The extensive winelist emphasises local wines.

Greyton

Greyton Lodge 46 Main Street • African/Continental • Open Mon-Sun 7:30–23:30 • Closed for lunch Mon • Booking advised • Corkage R10 • Children welcome • Major credit cards accepted • Non-smoking section (cigar-friendly) • Tel (0282) 549-876 • Fax (0282) 549 672 • E-mail greytonlodge@kingsley.co.za

Revel in the historic surroundings created by hospitable owners Philip and Sandra Engelen. Emphasis is on refined country cooking, complemented by award-winning winelists (Diners Club Winelist awards for 93, 96, 97 98, 99 & 00). In summer, breakfast and lunch are served in the garden, while in winter you can dine by candlelight beside one of the cavernous log fires. Nailed to the ceiling in the Royal Bar are some 15 000 corks, while on the wall are signatures of winemakers and wine industry luminaries (including John Platter). The 17 rooms and suites make the lodge an ideal relaxing getaway or conference breakaway.

Groot Drakenstein

Boschendal Restaurant Pniel Road (R310), 1,5km from junction with R45 • Cape-French cuisine with extensive buffet • Open 7 days a week, 12:15 for 12:30, guests to be seated by 13:30 • Closed Good Friday, 1 May, 16 Jun • Booking advised • Corkage R15 • Children welcome (half-price for ages 2–10) • Wheelchair-friendly •Major credit cards accepted • Non-smoking • Smart-casual dress code • Tel (021) 870-4274 • Fax (021) 874-2137 • E-mail reservations@boschendal.com • Website www.boschendal.com

Housed in the original cellar, the Boschendal Restaurant serves delicious buffet-style lunches. Heap your plate with expertly prepared Cape-French cuisine, steaming roasts, local seafood specialities, imaginative salads and sinful desserts from tables groaning with these tantalising treats, complemented by fine Boschendal wines, including the Jean le Long range, available only in this restaurant. (Diners Club Winelist awards for 98, 99 & 00.) Beautifully restored and well appointed, this is an ideal place to settle back and savour the food, the ambience and the company. The Manor House is a National Monument and museum with fascinating artworks, Cecil Rhodes memorabilia, Kraak porcelain, furniture and displays.

Le Café at Boschendal Pniel Road (R310) • Cape-French light lunches • Open Mon-Sun, 10:00–17:00 • Closed Good Friday, 1 May, 16 Jun & Christmas Day • No bookings accepted • Corkage R15 • Special children's menu • Wheelchair-friendly • Major credit cards accepted • Indoor-outdoor seating • Tel (021) 870-4274/82/83 • Fax (021) 874-2137

Tucked away in the original slave quarters, Le Café serves tasty light lunches and country-style teas with the best scones and muffins in the valley. Enjoy traditional bobotie in the cosy restaurant in winter; in summer, relax outdoors with a glass of wine, a slice of quiche or a baguette and a salad under the dappled shade of ancient oaks.

Le Pique-Nique at Boschendal off the Pniel Road (R310) • French-style picnic hampers • Open Mon-Sun, Nov-Apr, 12:15–13:30 for collection of baskets • Closed May-Oct & Good Friday • Booking advised • Corkage R15 • Special children's hampers • Wheelchair-friendly • Major credit cards accepted • Tel (021) 870-4274 • Fax (021) 874-2137 • E-mail reservations@boschendal.com

During the summer months Le Pique-Nique, at the foot of the majestic Simonsberg mountain, provides the perfect setting for an al fresco lunch. Collect your hamper filled with pâtés, French baguettes, home-cooked cold meats and crispy salads from the gazebo and spread your picnic at tables in the shade of fragrant pine trees or on the lawn beside a pond. For those who can't resist, ice-cream and coffee are served from the gazebo. Guests may linger in the gardens as long as they wish.

Hermanus

The Pavilion Restaurant Marine Drive • Global cuisine • Dinner Mon-Sat 19:00–22:00 • Closed Jun, Jul, Aug • Booking advised • Corkage R25 • Children from age 12 • Wheelchair-friendly • Major credit cards accepted • Non-smoking • Tel (021) 313-1000 • Fax (021) 313-0160 • E-mail marine@hermanus.co.za • Website www.marine-hermanus.co.za

The Pavilion is situated at the five-star Marine Hotel — part of The Collection by hotelier supreme Liz McGrath. The restaurant, which has views of the ocean and courtyard through sweeping arches, dishes up only the freshest ingredients from local markets. The menu offers contemporary continental cuisine, from hot smoked salmon trout, tempura crayfish on Asian greens, or wok-fried duck with green papaya salad, to roast leg of springbok with sweet potatoes.

Seafood at the Marine Marine Drive • French-local seafood • Open 7 days a week, lunch 12:00–15:00; dinner 19:00–22:00 • Booking advised • Corkage R25 • Children from age 12 • Wheelchair-friendly • Major credit cards accepted • Non-smoking • Tel (021) 313-1000 • Fax (021) 313-0160 • E-mail marine@hermanus.co.za • Website www.marine-hermanus.co.za

Located at the famous Marine Hotel, a member of the prestigious Relais & Chateaux, Seafood at the Marine is contemporary and cool, with the emphasis on fresh fish from the kitchen theatre. Savour the finest seafood soup in the Cape or a sublime pot au feu of linefish. This is award-winning marine cuisine, served with loving perfection.

Paarl

Bosman's Grande Roche, Plantasie Street • Global cuisine with 'Flavours of the Cape' menu • Open daily, all day • Closed Jun, Jul & Aug • Booking essential • Children over 7 • Wheelchair-friendly • Major credit cards accepted • Non-smokers accommodated • Tel (021) 863-2727 • Fax (021) 863-2220 • E-mail reserve@granderoche.co.za

Wind your way through the winelands and stop at Bosman's for light, elegant, informal lunches complemented by splendid wines from the superbly stocked cellar (Diners Club Winelist Diamond award in 00). Bosman's is a world-class restaurant providing contemporary Cape gourmet cuisine in the refined atmosphere of a magnificent manor house. The Grande Roche, a five-star estate hotel (see separate Stay-Over entry), has become a legend on the hospitality scene, winning a formidable array of awards and culinary accolades. Latest achievements include being ranked among the 10 top wine country hotels of the world in America's Food & Wine magazine and Satour's first Hotel of the Year award for its "incredible attention to detail, impeccable grounds, excellent food and superb levels of luxury". The first and only hotel-restaurant in Africa to achieve Relais Gourmand status, one of the world's highest Relais & Chateaux culinary appellations.

Il Casale Ashanti Wine Farm, Klein Drakenstein • Mediterranean & SA influences • Open Sep-May, 7 days a week for lunch, Wed-Sat for dinner • Closed Jun, Jul & Aug • Booking advised • Corkage R20 • Children welcome • Wheelchair-friendly • Major credit cards accepted • Non-smoking section • Tel (021) 862-6288 • Fax (021) 862-2864/863-3325 • E-mail casale@intekom.co.za

An exciting new venue on a very Mediterranean note, Il Casale offers breathtaking views of the Drakenstein mountains from the heart of Ashanti wine farm. Marc Friederich and his team use the freshest ingredients and some very typical South African delights to produce a tasty combination of Italian and Provençal cuisine. Home-made bread is baked daily. In winter, the fireplace creates a very warm and relaxed atmosphere in the arty lounge. In summer, the lovely terrace and lawn overlooking the 25ha dam makes it the ideal setting for lazy lunches and weddings.

Laborie Restaurant Taillefert Street • Traditional SA dishes & Mediterranean-style cuisine • Open Mon-Sun, lunch 12:00–14:00; Tue-Sat, dinner 19:00–21:00 • Booking advised • Children welcome • Wheelchair-friendly • Major credit cards accepted • Non-smoking • Tel (021) 807-3095 • Fax (021) 807-3094 • E-mail brand@kwv.co.za • Website www.kwv-international.com

Laborie Restaurant, on the beautiful Laborie Estate in Paarl, presents delicious summer and winter menus. Traditional Cape dishes and others with a Mediterranean flavour, served at elegantly appointed tables, go hand in hand with efficient service. Special functions can be catered for. (See separate Stay-over entry.)

Rhebokskloof Restaurant Rhebokskloof Wine Estate, Wine Route No 8 • Global cuisine • Open 7 days a week, Nov-Mar, Thu-Mon 11:30–late; Tues 11:30–17:00; Wed 11:30–17:30 • Apr-Oct, closed Wed • Booking advised • Tel (021) 863-8606 • Fax (021) 863-8906 • E-mail rhebok@iafrica.com • Website www.rhebokskloof.co.za

Rhebokskloof Restaurant offers an opportunity to enjoy top quality wines from a award-winning winelist that highlights Rhebokskloof Estate's wines, accompanied by superb global cuisine (one of South Africa's top 100 restaurants), all in one of the most stunning settings in the Cape winelands.

The Olive and Vine Suid-Agter Paarl Road, between Landskroon & Fairview • Traditional SA • Open Mon-Fri 11:30–14:30; Sat-Sun 11:00–15:00; closed Christmas Day & Good Friday • Booking advised • Children welcome • Wheelchair-friendly • Major credit cards accepted • Non-smoking • Tel (021) 863-3495/6, Fax (021) 863-3797 • E-mail ebr@new.co.za

This underground restaurant/deli is spot-on for any occasion. Indulge in a variety of organic foods from the deli. Soak up a wonderful winelands experience inside the underground cellar or outside surrounded by magnificent mountain scenery, while you relax and enjoy traditional South African food, including snoek pâté, bobotie and home-baked chicken pie. Picnic baskets are available on request. (Closed for dinner, except for pre-booked groups of 15 upwards, or special functions.)

Wagon Wheels 57 Lady Grey Street • Steakhouse par excellence • Tue-Fri 12:00–14:00; Tue-Sat 18:00–late • Closed Sun-Mon • Dinner only public holidays • Booking advised • Corkage R7,50 • Children welcome • Wheelchair-friendly • Major credit cards accepted • Non-smoking section • Tel (021) 872-5265 • Fax (021) 872-0062

Robert and Gabi Christianus' famous Wagon Wheels is no ordinary steakhouse. For years, this ultra-stylish couple has served the most extraordinary steaks in the winelands, and they're still at it, impeccably grilling sumptuously matured cuts with accompaniments to faint for — awesome chips, unbelievably crisp (and elegant) garden salads, superb alternatives for the carnivorously-challenged, and a decidedly classy winelist featuring local heroes and some high-powered non-citizens. Plus a relaxed, friendly ambience much-loved by locals and international wine visitors. Next door (and interleading) is **Gabi's Bar**, with its sleek French café-bar ambience. Immaculate espresso (alone worth the visit) and welcoming smiles for children complete the uncommon picture.

Robertson

Fraai Uitzicht 1798 Klaas-Voogds East (R60), between Robertson & Ashton • Country fare • Open for lunch & dinner, Wed-Sun • Closed in June • Booking advised • Corkage R10 • Major credit cards accepted (excl AmEx) • Non-smoking inside • Tel/fax (023) 626-6156 • E-mail fraai.uitzicht@lando.co.za • Website www.lando.co.za/fraaiuitzicht

This historic wine and guest farm (see separate Stay-over entry) was recently restored and a restaurant opened, much to the delight of local residents. Attentive hosts provide a friendly, relaxed ambience for fine dining. The varied menu consists of hearty home-cooked dishes using fresh produce from their vegetable and herb garden. Starters such as Black Forest rolls with spinach, ham and feta, or springbok carpaccio, main dishes that include tequila chicken, braised lamb in phyllo pastry or fillet Fraai Uitzicht, followed by not-to-be-missed desserts, especially the chocolate mousse. The inside fireplace is a delight in winter, and the outside verandah has spectacular views across the Breede River Valley. The food is complemented by a winelist that incorporates some of the Robertson Valley's finest.

Somerset West

Die Ou Pastorie Restaurant 41 Lourens Street • Continental cuisine • Lunch Tue-Fri, dinner Mon-Sat; closed Sun • Booking advised • Corkage R15 • Children welcome • Wheelchair-friendly • Major credit cards accepted • Non-smoking (except in bar) • Tel (021) 852-2120 • Fax (021) 851-3710 • E-mail info@dieoupastorie.co.za • Website www.dieoupastorie.co.za

This characterful restaurant has been offering consistency in service and quality of food for many years. The combination of good food, excellent service and dedication to guests' satisfaction are the cornerstones here. Owner Garry Roberts, aided by chef Conan Garrett, provides an innovative modern-styled à la carte menu, which changes seasonally, with flavours and textures that are harmoniously blended. This has earned Die Ou Pastorie the reputation of being one of the top restaurants in the Western Cape. It also features an award-winning winelist (Diners Club Winelist awards in 96, 97, 98, 99 & 00). This elegant restaurant, set in the historic former Dutch Reformed Church parsonage (circa 1819), offers the warmth, elegance and tranquillity of a bygone era and ensures an unforgettable experience. (See separate Stay-over entry.)

Lady Phillips Restaurant Vergelegen Farm, Lourensford Road • Cosmopolitan cuisine • Open Mon-Sun, lunch 12:00–14:30; tea 10:00–11:30, 15:00–16:00 • Booking advised • Corkage R10 • Children welcome • Wheelchair-friendly • Major credit cards accepted • Non-smoking • No cellphones • Tel/fax (021) 847-1346 • E-mail ladyphillips@vergelegen.co.za • Website www.vergelegen.co.za

A delightful daytime venue all year round, with open-air patio and newly redecorated interior, filled with fresh flowers. The small innovative à la carte menu makes imaginative use of the large variety of herbs picked daily from the garden. Country lunches range from quiches to home-made gourmet pies and pastas, as well as continental dishes. Interesting vegetarian dishes are also a feature. In summer, from Nov to Apr, 9:30–16:00 daily, the nearby **Rose Terrace** is open for alfresco lunches of pâté, salads and baguettes.

L'Auberge du Paysan Off the R44 between Somerset West & Stellenbosch; turn into Winery Road, follow signs into Raithby Road • French cuisine • Lunch Tue-Sat, dinner Mon-Sat • Booking advised • Corkage R15 • Children over 10 • Wheelchair-friendly • Major credit cards accepted • Tel/fax (021) 842-2008 • Website www.aubergedupaysan.co.za

Patron Frederick Thurmann's style and panache highlight the discreet charms of this chic French country restaurant, among the finest in the country. The elegant appointments, decor and ambience complement the traditional classic French menu with specialities from Alsace and Provence. In summer, sip pre-dinner drinks on the shady patio, and in winter, wine and dine in the romantic warmth of the open log fire. Tempting terrine of pheasant Cumberland, a casserole of fruits de mer or delicate and piquant quails followed by a finalé of crème brulée are specialities of the house. In winter, oysters, venison and duckling, and in summer, crustaceans and fresh Stellenbosch berries are seasonal delights. You may want to treat yourself to crêpe Suzette or sabayon prepared at your table by the patron. Superb winelist with L'Auberge du Paysan Pinotage now available.

Willowbrook Lodge 1 Morgenster Avenue, off Lourensford Road • French gourmet • Open 7 days a week, lunch & dinner • Closed Jun-Aug • Booking advised • Corkage R25 • Children over 12 • Wheelchair-friendly • Major credit cards accepted • Non-smoking section • Tel (021) 851-3759 • Fax (021) 851-4152 • E-mail willowb@iafrica.com • Website www.willowbrook.co.za

French owners Janik and Serge Olchanetsky preside over an intimate restaurant at this elegant country house (see separate Stay-over entry), a member of the prestigious Relais & Chateaux group. It's a place where fresh flowers, antiques, works of art and paintings create a refined ambience of exceptional comfort and warm hospitality in which to enjoy French-inspired cuisine. Head chef Loran Livesey combines wonderful fresh local ingredients with the rigours of traditional French haute cuisine for the seasonal à la carte menu at one of the 10 best tables in the country. Award-winning estate winelist.

96 Winery Road Restaurant Zandberg Farm, Winery Road (off the R44 between Somerset West & Stellenbosch) • Country fare with Cape, Provençal and Eastern influences • Lunch Mon-Sun, dinner Mon-Sat; lunch only Sun • Booking advised • Corkage R10 • Children welcome • Wheelchair-friendly • Major credit cards accepted • Non-smoking section • Tel (021) 842-2020 • Fax (021) 842-2050 • E-mail wineryrd@mweb.co.za

Well-known restaurateur Ken Forrester believes eating out should be fun. The result: a bright, buzzing venue in the winelands which is, unsurprisingly, immensely popular. A sort of foodie HQ for, in particular, local and international wine luminaries. Won, among other awards, bronze in the SFW Food and Wine Challenge. Food is fresh, colourful, unpretentious and zingily flavoured country fare. The menu changes frequently according to the whim and creativity of Chef Natasha Harris and Mother Nature. Winelist is extensive with choices from the Helderberg region, also the rest of the world with something to suit every pocket and palate. Diners Club Winelist awards in 97 & 00.

Stellenbosch

Le Pommier Helshoogte Pass, Banhoek • Country fare • Lunch/dinner Tue-Sat; lunch only Sun • Closed Mon out of season • Booking advised • Tel (021) 885-1269 • Fax (021) 885-1274

Rooted high up on the Helshoogte Pass overlooking the lush Banhoek Valley, you'll find Le Pommier Restaurant. This old converted farm-shed offers not only spectacular views but also a sense of timeless charm, warmth and personality. Like the mountains, forever suggesting different moods, Le Pommier offers cosy log fires in winter with snow-capped mountains in the distance and cool rolling greenery in the endless summer. These allures, combined with personal service, add to a sense of wellbeing not often experienced. Facilities include a conference/function centre, art gallery and guesthouse.

Oude Libertas Restaurant & Conference Centre Oude Libertas Road, opposite SFW off Adam Tas Road • Intercontinental cuisine • Lunch Mon-Fri 1200–15:00, dinner Mon-Sat 18:00–22:00 • Closed Sun • Booking advised • Corkage R16 • Wheelchair-friendly • Major credit cards accepted • Tel (021) 808-7429 • Fax (021) 886-6908 • E-mail oudelib@adept.co.za • Website www.oudelibertas.co.za

Seated in an intimate alcove at Oude Libertas Restaurant Cellar, surrounded by 7 000 bottles of maturing red wine, you can prepare for an eating experience that will excite the palate. You will be treated to the best of intercontinental cuisine, complemented by your choice of award-winning Zonnebloem and Nederburg wines. Oude Libertas Restaurant provides the ideal venue for a relaxed meal, business lunch or romantic dinner. In the Vineyard Hall, they cater for exquisite weddings, corporate functions and gala dinners. Oude Libertas conference centre consists of a theatre-style auditorium that will meet all your conference needs.

The Duck Pond R310, Welmoed Winery, Lynedoch • Country fare • Open 7 days a week in summer for lunch, 13:00–15:00 • Closed Mon during winter • Booking advised • Fully licensed • Corkage R9 • Children welcome • Wheelchair access • Major credit cards accepted • Non-smoking section • Tel (021) 881-3310 • Fax (021) 881-3310

The Duck Pond serves country-style food focusing on a lighter, healthier approach and using the freshest ingredients sourced from the area. Known for its personal friendly service and lovely setting — children especially love the ducks at the pond — it is the perfect place for long, lazy lunches. Specialities include ostrich bobotie, fragrant chicken and mushroom pie, and fresh mussels. The restaurant is fully licensed and promotes Welmoed's award-winning wines at very reasonable prices.

The Green Door Restaurant Delaire Wine Farm, Helshoogte Pass • Cosmopolitan • Mon-Sat 12:00–22:30; Sun 12:00–18:00 • Booking advised • Corkage R15 • Children welcome • Wheelchair-friendly • Major credit cards accepted • Non-smoking section • Tel (021) 885-1149 • Fax (021) 885-1685 • E-mail greendoor@mail.com

This country restaurant, high up on the Helshoogte Pass between scenic Simonsberg mountain and Botmaskop, boasts one of the most breathtaking wraparound views in the winelands and offers a small cosmopolitan à la carte menu which changes every 6 to 8 weeks according to seasonal availability. Leave that diet behind — wickedly delicious desserts encourage wayward behaviour. Dining is on the terrace or in a converted wine cellar according to the vagaries of the weather. Weddings, anniversaries, birthdays and other celebrations are catered for.

The Vineleaf Devon Valley Hotel, Devon Valley Road • Innovative Cape cuisine • Booking advised • Corkage R12 (no charge on rare/unusual wine)• Children welcome • Wheelchair-friendly • Major credit cards accepted • Non-smoking section • Tel (021) 882-2012 • Fax (021) 882-2610 E-mail devon@iafrica.com

The Vineleaf at the historic Devon Valley Hotel (see separate Stay-over entry) serves innovative Cape cuisine, with the emphasis on home-grown and organic produce. The menu changes daily to highlight whatever is fresh, exciting or seasonal. Head chef Isaac Monaheng, just back from a two-month stint as guest chef at one of Zurich's top restaurants, aims to combine the best of South African ingredients with originality and style — just-caught stumpnose on home-made squid-ink tagliatelle in a saffron broth gives you a taste of what to expect. In summer, enjoy a light lunch on the patio or enjoy a winelands pizza prepared in the wood-fired oven. In winter, savour one of their own Sylvanvale wines in front of the roaring log fire — the award-winning winelist (Diners Club Winelist merit awards in 98, 99 and Diamond award in 00) offers the full range of Devon Valley wines together with a representative selection of the Cape's finest.

Stellenbosch/Kuils River

Hermitage at Hazendal Bottelary Road, Kuils River • Unique combination of SA, Russian and Mediterranean cuisine • Picnics during season (Nov-Mar) • Open Sep-Apr, Mon-Sun, 12:00–14:30 • Open May-Aug, Tue-Sun, 12:00–14:30 • Closed Good Friday, Christmas Day, New Year's Day • Booking advised • Children welcome • Wheelchair-friendly • Major credit cards accepted • Non-smoking • Tel (021) 903-5112 ext 210 • Fax (021) 903-0057 • E-mail info@hazendal.co.za

This intimate restaurant is situated between the original cellar, which has now been renovated into a tasting centre and restaurant, and the new state-of-the-art cellar, built in 1996. A lovely fireplace in the lounge creates a warm welcome, and is a great place to relax after mealtimes. There's seating for about 50 people in the restaurant, with two adjoining courtyards. Outdoor seating on the patios affords beautiful views of the surrounding mountains and hills. Meals vary from light fresh salads, hearty home-made soups and specialities, to pasta and traditional Cape Malay dishes. Hazendal also offers this superb venue for functions. Russian-born owner Dr Mark Voloshin's passion for his homeland's culture saw him establish the Marvol Museum of Russian Art, which is situated inside the wine cellar, along with the conference facility, which can host up to 40 people. Here you can see a display of Russian icons and paintings by well-known Russian artists — Mark Voloshin's private collection of Fabergé eggs and jewellery are also on permanent display.